50 years **Berlinale**

Internationale Filmfestspiele Berlin

Berlinale
50. Internationale Filmfestspiele Berlin
Eine Veranstaltung der Berliner Festspiele GmbH
9.–20. Februar 2000
Potsdamer Straße 5 · 10785 Berlin
Tel. 259 20 920
http://www.berlinale.de

Wolfgang Jacobsen

50 years Berlinale

Internationale Filmfestspiele Berlin

nicolai

50 years Internationale Film-
festspiele Berlin
Published by Filmmuseum
Berlin-Deutsche Kinemathek
in collaboration with the
Internationale Filmfestspiele
Berlin

Chief editors:
Helga Belach,
Catherine Kerkhoff-Saxon

Editors:
Michael S. Cullen,
Jane Paulick

Translated by:
Catherine Kerkhoff-Saxon,
Robin Benson
Additional contributions
translated by:
Cheryce Kramer, Jane
Paulick (from German);
Louisa Dureau, Regina Guhl,
Eberhard Spreng (from
French);
Gabi Schilling, Helma
Schleif (from Italian);
Marianne Mielke (from
Dutch),
Hans-Joachim Schlegel
(from Russian/Polish)

Index:
Regina Hoffmann,
Gabriele Jatho

Design and layout:
Volker Noth Grafik-Design

Typeset:
LVD GmbH, Berlin

Print and binding:
Heenemann GmbH, Berlin

ISBN 3-87584-906-X

At a glance

Pieces of the mosaic

In asking Wolfgang Jacobsen to update the history of our Festival that he initially wrote in 1989, our hope was that he would now be able to access information previously off limit. Let's face it, in 1989 the Berlin Wall was tumbling but the communist regimes were still in place. The delicate political balance behind the »West Berlin« Festival and the need to take the susceptibilities of our nervous Eastern partners into account was indeed still there.

Ten years later, Berlin is a unified town again, the Soviet Union has collapsed and many archives have meanwhile been opened, thus allowing access to previously unknown material and certainly a new perspective on known or less known events. Wolfgang Jacobsen could largely profit from this gold mine, which makes this new edition of the Festival's history far more than just an update. The mood today might be more for stars, glamour and entertainment, but the so unique »political« past of this Festival and of this town cannot be ignored.

His task was however not easy. First, as a historian he was faced with a personal problem: in the last decade he has become a respected member of the advisory selection board of the Festival, and thus feared he might have lost the needed neutrality for the job. Then, as any researcher, he became more and more aware that archives and newspaper articles do not always give the full story, not to say the complete truth. We greatly admired Wolfgang Jacobsen for the way he exposed his problem to us and would like here to stress that we gave him full and unrestricted access to our archives and tried in no way to infringe on his independence as an author.

His second problem is indeed that of all historians. Truth is complex and even written material can lie or silence important aspects of an event. Much of the Festival history remains unwritten and undocumented: important deals and decisions are often made during meetings, phone conversations or through electronic mail, thus leaving no traces. The choice to rely primarily on written material is probably just as unsatisfactory as relying on the memory of witnesses who are too often inclined to embellish to their advantage. The history of this Festival is so rich in emotions, conflicting interests and contradictions that its complexity can hardly ever be fully told. The effort made by Wolfgang Jacobsen to penetrate into this labyrinth is therefore quite exceptional and calls for our respect.

Reading these pages, brought back to memory events I had long since forgotten. My task is to make the present and plan the future of the Festival, not to ponder over its past. But looking back can be healthy and help going forward. What most shocked me was to realize how apparently insignificant events suddenly gain importance as time passes, while others, at the time so dramatic, hardly merit to be mentioned today.

Making a festival is also an emotional job, but not all emotions survive time. Even some films that we once loved hardly survive historical evaluation. How many of them, considered at the moment to be masterworks, have disappeared into nowhere. When events fall into their historical perspective, other values appear. It is the merit

Ulrich Gregor,
Wolf Donner,
Moritz de Hadeln,
Alfred Bauer

of Wolfgang Jacobsen to have tried to put together these fascinating pieces of the mosaic, and I remain convinced many will find his book a unique view behind the scenes. It is also a tribute to those who made the last 50 years of this event something we can all be proud of.

Moritz de Hadeln

The beginnings

1951

June 6th–18th, 1951

First there was music. The Berlin Philharmonic Orchestra conducted by Leo Blech played the overture to Carl Maria von Weber's opera »Euryanthe«. Speeches followed. Then awards. Finally a film. Yet even it was only part of the introductory program. Nevertheless the crowds remained patient. Tension was mounting on that Wednesday evening in the Titania Palast. Then the time had finally come: for the first International Film Festival Berlin to be opened.

It was June 6th 1951, six years after the end of the war; life in Berlin was still not back to normal. But the city was exerting more and more pressure to reestablish its presence in all domains of society, to revitalize its function as a European art metropolis, as it had been in the first third of the century. It was within this context that the International Film Festival Berlin was established. It was called for short the »IFB« or the »Berlinale«, the latter to the regrets of the founding fathers, as they had wanted their festival to contrast to Venice's »Biennale« and not to sound as if it were related. But this term coined at the very beginning by the cabaret performer Tatjana Sais has survived all other attempts (e. g. »Film Olympics«) of naming the festival.

The establishment of the Film Festival was, at least for the history of Berlin, an event of significance and consequence. How had it all come about? The situation of the film industry in Berlin at that time has not been adequately examined. Of course Berlin had lost its importance as a center of film. The idea of doing something for Berliners and for the film industry by presenting an impressive series of events certainly came to several minds at once, so that the dispute as to who was first is pointless. But as time passed, memories faded, and legends took on substance, the discussion became embittered and led in part to strange animosities, which shall – at least marginally – be dealt with here.

No matter how widespread the idea of a film festival in Berlin modeled after the ›classical‹ festivals in Cannes and Venice might have been, crucial were the conception and initiative of Film Officer Oscar Martay of the Information Services Branch under the American High Commissioner McCloy. Martay had come to Berlin in 1948 as film advisor of the US State Department. After several talks with the responsible members of the city council of Greater Berlin (which as of the end of 1948 ran only the three Western Sectors) and with representatives of the Berlin film industry, a preliminary committee was set up on the initiative of Oscar Martay. It began its consultations in the fall of 1950. Its members were:

- Government Supervisor Theodor Baensch, head of the Film Section in the Division of Art in the Berlin Department of Education;
- Manfred Barthel, film editor for the Berlin daily »Der Abend«;
- Max Büttner, film distributor, member of the board of the Berlin branch of the Verband deutscher Filmverleiher e. V. and proprietor of Central-Film-Verleih;
- Oswald Cammann, managing director of the Spitzenorganisation der Berliner Filmwirtschaft (commonly called the »Spio Berlin«, the Berlin branch of the top organization of German film industries);
- Dr. Hans Cürlis, producer of documentaries and chairman of the Bund deutscher Kulturfilmhersteller e. V.;
- Ernst Hasselbach, producer of feature films and chairman of the Vereinigung Berliner Filmproduzenten e. V.;
- Oscar Martay;

In the first postwar years, *Oscar Martay,* as American Film Officer, saw to it, using unconventional methods, that film printing facilities were supplied with basic materials for the synchronization of foreign films. Later on, he was also the one to enable 21 district movie houses lying along the sector borders to East Berlin and the GDR to offer showings at reduced rates for East Berlin movie-goers, as well as for screenings in the Titania-Palast in Steglitz and the Waldbühne for Soviet Sector residents at greatly reduced prices. These performances were seen by thousands and thousands of visitors over the years. In 1953, Martay resigned from his position in the US State Department; until 1955, he was in a German production company, until 1957, with a distributor. Today he is head of his own film production company. For his services in establishing the International Film Festival, he received a Golden Bear in 1951.

The journalist *Manfred Barthel* from the Berlin tabloid »Der Abend«, who, having been impressed by the festival in Cannes in 1950, had called for a »Film Olympics« in Berlin, was not the only one to have claimed the idea of the Film Festival Berlin to have been his own. Barthel did in fact in the course of events help to establish the Film Festival.

There was also the cameraman *Gerhart Ottow,* who insisted on having given Greater Berlin a manuscript as early as 1949, from which the Film Festival had taken over all of his proposals as such. He was so convinced of having fathered the International Film Festival Berlin, that he applied for legal aid from the 17th Division of the Superior Court of Berlin with the intention of filing suit; when rejected, he lodged an appeal, which in turn was also rejected. On March 5th 1955 – the correspondence between Ottow and the city authorities had been dragging on for more than

- Government Supervisor Schneider of the Berlin Municipal Department of Tourism;
- George Turner, British Press and Film Officer.

At the first meeting of this committee on October 9th 1950, the course was set and the first organizational plans made. Oscar Martay saw to it that rooms were put at the committee's disposal in the Amerika Haus, Kleiststr. 10-12 (site of the Urania today); the Waldbühne (Berlin's largest open-air theater) was envisioned as an important location for events; and the dates were set from June 6th to 17th 1951. Furthermore, the following proposal of Martay was recorded: »We could give each visitor buying a ticket an evaluation sheet, which is later dropped in a special box at the exit. As prize we could, perhaps, award a silver Berlin Bear with the inscription ›Film Festival Berlin 1951‹.« And it was Manfred Barthel who named the event as it is still called today: International Film Festival Berlin.

At this meeting, the first questions of personnel were discussed. It is surprising that Oswald Cammann was foreseen as director, responsible for the program and organization, including advertising; Schneider was to be responsible for matters concerning tourism and for advertising as well; Oscar Martay and Max Büttner for the procurement of films; Manfred Barthel for the press; Dr. Cürlis was to take on the section for documentary films.

These ›first men of the moment‹ gave great consideration to the question of financing without, however, finding a solution. All possible sources were discussed, from ›tapping‹ the funds from the liquidation of the Ufa (Universum Film Company) to self-financing out of the proceeds from ticket sales. From today's point of view, even bizarre ideas were discussed seriously. Ernst Hasselbach proposed asking each participating country to send a documentary film to Germany, which could then be shown in the accompanying program of a cinema. »The profits from these documentary films«, he suggested, »could then flow into a fond for the financing of the Festival.«

They already had a good idea of how many films and which countries were to be invited: three films each from the USA and England (here the influence of the two film officers of the Allied Forces could be felt); two each from France, Italy, Austria and Germany; and one film each from the Netherlands, Denmark, Sweden, Finland, Israel, Egypt, India, Mexico and Australia. The participation of Japan, Turkey and Portugal was at this point still questionable. This selection made noticeable omissions. It is clear which countries were considered undesirable: »In conclusion to a discussion, the application for the admission of Eastern bloc countries was rejected by 7 votes«, the minutes record laconically. Yes, it was the time of the Cold War.

The members of this preliminary committee were not to vary substantially in the following meetings. It was not until it became a planning committee that everything changed. It was realized that with a relatively loose group of people – who moreover did not have adequate funds – it was hardly possible to plan such a series of events with the desired high standards. Especially the procurement of a competent organizer and director was difficult; it had become all too clear that Oswald Cammann with all his other activities (he was also business director of the Verband Berliner Filmtheater e. V. and of the Deutsche Filmexport GmbH, that is a classic example of a multi-functionary) could not manage this additional responsibility.

It was in connection with these considerations that Dr. Alfred Bauer was mentioned, whose »Deutscher Spielfilm Almanach 1929-1950« – even today a standard work in the field of the history of film – had just been published. Moreover, on July 7th 1950 Bauer had presented Mayor of Berlin Ernst Reuter, the three allied Commandants of the city and the Arbeitsgemeinschaft der Berliner Filmwirtschaft (forerunner of the Spio Berlin) with a »memorandum on the establishment of a Berlin film institute«, which also included the idea of organizing a festival. According to item 4, the function of this institute was to be also in »the preparation of film shows and the organization of a film festival week occurring yearly in Berlin (similar to those in Venice, Locarno, Brussels, etc.), in turn promoting tourism and visitors from abroad to Berlin, in cooperation with the Municipal Department of Tourism«.

four years – the verdict of the 5th Division of the Superior Court of Berlin was announced: »The appeal according to §§ 127 567 ff. ZPO is admissable. Yet it is not justified.« Ottow had not, according to the interpretation of the court, been able to bring in evidence to support his assertions. »In giving its reasons for this decision, the Superior Court has pointed out, and with reason, that the plaintiff can only claim copyright for the manuscript itself, but not for his ideas on how to carry out a film festival in Berlin.« Be it as it may, Ottow shall also be named here as one of the spiritual fathers of the Film Festival.

Titania-Palast. The opening of the first International Film Festival Berlin

Manfred Barthel

Oscar Martay

Alfred Bauer was born on November 8th 1911 in Würzburg. After studying law and art history, he received his Ph.D. in 1938 with a dissertation on film law. A year later, he passed the second state exam. After three years in the war, he joined, in 1942, Universum Film AG (Ufa); he was responsible for drawing up: disposition plans for the production of German feature films, monthly reports on films in production, as well as appraisals on legal and financial questions pertaining to film. He was active in the Reichsfilmkammer of the German Reich. From September 1st 1945 till June 30th 1948, he was, as film expert, advisor in the Film Section of the British military government, from July 1st 1948 to November 1st 1950, advisor of this Section in Berlin. As of 1951, he was director of the International Film Festival Berlin, retiring in 1976.

Alfred Bauer took over the organization of the Film Festival in the middle of November 1950, even though as late as October 31st of that year a list of the intended members of staff with Cammann as chairman was released to film magazines and newspapers. Cammann's withdrawal however opened up the way for Alfred Bauer.

The working conditions during this first period were anything but ideal, which was primarily a result of insufficient funding by the city, and a faltering flow of subsidies in general. For a long time Bauer worked alone in his office, and was backed only by the organizational committee, whose activities limited themselves primarily to their periodic meetings. De-jure, Bauer's and the committee's work first became official through a senatorial decree, Number 52 of Februar 19th 1951. It states: »For preparation a committee will be set up consisting of one appointee each from the Departments of Education, Commerce, Traffic and Public Enterprises, and Finances; and Messrs. Hasselbach as film producer, Büttner as distributor, Jacob as movie house proprietor, Dr. Cürlis as documentary filmmaker and Barthel (›Der Abend‹) as film journalist.« Only Karl Jacob, chairman of the Verband Berliner Filmtheater e. V. had not been a member of the preliminary committee constituted in the autumn of 1950.

Yet even as late as April 2nd 1951, that is about two months before the festival was to begin, Bauer had complained to Baensch: »I've been working for the city for nearly half a year now and I still don't have a contract. I think this is the craziest thing that has ever been done to me.« In his final report on this first festival he pointed out that until April the management had only had one employee at its disposal and that expenses had been covered in part by a private loan he had taken out. In this first year he was able to make it by with such a small staff, that it can nowadays only arouse admiration and compassion. He was assisted by:

- a press officer for three months (Jochen Severin from the »Neue Zeitung«);
- an advertising and special events-manager for three months (Karl-Heinz Bergmann);

Alfred Bauer died on October 19th 1986 in Berlin. In his honor, the International Film Festival 1987 established the Alfred Bauer Prize, to be given to a film opening up new perspectives in the art of cinematography.

Joachim Tiburtius, Alfred Bauer

- an expert on documentary films and film management for five months (Wilhelm Schäfer);
- in addition there was a manager for advanced ticket sales for six weeks, an interpreter and a translator for seven months and two secretaries for five and eight months respectively. For mass events there was a special manager, Herbert Weidner.

The budget

In the first three years the IFB was not a permanent institution, which meant that each year the Berlin Senate had to pass a new resolution, which in turn had to be formally recognized by the Berlin Parliament. It was not until the parliamentary decision of October 15th 1953, that the IFB (in combination with the Berliner Festwochen) became a permanent establishment, budgeted together under the heading »Festivals«.

For the first fiscal year, Alfred Bauer calculated with proceeds of DM 153 360, which were to balance expenses of DM 156 560. Following a number of revisions made by the Department of Finances, the budget for the Film Festival was set by the city at DM 130 000 for proceeds and DM 150 000 for expenses. In a senatorial decree, Number 52 from February 19th 1951, the actual date of birth of the IFB, these sums were confirmed; the House of Representatives gave its approval on May 4th.

It is therefore somewhat surprising that even though the difference in returns and outlay calculated had amounted to a deficit of only DM 20 000, the Berlin Senate

Internationale Filmfestspiele Berlin 1951
- Geschäftsführung - E. 16/4.51 # 199 16/4

13. April 1951

Mr. Oscar M a r t a y
Berlin-Zehlendorf

Sehr geehrter Mr. Martay,

nachfolgend geht Ihnen die gewünschte Erklärung über die katastrophale Lage unserer Filmfestspiele zu:

Für die Finanzierung der Filmfestspiele Berlin 1951, denen als kulturpolitisch wichtige Schaufensterveranstaltung des westlichen Films gegenüber dem Osten eine besondere Bedeutung zukommt, stehen lediglich 40.000.-- DM zur Verfügung, die aus Mitteln der Stadt Berlin gegeben wurden. Wenn die Filmfestspiele ein Erfolg werden und ihren politischen Zweck erfüllen sollen, muss noch eine Subvention von mindestens 100.000.-- DM zur Verfügung gestellt werden. Die Gesamtsumme von 140.000.-- DM wird benötigt für Werbezwecke in der gesamten westlichen Welt (allein die Plakatkosten betragen über 25.000.-- DM), ferner für Aufenthalt und Unterkunft der geladenen prominenten Gäste, Unterhaltung des Festspielbüros für ca. 6 Monate und Risiko-Reserve für den Fall, dass in der "Waldbühne", die als Hauptfinanzier der Filmfestspiele anzusehen ist, keine Vorführungen stattfinden können.

Ich darf in diesem Zusammenhang darauf hinweisen, dass zur Finanzierung für die allgemeinen Kulturfestspiele im Herbst d.J., die sich hinsichtlich ihrer politischen Bedeutung niemals mit den Filmfestspielen messen können, das Zwanzigfache des Betrages, nämlich 800.000.-- DM (davon allein 300.000.-- DM von alliierter Seite) bereitgestellt wurden. Auch für die Ruhrfestspiele wurde durch die Alliierten eine Spende von 50.000.-- DM ausgeworfen.

Wenn nicht in kürzester Frist für die Filmfestspiele die benötigten weiteren Mittel bewilligt werden, die es gestatten, eine der grossen Veranstaltung entsprechende Planung auf weite Sicht durchzuführen, muss ernstlich mit dem Scheitern der Filmfestspiele gerechnet werden.

Mit vorzüglichster Hochachtung

gez. Dr. Bauer

- - - - - - - - - - - - - - -

Letter from Alfred Bauer to Oscar Martay concerning the Film Festival's catastrophic financial situation

(which formed the municipal government since a new constitution and elections in January) approved of a sum as high as DM 40 000. This discrepancy turned out to be quite a blessing.

Furthermore the funds available were covered by DM 50 000 put up by the Office of the Allied Kommandatura in the form of a loan on the assets from the Ufa-liquidation. The only condition made was that the Senate put up a guarantee for this amount and if needed balance the account when the Festival was over. In fact the Senate did have to pay the Allies a sum of DM 20 700 out of the budget of 1952.

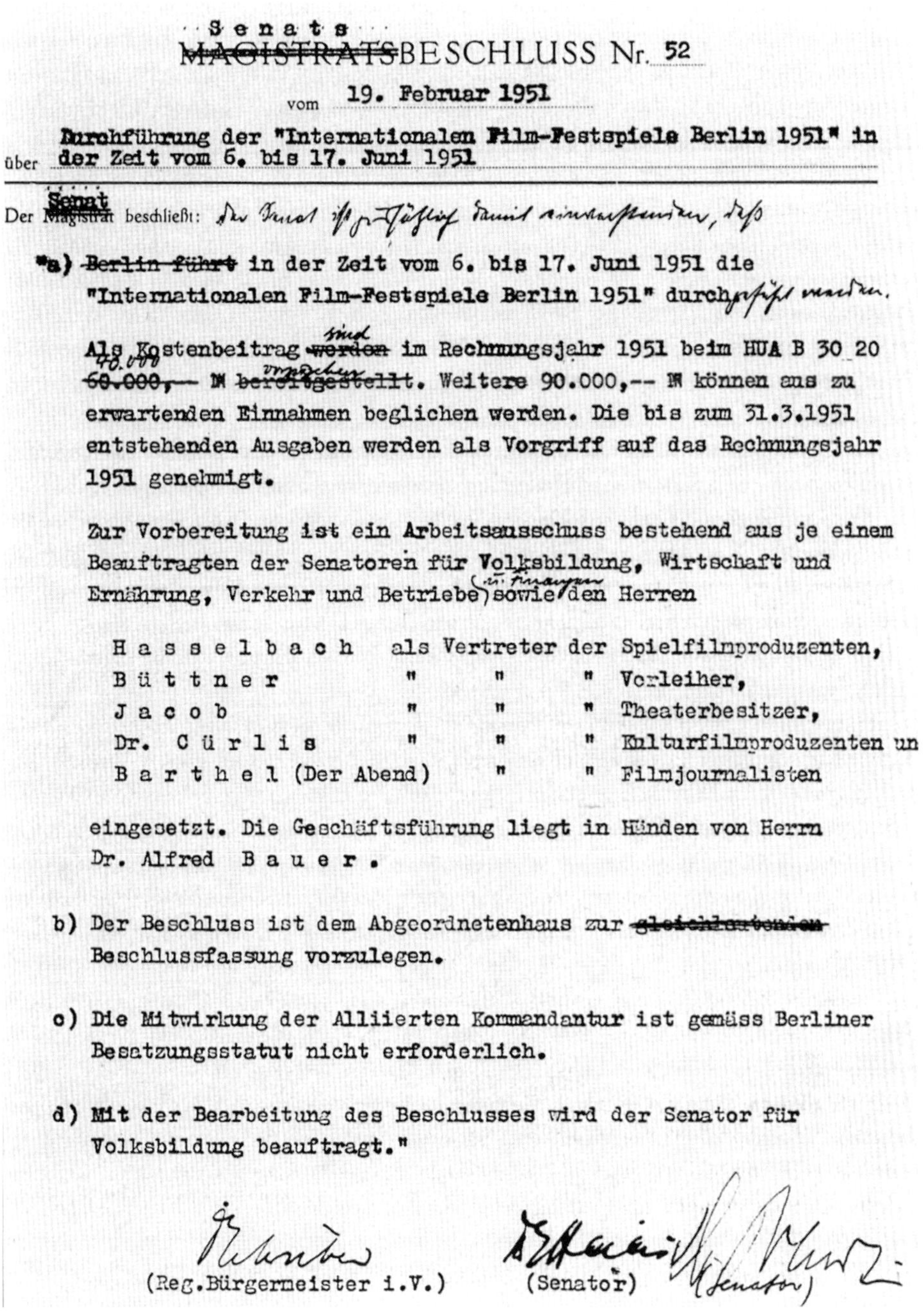

Senats ~~MAGISTRATS~~BESCHLUSS Nr. 52

vom 19. Februar 1951

über Durchführung der "Internationalen Film-Festspiele Berlin 1951" in der Zeit vom 6. bis 17. Juni 1951

Der Senat ~~Magistrat~~ beschließt:

"a) ~~Berlin führt~~ in der Zeit vom 6. bis 17. Juni 1951 die "Internationalen Film-Festspiele Berlin 1951" durch

Als Kostenbeitrag sind ~~werden~~ im Rechnungsjahr 1951 beim HUA B 30 20 40.000 ~~60.000,--~~ DM vorgesehen ~~bereitgestellt~~. Weitere 90.000,-- DM können aus zu erwartenden Einnahmen beglichen werden. Die bis zum 31.3.1951 entstehenden Ausgaben werden als Vorgriff auf das Rechnungsjahr 1951 genehmigt.

Zur Vorbereitung ist ein Arbeitsausschuss bestehend aus je einem Beauftragten der Senatoren für Volksbildung, Wirtschaft und Ernährung, Verkehr und Betriebe sowie den Herren

H a s s e l b a c h	als Vertreter der	Spielfilmproduzenten,
B ü t t n e r	" " "	Verleiher,
J a c o b	" " "	Theaterbesitzer,
Dr. C ü r l i s	" " "	Kulturfilmproduzenten un
B a r t h e l (Der Abend)	" " "	Filmjournalisten

eingesetzt. Die Geschäftsführung liegt in Händen von Herrn Dr. Alfred B a u e r .

b) Der Beschluss ist dem Abgeordnetenhaus zur ~~gleichlautenden~~ Beschlussfassung vorzulegen.

c) Die Mitwirkung der Alliierten Kommandantur ist gemäss Berliner Besatzungsstatut nicht erforderlich.

d) Mit der Bearbeitung des Beschlusses wird der Senator für Volksbildung beauftragt."

(Reg.Bürgermeister i.V.) (Senator)

Senatorial decree concerning the establishment of the International Film Festival

Even more clearly than in this loan, the interest of the American forces in the Film Festival can be seen in their direct donation of DM 35 000, which was later used to cover certain miscalculations. In the final accounts, expenses of DM 214 000 were set against returns of DM 187 000; these had come in as proceeds from the events themselves, as a grant from the Senate of DM 42 000, and as the above mentioned donation from the American military authorities. The greater portions of expenses were DM 63 500 for advertising, DM 30 000 for payroll and DM 27 000 for accommodating the guests of the IFB. A deficit of approximately DM 25 000, which at first the Americans planned to cover, was apparently assumed by the Senate.

A look in the future: it was this deficit (which, considering the impossibility of making an accurate estimate in this first year, was hardly astounding) that was decisive in setting the level of subsidies needed for the next year at DM 70 000. In addition there was a donation from Berolina-Film and grants from both the Federal Ministry of All-German Affairs and the Office of the Allied Kommandatura, so that the total sum available (not including proceeds from the Festival itself) was DM 100 000. As the years passed, the funds increased continually; by 1956, the year the Festival was given official »A«-level status, they had reached approximately DM 400 000.

Numbers can be deceiving. Their meaning can only be understood by analyzing their relationship to inflation and to the changing capacities and aims of the Festival. The budgets of the first years were tight, yet not to such a degree that Bauer and the other organizers were not able to succeed, even in this very first year, in bringing about an impressive – and internationally recognized – festival, created so to speak »from scratch« and having had little time to make arrangements.

To the same degree as the Allies (especially the Americans) were interested in the success of the IFB and the Senate of Berlin committed, the film industry had its reservations and was even in part disapproving – in particular the Spitzenorganisation der deutschen Filmwirtschaft (Spio) with its headquarters in Wiesbaden.

No support from the Spio

On January 12th and 13th 1951, the Spio met in Berlin. The board was informed officially of the Festival and asked to take part – to no avail. A letter from the Verband deutscher Filmproduzenten, the most influential branch of the Spio under the chairmanship of Walter Koppel, summed up on March 19th 1951 all the film industry's qualms and misgivings. In essence they substantiated the crisis of the German film industry, which »as a result of the film politics of the Allies, put German film production at a serious disadvantage vis-à-vis foreign productions«. Consequently, it was concluded: »Out of our responsibility to the struggling German film industry, we have not been able to decide to advise production companies to participate.«

Fédération Internationale des Associations des Producteurs de Film (FIAPF)

The job was complicated by other matters as well. Especially the Fédération Internationale des Associations des Producteurs de Film (FIAPF), which had a quasi monopoly on international film festivals, was long uncooperative. At their conference during the film festival in Venice in September 1950, they passed a resolution stating that national productions included as of 1951 were only to participate in the festivals at Cannes and Venice. As unpleasant as this decision of the FIAPF was for Berlin, it was to a certain degree understandable; there was the danger – with the growing interest particularly of socialist countries in establishing such events – of an overabundance of festivals, a saturation of the market, which in turn would mean a decline of the general interest in such festivals.

Such was the situation with which Bauer saw himself confronted when he addressed the Centre Nationale de la Cinématographie in Paris on November 15th 1950. He announced the dates of the IFB for the coming year and in an official communiqué solicited for the participation of French film productions. After consulting the French film industry organizations, the Centre Nationale agreed to participate, but only if the festival were not a competition. Which was exactly what the organizers and the Senate intended; although the audience was to choose its favorite film by ballot, they still, as at any proper festival, did not want to do without a jury. This issue is not as superficial and vain as it might at first seem; it concerned in principle the question of the status of the first IFB. And so far Berlin had been denied so called »A-status«.

Not only France, but Italy as well refused official participation in the IFB; Venice and Cannes were hereby sufficiently protected. Nevertheless the producers' associations of both countries permitted their members to send films to Berlin, and so the conflict ended in a compromise. In Berlin one tried to relieve tension by setting up a German jury instead of an international one and by using different categories for the awards than customary in Venice and Cannes. Australia, England, Ireland, Switzerland, Spain and, most important, the USA had all spontaneously accepted the invitation to participate; by March twelve other countries joined them. On behalf of the president of the MPAA, Eric Johnston, the representative of the Motion Picture Association of America Inc. in Germany, Marc M. Spiegel (Frankfurt) assured »that it will be a pleasure for the member firms I represent to take part in the International Film Festival Berlin 1951. The American film industry will be represented by creations of most recent production; some films shown will not yet have had their world première.« (Letter, April 25, 1951.)

Marc M. Spiegel

Still, the complications of this initial phase were not over. Unexpectedly the Spio released a statement to the press claiming that in parliamentary circles in Bonn the postponement of the Festival until October was being considered. Bauer and the organizational committee were appalled, and even the Berlin branch of the Spio Wiesbaden, an independently registered organization, was quite irritated by this announcement.

Setting the dates

Whether or not this press release was a deliberate attempt of the Spio Wiesbaden to hinder the Festival, or in fact a demarche of parliamentary circles – the matter of setting the dates for the approaching Festival had already been discussed in such great detail that a postponement at this point was out of the question. As early as the beginning of December 1950, Walter May, city councillor in the Department of Education, had urged Oscar Martay to put off the Festival until September 1951. In reply, Martay had listed off all the reasons which the organizers had found to speak for a scheduling in June: First of all, one wanted to be accommodating to the other German cities (Martay mentioned Wiesbaden, Munich, and Cologne) which were also planning film festivals for the summer and fall of 1951. In addition, it was possible that a September scheduling would coincide with or be too shortly before the Film Biennale in Venice. Furthermore, September would bring in an unpredictable element, the weather – which was, considering the significance of the open air events in the Waldbühne for the budget, an important argument. Besides, by this time, that is by December 1950, contact had already been established with the countries which were to be invited to the Festival. The last of Martay's arguments for a scheduling in June shall be quoted directly: »It seems to me that as one of the most important reasons for the dates in June is the fact that shortly after we announced the Berlin Film Festival in the media, the press in East Germany announced for summer 1951 in East Berlin, the ›Welt-Jugend-Festspiele‹ (World Youth Festival), which will be built up around a meeting of the ›Weltbund der Demokratischen Jugend‹ and organized by the ›FDJ‹ (the official East German youth organization). I believe that it is exactly this political aspect which makes it imperative to hold the Berlin Film Festival in June, creating the necessary counter-event, that is *the* attraction for East Berliners and residents of the Eastern bloc, not to mention for the youth of these socialist countries.« (A comment here: Of relevance was not only the competitive relation-

The Waldbühne – over years a popular location for Festival events

ship to the 3rd Weltfestspiele der Jugend und Studenten which, by the way, did in fact affect attendance to the International Film Festival Berlin positively, but also the existence in East Berlin of a film festival – albeit small – of its own as soon as the IFB was over: the »Festwoche des volksdemokratischen Films« in July 1951, at which six films, one each from Poland, Czechoslovakia, Rumania, Hungary, Bulgaria and the People's Republic of China were shown.)

Irritation continued over the »Bonn announcement«. Alfred Bauer remarked curtly: »Either our film festival is being sabotaged or West Germany wants to take charge.« In the end, nothing came of it.

Patronage

In the meantime preparations for the actual events were proceeding. As early as December 1950, Alfred Bauer had shown concern with the sponsorship of the Festival and had written to the President of the Federal Republic of Germany, Theodor Heuss, requesting his patronage. It was not until March 9th 1951 that an answer was received from the Office of the President, in which the personal assistant of the President, Hans Bott, passed on the suggestion of »offering the patronage of the International Film Festival Berlin 1951 to Federal Minister of the Interior Dr. Lehr, as it is this ministry which deals with all matters relevant to film«. The Federal President was only interested in being an honorary patron if he could actively participate himself. Bauer had by-passed official channels to make these arrangements, which annoyed the Senator for Education, Professor Dr. Joachim Tiburtius. To appease him, Bauer proposed offering the patronage to Mayor Ernst Reuter – a suggestion which Tiburtius more or less ignored, inviting instead Dr. Lehr only to the opening of the International Film Festival. Dr. Lehr accepted: »It is necessary to set off the Berlin Film Festival properly from similar events in the Eastern Zone. On the other hand – as you know – I intend on this occasion to award the German Film Prize for 1950 in a solemn manner to the different deserving winners. Only then will it be possible to lend the German Film Prize the public esteem which is needed to create real incentives for quality productions. Therefore, I would like the presentation of the German Film Prize to be appropriately emphasized in the announcements, program, and in the arrangements for the evening [i. e. of the opening of the International Film Festival].« (Letter, May 29, 1951.)

German Film Prize

As a result the Federal Government was unexpectedly on hand with an ›event within an event‹ in Berlin, and it is certainly not a mere accident that the presentation of the first German Film Prize (later called the Federal Film Prize) should coincide with the beginnings of the International Film Festival. And they continued to coincide for decades to come (except in 1952, when the prize was awarded in Bonn): two independent events having the same backdrop; a circumstance which was seen by the socialist countries again and again as proof of the presence of the Federal Republic of Germany in Berlin. It is not until 1978 with the rescheduling of the Film Festival that these two events take place independently from one another.

The jury

One of the last decisions that Bauer had to make before the opening of the Film Festival was the appointment of a film jury. Fritz Podehl, head of the Commission for the Voluntary Control of Standards in the German Film Industry, was appointed president of the jury. The other jurors were:

- Dr. Emil Dovifat, professor for political journalism at the Free University of Berlin;
- Werner Eisbrenner, composer;
- Günter Geisler, journalist and critic for the »Berliner Anzeiger«;

- Walther Karsch, critic, co-publisher of the »Tagesspiegel« and chairman of the Berliner Kritikerverband;
- Hilde Lucht-Perske, city councillor;
- Tatjana Sais, actress, cabaret performer and member of the »Insulaner«;
- Paul Heimann, lecturer at the Teachers' College, Berlin;
- Johannes Betzel, movie house owner and chairman of the Spio.

The jury had twelve awards at its disposal for films classified in the following four categories: dramatic films, comedies, crime and adventure films, as well as musicals. According to the regulations, the jury had to give away all the awards (which in fact it did not do: two »Bears« were not awarded). Ratings were given according to a fixed scale, ranging from 0 for »poor quality«, 1 for »below average«, 2 for »average« and 3 for »high quality«. An additional clause stated: »At request of a member of the jury, a discussion as to the final evaluation may take place. Otherwise the scale of ratings is decisive in the determination of the highest qualifications.« These rigid regulations left the presentation of the awards wide open to criticism, and in fact there were but few reporters from the daily papers who spared the Film Festival jury and its decisions in their final resumées of the IFB.

In addition there were awards in the categories of long documentary, documentary, art and science films. Specical prizes were awarded by the City of Berlin, and the movie-goers could choose their own favorite by filling out an evaluation sheet. For the main categories the trophy was – as Oscar Martay had suggested at the very first meeting of the IFB's preliminary commission – a Berlin Bear, in either gold, silver or bronze; for short documentary films there were the appropriate plaques, and for the audiences' favorites large and small bronze plates.

The opening gala

So much for the planning. The evening of June 6th had finally arrived. The enthusiasm of Berliners seemed to know no bounds. Outside the Titania-Palast the mood was euphoric. When the stars arrived »all hell broke loose«. This spectacle was captured in an article by the Berliner journalist Dora Fehling:

»Everyone in Steglitz was going crazy. Or rather, they were standing in line. Or behind barricades. The police had closed off whole blocks, as if highly explosive mines were strewn about the area. The crowds were getting their money's worth, at least of German stars: those from abroad, who were to fill hotels, were not to be seen. But then the Festival-show had only just got off the ground.

Stars in flesh-and-blood

Pouring into a Titania-Palast surrounded by flags were: a suntanned Hans Söhnker; a very slender and pale Dorothea Wieck with bandages on her wrists; Hilde Körber with one of her daughters; Loni Heuser looking very feminine; and eternally young Olga Tschechowa making her way in followed by her latest partner. Karin Hardt, Hilde Sessak, Gretl Theimer, Karin Evans, Eva-Ingeborg Scholz, Margot Hielscher, Käte Haack and Winnie Markus also received due admiration. To illustrate the range of personalities: neither School Superintendent Weigel, nor Waldbühnen director Tuntsch with his inevitable menthol cigarettes were absent.

Heads bowed, the critics were approaching: for a span of nearly two weeks, they had bidden farewell to both house and home, not to mention to all other human bonds. Two Viktors were present: the huge and corpulent Janson and the ›peaceful‹ de Kowa, who was accompanied by his delightful wife, Michi Tanaka, wearing such a sophisticated combination of modern-Asian garments and a pitch-black ponytail, that the astonished crowd let out their first cries of »Oh, how cute!«. The Meisels were represented by: Kurt, the actor, and Willi, the composer. Theo Lingen, five

Jury members Johannes Betzel, Günter Geisler (standing), Fritz Podehl, Walther Karsch (standing), Hilde Lucht-Perske, Emil Dovifat, Werner Eisbrenner

pounds overweight or at least heavier, arrived and put everyone in a great mood; and for the time being Walter Franck had shaken the Western dust (from the Federal Republic) off his feet; and Carl Raddatz contrasted so to say purely superficially to Ernst Wilhelm Borchert: crook contra ›Faust‹, that is, so to speak, from the stage or cinema point of view.

Outside the Titania-Palast newspapers and magazines were being given away in such quantities, that one would have needed a rucksack to carry them home. And there were teeny-weeny bottles of perfume around to improve the air of which there was so little in the relatively large Titania-Palast, that instead of evening dress, a bathing suit would have been more appropriate. Apropos space: the Titania-Palast wasn't a movie house for long. Who knows what has happened to the rows of seats since then.« (Telegraf, June 8, 1951.)

In the auditorium, Senator Tiburtius greeted the guests; then Undersecretary of the Federal Ministry of the Interior Dr. Wende, representing Minister Lehr who had unexpectedly cancelled his appearance, awarded the German Film Prize of 1950. A film compiled of excerpts from films which had been nominated for the Silver Laurel Award established by David O. Selznick set the stage for the awarding of this prize to HERRLICHE ZEITEN (»Wonderful Times«), directed by Erik Ode. The award was accepted by Günter Neumann, the author of the film and leader of the Berliner cabaret show »The Insulaner«.

Mayor Reuter spoke a word of greeting, called Berlin an »oasis of liberty and independence, surrounded by a system of violence and oppression, which uses art for the purpose of propaganda«, and beseeched the city to be »a bastion which the totalitarian powers storm in vain.« Yes, not only the International Film Festival, but also a bit of the self-image of this city divisioned in sectors was presented: in a language harsh and full of slogans.

Joan Fontaine

The opening film was hors concours – Alfred Hitchcock's REBECCA starring Laurence Olivier and Joan Fontaine, who was the most jubilantly received guest of this first Film Festival: her drive from the airport into the city turned into a triumphal procession, reflecting how the Berliners craved for glamour and international prestige. For the time being, the interest of foreign movie-people to put in an appearance in Berlin was not great; which was no wonder considering the still existing resentments against Germany and the newness of the Festival, whose course could not yet be known. Nevertheless some producers, directors, actresses and actors did accompany their films to Berlin: among them the English director Anthony Asquith, Jean Delannoy from France, the Mexican actress Rosaura Revueltas, who played a leading role in the remake of the German film MÄDCHEN IN UNIFORM [Girls in Uniform], and the directors Göran Gentele and Alf Sjöberg, as well as the actress Anita Björk (as FRÖKEN JULIE (»Miss Julie«), though one of the public's favorites, not in the Competition) and Ulf Palme from Sweden. Bernard Blier and Suzy Delair were also among these first guests.

Curzio Malaparte

Another prominent guest was the controversial Italian writer and director Curzio Malaparte, who had been closely affiliated with Italian fascism, and had come to Berlin to present his film IL CRISTO PROIBITO (»Forbidden Christ«). Master in the art of promoting himself, he provided the first small scandal of the Film Festival: at the very first jury session he had his production company put a plate on the table on which was engraved a text which can no longer be given word for word, but which as far as jury member Walther Karsch can remember ran something like: »Grand Prize of the Berlin Film Festival for Curzio Malaparte's film ›Forbidden Christ‹«.

The stars were of course important for the public; yet more important internally, economically and politically, were the representatives of the foreign film associations, whose presence could be seen as indicators of the significance of the Film Festival itself. And here the tendency was clearly towards an interest in the German market on the part of foreign producers and importers.

German entries

Whereas the foreign entries drew applause from the audiences and were written up well in reviews by the critics, the three German entries were received poorly. Not only Erich Engel's DAS SELTSAME LEBEN DES HERRN BRUGGS [The Strange Life of Mr. Bruggs] was a failure, but also Rolf Hansen's DR. HOLL (although it did at least receive an honorary mention for outstanding acting) and TALENT ZUM GLÜCK [A Talent for Happiness] by Helmut Weiß. The co-production DAS GESTOHLENE JAHR [The Stolen Year] caused, as Werner Fiedler wrote, »shrill discord«. This apparently very pompously made film »was received by boos, voices were repeatedly heard calling for the screening to be discontinued, and certain scenes were drowned out by contemptuous laughter. The critical cineast was, however, in no mood for laughter. Rather he was angry at the lack of instinct shown in playing such a film in such an international context.« Fiedler combined his criticism with an appeal to the audience to restrain itself despite the irritation »in consideration of the foreign guests«. »The Competition should not be degraded by a rowdiness which from the outset does not give a film a fair chance.« For: »in the end it is a question of survival for German film productions – a desperate struggle; and the honestly critical person will become more and more distressed as one German movie after another hits bottom.« (Der Tag, June 12, 1951.) German films were having a hard time taking off at the first International Film Festival Berlin: this would remain the case for several years to come. And audiences in Berlin were going to be a ›nightmare‹ for certain German directors.

Margot Hielscher,
Helmut Käutner,
Joan Fontaine

The awards

And the awards? The first Golden Bear went to the Swiss entry by Leopold Lindtberg DIE VIER IM JEEP (»Four in a Jeep«) (category dramatic film), further Golden Bears were awarded to SANS LAISSER D'ADRESSE [Without Leaving an Address] from France for the best comedy (directed by Jean-Paul Le Chanois), André Cayatte's JUSTICE EST FAITE (»Justice is Done«) for the category crime and adventure film; best musical was the Disney production CINDERELLA, which also received the Audiences' Choice Award; the Golden Bear for the best documentary film went to a Disney production as well, BEAVER VALLEY. In the »Tagesspiegel«, Karl Walther Kluger came to the following critical conclusions: »It is not all that easy to criticize the decisions of the jury, as they have had to keep to the assigned categories, which were not able to do justice to the films presented, and if we look at the distribution of the awards more closely, it was in some instances a case of rape by a very inflexible system. If,

IL CAMMINO DELLA SPERANZA (»The Path of Hope«): a scene with Raf Vallone

REBECCA: Joan Fontaine, Judith Anderson

The Awards of the German Jury

Feature Films
Dramatic Films
Golden Berlin Bear
DIE VIER IM JEEP
Switzerland, directed by Leopold Lindtberg

Silver Berlin Bear
IL CAMMINO DELLA SPERANZA
Italy, directed by Pietro Germi

Bronze Berlin Bear
THE BROWNING VERSION
Great Britain, directed by Anthony Asquith

Comedies
Golden Berlin Bear
SANS LAISSER D'ADRESSE
France, directed by Jean-Paul Le Chanois

Silver Berlin Bear
LEVA PA »HOPPET«
Sweden, directed by Göran Gentele

Bronze Berlin Bear
THE MATING SEASON, USA
directed by Mitchell Leisen

instead of creating rigid categories – dramatic films, comedies, crime and adventure films, and musicals – the jury had been given four Golden, four Silver and four Bronze prizes to award, the results would have been more satisfying and more individualistic.« (June 19, 1951.)

The Film Festival was a hit with Berliners. They cast their ballots and flocked to the larger events in the Waldbühne and at the Funkturm (radio tower and city landmark). The open-air screening of DAS SELTSAME LEBEN DES HERRN BRUGGS was one of the entertaining weekend events in June. Gustav Fröhlich greeted the audience, Bruno Fritz moderated the program, Gustav Knuth, Carl Ludwig Diehl, Dorothea Wieck, Jakob Tiedtke and Carsta Löck were also on hand. The »Black-Watch« Regiment Bagpipers played, and as a finale there were fireworks. The following Sunday afternoon, at 3:30 p.m. in the »Sommergarten am Funkturm«, one could for 1.50 Marks (East or West) marvel at the »International Star Revue« with more than »300 actors and actresses from inland and abroad«. The highlights of the program were a grand performance of the City Opera Ballet which danced Johann Strauss' Emperor Waltz, the numbers sung by the soloists Gretl Theimer, Ilse Hülper, Margot Hielscher, Margarete Slezak and the Sunshine Quartet; and then there was a parade with flower-covered cars which was expected to arrive at 4:20 p.m. at the Funkturm after having travelled half way through the city – from the Gedächtnis-Kirche (Memorial Church) to the Südstern, from the Platz der Luftbrücke (both large squares) to Rathaus Steglitz (district town hall), from the Bundesallee (main avenue) to the Halenseebrücke (a bridge). Around 30 000 film enthusiasts had not wanted to miss these special events. As Dora Fehling had written: Berlin had gone crazy!

Yet, it was also this same audience that exhibited a political alertness in regard to the films; in listing a few details, »Zeitgeist« becomes tangible: »... it was neither the selection of interesting films, nor the open response of the audience, neither the big

laughs, nor the spirited demonstrations of displeasure which I had especially appreciated. The likes of these can be found elsewhere as well. Unique was: this spontaneous, thundering, demonstrative applause for all scenes showing man in his dignity and in freedom. More precisely: a French patrolman lets some poor Italian immigrants cross the border… (CAMMINO DELLA SPERANZA) - a white person asks a black: ›Shall we be friends?‹… (BRIGHT VICTORY) - a French-woman makes it absolutely plain to some fellow countrymen who have come on a house search what is to be thought of such authorized measures… (DIE VIER IM JEEP) - and each time the audience broke out into a roar of applause and loud cheers, powerful, long and from the heart.« (Edmund Luft: Applaus für die Berliner; in Filmblätter, No. 25, May 22, 1951.)

Nevertheless, the problems of the IFB due to the political situation of the city and the conflicting interests of the four victorious powers must also be mentioned. Ernst Reuter's emotional words of greeting at the opening night of the International Film Festival Berlin had indisputably shown the boundaries, established the limits. A commentary printed in the East Berlin »Tägliche Rundschau« on June 23rd, although ideologically in contrast, is similarly pointed. Entitled »West Berlin's decadent film-facade«, the adjective »international« which had been used »even though one had restricted participation to films from Western countries« was treated with irony.

The judgement passed on West German films was particularly harsh: »terribly low-level.« And the article continues with: »West Berlin films have given clear proof of the state of affairs of film production in capitalistic countries, especially of the situation in a country occupied by Americans: decadent in content, with petit-bourgeois and placating sentimentality, monstrously dollied-up kitsch, anti-soviet tendencies and warmongering, nihilistic emptiness and pathological excesses.«

Crime and Adventure Films
Golden Berlin Bear
JUSTICE EST FAITE
France, directed by
André Cayatte

Silver Berlin Bear
- not awarded -

Bronze Berlin Bear
DESTINATION MOON
USA, directed by
Irving Pichel

Musicals
Golden Berlin Bear
CINDERELLA
USA, a Walt Disney production

Silver Berlin Bear
TALES OF HOFFMANN
Great Britain, directed by
Michael Powell,
Emeric Pressburger

Long Documentary Films
Golden Berlin Bear
BEAVER VALLEY, USA,
a Walt Disney production

Silver Berlin Bear
- not awarded -

Bronze Berlin Bear
THE UNDEFEATED
Great Britain

Special Prizes of the City of Berlin for outstanding achievements in film

IL CRISTO PROIBITO
Italy, directed by
Curzio Malaparte

DIEU A BESOIN DES HOMMES
France, directed by
Jean Delannoy

Honorable Mention
DR. HOLL
FRG, directed by
Rolf Hansen

Audiences' Choice

Large Bronze Plate
CINDERELLA, USA

Small Bronze Plate
THE BROWNING VERSION
Great Britain

Die Vier im Jeep: Viveca Lindfors, Ralph Meeker

In retrospect: no matter how contrary the points of view were in East and West, and even if no one wanted to admit to some degree of agreement in their verdicts, there was a consensus in writing up a balance of this first Film Festival. Senator Tiburtius stated: »The apparently low standard of German films in comparison to foreign works will be the topic of much discussion. I refuse to believe that this situation has been caused by economic problems alone, however urgently these may be felt. The artistic formulae we are used to employing in our studios no longer work. We have once again been given absolute proof.« (Festival-Bulletin 10/11, 1951.) These arguments could have formed the basis for a dialogue, but such a dialogue was still a long way off.

After the success of this first Film Festival, the organizers and the Berlin Senate began considering year Number Two. A start had been made.

The setting

In the first year of the International Film Festival Berlin, the German film industry was in the middle of a serious crisis, for which there were several causes. The film business in Berlin was affected as well.

Nearly all of the production facilities had been destroyed or damaged during the war; those which had survived were later confiscated or dismantled. In the Eastern Sector of the city, under the supervision of the Soviets, the Defa was founded; in the Western Sectors the studios were quite make-shift. Until well into the fifties, it was only possible to work in two studio-complexes: one in Tempelhof, Oberlandstrasse 29-34, in which »Studio 45« under the direction of Ernst Hasselbach and Alfred Schönnenbeck began production in 1945; and the other, in C.C.C. (Central Cinema Company GmbH)-Atelier at Verlängerte Daumstrasse 16 in Spandau-Haselhorst, for which Artur Brauner had received a license in 1946, but did not begin business until 1949.

The situation of the film industry in Berlin after the war was closely related to the role that the Ufa-concern had played in the thirties and forties. In 1942, Joseph Goebbels had restructured Ufa Syndicates, bringing it together under the parent organization Ufa-Film GmbH. The German film industry had thus been coordinated and nationalized.

After the war a solution for the property of the Ufa had to be found. All property in possession or under the control of the German Reich on May 8th 1945, and had been used for the production, distribution, and screening of films, or other related activities, was, for the time being, confiscated – as was the case with all property of the Reich – by the military government of the Allies. Military Law Number 52 subjected the property involved to the »confiscation, direction, administration, supervision or to other controls« by the military government. For the enforcement of Law Number 52, Property Control Branches (in the American and British zones), and the Department Contrôle des Biens (in the French zone) were formed by the indiviual military governments. For administrative tasks associated with the former property of the Ufa, German trustees were appointed. In an attempt to lessen confusion, the Ufa-Film GmbH was also called the Ufi.

The reestablishment of a German (and Berlin) film industry was not only a question of capital, but also one of structure and organization. The Ufa-concern was a strictly »vertically« constructed multi: production, printing, and synchronization facilities, distribution, movie houses and other enterprises (technical laboratories, and publishing house) were all part of an integrated network. As a result, a taut economic and political management was possible.

The concern's integrated organizational system must have been greatly disliked by the Allies, especially its political dimension. It was above all the Americans who pursued the decartelization of this industrial political power. The so called »Monopoly Ordinance No. 1« prohibited any sort of concentration of economic power. Step by step, the assets of the Ufa/Ufi were to be liquidated, the different branches decentralized. In accordance with the allied democratizing policy, the old Ufa-concern was to be dissolved; naturally, solid economic interests on the part of the Allies also played a role.

On September 28th 1949 Ernst Reuter, received an order »concerning the property of the film industry once belonging to the Reich« from the Allied Kommandatura

(BK/O(49) 206; O stands for »order«). In this order the »ownership of the property found in Greater Berlin, which had belonged to or been under the control of the German Reich on May 8th 1945, and had been used for the production, marketing and screening of films (...) or in connection with the like«, was handed over to a »liquidation committee«, acting as trustees. The essence of this order: All property of the former Ufa-concern was to be disposed of within 18 months to the highest bidder. A few terms of sale were set, one of which was that the authorities, civil servants and other government employees, political parties, and non-rehabilitated Nazis, the liquidators themselves (if still in office) and investment groups with more than 25% foreign holdings, were excluded from the auction.

This order was received by the German authorities with resistance. An SPD petition, in which the Federal Government was asked to examine this law and to use all legal means for invoking a revision, was supported unanimously by the Bundestag. In Berlin at the beginning of October, the city government commissioned a committee to investigate the effects of the order and decided on April 3rd 1950 »to contact the responsible authorities of the Allies, in order to bring about the participation of the German authorites in the liquidation of the property of the Ufa, and in particular the consultation of representatives of the city government by the liquidation committee«.

The city wanted to guarantee that it would have a say in the redistribution of Ufa property, which brought it into a conflict of interests with the Spio in Berlin: it suspected the city of aiming at »a cold socializiation«, i. e., a government-run Berlin film industry. The city on the other hand feared a further exodus of the employees of the film industry and of the industry itself to West Germany, where – at least from Berlin's point of view – an alarming concentration of film capital had already accumulated.

BK/O (49) 206 was replaced about a year later, on September 30th 1950 (coming into force on October 20th) by Law Number 10: »concerning the disposal of property previously having belonged to the Reich«. It did, though, not differ greatly from the order which had been in effect until then. Instead of a liquidation committee, there was now a »decentralization committee« which was to be made up of three or more German citizens appointed by the Allied Kommandatura« and instructed »to dispose of all property falling under this law by January 1st 1952«.

New was that the German authorities were given a certain advisory role. In a letter (BK/L (50) 130, L stands for »letter«) to Ernst Reuter from the September 30th 1950, the presiding Chief of Staff of the Allied Kommandatura Berlin (AKB), Commandant Gaugain, announced that the formation of a »German committee for the reorganization of the motion picture industry« was planned; the Chancellor of the Federal Republic of Germany was requested to name ten delegates for this committee. Two delegates were to come from Berlin.

The first conference between the newly formed German Film Industry Reorganization Advisory Committee (GFRAC) and the Film Industry Reorganization Committee (FRC) of the Allied Forces was held on January 30th 1951 at the Petersberg, residence of the Allied High Commission. At this conference, the Film Festival Berlin came up. That is the chairman, British Film Officer Dow, asked, »if West Berlin should be granted a loan out of the assets of the Ufa to the amount of DM 50 000 to finance a film festival which was to take place in June 1951«. (Memorandum of the Federal Minister of Economic Affairs, Gesch.-No. IB7, Feb. 2, 1951.)

At the subsequent meeting of the GFRAC, producer Georg Witt and distributor Herbert Tischendorf spoke out against a loan, »as it would not be possible to show any new and remarkable German films in June«. Hence, Witt proclaimed, the association of producers would not take part in the film festival, moreover »it would virtually only serve the purpose of propagating foreign films« (Minutes of the meeting). It was only after the intervention of the delegates from Berlin, who stressed the significance of a film festival for West Berlin, that the committee decided to grant the loan, »on condition that the amount of the loan would be repaid in full, even if, in the course of the festival, a deficit should show«.

Yet the disputes caused by the winding-up or the restitution of the one time Ufa-concern were still long from over. The intended liquidation of Ufa/Ufi property was not successful. The so called »Lex Ufa (Ufi)«, that is Order Number 52 of the Allies, was replaced by a corresponding German law on June 6th 1953, which seemed to take the demands of the Allies into account, but in fact encouraged the re-integration of the Ufa; by 1956, it had been absorbed by a syndicate under the direction of the Deutsche Bank and re-consolidated under two parent corporations, »Universum-Film AG« and »Ufa-Theater AG«.

The hopes of the German film industry of receiving financial aid out of the Ufa/Ufi assets were not fulfilled. The economic situation grew even more critical for two other reasons; they could be labelled »regulation of quotas« and »fixation of quotas« – for the interest of the Allies was not exclusively – as stated in the preamble of BK/O (49) 206 – in the »stimulation of a healthy, democratic and privately owned film industry«. (The word »democratic« was then nowhere to be found in the actual text of the law.) Their interest was also determined by a healthy, privately owned American film industry. For this reason, the German film industry continued to plead for a regulation of quotas. Similarly as practised in other European countries, the number of imported foreign films could be regulated annually by the government.

Sehr gut 12. Juni 1951

Gut 12. Juni 1951

INTERNATIONALE FILMFESTSPIELE BERLIN

6.-17. Juni 1951

Publikums-Abstimmung.

Die vier perforierten Ecken tragen die Bezeichnung

„sehr gut" „gut" „mäßig" „schlecht".

Trennen Sie bitte die Ecke ab, die nach Ihrer Meinung auf den Film zutrifft und werfen Sie bitte die abgetrennte Ecke am Ausgang in die bereitgestellten Abstimm-Urnen.

Am Schluß der Filmfestspiele werden zwei Preise für die publikumswirksamsten Filme vergeben, die Sie durch diese Abstimmung ermitteln.

Wir danken Ihnen für Ihre freundliche Mühewaltung.

DAS ORGANISATIONSKOMITEE

Schlecht 12. Juni 1951

Mäßig 12. Juni 1951

The audience's ballot

Tatjana Sais presents one of the first Golden Bears.

And lastly, the Berlin film industry had been particularly badly affected by the nearly one year long Soviet blockade of land routes and water ways from the Federal Republic of Germany to Berlin in 1948/49. The political situation and the drastic shortage of energy led to many producers renting studios in West Germany. For a short time, the Berlin film industry came to an almost complete standstill; films produced during the blockade in Berlin began by showing a Berlin Bear in chains, a forceful metaphor of Berlin's will to survive.

It is in this context that the reservations of the Spitzenorganisation der deutschen Filmwirtschaft (Spio) to the establishment of the International Film Festival are to be seen (and are perhaps then not incomprehensible). Walter Koppel spoke of an »international ordinance apparatus«, which was stifling the competitive capacity of German film production. Consequently the situation remained as follows, at least for this first year: the Spio would not officially participate in the Film Festival, and yet at the same time, it would not - although it could have - stand in its way.

The second summer

1952

June 12th–25th, 1952

He inspired one with courage; he believed in a German film renaissance: Billy Wilder – totally unmistakable, with his cap, and friendly banter. »If we can help a bit, that would be wonderful. The whole world is waiting for a German film«, he remarked in a talk with a reporter from the »Welt«. »When they begin copying Hollywood, then it's all over.« (June 22, 1952.)

So far no one had wanted to put in a good word for the German Festival entries. Rather, it was regretted that so few American films were participating, for which there were reasons. Originally the Americans had wanted to show Anatole Litvak's DECISION BEFORE DAWN in Berlin, but had withdrawn it after the Bavarian government had intervened during the shooting and insinuated that the film was anti-German. And then there was the so-called »Welles Affair«. During a visit in 1950, Orson Welles had been critical of attitudes in Germany. Therefore, when during the planning of the second International Film Festival the possibility of inviting Orson Welles' OTHELLO came up, a controversy broke out in the committee (4th meeting,

The Orson Welles affair

Eva-Ingeborg Scholz, Siegfried Breuer, Françoise Rosay

Billy Wilder with his wife, Judith Eribe, and William Holden with his wife, Brenda Marshall. To the left behind them, Rhada from India, leading actress in THE RIVER

The Festival's first home in the city, the Delphi movie house on Kantstraße

May 23, 1952). These comments of the director, it was felt, had been anti-German. Only after long deliberation was the decision made to send an invitation, which Welles however declined. Nonetheless, on the evening of June 12th when Reuter and Senator Tiburtius opened the 2nd International Film Festival in the Delphi-Kino, the turbulences of the planning stage, the internal difficulties and the external power struggles were a thing of the past. It was clear that, despite a few points of disagreement, the Senate's policy towards the Festival had become stable, Alfred Bauer's position established more firmly and the whole organizational structure solidified.

The success of the première in 1951 had been registered favorably by the Senate. Bauer had presented a program which could hold its own with the already established film festivals; Berlin had made the headlines, and the population had played its part enthusiastically. Yet as everyone involved realized, without the cooperation of producers and in particular of the FIAPF, it was not possible in the long run to establish the Film Festival. Which meant the rigid attitude of the Spio would have to be worked on. Bauer had tried as early as July 1951 to get support for the 1952 Film Festival from Renato Gualino, President of the FIAPF. Gualino called his attention to the next FIAPF conference during the Biennale in Venice, at which the question of the number of festivals in the coming year to receive official support from the FIAPF would be decided. He recommended informing the German delegation of producers and having them represent Berlin's interests. Not that anyone expected Berlin to be given equal status to Cannes and Venice. In fact, the FIAPF had already, a year earlier, agreed on allowing only one festival of the so-called »A-category« (officially this term does not exist in the FIAPF regulations), namely Cannes; if two had been allowed, the other would certainly not have been Berlin. Yet for Berliners what primarily mattered was to win the favor of the international parent organization (i. e. the FIAPF) and hereby influence producers at home and abroad.

Pokering for the backing of the Spio

Senator Tiburtius therefore appealed at the beginning of August to the two German representatives to the FIAPF conference, Dr. Günter Schwarz and Dr. H. B. Baum, from the Verband deutscher Filmproduzenten e. V. (the association of German film producers); and to back them, to Dr. Lüders from the Federal Ministry of Economic Affairs, who belonged to the delegation from the side of the government, as well as to the influential chairman of the Freiwillige Selbstkontrolle der Filmwirtschaft (board for the voluntary control of standards in the film industry) Fritz Podehl – all in Wiesbaden. It was indeed a curiously roundabout route which was necessary here: to attain the support of the Spio, Tiburtius availed to the FIAPF, which in turn referred him back to the Spio.

Schwarz's and Baum's stance was not as harshly unfavorable as in the year before; even though Baum openly demanded direct »subsidies instead of guarantees and loans«, promising in return »between three and five German films of exceptional content and form in the course of each year of production«, Schwarz in his reply assured Tiburtius, that he would plead for the approval of the application of the International Film Festival Berlin 1952 in Venice and did in fact see to it being put on the agenda of the general assembly.

The congress met on September 4th 1951. Its most important decision: »The general assembly has examined (...) the situation of all film-related events in 1952 and has decided to officially recognize for 1952, the international festival in Cannes, planned for the month of April, and the film show in Venice, to take place in August. And for the others: »As far as the remaining film events are concerned, the general assembly of the International Federation of Film Producers has endorsed a formal request asking its members to appeal to their respective governments or other interested parties, in order to make sure that no further film events having an international competition are held. Accordingly, all members are requested to participate only at those events not having the character of a competition.«

On the one hand, the FIAPF definitely tended towards a restrictive policy allowing only one festival with an international jury and awards, yet on the other hand, it had agreed, out of consideration for the tradition and advanced stage of planning of the events in Cannes and Venice, to allow two in 1952; at the same time though, it did recommend the governments of France and Italy to negotiate bilaterally on the organization of one single festival of this kind for 1953.

Consolation for the »Berlinale« from the FIAPF

For Berlin there was a consolation. The resolution explicitly stated: »Subject to the foregoing regulations, the festival of the City of Berlin has been approved.« Dr. Schwarz, it appears, had represented Berlin's interests with verve. As a consequence these decisions meant for the IFB: if Berlin dispensed with a jury and the presentation of awards, the producers would then have no objections to a continuation of the Berlin Film Festival.

All that was still lacking then was the official backing, that is of parliament, in the city of the Festival itself: a backing which could only be obtained through decrees - of the Senate, of parliamentary committees, and of the House of Representatives. Senate Bill 1212, drawn up at a session on December 10th 1951, passed on to the Committee of Education on December 20th by the House of Representatives at their 31st (ordinary) and 32nd (extraordinary) sessions, and approved by them after some revisions on January 17th 1952, introduced some changes and innovations to the original concept. The first estimate, which had been made already in early November 1951, had set the finances at DM 180 000 each for revenues and expenses, of which the Senate was to put up DM 90 000. This proposal was rejected and reduced by DM 20 000, affecting in particular the funds reserved for promotion activities; the Senate subsidy was in other words cut to DM 70 000.

The change with the most far-reaching consequences was that brought about by the Education Committee. At first a relatively small working committee was envisaged which was to include:

- the directors of the Department of Education, of Finance, as well es Economics and Nutrition;
- representatives of the allied military governments and
- representatives of the film industry associations.

But the interest of diverse associations in the Film Festival had meanwhile been aroused. A number of »socially relevant groups«, such as the German Trade Union Federation (DGB), had approached the Senator and complained to the fact that they had not been invited to participate in the preparation and arrangements for the Festival. The Senate finally gave way to the lobbyists. In 1952 a new feature was that a bill for the House of Representatives provided for the involvement of a representative of the DGB as well as delegates of the association of critics and the association of employees of the film industry in the organizational committee; even a representative of the Senator for Traffic and Public Enterprises worked his way into the committee. Finally the parties also made their demands known so that three members of the House of Representatives were proposed for the organizational committee.

However, that was not enough either. Although the Education Committee recommended to the House of Representatives that it votes for the bill, this was linked »with the proviso that the number of deputies to be elected to the organizational committee should be raised from three to seven, and, moreover, that a representative of the Freie Volksbühne should belong to this organizational committee«. (Resolution of Jan. 2, 1952, document of the Berlin House of Representatives, No. 851, issued on Jan. 12, 1952.)

The organizational committee had been considerably enlarged. At its first regular meeting on February 15th 1952, 25 men and women met in the offices of the Department of Education, Messedamm 4-6 in Charlottenburg:

- Senator Tiburtius as chairman;
- Dr. Hans Cürlis for the documentary film producers' association and the Spio Berlin;
- Ferdinand Buttkus (Allianz/Pallas) for the distributors' association;
- Karl Jacob (Marmorhaus) for the movie house association;
- Adolf Kandziora for the association of film technics enterprises;
- D. C. Travis, Chief Information Service Branch, HICOG;
- Oscar Martay, Film Officer of the ISB, HICOG;
- Mr. Kessler, British Information Service;
- Hilde Lucht-Perske, MHR (Member of the House of Rep.) (SPD);
- Willi Hübner, MHR (SPD);
- Albert Horlitz, MHR (SPD);
- Wilhelm Padberg, MHR (CDU);
- Ruth Hahn von Dorsche, MHR (FDP);
- Wilhelm Bennecke, MHR (FDP);
- Professor Kurt Landsberg for the Freie Volksbühne;
- Thea von Harbou for the association of employees of the film industry;
- Ernst Walter David for Berlin's press association;
- Dr. Hans Hirschfeld, head of the Senate Press and Information Services Office;
- Friedrich Lange, supervisor in the Department of Finances;
- Heinz Schneider from the Department of Traffic and Public Enterprises;
- Dr. Franz Wallner-Basté from the Department of Education;
- Mr. Hartmann from the Department of Education;
- Reinhard Elsner from the Department of Education;
- Theodor Baensch, head of the Film Section of the Department of Education;
- Dr. Alfred Bauer as managing director of the International Film Festival.

Despite the large committee: the realities of the situation determined the course of events. In the committee much was discussed, but little decided. The organizational work was in the end accomplished by Alfred Bauer. He prepared the decisions which the committee later made.

Festival movie houses

One of the main points debated and then decided concerned the new Festival movie house, or rather new Festival movie houses. They were unanimously dissatisfied with the Titania-Palast in Steglitz with its some 2000 seats, and needed two movie houses to replace it, if revenues were to remain at about the same level as in the previous year. Besides, most were interested – especially in film industry circles – in bringing the Festival to the Kurfürstendamm. The proximity of the movie houses to the organizational offices of the Festival which had been moved to Budapester Str. 23 in April was another argument. At the beginning of February,

Bauer wrote a paper with the sole purpose of weighing the pros and cons, and came to the conclusion that the Delphi in the Kantstraße, quite near the Kurfürstendamm, and the Capitol at Lehniner Platz (built by Mendelsohn, once the Universum movie house and today the residence of the Schaubühne theater) were the most suitable and in addition promised to bring in higher returns. The committee followed Bauer's suggestion: the new locations for the Festival had been found.

There were debates as well on the topic of screenings in so-called peripheral or district movie houses. The Christian Democratic Senator was enthusiastic about the idea of showing the films after the Festival in the districts of Wedding and Neukölln.

The Capitol
at Lehniner Platz

Bauer objected to this proposal and with him the representatives of the film industry. First of all, he argued, it was not usual to show the films other than in the Festival movie houses; secondly, the producers, who made their films available free of charge, would suffer losses from a further showing; and thirdly, the Festival budget would be burdened by additional expenses with which were not originally calculated. The minutes of the 1st meeting on February 15th record Tiburtius' dismissal of these objections: »The Senator was of the opinion that a way must be found to overcome these problems.« After a heated discussion, he specified his interests in »that it be, after all, a political necessity to bring the Festival to the workers' districts«.

Although it is true that the Senator's concept was carried out, the screenings in Wedding (Corso am Gesundbrunnen) and in Neukölln (Metro-Palast) were more or less token-showings. Furthermore, in the committee itself the discussion arose as to which films, even though they did not have the consent of any of the producers yet, could be shown to a »workers' audience« in these districts; one was of the opinion that Vittorio De Sica's Miracolo a Milano (»Miracle in Milan«) was not appropriate. As a result, movie fans in Neukölln were able to see Gino Cervi and Gina Lollobrigida in Moglie per una notte (»Bride for a Night«) by Franco Brusati, and the audiences in Wedding, Erich Engel's Die Stimme des Anderen [The Other One's Voice] (which ran later under the title of »Unter den tausend Laternen«), as well as Un grand patron (»A Big Boss«) by Yves Ciampi.

Alfred Bauer appoints a press spokesman.

The 2nd International Film Festival was coming up soon and the position of press spokesman was still vacant. Many different names came up at the committee's meetings, including: Dr. Fritz Olimsky, formerly film critic for the »Berliner Börsen-Zeitung« and employee of the Deutsche Presseagentur; Dr. Wilfert from the »Tagesspiegel« or Karl-Heinz Bergmann from the Berlin Film-Club; Jochen Severin, who had already done press work for the IFB in 1951; the film journalist Edith Hamann or the critic Georg Herzberg, previously editor of the »Film-Kurier« and

Miracolo a Milano: a scene with Francesco Golisano (on the left)

then on the editorial staff of the »Film-Echo«. The committee's members were not able to agree on one candidate, and were therefore all the more surprised and a bit annoyed when Bauer, without any further consultation, chose Georg Herzberg and confronted them with a fait accompli. Yet it can be presumed, if one judges from the debates in the minutes, that the IFB would have had to do without a press spokesman, if Bauer had waited for the decision of the committee. For instance the following conflict about Karl-Heinz Bergmann was unpleasant and typical of the times: Bergmann had been a member of the board of the Defa (association of East German film enterprises), a fact one did not want to ignore at this time. Yet, first he was promised the vacant position, and then put off for a month. By the time the month was over, Herzberg was already on the job. The German critics' association intervened and a position was found for Bergmann, who was made responsible for all secondary events. The third man at Bauer's side was again Herbert Weidner, who, as in the year before, was in charge of mass events, as well as of publicity.

Hon dansade en sommar: Folke Sundquist, Ulla Jacobsson

RASHOMON: Toshiro Mifune, Machiko Kyo

HON DANSADE EN SOMMAR
»One enjoys letting oneself be captivated again here by the love of a student to a country girl, by the magic of a midsummer's night and the beautiful harmony of Northern nature to the straightforward events told in the subdued tone of a ballad. One is even pleased with the disturbing chastity to be found in those daring scenes showing, for example, a naked couple bathing and accepts, as fitting to the context, the village pastor who wants to have nothing to do with such modern adolescents.«
Walter Lennig in:
Der Tagessspiegel,
Juñe 21, 1952.

Unfortunately the weather at the open-air events was not very acquiescing. It rained, it was unpleasantly cool, so that the public did not crowd to the picture shows in the Waldbühne as had been hoped; the Waldbühne was merely a fifth full. Only at the concert, which the Film Festival had sponsored with the RIAS (»Radio in the American Sector«) was there a full house. On that day the sun was even accommodating, so that film director Robert A. Stemmle was able to take the outdoor shots for his musical HEIMWEH NACH DIR [Homesick for You]. When the Festival came to an end on Wednesday June 25th 1952, everyone agreed – despite all criticisms to details – on one thing: the Festival should be continued. There had been no jury that year; the awards were determined by the audiences. The Golden Berlin Bear went to the Swedish film HON DANSADE EN SOMMAR (»One Summer of Happiness«) (which had a nude scene felt to be extremely indecent). To Akira Kurosawa's RASHOMON, as well as to Jean Renoir's India film THE RIVER, the public paid little attention. One was interested in stars, and preferred light entertainment; one did not have an eye for the unknown. Even the West German critics only registered RASHOMON and THE RIVER in passing.

To mention the setting of another event: for the first time a film fair was held, which was, at this point, initiated and managed by the Berlin film industry itself, in the Studio at Lehniner Platz (a small cinema in the Mendelsohn building), from June 16th–24th. This first fair must be seen as the beginnings of this important branch of the IFB.

At the 6th meeting of the organizational committee on July 10th, shortly after the Festival, the members were unanimously of the opinion that they had been successful in their work. Yet, at the same time, they agreed that the Festival had lasted too long. Senator Tiburtius reported on the effects he had observed this to have:

The River: Patricia Walters, Rhada, Arthur Shields

Visiting East Berlin: yes or no?

when too much time elapsed between events, then some of the visitors simply went to the Defa and saw films there. »There is«, the minutes of the meeting record, »nothing to say against visiting the Eastern Sector, it is even welcomed, and yet it must be the responsibility of the Festival to give the audience direction and to keep them occupied.« Friedrich Luft described the problem similarly in his final resumée: »The visiting journalists were given so little to do, that out of pure curiosity, invitations in their pockets, they spent much time at the Defa. The events had in no way formed a whole; there was neither a center nor a place for friendly exchanges between the participants to crystallize.« (Neue Zeitung Berlin, June 27, 1952.) And yet the Senate itself was, in fact, considering officially arranging showings of Defa films. Then again, the harshness of the situation can be best seen in the following: »Independently from the actual Film Festival program, the Federal Ministry of All-German Affairs showed the press in the documentary Film hinter dem Eisernen Vorhang [Film behind the Iron Curtain], an informative arrangement of cuts from feature films and newsreels from Soviet Russian and East German Defa productions, hereby giving insight into the Soviet Russian methods of propaganda.« (Alfred Bauer in the final report of the 2nd IFB.)

The Festival closed with returns of DM 202 554.22 and an outlay of DM 220 324.47, that is, with a deficit of about DM 17770, which was covered by the promised deficiency guarantee of up to DM 30 000 from the Allies. As a result of the budget having been overdrawn rather heavily, appropriation for 1953 was set at DM 213 000, of which the Senate was to take part with a subsidy of DM 100 000. This time DM 20 000 was made immediately available for the management. These decisions received final approval from the House of Representatives at its 60th (ordinary) session on December 18th.

Audiences' Choice

Golden Berlin Bear
HON DANSADE EN SOMMAR
Sweden, directed by
Arne Mattson

Silver Berlin Bear
FANFAN, LA TULIPE
France, directed by
Christian-Jaque

Bronze Berlin Bear
CRY THE BELOVED COUNTRY
Great Britain, directed by
Zoltan Korda

Even those who had been participants themselves, could not help but notice the unfortunate role the organizational committee had played. They came to the conclusion that for 1953 two bodies having separate spheres of competence should be established: an advisory board with seven members from the House of Representatives and the Departments of Education, Finances, Economic Affairs, Nutrition, Traffic and Public Enterprises; and a working committee made up of members from the advisory board and »a selection of experts, as suggested by the Senator of Education who is the responsible person in charge.«

FANFAN, LA TULIPE:
Gérard Philipe

Alfred Bauer resigns

1953

June 18th–28th, 1953

Gary Cooper in Berlin

The Waldbühne. A warm summer night. In a tuxedo and a neat bow tie, in his left hand a small Berlin Bear, in his right a long matchstick: the Hollywood star. A Berlin policeman, in those days with a shako, lights the match. Thousands are already burning. Charming and lanky, Gary Cooper, who had come to Berlin with his wife, daughter and mother-in-law, put in an appearance. A portrait of a family and a star in one, or: the Western hero as gentleman. Hannerl Matz, Margot Hielscher and Barbara Rütting had their photos taken with him, and Berliners crowded round hunting for autographs. Excitement was caused by Cooper's meeting with union members and his clear statements to the domestic political situation in the USA. Without flinching, he condemned McCarthy's »hunt on communists«. Cooper himself had been in Germany once before in 1938, and the degree of surveillance then he found reminiscent of the prevailing climate in the States. His words were clear, and that did not only make him friends in the Federal Republic of Germany.

Political uprising in East Berlin

Yet, during the 3rd Film Festival, sensational appearances were a rarity. Instead the mood was quite subdued. On June, 17th 1953, on the evening before the Festival's opening gala, there had been a riot, a political uprising, in the Eastern Sector of Berlin. As a result, the city was charged with tension, and the atmosphere at the opening of the IFB depressing. Yet, aside from a few short notice cancellations, in particular from abroad, and of the planned reception for the Senate (the money from which was instead donated to charities), the evening remained as planned. In his opening speech, Senator Tiburtius spoke in memory of those killed in the uprising, and prayed for the effect of film in bringing an understanding between nations. The course of events of the Festival itself was hardly affected. However, attendance from the Eastern Sector did fall drastically, causing heavy losses. »If«, as Bauer stated in his final report, »the Eastern population had not been prevented from attending events by a ban on border traffic, (20% of seating had been calculated for fans from the East) the number of visitors originally estimated would certainly have been attained (...) Poor attendance at the B.T.L. (cinema on Potsdamer Strasse), which had been rented exclusively to accommodate residents of the East, can be attributed to the closing off of the border.«

Truly causing a sensation was Minister of the Interior Lehr's cancellation of his appearance at the Film Festival for the third time, and that his replacement, Undersecretary Bleek, had to award the German Film Prize at the opening ceremony. This incident was noted by many and met with the mistrust common to Berliners in those days to all matters concerning the bonds between the City of Berlin and West Germany. In an unusually biting letter, the Spio Berlin, for example, criticized the absence of the Minister, who in turn immediately, although somewhat nonchalantly, justified his behavior with »the difficult and significant negotiations on electoral law« in Parliament in Bonn. Still a bit pressed for justification, Lehr tried, in a letter to Tiburtius, to explain his absence, and expressed regret at having been detained »in exactly those days of the past week which have been so fatefully significant for Berlin and Germany as a whole.« Lehr expressedly points out that he would welcome a continuation of the awarding of the Federal Film Prize during the Film Festival as »proof of the close and indissoluble ties between the City of Berlin and the Federal Republic of Germany« (Letter from the Minister, June 25, 1953).

If one gives credence to commentaries in the press and to observers, routine was making itself felt for the first time. That which had been earlier received with criticism, i. e. the initial insecurities of the organization, was almost longed for at this stage. Friedrich Luft wistfully lamented the »improvised spirit« of the first Film Festival. General opinion of the quality of the program was also reserved. Here a few lasting impressions: the brutal realism of the Brazilian film O Cangaceiro [The Bandit], shocking and unnerving; an elegiac love story from Japan of a romance on the edge of town – Entotsu no mieru basho [Where Chimneys are Seen], giving a feeling for one style of Japanese cinema; and the other: Sengoku Burai [Soldiers], using historical material in the tradition of Kurosawa's samurai films; Jacques Tati in Les Vacances de Monsieur Hulot (»Mr. Hulot's Vacation«), much more than the mere »Chaplinesque playfulness« seen by contemporary critics, but rather the comic assertion of an innocent intelligence in a malcontent world; and the pessimistic and coarse men's film Le Salaire de la peur (»The Wages of Fear«) with Charles Vanel, Yves Montand, Peter van Eyck and Folco Lulli, which received as Audiences' Choice the Golden Berlin Bear, that is, that Bear which had been newly created by the sculptress Renée Sintenis. The Special Prize of the Berlin Senate was awarded by an international jury of delegates, whose members were from those countries who had entered full-length feature films in the Festival – also a première. Three films »best fulfilling the ideals of a world oriented towards freedom« received the prize: Elia Kazan's Man on a Tightrope, telling of the flight of a Czech circus director to the West (in reality a »cold war« film), Luigi Zampa's Processo alla città [City on Trial] about the corruption of law and society, and Heinosuke Gosho's Entotsu no mieru basho. Post scriptum, but still of importance, a reference to an African film, which was entered in the Competition by the Gold Coast: Sean Graham's The Boy Kumansenu, a story told in an almost documentary style, about a young black man who, having grown up in a village, has to learn to hold his own in the city; the film was an outsider which, irritating and forlorn within the framework of the Festival program, attracted the attention of a few critics.

Le Salaire de la peur
»This film is without a ray of hope for the humanitarian. It is, no matter how brillantly conceived and then executed – basically inhuman (...) A cold-bloodedly filmed thriller, aiming for suspense, death and ruin, which, as Clouzot stressed at a press conference, wants to politically and morally orient against those monopolies and trusts which permit such deadly rides on nitroglycerine to happen.«
Friedrich Luft in: Die Neue Zeitung, June 30, 1953

Gary Cooper with his wife and daughter at the Waldbühne

The verdict on the two German entries was once again devastating. Martin Schlappner wrote of »the Germans«: »With DER KAMPF DER TERTIA (»Fight of the Tertia«, directed by Erik Ode) they indulge in a somewhat dubious glorification of a leader, by youths in a reform school; and with EIN HERZ SPIELT FALSCH (»A Heart's Foul Play«) they once again prove that they can be devious on other accounts: everything is washed away by tears, wasting the good performances of the actors, and giving a talented director, Rudolf Jugert, the opportunity of ruining his taste for the artistic.« (Neue Zürcher Zeitung, Juli 1, 1953.)

And such were the reactions even though the organizers, foremost the Senate and the film industry, had come up with a new way of selecting the German entries. A commission for the selection of German films for the IFB had been constituted specially that year. Its members were identical with those of the so-called Parity Commission for the selection of German films for the Biennale in Venice, yet in addition complemented by four representatives from Berlin, that is by:

- Ruth Hahn von Dorsche, MHR (FDP) as spokeswoman for both the Senate and the House of Representatives;
- Alfred Bittins, chairman of the Berlin film producers association;
- Ferdinand Buttkus for the Berlin film distributors' association; and
- Karl Jacob for the Berlin movie house association.

The Parity Commission members were representatives of:

- the film industry (Amelung/Munich; Beck/Munich; Bittins/Berlin; Dr. Hossfelder/Wiesbaden; Jacob/Berlin; Lavies/Wiesbaden);
- the Commission for the Voluntary Control of Standards (Fritz Podehl/Wiesbaden);
- the Standing Committee of the Ministry of Cultural Affairs (Dr. Burkart);
- the State Film Assessment Boards (also Dr. Burkart);
- the Bundestag Committee for Press, Broadcasting and Film (Dr. Vogel/Bonn);
- the Federal Ministries (Foreign Affairs/Dr. Salat; the Interior/Dr. Lüders; Economic Affairs/Ockhardt; All-German Affairs/Dr. Schyla;

Eric Johnston signs the Golden Book of the City of Berlin; around him, near the table: Senatorial Press Spokesman Dr. Hirschfeld, Paramount president George Weltner, German representative of the MPAA Marc M. Spiegel, Warner Bros. press spokesman Dr. S. H. Fuehr, Mayor Ernst Reuter

– the film journalists' association (H. C. Opfermann/Düsseldorf; Hannes Schmidt/Düsseldorf).

Chairman was Legation Councillor Salat from the Ministry of Foreign Affairs.

After two days of showings and discussions in Remagen at the beginning of June, this commission gave out the following recommendation – and that is all that it was – to the Berlin Senate, for: a single feature film, the Georg Witt production Ein Herz spielt falsch [A Heart Cheats], and several documentaries. The following comments to two of the documentary films, Lieber Leierkastenmann [Dear Organgrinder] (Neue Wochenschau GmbH, Hamburg) and Endstation Freiheit [Freedom Terminal] (Dokumentar-Film, Berlin), characterize the nature of the discussions held at these meetings. »Speaking against both films are a number of political arguments, to which the commission does not see itself authorized to judge. The spokesman from the Office of Foreign Affairs has pointed out that the film Leierkastenmann, bringing forth memories of the marching troops in 1933 and of Hitler, might be misinterpreted by the Festival's foreign guests. Regarding the film Endstation Freiheit, there are second thoughts concerning the politics of the producer Johannes Häusler. The commission therefore advises caution with these two films, yet leaves it up to Berlin to assess the political arguments.« (Dr. Lüders, Ministry of the Interior, to the Senate, June 3, 1953.) As a result, the German entries were nominated only very reluctantly.

Structural and financial questions

An important decision was made shortly before the beginning of the Festival. Senatorial decree Number 3302 from May 26th 1953 had ordered the »reclassification of the Berliner Festwochen and the International Film Festival as permanent institutions« in 1954. Yet contrary to expectations, this decree did not have positive effects only, as Alfred Bauer was soon to find out; the closer connection resulting between these two institutions caused friction in the appointment of staff, which in turn

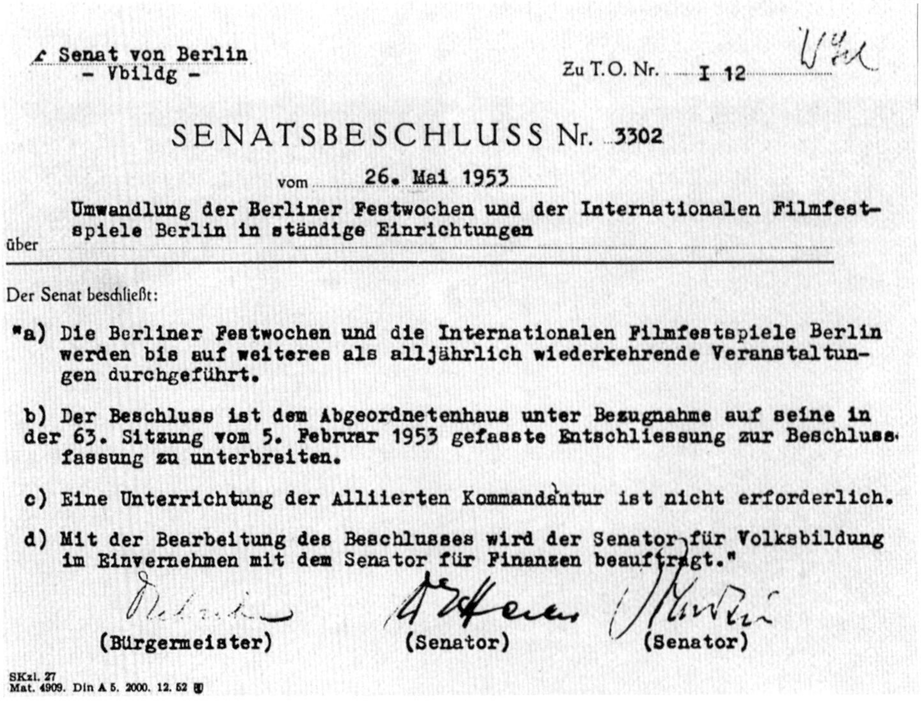

Senat von Berlin
– Vbildg –

Zu T.O. Nr. I 12

SENATSBESCHLUSS Nr. 3302

vom 26. Mai 1953

über Umwandlung der Berliner Festwochen und der Internationalen Filmfestspiele Berlin in ständige Einrichtungen

Der Senat beschließt:

"a) Die Berliner Festwochen und die Internationalen Filmfestspiele Berlin werden bis auf weiteres als alljährlich wiederkehrende Veranstaltungen durchgeführt.

b) Der Beschluss ist dem Abgeordnetenhaus unter Bezugnahme auf seine in der 63. Sitzung vom 5. Februar 1953 gefasste Entschliessung zur Beschlussfassung zu unterbreiten.

c) Eine Unterrichtung der Alliierten Kommandantur ist nicht erforderlich.

d) Mit der Bearbeitung des Beschlusses wird der Senator für Volksbildung im Einvernehmen mit dem Senator für Finanzen beauftragt."

(Bürgermeister) (Senator) (Senator)

SKzl. 27
Mat. 4909. Din A 5. 2000. 12. 52

Senatorial decree on the reclassification of the Berliner Festwochen and the International Film Festival Berlin as permanent institutions weighed heavily on the tight budget of the Film Festival. For example, out of the joint costs for the staffs of the two organizations, approximately DM 160 000, more than half were booked to the IFB, even though some of the employees involved (head of ticket sales, accountant, cashier, administrative assistants) were needed by the IFB for much less than half the year, if at all. On the good side, however, was the fact that Bauer was no longer employed by a contract limited in time, but on a permanent basis. It should be mentioned, however, that the following unpleasant incident had first had to occur for Bauer to attain an upgrading of his person and function.

Since its beginnings, the Berlin Department of Finances had regarded the Film Festival with reservations. In particular, the responsible official, Friedrich Lange, who was especially thrift-oriented, found fault in Bauer's unconventional budget management, which did not always conform to the regulations. Be it as it may, in reading the minutes it is not possible to overlook that Lange's restrictive attitude towards the Film Festival was not always objective. Indeed, it is to him that the draft of a contract of employment for the 4th International Film Festival can be attributed, which Bauer received from the personnel department of the Department of Education on December 23rd 1953. In this version of the contract, he was expected to accept a cut in salary and – despite a verbal agreement to the contrary, promising indefinite validity – a term of contract »until a cut-off date of September 30th, 1954«.

Alfred Bauer resigns.

Bauer, for whom this draft of the contract must have been an affront, reacted spontaneously. Immediately after Christmas, he resigned from his office as director of the Film Festival. His action (backed effectively by the film industry) had the desired effect. At a meeting after the turn of the year, Baensch, head of the Film Section, promised Bauer support in the essential items. Bauer, however, who was no longer so trusting, demanded his statement in writing, which Baensch, in turn, interpreted as a breach of confidence. It was not until Senator Tiburtius put in a good word that the matter was straightened out; Bauer took up office again on January 4th 1954.

At the budgetary meeting on December 11th 1953, at which Bauer had not been able to participate, the staff was considerably reduced; for Bauer most irritating of all must have been that the position of manager for secondary events, which Gerd Grassmé had supervised for two years, was no longer provided for in the budget of 1954, as well as that several periods of employment (for an interpreter and a press assistant) were shortened.

This whole incident is symptomatic of the first years of the Festival: financially and organizationally, the Festival direction repeatedly suffered interference and considering the amount of prestige the Senate attached to the Festival, financing was meager. In general, the Senate's line was to make as many decisions as possible itself, leaving Bauer little leeway. The director's determination and endurance in encountering incessant obstacles – no matter from which side they came – has to be admired, not only in these first years, but in the years to come as well.

At a meeting in late December, it had been agreed that the office of the organization must remain near the Kurfürstendamm, as only then could a smooth management of the Festival be guaranteed. Yet in January – in Bauer's absence – on the initiative of Lange, notice was given on the old offices and a new space rented in Dahlem, Am Hirschsprung 4. On his return, Alfred Bauer was confronted with the accomplished fact; he had no choice but to accept the situation. Organizationally, the year of 1954 was not getting off to a very good start.

Les Vacances de Monsieur Hulot: Jacques Tati, Michelle Rolla, Nathalie Pascaut

O Cangaceiro

Audiences' Choice

Golden Berlin Bear
Le Salaire de la peur
France, directed by
Henri Clouzot

Silver Berlin Bear
Magia verde
Italy, directed by
Gian Gaspare Napolitano

Bronze Berlin Bear
Das Pestalozzidorf
Switzerland, directed by
Leopold Lindtberg

International Delegate-Jury

Special Prize of the
Berlin Senate
Man on a Tightrope
USA, directed by
Elia Kazan

Processo alla città
Italy, directed by
Luigi Zampa

Entotsu no mieru basho
Japan, directed by
Heinosuke Gosho

Le Salaire de la peur:
Yves Montand, Folco Lulli

Rencontre with Lotte Eisner

By Kashiko Kawakita

It was 1953 when we first took part in the Berlin Film Festival. My late husband, Nagamasa Kawakita, had founded Towa Shoji GK, a foreign film import and distribution company in 1928, mainly importing high quality German films such as METROPOLIS, DIE NIBELUNGEN, MÄDCHEN IN UNIFORM, DER KONGRESS TANZT *etc., so Berlin was almost our second home.*

When we saw the ruins of the Kaiser Wilhelm Memorial Church and Kurfürstendamm, we were speechless though we had the same experiences of the war in Tokyo.

My husband, who was on Board of Directors of Toho Co., was the chief delegate of the Japanese delegation and presented two feature films from Japan: SENGOKU BURAI *[The Soldiers] a period play by Hiroshi Inagaki, and* ENTOTSU NO MIERU BASHO *(»Where Chimneys are seen«) a modern play by Heinosuke Gosho. A few actors and actresses were also present and their Kimono styles were much admired. Michiko Tanaka, wife of Victor de Kowa helped us greatly. They invited all the staff to their house and served us delicious Japanese food.*

In those days the US were very eager to encourage the Berlin Film Festival because of the cold war with the USSR. They sent Gary Cooper and William Wyler to the Festival, and Eric Johnston, head of MPAA, was the chief delegate. We were very happy that »Where Chimneys are seen« had won the prize.

During the Festival, the most significant rencontre for me was with Lotte Eisner, curator of La Cinémathèque Française. The moment I was introduced to her, we became friends. She was busy collecting posters, stills, seeing film after film, negotiating with the producers to show their films at the Cinémathèque. She taught me everything necessary to run a Cinémathèque. Later on in Paris she introduced me to Henri Langlois and I found in him a genius and an ardent film lover. He helped me to organize my small Cinémathèque Japonaise - now Kawakita Memorial Film Institute.

In 1956 I was appointed juror of the Festival. Marcel Carné was the president. He was serious and patient. He listened to each member of the jury and tried to understand his or her point of view. At the same time he had his own opinion and standpoint which he kept firm. He was fair and kind. I learned much from him about how to behave as a juror. He seemed to appreciate me too. He introduced me to Mme. Arletty, saying: »This is a most capable assistant of mine«. We have continued our friendship ever since.

Starting from the Berlin Film Festival, I have served on juries at 25 different film festivals. I always remember my first experience in Berlin dearly.

ALEC GUINNESS

Kettlebrook Meadows
Steep Marsh
Petersfield
Hampshire GU32 2BD

3 July 1989

Dear Herr Hadeln

Thank you for your letter of 27 June. I am honoured by your suggestion that I should write a short piece about the Berlin Film Festivals I have attended but I am afraid I cannot. They were most pleasant affairs and I received fine hospitality but I can find nothing interesting or amusing to say. Please express my regrets and apologies to Herr Jacobsen. I appreciate your having approached me.

Yours sincerely

Alec Guinness.

The glamour of it all

1954

June 18th – 29th, 1954

A man in a white jumpsuit, a tasseled cap on his head, climbs the front of a hotel on the Kurfürstendamm. It is mid-summer, 35° C. Down below in the street, pedestrians crane their necks. Using window sills, ledges, and balcony railings, the facade climber inches his way up higher and higher. At the top, a woman waits for him. On his jumpsuit is printed »Berlin greets Paula Wessely«. The cat man, a true Berlin character, en route to his star. Can you guess what he hands over the edge? A Berlin Bear, of course.

A snap shot from the Film Ball: three women, a bouquet in front of them, pose for the camera. Three actresses, or as was said during the fifties, three film goddesses:

Sophia Loren, Yvonne de Carlo, Gina Lollobrigida at the Film Ball in »Prälat Schöneberg«

Paula Wessely and the »cat man«, a true Berlin original

Alfred Bauer,
Gina Lollobrigida

Eva Bartok, Curd Jürgens

Sophia Loren, Yvonne de Carlo and Gina Lollobrigida. It turned out to be the only photo showing the Italian rivals together, with Loren who was hardly known as yet and the celebrated »Gina nazionale«.

Stories of the stars

More stars than ever before had arrived at the 4th Film Festival. Today it is almost impossible to imagine how greatly the Festival gave the city a different flair. In front of hotels, impatient Berliners waited – wanting to see Vittorio De Sica, cheering at Jean Marais as he threw his ties out the hotel window down to the crowd below, pushing in around Curd Jürgens and Eva Bartok, whose adventures filled the gossip sheets, and when Gina Lollobrigida appeared, their enthusiasm knew no bounds. A

Festival advertisement near the border to the Eastern Sector at Anhalter Station

loud-mouthed Berliner cried impishly: »Who's that there? My, if it isn't our Hildegard!« and paper and pen were pulled out for an autograph from Hildegard Knef.

An eye-witness reports: »Remember how it was last year? Black crepe banners waving above the Berlinale flag, the shots of the June Uprising still ringing in the loudspeakers, and many guests had cancelled their visits. This time, many more had come than were expected, and along the Kurfürstendamm life was flowing as it had not done since before the war. Fans of both sexes and all ages crowded in around the large hotels, breaking through police lines to storm Richard Widmark, Vittorio De Sica or Jean Marais, Wessely or Françoise Arnoul for autographs; and when they wanted to see their favorite star of the Festival, Gina Lollobrigida, at her window, they shouted in chorus, bringing back strange memories…« (Hugo Hartung, Deutsche Zeitung und Wirtschaftszeitung, July 3, 1954.)

The atmosphere of the Film Festival in the fifties was determined by the enthusiasm of the residents of Berlin, and their desire to be carried away by the glamour of it all; they wanted to stand in line, to applaud and cheer, to give a star a friendly pat on the back or a hug. It had turned into a festival for the »man on the street«, and the feeling of a new era was in the air: a Berliner was someone again – or at least wanted to be someone again. In 1954, the Film Festival was able to make a breakthrough, receiving greater international recognition. It was able to establish itself as a social event similar in importance to those in Cannes and Venice. Berlin could now be radiant – and the public along with it.

Films: hits and misses

Several films had been misunderstood: e. g., Douglas Sirk's melodrama MAGNIFICENT OBSESSION with Jane Wyman and Rock Hudson, and IKIRU [To Live] by Akira Kurosawa, a lonely film about a lonely man, and the happiness to be found in parting and the stillness to be found in movement: a man, deathly ill on a swing hanging still, finds pleasure in the wild swinging movements of a young woman. These images were too soft for the boisterous Festival of 1954.

Again the prizes were negotiated by the audiences' evaluation. And two films with lots of big names outscored the others by far: HOBSON'S CHOICE by David Lean with the lustful Charles Laughton as house tyrant, and the Italian entry PANE, AMORE E FANTASIA (»Bread, Love and Dreams«) with Vittorio De Sica and Gina Lollobrigida by Luigi Comencini: »an emotional fruit punch« was the journalist Bodo Kochanowski's comment (Neue Presse, July 2, 1954).

Once again a failure was the German entry, the German-American co-production RUMMELPLATZ DER LIEBE/CARNIVAL STORY by Karl Neumann, which had its première in the Waldbühne to an audience of 25 000 and was mercilessly booed at, which not even the stars of the film, Curd Jürgens and Eva Bartok, had been able to hinder. The Berliners retitled the film the equivalent of »Scrap-yard Story« – capturing the mood of this disastrous evening.

Financial problems all over again

Even though this flop could not curb the popularity of the Film Festival, there was no way for it to be held without some organizational disputes. This was the first year in which the Federal Government had contributed financially to the Festival. This development had been preceded by statements from the Spio Berlin as of fall 1953, as well as from the Berlin Senate and House of Representatives. With a memorandum (Sept. 9, 1953), the Spio Berlin had reacted to rumors saying that the budget of the next Film Festival was to be cut. »If the House of Representatives endorses funds amounting to only DM 500 000, it will mean a reduction of the sum which goes to

Jigokumon (»Gate of Hell«): Machiko Kyo, Kazuo Hasegawa

the IFB 1954 to less than DM 100 000, and would as a consequence greatly endanger the Festival's aspirations internationally.« As always those bodies having political influence reacted slowly; Oswald Cammann for the Verband der Berliner Filmtheater e. V. wrote in a letter to the Spio Berlin »that our association will not be able to work in cooperation with future Film Festivals, if the amount made available by the Senate in the budget is not raised above DM 100 000« (Nov. 20, 1953).

It was in this predicament that the Federal Government decided to help out, and at that with a grant of over DM 100 000, of which the larger portion of DM 70 000, came from the Federal Minister for All-German Affairs, at that time Jakob Kaiser; the Ministry of the Interior contributed DM 25 000, and the Federal Office of the Press, DM 5 000. The growing interest of the Federal Government was emphasized by the fact that the Federal Minister of the Interior, who was now Gerhard Schröder, awarded the Federal Film Prize personally for the first time, and in that nearly all members of the Federal Committee for Press, Broadcasting and Film Affairs were present in the city for several days during the Film Festival.

This visit caused – in its aftermath – troubles, as the committee did not feel it had been treated as it should have been by the authorities in Berlin. Their complaints stirred up quite some excitement in Berlin, which did not subside until a conciliatory letter was sent from the Senator for Education to the committee's chairman, Paul Bausch. An increase in institutional ties meant an increase in the demands made: a fact one would have to get accustomed to in Berlin.

A question of competence between the Berlin Senate and the Spio

If one reads the records and correspondence, it becomes quite clear that the tactics of the Senate were to not take the film industry too closely into account when making IFB decisions; this meant that the passage in the IFB regulations, identifying »the organization of the German film industry« as co-organizer and sponsor of the Festival, was hardly fulfilled. On July 24th 1954 the business manager of the association of Berlin film producers drew up a »report on the lack of cooperation of the

Pane, amore e fantasia: Gina Lollobrigida, Marisa Merlini, Vittorio De Sica

Senate of the City of Berlin with the Berlin film industry, especially on the occasion of the IFB 1954«, which was then endorsed by all of the other individual associations as well. The central point of this complaint was that the Spio had been excluded from the preparations to the 4th International Film Festival. It is true that there was no representative of the Spio in the advisory board; after the called-for demarche, they were merely consoled with the promise that one of their representatives would be consulted in pertinent issues. De facto, they were never consulted.

Weg ohne Umkehr (»No Way Back«): Ruth Niehaus

Audiences' Choice

Feature Films
Golden Berlin Bear
Hobson's Choice
Great Britain, directed by
David Lean

Silver Berlin Bear
Pane, amore e fantasia
Italy, directed by
Luigi Comencini

Bronze Berlin Bear
Le Défroqué
France, directed by
Léo Joannon

Long Documentary Films
Large Golden Plaque
The Living Desert
USA, directed by
James Algar

Large Silver Plaque
Det stora aventyret
Sweden, directed by
Arne Sucksdorff

Large Bronze Plaque
Un siècle d'or
Belgium

International Delegate-Jury

Special Prize of the
Berlin Senate
La grande speranza
Italy, directed by
Duilio Coletti

Sinha Moca
Brazil, directed by
Tom Payne

Ikiru
Japan, directed by
Akira Kurosawa

Walt Disney
for supporting the Film
Festival over the years with
the best of his productions

The Senate's stance, which from a political point of view was understandable, caused Alfred Bauer, who personally had nothing against a greater participation by the film industry and had in precarious moments always received their support, difficulties as director of the Film Festival. He had to ward off the accusation, brought in by the business director of the association of German film producers, Alfred Jurisch, a lawyer, of having neglected contact with the Spio.

The stubborn insistence of the Spio, whose primary aim was the joint appointment of both the city administration (i.e. the Senate) and the film industry to the governing bodies of the Festival, did not pay off as well as had been hoped. Again the Senate found a way to limit the Spio's influence. The Spio was to be represented in the organizational committee, but not in the advisory board, where most of the decisions were actually made; in the fundamental set-up of having both an advisory board and an organizational committee nothing was altered. One could in no way speak of the aspired parity. For the first time, this division was also ankered in a senatorial decree. There could be no doubt that this round had been won by the Berlin Senate.

The Living Desert

Gold for West-Germany

1955

June 24th–July 5th, 1955

In front of the Filmbühne Wien and the Gloria-Palast on the Kurfürstendamm, the lanes had been marked off with traffic cones as a precautionary measure. There was one lane for through-traffic, the other two for Festival guests. The police were expecting five to six hundred cars for the opening. The somewhat chaotic circumstances of the year before, when spirited Berliners had stormed Festival stars, were not supposed to be repeated. In addition the police formed »living fences«, barriers against autograph hunters. Yet this year, as it turned out, Prussian thoroughness had been exaggerated. For although the enthusiasm and the involvement of the residents of Berlin remained great, there were few opportunities for them to direct this enthusiasm at stars. A whole range of German movie celebrities, from Maria Schell to Romy Schneider, from O. E. Hasse to Curd Jürgens were on hand – but from Hollywood there was only a young actor named Edmund Purdom, and Ann Miller, a »Hollywood Belle«, as one said in those days. Karena Niehoff had summed it up well: there were »...no important stars from abroad for the fans. Yet it had always been exactly this easily-arranged feature which had made the Berlin Film Festival unique; that is, that it was enacted in front of a human backdrop such as is affiliated with film, a setting which was not just ornamental, but also social and physical. From the Festival management's explanation, that the stars were all ›busy‹, one can only infer that last year, when everybody who was anybody had heeded the call, general unemployment among international stars must have been rampant. Perhaps, these precious ladies and gentlemen have not yet been convinced adequately enough of the fact that not only Berlin needs them, but they need this big city, which works harder to increase their market value than small and delicate Cannes or debaucherous Venice.« (Der Tagesspiegel, July 10, 1955.)

Lookers-on applaud...

Cannes and Berlin: competing for dates

By the way, speaking of Cannes and Venice: on an international level there had been a wrangling for dates. In 1954, Cannes' organizers, perhaps not unimpressed with the success of the IFB, had resolutely rescheduled their festival dates for 1955, from the end of March to May, and then, after another change, to April 25th till May 10th.

The Berlin Film Festival, originally planned for June 18th-29th, had then also to be rescheduled, so that it would not land on a date too near (and forbidden by the FIAPF) the festival in Cannes. To top it off, June 18th, a Saturday, was not suitable for an opening, and June 17th had in the meantime been elevated to a national commemoration day (the June Uprising). Other limiting factors were the commencement of the summer holidays at the beginning of July and the dates of the Biennale in Venice, so that the organizers finally agreed to the period from June 24th to July 5th 1955. These dates were approved of by the administrative board of the FIAPF in Madrid in October 1954; at this same meeting the regulations of the Federation were revised, bringing, however, no alterations of relevance for the IFB – with the exception of one item: »The Fédération cannot recognize any festival which is, in the character of its prizes, the wording of its invitations, or in any other respect in some way politically inclined.« This restriction rested on the unanimous decision of the FIAPF's general assembly in Locarno that same year.

The awards are restricted by the FIAPF.

Dr. Günter Schwarz from the Export-Union of the German film industry, and the German delegate to the FIAPF, informed Alfred Bauer on November 12th 1954: »With reference to this regulation, the administrative board has decided to ask the Berlin Film Festival to refrain from awarding prizes having a political character.« Yet it had been only at the last Festival in 1954 that they had created a prize for those films which – so item 11 of the IFB regulations – »best fulfilled the ideals of a world oriented towards freedom«. And now exactly this prize could no longer be awarded.

Rains could not hold them back – spectators at the Waldbühne.

The audiences' choice remained for the last time the basis for a Berlin »prize«, which according to the FIAPF was at any rate merely a »certificate«.

The Golden Berlin Bear: for the first time the Grand Prix went to a German production – to Robert Siodmak's DIE RATTEN [The Rats]. Maria Schell (»...even her step whispers of her soul«, as one critic wrote) plays the abused Pauline Piperkarcka in postwar Berlin, in a quite topical filming of the tragicomedy by Gerhart Hauptmann. The Polish maid becomes the »Eastern refugee« Pauline Karka, who in dire need sells her child; hence this film is also a document of the conflict of an emigrant, and of the director Siodmak himself, with the political situation of Germany in the wake of National Socialism. Berlin is shown both lucidly and realistically; the destroyed city and its destroyed inhabitants have presence, the documentary background disillusions. The public was affected by the film's relevance, more so than the critics; they had in the end been even more impressed with it than with Otto Preminger's CARMEN JONES, the only film to have been sold out in advance – tickets were traded on the black market at top prices. »The spectrum of reactions ranged from wild enthusiasm to strong distaste; I had felt both extremes and their relationship to one another while watching this extraordinary experiment: enthusiasm for the vitality and great composition of the mass scenes, the screen jam-packed and full of vaporous colors; and distaste at the pedantic conscientiousness with which the grand ›numbers‹ from Bizet's famous opera were stowed away, piece by piece, in the turbulent events of the story.« (Sabina Lietzmann, Frankfurter Allgemeine Zeitung, July 9, 1955.)

Maria Schell, Barbara Rost, Robert Siodmak

Controversy over Falk Harnack's DER 20. JULI

The second German entry was Falk Harnack's DER 20. JULI [July 20th], to which the Selection Commission for German Film Entries could not make up its mind. On June 14th, the commission's chairman, Dr. Lüders from the Federal Ministry of the Interior, explained to Bauer that the commission had only been given an unfinished, not edited copy, to which no decision could be made and recommended another screening after the completion of the film. Furthermore, the head of the Berlin Film Section, Theodor Baensch, reported to the Senator for Education: »The second thoughts of the majority of the commission were apparently determined by considerations involving a film from Munich on the same topic. Whether some of the members had other reasons which were not expressed cannot be said.« (June 15, 1955.) The production from Munich to which Baensch makes reference was G. W. Pabst's ES GESCHAH AM 20. Juli [It Happened on July 20th] which had been submitted under the title of »Die Stunde der Versuchung« but then later withdrawn.

In fact, preluding the nomination of Harnack's film, a political tug-of-war had ensued. The widow of General Fromm had petitioned for a warrant to prohibit the film's distribution (by Herzog-Film) for its »denigrating portrayal of the General«. In turn, a dispute broke out in the press to the cuts which had been made by the FSK; such intervention was felt to be the equivalent of censorship. Reinhard Goerdeler protested on the behalf of the families of Beck, Goerdeler and Stauffenberg and for the members of the organization »Aid for the Victims of July 20th 1944« who were all against adoption of this film in the Festival program, as they had basic qualms to a filming of these events and were of the opinion – and this statement makes reference to G. W. Pabst's ES GESCHAH AM 20. Juli as well – »that the two films do not adequately give expression to the concerns of the resistance movement and its spiritual, moral and legal significance«. (Statement to the press, not dated.) Theodor Baensch assessed the situation as follows: »In my opinion, it is doing too much of a

Die Ratten: Maria Schell

good thing when one involves the ministries, Parliament and film industry associations, amongst others, in the selection of the German entries to the Festival. At the session in Wiesbaden there were present from Bonn alone: two ministerial secretaries, plus one representative each from the Ministries of Foreign Affairs and Economic Affairs, as well as from the Office of Press and Information Services. The commission of 16 members (8 representatives from the film industry and 8 from the federal and state governments) is in this constellation and size, crassly out of proportion to the mission entrusted to it.«

Co-organizers and sponsors

Two more matters of internal importance: In 1955, that which had been merely alluded to the year before was enacted – a new co-organizer and sponsor of the Festival was mentioned for the first time in the regulations. Item 2: »The organizers and sponsors of the event are the Berlin Senate together with the government of the Federal Republic of Germany, in cooperation with the organizations of the German film industry.« An oddity of the financing was that one organizer and sponsor supported the Festival with funds appropriated for specific purposes, and yet these funds were still regarded, as far as the budget was concerned, as »donations from a third party«. The funds from the Federal Government should have in fact been part of the regular budget, but this apparently could not be arranged at such short notice. Yet this was not the only peculiarity: members of the Festival's advisory board were in part also members of the organizational committee and both bodies were headed by the city's Senator for Education. The procedural regulations of the advisory board, for example, allowed for the following situation: first of all, the advisory board advises the Senator for Education, secondly the Senator for Education is a member of this same board, and thirdly the Senator for Education presides over this board as chairman. Ergo: the Senator for Education advises himself under his very own chairmanship! (The author of this ironic observation was Senatorial Supervisor Wallner-

Carmen Jones: Dorothy Dandridge, Harry Belafonte

THE SEVEN YEAR ITCH: Tom Ewell, Marilyn Monroe

Basté, who noted his discovery on May 3rd 1955, yet supplemented it with the resigned and mitigating sentence: »Since, as has often been the case, little offence is felt by such circumstances, I shall refrain from suggesting a change.«) It can be concluded: the Senator for Education made use of his influence on the IFB.

The Festival brochure: a scandal

As the 5th Film Festival was approaching, which, by the way, was to be turned into a small jubilee celebration, a problem arose which almost led to a scandal. It concerned the publication of the official program. Robert Scheuer, who had been editor up till then, had criticized the Film Festival in part in his journal »Filmblätter«. Especially upsetting was the Filmblätter's »Special Issue of Slip-ups« in which Scheuer found fault with a whole series of things which, in his opinion, had gone wrong at the last Film Festival. Among other things, he had taken up the affair concerning the Bundestag committee, criticized that the performances for Eastern visitors in the B.T.L. movie house on Potsdamer Strasse had doubled in price over the year before from 25 to 50 pfennigs, and that his program brochure was not subsidized for sales to Eastern visitors. All these criticisms gave Alfred Bauer enough reasons to take the exclusive rights which Scheuer enjoyed as editor away from him and to divide them between all four of the existing film journals. Scheuer reacted furiously and an angry correspondence ensued.

A typical detail for the times might be illustrative here: the Press Spokeswoman for the IFB, Annemarie Schmidt, reported in a letter to Scheuer that inquiries had been made at the offices of the Film Festival as to »why we allowed a magazine printed in the Eastern zone to be handed out at the Festival«. (Feb. 15, 1955.) The magazine meant is exactly the special issue of the »Filmblätter« mentioned above, which she designates moreover as »anti-Berlin«. In a rage, Scheuer wrote to the head of the Berlin Film Section, Theodor Baensch, making the already nonsensical accusations even worse. He has gone down for having stated that »the (supposedly unobjective) Filmblätter critique of the Festival had been interpreted by Festival guests as ›communist‹« (Feb. 20, 1955). In the fifties no accusation imaginable was worse than being suspected of quasi »subversive communist activities«. After this statement all composure was lost, and a rather marginal quarrel escalated in denunciations. No one could afford to insinuate that someone was hostile towards Berlin – that was to touch on sore spots in the German's conception of himself. It was Senator Tiburtius who was able to de-escalate these more than personal attacks. On his suggestion a contract was drawn up between the publishing company concerned and the Film Festival, which, on three tightly packed pages and in 14 items, was to regulate the tiniest detail of this future joint venture. It was on March 3rd that the adversaries signed the paper.

The efforts made by Alfred Bauer and his team to promote the Film Festival visually were enormous. They used as advertising media: 19 000 standard posters in different sizes and languages, and 210 000 leaflets, distributed throughout West Germany, as well as in abundance abroad. Sculptured works and banners were displayed as publicity at the Hannover Fair and in innumerable other places in West Germany; special posters were hung in the Berlin inner city and at Tempelhof Airport. The Kurfürstendamm, which had been freed from street-car tracks that year and now offered thousands of cars parking space in the center lane, was decorated along both sides with flags from all participating nations; lights were strung across the street; many public buildings (not damaged by the war) – district city halls, memorial churches, major banks and department stores – were lit up at night; all West Berlin public transportation, as well as all public buildings in the city were beflagged. And there were 120 billboards hung with 480 posters – facing eastwards – which could be easily viewed from East Berlin. Yes, they had been willing to put out DM 60 000 for advertising alone.

Audiences' Choice

Feature Films
Golden Berlin Bear
Die Ratten
FRG, directed by
Robert Siodmak

Silver Berlin Bear
Marcellino, pan y vino
Spain, directed by
Ladislao Vajda

Bronze Berlin Bear
Carmen Jones
USA, directed by
Otto Preminger

Long Documentary Films
Large Golden Plaque
The Vanishing Prairie
USA, directed by
James Algar

Large Silver Plaque
Continente perduto
Italy, directed by
Leonardo Bonzi

Large Bronze Plaque
Im Schatten des Karakorum
FRG, directed by
Eugen Schuhmacher

IFB advertising on billboards, easily seen from the East

Publicity parade on the Kaiserdamm in Charlottenburg for A Prize of Gold with Richard Widmark. The British entry in the Competition was to crown events at the Waldbühne.

In the top three

1956

June 22nd–July 3rd, 1956

The 1st International Film Festival Berlin had started off with a jury, even if it had not been an international one. Yet having neglected to make an agreement with the FIAPF, the international parent organization for the film producer's associations which wanted to reserve the privilege of determining the regulations for film festivals for itself, it had been reprimanded and forbidden the continued appointment of a jury.

In Berlin they had made a virtue of necessity and had declared the viewers »the jury«. A verdict was given with one's entrance ticket: depending on where one tore it, the evaluation was either »very good«, »good«, »average«, or »poor«. »The jury, the people of Berlin«, proclaimed Mayor Ernst Reuter in 1952, »is as tolerant as it is competent in judgement. An official assessment of the most popular film by audiences in Berlin shows that public taste, as ill-reputed as it is, has in fact the same status as the official presentation of an award.« As a matter of fact, the choice of the films by the audience had an important function as publicity, inviting the involvement of Berliners, and it can be presumed that the »Berlinale« would not have become as popular so quickly if public opinion had not been an integral part of the Festival.

The »Berlinale« receives »A-status«.

Nevertheless, in Berlin they had never ceased to hope for an official international jury. At the FIAPF conference in 1955 in Washington, the Berlin Film Festival was finally given the yearned for »A-status«, which put Berlin on the same level, at least on paper, as the other two festival cities, Cannes and Venice. (However catchy the term »A-status« might be, it is nowhere to be found in the actual guidelines of the FIAPF. Yet it was used to designate those film festivals which were recognized in the fifties by the FIAPF, and which were supplied with films by the national producers' associations; these festivals had permission to set up an international jury and were allowed to award prizes. Nowadays the FIAPF guidelines merely distinguish between those festivals which hold no competition and those which do, either specialized or non-specialized.) Even after the decision had been made in Washington, the prizes

High expectations despite the rain: passers-by in front of the Filmbühne Wien on Kurfürstendamm

the prizes for the audiences' favorites continued to be awarded, as they »are highly valued by producers and distributors the world over as a means of researching public taste and for market analysis, and they represent a unique way of measuring a film's international value«, as was asserted in an official declaration.

The movie-goers and the film industry, which were dependent on each other, were the two pillars, or perhaps one should say parameters, of the first years of the IFB. The Film Fair, which had also existed from the very beginning, was not a new innovation. Already in 1956, transactions amounting to millions of German marks bore witness to the growing reputation of the Festival in international trade, and the presence of representatives from all larger production and distribution companies from overseas and Asia attest to this fact impressively as well. That these companies paid more attention to the opinion of the audiences than to the decisions of the jury goes without saying.

Talk about town

At the time of this year's Film Festival, topics of interest around Berlin were the Senate's decision to build a new Opera House on Bismarckstraße and the expropriation of property for this project; the introduction of new license plates (B–A1 to B–Z999) at the exorbitantly high fee of DM 20; the traditionally big sports event was the final match in the German football championship in Olympic Stadium, at which Karlsruher SC, having no chance, lost with a score of 1 to 4 against Borussia Dortmund (for insiders: the Dortmund forward line consisted of the three »Alfredos«, the strikers Niepieklo, Kelbassa and Preissler). And the »Tagesspiegel« brought a report on July 1st about an »existentialist cellar« – the legendary »Eierschale« – at Breitenbachplatz, a meeting place for teenagers, rowdies, and motorcycle gangs who, nonetheless, practised »self-discipline«. Only once did an incident clash with the events of the Festival, when the leftist youth organization, »Die Falken«, laid down a wreath at the bottom of the Spanish flagpole on the Kurfürstendamm – »For the victims of the Franco regime«. For a moment it seemed as if the harmony of the Festival was in danger, a crowd gathered and harsh words were exchanged between passersby and »Falken«, who »as political greenhorns had once again missed the point« (Der Tagesspiegel, June 29, 1956). In the end, the police showed up and removed the wreath. The political climate, felt also in the daily course of the Festival, revealed itself to be strangely contradictory.

At odds over films of the Defa

The Heinrich-Zille Gesellschaft e. V. had planned to show two Defa films at the Filmbühne am Steinplatz during the Festival, namely, DIE BLAUEN SCHWERTER [The Blue Swords] by Wolfgang Schleif and Kurz Maetzig's DIE BUNTKARIERTEN. When Alfred Bauer heard of their intentions, he addressed a letter of protest to the Berlin Department of Education (June 4, 1956), which then attempted, through the movie house association, to cancel the arrangements for the showings, even though they had no legal grounds to do so. The chairman of the Heinrich-Zille Society, Joachim Albitz, gave in to the policital pressure in the end; in a letter to the Film Section of the Department of Education, Albitz wrote that with the cancellation of the screenings, the intended donation of the proceeds to a charity organizing holidays for needy Berlin children in the country would unfortunately have to be dropped; in another letter he makes reference to a speech »given during the Zone-Debate in the Bundestag« by Herbert Wehner, and then cites Federal Minister for All-German Affairs Jakob Kaiser for saying that, the Federal Government welcomed and supported all efforts giving young people an opportunity to get to know each other and of experiencing the countries and peoples on both sides of the zonal boundaries.

The following incident gives further indication of the political climate surrounding the Festival: during the film festival in Cannes, the film NUIT ET BROUILLARD [Night and Fog] by Alain Resnais, a documentary about the concentration camp in Auschwitz, caused absolute furore. (The film commentary was by Jean Cayrol, the German adaption by Paul Celan and the music by Hanns Eisler.) The German ambassador in Paris, von Maltzan, protested on behalf of the German Federal Government against the showing of this film, as according to the statutes for festivals (Article V), only such films could be shown - so in this case the disgraceful reasoning - which did not injure the feelings of the people of another nation, or interfere with their peaceful co-existence. As a consequence and after the intervention of the French Ministry of Foreign Affairs, Industry and Trade, the film was withdrawn from the festival, and was shown at a later date only to invited guests at special screenings. The screenwriter Jean Cayrol, survivor of the concentration camp in Mauthausen, wrote a letter to Heinrich Böll, in which he condemned the Federal Government's course of action. The consequences of this affair were also felt in Parliament. At the Bundestag session on April 18th 1956, the Office of Foreign Affairs verified on request of member Annemarie Renger that the Federal Government had intervened in Cannes.

The Federal Government intervenes in Cannes, against Alain Resnais' NUIT ET BROUILLARD. The Berlin Senate gives its consent to a special showing during the Film Festival.

These events were also discussed by the advisory board of the Film Festival Berlin in its 4th meeting on May 25th 1956. Günter Schwarz, delegate of the German producers' association to the FIAPF, gave a report on the incidents in Cannes, voicing his opinion as well on the rejection of the German entry, Helmut Käutner's HIMMEL OHNE STERNE (»Sky Without Stars«), which had initially been accepted in Cannes and then, presumably after protest on the part of the Soviet delegate, was told it could not participate. (»The Russians had explained that they could not comment on the matter«, to quote the minutes taken at the meeting; later this passage was omitted from the official version.) This controversy was in the end a question of Article V, »whether one should allow any political films dealing with the past 50 years« (as cited in the minutes). Senator Tiburtius advocated a liberal interpretation of the regulations and urged for the organization of a special screening of NUIT ET BROUILLARD in Berlin. The advisory committee decided to adopt his proposal, yet following a suggestion made by Bauer, this screening was not organized by the Film Festival itself, but by the »Congress for Cultural Freedom«. As early as May 24th 1956, that is before the advisory committee meeting, the Senator for Education had instructed his assistant in Bonn, Dr. Herbert Antoine, to look into the affair. An excerpt from Antoine's report to Tiburtius reads as follows: »As instructed, I contacted Dr. Rowas from the Office of Foreign Affairs, who after consulting Mr. von Trützschler and the Undersecretary, declared that the Office of Foreign Affairs wanted to basically adhere to its position, taken in Cannes on the film NUIT ET BROUILLARD. However, Dr. Rowas was of the opinion that in the end it was up to the Berlin Senate to decide its own course of action. I then pointed out that all of the Berlin authorities which had looked into the matter had been in agreement, the film should be shown in Berlin on an especially worthy occasion. Mr. Rowas replied that he believed one had to have first seen the film to understand how devastating its whole contents were, and that it should not be shown within the framework of a film festival. I explained that we Berliners hold the viewpoint that one cannot be reminded too often of what happened [in the War] and that we believe today's Federal Government cannot be associated with the events of the Nazi period. I told him I did not feel it proper to

Michèle Morgan,
O. W. Fischer

Artur Brauner, Hans Albers,
the producer and his star
(VOR SONNENUNTERGANG)

pass responsibility on to the Berlin Senate alone, especially after we had emphasized again and again that we wanted to act jointly with the Federal Government in the Film Festival in Berlin. When I asked if the matter could be reconsidered, Mr. Rowas finally stated plainly that the Office of Foreign Affairs was against showing the film.«

The Berlin Senate however was able in the end to take action regardless of these »reservations«. On July 1st 1956, NUIT ET BROUILLARD was shown at Capitol cinema. The President of the Berlin House of Representatives, Willy Brandt, spoke an opening word and pointed out that »the German people should not be allowed to forget, so that others can«. The film was shown again on July 2nd and 3rd.

Finances and publicity

As far as finances and publicity go, the Film Festival was now, after five years, able to hold its own, as can be illustrated in the following names and numbers: 34 nations, including the United Nations, had entered films in the Competition, in addition, five countries had sent delegates or observers. With more than 1100 official festival participants, including over 500 journalists, the number of guests compared to the year before had more than doubled. Also arriving in great numbers were the celebrities, who were idolized so greatly during these first years in Berlin – to exemplify, here are seven names: Gary Cooper, Trevor Howard, Michèle Morgan, Jeanne Moreau, Silvana Pampanini, Arletty and Bob Hope – all illustrious enough to prove the respectability of the Festival. These names and numbers certainly also had to do with the Festival's »promotion« to »A-status«.

Even if the proceeds were high and the splendor of the prominent guests was not to be overseen, 1956 was not a good film year – as was also the case for ten years of German postwar films. That which after 1945 had initially seemed promising – Wolfgang Staudte's DIE MÖRDER SIND UNTER UNS (»Murderers Among Us«), the first postwar film from Berlin should be remembered here – had long since been forgotten in the wave of banal comedies and »Heimatfilme« (sentimental films with lots of local color), hence it is hardly astonishing that in searching for films of a higher standard, with which one wanted to be seen at an international festival, one resorted to those based on literature. Last year's entry had been Robert Siodmak's DIE RATTEN; this year's was Gottfried Reinhardt's VOR SONNENUNTERGANG [Before Sundown]. Works by Hauptmann were the favorites.

Festive opening at the Gloria-Palast.
In the foreground, a star: Carla Hagen

The foreign entries were also not particularly remarkable. Only a Finnish film entitled Tuntematon sotilas [The Unknown Soldier], which was run at the Festival under the title of »Trommelfeuer in Karelien« and in the movie theaters under the distributor's title of »Der unbekannte Soldat« caused a stir. This film about the Finnish-Soviet War, made using two former privates of the Finnish army as amateur actors, based on a novel by Väinö Linna, and not shown in Cannes as the festival management there had had certain qualms, received in Berlin much recognition for its clearly anti-war stance (for which it was compared to All Quiet on the Western Front) and its sensitive characterization of the enemy. Yet it did not receive an official Festival award, which is not in fact surprising. Were the reasons political? No matter, the jury of the International Catholic Organization for Cinema (OCIC) with members from Egypt, Belgium, the Federal Republic of Germany, England, France, Luxembourg, Austria and Spain awarded their prize to this entry and directed expressed attention to the wording of their statutes calling for the presentation of their award to a film which »in contents and form encourages spiritual improvement and human values most.«

Tuntematon sotilas
»Finland's contribution to the Festival, a war movie which in no way takes sides, showing as in All Quiet on the Western Front, simple soldiers, whose fate is war and who, although of average character, are on occasion capable of self-sacrifice for a comrade. It is a harsh men's film, interspersed with excerpts from weekly newsreels. Dying people, dying forests – not a film made to please the audience, but a warning, which will hopefully be heard here and everywhere.«
Ethel Schwirten in: Frankfurter Rundschau, July 6, 1956

It must have been difficult for the first international jury with Marcel Carné as president to award the prizes, as can be inferred from the reactions in the press. It was able to come to a rough agreement in awarding the Golden Bear to Invitation to the Dance by Gene Kelly, but otherwise dissatisfaction prevailed. Yet it was not so much that the films themselves, which received major awards, special prizes or honorary mentions, reaped criticism, but rather that there was general failure to understand the fact that several films which had been received well by the viewers, had received no recognition at all from the international jury. Such was especially the case with the Spanish entry Mi tio Jacinto (»Pepote«) and the Danish comedy Kispus. For example, Wilhelm Mogge, editor of the »Kölnische Rundschau« and member of the

International Jury for Feature Films
Marcel Carné (France, president)
W. G. Luckwell (Great Britain)
G. v. Sampieri (Italy)
Kashiko Kawakita (Japan)
Leo J. Horster (USA)
Ilse Urbach (FRG)
Ludwig Berger (FRG)

International Jury for Documentary and Short Films
Otto Sonnenfeld (Israel, president)
Sarukkai Gopalan (India)
J. Hulsker (Netherlands)
D. Gualberto Fernández (Uruguay)
Fritz Kempe (FRG)

The Awards of the International Jurys

Feature Films
Grand Prix of the 6th IFB
Golden Berlin Bear
INVITATION TO THE DANCE
USA, directed by Gene Kelly

International Prize
Silver Berlin Bear
RICHARD III
Great Britain, directed by Laurence Olivier

Silver Berlin Bear for the best director
Robert Aldrich
for AUTUMN LEAVES
USA

OCIC jury combined his objections to the decisions of his colleagues on the international jury in a declaration of love to the viewers: »Joe Doakes – this creation, this scapegoat of the film industry – has proven to have much more understanding of art and the metier than the experts in the jury, who were lacking it seems in the critical component. Joe Doakes had his big moment and saw himself – probably to his own great surprise – on the same, even if not quite identical, front as the competent reviewers in the papers.«

It was the German entry VOR SONNENUNTERGANG, given first place by the audiences, which made sure that there was not agreement with the critics on all counts. Yet this one decision was considered merely an oversight, and excused in reviews with the weakness of Germans for the leading actor Hans Albers.

INVITATION TO THE DANCE: Gene Kelly, Tamara Tumanova

However, the audiences and the jury were in total agreement when it came to awarding the prizes for long documentaries, and it was noted with pleasure that both had given preference to the German entry KEIN PLATZ FÜR WILDE TIERE [No Space for Wild Animals], rather than to the Disney production THE AFRICAN LION.

No matter, expert jury-opinion (and the distribution of the prizes) or the public's taste: the very fact that opinions were so divergent indicates that there were no exceptional films that year. And it was exactly in this point that there was an absolute consensus: it had been a poor film year, which had not been able to bring forth any outstanding films for the Festival in Berlin, especially as Cannes and Venice had already taken the pickings. Friedrich Luft put it all in a nutshell: »The movie business is flourishing. Movies are stagnating.« (Die Welt, July 7, 1956.)

Silver Berlin Bear
for the best actress
Elsa Martinelli
in DONATELLA
Italy

Silver Berlin Bear
for the best actor
Burt Lancaster
in TRAPEZE
USA

1st Special Prize
Silver Berlin Bear
THE LONG ARM
Great Britain, directed by
Charles Frend

2nd Special Prize
Silver Berlin Bear
LA SORCIÈRE
France, directed by
André Michel

Honorable Mention
for the best director
Alfonso Corona Blake
for EL CAMINO DE LA VIDA
Mexico

Honorable Mention
for the colors in
HAKUFUJIN NO YOREN
Japan, directed by
Shiro Tanaka

Honorable Mention
for the best comedy
PANE, AMORE E...
Italy, directed by
Marcello Girosi

TUNTEMATON SOTILAS –
a scene from the Finnish
entry in the Competition

Long Documentary Films
1st Prize
Golden Berlin Bear
Kein Platz für wilde Tiere
FRG, directed by Bernhard and Michael Grzimek

2nd Prize
Silver Berlin Bear
The African Lion
USA, directed by James Algar

Audiences' Choice

Feature Films
Golden Berlin Bear
Vor Sonnenuntergang
FRG, directed by Gottfried Reinhardt

Mi tio Jacinto
Spain, directed by Ladislao Vajda

Trapeze
USA, directed by Carol Reed

Long Documentary Films
Large Golden Plaque
Kein Platz für wilde Tiere
FRG

The African Lion
USA

Zauber der Natur
FRG

Richard III:
Laurence Olivier

The »Zoo-Palast« at the heart of Berlin

1957

June 21st–July 2nd, 1957

Berlin was having an attack of building fever. Ruins were being torn down in all districts, and new buildings were under construction. Lehrter Station, a partial ruin, was supposed to be dynamited, but its destruction originally planned for the beginning of June, was postponed because an American film company wanted to use the bombed facade as a backdrop. And in the district of Tiergarten, a whole new quarter had been erected; that is, within the course of the International Architecture Exhibition (»Interbau«), the Hansaviertel had been developed, for Berliners a place of pilgrimage and the epitome of modern living. The high rises were spectacular, the functional architecture exciting, the only question was whether one could afford to live there. The official opening of the »Interbau« was on July 6th, four days after the closing of the Film Festival.

Berlin has a bout of building-fever.

The motto of this 7th Berlinale was »the Film Festival in a new Berlin«. The guests' limousines did not drive up on the Kurfürstendamm, but in front of the new Zoo-Palast movie house, whose wide front was decorated with flags. Lookers-on crowded round the glass doors of the entrance, and marveled at the generously proportioned lobby; everyone was proud of the air conditioning and of the modern projection equipment. Although the Zoo-Palast was not the Festival center which Alfred Bauer had tried to get approved of by the Berlin Senate, it was also not a stopgap solution, but finally a true Festival movie house. Even today, the Zoo-Palast is the major building of the Festival, that is, for Berlin a kind of movie house focal point.

Legitimation pressure

Yet so far, the Festival itself had not undergone any substantial changes to correlate with these external changes, even though the Film Festival was incessantly under a certain pressure to legitimize itself. The internationality of the Festival was in doubt; the voices in the press admonishing the absence of Eastern bloc countries were becoming louder and louder. And within the management itself as well, at the meetings of the organizational committee, the question of the participation of, for example, Czechoslovakia, which had signalled its interest, and an invitation to the Soviet Union, followed by one to the GDR were vehemently debated. At this point, however, there was opposition, coming primarily from Bonn.

The position of Berlin vis-à-vis the socialist countries had also become precarious as a consequence of a decision which had been made in Cannes, allowing all countries to participate in its festival, even those maintaining no diplomatic relations with France. This new ruling in Cannes stated that those countries maintaining diplomatic relations with France would continue to be invited by the Ministry of Foreign Affairs, the other countries – such as the Peoples' Republic of China and the German Democratic Republic – were to be invited by the producers' association.

Moreover, Berlin was now competing strongly with the film festival in Karlovy Vary, which had also been conferred »A-status« and was making preparations for its tenth »jubilee festival«. To top it all off, it could boast of a contract which had been drawn up between the American Syndicate of Independent Motion Picture Producers (SIMPP) and Czechoslovakian National Film Productions for the export of twelve independently produced American films, hereby having secured the participation of the Americans in its festival.

Faced with these politico-cultural changes, the Film Festival Berlin was somewhat isolated, especially as the argument used, in particular by the Office of Foreign Affairs, of not maintaining diplomatic relations with the Soviet Union, was, as of 1956, no longer based on fact. Moreover, the Federal Republic of Germany itself was to be represented in the competition of 1956 in Karlovy Vary, even though it did not maintain diplomatic relations with Czechoslovakia. And that Berlin was »a bastion of freedom«, as it was so popularly called in the fifties, seemed quite questionable, especially if one considered that no one had raised any objections to the participation of Franco-Spain. West Germany was the one to use arguments which were determined by the idea of demarcation; commentary from the GDR was quite »all-German« during this period.

The Film Festival for the first time at its new location in the center of town

Several commentators were to quite deliberately make reference to Article II of the amended guidelines of the Berlin Film Festival: »The Film Festival should give proof of the development of cinematographic art to a large audience, bring together leading personalities of the film world for an exchange of ideas in Berlin, and contribute to the understanding and friendship between the peoples of different nations.« The newly acquired »A-status« of the Berlin Film Festival made political correction necessary.

The basic tenor of critique to this year's Festival was that it had been a disappointing film year. The Golden Bear went to TWELVE ANGRY MEN by Sidney Lumet; Henry Fonda accepted the award on his behalf. As a result of pressure from the producers' association, the Audiences' Choice Award was no longer presented. Alfred Bauer had not had an easy time in deciding to eliminate this award, as this evaluation by the viewers had been an original component of the Berlin Festival. It was in this year, 1957, that the Fédération Internationale de la Presse Cinématographique (FIPRESCI) awarded its »Prize of the International Federation of Film Journalists« for the first time (to the English entry WOMAN IN A DRESSING GOWN); it also held its annual conference in Berlin, no doubt signifying a certain acceptance towards the IFB. Nevertheless, the relationship between the Festival and the FIPRESCI was to become quite strained in the years to come.

JONAS - a new kind of West German film in the Competition

West Germany was represented in the Competition by an astonishing film: JONAS by Ottomar Domnick. The selection commission for German Entries had recommended this first feature film by Domnick for the Competition, as well as Rolf Hansen's conventional crime-melodrama DIE LETZTEN WERDEN DIE ERSTEN SEIN [The Last Shall Be First]. JONAS can be seen, within the realm of possible German film productions that year, as an experimental long shot; a singular, monolithic film, forerunner of the »New German Cinema« and of the »Autorenfilm« (films written and directed by the authors themselves). Domnick, by profession a neurologist, breaks with the tradition of narrative cinema and choosing a fragmentary, associative form, is at times committed to a rather dubious psychological structure which turns in and around itself. Hans Magnus Enzensberger had written the text to the film.

The film tells of unrequited love, and makes a subject of existential fear and isolation. The German film critics reacted, for the most part, quite reticently to this experiment, some even harshly dismissive. »Attempts at essentiality« is the title of an essay by Rolf Becker on the critique to be found in German films on contemporary issues; here Becker attributes to JONAS a »stylish modernity and modernistic chic«: »...so to say the filmic vinyl-topped table of the fifties. This ›avant-gardism‹ – in truth arrière-gardism – which is marveled at by some intellectuals who see the cinema ›finally elevated to art‹, and often in its avant-gardistic pervasion unconsciously comic, makes no commitments and is of no consequence for German cinema as a whole.« (Der Monat, No. 130, July 1959.) In the rigorousness of its means, the film is an affront to the cinema of the Federal Republic, and in style to a great degree inconsequential, yet still a signal, especially within the context of the selection of German films for the Film Festival. The film did however leave the selection commission in need of an explanation.

That is, their decision, in itself courageous, had to be justified. Alfred Bauer had been told that the film was difficult to understand and that the members of the selection commission had only understood the film after »Ministerial Supervisor Mrs. Spangenberg had clarified the meaning and contents of the film« (letter to Bauer,

May 27, 1957). The commission recommended that the Festival management therefore arranges a special press conference for the film and an introductory lecture before the showing. The director was asked for his consent, which would allow »an uninitiated audience« to understand ». . . the psychoanalytical symbolism of the film«. Domnick had no objections, and on his own initiative, added an introduction in English and French giving information to the contents of the film, and making a subtitling of the whole film superfluous, which at any rate had not seemed opportune for aesthetic reasons. Despite all these pedagogical measures, JONAS did not receive a prize. Yet it had been a gallant attempt to break with the wishy-washy traditions of the selection committee.

In contrast to the above: Helmut Käutner's HAUPTMANN VON KÖPENICK (»The Captain from Koepenick«) received six prizes at the Federal Prize Awards, including the Golden Cup as »best full-length feature film of international standard«.

The arrival of a star

Berliners still took a fancy to big names: Henny Porten was given thundering applause on her arrival at the Zoo-Palast; Vico Torriani doled out kisses to the backs of many a hand; Hildegard Knef and Peter van Eyck were swallowed up by the crowd; infatuation was felt for Trevor Howard, who had a reputation for being a man who held his liquor well, and Henry Fonda; and then Errol Flynn and Patricia Wymore arrived: »It is seven twenty-five p.m.: the plane from Frankfurt touches down, and taxis in. Are you ready? The time has come! Dr. Bauer, the Film Festival director instructs the musicians: fanfare for Errol and fanfare for Patricia, his wife who is arriving with him. But on board there are more very important persons: the Minister-President of Saarland and his wife. The President of the Berlin House of Representatives, Willy Brandt, Chief of Protocol Dr. Klein, and a giant bouquet of carnations are there to greet them. Politics comes first – which goes without saying... But as soon as greetings have been exchanged between the Saar and the Spree, and the landing strip left, a sun-tanned man with wavy brown hair appears at the

JONAS: Robert Graf, Elisabeth Bothaty

cabin door at the top of the gangway, looking exactly like that ›devilish guy‹ who had enabled Errol Flynn to win a million hearts.

Fanfare, cheers, hellos and ahs – beside Errol, Patricia Wymore appears in a white jersey suit. For seconds the couple remain at the top of the stairs. Journalists from the Bild newspaper ›shoot‹, no ›fire‹ their cameras. Patricia cuddles up to Errol and gives him a kiss, how could one ask for more!

The music blares. Errol nearly dies laughing at the brass instruments clustering round at the foot of the gangway, like sharks round a swimmer. ›Today's your birth-

TWELVE ANGRY MEN
»America's ›Twelve Angry Men‹ was made contrary to the traditionally strict principles of film. Only one location is used, the chamber of the laymen jury in a common court house. Here one sees twelve men, who by chance have become the jurors in a murder trial. The time-span covered lasts only as long as it takes for these twelve members of the jury to discuss their thoughts, prejudices, suspicions and to come to a verdict. There are no flashbacks, no interludes. The film merely takes these twelve men in this stuffy, shabby room and shows how their individual characters are revealed and take on form, as they talk, quarrel, almost beat each other up, and then reach agreement. This film is a great intellectual pleasure.« Friedrich Luft in Süddeutsche Zeitung, July 4, 1957

TWELVE ANGRY MEN: Henry Fonda

day, Mister Flynn, isn't it?‹ – ›Yes, that's right – forty-eight years old!‹ he cries out cockily and shakes and kisses hands, gazing into the women's eyes, yet never leaving his wife's side, so to say side by side, or rather foot to foot, that is: crocodile leather pumps to crocodile leather shoes.« The on-the-spot reporter is Ilse von Scotti, for the first number of the Festival paper »Film in Berlin«. Everything was registered in Berlin at a glance: pumps to low shoes – crocodile – as said; as well as bad manners: in the press it was indignantly noted that Flynn attended some of the receptions

Reception at the airport: Brigitte Succar, Alfred Bauer, Patricia Wymore, Errol Flynn

PR idea: reception of the Gloria on the Havel river, Grethe Weiser, Winnie Markus, Maria Brauner, Maria Holst

hardly shaven. But Berliners are forgiving, especially when an American speaks broken German.

Boxers and movie stars

On June 29th at the Sportpalast, Peter Müller, the champion, and the young challenger Gustav »Bubi« Scholz fought in the German middle-weight championship. At the ringside: O. E. Hasse, Heinz Rühmann, Hildegard Knef, Nadja Tiller and Ulla Jacobsson. The fight was short; the local hero »Bubi« Scholz was able to win his knock-out victory. And it was he who was the talk of the town at the Film Ball.

Hildegard Knef,
O. E. Hasse

International Jury for Feature Films
Jay Carmody (USA, president)
Jean de Baroncelli (France)
John Sutro (Great Britain)
Dalpathal Kothari (India)
Fernaldo Di Giammatteo (Italy)
Bunzaburo Hayashi (Japan)
Miguel Alemán jr. (Mexico)
Thorsten Eklann (Sweden)
José María Escudero (Spain)
Edmund Luft (FRG)
Ernst Schröder (FRG)

International Jury for Documentary and Short Films
Adolf Hübl (Austria, president)
Paul Louyet (Belgium)
Yrjö Rannikko (Finland)
Norman McLaren (Canada)
Ahmed Sefrioui (Morocco)
Karl Naef (Switzerland)
Paul Heimann (FRG)

The Awards of the International Jurys

Feature Films
Grand Prix of the 7th IFB
Golden Berlin Bear
TWELVE ANGRY MEN
USA, directed by Sidney Lumet

Silver Berlin Bear
for the best director
Mario Monicelli
for Padri e figli
Italy

Silver Berlin Bear
for the best actress
Yvonne Mitchell
in Woman in a Dressing Gown
Great Britain

Silver Berlin Bear
for the best actor
Pedro Infante
in Tizoc
Mexico

Special Prize for the best music
Silver Berlin Bear
Ravi Shankar
for Kabuliwala
India

Special Prize
for its most remarkable solution to the dramatic structure and its cultural-historical portrayal
Silver Berlin Bear
Amanecer en puerta oscura
Spain, directed by
José Maria Forqué

Long Documentary Films
1st Prize
Golden Berlin Bear
Secrets of Life
USA, directed by
James Algar

2nd Prize
Silver Berlin Bear
L'Ultimo paradiso
Italy, directed by
Folco Quilici

Ingmar Bergman

Disney-City

1958

June 27th–July 8th, 1958

The »Building Senator's sandbox« extended out all around the Memorial Church: a new stretch of subway and the Café Kranzler-Eck were under construction. Visitors could hardly get through to the Zoo-Palast. The advice given in the Festival paper was: »Leave your cars at home and come instead on foot equipped with a rag to clean your shoes.«

Opening in the new Kongreßhalle in Tiergarten District

For the invited guests of the 8th International Film Festival, however, there was no problem. They met in the green Tiergarten District away from the Kurfürstendamm, in the »glittering« Kongreßhalle. The residents of Berlin had flippantly nicknamed this new architecural feat the »pregnant oyster«. And despite pouring rain, thousands pilgrimaged to Tiergarten on this June 27th, to catch in passing a glimpse of the arriving stars.

Willy Brandt, the new Mayor of Berlin was able to welcome many illustrious guests: Jean Marais, who was also a member of the international jury and to whom Berliners gave a big hand, had arrived from France; seated in the auditorium as emissaries of the Italian film world were Valentina Cortese, Federico Fellini and Giulietta Masina; the Argentinian actor Carlos Thompson was on the list of guests, as were Bibi Anderson from Sweden, Eisuke Takizawa from Japan and – for Austria – Rudolf Forster. Frank Capra, who was to preside over the jury, Stanley Kramer and Peter van Eyck had all come, as of course had many German stars – Winnie Markus, Nadja Tiller and Walter Giller, Dieter Borsche, O. E. Hasse, Martin Held, Paul Klinger, Gerhard Riedmann and Curd Jürgens.

Berlin, politically the point of intersection between East and West

In his opening speech, Brandt emphasized the multifariousness of international film – and drew much applause. »Hence some films will strike us as odd or strange. The standards used from country to country for measuring the quality of a film or the actors' performance are hardly less diverse than the languages and customs of their peoples. That which is seen on one continent as perfect, will not always appeal to us here in Europe. Yet this fact should not as a consequence entice us to be petty. I have confidence in the openmindedness of this city and that we shall be spared manifestations of intolerance on the one hand, and oversensitivity on the other.« And, of course, the political appeal was not forgotten: »Here, right through this city, a boundary has been imposed, seeking to sever the residents of Berlin from each other, a boundary which not only divides Germany, its people and the nation, but also symbolizes that rift which is the basis of the international crisis causing us all such anxiety.« It is also as a political point of intersection that Brandt attached the significance of the Festival, for the »films of the peoples of different nations shall be shown to the residents of the whole of Berlin, that is, also to our fellow citizens from the Eastern Sector and our countrymen from the surrounding areas«. The Federal Minister for All-German Affairs, Ernst Lemmer, was seated in the auditorium as well.

Jean Marais, surrounded by fans at Mariendorf harness race course

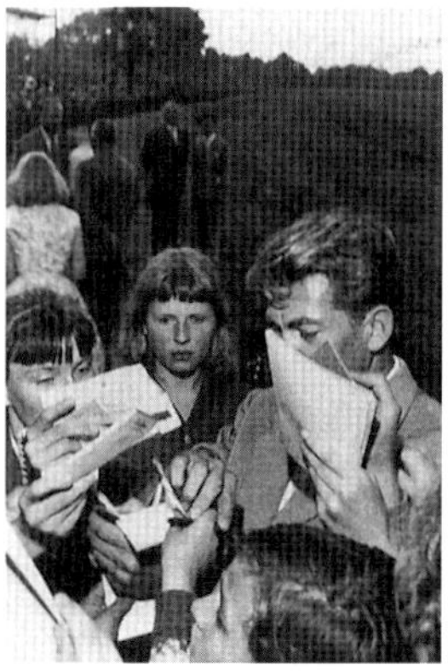

Karena Niehoff, a critic who was not only souverain, but also alert to political implications, wrote that »the nervous boldness of the ›stubborn city on the front‹ is – fortunately enough – no longer Berlin's greatest attraction.« Many commentators stressed the special political position of West Berlin and also attributed the Film Festival with a function as a cultural as well as political crossroad for East and West. The Soviet Union had been sent an invitation for participation in the Film Festival; most had expected them to accept, which however was not the case; they declined in protest to an error in form. The Berlin Film Festival had ultimately been given a new role, which was also now being acknowledged by more and more of the public at large. »In the meantime, one no longer expects spite and stubborness from Berlin, but vitality, flexibility and openess; when the Festival took place for the first time in 1951, it was as a political demonstration of western cultural life which was to make the differences to the Soviet zone visible – which made sense at the time, but has gradually taken on the form of anachronistic self-righteousness.« (Der Tagesspiegel, Jan. 11, 1958.)

SMULTRONSTÄLLET
»Even though the Indian Film DO ANKHEN BARAH HAATH was only awarded the 2nd prize by the official jury, it outclassed all the others. The Golden Bear went to Sweden's problematically artificial sequence of images, ›Wild Strawberries‹, which, however, was less convincing in the more optimistic variations of Ingmar Bergman, than in the performance of the 78 year old Victor Sjöström.«
Werner Jungeblodt in: Echo der Zeit, July 20, 1958

And now to the films: SMULTRONSTÄLLET (»Wild Strawberries«) by Ingmar Bergman, which ran at the Festival as »Am Ende des Tages« and then later was distributed under the title »Wilde Erdbeeren«, received the Golden Bear, a decision with which the critics were not all in agreement. Sidney Poitier was awarded the prize for best actor, for his portrayal of a convict in Stanley Kramer's anti-racist film THE DEFIANT ONES. This role and the distinction received by Poitier in Berlin, were his breakthrough as an international star. The other two American entries were WILD IS THE WIND by George Cukor with Anna Magnani, which received a Silver Bear, and Douglas Sirk's A TIME TO LOVE AND A TIME TO DIE, which raised objections in the Festival committee, as there was disagreement as to its »artistic significane«. The Swiss entry was a film adaption of Dürrenmatt's ES GESCHAH AM HELLICHTEN TAG (»It Happened in Broad Daylight«) by Ladislao Vajda with Heinz Rühmann and Michel Simon. Receiving positive reviews were the Indian film DO ANKHEN BARAH HAATH [Two Eyes – Twelve Hands] by V. Shantaram, and in particular, the Japanese film by Tadashi Imai, JUN-AI MONOGATARI [A Story of Pure Love], on which Wolfgang Schimming commented in the »Rheinische Post«: »New contents and images seem only to thrive and reach maturity in the distant young film nations, this is hardly the case in the classical film countries, where contents have become stale and the technical qualities slicker and slicker. In JUN-AI MONOGATARI, Japan has taken up the case of a young working woman living in a welfare home who, suffering from the effects of radioactivity, has incurable leukemia. In the hospital scenes and the seriousness of

Jubilant crowds in front of the Kongreßhalle, site of the »ceremonious opening«

their portrayal, one becomes conscious of that reality which is tragically experienced as a result of the atomic bombs.« (July 12, 1958.) By and large, the distribution of prizes by the jury under the presidency of Frank Capra met with the approval of the critics. Belonging to the jury for the Germans was, among others, the Berliner director Gerhard Lamprecht, as well as Willy Haas, who had already, in the twenties, been editor of the »Film-Kurier« and the »Literarische Welt«, and was one of the most versed reviewers of international film, having also written screenplays for Friedrich Wilhelm Murnau and G. W. Pabst.

Commotion is caused by the West German film entry.

In 1958, German cinema had still not recovered from its low. At a meeting on June 3rd, the selection commission nominated only one film as official German entry, Hans Domnick's TRAUMSTRASSE DER WELT [Dream Road of the World], a documentary film. Theodor Baensch informed his boss, the Senator of Education, that no feature film worthy of the Festival had been found among those submitted for a viewing. »Dr. Bauer will clarify whether or not the German program can be extended to include the feature film of the Bavaria, TAIGA (about the fate of prisoners of war) which is most likely quite good.« (The film referred to here was a film by Wolfgang Liebeneiner based on a book by Herbert Reinecker about a German woman doctor who is a prisoner of war played by Ruth Leuwerik, in a Sibirian labor camp.) Submitted and rejected had been the following films: DER ACHTE WOCHENTAG (»The Eighth Day of the Week«) by Alexander Ford, a German-Polish co-production from CCC Film; Leo de Laforgue's KANAILLEN which imitated neorealistic stylistic means; and for the time being, POLIKUSCHKA based on a Tolstoy novella, a CCC production too, directed by Carmine Gallone. Discussed in passing was also Wolfgang Staudte's KANONENSERENADE (»Always Victorious«) with Vittorio De Sica. It was only shortly before the Festival began that POLIKUSCHKA was nominated as the second German entry and programmed for July 8th, the last day of the Festival. On July 7th, Alfred Bauer notified Senatorial Supervisor Wallner-Basté that »the program for the closing night would have to be altered in a hurry«. Artur Brauner, the responsible producer

Friedrich Dürrenmatt and Michel Simon at the Film Ball in the Palais am Funkturm

Giulietta Masina and Federico Fellini in front of the Kongreßhalle

International Jury for Feature Films
Frank Capra (USA, president)
J. Novais Teixeira (Brazil)
Jean Marais (France)
Raul Rotha (Great Britain)
L. B. Rao (India)
Duilio Coletti (Italy)
Michi Tanaka (Japan)
Gerhard T. Buchholz (FRG)
Willy Haas (FRG)
Gerhard Lamprecht (FRG)
Leopold Reidemeister (FRG)

International Jury for Documentary and Short Films
Wali ed-Din Sameh (Egypt, president)
Edward Toner (Ireland)
A. Koolhaas (Netherlands)
Jan-Olof Olsson (Sweden)
A. Forter (Switzerland)
Günther Birkenfeld (FRG)
Werner Eisbrenner (FRG)

had informed Bauer that the synchronization of the film could not be completed in time; as a substitute, he offered the Film Festival Geza von Radvanyi's remake of MÄDCHEN IN UNIFORM [Girls in Uniform], which Press Spokesman Dr. Hans Borgelt and Dr. Georg Hossfelder, business manager of the Spio and delegate of the German film industry, took a look at on July 7th. They were in favor of the substitutional nomination and Bauer accepted their decision. This change in program was not all that inopportune, as there had anyway been objections to the selection of POLIKUSCHKA as a German entry; it was a German-Italian-French co-production, with an Italian director (Carmine Gallone) and actors and actresses from all three countries (Folco Lulli, Ellen Schwiers, Antonella Lualdi, Ivan Desny and Gabrielle Dorziat). As Alfred Bauer stated in addressing Wallner-Basté: »German film-makers seem to me to be represented better in MÄDCHEN IN UNIFORM than in a German-French-Italian co-production about whose appropriacy the committee of the 8th International Film Festival Berlin could not reach a hundred percent consensus.« In the press there were also rumors that POLIKUSCHKA was taken out of the program for being »all too Italian«. Just the same, MÄDCHEN IN UNIFORM was not able to make up for the general low quality of German film productions, which Federal Minister of the Interior Dr. Gerhard Schröder described in his speech at the presentation of the German Film Prize; and as a consequence, he encouraged the film industry to have the »courage to use so-called unpopular means«, much to the indignation of the representative of the Spio, Walter Koppel, who then voiced opinions contrary to Schröder's remarks.

»Congratulations! The ›Eighth‹ was a success!« stood in the »Abend« (July 9, 1958) and most of the other papers as well reported of a film program with an amazing number of unusual films worthy of discussion, and of the many guests, who were always a yardstick of the popularity of the Festival. The Golden Book of the City of Berlin was signed by Walt Disney, whose films had been shown in Berlin since the

THE DEFIANT ONES: Tony Curtis, Sidney Poitier

The Awards of the International Jurys

Feature Films
Grand Prix of the 8th IFB
Golden Berlin Bear
Smultronstället
Sweden, directed by
Ingmar Bergman

Silver Berlin Bear
for the best director
Tadashi Imai
for Jun-ai monogatari
Japan

Silver Berlin Bear
for the best actress
Anna Magnani
in Wild is the Wind
USA

Silver Berlin Bear
for the best actor
Sidney Poitier
in The Defiant Ones
USA

Special Prize
Silver Berlin Bear
Do ankhen barah haath
India, directed by
V. Shantaram

Long Documentary Films
1st Prize
Golden Berlin Bear
Perri
USA, directed by
N. Paul Kenworthy jr.,
Ralph Wright

2nd Prize
Silver Berlin Bear
Traumstrasse der Welt
FRG, directed by
Hans Domnick

Smultronstället:
Victor Sjöström

very first Festival and who had almost regularly received awards. Disney belonged to the Berlin Film Festival and for this one day the Festival belonged to Disney. He was like a father figure from the Promised Land of Movies, and even other celebrities waited in line for his autograph. As Disney was signing the guest book, Willy Brandt was heard to say: »Our children are constant reminders of your characters.« Sympathy, it seems, was mutual indeed.

Walt Disney – Berlin's darling

Reception at the Mayor's: Walt Disney receives a porcelain bear from Willy Brandt.

Walt Disney

Politics and the Nouvelle Vague

1959

June 26th–July 7th, 1959

Football fans in Berlin: in Olympic Stadium, Eintracht Frankfurt played against the Offenbacher Kickers in the German Football Championship. The »Main Derby« on June 28th was won by the team from Frankfurt in extra time, 5 to 3.

Politicians in Berlin: the Federal Assembly met for the election of the President of the Federal Republic of Germany. On July 1st, Dr. Heinrich Lübke was elected new Federal President in the second ballot. Defeated were Carlo Schmid and Max Becker. The election had been broadcast live on TV.

Movie stars in Berlin: Sophia Loren was wearing a white tulle dress at the opening gala, a mink cape when visiting the Mayor at City Hall in Schöneberg, and a lacy summer hat on the Kurfürstendamm: such hats were irreverently called »wagon wheels«. Jean-Claude Brialy's bow tie was also marvelled at – not the traditional »propeller«, but the fashionable »shoe string«. David Niven looked smart and distinguished, Rita Hayworth played the lady with sex appeal, Van Heflin grinned both amiably and uncouthly, Giulietta Masina beamed, Esther Williams rode – on top of a wave of enthusiasm. Grand entrances, airs and escapades: Elsa Maxwell, the gossipy sharp-tongued columnist, kept her eyes open, as eyes were kept on her. Photographers took snap shots of Elsa Maxwell with... Such was everyday life at the Festival of 1959.

The organizers registered, not without pleasure, that 53 countries were participating in the 9th International Film Festival Berlin, more than ever before. Also the number of guests, delegates, artists, film executives, politicians and journalists was beyond all expectations. This positive balance was not to be taken for granted this year, the year of the second Berlin Crisis – the first being the Blockade in 1948/49. In November 1958, Nikita Khrushchev had declared an end to Berlin's Four-Power-Status and demanded a demilitarized »Free City of West Berlin«. At the Geneva Conference of Foreign Ministers, a plan for freedom, from the vantage point of the West, was discussed, which was also to guarantee unity for Berlin. Within this political context, it was in no way astonishing that the speakers of the Film Festival, as well as journalists from Berlin and West Germany spoke out for an »acknowledgement of a free Berlin in the heart of Europe by all free peoples« when the Film Festival was opened on June 26th. Willy Brandt in his speech also went into the international efforts towards finding a solution to the Berlin crisis: »One could almost assume that the conference of foreign ministers in Geneva was interrupted to please our Dr. Bauer. In any case, the curtain of the international political stage was lowered before the curtain for the Film Festival Berlin could be raised this evening.«

The Film Festival overshadowed by the second Berlin Crisis

In East Berlin banners could be seen hanging across the streets on which were written: »The bear is growling, be sly and make Strauss' fur fly.« This slogan alluded to Minister of Defence Franz Josef Strauss and his politics, which strived for a reestablishment of the West German armed forces, as well as for atomic armament in the Federal Republic.

Yet despite such political conflict and the polemic tones in the press of the GDR, the off-stage political dialogue between East and West had not come to a standstill. As in the year before, foreign and West German journalists informed themselves in East Berlin about Defa productions; they visited Defa Studios in Babelsberg and followed up invitations to visit the East Berlin film club the »Möwe« during the »Berlinale«.

Alexandre Alexandre on the »Nouvelle Vague«

The Festival paper »Film in Berlin« published a short essay by Alexandre Alexandre on the »Nouvelle Vague« and its origins; it was one of the first articles to appear in German calling attention to Truffaut, Chabrol, as well as Louis Malle. In Cannes, François Truffaut had captured attention with LES QUATRE CENTS COUPS (»Four Hundred Blows«), hors concours. Alfred Bauer had also been impressed by this film. Bauer's informant in France, as well as confidant, was the journalist Alexandre Alexandre, emigrant from Berlin. Bauer entrusted him with the preselection of French films for the Festival. Alexandre used the leeway allowed him by Bauer to also suggest films which went against the trends, contrasting to big name movies, or ambitious entertainment films. In a letter to Alexandre (April 13, 1959), Bauer remarked on the films which Alexandre had proposed for the 9th IFB: ARCHIMÈDE LE CLOCHARD (»The Magnificent Tramp«) by Gilles Grangier – »Gabin is very popular in Germany; if this film is up to the Festival, it ought to be a success . . .«, which was the case and Jean Gabin received the Silver Berlin Bear for the best actor. ORFEU NEGRO (»Black Orpheus«) by Marcel Camus – »would, perhaps be a valuable contribution«; the film was however run in Cannes. HIROSHIMA MON AMOUR by Alain Resnais – »a touchy subject«. LES QUATRES CENTS COUPS by François Truffaut – »also here I have some second thoughts as to the theme«. LE CHEMIN DES ÉCOLIERS [Student's Road] by Michel Boisrond – »important alone for the outstanding directing and casting«; roles in this film were played by Françoise Arnoul, Bourvil, Alain Delon and Lino Ventura. POURQUOI VIENS-TU SI TARD? [Why Do You Come So Late?] by Henri Decoin – »I am very interested in this film, if it's any good«. Bauer himself then brought three more titles into play: Geza von Radvanyis German-French co-production DOUZE HEURES D'HORLOGE/IHR VERBRECHEN WAR LIEBE [Twelve Hours By the Clock], the Pierre Fresnay film LES PÉTROLEURS and Albert Lamorisses's LE VOYAGE EN BALLON (»Stowaway in the Sky«).

Sophia Loren

Alfred Bauer, Esther Williams

Willy Brandt, Rita Hayworth

The success of Truffaut's film in Cannes gave the impulse for the acceptance of a »Nouvelle Vague« film in Berlin. Bauer was also acting upon the enthusiasm of Alexandre for the films of these young directors. Yet none of the initially disputed titles was then invited to Berlin, instead they chose Claude Chabrol's LES COUSINS (»The Cousins«). »The young Claude Chabrol has taken up the moral offensive against the ›modern world, which stifles innocence‹, as he recently declared in connection with his film LES COUSINS, and in his pale totality he is a playmate of Evilness and Godlessness, setting out to bring the moon down from the sky when it darkens the sun. Chabrol is in league with Baudelaire, with Flaubert, Balzac and Ionesco.« (Karena Niehoff, Der Tagesspiegel, July 12, 1959.) The jury awarded the Grand Prix of the Film Festival to Chabrol. In the years to come, the directors of the »Nouvelle Vague« were able to show their films in Berlin again and again. Truffaut, Chabrol, Godard – in the Berlin Film Festival they had found their forum.

The Golden Bear for Claude Chabrol's LES COUSINS

Although the selection of films had attained general approval in this year – in the Competition were films by Akira Kurosawa, Leopoldo Torre Nilsson and Fons Rademakers – the organizers were quite critical of their own success. More than anything else, a further improvement in the selection procedure was discussed. In a letter to Alfred Bauer, Senator Tiburtius asks: »Is it possible to be more selective in choosing both foreign and German feature films, without violating an international regulation?« (July 13, 1959.) This was in fact a problem, as the selection of the films was made in the respective countries and the possibilities of the Festival to reject an film already nominated were limited. Bauer suggested making more visits to the individual countries, in order to get on-the-spot information and to assure an influence in the selection early on. He had had good experience with Alexandre Alexandre, his confidant in France. However, these plans were thwarted by a lack of funds. Bauer's attempt to attain an increase in Federal funds, to DM 300 000, was not successful.

Jean Renoir, Willy Brandt

Robert Aldrich, Edmund Luft, Ignazio Silone

Wine-tasting at the Hotel Gehrhus: Willy Brandt, Rita Hayworth, James Hill, Rut Brandt, Van Heflin

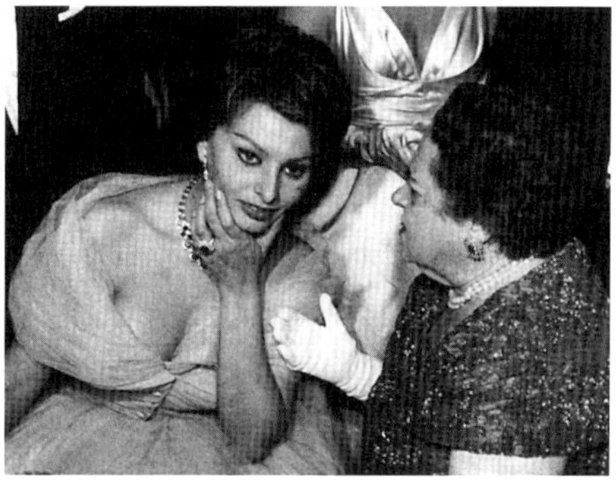

Sophia Loren with Hollywood's famous gossip columnist Elsa Maxwell

International Jury for
Feature Films
Robert Aldrich
(USA, president)
Johan Jacobsen (Denmark)
Charles Ford (France)
John Bryan (Great Britain)
Ignazio Silone (Italy)
Shigueo Miyata (Japan)
Waley Eddin Sameh (UAR)
O. E. Hasse (FRG)
Gerhard Prager (FRG)
Fritz Podehl (FRG)
Walther Schmieding (FRG)

International Jury for
Documentary and
Short Films
Curt Oertel
(FRG, president)
Paul Davay (Belgium)
Katina Paxinou (Greece)
M. D. Bath (India)
Odd Hølaas (Norway)
Alfonso Sánchez (Spain)
Hans Cürlis (FRG)

The Awards of the
International Jurys

Feature Films
Grand Prix of the 9th IFB
Golden Berlin Bear
LES COUSINS
France, directed by
Claude Chabrol

Silver Berlin Bear
for the best director
Akira Kurosawa
for KAKUSHI TORIDE NO
SAN-AKUNIN
Japan

Silver Berlin Bear
for the best actress
Shirley MacLaine
in ASK ANY GIRL
USA

DER REST IST SCHWEIGEN:
Ingrid Andree,
Hardy Krüger

When Sophia Loren is asked at a press conference: »›Have you ever seen any German postwar films and if so, what were your impressions?‹« – she answers, »›I rarely go to the movies.‹ As there is laughter, she hesitantly adds: ›I've surely seen a few, but I can't remember.‹ – So much for German postwar films. It would however be unfair to overlook those which did make the mark.« (Münchner Merkur, June 8, 1959.)

Silver Berlin Bear
for best actor
Jean Gabin
in ARCHIMÈDE LE CLOCHARD
France

Special Prize
for outstanding single performance
Silver Berlin Bear
Hayley Mills
in TIGER BAY
Great Britain

Long Documentary Films
Golden Berlin Bear
WHITE WILDERNESS
USA, directed by
James Algar

And yet it was this year's German entry, Helmut Käutner's DER REST IST SCHWEIGEN (»The Rest is Silence«), which contrary to all expectations did not receive an award, that was one of the most remarkable films of the Competition. The selection commission had clearly had reservations on the film, and quasi as compensation for its »difficult« subject matter had invited instead the comedy UND DAS AM MONTAGMORGEN [And That on Monday Morning] as opening film. It was therefore all the more surprising that Käutner's film was a success in the reviews which discussed this film more than any other. The film, a modern adaptation of Hamlet, set in the industrial milieu of the Ruhr District (about a fratricide in the last year of the war and its discovery in 1959), was considered by Walther Schmieding in the Essen »Ruhr Nachrichten«, »the greatest and most ambitious venture« of the 28 feature films of the Festival: »In this formally often brilliant film, there are two thoughts which set it apart from all the others. For one there is the confrontation with National Socialism and the ›coming to terms‹ with one's own past, which is at least begun here using the material of ›Hamlet‹ as a model. For the other, there is Hamlet's decision to no longer kill, since the problems of the world are not to be solved by murdering and murdering in return.« (July 19, 1959.)

PARADIES UND FEUEROFEN: a documentary film about Israel up for discussion

Controversial as well was the West German documentary PARADIES UND FEUEROFEN [Paradise and Oven of Fire] by Herbert Viktor, a reportage on the State of Israel. On April 8th 1959, IFA-Productions Frankfurt/M. addressed a letter to Senator Tiburtius, in which it called attention to the fact that the film had been submitted as a German entry to the 9th Film Festival Berlin, and simultaneously – and this was the unusual – pointed out in detail, that the film fulfilled »all requirements of the regulations«, and in particular »the guidelines set down in Article 8. This film about Israel was

LES COUSINS: Juliette Mayniel, Claude Cerval, Jean-Claude Brialy

The beginning of a career: admirers smashed champagne glasses for ›starlet‹ Barbara Valentin.

produced in an effort to ›contribute to the understanding and friendship between nations‹, and especially to awaken in us Germans, after the tormenting experiences of the past, a new understanding between us and the Jewish people, without insulting the feelings of other groups.« In closing the IFA adds: »Therefore we believe that nothing should be left undone to enable a Berlin screening of the film Paradies und Feuerofen. It should be coordinated under the auspices of the Berlin Film Festival, in order to allow the première of this film in Germany to become the event it deserves to be, almost exactly 20 years after the world première of the film Jud Süss at the same location.« This reference to Veit Harlan's anti-semitic, Nazi propaganda film Jud Süss in this context is quite shocking, yet what is meant by this unfortunate statement is nothing more than that this Jew-baiting film should be countered by a bit of filmic correction and »reparation«, a desire which should be understood within the context of the political efforts being made in the Federal Republic of Germany to come to terms with the Nazi atrocities and the war crime trials in process since 1958 against Nazi criminals.

In trying to decide whether the film should participate, the persons responsible proved themselves quite insecure. The head of the Berlin Film Section, Herbert Antoine, criticized the rating of »highly commendable« which had been conferred upon the film by the Film Assessment Board (FBW). Both he and Senator Tiburtius pointed out that in their opinion the picture presented of Israel was too subjective, and they found certain shots and sequences »arbitrary and not always dictated by the best of taste«. Hence, and because they suspected that at least some of the scenes had been shot without an official Israeli permit, they came out against the film. Otherwise they feared there would be protest from the Israelis (noted by Antoine, April 20, 1959). Their appraisal was in contrast to the assessment of the FBW, which had found the film outstanding in its »dramaturgically well-thought out form«, in its »objective portrayal« which does not shy from being critical, and in that the authors do not deny having »a decisive opinion on the subject of their report themselves« (Film Assessment Board Wiesbaden, statement of reasons, Sept. 11, 1958).

In this difference of opinion between the Berlin Senate, the Festival management and the selection commission, the advocates of the film were able to assert themselves. The film was accepted as the official German entry in the category of full-length documentary films and received – under the protest of the Egyptian jury member, Mary Ghadban – the prize of the International Catholic Organization for Cinema (OCIC). The critics also praised the film in their reviews. And yet: international protest was not long in coming. In »Al-Alam« an »independent daily paper for the arab world« published in Damascus, there is much sharp polemics against the film and reference is made to the unsettled problem of Palestine. Nevertheless that which caused even more surprise in Berlin was the announcement that Paradies und Feuerofen, after an elite circle, including President Isaak Ben Zwi, Prime Minister David Ben Gurion and Foreign Minister Golda Meir had seen the film, was not to be released in Israel for showings to the public. The Berlin paper »Der Tag« summed it up: »With this decision, the much feared response has been given to a question concerning all Germans: what good could come from a film about Israel when it has been made by Germans, of all people.« (Aug. 11, 1959.)

A letter

By Toshiro Mifune

Dear Mr. Moritz de Hadeln,
When I was informed that Berlin's International Film Festival would celebrate its 40th anniversary, several of my memories concerning this festival came to my mind. It was thirty years ago (probably in 1959) when we participated in the nineth Berlin International Film Festival with KAKUSHI TORIDE NO SAN-AKUNIN *(»The Hidden Fortress«) by director Akira Kurosawa. We were honored with the »Fipresci Award«. The films presented to the festival were played in the theater which was situated near the Brandenburg Gate in East Germany. I was deeply moved to know that the city had been divided into West Berlin and East Berlin, and that it had forced many families, couples, brothers and sisters to live separately. These reminiscences made me look around the drawers and shelves in my study to find one picture.*

*In the picture, there are Mr. Nagamasa Kawakita, Mrs. Kashiko Kawakita, Ms. Michiko Tanaka, and the director of the festival, Mr. Alfred Bauer. We were all much younger having a good time talking. Mr. and Mrs. Kawakita, who imported and introduced »Kaigi wa odoru« (*DER KONGRESS TANZT*) and many other German films into Japan in the golden age of the German »Ufa Film Company«, spoke German, English and Chinese fluently. Mr. Kawakita has passed away. Ms. Michiko Tanaka moved to Munich in 1980, but last year (in 1988), I received the letter telling me of her death.*

Today, film industries in many countries are having a difficult time due to the development of television, video and other leisure industries. In Japan, nowadays, films can draw only ten percent of the audiences of its glorious days. However, we believe that a good film attracts many human hearts. And this belief in films still encourages us to keep producing one.

Sincerely yours,
Toshiro Mifune

Michiko Tanaka,
Alfred Bauer, Kashiko and
Nagamasa Kawakita

Karin Baal on her way to
the Film Ball
in the Palais am Funkturm

The Festival in the district
of Wedding: special
screenings for »visitors from
the East« in the Corso
movie house

The jubilee: an average affair

1960

June 24th–July 5th, 1960

At Tempelhof Airport Cary Grant answers reporters questions. When asked how he manages to look so young he replies: »Well, I don't know. It's just me«. On arrival all guests receive the obligatory miniature stuffed bear and a bottle of champagne; in years to come an instant coffee set was to be presented.

Thousands of Berliners gather at Bahnhof Zoo (the central railroad station) and buy a platform ticket for 20 pfennigs in order to give Jean Gabin a triumphant reception. The man with the cap disappears in the delighted crowd. Where is the star and where are the Berliners? Finding the reporters too pushy Trevor Howard comments: »All Berlin is crazy!«.

Male stars and no »Sexival«

It is the male stars who dominate at the decennial. Vittorio Gassmann, Jean-Paul Belmondo, Gene Kelly, Richard Widmark, and Richard Attenborough. They also get the Berliners lining up to see them. Hans Borgelt, press manager of the IFB, makes a virtue out of a necessity and points out that the International Film Festival Berlin is no »Sexival« – a reference to Cannes and to the previous year in which Barbara Valentin »indecently« – as it was called at the time – made her bid for the top in Berlin. »The lack of glamour, spice and fashion (which really isn't so bad, after all) is nothing to be proud of« wrote Karena Niehoff, »and if the dirty career operations performed by the actresses bear more modest (or rather hidden) fruits than the well ordered male film industry, that may well be valuable in some respects – but it doesn't say anything about the quality of the films, nor does it improve them one iota.« (Der Tagesspiegel, July 10, 1960.)

When the 10th International Film Festival Berlin ended on July 5th, with the closing ceremony traditionally hosted by the Federal Press Spokesman, Undersecretary Felix von Eckhardt, feelings were mixed. The weather had been wet and cold, the films had disappointed almost everybody, and the jury's decisions left nearly

Cheers for Jean Gabin at Zoo Station

THE ANGRY SILENCE: Richard Attenborough

THE ANGRY SILENCE
»A courageous topic, which raises questions as to how far the individual can assert himself in the face of mass decisions, even though – or because – he has nothing but his common sense to help him. (...) The individual characters are depicted in a clear and powerful manner: the ambitious trade union secretary, the old, resigned fighter, the young members who are ›in it‹ because they don't know any different, and the loners who haven't yet lost a sense of the necessity of personal freedom. There is no attempt to protect the employer's side, either.«
Else Goelz in: Stuttgarter Zeitung, July 8, 1960

everyone perplexed. It had been no more than a »festival of work«. Although the Festival had been able to hold its own vis-à-vis Cannes (whose 1960 competition had not been convincing either) there could be no talk of a dazzling jubilee, which had, in fact, been the aim. »Cinema Disaster« was the pungent title in the »Frankfurter Rundschau« (July 7, 1960). It was, above all, the distribution of the prizes which caused displeasure, both among the guests of the International Film Festival Berlin, and among the journalists and the Berlin audiences. The latter clearly expressed their disapproval when it was announced that the Grand Prix was to be awarded to the Spanish film EL LAZARILLO DE TORMES (»Lazarillo«) by César Ardavin. This was a ballad based on a 16th century picaresque novel about the corruption of childhood innocence. »This jury stands accused; it has proven to be the worst in years. Its decisions testify to its bankruptcy and are a disgrace to the Berlin Festival« commented Karl-Heinz Krüger in the Berlin newspaper »Abend« on July 6th. He was not the only one to attack the jury. The feeling was that the decision to award the prize was a poorly conceived joke on the part of the jury, which was presided over by the American actor Harold Lloyd. It had been expected that an award would be given for the British film THE ANGRY SILENCE made by the young director Guy Green, with Richard Attenborough playing the part of a young worker who resists the pressure of the collective, which has decided to go on strike in a factory. However, this film did receive the prizes of the OCIC and FIPRESCI, a fact which did help to cool raised tempers somewhat when the prizes were awarded.

What had started as an expedient demonstration in 1951 – in his opening speech Willy Brandt called the first Film Festival in Berlin a political affair – had developed, a decade later, into an institution. Berlin's cultural life was no longer conceivable without it. Yet even so, during the first decade the Film Festival had not succeeded in freeing itself from the shadow of Cannes. This could not simply be explained in terms of a crisis in international film production, in which the only outstanding films were those made in France; it was also a symptom of the stagnation in Berlin. The guidelines imposed restrictions on the selection procedure. Films could not be rejected unless they hurt the national pride of a country.

From its very inception, Alfred Bauer had invited the participation of films from the Third World in the Berlin Festival. Films from Egypt had appeared continuously in the Berlin program, and contacts to India had also been good. The high representation by Asiatic countries in 1960 was accounted for by Japan (a traditional film country which participated with two films), Pakistan, the Philippines, Korea, Thailand, and India. Contemporary critics were severe in their judgement of films from the so-called developing countries. »The screen was simply flooded with experiments from countries with underdeveloped film industries. They were harming themselves by presenting their local products for comparison. It was impossible not to be bored watching this completely uninhibited, overabundance of exotic images. Annoyance at so much wasted effort was only alleviated by pity for those who had been so ill-advised.« (Dora Fehling, Telegraf, July 7, 1960.) In spite of such objections Bauer adhered to his policy of including films from the Third World in the Competition. From 1965 on an additional forum was established with countries giving a representational show. On January 29th 1960, at the 7th session of the advisory board, Senator Tiburtius reduced this policy to a simple formula: »Win over the underdeveloped countries for Berlin. Don't let them be tempted by the East.« (Quoted in the minutes.) The selection commission also had to put up with critical

KIRMES [The Fair]: a scene with Hans Mahnke, Juliette Mayniel, Wolfgang Reichmann

comments regarding the short films, whose standard had been a constant cause for complaint in the previous years. »Nothing provocative, nothing imaginative, no élan« noted Dora Fehling (Telegraf, July 7, 1960). Ethel Schwirten could only recall »countless little films« which had not been much more than travel brochures and factory reports (Frankfurter Rundschau, July 7, 1960).

All that remained was one great film from France, whose formal and thematic rigor had shocked many, yet which nevertheless received the Silver Berlin Bear for the best director – even if Else Goelz, writing in the »Stuttgarter Zeitung« (July 8, 1960) found the decision »had been made on the basis of some mysterious brain twister«. Jean-Luc Godard impressed the 10th International Film Festival Berlin with his film A BOUT DE SOUFFLE (»Breathless«), leaving the critics speechless. Not one of the reviewers dared to deny that Godard's film had »formal qualities«. In »Die Zeit« Thilo Koch wrote that »superficially the film used very modest means (. . .) but the acting performances of Jean Seberg and Jean-Paul Belmondo accomplish more than would be the case with a wide screen and technicolor. Decisive, however, is the fact that Godard (. . .) mainly tells his story with the camera and with a dramatic sense which is in the best French tradition too.« (July 8, 1960.) Several critics were shocked by the infringements of moral codes. The indignation of Berlin critic Irene Pulst was aroused because »of the trickery being played with the magic word New Wave, of which we no longer want any part, because elements ripe for jail are being given the attributes of the New Wave« (Spandauer Volksblatt, July 8, 1960). She also included Robert Bressons's PICKPOCKET in her critique. Heinz Mudrich, commenting in his »Berlinale« concluding report, discovered »Love, thieves, people, and masses«, plus a »criminal wave of the brand ›steal if you can‹. First of all there was the pickpocket, in which the French do-it-yourself picture-maker Robert Bresson really does not show much more than a pickpocket, and a glamorous one at that (. . .) not to mention the morbid Michel in A BOUT DE SOUFFLE, who breaks open cars the way others break open nuts.« And he did not find »one single word on morals« when commenting on the award which went to Godard. (Die Zeit, July 15, 1960.)

International Jury for Feature Films
Harold Lloyd (USA, president)
Georges Auric (France)
Henry Reed (Great Britain)
Sohrab Modi (India)
Floris Luigi Ammannati (Italy)
Hidemi Ima (Japan)
Joaquin de Entrambasaguas (Spain)
Frank Wisbar (FRG)
Georg Ramseger (FRG)
Werner R. Heymann (FRG)
Eva Staar (FRG)

International Jury for Documentary and Short Films
Johannes Eckardt (FRG, president)
Roberto Alejandro Tálice (Argentina)
Ludwig Gesek (Austria)
Lars Krantz (Sweden)
Semih Tugrul (Turkey)
Tahar Cheriaa (Tunisia)
Edwin Redslob (FRG)

The Awards of the International Jurys

Feature Films
Grand Prix of the 10th IFB
Golden Berlin Bear
El lazarillo de Tormes
Spain, directed by
César Ardavin

Silver Berlin Bear
for the best director
Jean-Luc Godard
for A bout de souffle
France

Silver Berlin Bear
for the best actress
Juliette Mayniel
in Kirmes
FRG

Silver Berlin Bear
for the best actor
Fredric March
in Inherit the Wind
USA

Special Prize
for the best comedy
Silver Berlin Bear
Les Jeux de l'amour
France, directed by
Philippe de Broca

Long Documentary Films
Golden Berlin Bear
Faja Lobbi
Netherlands, directed by
Herman van der Horst

Special Mention
Mandara
Switzerland, directed by
René Gardi

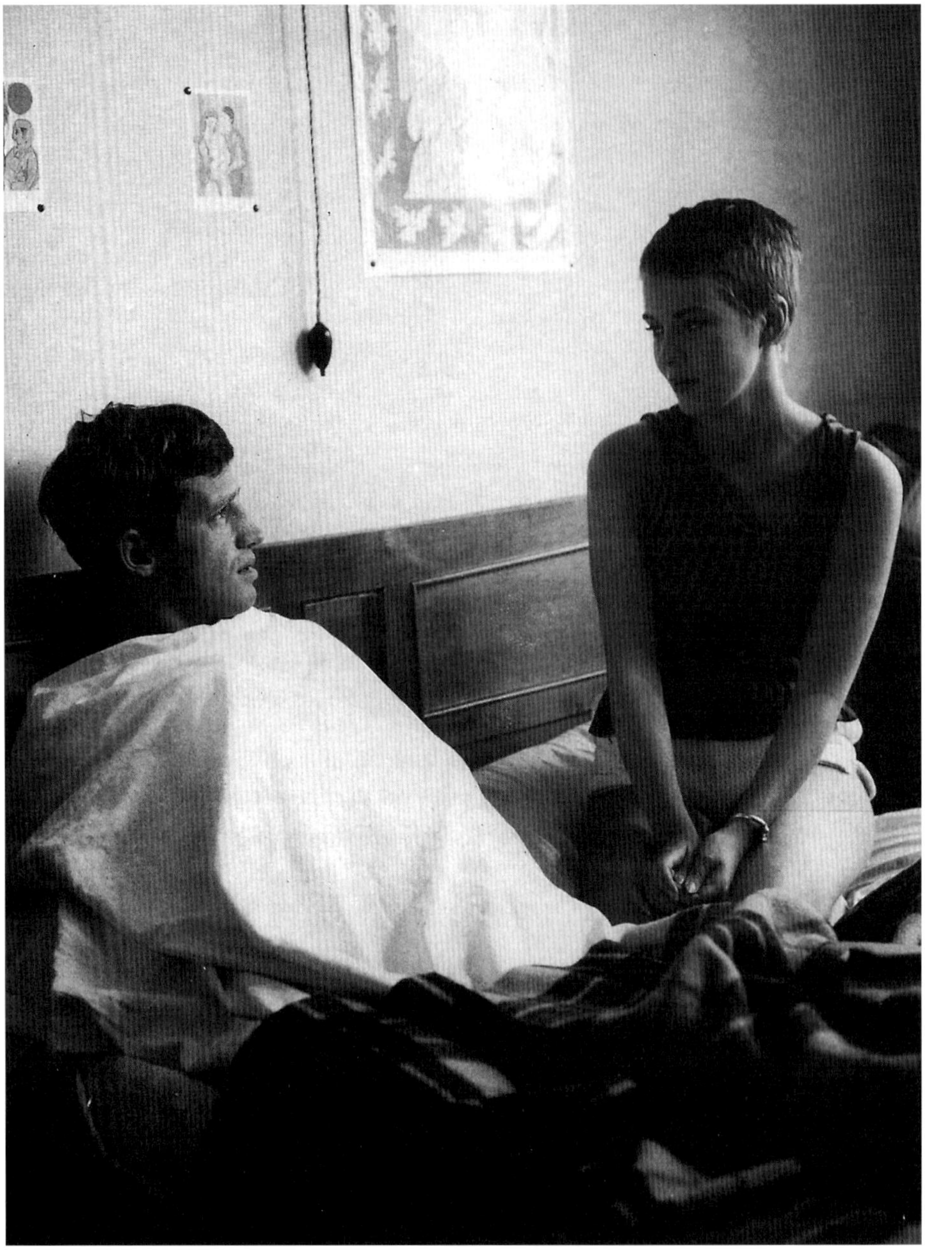

Friedrich Luft (Süddeutsche Zeitung, July 7, 1960) showed a much more detatched attitude in an article which was also an attempt to vindicate the jury: »The jury did not have it easy today. There was nothing exceptional. Awarding the talented French director Jean-Luc Godard the prize for the best director for A bout de souffle was correct and courageous. He broke through a wall of convention. It is a tribute to the jury.« Thus, in the jubilee year there was one film at least which – retrospectively – has long since become a classic.

A bout de souffle:
Jean-Paul Belmondo,
Jean Seberg

A lucky strike for the jury

1961

June 23rd–July 4th, 1961

Although 53 countries were represented at the 11th International Film Festival Berlin – of which 46 showed feature films, documentaries, or short films, and seven sent delegates – the number of films competing was limited for the first time. A decision was made by the FIAPF permitting each country to show only one full-length film as its official contribution. To be sure, the Festival director was allowed to invite additional films from any country, but the FIAPF felt that each country should be represented in the program with a maximum of two films. Thus the 1961 Competition focused on 23 films, five of which had been invited by Alfred Bauer: Michelangelo Antonioni's LA NOTTE (»The Night«), Jean-Luc Godard's UNE FEMME EST UNE FEMME (»A Woman Is a Woman«), Stuart Rosenberg's QUESTION 7, Ralph Thomas' NO LOVE FOR JOHNNIE, and the West German documentary TRAUMLAND DER SEHNSUCHT [Dreamland of Longing] by Wolfgang Mueller-Sehn.

Scepticism

There was great scepticism following the weak year of 1960. Reservations were not only voiced by the critics, they were also prevalent among the organizers. Objections were primarily directed at the selection procedure. There was an intensified urge to travel, to participate in the previews in other countries; furthermore, the culture attachés of the German embassies were to be drawn into the selection of the films. The minutes of the organizational committee constantly made allusions to so-called »artistic films«, which was little more than phrasemongering, for there was hardly any exchange of arguments. At best there were emotional reservations and a widespread moralizing attitude towards films such as Bresson's PICKPOCKET the year before. New aesthetic tendencies were accepted only hestitantly and rather reluctantly, as was the case with the French »Nouvelle Vague«, which Bauer had invited to Berlin, or with Antonioni's aesthetically very stringent and rigid camera style in LA NOTTE in 1961. These films, which remained alien to many on the organizational committee, were branded »nihilistic« – even by critics. The »Berlinale« had difficulty in recognizing the signs of the times. Nevertheless some films still managed to break through the hard shell, albeit inconspicuously at first, for it was increasingly apparent that the Film Festival was slipping towards a crisis that would break out in the next few years.

In Berlin people were still clinging to a cinema of stars, and failed to notice that the social indicators were beginning to change. This year, too, the International Film Festival was host to its fair share of famous directors: Billy Wilder and Nicholas Ray, Jean-Luc Godard and François Truffaut, Ingmar Bergman and Satyajit Ray, Fons Rademakers and Elio Petri. For the general public, however, the glamorous names were missing; at best Toshiro Mifune, Anna Karina and Leslie Caron had those »star qualities« which the management of the Festival had wanted to offer. Bauer had invited 60 actors »of international standing«. Only a few of them accepted. According to Bauer, the actors had declined because they chose instead to accept an invitation to the film festival in Moscow »which, as we know, has invited the artists with all expenses paid including a sight seeing tour through the Soviet Union« (cited in the minutes of July 14, 1961).

Movie stars in Moscow?

So in 1961 the »show« in Berlin was left completely in the hands of Jayne Mansfield, which also later led to a scandal. Even the Film Festival magazine »Film in Berlin« showed an interest in having photos of Jayne Mansfield, even if less provocatively than was the case of the reporters working for the illustrated magazines such as

Photos of Jayne Mansfield

Scandalous: Jayne Mansfield poses for photographers.

»Stern«, »Quick«, »Neue Revue«, not to mention »BZ« and »Bild«. The following remarks are included in a commentary made by Bauer at the end of the Film Festival: »Things happened which were felt to be both out-of-place and disastrous: the ease with which some saw fit to display the bodily charms of the American actress Jayne Mansfield (who received DM 2000 in fees and refunded expenses for her participation), which was then accompanied by similiar, unpaid appearances by a ›starlet‹; together they earned the festival – at least during the first half – the sarcastic title of »Bosom Berlinale« in the entire German press, and in a part of the foreign press too.« In a letter (Aug. 2, 1961) to Dr. Gerd Bucerius, Bundestag member of the CDU and editor of »Stern«, Bauer complained about the reports on the International Film Festival. He dismissed accusations made by reporters that actresses participating in the festival had indulged in excesses. In his opinion the »incidents« were »the work of Bild journalists, without whose encouragement the ladies would never have exposed themselves«. He continued: »Your magazine fails to point out to the defenseless reader that, in spite of the critical politicial situation this summer, representatives of 47 nations from all over the world met in Berlin to participate in a peaceful film competition. »Stern« says nothing about the proven high quality of this year's Film Festival and the accompanying events, which constantly earned the attention of the serious daily press at home and abroad. Instead your magazine provides Eastern European propaganda with welcome material for the assertion that the ›hotbed of vice‹ of Berlin should be transformed into a ›clean, free city‹ as quickly as possible«. Thus Jayne Mansfield's exhibitionism was raised to the level of a political affair – a rather grotesque blunder in view of the third Berlin crisis which was now impending and which Bauer was alluding to.

Cute: Jayne Mansfield with »Mecki«

It was on the screen that the Festival experienced true moments of bliss: in Godard's Une femme est une femme the seriousness of life is foiled by the game, and

Anna Karina,
Jean-Luc Godard

A moment of bliss

the true-to-life imitation turns out to be a roguish trick played on celluloid. Anna Karina plays the striptease dancer Angéla. However, the big surprise came when the prize was awarded at the Zoo-Palast: Anna Karina received the Silver Bear for the best actress. Sighs of disbelief followed, make-up ran, there were curtseys, tears of joy, and all restraint was abandoned. For a moment life became cinema and cinema a gay science. There has hardly ever been a happier winner.

There was another image which remained unforgettable for audiences. A clip from Antonioni's LA NOTTE; Jeanne Moreau as Lidia – a black dress with thin straps, her naked arms hanging, her red mouth closed, questioning; her eyes wide open and concentrating behind her. Marcello Mastroianni – playing her husband Giovanni – goes past in a dark suit, his tie tightly knotted, head turned away, immersed in thought. Is there any escape from that mist-enshrouded situation in which one touches but does not feel anything? Heinz Ungureit in the »Frankfurter Rundschau« wrote: »A married couple who have become strangers to one another go out into the night, him staggering more than ever before, whilst she is even more bored by his submissive tendency. An embrace in which he saves the situation for himself could not be more repulsive or fatal. The film leaves us with this feeling of hopelessness, in which all relations are reduced to outward appearances and gestures.« (July 6, 1961.) The jury awarded Antonioni's film the Golden Berlin Bear. A good decision.

Kyogo Kagawa,
Toshiro Mifune

»A Film with horns and claws« was how Friedrich Luft described DAS WUNDER DES MALACHIAS [The Miracle of Malachias] by Bernhard Wicki. Horst Bollmann played the bareheaded, naive Father Malachias, who prays to God to remove a den of iniquity, a common pub from his parish. The miracle transpires; however, the consequences are quite different to those anticipated by Malachias: the path has now been cleared for hypocrites. Wicki's production reveals a sense of the grotesque: the film »is a thunderstorm. It wants to be a place for peace and quiet – but has no such

Une femme est une femme:
Anna Karina

qualities itself. It wants to show us how to breathe – but is itself constantly out of breath. It is so eager that it stands in the way of its own final goal. In the end it tragically takes on more than it can handle.« (Friedrich Luft, Die Welt, July 5, 1961.) Yet perhaps it was precisely this outstanding effort which was why the Silver Bear for the best director went to Bernhard Wicki.

Seldom before had a jury thought at such variance, and decided so boldly. Its members had included the directors Satyajit Ray, Nicholas Ray, and Falk Harnack. It had been a Film Festival of wonders although not without injury. »I love you, Berlin!« were the words with which Toshiro Mifune took his leave of Berlin – almost a wistful taste of things to come.

La notte: Jeanne Moreau, Marcello Mastroianni

Memo from…

By Satyajit Ray

I had accepted to serve as a juror at the Berlin International Film Festival in 1961, and my very first memory is of being received at the airport by Mr. Edmund Luft. I am six foot five, but Mr. Luft was a good two inches taller than me. I rarely have to look up to people when I am standing, but this time I did. My eyes obviously betrayed the question in my mind. »One metre ninety-nine centimetres«, informed Mr. Luft genially.

Film festivals are memorable not so much for the films one sees there as for the people one meets: directors, producers, critics, actors from all over the world. Film makers everywhere talk the same language, face the same problems, and even use the same equip-

International Jury for Feature Films
James Quinn (Great Britain, president)
France Roche (France, vice-president)
Marc Turfkruyer (Belgium)
Satyajit Ray (India)
Gian Luigi Rondi (Italy)
Hirotsugu Ozaki (Japan)
Nicholas Ray (USA)
Falk Harnack (FRG)
Hans Schaarwächter (FRG)

International Jury for Documentary and Short Films
W. de Vogel (Netherlands, president)
Else Goelz (FRG, vice-president)
Flavio Tambellini (Brazil)
Ingeborg Lyche (Norway)
Don Luis Gómez Mesa (Spain)
Mohammed Gamal Eldin Rifaat (UAR)
Max Lippmann (FRG)

ment. As a result, rapport is established in no time at all My most memorable meeting in Berlin was, however, not with a director, but with a producer: the legendary David O. Selznick. Selznick had written to me in Calcutta asking me to make a film for him. I had said I would give it a thought.

Early in the sixties I had won the Selznick award for one of my films, and the following year the award ceremony was to be held in Berlin. I was invited to hand over the prize to the winner.

I duly arrived, free from tension for a change, as I had no film in competition. The very next day I was invited by Selznick to lunch at the Hilton, where he was staying. We met, Selznick shook my hands warmly, and we took our seats at the table. All through lunch, Selznick regaled me with stories about stars and directors who had worked for him. I learned, for instance, that Gregory Peck was retained on the payroll not so much for his histrionic ability, but simply because of the enormous fan mail he received. I also learned that Ingrid Bergman was in the habit of falling in love with every director she worked with - »with the exception of Alfred Hitchchock« - Selznick was careful to add.

Gradually, Selznick broached the subject of the film he had offered. I had made up my mind to give him an honest answer, and I did. »Mr. Selznick«, I said, »I know about the memos you periodically send to directors. I am used to working in complete freedom with no interference from the front office. In fact there is no such thing as a front office in India.«

Selznick threw up his hands. »But you will surely get that freedom if you work for me«, he said. »It is only to directors who come unprepared on the set that I send memos. With you there will be no question of memos, I can assure you. Think about it, please.«
I said I would.

Lunch over, I took my leave, did some shopping, saw a movie and returned to the hotel. The ceremony was the same evening, and it was a formal occasion.

A retrospective of six films was dedicated to Akira Kurosawa, one of which is IKIRU with Takashi Shimura which had run in the Competition in 1954.

As I collected my key at the reception desk, I saw an envelope in my pigeon hole. I took it out and took out the paper it contained. It was a small slip at the top of which was printed »Memo from David O. Selznick«. Below it was half a dozen lines of typescript - the speech that it was desired that I should make that evening while handing the prize to Ingmar Bergman.

At the last minute

By Bernhard Wicki

Of all the times I participated in the »Berlinale«, the year 1961 remains unforgettable.

I had finished shooting my film Das Wunder des Malachias *that spring, - it was supposed to be premièred at the Berlin Film Festival, which back then still took place in the summer. I had promised this to my friend and producer, Jochen Severin, and the distributor Theo Osterwind, of the German Filmhansa. Osterwind had in the meanwhile become director of the Ufa as well, and it was particularly important to him to present this work at the Berlin Festival as the first film of the Ufa-Filmhansa. The director of the »Berlinale« at that time, Alfred Bauer, placed the date of the première as late as possible, that is, my film was the concluding film of the Competition. Cutting and synchronization were completed, the »Berlinale« began, we had just begun with the mixing. Time got shorter and shorter. We worked on, day and night. A complicating factor was that the visuals were being done in the copying lab at the Ufa in Berlin, the soundtrack in the copying lab of the Filmhansa in Göttingen. Our production director, Otto Meissner, now a well-known TV producer, was on the brink of despair. My cameraman and longtime friend Gerd von Bonin was, thank God, able to do the lighting adjustments in Berlin, so that I had the opportunity to interrupt the mixing, time and again, and participate in the process. Early in the morning of the day of the première the*

The Awards of the International Jurys

Feature Films
Grand Prix of the 11th IFB
Golden Berlin Bear
La notte
Italy, directed by
Michelangelo Antonioni

Silver Berlin Bear
for the best director
Bernhard Wicki
for Das Wunder des Malachias
FRG

Das Wunder des Malachias: Richard Münch, Horst Bollmann

Silver Berlin Bear
for the best actress
Anna Karina
in Une femme est une femme
France

Silver Berlin Bear
for the best actor
Peter Finch
in No Love for Johnnie
Great Britain

1st Special Prize
Silver Berlin Bear
Une femme est une femme
France, directed by
Jean-Luc Godard

2nd Special Prize
Silver Berlin Bear
Mabu
Korea, directed by
Dae Jin-Kang

Silver Berlin Bear
Makkers, staakt uw wild geraas
Netherlands, directed by
Fons Rademakers

Long Documentary Films
Golden Berlin Bear
Déscription d'un combat
Israel, directed by
Chris. Marker

Special Prize
Silver Berlin Bear
Traumland der Sehnsucht
FRG, directed by
Wolfgang Mueller-Sehn

last roll of mixing was finished. I was so exhausted, that I simply slept through the first screening of my film that afternoon. I would also have slept through the evening screening if Jochen Severin and Theo Osterwind hadn't dragged me out of bed.

The next day I was awarded the Silver Bear for best direction, the Golden Bear was awarded a film in which I had acted, Antonioni's La notte.

Nicholas Ray

After Oberhausen

1962

June 22th-July 3rd, 1962

There was no competition - in any sense of the word - for Wolfgang Neuss, cabaret performer, and film actor. He showed his film GENOSSE MÜNCHHAUSEN [Comrade Münchhausen] in a small movie theater, and introduced each showing with a cabaret performance, which many found incomprehensible at times owing to his (Berlin) dialect and perhaps because of his dialectics too (over to the left, where the heart beats!). »They say I want to undermine the Film Festival. Tell me now, with a standard that low how can you dig deep enough to undermine it?«

Once again the Film Festival took place in the shadow of political events. Following an ultimatum from Nikita Khrushchev, the international political debate about the status of Berlin among the world powers had come to a head, triggering off the third Berlin crisis. On August 13th 1961, the Chairman of the Council of State of the GDR, Walter Ulbricht, ordered the Wall to be erected between the Western Sectors and the Eastern part of the city.

August 13, 1961: the Wall is built.

The critical political situation led the Senate of Berlin and the management of the Festival to consider whether it was advisable, and politically justifiable, to hold the

Jean-Pierre Léaud, François Truffaut

12th International Film Festival Berlin. It was quickly decided not to stop preparations for the IFB. Thus on June 22nd 1962 the Film Festival was opened by Deputy Mayor Franz Amrehn on behalf of Mayor Brandt, who was in Bonn discussing the Berlin situation with US Secretary of State Dean Rusk. Brandt stated at a press conference during the Festival: »I must admit that I am among those who were afraid, on August 13th, that Berlin's streets could become the scene of a war, and that very careful considerations were necessary amidst the indignation which arose in us all at the time, and the responsibility which one had to bear for this city, for this people, and for peace in the world.«

A Kind of Loving
»With this film England has picked out the most appropriate film from its repertoire. Incidentally, as chance will have it, a combination of family nastiness and straight forward sex, but this time in a carefully aimed, and quite well-balanced composition. This country does not only produce bizarre, eccentric whodunnits from time to time, but repeatedly comes up with new directors, and a sensible, well-prepared piece of British reality, social critique, and to an even greater degree critique of individuals or of a social class, which shares responsibility for ›the conditions‹ and is certainly not always their victim. (...) This is John Schlesinger's first film, and, considering this fact, it has been made in a remarkably lapidary manner; no hypocrisy, no tricks, no strenuous theories of society and humanity. And both of the leading actors (Alan Bates and June Ritchie) operate in this directness with uncomplicated certainty.«
Karena Niehoff in: Süddeutsche Zeitung, July 8, 1962

This year, harsh criticisms were voiced soon after the first film performances. It was said that this was a »Berlinale« of low-quality films and nice people – among others Tony Curtis, Shirley MacLaine, and James Stewart. The critics only found three films of substance; John Schlesinger's A Kind Of Loving, Francesco Rosi's Salvatore Giuliano, and Ingmar Bergman's Samson i en spegel (»Through a Glass Darkly«). Apart from these films they only saw trivialities and embarrassments, as in the case of Helmut Käutner's Die Rote (»The Redhead«), adapted from the novel by Alfred Andersch. Both Käutner and Andersch were at odds at the press conference. The journalists showed no lenience. Ruth Leuwerik cried. Exhaustion and disappointment were apparent. However, Wolfgang Neuss took up the cudgels for Käutner: »You can see what can happen when a German cabaret performer enters film by taking a look, for example, at Helmut Käutner. And if you take the following remark ›Käutner is certainly more than just a cabaret performer‹ (and you can't get more than that!). Cabaret performers are (and Helmut Käutner is the best example) all-round talents who think, write, and act; moralists who are not tied down creatively. Humor, wit, and spirit are pretexts for getting the moral across.« (Film in Berlin. Official Festival Almanac 1962.)

In a radio commentary Friedrich Luft drew radical conclusions from the unsatisfactory Festival program and suggested that the Film Festival should do away with its »A-Status«, thus making possible a less restricted, and more carefully chosen selection of films. However, the Senate did not want to risk the international reputation which was linked to its classification as an »A-Festival«. Alfred Bauer, who had fought so hard for this international recognition, was even more reluctant to lose it. The only way out then, it seemed, was to improve the quality of the Festival by changing the selection procedure. Yet this was, again, a question of money, for trips abroad placed a heavy burden on the budget, which was so stretched that only a general increase in the subsidies from the Senate and the Federal Government could have remedied the situation. There was no sign of this happening. The financial situation was made more difficult by the fact that there were no more performances for visitors from the East, and, on the other hand, special events – e. g. at the Waldbühne – now attracted far less people. Thus discussions revolved endlessly around the consequences to be taken as a result of the overtly negative criticisms of the Festival. Hans Borgelt found words of encouragement for both himself and the general public: »A poor year is no reason for resignation« he wrote in the »Tagesspiegel« on August 5th. Manfred Delling's comment on the situation was more pragmatic: »More money is always good – but on its own it does not always solve questions of an artistic nature. In this case: an increase in the budget does not, unfortunately mean, as Professor Tiburtius seems to assume, that the standard of the Festival will improve as a result. The decisive thing is not whether colleagues can

Centers of Festival activities: Haus Wien (also location of press conferences), Film-Bühne Wien (Festival movie house, second to the Zoo-Palast) and the Hotel am Zoo (residence of the Festival management)

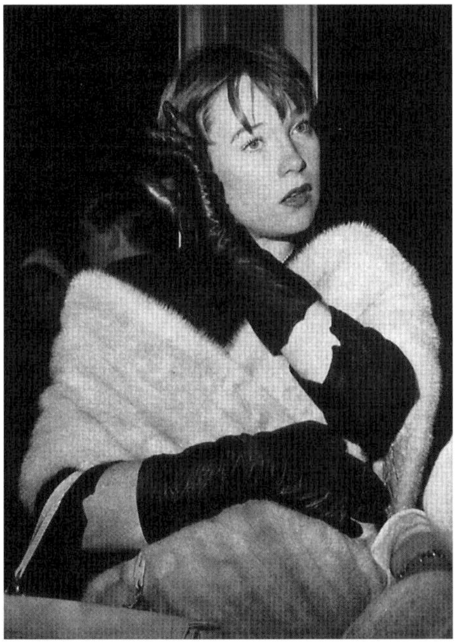

Arrival at Tempelhof Airport:
Shirley MacLaine

James Mason,
Gloria Stewart,
Alfred Bauer,
James Stewart

Jean-Paul Belmondo with his wife, Jean-Pierre Léaud, Françoise Arnoul and on the far right,
Alexandre Alexandre

travel, but, first and foremost, who travels. We had been assured beyond any doubt that the film entries received for this year's festival were considered by the selection commission to be films of very high quality and had been invited for this reason. However, they turned out to be minor catastrophes. This seems to be a more serious problem that an undersized budget.« (Die Welt, July 25, 1962.)

The Film Festival had to react to altered production conditions, and especially to asesthetic innovations by young directors. In individual cases this did in fact happen. France's »Nouvelle Vague« was respresented in Berlin. Antonioni and Bergman were also able to show their films. John Schlesinger and Francesco Rosi appeared as representatives of the cinema's emerging at the Berlin Competition. The crisis of the »traditional sectors of the industry«, which had determined the International Film Festival program in the fifties, became apparent, and with it the uncertainties on the part of those responsible for the film selection for the IFB. The necessary break with convention did not come easily. German participation had always been a special yardstick. This was to become even more apparent now, in the wake of Oberhausen.

Oberhausen and the consequences

During the 8th West German Short Film Festival in Oberhausen, in 1962, a group of 26 film-makers had read out a manifesto and proclaimed the intention of the undersigned »to create new German cinema«. February 28th, with the public pronouncement of the »Oberhausen Manifesto«, has been synonymous with the birth of the »New German Cinema« ever since. This movement among film-makers from the Federal Republic of Germany must be seen in the context of attempts being made by directors of the »Nouvelle Vague« in France or those of the British »Free Cinema«. This is also the start of the Autorenfilm (films conceived and made by the authors themselves) in the Federal Republic, of breaking with the production methods used by the »fathers«. It is surely no coincidence that the slogan »Papa's cinema is dead«, was taken from the title of a critique written by Louis Bory on Alain Resnais' L'Année dernière à Marienbad (»Last Year at Marienbad«).

Kohayagawake no aki [Late Summer] – a scene from Yasujiro Ozu's entry in the Competition. A year later, a Retrospective is dedicated to this Japanese director.

A precursor of the »New German Cinema« had already been run as the official West German contribution – without any great degree of success – at the festival in Cannes in 1961: Böll's adaptation of DAS BROT DER FRÜHEN JAHRE [The Bread of those early years] by Herbert Vesely, who now, one year later, was among those who signed the »Oberhausen Manifesto«. The selection commission had four German films to choose from for Berlin: Helmut Käutner's DIE ROTE and Ottomar Domnick's OHNE DATUM [Without Date] – whose film JONAS had caused a stir at the »Berlinale« in 1957 – were accepted for the Competition, whilst GENOSSE MÜNCHHAUSEN by Wolfgang Neuss, and a film by Wolfgang Staudte, the TV film DIE REBELLION, were rejected.

International Jury for Feature Films
King Vidor (USA, president)
André Michel (France)
Emeric Pressburger (Great Britain)
Hideo Kikumori (Japan)
Dolores del Rio (Mexico)
Jurgen Schildt (Sweden)
Max Gammeter (Switzerland)
Günther Stapenhorst sen. (FRG)
Bruno E. Werner (FRG)

International Jury for Documentary and Short Films
Olavi Linnus (Finland, president)
A. L. Srinivasan (India)
Dorothy Macpherson (Canada)
Abdallah Masbahi (Morocco)
Pia Maria Plechl (Austria)
Karl Otto (FRG)
Fridolin Schmid (FRG)

SALVATORE GIULIANO

»Nouvelle Vague« and the »Daring Wave«

Faced with this new movement of young film-makers the producer Artur Brauner tried to seize the bull by the horns. In an article in the Festival Berlin Almanac entitled »›Fathers‹ and ›Sons‹« he counterposed what he called his »Daring Wave« to the »Nouvelle Vague« as an attempt at a »revolution from above« linked with the offer to the »rebels« to make films with him as producer. De facto, however, it was a question of rights of possession. In another article in the Festival Almanac Joe Hembus saw the »Oberhauseners« as »searching for new truths« and took three films of the young generation as examples: alongside Vesely's Film, he also referred to TOBBY by Hansjürgen Pohland, and DIE PARALLELSTRASSE [Parallel Street] by Ferdinand Khittl and Bodo Blüthner. In the words of Boris von Borresholm (an initiator of the »Oberhausen Manifesto«), who rigorously described the »cinema of the authors«: »All responsibility to the film-maker, the innovator in the widest sense of the term. These authors insist on the primacy of subjects which are close to life, and on the truth of their inception. They are not outsiders in economic matters, nor are they adept in taking risks at any price. They know the price. The dream factory has gone bankrupt. The new film now has the say: the film of the authors.«

Whatever the case may be, these much discussed contributions placed the Film Festival Berlin at the center of the debate on film policy, and provided the adversaries with a forum. One may assume that the attitude of the Festival management was most aptly reflected in the aphorisms coined by Hans Habe under the heading »After ›Heimat‹ Films, Genius Films? How about Human Films?« appearing as a kind of closing comment on the other contributions in the Festival Alamanac: »Germany is a country of extremes. Extremes are just as little suited to film as they are to politics. Having placed one's bets on Heidi and the Alps they now want to ride a new wave which has already been swallowed up by a more recent one. For the »Film Festival Berlin« this means that »now that many of the best international films are coming to Berlin, the question arises as to how many of them come from Germany. From Jannings to Schell, from Lubitsch to Wyler. What is true for the balance of trade is true for film: a country which can export so many good things cannot be doing too badly. It would hardly be right if a renaissance did not develop out of the crisis.«

The balance for the 12th International Film Festival Berlin was very poor; the management indignantly noted the reserved reaction in the press. »Nobody does Berlin a favor by fiddling the books or by covering up the fact that we deserve more than international cinema, not to mention German cinema, has been giving us« to quote Dieter Hildebrandt (Frankfurter Allgemeine Zeitung, July 5, 1962).

The Awards of the International Jurys

Feature Films
Grand Prix of the 12th IFB
Golden Berlin Bear
A KIND OF LOVING
Great Britain, directed by
John Schlesinger

Silver Berlin Bear
for the best director
Francesco Rosi
for SALVATORE GIULIANO
Italy

Silver Berlin Bear
for best actress
ex aequo
Rita Gam and
Viveca Lindfors
in NO EXIT
Argentina

Silver Berlin Bear
for the best actor
James Stewart in
MR. HOBBS TAKES A VACATION
USA

Special Prize
Silver Berlin Bear
Jon Young Sun
in TO THE LAST DAY
Korea

Long Documentary Films
Special Prize
Silver Berlin Bear
GALAPAGOS
FRG, directed by
Heinz Sielmann

No resonance

1963

June 21st–July 2nd, 1963

Before the 13th International Film Festival Berlin started Alfred Bauer recalled the successes – in a »cultural and idealistic sense« and in terms of »economic significance« – of previous years in an article for the »Tagesspiegel«. It was more of a resumée than a perspective for the future, no reference was made to the critical objections raised over the past years. It held no prospects and was simply another tribute to the spirit of the founding years: »In addition to developing aesthetic standards and providing motivation for intensified achievement, film festival offer an immeasurably important chance to become acquainted with and grow closer to other countries through

John Huston with his daughter Anjelica

their films, be they documentary or feature films with descriptions of indigenous milieus and mentality.« (June 2, 1963.)

The Festival management, which had, incidentally, taken up a new residence in Bundesallee 1-12, the former Joachimsthalsche Gymnasium (secondary school), was rather lost for ideas about how to make the selection and organizational structure more flexible, and efficient, a fact which was reflected in the minutes and in the advisory board meetings. The Department of Education and the other board members had no recipe, either.

Thoughts are made on the selection and organizational structures.

Vague proposals for tightening up the Festival procedure were discussed, such as dropping certain special events. There was also general agreement that »experts« should be called in to help select the films, yet who was meant by this: the film critics perhaps? Nor was there any conception of how all these things were to be organized, not to mention the rising costs, which could not be covered by the current budget. A revision was necessary, but how was it to be effected? After the 13th Film Festival was over, »A-Status« was once again questioned, and the possibility of holding the IFB every two years debated. However, a study carried out by the Senator for Education that year pointed out that:

»This would render a continual documentation of the development of film-making impossible. Yet this is precisely the critical issue at the moment, because the questions raised by television and the emergence of a new generation of directors are increasingly bringing film back to its intrinsic artistic laws. If, however, the International Film Festival Berlin no longer gives a coherent impression of the state of international film-making, it will not provide any noticeable stimulus for making films either.« Thus, at the 34th meeting on November 5th 1963, the Senate decided to continue holding the Film Festival every year (senatorial decree No. 663/63).

Charles Aznavour, Eddie Constantine, Sidney Poitier, Alfred Bauer; behind them, Karl Friedrich Wohlrabe, Daphne Dale and IFB Chief of Protocol Ilse Urbach

Other possible changes in the Festival were discussed at this Senate meeting, e. g. a prize for »young film countries« in order to avoid the »imbalance« between American and European films on the one hand, and films from the Third World on the other; no more competitions for short films - owing to the rivalry from Oberhausen and Mannheim; a general reduction in the number of events held; cutting down the size of the advisory board and introducing standing rules for this committee; the introduction of a competition for film academies; the establishment of a representative German film fair; and participation of young film critics - this was primarily in reference to Ulrich Gregor and Enno Patalas, editors of the film magazine »Filmkritik«; in these two figures ardent and knowledgeable critics of the International Film Festival Berlin had emerged. »In our opinion film critics could certainly be won over for collaboration, especially as they must be interested in gathering practical experience by working for the Film Festival. The critics have frequently blamed those responsible for failing to involve them« (senatorial decree, Nov. 4, 1963). A decision on these points was postponed, as they first wanted to wait for the 14th Film Festival.

Cutting back the finances

Owing to the higher costs this year, the Federal Ministry of the Interior increased its subsidy by DM 50 000 to make a total sum of DM 350 000. This was a drop in the bucket because - almost as a counter-move - the Federal Minister of All-German Affairs, this was Dr. Rainer Barzel in Ludwig Erhardt's first cabinet, ordered the allowance for inviting journalists to be cut from DM 40 000 to a mere DM 20 000. This hit the budget of the 1963 Festival particularly hard because there were plans to develop the TV Film Review, which had been introduced in 1962, and broadcast in cooperation with Sender Freies Berlin (a Berlin broadcasting channel), to turn it into a competition. This was also conceived as a kind of »TV link« to East Germany. The new Berlin Senator for Science and the Arts, Adolf Arndt, thus filed a petition

Treffpunkt Haus Wien - Alberto Sordi, Michelangelo Antonioni

Mensch und Bestie: Götz George

(May 9, 1963) with the Federal Minister in which he described the disadvantages caused by cutting the funds, in particular for the project of the »TV Film Review«; yet his intervention was in vain. Rainer Barzel referred to the separation of competences between the Federal Press Information Services Office and his own ministry from whose budget funds could only be granted which were intended for the invitation of journalists from the Federal Republic. »A distinction, for example, between German speaking and other foreigners is not possible« (May 20, 1963).

TV link: Festival films are broadcast on TV for the inhabitants of East Berlin.

From June 27th on five feature films from the Competition and one review of cultural films were broadcast via the »TV link« on six nights, each being introduced by Friedrich Luft. This self-assertive propaganda measure was a reaction to the erection of the Wall; the shock at the division of the city ran very deep. The Senate and the Festival management felt politically obliged to maintain relations with the inhabitants of East Berlin. From the very inception of the Film Festival special screenings had been arranged for the inhabitants of East Berlin, especially at the Corso movie house in Wedding. These had to be stopped following the construction of the Wall. The »TV link« was an attempt to continue this tradition of the Festival in a different manner.

On the occasion of the first broadcast, Willy Brandt held a speech in which he recalled the performances at the Corso: »This encounter with the film nations of the world had become a positive tradition. The critical mind and openness of Berlin audiences, the overtly objective nature of the Festival and hence, at the same time, its ability to bring people together, the close contact between the art of film-making and contemporary events on the soil of the German capital were elements which had always lent the Berlin Film Festival a special character. The Wall, which has cut through our city since those August days, prevents you, my fellow citizens in East Berlin and in the Zone, from directly participating in the events at our Film Festival. So I am all the more pleased that it is possible, this year, to bring you into contact – at least indirectly – with the films from all over the world which are being shown here.«

VERSPÄTUNG IN MARIENBORN (»Stop Train 349«) by Rolf Hädrich, based on a book by Will Tremper, was the abortive opening film of this year's Film Festival. It related the story of an escape from the German Democratic Republic: Just before the border, a young man jumps onto an American military train, which is stopped by the Russians who have noticed the attempted escape. The train's passengers form two opposing groups. The larger of the two groups of travellers is willing to hand over the man – for selfish reasons.

»Daring Wave« founders.

However, both critics and audiences were even more merciless towards the second German film in the program: Edwin Zbonek's MENSCH UND BESTIE [Man and Beast], the first film from Artur Brauner's »Daring Wave«. Herbert Ihering's was one voice among many: »This was one of the most embarrassing mistakes in film history. Caine and Abel under Hitler. An SS officer pursues his brother, who has escaped from a concentration camp, through woods, drought, mountains, water, and ice, to the point of extermination. In between, there is a nurse and love. Is this told in a genuine and subtile manner? Everything is sold out to film routine. Sensationalism where the fate of an age should be portrayed. No matter how unbelievable it may seem, it is nevertheless true: the film-makers try to show a human tragedy in Nazi Germany using chase sequences characteristic of cowboy films. It is almost cynical that, at the end of the Berlinale, posters advertise a film festival of Western, which is to follow the 13th International Film Festival Berlin at the Berlin movie house Zoo-Palast.« (Die Andere Zeitung, Hamburg, July 11, 1963.)

John F. Kennedy visits Berlin.

It was not the Film Festival which held Berliners and visitors to the city in suspense this June. The big event which was understood as a political landmark was the visit of the American President, J. F. Kennedy, who arrived in Berlin on June 26th for a six hours' stay. On this particular day Nikos Koundouro's film MIKRES APHRODITES [Young Aphrodites], which was later awarded a Silver Bear, had its première. But the winner was »Ish bin ein Bearleener« (I am a Berliner – J. F. Kennedy).

The attraction lies, above all, in the element of surprise

By Alfred Bauer

Film festivals have gained a secure place in the cultural life of many nations during the past fifteen years. More and more countries, more and more cities hold film events on a national or an international basis. The major, officially recognized festivals in Venice, Cannes and Berlin are augmented by numerous smaller festivals and inofficial film events. The great number of these secondary festivals and similar events is detrimental to the interests of film, which is struggling desperately to survive; on the whole these threaten to largely abandon the original impetus for festivals, above all, where organizational motives – for example, considerations concerning tourism and the like – are valued more highly than the presentation of cinematic art.

The impulse for an international festival, which should be an artistic affair, should be primarily of an ideal nature. The director of the event has the responsibility of organizing a competition at which, by strict critical standards, the absolutely best artistic achievements in the realm of film of the various countries are to be determined. Since

International Jury for Feature Films
Wendy Toye (Great Britain, president)
Henri Sokal (FRG, vice-president)
Fernando Ayala (Argentina)
Jean-Pierre Melville (France)
Br. Chopra (India)
Guiglielmo Biraghi (Italy)
Masatora Sakurai (Japan)
Karl Malden (USA)
Günther Engels (FRG)

International Jury for Documentary and Short Films
T.O.S. Benson (Nigeria, president)
Charles Boost (Netherlands, vice-president)
Børge Høst (Denmark)
Carlos Fernández Cuenza (Spain)
Abdel Rahim Sorour (UAR)
Wolfgang Kiepenheuer (FRG)
Volker Baer (FRG)

a festival can exercise a strong attraction upon producers, artists and journalists only by screening most recent films, the major festivals define certain conditions in special guidelines for the inclusion of a film.

One of the most important and most difficult preparatory tasks for the artistic tour de force *consists of determining the outstanding films in large and small film countries and of winning their participation in the festival. Particular dispositions of the producers, economic considerations which demand the immediate release of a film on the world market and, last but not least, the decisions of national selection commissions can prevent the selection committee of a festival from including a valuable film in the competition.*

Along with the right of the large countries to officially nominate a film, a festival management has the possibility of inviting films of particular artistic quality, thereby enriching the program. To name but a few examples from recent years of films which were included in the program of the Berlin Film Festival by invitation and which, after Berlin, were acclaimed world-wide: THE DEFIANT ONES, LES COUSINS, A BOUT DE SOUFFLE, LA NOTTE. *The winners of the competition of a major festival, determined by a jury consisting of renowned persons from domestic and international cultural life, receive a trophy having a highly idealistic value. In a sense the Olympic Games provide a good*

Television Film Festival in the Haus des Rundfunks, a »TV-bridge« following the construction of the Wall

comparison. In a film competition, too, it is not victory alone but participation itself which is important, a maxim which the Berlin Film Festival has followed since its inception and which has brought it the unrestricted recognition of young Afro-Asian and Latin-American film countries.

Thanks to technology it is today no longer a problem for all film producing countries of the world to participate in the Competition. The high participation statistics of the Berlin Film Festival easily prove this. By inviting young film countries, a survey of world film production is provided. A cross-section of international film creation includes the films of these countries as well, even if they do not yet demonstrate the artistic quality of the top productions of the larger nations. Decisive is that the film be characteristic for its country of origin and that its content and style provide an interesting insight into the production of the country.

In addition to developing aesthetic standards and providing motivation for intensified achievement, film festivals offer an immeasurably important chance to become acquainted with and grow closer to other countries through their films, be they documentary or feature films with descriptions of indigenous milieus and mentality. At film festivals the world comes together, and it is up to the viewer to understand and correctly evaluate the works.

Many domestic and international critics share the opinion of the Berlin Festival management that not all films of a festival are to be measured and criticized by the same unbending standard; for up until now unfortunately, only few countries demonstrate development of a future-oriented cinema.

Throughout its history, the Berlin Film Festival has understood one of its duties as providing an opportunity, alongside the official program, to view or to re-view meaningful works of the past. Under the motto »Gems of International Cinema Art« classical film works are presented annually in the Retrospective which becomes more popular each year.

Because television films are also a component of international film production, they have been included in the festival programs in Cannes and Berlin for the past few years. This expansion of the program has the intention, above all, of furthering the aspired coexistence of film and television.

Film festivals are important not only in a cultural and idealistic sense, however, but have moreover a very great economic importance as well, not only for the festival itself, but also for film in general. Festivals conducted at an appropriate place and in the right framework are also an important meeting place for representatives of the film industry and a market for world film trade. A film which the jury awards a prize usually becomes interesting immediately and an economically important item. On the other hand, a film which receives bad reviews in the international press loses many export possibilities. An ambitious work of art, often unable to recoup its production costs on the domestic market, has a chance, by way of a film festival of becoming regarded as a model and characteristic product of its nation which can be sold to many countries. Many films are seen by specialists who would never, without the festival, have gotten to know the film. And many films which earn no prizes become through extensive reporting, inside-tips in many countries and later box-office hits. The exposure provided by the 400 to 500 journalists from all parts of the earth who participate in the major festivals render them a world-wide showcase for cinematic art.

The element of surprise is a distinct characteristic of film festivals. New artistic forms of film, young authors and directors, hopeful new actors quickly become subjects of discussion. What did Europeans know about Japanese film before RASHOMON *was shown*

The Awards of the International Jurys

Feature Films
Grand Prix of the 13th IFB
ex aequo
Golden Berlin Bear
BUSHIDO ZANKOKU MONOGATARI
Japan, directed by
Tadashi Imai

IL DIAVOLO
Italy, directed by
Gian Luigi Polidoro

Silver Berlin Bear
for the best director
Nikos Koundouros
for MIKRES APHRODITES
Greece

Silver Berlin Bear
for the best actress
Bibi Andersson
in ÄLSKARINNAN
Sweden

Silver Berlin Bear
for the best actor
Sidney Poitier
in LILLIES OF THE FIELD
USA

Special Prize
Silver Berlin Bear
THE CARETAKER
Great Britain, directed by
Clive Donner

Long Documentary Films
Silver Berlin Bear
DER GROSSE ATLANTIK
FRG, directed by
Peter Baylis

Jean-Pierre Melville

T.O.S. Benson, Minister for Information Services from Nigeria, with his wife

and celebrated at the Biennale in Venice? This Japanese success, both an artistic and economic triumph, prompted RASHOMON*'s success throughout the entire world. A similar case were the films of Ingmar Bergman, which are today exported in almost all countries after the film* SMULTRONSTÄLLET, *which won the Golden Bear in 1958, gained such great recognition. In this context one should also mention the surprising festival successes of Soviet, Polish or Indian films and of course numerous productions of major film countries rich in tradition.*

The film-related economic advantages which the festivals provide cannot be expressed in concrete figures. The fact that it is significant, however, can be clearly read in the constantly growing number of participants in the Berlin Film Festival.

In the contemporary struggle between film and a range of leisure time activities which keep the public from going to the movies, the opinion becomes ever firmer, that film festivals of international merit are, for many producers, a useful and important impetus to produce more valuable films and thus to win back film viewers who have fallen by the wayside. It stands equally beyond dispute, that the number of smaller film festivals must be reduced and brought into a reasonable relation to the availability of films mature enough for a festival. Only the major festivals, which have demonstrated their value in furthering film art and the film industry, will have a future. It is self-evident that those events best serve the film festival's purposes which are not exclusively for film experts but are also, as in Berlin, accessible to the public at large, who are the true basis of film production.
(In: Der Tagesspiegel, June 2, 1963)

Debacle and reform

1964

June 26th–July 7th, 1964

»Can we continue like this?« was the question Friedrich Luft asked in the »Welt« (July 11, 1964) and noted a general feeling of »the morning after the night before«. Ulrich Gregor quoted the German title of Sartre's book »No Exit« in the »Spandauer Volksblatt« (July 9, 1964): »The Game is Over«. »Bild-Berlin« wrote quite vividly, »The Berlinale is a trash heap«, and the author, Marianne Koch, commented with the airs of »We are somebody again«: »It simply is no longer enough for someone to turn up with something. If someone wants to offer us something, they have to pull something special out of the bag. This has got nothing to do with ingratitude. You can accuse poor relations of ingratitude if they refuse to accept a jacket which has been mended – we are not poor relations and don't want to be either.« (July 8, 1964.) Karena Niehoff's resumée was fairer but more wistful: »... And a Festival quietly dies ... What use is it to us if we do not tolerate communists here, if we are a reliable outpost of freedom, highly praised by the world for our sufferings, and if we are a cultural center; incidentally, not a city and not even just a pleonastic, international metropolis, a complacently made-up primadonna, but an emblem stylised with heraldry, with rituals and crusaders' flag, which even the last remaining, remote Kraal inhabitant and the first best Texan cowboy support, patting the Germans on the back as they do so. It is of no use whatsoever if Berliners always remain true to themselves: people won't send us better films because of this.« (Christ und Welt, July 17, 1964.) The most biting attack, however, was probably that launched by Enno Patalas in the August edition of »Filmkritik«: »The time is up, Dr. Bauer!«.

»... and a Festival quietly dies.«

The political and polemical squabbling surrounding the 1964 Film Festival started at the beginning of the year. Tension became increasingly apparent. The reputation of the IFB was no longer unquestioned, and other West German cities would have gladly staged the Festival. In the magazine »Münchner Leben« (Dec., 1963) the journalist Karl H. Kaesbach pleaded for the Film Festival to be moved to Munich, or at least »the Film Festival could alternate between Berlin and other German cities especially predestined for it, e. g. Munich, Düsseldorf or Baden-Baden.« This polemic became a political issue because Kaesbach believed that by moving the Festival to cities in West Germany the socialist countries could be induced to participate – this touched a sore spot as far as Berlin's and the »Berlinale's« status was concerned. Furthermore, he underlined his arguments by pointing out that the cities of Munich and Berlin would agree »in a loyal manner« to the »dual seat« of the Deutsche Film- und Fernsehakademie (German Film and TV Academy), the establishment of which was the subject of public discussion at the time. Volker Baer, film editor of the »Tagesspiegel«, countered Kaesbach's article: »And finally, Mr. Kaesbach is also wrong in thinking: ›The precondition for examining this suggestion ... would be the more or less spontaneous, consent by Berlin to this kind of common action.‹ Well, with all reservations towards the word spontaneous, we give our spontaneous consent to Berlin and reject K. H. Kaesbach's proposals.« (Nov. 14, 1964.) Kaesbach's article also caused unrest at a political level. The Senator for Science and the Arts, Adolf Arndt, wrote to his party colleague, Dr. Hans-Jochen Vogel, then Mayor in Munich. In his letter (Jan. 15, 1964) he drew special attention to the fact that the magazine »Münchner Leben« was an »official organ« and that this had caused »ill-feeling« in Berlin.

Munich – a rival city?

Arndt's subsequent arguments make it quite clear just how much Kaesbach's pro-

Claudia Cardinale, Alfred Bauer

posals questioned the way in which Berlin conceived its political role. Arndt gave the status of Berlin as a German capital and the outstanding status of the city vis-à-vis other West German municipalities thorough consideration: »Actually, one ought to believe that Germany gathers its strength in its oppressed capital more than is the case with any other country. It is with bitter disappointment that I am forced to say from my experience in office that precisely the opposite is true here, and that is suicidal. This is compounded by the fact that Berlin is erroneously treated as a municipality by the other municipalities, whereas Berlin really ought to stand out among the realms of the municipalities both as the capital city of Germany and as a federal state of the Federal Republic of Germany. To be quite frank, therefore, I do not wish to recognize that there could be a parity between Berlin and other major cities.« Thus, Berlin's position was unequivocally stated. One may also suspect that the excursus dealing with the fundamental significance of Berlin, which retrospectively almost reads like a tactical distraction from the discussion – which was actually quite concrete – about the continuance of the Film Festival, stopped further debate over the IFB.

On the other hand, the political committees were more critical towards the Film Festival in Berlin than ever before, even though there was no change in plans. For the time being, the 14th International Film Festival Berlin would be held in the same old form, and considerations about reforms remained quite general. This hesitant attitude produced the reaction it deserved, as quotations from the press reveal. The 1964 Film Festival was an artistic disaster. However, perhaps it was precisely this debacle which led to energetic steps to make reforms ready for the 15th IFB. Furthermore, the structural proposals of the »young film critics« who had been disregarded up to this time, were now taken seriously. At least a dialogue over contents started up and positions were formulated. One could say that the International Film Festival Berlin became more democratic after 1964.

Alfred Bauer and Sidney Poitier at a reception put on by the Senegalese Delegation

When selecting films for the Competition program films already submitted were rejected. Furthermore, Alfred Bauer made decisions which met with surprise in France and Sweden as well as with the German selection committees. The atmosphere had already suffered during the preparations. For instance, Alfred Bauer had turned down the French contribution BANDE À PART (»Band of Outsiders«), the latest Godard film, which then received its first showing in »Woche der Kritik« run during the Film Festival and organized by the Club der Filmjournalisten (Film Journalists' Club) as well as by Kurt Habernoll and Ulrich Gregor. (Incidentally, Ulrich Gregor was taken on in 1964 and made responsible for »cinema art related affairs« in the Festival newspaper, where he – together with Gero Gandert, who now works for the Stiftung Deutsche Kinemathek – took care of the »Panorama« pages, which included interviews with young directors as well as articles on film history.)

Uproar surrounds the rejection of Vilgot Sjöman's film 491.

Malcontent arose in the early stages, however, due to the rejection of the Swedish film 491 by Vilgot Sjöman, a decision in which Bauer nonetheless received the backing of the Senate. Sjöman's film – which was based on fact – portrayed the fate of six maladjusted youths. Supervised by the youth welfare office, they are put in an apartment which they then share. One of the social workers sexually abuses the boys, whilst the boys themselves force a girl to take up prostitution, and set a dog on to her, with sodomite intentions. It is their 491st sin, against which the reverend had already warned them: »You will be forgiven for 490 sins. On the 491st the devil will come and fetch you.« This film had been nominated by the Swedish Producers' Association together with the Svenska Filminstitutet (Swedish Film Institute) although, or rather because, the film had only been given conditional release by the censor in Sweden, the reason being that it was »unsuitable« for showing to the general public »from the standpoint of ›mental hygiene‹«. The Svenska Filminstitutet had lodged a protest against this measure, yet no decision had been reached at the time the film was nominated for the Film Festival. »The decision of the

491: a scene with Lena Nyman

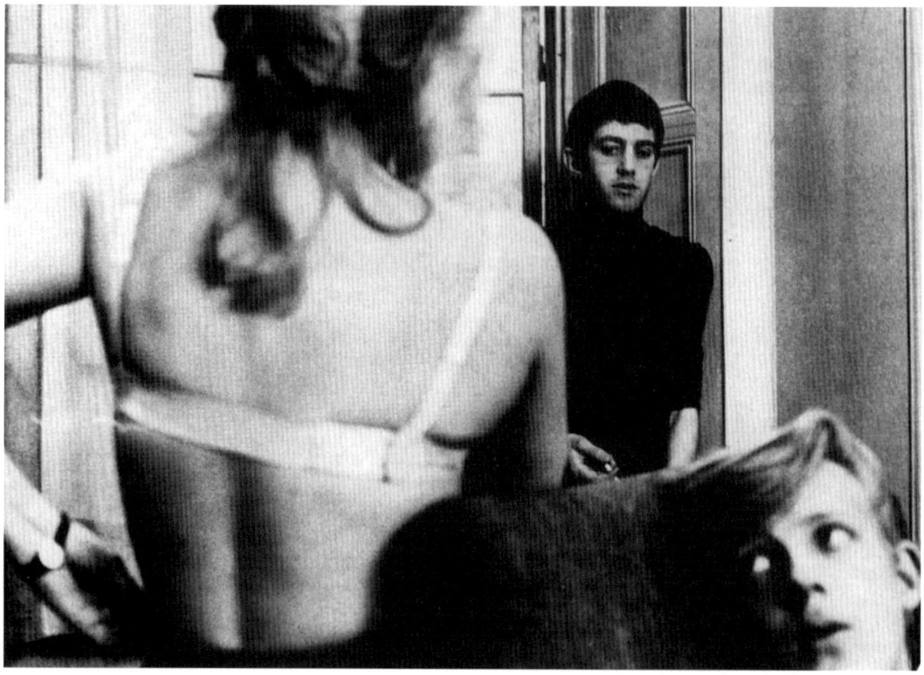

Swedish Producers' Association and the Swedish Film Institute to show the film 491 at the Berlin Festival has, however, been made completely independently of the decision of the government on the question of censorship. In making its decision the Film Institute was guided by the same principles as those described in §7 of the guidelines: ›The sole and exclusive criterion determining the selection of a film must be its artistic value.‹« (Quoted from the translation of a letter from Harry Schein, Svenska Filminstitutet dated Feb. 3, 1964 to Alfred Bauer; the original has disappeared.)

This reference to the Festival's guidelines placed Alfred Bauer in a difficult position since he had no right to refuse the film as an official contribution. Shocked by a report in the »Spiegel« magazine at the beginning of April, the Film Commissioner of the Evangelical Church in Germany, High Consistory Dr. Hermann Gerber, and the Catholic Film Commissioner of the Church Main Office for Visual Arts and Film, Monsignor Anton Kochs sent letters (both dated April 17, 1964) to the newly appointed Senator of Science and the Arts, Dr. Werner Stein, calling on him to examine whether it was permissible to show the film 491 at the International Film Festival. It was a question of far more than just »grave misgivings about the effect on the public, the church, and the standard of the Film Festival« to quote Hermann Gerber; the letters also pointed out quite unequivocally that the churches were likely to withdraw their juries from the Festival if a decision was made in Berlin to run the films. The churches took their arguments from the heated debates which had surrounded Ingmar Bergman's film TYSTNADEN (»The Silence«) and which had been shown in the Federal Republic in January 1964; both letters contained references to Bergman's film. Indeed, Gerber even cited Ruy Guerra's OS CAFAJESTES [The No-Good Ones] shown in Berlin in 1962 – and the Greek film MIKRES APHRODITES by Nikos Koundouros, which had been shown at the IFB in 1963, and had won the prize for best director (Silver Berlin Bear).

Kanajo to kare (»She and He«): Sachiko Hidari

Faced with this response, the Senate and the Festival management resorted to a trick. The Swedish producers had run 491 in several closed showings for the press and other interested parties during the Cannes festival in 1964, a procedure which was by no means unusual. According to the interpretation prevailing in Berlin, however, – § 8 of the guidelines – the Swedish film thus no longer fulfilled the requirements for participating in the Berlin Festival. The guidelines stated that only those films which had not been shown anywhere in Europe outside their country of origin and/or at other film festivals, or at similar events, were to be allowed to compete at the Berlin Festival. Film Section advisor Frank Schwerin expressly stated in a memorandum to his Senator that »the question of excluding youths aged between 18 and 21 should no longer be considered as a reason for rejecting entries«. On May 25th Alfred Bauer informed Fenne Fant of Svensk Filmindustri that the film had been rejected. This led to a very strong reaction in Sweden, and even to letters of protest to Mayor Willy Brandt.

Controversy over the German entries

Bauer's high-handed decisions also led to discontent in the case of the nominations of the German entries. Alfred Bauer had invited Wolfgang Staudte's HERRENPARTIE [Stag Party] of his own accord, thus bypassing the vote of the selection commission which had favored Rudolf Jugert's KENNWORT: REIHER [Password: Heron]. The background to this dispute over areas of competence seems to have been »certain doubts« (not specified in any greater detail) on the part of the then Federal Minister of the Interior, Hermann Höcherl, about Staudte's film, which presented an encounter between German tourists and the inhabitants of a Yugoslavian village, who were unable to forget the shooting of hostages by the German Wehrmacht during the Second World War. Following a talk with Ministerial Supervisor Fuchs at the Federal

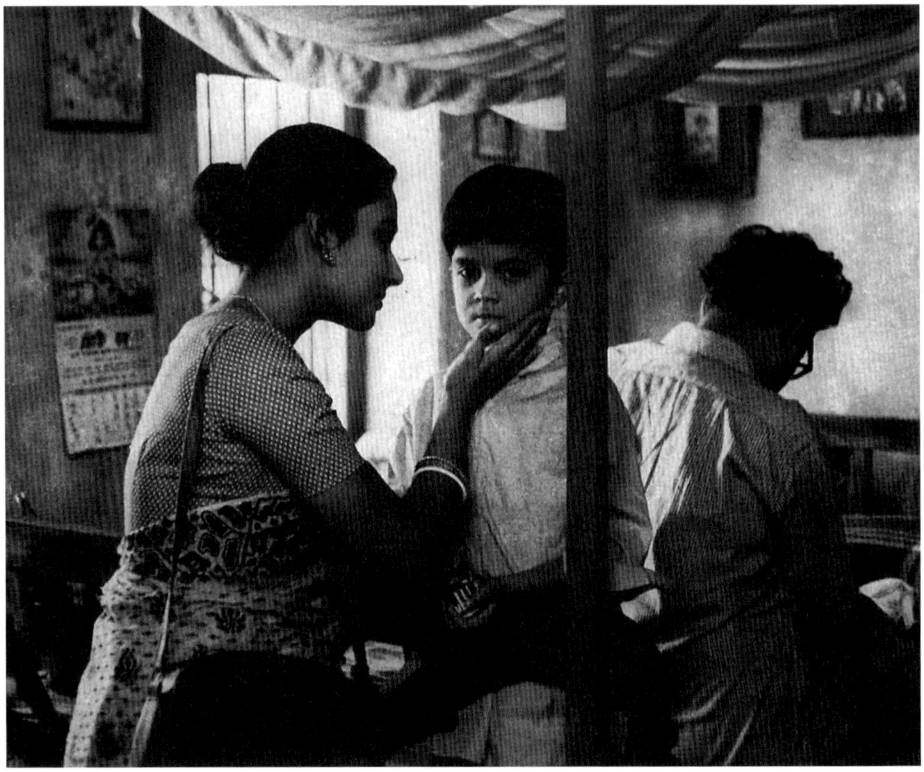

MAHANAGAR [The Big City]: Madhabi Mukherjee, Avil Chatterjee (in the background)

Ministry of the Interior on May 13th 1964, Schwerin, advisor of the Film Section, noted that there was even the possibility of Höcherl »visiting Berlin during the IFB«. Schwerin wrote: «We promised Mr. Fuchs that HERRENPARTIE would definitely be shown following the Federal Film Prize Awards«. The invitation for Staudte's film was not cancelled. The selection commission also nominated Thomas Fantl's film ZEIT DER SCHULDLOSEN [Time of the Innocent] based on the play written for theater and radio by Siegfried Lenz. KENNWORT: REIHER, Jugert's film about the Resistance during the Second World War, was shown in »Woche der Kritik«.

Bauer's tendency in 1964 to choose the safe path through the middle, to concede to films »which address themselves to the public as a whole« lowered the standard of the program, and produced a dull festival. The jury, presided over by the American director Anthony Mann, made a surprising choice in the Turkish film SUSUZ YAZ [Waterless Summer] by Ismail Metin. This contributed to the fact that critics later labelled the Festival »provincial« and declared the awarding of the Grand Prix, which was primarily made at the instigation of Jacques Doniol-Valcroze, to be a blatant mistake. Ulrich Gregor wrote in the »Spandauer Volksblatt« that the film was »so overloaded with false and naively presented folklore that the best one could have done with the film would have been to pass over it in silence. Placing this botch-up, which was evidently produced with a great deal of speculation, calculating on a European preference for sweet oriental imagery, above a film like Hani's »She and He« which – if there was any justice – would have been entitled to the first prize, is tantamount to deriding the public.« (July 9, 1964.)

A surprise in the distribution of awards

The negative response to the 14th Film Festival led, at first, to hectic activity within the Senate and the Festival organization. Whilst Alfred Bauer tried to save

OS FUZIS [The Guns]

what could be saved, and used the language of appeasement in his closing report, the dominant opinion held by the Senate and the Senator for Science and the Arts responsible was that far-reaching measures to restructure the Festival were necessary. Bauer's position as Festival director was no longer unquestioned either. In any case, his competence with respect to the choice of films was to be restricted. Whereas Bauer initially put up resistance to plans of reform, he was soon forced to see that he no longer had such a strong position, and that he could not assert himself vis-à-vis the Senate and critics of the Film Festival. Consequently, his attitude, so rigid at first, softened, giving way to a willingness to engage in dialogue, so that he too became involved in making proposals to restructure the Festival.

Reform

On August 28, 1964, he presented the Senate with a 10-point program to improve the Festival. This program included the following suggestions: the introduction of an autonomous status for the Film Festival so that it could send invitations directly to the socialist countries; a diminution in the size of the organizational committee (previously consisting of 18 members) responsible for selecting Festival films and receiving criticisms this committee should now consist of six people with the director of the Festival making the number up to seven (he proposed the following by name: the critics Volker Baer, Ulrich Gregor, and Ilse Urbach, the sculptor Professor Erich Reuter, the writer Uwe Johnson, and the film producer and director Hansjürgen Pohland); a change in the IFB's guidelines enabling it to invite films to participate in the Competition even if they had already been shown outside their country of origin or at another festival (interestingly enough, Bauer refers to the case of 491); financial allowances for Festival films, i. e. on the one hand a grant for Festival films (including foreign productions with German distributors) by means of the premium of at least DM 100 000 in accordance with the Law on Film Grants, which had not been passed but was still in the discussion phase at this time, and, on the other hand, the exemption of Festival films, which were commercially exploited,

Ulvi Dogan, producer, author and leading actor of the Turkish film SUSUZ YAZ, receives the Golden Bear from Anthony Mann

Sidney Poitier, Begum Aga Khan

Anthony Mann's wife, Maria Gladys, congratulates Ruy Guerra

from value-added tax; the creation of a prize and a separate Festival section for »young film countries«; a new status for the jury either by doubling the number of German members in order to have more influence on decisions, or replacing the »official« jury (in accordance with FIAPF guidelines) by a »press-jury« – a »revolutionary measure«; the continuation of »Woche der Kritik«; the introduction of an »International Amateur Film Festival« running concurrently; winning over new audiences; bringing the Film Festival »closer to the people« by re-introducing audience evaluation or by means of »folklore evenings«.

While some of these proposals coincided with ideas brought up by the Senate, especially those aiming at tighter organization, others, such as allowances and grants for Festival films which were to be distributed were out of the question. Such an incentive would hardly have resulted in producers – as Bauer believed – sending their best films (i. e. from the artistic standpoint) to Berlin; and as far as the attraction of the Festival for the public was concerned, Bauer was adhering to ideas which now – in the middle of the sixties – seemed rather outdated.

Critics join the organizational committee.

Some took a counterposition: there were critics who rejected participation on jury and festival committees, because they wanted to remain unbiased and independent in their coverage of the »Berlinale«.

On November 10th 1964, the Senate presented its opinion, via Schwerin – advisor of its Film Section – of Bauer's catalogue of proposals, which was basically in line with the assessment given above. Furthermore, representatives of the Senate (including Senator Werner Stein and Senatorial Executive Harald Ingensand, one of Bauer's most outspoken critics), the Film Festival (Alfred Bauer, Hans Borgelt) and the film industry met with some film journalists, who included Karena Niehoff, Ilse Urbach, Klaus Hebecker, Volker Baer, Ulrich Gregor, Enno Patalas, and Friedrich Luft, in order to discuss the reform proposals for the Film Festival. One major result of the talks was the intention to take advantage of the expert opinions offered by the critics when selecting the films. The minutes also noted the following point: »The Senator raised the question as to whether the existence of various ›schools‹ was to be taken into account when choosing films. The journalists replied that supporters of the various camps, i. e. ›literary‹ versus ›sociological‹ film criticism, had always been in agreement with respect to the quality of the films, so that differences in the assumptions underlying their observations were not substantial.« With that, one crucial aspect of the reform strategy had been realized: the competence of the critics was incorporated into the organizational committee, thus creating a counterweight to the state representatives and the associations' functionaries. Furthermore, the critics declared their willingness to participate in the international jury (Karena Niehoff and Hans-Dieter Roos were to take part in 1965).

The Senate Department responsible was not able to gain acceptance of another consideration, i. e. rescheduling the date of the Film Festival to late fall. On this question Alfred Bauer assured himself of the support of his confidants and foreign representatives. The Department's suggestion was received negatively on the part of: C. C. Schulte in Rome, Bert Reisfeld in Los Angeles, Alexandre Alexandre in Paris, Pem (i. e. Paul Marcus) in London, and Wilhelm Petersen in Madrid; Spio also dismissed the suggestion of switching dates. Alfred Bauer summarized these views in a letter to Harald Ingensand: »Berlin would have to become – nolens volens – a reenactment of the other festivals.« (Oct. 19, 1964.) The Senate gave way on this issue.

One other point remained open: as early as 1956 the first cautious speculation could be heard concerning the establishment of a limited company for the Festival. In a discussion following the 1964 Film Festival these ideas became acute again. It was primarily a question of finding an organizational form which enabled the socialist

International Jury for Feature Films
Anthony Mann (USA, president)
Hermann Schwerin (FRG, vice-president)
Lucas Demare (Argentina)
Jacques Doniol-Valcroze (France)
Georges Tzavellas (Greece)
Richard Todd (Great Britain)
Takashi Hamama (UAR)
Gerd Ressing (FRG)

International Jury for Documentary and Short Films
Girja Mookerjee (India, president)
Ferdinand Kastner (Austria, vice-president)
Roland Verhavert (Belgium)
Aud Thagaard (Norway)
Burhan Arpad (Turkey)
Peter Schamoni (FRG)
Hans-Joachim Hossfeld (FRG)

countries to accept invitations to the Competition without coming into conflict with their own fri-partite theory. Senator Stein wrote to Bauer and commented on his demand for »autonomous« status for the Film Festival: »We agree on the advantages to be had by transforming the International Film Festival Berlin into a legal person. This could be done most expediently in connection with the Berliner Festwochen. The draft of a partnership agreement for a non-profit-making limited company whose partners should be Berlin and the Federal Republic will be completed at the end of this year.« However, he went on to say that »the Federal Republic was not at all in favor of the idea of transforming the Film Festival into a limited company. (...) Under these circumstances this new organizational structure could be planned for 1966 at the earliest. I shall do my utmost to ensure that considerations of foreign policy do not tip the scales in the decision-making process.« (Dec. 10, 1964.) Owing to this decision the Eastern bloc countries continued to be excluded from the Festival Competition. Foreign policy won the day. However, a new start had been made.

25 times Berlin

By Freddy Buache

My first trip to Berlin took place on the occasion of the Film Festival in which I participated: that was in 1964. I discovered the film event and at the same time a city which had dominated my dreams for a long time. Because when I had begun to occupy myself systematically with the seventh art, the directors of that great epoch of German film (between 1919 and 1933) had immediately drawn my attention. Lang, Pabst and Lubitsch, for example, quickly occupied a preferred place among the small group of my favorite directors, and therefore Berlin, a magical place in that specific time, awakened in me the love of a culture which the teachers of my youth had all too often left in the dark. German theater, writing and, above all, painting (romanticism, which is so poorly known in the Romance countries, and expressionism) became for me through reading, visits to exhibitions and theater productions unusually important sources of emotion and reflection.

That is to say, when I came to the Film Festival as a journalist for a daily newspaper, as the person responsible for the Swiss Cinémathèque and from 1964 (to 1969) the codirector of the Locarno Festival, always searching for appropriate films to complete our own program (which took place some weeks, then some months later), I naturally had to concentrate my attention mainly on the screenings, particularly on those which took place on the margin of the official Competition. Yet this professional obligation never kept me from strolling along the streets or canals (where red roses suddenly allowed my thoughts to wander back to Rosa Luxemburg) or to seek in other places certain traces of old memories of this wounded city, to visit the museums, the galleries, the opera, the zoo and, of course, the typical Berlin restaurants or cabarets.

During this first visit, I was struck by the lively and collegial warm-heartedness of Dr. Alfred Bauer, and the memory of his discreet presence combines itself with the sunny moments of those days; for the Film Festival took place in June back then, a season which invited to meetings and discussion on terraces, to excursions to the lakes... The joy which this caused was increased by the circumstance that here, far away from their usual environment, I met my Parisian colleagues Henri Langlois and Lotte Eisner. Lotte return-

ed after a very long exile for the first time to the place of her childhood and youth, and with her - what an extraordinary privilege - I retraced step by step the (so mythical) Berlin of yesteryear in the (so painfully and poorly healed) Berlin of the year 1964. In this unusual situation other permanent friendships were made, and I will not forget one of the most joyous, most generous ones, which was given to me by Gerhard Lamprecht.

Above all else which this beloved city gave me year in and year out, the Film Festival taught me much, especially with its wonderful Retrospectives, and I do not only refer to those with an obvious and serious »cultural« claim. (Ah! The pleasure of hearing and seeing Lilian Harvey!) In 1973 I was a member of the jury and was very happy to be able to present the Golden Bear (finally!) to Satyajit Ray - for ASHANI SANKET. *In short: For twenty-five years I have been loyal to Berlin and its festival, and that, more than my words, is an expression of my thanks to all the ladies and gentlemen who with Moritz de Hadeln, Ulrich Gregor and their wives produce so much diverse information about film and do it with such sensitivity and competence, so that the great tradition of warm reception and common pleasure may continue.*

The Awards of the International Jurys

Feature Films
Grand Prix of the 14th IFB
Golden Berlin Bear
SUSUZ YAZ
Turkey, directed by
Ismail Metin

Silver Berlin Bear
for the best director
Satyajit Ray
for MAHANAGAR
India

Silver Berlin Bear
for the best actress
Sachiko Hidari
in KANAJO TO KARE
Japan
and
NIPPON KONCHUKI
Japan

Silver Berlin Bear
for the best actor
Rod Steiger
in THE PAWNBROKER
USA

Special Prize
Silver Berlin Bear
Ruy Guerra (director)
for OS FUZIS
Brazil

Long Documentary Films
Golden Berlin Bear
ALLEMAN
Netherlands, directed by
Bert Haanstra

THE KNACK ... AND HOW TO GET IT: Richard Lester's Competition entry with Rita Tushingham

A happy year

1965

June 25th – July 6th, 1965

A boy destroys a photograph on his father's desk. It is a photograph of Konrad Adenauer. An idol. A son takes his revenge on his father by getting rid of *his* »model father«; a revelation and a disappointment. The opening film at the 15th International Film Festival was PARIS VU PAR ... (»Six in Paris«), an episodic film by Jean Douchet, Jean-Luc Godard, Jean-Daniel Pollet, Eric Rohmer, Jean Rouch and Claude Chabrol. Their entry was censored when it was shown in Berlin. The action goes even further: The boy pokes out the eyes on the photo. This scene had been cut, out of consideration for the host country. Prominent politicians were sitting in the parquet. Willy Brandt was the chancellor candidate of the Social Democrats in opposition. The election campaign was underway.

The Festival: three parts

This year the Festival was divided into three parts. It consisted of the Competition, an Information Show for films not competing for the »Berlin Bears«, because they had already been shown at other festivals, or because the selection commission felt that it would be better to run them outside the Competition, and a Representational Show for the countries participating in the Film Fair making films available which had been selected by delegates and producers of the various nations – acting on their own responsibility. This show was open to the public.

The Festival management and those in the political hierarchy responsible had learned from the debacle of the IFB in 1964, even if it had been necessary for the Senator for Science and the Arts, Professor Dr. Werner Stein, to do some persuading with the Federal Ministry of the Interior. Agreement had been reached on the following measures: tightening up the Competition program, supplementing it with the Information and Representational Shows, reducing the number of prizes, and having the jury members nominated by the Festival management instead of by the individual countries. Above all, the selection commission, which had hitherto been composed almost exclusively of representatives of the authorities or spokesmen of interest groups, was to be extended to include specialists, which in this case meant five film critics. These proposals had been agreed upon by Alfred Bauer and the Senate. Bauer himself had already tried to take the wind out of the critics' sails in August 1964 with a ten-point program on reforming the IFB. This move had shored up his position. Bauer soon found an ally in Senator Stein who had recognized the lack of structure in the Film Festival. Together, they worked on a new version of the guidelines which, however, had to be accepted by the Federal Minister of the Interior. This created some problems. At first, the Minister only gave his consent to some of the reform proposals: i. e. reduction in the number of Competition films and the selection of jury members (letter of Dec. 15, 1964). In Bonn objections were directed, in particular, against the intention to tighten up the selection criteria, and only to accept »films of artistic value« (Article 1 of the guidelines). The Federal Minister of the Interior, Hermann Höcherl, underlined the importance of the Festival with respect to foreign policy and the film industry, fearing diplomatic discontent if a film from another country was rejected. In his reply Senator Stein argued: »I cannot accept the fact that the Federal Republic of Germany is frequently not represented at Film Festivals abroad because no suitable film has been found, nor can I accept the opposite situation, i. e. that the International Film Festival Berlin has to take every film simply because it comes from a country which (...) produces more than 50 films a year.« (Jan. 22, 1965.) Stein also defended the Berlin decision to improve the selection

The Federal Ministry of the Interior states its case.

commission by having film critics participate in it and to exclude Senate representatives from it in the future as »the executive is principally not entitled to pronounce aesthetic value judgements«.

As far as the question of the rights on inviting films was concerned, Stein found a compromise which, on the one hand, did not restrict Alfred Bauer's field of competence, and, on the other hand, included him in the new modes of decision-making and selection. The guidelines stipulated that the Festival director had the right to invite films. However, he was only entitled, in exceptional cases, to issue an invitation of his own accord without informing or consulting the selection commission. (Exceptional cases arose immediately, of course, when for example producer Franz Seitz pushed Bauer to nominate Rolf Thiele's WÄLSUNGENBLUT for Berlin because otherwise Rolf Thiele would choose Cannes or Venice. This was all at very short notice, of course.)

The Federal Minister of the Interior took his time in replying to Stein's letter, so that the latter finally sent a telegram on February 12th calling for a decision, since otherwise the 15th International Film Festival Berlin would be »jeopardized«. He received a reply four days later. Hermann Höcherl gave his consent to the Berlin reform proposals, although not without pointing out differences. »My opinion that paying too much consideration to artistic criteria is confirmed by the experience which the international film festival in Venice has had with this procedure recently. (...) I leave it to your discretion to decide to what extent you wish to give artistic criteria priority over other considerations when choosing the films. However, I would ask you to show understanding for the fact that the Federal Government, which must make good any diplomatic discontent arising, will distance itself if necessary and leave responsibility in the hands of the Berlin Senate.« (Feb. 16, 1965.) Hence, the new guidelines were enacted in time by the Berlin Senate on April 27th 1965. This may not have been a particularly thorough reform, yet this year did mark a certain new start in the history of the International Film Festival Berlin.

Koji Wakamatsu, Takao Yoshizawa

Joachim Tiburtius, Ulrich Gregor

Werner Stein, Willy Brandt

Participation of critics in the selection of the films proved to be a good idea even though there were difficulties at first because schedules were frequently planned at short notice. Werner Fiedler, Ilse Urbach, Kurt Habernoll, and Ulrich Gregor from Berlin, and Enno Patalas from Munich were placed on the commission. Whereas Fiedler and Urbach represented the »older generation« of critics, Gregor and Patalas represented new positions among film critics, positions with an avant-gardist orientation combined with social criticism. Between these poles, Kurt Habernoll was more or less assigned the role of mediator. Other critics like Friedrich Luft and Karena Niehoff toured abroad looking for films for the Festival, Luft in England - he obtained Polanski's film REPULSION - and Niehoff in India. By including films by Jean-Luc Godard, Agnès Varda, Palle Kjaerulff-Schmidt, Bo Widerberg, Koji Wakamatsu and Roman Polanski, the Competition offered a spectrum of the new generation of film-makers, not to mention films by Georges Franju and Satyajit Ray.

Critics participate in selecting the films.

The Federal Republic was represented at the Competition with WÄLSUNGENBLUT, based on a novel by Thomas Mann. Kurt Hoffmann's DAS HAUS IN DER KARPFENGASSE [The House in Carp Lane] which had received the most West German film prizes, yet had been rejected in Cannes for lacking in artistic quality, and NICHT VERSÖHNT ODER ES HILFT NUR GEWALT, WO GEWALT HERRSCHT [Not Reconciled] by Jean-Marie Straub and Danièle Huillet were shown at special performances in the Information Show. The latter film was also entered for the Competition but unanimously rejected by the selection commission with the exception of one abstention by Enno Patalas. However, the commission members agreed to invite the film for the Information Show which would be linked with a discussion. On July 4th the film was premièred at the Atelier am Zoo under the heading »New Narrative Structures in Film«. Gideon Bachmann chaired the discussion and Alexander Kluge, Michel Delahaye, Enno Patalas and Straub where on the podium. It was a very lively discussion. Members of the audience accused Straub of dilettantism and criticized the dialogue for being monotonous. What they had failed to notice was the music score underlying the

»New Narrative Structures in Film«

Famous for her gossip column and radio shows: Hedda Hopper

ALPHAVILLE:
Eddie Constantine,
Anna Karina

visual images, and the language. Michel Delahaye said: »What we have seen here is one of the best films since Murnau and Fritz Lang.« He was quite right.

This year, the Festival organizational team resided in Berlin's new city center. In any case, the Europa-Center – which was ceremoniously opened in 1965 and triumphantly dominated the ruins of the Memorial Church – was considered to have metropolitan status. The Royal Palast, the movie house complex connected to it, was made into a Festival movie theater, since the Filmbühne Wien was held to be obsolete. The atmosphere during the presentation also reflected the new start. The suggestion was even made to drop the Zoo-Palast in favor of the Royal-Palast. But it did not come to this, fortunately.

You will be gripped by REPULSION

All around the Europa-Center, set in the sidewalk in white paving stones or simply – depending on the sidewalk-artist – written in chalk, there was a mysterious message, four capital letters: EKEL (repulsion). This was how the distribution company Atlas-Filmverleih advertised Roman Polanski's film. A subversive slogan accompanied this piece of PR work: »You will be gripped by REPULSION«. The opinions of the critics and audiences were divided over this film as had seldom been the case with any other film shown at the Berlinale in the past. For some, Polanski's film was a flippantly made and cynically calculated horror strip, yet the film left a strong impression among the majority of the critics. Peter W. Jansen was gripped by REPULSION. »The film presents a rich juxtapositioning of imagery, showing desire and pain, growth and disintegration, lust for life and passion for murder (...) A film which, on the face of it, seems to be a thriller and shocker in which repulsion is implicit, and which is created with all the means available to film-makers, of directing people and composing images, of architecture and sound; it is in fact a work of great, moral seriousness. REPULSION is, not least, an angry and indignant response to the total sex-

Le Bonheur:
Marie-France Boyer,
Jean-Claude Drouot

ualization of life, which is only a symbol of the death of dialogue and an absence of communication. Repulsion will be talked about for a long time.« (Frankfurter Allgemeine Zeitung, July 1, 1965.)

One could see and read Agnès Varda's Le Bonheur [Happiness] almost as an involontary counterweight to Polanski's Repulsion. A newly wed husband loves his wife and another woman; his love is enough for two, and his happiness is the happiness of the women. Varda counters the harsh abruptness of Polanski's universe with a cosy, naive interior. Happiness is unique like love itself, or it is not - like life itself. In Berlin, Le Bonheur confused many people and angered few.

Charulata [The Lonely Wife] by Satyajit Ray, a film based on a novel by Rabindranath Tagore, has a similar constellation to Le Bonheur but the symbolism is reversed. A woman feels increasingly lonely with her husband (an idealistic journalist). She finds an escape in literature and in a hypotrophic love for her brother-in-law. In the end, the married couple, both workaholics who have lost sight of themselves and who experience neither life nor love, are left empty-handed. The final picture freezes as they reach out for one another. But they do not establish contact - like a scene from Michelangelo. The audiences liked its novelette character.

Science fiction located in the present: In Godard's film Alphaville, Lemmy Caution, the comic-strip agent, is victorious and falls in love. Lemmy Caution lives in opposition to the times, in which feelings, love, and sadness have been eliminated. For the cinema, living in opposition to the times means that the clocks run differently. Howard Vernon plays Professor von Brown who designs a powerful computer for giving commands; he had already appeared in films by Fritz Lang and was also to play various parts in films by Straub/Huillet. Incongruence - the 1965 Festival thrived on it.

A meeting of the jury: Frank Schwerin, Alexander Kluge, John Gillett, Karena Niehoff, Edmund Luft

Lee Marvin taking a »ride on an steamship«, a tradition in summer for the Film Festival guests

Six critics sat on the jury (John Gillett, Ely Azeredo, Monique Berger, Kyushiro Kusakabe, Karena Niehoff, and Hans-Dieter Roos) together with one producer (Jerry Bresler) and two German film-makers (Hansjürgen Pohland and Alexander Kluge). »After two hours someone asks: Do we only announce the number of votes for and against anonymously? Or do we give our names, too? Three hours later: Shall we mention them if we have minor disagreements, or only if we have pangs of conscience? A little later: who is to draw the line between ›acceptable nuances‹ and ›fundamental opposition‹? Those affected or the jury president? But how is he supposed to sort out the stones which have been put in his path. We came to an agreement, in spite of everything, about how the souls of the underdogs were to remain intact if the worst came to the worst – and then the casus belli did not even arise. The passion of this or that person for his one or two favorites no matter how absolutely impossible or even weak was rapidly extinguished: do we award the Golden Bear to LE BONHEUR or ALPHAVILLE? Those were the two fervently defended camps.« (Karena Niehoff, Der Tagesspiegel, July 10, 1965.)

Jean-Luc Godard received the Festival's Grand Prix. The Silver Bear for the best director went to Satyajit Ray, and, as there were so many films worthy of awards, the jury presented special prizes to Agnès Varda and Roman Polanski. Some observers regretted the fact that Bo Widerberg's Swedish entry KÄRLEK 65 [Love 65] did not receive a prize. Apart from this, however, there was no haranguing of the jury or the Festival.

»Affairs within Walls«: friction over the Japanese entry.

Nevertheless, the Japanese Association of Film Producers did complain to the Foreign Ministry and the Consulate General in Berlin about the screening of the film KABE NO NAKANO HIMEGOTO [Affairs within Walls] by the young director Koji Wakamatsu – who worked independently of the studios. The film, which was both a voyeuristic masterpiece and full of social criticism, did not have the blessing of the

Japanese studio bosses. It was argued that he had hurt Japanese national pride, and that the organizers in Berlin had not reacted to early protests. As a consequence, Japan would no longer participate in the Film Festival. This forceful protest was triggered off, on the one hand, by the fact that not one of the films of the five big Japanese studios had been selected, and, on the other hand, by the disconcerting and dismissive attitude of audiences when the film was shown. The Japanese Association of Film Producers failed to mention the fact that the Berlin selection commission had, in fact, tried to get other productions from Japan, having been advised by the English critic Donald Richie, an expert on Japanese cinema. However, either the quality of the films did not meet the selection criteria or the Japanese film producers sent films which the Berliners had voted for at other festivals, e. g. Kurosawa's AKAHIGE (»Red Beard«) or a new film by Susumu Hani. The arguments presented by the Japanese gave the impression that there were two different kinds of film: those which were intended to be shown officially, and those which were only intended for home-viewing. (In the program Wakamatsu's film was not announced as the »official« Japanese entry, but as a film which had received an »invitation«.) However, summa summarum, this was a scandal behind walls.

One »official« film, which certainly was a scandal, was shown in the Representational Show. ASSEGAI TO JAVELIN, a documentary film from South Africa, which related how the black population was casting aside the warrior's spear (assegai) and turning to the sport of throwing the javelin. The basic attitude behind the film was that apartheid did not exist. Both screenings had to be interrupted owing to massive protest, primarily on the part of students. The police intervened.

This had been the only political disaster – and a necessary protest – in a happy year.

International Jury
John Gillett
(Great Britain, president)
Alexander Kluge
(FRG, vice-president)
Ely Azeredo (Brazil)
Monique Berger (France)
Kyushiro Kusakabe (Japan)
Jerry Bresler (USA)
Karena Niehoff (FRG)
Hansjürgen Pohland (FRG)
Hans-Dieter Roos (FRG)

The Awards of the
International Jury

Feature Films
Grand Prix of the 15th IFB
Golden Berlin Bear
ALPHAVILLE
France, directed by
Jean-Luc Godard

Special Prize of the Jury
Silver Berlin Bear
LE BONHEUR
France, directed by
Agnès Varda

Special Prize of the Jury
Silver Berlin Bear
REPULSION
Great Britain, directed by
Roman Polanski

Silver Berlin Bear
for the best director
Satyajit Ray
for CHARULATA
India

Silver Berlin Bear
for the best actor
Lee Marvin
in CAT BALLOU
USA

Silver Berlin Bear
for the best actress
Madhur Jaffrey
in SHAKESPEARE-WALLAH
India

Special Mention
Walter Newman,
Frank Pierson
authors of CAT BALLOU
USA

Cul-de-sac:
Lionel Stander,
Jack MacGowran

Not a dead end

1966

June 24th–July 5th, 1966

»How can one even speak of a reestablishment of the German film industry? It's not enough to merely give it celluloid and some food. Screenwriters need cigarettes and coffee most of all, and these have become currencies in Germany. So long as I can't supply them with something to smoke and with something stimulating to drink, everything is hopeless.« A memory. A bit of reality packed into an anecdote. Paul Marcus, emigrated Berlin journalist, who became famous under his initials »Pem«, cites Erich Pommer, the German producer, who was responsible as American Film Officer for the reestablishment of the film industry in the Western zones after the war. On May 8th of this year, Pommer died in Hollywood; Pem is holding a speech in the Urania, it is very personal and very much in friendship. The Film Festival is presenting – in Pommer's honor – his film LILIOM made in exile and directed by Fritz Lang. Lotte H. Eisner speaks a few introductory words. The Film Festival Retrospectives tell of losses.

Memories of Erich Pommer

In a conference room at the Europa-Center, seven directors are seated. They are to discuss the topic »Does cinema have a future?« Peter Schamoni, Roman Polanski, Pier Paolo Pasolini, Satyajit Ray, Jean-Paul Rappeneau and Volker Schlöndorff are the guests, Erwin Leiser is the host. This event has been organized jointly by the Film Festival and the ZDF (German television Channel Two). The interest of the public is great, the desire of the directors to contemplate the future of film is small. The very existence of film is endangered; little has changed here – even if film festivals do have a future. Joe Hembus reports on this discussion: »Peter Schamoni felt that involvement was the key. Polanski found the question to the future of film ›a very difficult question‹ and felt incompetent to offer any theories; as punishment, he was asked no further questions – and fell into complete silence. Pasolini offered his concept of a ›spiritualized reality‹. Schlöndorff gave him a big hand, and rejected the primacy of commitment (›art comes before commitment‹), assigning film-makers the realm of their own small worlds instead of the world at large. (›Films should communicate the thoughts one person has about his fellow men‹). Ray spoke of the difficulties in making films in India (...). Suddenly there was talk of the costs of production. Polanski woke up.« (Film International, No. 10, July 3, 1966.) At the end the listeners applauded, especially those imploring sentences stating that films do not belong so much on TV as in movie houses. At times one could believe that the present perpetuates itself, without having a future.

Does cinema have a future? Six directors search for answers.

At a third event, Erwin Leiser and Dr. Heinz Rathsack are available for questions from the public. They are the first directors of the Deutsche Film- und Fernsehakademie Berlin (German Film and Television Academy, also called the dffb). In June 1965, after long and strenuous discussions, the Federal Government and Berlin had come to an administrative agreement on the dffb. In July 1966, the government of Bavaria decided to establish a college for television and film (the HFF) in Munich. The broad topic up for debate was: »A film and television academy – what for?« For the dffb the future had just started. On September 15th 1966, instruction began. In the years to come, films by graduates were to be found in the Film Festival program again and again.

The German Film and Television Academy

Informal conversations, rather than the actual »Berlinale« themes and the discussions about films in the Competition and elsewhere, and even chitchat had often more substance: in them lay the mood and atmosphere of the times, a voice could be heard, a curious glance became visible – lines of communication, sometimes even a network.

New Festival movie houses in the Europa-Center on Tauentzienstrasse

Press conference with Lionel Stander, Jacqueline Bisset, Roman Polanski

Podium discussion with Peter Schamoni, Roman Polanski, Pier Paolo Pasolini, Erwin Leiser, Satyajit Ray, Jean-Paul Rappeneau, Volker Schlöndorff

Press conference with Geraldine Chaplin, Claude Briac, Hans Borgelt

A change in audience

The Festival had changed. It had become more detached, more business-like. Fans no longer gathered round outside of the movie houses. Friedrich Luft found that everything had become a bit too »chilly«. »Autograph albums no longer exist. The stars, although they are probably much more intelligent today than those who were so wooed then, don't even have to know how to write their names. No one asks them to do so in public.« (Die Welt, July 9, 1966.) The gossip sheets took to actor Edd Byrnes, whose real name no one knew, everyone calling him »Cookie«, from his role as private detective in the American TV series 77 Sunset Strip, which West Germans loved watching on weekends. But even on television »Cookie« was not Edd Byrnes. He existed in the voice of the German actor dubbing him, Hans Clarin, in a thin breaking teenager's voice chirping innocently silly redundant nonsense. The stars of the »Berlinale« were having identity problems. The movie theater was now in one's home, bathrobe, sofa, and all. The old audiences had gone astray. And the Film Festival was playing both ends to the middle. Young people thronged to the movies, questioning both directors and screenwriters; they had a feeling for complications. Friedrich Luft: »The movie houses were filled with an extremely lively and knowledgeable audience. They did not blindly accept the well-construed cynicisms of Roman Polanski, and they warned Jean-Luc Godard not to ruin his otherwise wonderfully sensitive and correctly portrayed picture of the youth of the sixties with trivialities and let him hear, with reason, that they had scruples - never before had we received such a self-confident response.« This is to be read as the observations of one of the older generation in his comments on the beat generation, who he had also once called »long haired howlers at microphones«. Yet he is not unattentive to them, and he does show sometimes an ironic sympathy, especially for the intelligence of those films in search of a completely different tradition than prevalent in the early years of the »Berlinale«.

The Film Festival Berlin was searching: searching for an audience and for films. The reform euphoria of the previous year seemed to have been curbed. Behind the scenes there had been disputes; especially to the constellation and competence of the critics for the selection commission. Alfred Bauer had demanded that the members be replac-

Jean-Pierre Léaud receives an award as best actor.

Nino Davoli, Pier Paolo Pasolini

Douglas Fairbanks jr.

ed completely, which the Senate had refused to do. Senator Stein wanted continuity - keeping, of course, reform in mind. Raimund Le Viseur, film critic for the »Abend«, was to be appointed to the position vacated by Ulrich Gregor, who had been transferred to the advisory board. But the Federal Ministry of the Interior raised objections, because it saw the requirement that members be sworn to secrecy endangered, as the »Abend« supposedly did not accept such an oath for its critics. The Ministry suggested Dieter Strunz, critic for the »Berliner Morgenpost«. Yet Enno Patalas argued against him publicly in the March issue of the »Filmkritik«, which then affected work in the selection commission.

Polemic among the critics

The feud between Patalas and Strunz was determined by opposing aesthetic, film critical and conceptional positions and it was Alfred Bauer, the Berlin Senate, and the Federal Ministry of the Interior who became involved, mediating using subtle tactics, yet also sometimes aggravating the situation. Patalas' competence, however, was not doubted; he used his influence, argumenting - often rigorously, and yet not in a conciliable way - against the Festival management, but with a passion for films, the cinema, and for the Film Festival Berlin. »For fifteen years now those responsible for the Berlinale have been drooling over the spectacular examples set by Cannes and Venice, and which here in Berlin will never be achieved - instead of grasping that as a festival of another style, Berlin could be superior to both«, writes Patalas. »As a festival for the audiences, instead of for the consumers. As a festival of the authors, not of the stars. As a festival of discussion, rather than a festival of prestige; as a place for confrontations, not for exchanging compliments. As a show-ground for new cinema, instead of a parade of the well-established.« (Filmkritik, August 1966.) Patalas was willing to attack, where others did not dare to show their colors; and he denounced the hesistant efforts towards reform - »two steps forwards, one step backwards: the reform of the ›Berlinale‹ progresses at the tempo of the procession of the Echternach pilgrimage.« And by insistently and incessantly criticizing, he accelerated the Film Festival's progress. Alfred Bauer once called Patalas, an »extreme cineast«: evidently a compliment, even if made with a certain aloofness.

Schonzeit für Füchse [Closed Season for Fox Hunting]: Christian Doermer, Helmut Förnbacher

La Caza (»The Hunt«): Ismael Merlo, Alfredo Mayo, Emilio G. Caba

Cul-de-sac: Lionel Stander

News from the jury

The jury, which was presided over by the French producer Pierre Braunberger and to which Pier Paolo Pasolini had been appointed on the explicit wish of Bauer, favored two films for the Golden Berlin Bear: Polanski's Cul-de-sac and Satyajit Ray's Nayak [The Hero]. They debated for two hours. At an interim ballot, the American critic

Hollies Alpert and the German jury members – Franz Seitz, Helmuth de Haas and Kurt Heinz – voted for Polanski, the other five members for Ray. According to the minutes of the jury, the Swedish writer and critic Lars Forssell changed »his mind suddenly at 10:15 p.m.« and voted for Polanski. Bauer and de Haas suggested awarding Ray's film and his complete works a Special Mention, which was then discussed; aside from Pasolini, who felt such an award to be an insult to Ray and proposed as a compromise awarding Polanski and Ray ex aequo the Golden Bear, the jurors accepted their suggestion. All other decisions were reached with clear majorities.

The awards had brought no surprises. It had merely been an interplay between Ray, Polanski and Godard, whose protagonist from MASCULIN FÉMININ, Jean-Pierre Léaud, received the award as best actor.

A telegram

from Jean-Pierre Léaud

here is the comment you requested stop i received the best actor award at the international berlin film festival for masculin féminin by jean-luc godard stop i have very pleasant memories of the festival in berlin stop best wishes
jean-pierre léaud

International Jury
Pierre Braunberger
(France, president)
Franz Seitz
(FRG, vice-president)
Emilio Villalba Welsh
(Argentina)
Khwaja Ahmad Abbas
(India)
Pier Paolo Pasolini (Italy)
Lars Forssell (Sweden)
Hollies Alpert (USA)
Helmuth de Haas (FRG)
Kurt Heinz (FRG)

The Awards of the
International Jury

Feature Films
Grand Prix of the 16th IFB
Golden Berlin Bear
CUL-DE-SAC
Great Britain, directed by
Roman Polanski

Silver Berlin Bear
for the best director
Carlos Saura
for LA CAZA
Spain

Silver Berlin Bear
for the best actress
Lola Albright
in LORD LOVE A DUCK
USA

Silver Berlin Bear
for the best actor
Jean-Pierre Léaud
in MASCULIN FÉMININ
France

Special Prize of the Jury
Silver Berlin Bear
SCHONZEIT FÜR FÜCHSE
FRG, directed by
Peter Schamoni

Special Prize of the Jury
Silver Berlin Bear
Lars Passgard
in JAKTEN
Sweden

Special Mention
Satyajit Ray
for NAYAK
and his complete works

PARAMOUNT PICTURES CORPORATION
WEST COAST STUDIOS
5451 MARATHON STREET — HOLLYWOOD, CALIF. 90038
AREA 213 469-2411 — CABLE ADDRESS "FAMFILM"

June 20, 1967

Internationale Film-Festspiele Berlin
Eing.: 23. JUNI 1967
Anlagen:

Dr. A. Bauer
Filmfestspiel
Bundesallee 1-12
Berlin 15, Germany

Dear Dr. Bauer:

I was very pleased to learn that you have invited my latest film, "The Fearless Vampire Killers", to the Berlin Film Festival. It goes without saying that personally, I would have been very happy to have this film shown at this festival, as I have spent over a year working on it, and I think it is one of my best.

Unfortunately, I understand that you may not be getting the picture from M-G-M, and the reasons for this are as follow:

Our American partner in this picture, Mr. Ransohoff, had the right to alter the film for the U. S. A., and at this moment is still re-cutting and re-dubbing my final version. I understand that some twenty minutes were cut out of the film, and I am very skeptical as far as the result of this operation is concerned.

Although my final cut prevails outside the U. S., Mr. Ransohoff put forth a suggestion that his version, and not mine, should be presented at the Berlin Film Festival. Alternatively, the suggestion was made that in return for my version being shown in Berlin, I should agree to Mr. Ransohoff's cut to be shown world-wide.

I hope you understand that I could not agree to either one of these suggestions.

I wish you, as ever, all the success at this very worthwhile event.

Yours,

Roman Polanski

RP:tr

Festivals-Ltd.

1967

June 23rd–July 4th, 1967

It looked as if the Film Festival would have to look around for another movie house. And all because of DOCTOR ZHIVAGO. In November 1966 the film had had its Berlin première at the Royal-Palast. It became a box-office draw, a hit. Everyone was whistling »Lara's Theme«, the film melody. And now the dates for the Festival in June were coming up, and the film was still playing to an almost sold-out house. The Royal-Palast was – as in the year before – planned as the IFB movie house. Yet since the Film Festival – differently from Cannes – did not have its own movie house, one was dependent on the cooperation of the proprietors of the theaters, as well as of the distributors. Would MGM take DOCTOR ZHIVAGO out of its program for the benefit of the Film Festival? The Festival management was beginning to get somewhat nervous, and began to consider an alternative location. And the possibilities were limited in Berlin. Then finally MGM took a stance: for the length of the Festival, the screenings of DOCTOR ZHIVAGO would be interrupted. Afterwards, Omar Sharif was to get off to a new start – which he did, for two more years. In 1968 and 1969, MGM also discontinued their showings of DOCTOR ZHIVAGO for the length of the Festival.

DOCTOR ZHIVAGO and the »Berlinale«

Preparations for the IFB were underway and hopes were high. Yet matters in the end turned out to be quite sobering. For these hopes had been based on the »Berliner Festspiele« being transformed into a private limited company: Festivals-Ltd, which meant a kind of »denationalization« of all the different festivals in Berlin – the Theatertreffen, Festwochen, Jazz-Festival, Television Competition and Film Festival. This far-reaching proposal had been preceded by a number of events, the first, at least as far as the Film Festival was concerned, was in the year 1956. The »Berlinale« had just been recognized internationally and conferred with so called »A-status«. However because of the controversial status of the city, the socialist countries still did not participate in the Film Festival. Invitations were sent out via the Office of Foreign Affairs in Bonn, and this fact had frustrated all attempts made by Berlin. As a consequence, the members of the organizational committee of the IFB 1956 came up with the idea of founding a private company, which would give the Film Festival an independent status, and more freedom in their policy of inviting different nations: i. e., some leeway.

Festivals-Ltd.: a new organizational structure for Berlin's festivals

At the meeting on December 18th 1956 a plan was drawn up for the establishment of the Festivals-Ltd.; one hoped to bring the plan into effect by 1958. It remained however a mere wish. Unsolvable financial problems and also general and obtrusive clashes of competence, particularly in the question of the sponsorship of the company, caused the project to be shelved. Yet this concept was at no point completely forgotten. About nine years later, the idea of a private limited company was revived by Berlin.

After more than two years of negotiations, the Federal Government and Berlin agreed to a new organizational structure for the Berlin Festivals. The Federal Government and Greater Berlin became the sole partners of the Festivals-Ltd. There were to be four representatives each from Bonn and Berlin on the supervising board of curators. Even though artists from »Eastern bloc countries« had already performed during the »Festwochen« and at the Jazz-Festival, the presentation of films from these countries in the Competition of the IFB had always been thwarted by the invitation procedure. Now there was hope that everything would change. As early as 1966, when the plans for the company became public, Senatorial Executive Harald Ingen-

Glauber Rocha,
Rodolfo Kuhn

sand from the Department of Science and the Arts had replied in an interview to the question of whether such a company would ensure the participation of the socialist countries in the »Berlinale«: »We do hope that such a company will relieve these problems as well. Yet more important than this question is the reduction of the number of government-run institutions in Berlin as a general politico-cultural goal, which has developed out of the plain conviction that much of that which has unavoidably come under the jurisdiction of the administration of Berlin in the past ten or fifteen years should be privately run, i.e., left to the influences of society. And it is possible indeed, that the controversial questions between the East and the West will also become less relevant if the sponsorship and organization is determined privately.« Hopes were high; yet the leopard did not want to change his spots so quickly, which had its consequences for the GDR. Harald Ingensand continued with: »The ›other side‹ will not be invited. We do hope however that the other Eastern bloc countries will accept the invitations received from Berlin Festivals-Ltd.« (Interview by Christa Maerker, Spandauer Volksblatt, Nov. 20, 1966.) It was feared that an invitation to the GDR could be interpreted as a first step towards official recognition – and at any rate it was not believed that the GDR could exert so much pressure on the other socialist countries that they would make their presence dependent on the GDR's. Tension between the East and the West had not yet let up. It would not be until Willy Brandt's political initiative, that is with the signing of the 1972 treaties with the Eastern bloc states, that a new trend in the policy of the Festival would be felt. The dependency of a festival on politics is greater than often assumed.

The board of curators is constituted.

On April 17th 1967, the board of curators of Berlin Festivals-Ltd. met for its first meeting. From the Federal Government were: Parliamentary Undersecretary Ernst Benda, as spokesman for the Federal Minister of the Interior; Ministerial Assistant Secretary Dr. Heinz Gefaeller, for the Federal Minister for All-German Affairs; Ministerial Assistant Secretary Dr. Karl Schmitt, as representative of the Federal Minister for Finances; and Legation Councillor Dr. Gerhard Kramer for the Office of Foreign Affairs. On the board for Berlin were: Senatorial Executive Horst Grabert as head of the Office of the Senate, Deputy Mayor and Senator for Finances Heinz Striek, Senator for Science and the Arts Professor Dr. Werner Stein and Dr. Hermann Schwerin, who had been appointed by the Senate to represent the film industry. Senator Stein was elected chairman of the board, and Ernst Benda vice-chairman. Resolutions were drawn up for the transition of the IFB and the Festwochen into Berlin Festivals-Ltd. Senatorial Supervisor Reinhard Wilke, acting business manager, was authorized to carry out negotiations with Dr. Rolf May – till then public relations director of the Springer newspaper corporation – for the position of executive manager of Festivals-Ltd., with Dr. Peter Löffler – presidential secretary of the Academy of Art – for the position of director of the Berliner Festwochen, and with Dr. Alfred Bauer for the renewal of his contract as director of the Film Festival.

Press conference with
Christof Wackernagel,
Johannes Schaaf,
Rob Houwer

For the Film Festival this new organizational form did not in the end bring many advantages; nor did the fact that it could now issue invitations itself. The USSR, Hungary, Bulgaria, Rumania, Poland, Yugoslavia and Czechoslovakia were all asked to participate. But only non-aligned Yugoslavia accepted the invitation to the Competition of the Film Festival, which was anyway nothing new – Yugoslavian films had been shown in Berlin between the years of 1953 and 1957. Czechoslovakia did show a film by Jiří Menzel in the Representational Show. There is a note by Alfred

Edith Evans, Michel Simon

Bauer on file stating, »that on Tuesday April 4th, in East Berlin, an assembly for all managers of state film industries of Eastern bloc countries was held. At this meeting, the spokesman of the GDR urged his colleagues to neither attend the Film Festival in West Berlin, nor to send films. This request was received with silence, neither acceptance nor rejection were expressed by the assembly. A discussion of the matter did not take place. This was in fact astonishing, as up till then all important procedures had been formulated in unanimously reached resolutions by the managers of the Eastern film industry.« (April 6, 1967.) It cannot be verified whether or not Bauer's informant reported what happend correctly or not. Just the same the disappointment in Berlin to the renewed absence of the socialist countries was great. »Nothing more could have been expected«, wrote Uwe Nettelbeck. »There was talk here of a trick with which one hoped to win over some of the Eastern bloc states for the ›Berlinale‹. It is therefore no wonder, that the Eastern bloc states also spoke of a trick and stayed away. Only the Yugoslavians were willing to let the trick be a trick and came.« (Die Zeit, July 7, 1967.)

Shattered hopes

Tätowierung: Helga Anders, Christof Wackernagel

Le Départ: Jean-Pierre Léaud

La Collectionneuse: Patrick Bauchau, Haydée Politoff

It seemed as if the »Berlinale« could not make much headway. All efforts for reform had come to nothing. Discussions went nowhere, impulses were not carried out or only half-heartedly. There were, however, single films in the program, justifying the existence of the Festival: Johannes Schaaf's Tätowierung [Tattooing] for instance, which was received with much controversy, or Jerzy Skolimowski's Le départ [The Departure], »a harmonious film, thematically rigidly composed, its

comic element taking on substance, not becoming ridiculous or compromising the standard it had set itself.« (Wolfram Schütte, Frankfurter Rundschau, July 3, 1967.) Yet the Berlin Film Festival was still seeking a new profile. And there were guests, who departed in disappointment: Jean Marais furiously packed his bags on the third day. He as well had not been received very enthusiastically; he was no longer such an idol. He had found the Film Festival »boring« and spoke of a »third rate festival«. Tempi passati!

There were however good moments. Uwe Nettelbeck reports of Eric Rohmer's La collectionneuse [The Collector]: »At this point, his film does seem to have come from another planet or from another, future space in time. The happiness which it promises still sounds quite outrageous - which would not have to be the case, and one day will no longer be.«

International Jury
Thorold Dickinson
(Great Britain, president)
Rüdiger Freiherr von Hirschberg
(FRG, vice-president)
Knud Leif Thomsen
(Denmark)
Michel Aubriant (France)
Sashadhar Mukerjee (India)
Aleksander Petrović
(Yugoslavia)
Willard Van Dyke (USA)
Manfred Delling (FRG)

The Awards of the International Jury

Feature Films
Grand Prix of the 17th IFB
Golden Berlin Bear
Le Départ
Belgium, directed by
Jerzy Skolimowski

Silver Berlin Bear
for the best director
Zivojin Pavlović
for Budjenje pacova
Yugoslavia

Silver Berlin Bear
for the best actor
Michel Simon
in Le Vieil homme et l'enfant
France

Silver Berlin Bear
for the best actress
Edith Evans
in The Whisperers
Great Britain

Special Prize of the Jury
Silver Berlin Bear
La Collectionneuse
France, directed by
Eric Rohmer

Special Prize of the Jury
for the idea and screenplay
Silver Berlin Bear
Michael Lentz
Alle Jahre wieder
FRG

Week-End: Mireille Darc

A la Grande Salle! or: student protest

1968

June 21st – July 2nd, 1968

Student protest

At the Free University Berlin, students have taken over the offices of the rector and declared him out of a job. In the »Audimax« (auditorium maximum – the main auditorium on campus), Daniel Cohn-Bendit and students discuss the protest movements in France and in Berlin. At another gathering, Fritz Teufel, spokesman of the APO (extraparliamentary opposition) and communard, appoints himself new rector of the university, and hands over its institutes to the students.

WEEK-END by Jean-Luc Godard

Yet another location, a movie house: a couple in a sports car gets caught in traffic. Submissively, everyone waits. Except for the couple, who pull out of line and pass the others. There's aggression, blood, an accident – a burning wreck, corpses on the turf. No one takes much notice. Later: in a meadow, a man is reading Rousseau's »Contrat social« out loud. He is wearing a costume. It is the actor Jean-Pierre Léaud. Another man is playing Mozart on a grand piano at a farm. Just as the images are extreme, so are the movements of the camera. Passing the line of traffic had been frighteningly long, never ending. At the farm, the camera scans 360 degrees several times. And then the film continues: a woman is being raped, her husband does not intervene. He smokes and waits. A garbage collector lectures on capitalism and nationalism. Everything ends up in a cannibalistic ritual. Man and animal in one pot, slaughtered, for feed. A written title is projected into the sound film, reading »Totem et Tabu«. The film is by Jean-Luc Godard and called: WEEK-END. In the Zoo-Palast, where the films for the Competition are being shown, there are irritated, and disturbed catcalls, some viewers flee, others remain, mesmerized. Godard closes with the line: »The end of the story. The end of the cinema.« It is as polemic as it is ironic. Godard's film is a continuation of reality in the cinema, using other means. And everything could have evolved differently – in this June of 1968 in Berlin.

WEEK-END: Mireille Darc, Jean Yanne

Rally in front of City Hall in Schöneberg, Feb. 21, 1968: differences with Eberhard Diepgen (CDU), later Mayor of Berlin

SPD rally in protest to US involvement in Vietnam, Feb. 18, 1968

Student demonstration with Rudi Dutschke (middle) and Fritz Teufel (sixth from the left)

In the Audimax of the Free University, students show the first part of a Defa film for television, PILOTEN IM PYJAMA [Pilots in Pyjamas], on sheets of paper which they have lined up one after another. The GDR team, the documentary film-makers Heynowksi and Scheumann, had filmed in North Vietnam: US pilots in a prisoner of war camp. The film itself cannot be shown, because students of the Film and Television Academy have painted the screen red. Someone calls out for the »Red Screen« to take action. The Film Festival comes to mind.

A la Grande Salle! The film festival in Cannes is discontinued.

The ›unimaginable‹ had taken place in Cannes. Festival director Favre Le Bret had announced the discontinuation of the festival at half-time. On May 17th, in the Paris School of Film Technics, thousands of movie people had gathered to show their solidarity with the striking workers and students. They had called for the end of the film festival in Cannes where François Truffaut and Jean-Luc Godard then declared their support. A demonstration was formed and they marched to the large auditorium of the festival, following Godard's cry of »A la Grande Salle!« The auditorium was taken over. The authors and producers withdraw their films; and even though, according to the regulations, there was the possibility of ignoring this step, Favre Le Bret decided to do without these films and declared the competition over.

No one believed that the »Berlinale« would remain untouched by these incidents of political and social protests. There had been protests at the Experimental Film Festival in Knokke; at the West German Short Film Festival in Oberhausen there had been an exodus of German film-makers; and at the Festival of Young Cinema in Pesaro it had been no different, except that it had all ended by the police taking action. It seemed only logical, that the Film Festival in Berlin would be »politicized« too. Particularly as the structures in Berlin were similar to those in Cannes. Enno Patalas reflected in »Die Zeit«: »On the other hand, in a city of the size of Berlin – and in Berlin in particular – the conditions essential for a remodelling of the Festival could be created. The catchphrases ›festival populaire‹, the peoples' festival, and the critical festival-analogue the ›critical university‹ – which were coined in Cannes, could take on concrete meaning in Berlin. (...) Naturally, much is dependent on what position the students in Berlin take to the Festival. They would certainly be blind not to see that it offers them an opportunity to demonstrate. It would, however, be naive, if they perceived cinema solely as a fitting excuse to demonstrate, and did not perceive the object from which they should demand changes. (...) To disrupt the Festival alone would only be a debatable success. It would be better to force the creation of a new Festival.« (May 31, 1968.) A left-wing critic examines experiences made in Cannes, checking them for their validity for the »Berlinale«, only, in the end, to become caught between the two fronts.

Geraldine Chaplin, Carlos Saura

Director Susumu Hani with his wife, actress Sachiko Hidari (on the right), and Kuniko Ishii at the opening gala in the Kongreßhalle

Press conference with Peter Brogle, Werner Herzog, Wolfgang von Ungern-Sternberg, Hans Borgelt

Disruptive discourse: students contra critics and film-makers

At an event on June 23rd, in the Audimax of the Technical University, young German film-makers – Alexander Kluge, Edgar Reitz, Christian Rischert, Johannes Schaaf – and the film critic Patalas wanted to come to an agreement with the students, in particular with those from the German Film and Television Academy, on a mutual basis for action. But the discussion took a different turn. They all voiced their dissatisfaction with the German film scene, but the students could not be persuaded that the podium guests were truly committed. The students accused them of having come to terms with the situation, and called them »the establishment's flunkies«; another accusation was that they were »left-wing reactionaries«. Kluge, Patalas and the others were then bombarded with eggs. The opposition was fighting within its own lines, the fronts having become diffuse. The revolution did not happen. Instead there were non-stop discussions. The Festival itself remained unmolested. A chance had been missed, and exactly at that moment when the possibility of influencing the Festival, of forcing a restructuring of its contents, and even the chance of establishing a counter-festival, had been greater than ever before. Moreover, the Senate and the Festival management had been expecting disturbances and demands. And they would have had to react, which they would have done in order to preserve the Festival, which for years now had taken on a central function in the cultural policies of the city. Yet when these protests dissipated in actionism, the traditional structure of the »Berlinale« was able to consolidate itself once again – that is, until two years later when it came to a huge scandal, breaking up the Festival completely, and resulting in the establishment of the International Forum of Young Cinema.

The necessary reforms were once again left in the hands of the organizers, and they settled themselves back in. There were proposals existing which were worthy of discussion, similar to those made in Cannes: i. e., to eliminate the Competition,

LEBENSZEICHEN: Wolfgang Reichmann (standing), Wolfgang von Ungern-Sternberg, Athina Zacharopoulou, Peter Brogle

and in consequence the awards; to distinguish between commercial and artistic films; to no longer feature the producers, but the film-makers (directed against the influence of the FIAPF); to stop representationalism and to introduce entrance fees free of charge for all interested.

Squandered reforms

The problem with these suggestions was that one could not realize them isolated in only one city, whether it be Cannes, Berlin or elsewhere. These large film festivals were subject to the regulations of the FIAPF, from which one could not break so easily, without risking the loss of »A-status«, which meant forfeiting one's chance of getting important films. Therefore the FIAPF was also called upon to react to this situation, to reconsider its regulations and to get rid of anachronistic organizational and representational structures. It no longer made sense to pretend that nothing had changed and that everything could remain as it was.

There was another event on June 23rd. The association of film journalists organized a public discussion in Humboldt Auditorium at the Urania: »What are the Berlinale's chances?« The panelists were Ulrich Gregor, Enno Patalas, Heinz Ungureit, Hermann Schwerin, Peter Schamoni, O. F. Gmelin, Ulrich Pöschke, and Alfred Bauer. Walther Schmieding, who was leading the discussion, acted as a buffer in the harsh exchange of blows between the podium and the auditorium. The audience, mostly students, demanded – backed by Gmelin – e. g., the expropriation of Constantin and Bertelsmann distribution companies and the elimination of entrance fees.

The arguments were political, yet the reactions were sometimes purely actionistic. The »Tagesspiegel« wrote that the discussion was »garnished with hoots, and howls, laughter and moderate insults« (June 25, 1968). But this event did have some effect. Bauer proposed that, »constant public discussions« be held daily during the Film Festival and it was agreed upon to show dffb-films.

Chronik der Anna Magdalena Bach: Christiane Lang-Drewanz

A long shot shows a valley full of windmills, blades turning. A man is on high ground, he is a German soldier going berserk, shooting wildly about, having declared war on everyone. He is a member of the occupying forces in Greece. Another long shot, again taken from above: people are fleeing; the soldier is shooting at them. In the middle of the square lies a dead donkey - a victim. Werner Herzog was showing his first full-length feature film in the Competition. By acting independently, his hero becomes an outsider. In Herzog's film, signs of going crazy, of insanity, become signs of life (Lebenszeichen) - also the title of the film. Lebenszeichen (»Signs of Life«) - could have also been the impassioned motto of this Film Festival. »In his revolt against everyone, he had begun something titanic, for his opponent was hopelessly more powerful. And so he had miserably and shabbily failed, as all others like him.« Such was the concluding commentary in Herzog's film. Werner Herzog did not only show his film in the Zoo-Palast. Privately, he organized the screening of Competition films in one of Berlin's outer districts, as had been done once years before. Yet this time round, the stars were not in the limelight, but the films and their authors were. People wanted to talk and in the »Rollkrug« movie house in Neukölln such a dialogue was possible. Film-makers and audience conversed. It was here as well that Jean-Marie Straub's Chronik der Anna Magdalena Bach (»Chronicle of Anna Magdalena Bach«) was presented.

Straub's film was playing in the Competition, although Straub himself had not come to Berlin. In a letter to Alfred Bauer, he had given the reason for his absence, »because I have no desire to put myself up for trial in a court which sentenced my last film Nicht versöhnt oder Es hilft nur Gewalt, wo Gewalt herrscht [Not Reconciled] to death -in a closed session.« As a reminder: Nicht versöhnt had been run in 1965 in the Info-Show. But Straub did want to show his new film, the Chronik, in Berlin, »for Berliners, who then will be able to see it on a large screen (although

International Jury
Luis Garcia Berlanga (Spain, president)
Peter Schamoni (FRG, vice-president)
Alex Viany (Brazil)
Georges de Beauregard (France)
Alexander Walker (Great Britain)
Domenico Meccoli (Italy)
Carl-Eric Nordberg (Sweden)
Gordon Hitchens (USA)
Karsten Peters (FRG)

The Awards of the International Jury

Feature Films
Grand Prix of the 18th IFB
Golden Berlin Bear
OLE DOLE DOFF
Sweden, directed by
Jan Troell

Special Prize of the Jury
Silver Berlin Bear
NEVINOST BEZ ZAŠTITE
Yugoslavia, directed by
Dušan Makavejev

Silver Berlin Bear
for the best director
Carlos Saura
for PEPPERMINT FRAPPÉ
Spain

Silver Berlin Bear
for the best actress
Stéphane Audran
in LES BICHES
France

Silver Berlin Bear
for the best actor
Jean-Louis Trintignant
in L'HOMME QUI MENT
France

Special Prize
Silver Berlin Bear
COME L'AMORE
Italy, directed by
Enzo Muzii

Special Prize as director
of his first feature film
Silver Berlin Bear
Werner Herzog
for LEBENSZEICHEN
FRG

it has neither predicate nor distributor); and because I believe that this film is (also) a protest, a strike against laws meant to promote film and the Emergency Powers Act, and an appeal to those social and economic structures which would make films accessible« (June 28, 1968). Straub's letter, his position and his film were a form of protest, even more, they were the defense of a form. His shots are insistingly calm, perceptive. One is forced to see, for example, how an instrument is played, forced to perceive the movements of the hand, and to hear it reflecting the wind in the silence. Such qualities also belonged to the political protest of 1968.

Alfred Bauer had wanted to show Polanski's ROSEMARY'S BABY and Stanley Kubrick's 2001: A SPACE ODYSSEY in the Competition. However, he was not able to get these films. Of YELLOW SUBMARINE, the Beatles' animated film, he was sceptical and did not want it. There, he might have found a taste of the future; he had obviously closed his mind to it.

The Golden Bear 1968 went to OLE DOLE DOFF [Eeny Meeny Miney Moe] by Jan Troell. It was a compromise - as was the whole Festival. Yet it was a good one. Such was the here and now in 1968.

Protest

By Jean-Marie Straub

Dear Dr. Bauer,
Thank you for your invitation, but I won't be coming to Berlin:

- *since I have no desire to place myself before a court which only three years ago at the same location (in an executive session) pronounced the death sentence against my previous film* NICHT VERSÖHNT ODER ES HILFT NUR GEWALT, WO GEWALT HERRSCHT;
- *and since I don't like police dogs and criminal police (even in civilian clothing) and the whores who hang around such festivals in droves (usually, alas, they are writers), and the parasites and pimps of an industry which demonstrates ever less imagination (even of the capitalistic variety) and ever more cynicism. And yet I am glad (despite the absurdity of every competition) that the* CHRONIK DER ANNA MAGDALENA BACH *will be shown within the framework of the Festival: for Berliners, who will then be able to see it on a large screen (although it has neither predicate nor distributor);*
- *and because I believe that this film is (also) a protest, even a strike against laws meant to promote film and the Emergency Power Act and an appeal to those social and economic structures which would make films accessible to e v e r y o n e.*

Sincerely,
Jean-Marie Straub
June 28th, 1968

Unfulfilled wishes

1969

June 25th – July 6th, 1969

Wishes and reality: the lacklustre awards

On July 1st, Gustav Heinemann was sworn in as Federal President, on the same day in London, Charles, as successor to the throne, was proclaimed the »Prince of Wales«. A week later, in Berlin, the prizes were awarded. Jury president Johannes Schaaf presented the Golden and Silver Bears. Yet it was all neither ceremonious nor festive, but rather plain and casual: »The few evening dresses and dinner jackets seemed like remnants of past celebrations. And photographers, for whom the missing commotion caused no end of trouble, had to make great efforts to be able to shoot a few quick portraits of the prize-winners. The directors, having won their awards, fetched their metal bears to moderate applause and just as moderate heckling, and disappeared instantaneously out of the limelight.« The International Film Festival Berlin was caught between its wishes and reality. »Wünsche und Wirklichkeit« (wishes and reality) was also the Festival title of the episodic film AMORE E RABBIA [Love and Anger] by Carlo Lizzani, Bernardo Bertolucci, Pier Paolo Pasolini, Jean-Luc Godard and Marco Bellocchio. The latter's contribution was politically straight forward, a fictitious discussion, a kind of play between revolutionary students, lecturers and policemen. The conflicts of the year 1968 had remained topical. Alf Brustellin, critic and later film director, closed his report on the presentation of the awards in Berlin with: »The whole thing was a quick, business-like procedure, reflecting the mood of the Festival precisely. Yet in this case, it was appreciated. This branch with its cult traditions has hardly left any believers; the image promoted by the industry has not been functioning as it should for ages now.« (Süddeutsche Zeitung, July 9, 1969.) The »Berlinale« oscillated back and forth between »Love and Anger«. It was therefore only natural that some wishes had to remain unfulfilled.

Rainer Werner Fassbinder

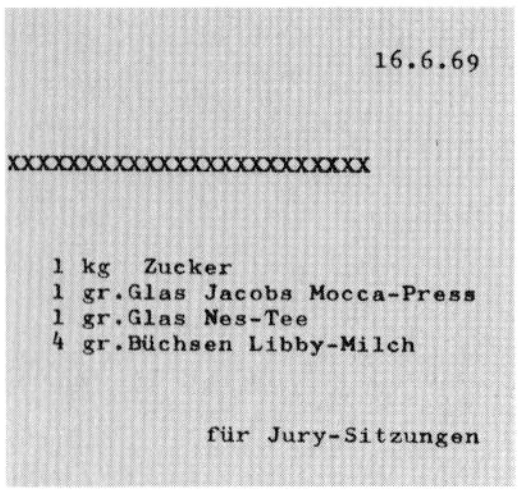
16.6.69

xxxxxxxxxxxxxxxxxxxxxxxx

1 kg Zucker
1 gr.Glas Jacobs Mocca-Press
1 gr.Glas Nes-Tee
4 gr.Büchsen Libby-Milch

für Jury-Sitzungen

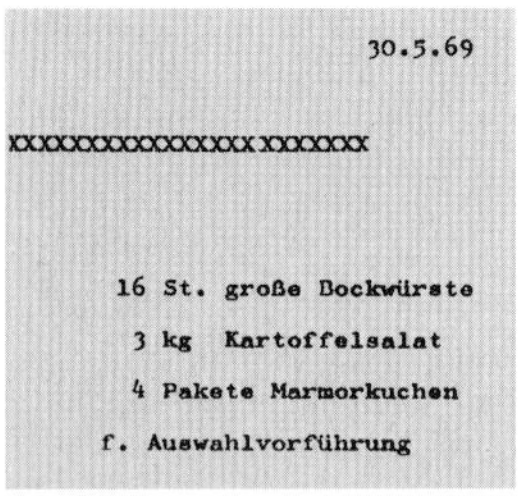
30.5.69

xxxxxxxxxxxxxxxx xxxxxxx

16 St. große Bockwürste
3 kg Kartoffelsalat
4 Pakete Marmorkuchen
f. Auswahlvorführung

Tidy bookkeeping...

An American Competition entry, John Schlesinger's MIDNIGHT COWBOY, the story of a friendship between two men, a young male prostitute and a small-time gangster, which had from the start been treated as a »sure candidate« for a prize and which was also clearly the public's favorite, went empty-handed when the »Bears« were distributed. Jon Voight and Dustin Hoffman were not even to receive prizes for their outstanding performances (the 1969 jury did not award any prizes at all for acting performance). United Artists, the distributor of the film was so appalled that it decided to boycott the IFB in the future – a decision which it upheld for ten years.

First films by Brian de Palma and Želimir Žilnik

The second American film, a debut, was a low-budget film made for $ 43 000. Its subject matter was Vietnam, the American trauma. Three young men try to get out of the draft. One of them behaves like a right-wing radical in front of the draft board, in the belief that he will then be able to avoid his induction order. But it is he who is found fit for service and sent to Vietnam. Later a war-correspondent interviews him just as he is aiming at a Vietnamese woman. This GI had turned reality around, developing a macabre, revealing, and bloodily serious game: staging scenes for TV. The images are not desperately homesick postcards, but pictures which are true because they lie. It was a disrespectful, cynical, sometimes hippie-esque and satirical film from the underground: GREETINGS by Brian de Palma.

Another first work came from Yugoslavia: Želimir Žilnik's RANI RADOVI (»Early Works«) about a group of young revolutionaries who fail to get their ideas across in the country, as well as in factories, to farmers and to workers. They are paid no attention at all, until the police haul them in and cut off their hair. The only girl among them, Yugoslava, returns home discouraged and disappointed, she has to »accept her food at the doorstep like a dog«. The final shot: »The others are shown sleeping or lying about; the camera moves along their motionless bodies as if they lay in state: the living dead. Yet the girl is still seen as a provocation. So they shoot her, drench her with gasoline and set her on fire. A quote from Saint-Just at the end: ›Revolutionaries who carry out the revolution only halfway, dig their own graves‹.« (Wolfram Schütte, Frankfurter Rundschau, July 7, 1969.) Žilnik's film portrays society using a farce as its means; it is critical of the orthodoxy of the older generation, self-critical of the verbal radicalism of the younger – and of the left, to which Žilnik himself belonged.

A political radicalism of themes and an anarchistic angle used in setting the films, characterized a number of the films shown at the »Berlinale« in 1969. A trend was visible; a change was in the air, which included self-reflection as well, without sacrificing political positions. Yet everything also seemed like a game: the staging used means from genre films, combining slapstick with Western, surrealistic effects with documentary material – an anarchy of means, but in itself a style.

In the line of fire: Peter Zadek's ICH BIN EIN ELEFANT, MADAME

Peter Zadek's hero in ICH BIN EIN ELEFANT, MADAME [I Am an Elephant, Madame] is Rull, a school boy from Bremen, who rebels against the conventional methods of education. Zadek takes sides; the film is full of contradictions, it is anarchistic and artistic. Zadek wants to shock. Wolf Lepenies notes ironically, that »the rejoicing of the audience shows: Zadek has filmed the ›burnt punch‹ of the sixties« (Frankfurter Allgemeine Zeitung, July 7, 1969). He did however, receive the mockery from his very own target group, i. e., a jury of young adults awarded him the »Rusty Film-Reel-Container Ribbon«, because in his film he had »exploited commercially the presently popular kind of series about young ruffians to an even greater degree by enriching this genre with pseudo-political phrases« and »adolescents who are familiar with the subject matter can only stand it all by feeling disgusted«. Approval and rejection lay near one another – and it was not merely a question of generation. The jury had found all three films worthy of awards – the Grand Prix of the Festival went to RANI RADOVI, de Palma und Zadek received Silver Bears.

LIEBE IST KÄLTER ALS DER TOD: Hanna Schygulla, Ulli Lommel

RANI RADOVI: Milja Vujanović waves the flag

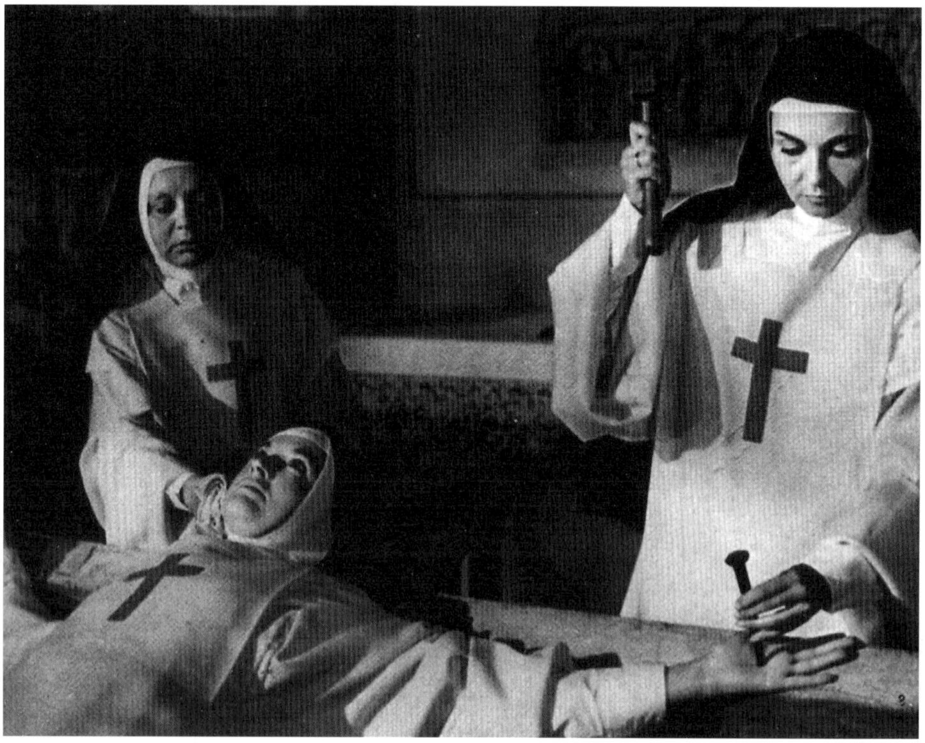

LA VOIE LACTÉE: Augusta Carrière (being crucified)

The fact that the wishes of some of the critics and viewers went unfulfilled was then blamed on the selection commission, which was made up of two groups who voted independently: delegates of the Federal Ministry of the Interior, the Berlin Senate, and the film industry, and the Festival director; as well as a group of five critics. Three of the ten members responded to these accusations. Ulrich Schamoni, Kurt Habernoll and Christa Maerker, in an article for the Festival paper, »Film International« (No. 9/1969) pointed out that eight of the twenty-two films had been accepted for the Festival program without a vote by the selection jury; they also criticized that the independence they had been promised was not worth much. As a consequence, after the Festival was over, new procedural regulations for the commission were adopted (Dec. 15, 1969). There were two essential changes: the abolishment of the two-chamber system and a reduction in the number of members. The separate commission for the selection of German films was also eliminated. (Although it must be said here that it had been the members of the general selection commission who had chosen the German entries for the IFB in 1969. Besides Zadek's film, which ran as the official German entry, they had chosen Rainer Werner Fassbinder's LIEBE IST KÄLTER ALS DER TOD (»Love is Colder than Death«), after Peter Fleischmann's initially nominated JAGDSZENEN AUS NIEDERBAYERN [Hunting Scenes from Lower Bavaria] had been withdrawn by its producers. In addition, there was talk of Rudolf Thome's DETEKTIVE [Detectives], Hansjürgen Pohland's AUF SCHEISSER SCHIESST MAN NICHT [You Don't Shoot Jerks] and Gustav Ehmck's SPIELST DU MIT SCHRÄGEN VÖGELN [If You Play with Crazy Birds]).

German films up for selection

The »Berlinale« 1969 ended with LA VOI LACTÉE (The Milky Way«) by Luis Buñuel. Peter Handke in an interim report for »Die Zeit« (July 11, 1969) came out particularly in favor of Godard's LE GAI SAVOIR [The Gay Science]. And, to the second Godard

MIDNIGHT COWBOY: Dustin Hoffman

film which was being shown in the Info-Show, he noted: »In ONE PLUS ONE Brian Jones is mostly seen from the back, much like the moribund in Wim Wender's ALABAMA. And the ends of the guitar strings stand out so far from the guitar's neck, that at first one thinks they are hairs. ONE PLUS ONE has already become a legendary film.«

Unfulfilled wishes and »Sympathy for the Devil«.

International Jury
Johannes Schaaf (FRG, president)
Agneša Kalinova (Poland, vice-president)
José Dominianni (Argentina)
François Chalais (Belgium)
John Russel Taylor (Great Britain)
Giovanni Grazzini (Italy)
Masaki Kobayashi (Japan)
Archer Winsten (USA)
Ulrich Gregor (FRG)

The Awards of the International Jury

Feature Films
Grand Prix of the 19th IFB
Golden Berlin Bear
RANI RADOVI
Yugoslavia, directed by Želimir Žilnik

Silver Berlin Bear
BRASIL ANO 2000
Brazil, directed by Walter Lima jr.

Silver Berlin Bear
MADE IN SWEDEN
Sweden, directed by Johan Bergenstråhle

Silver Berlin Bear
ICH BIN EIN ELEFANT, MADAME
FRG, directed by Peter Zadek

Silver Berlin Bear
GREETINGS
USA, directed by Brian de Palma

Silver Berlin Bear
UN TRANQUILLO POSTO DI CAMPAGNA
Italy, directed by Elio Petri

o. K.: Friedrich Thun,
Eva Mattes, Hartmut Becker

The crisis

1970

June 26th–July 7th, 1970

The international jury stepped down, the Festival director and managing director of Festivals-Ltd. handed in their resignations, the Competition was broken off and in turn, no prizes were awarded – these were the symptoms of the 1970 crisis. The International Film Festival Berlin was on the verge of disintegrating.

It was now evident how high a price would have to be paid for the fact that the plans for a reform of the »Berlinale« had gotten caught in the cogs of the administrative machinery of the Senate, the Festivals-Ltd., the board of curators and the Festival management. How had such a development come about? Even in retrospect – or maybe exactly in retrospect – it is almost impossible to find one's way through the jungle of official statements, resolutions, positions and memories of those concerned. The whole atmosphere was too polluted with insinuations, open and hidden animosities, interspersed with concrete commercial interests. And to top it off, there was an exalted nervousness in Berlin this year, the year in which student unrest reached its peak, having long since left the campus, making itself felt in all sectors of society. The Festival was not immune to this mood, and it was not from nowhere that the actual scandal ignited over a film which had as its subject matter a (authentic) war atrocity which had been carried out by American soldiers in Vietnam – the rape and murder of a Vietnamese girl. It is nearly impossible to follow how profound the problems of communication were between the quarreling parties, how quickly everyone was ready to believe rumors and insinuations, and how little composure and tolerance were to be found in the face of discussion. In principle, one no longer spoke the same language.

In retrospect, it is self-evident that the »Berlinale« was a kind of relic, or at least an anachronism, in its demands and structure. Since its beginnings it had changed little. It had continued to persevere in the glamour of the past decades, until being abruptly confronted with a development which had already established itself in society. In this respect, the incidents were not surprising. They had a certain inevitability, that astonishingly had not all come about sooner.

First of all, an attempt will be made to reconstruct the course of events.

The films of the first four »Berlinale« days cause disappointment and annoyance. Especially the opening film, KLANN/GRAND GUIGNOL by Patrick Ledoux, which was greated with catcalls. L'URLO [The Cry] by Tinto Brass, L'EDEN ET APRÈS [Eden and After] by Alain Robbe-Grillet, and DIONYSUS IN 69 by Brian de Palma were also unable to raise spirits. Only Rainer Werner Fassbinder's WARUM LÄUFT HERR R. AMOK? (»Why Did Herr R. Run Amok?«) and OUT OF IT by Paul Williams received positive reviews; and there was immediate talk that Fassbinder's film would be one of the prize-winners.

The première of Michael Verhoeven's O.K.

Then on Tuesday, June 30th, at 3:00 and 9:00 p.m., Michael Verhoeven's O.K. was shown. The viewers reactions in the Zoo-Palast were divided: there was sporadic yet boisterous protest, although admittedly, the majority was approving and even enthusiastic. An eyewitness, Kurt Habernoll, noted, »Several people walked out in protest. Among them was the German jury member Manfred Durniok.« (Vorwärts, July 9, 1970.) The producer of the film describes it as being, »about a young Vietnamese girl, Mao, who had actually existed – that is, until November 18th 1966. On this day she was dragged off and raped, stabbed and then shot by four American soldiers. A man named Eriksson was also present. He was the fifth man. He could not help the girl.

Discussion in Schöneberg City Hall: Alfred Bauer, Véra Volmane, George Stevens

Walther Schmieding, Gunnar Oldin, David E. Neves, Billie Whitelaw, Dušan Makavejev, Alberto Lattuada, Manfred Durniok, Edmund Luft

Walther Schmieding

In the auditorium: film-makers, Festival-makers and above all journalists

But he did go to his Captain and report the incident. Eriksson was rebuffed, the charges were suppressed. The film o.k. tells of Mao's suffering. The day of her death is moved to Easter Monday and the incidents are restaged in the modus of a Bavarian Passion Play. Thus the observer is given distance, forcing him to reflect, and simultaneously the true backdrop is moved vividly close to a familiar mentality.« (Statement of the producer.)

In the reactions in the press – in both conservative as well as liberal papers – o.k. did well. It was held to be a politically provocative film, moving and passionately moral. Whether or not it was a success artistically, however, is debatable. Opinions were divergent. Yet the questions involved here were not ones of aesthetics.

A day later, the jury convened. And the decisions made at this meeting were the initial sparks that setting off the conflicts which follow.

German apologies

Wednesday, July 1st, before the meeting begins, the German jury member Manfred Durniok apologizes to the president, the American George Stevens, for the fact that the Federal Republic of Germany has entered and shown a film like o.k. The jury then meets. After controversy over o.k., the journalist, Klaus Hebecker, to whom George Stevens has temporarily handed over the presidency, informs the selection commission in a letter (of which a copy also goes to the Senator for Science and the Arts), that the jury, with a majority of six to three votes, feels itself »obliged to neutralize the German Competition entry by Michael Verhoeven, until the selection commission is put in the position of having to reconfirm that the film fulfills international festival regulations.« The objections of the jury are in reference to a controversial item in the International Film Festival Berlin guidelines – subject to the requirements of the FIAPF – which states that the participating films should »contribute to the understanding and friendship between the peoples of different nations«.

The members of the 1970 selection commission were: journalists Dr. Ingeborg Keller, Dr. Hans Borgelt, Dr. Georg Ramseger, Gerhard Schoenberner, movie house

Discussion in the Royal-Palast: Michael Verhoeven

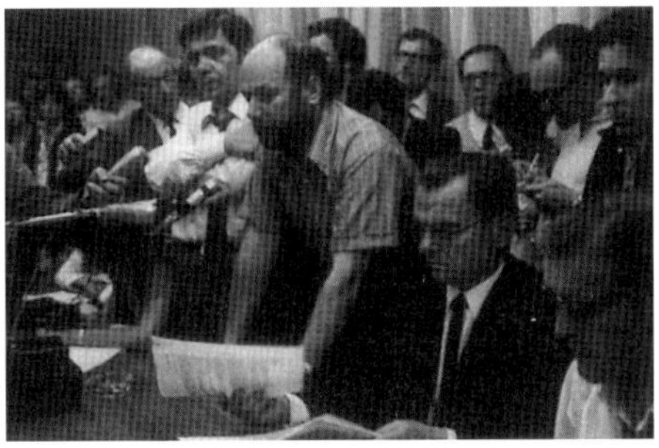

Walther Schmieding, Dušan Makavejev, Alfred Bauer, Gunnar Oldin, and in the background, Enno Patalas (fourth from the right)

Alexander Kluge, Gerhard Schoenberner, Peter B. Schumann, Roland H. Wiegenstein, Walther Schmieding

Rainer Werner Fassbinder, Rudolph Ganz, Karsten Peters, Ingvelde Geleng, Walther Schmieding

proprietor Kurt Broschke, producer Rudi Flatow, as well as Dr. Alfred Bauer as chairman. The members had been appointed – as was now custom – by the managing partners of Berlin Festivals-Ltd. and by its co-organizer and sponsor, the Spio.

Makavejev's position

Thursday, July 2nd. The juror Dušan Makavejev, film director from Yugoslavia, who had won a Silver Bear two years earlier for his film NEVINOST BEZ ZAŠTITE [Innocence Without Protection], addresses a letter to the director of the IFB, in which he accuses the jury of having taken »the route of a censor (...) towards both the program itself as well as towards the policies of the program and the Festival management«. Hence the jury had overstepped »drastically the procedural rules as also their jurisdiction«.

Makavejev, who at the jury meeting the day before had classified O.K. as anti-militaristic, but as not anti-American and was supported by the Brazilian director and juror David Neves, makes clear reference in his letter to the rules of procedure set down on June 26th at the first meeting of this IFB jury. Item 2 reads: »The jury evaluates the artistic value of a film but it does not indicate whether it fulfills the requirements for participation in the Competition. This is the duty of the Festival director and the selection commission.« Furthermore, Makavejev disassociates himself from the letter written by the jury to the selection commission and asks Dr. Bauer if he may read both his and the other letter at the next press conference.

It was most likely on the same day, that Makavejev told the producer of the film, Rob Houwer, and the director about the events at the jury meeting. It is unclear whether the rumor that O.K. had been disqualified from the Competition – which spread like wildfire and was sent out by news agencies the next day – had its origins here, i. e., with Makavejev, or if this version can be attributed to Houwer and Verhoeven. The accusation that Makavejev had formally broken his oath – he had been sworn to secrecy as a jury member – by telling Houwer and Verhoeven is immaterial. Of more consequence is that in this situation, everyone involved had overlooked the fact that the jury lacked the authority to exclude a film from the

Competition. That Alfred Bauer did not immediately counter the rumor, can, in retrospect, only be explained by the hectic events or by unfortunate tactical considerations on his part.

Press conferences and resolutions

At any rate, the same evening a meeting was held at which the following resolution was adopted at midnight: »Assuming that the information which has been received is correct – the participants and journalists of the 20th International Film Festival Berlin gathered together on this 2nd of July, 1970, at 12:00 a.m. protest most vehemently to the behavior of jury president George Stevens and a majority of the other jury members to O.K., the German entry for the Competition. Those gathered here tonight regard a jury which understands itself as having the final say as censor as intolerable and demand its resignation.«

Friday, July 3rd. Using circulars and leaflets, Michael Verhoeven and Rob Houwer give out invitations for a special press conference, at 2:00 p.m., in the Cine-Center, because »the international jury has disqualified the German Festival entry O.K. from the Competition«. At the same time, the jury disavows the press release concerning the disqualification of O.K. and stresses that all jury members have been sworn to secrecy, which means that they are not to pass on any information to the public.

Alfred Bauer's rescue attempt

At this press conference, Alfred Bauer reads a statement declaring his position, in which he points out that the selection commission alone is responsible for the acceptance of O.K. in the Competition, and that according to the rules of procedure the jury does not have the right to disqualify a film – hence, O.K. is still in the Competition. This declaration comes too late and does not seem convincing. It is insinuated that he is only trying to cover up for the »jury's censoring«.

Moreover, in a notarized and deposited statutory declaration, Verhoeven and Houwer assert that they were informed on July 2nd by a jury member, who wanted to remain anonymous, that the president of the jury, George Stevens, had issued an ultimatum: either the German film entry for the Competition, O.K., be disqualified, or he would resign. Evidently he had then put the matter up to vote immediately: his motion was then supported by both German jurors, Hebecker and Durniok; furthermore, Stevens had stated that his actions were purely politically motivated.

The jury meets again and confers until 11:40 p.m. Afterwards, a second press conference is held in the Cine-Center, at which three jury members are present: Dušan Makavejev, David Neves and the Swedish critic Dr. Gunnar Oldin. Shortly before, Walther Schmieding, in his capacity as director of Festivals-Ltd., had declared the jury to be no longer sworn to secrecy, so that they could take a public stand regarding the events and accusations.

The jury is released from its oath.

Saturday, July 4th. It is the second half of this same midnight conference, and Schmieding declares at 12:45 a.m. that he and Alfred Bauer shall immediately request the Senate to relieve them of their duties, and that before they step down they will demand the jury's resignation. In the morning, they carry out their intentions. Schmieding issues a three-page statement in which he announces that he has »asked the jury of the Film Festival to no longer officiate«. An »atmosphere dominated by accusations, insinuations and incessant protests« has made the continuation of the jury's activities seem »senseless«. In addition, he announces that he and Dr. Bauer have offered the board of curators of Festivals-Ltd. their resignation, and gives a short summary of the incidents up till then.

Alfred Bauer and Walther Schmieding offer to resign.

Following publications of the contents of this declaration, a meeting of the jury members is held in which Schmieding and Bauer also take part. Stevens and

Makavejev reaffirm their positions. Schmieding then explains that the jury has been the victim of an inadequate information policy on the part of the Festival management, and expresses the opinion that Makavejev should be excluded from the jury for formal reasons, even if he personally »understands the reasons, which caused him to break his word of oath.«

After a debate, which here and again oversteps certain limits and becomes too personal, the jury demands an audience with the chairman of the board of curators, Senator Stein.

This conference begins at 6:00 p.m. in the office of Dr. Bauer in the Europa-Center. The outcome of this discussion is made public in a communiqué: the Film Festival is to be continued, the jury – subject to the international statutes – has declared its willingness to remain in office, and Schmieding and Bauer are to continue to supervise the management, until the board has come to a decision concerning their letters of resignation. As to the consequences of these incidents on the planning of future Film Festivals, consultation is to follow after the 20th IFB is over, and consequently free from the pressure caused by the conflicts of the moment. These resolutions turn out to be mere wishful thinking.

At the next press conference in the City-Filmpalast, at 11:00 p. m., the results of these negotiations are made public. Alfred Bauer does not appear at the press conference, Walther Schmieding does. The decisions are read out by Hans Borgelt. The communiqué triggers a storm of indignation. Schmieding, the Festival management and the Senate are vigorously attacked. There is even a call to take over the Zoo-Palast. The discussion drags on into the wee hours of Sunday.

Sunday, July 5th. In the course of the debate, the journalist Rudolph Ganz reads out a resolution, which is then put up for vote. This resolution states that the jury has only been asked to remain in office because of pressure from the Senate, »even though the jury has clearly disqualified itself by violating the conditions of the regulations, showing political bias, repeatedly misleading the public and by the members' inability to communicate with each other.« And it is for these reasons that the resolution asks: the jury to resign, the directors and producers to withdraw their films, Senator Stein to receive a delegation, and Alfred Bauer to step down. A large majority accepts the resolution. Some participants subsequently protest that the number of votes against the resolution were not counted and that the whole situation had been premeditated and staged by a few. Accusations were made at all levels in 1970. In the course of the day films are withdrawn from the Festival program: i. e., all Chilean and Brazilian films, as well as BALTUTLÄMNINGEN [A Baltic Tragedy] by Johan Bergenstråhle (contrary to the will of the producer), WIE ICH EIN NEGER WURDE [How I Became a Negro] by Roland Gall, WARUM LÄUFT HERR R. AMOK? by Fassbinder, O PROFETA DA FOME [The Prophet of Hunger] by Maurice Capovilla and both of the Dutch short films DE BABY IN DE BOOM [The Baby in the Tree] by Nouchka van Brakel and REMBRANDT VOGELFRIJ [Rembrandt Outlawed] by Ernie Damen.

The jury steps down.

At 3:00 in the afternoon the jury meets for a last time. The members are so at variance that it is no longer possible to continue working. At 6:00 p.m. the jury announces to the Senator that they will no longer convene. The Italian director Alberto Lattuada gives his reason for this decision: he can no longer justify passing judgement on the films of his colleagues. At 7:00 p.m. in the City-Filmpalast, Walther Schmieding announces the decision of the jury and reads out a statement from the Senator, »with this resolution of the jury, the Competition is terminated. (...) Effec-

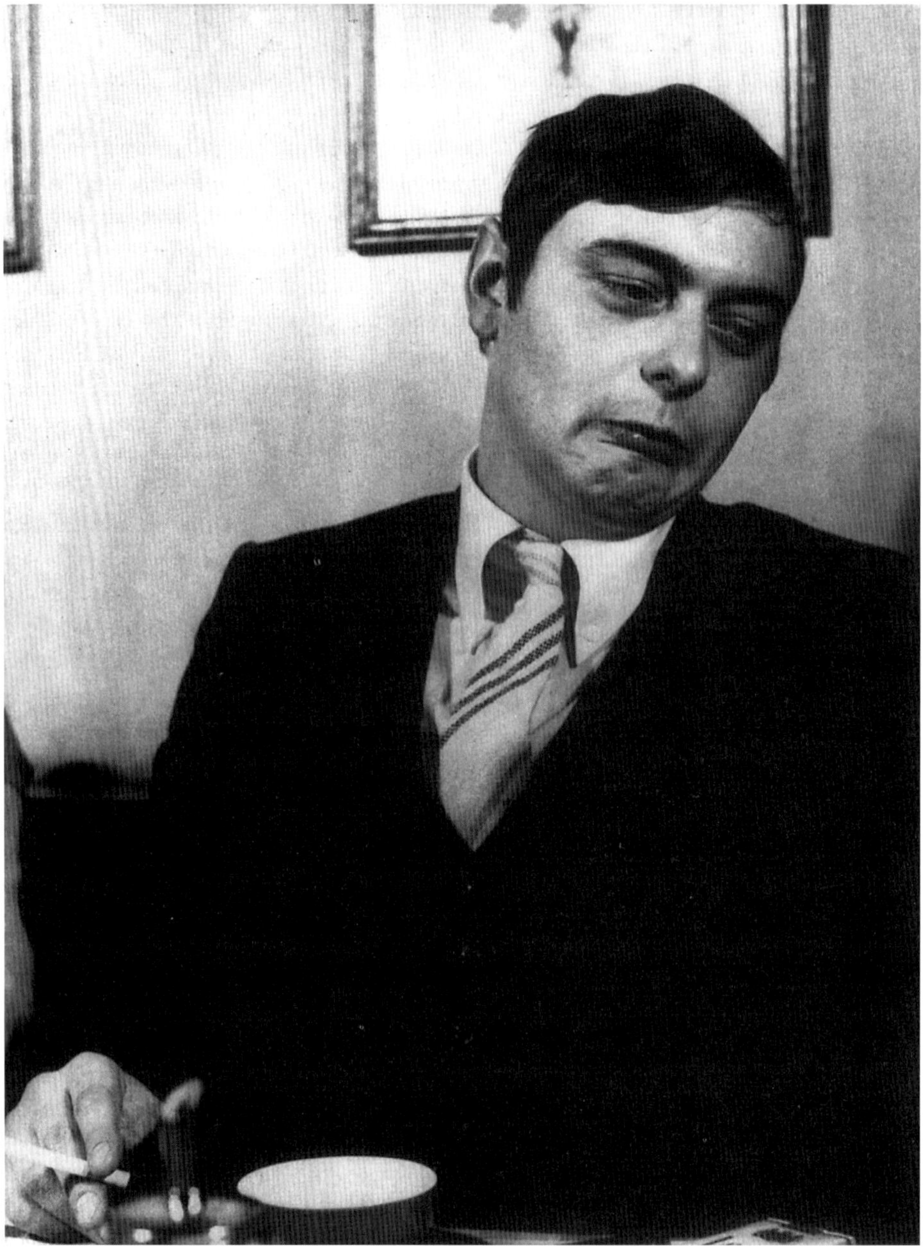

Warum läuft Herr R. Amok?: Kurt Raab

tive of this moment, there will be no more showings of the 1970 Competition films. The Film Retrospective and Info-Show will be continued with their programs as planned.«

The Competition is discontinued.

The news that the jury had resigned was received with applause in the City-Filmpalast. The decision not to show any more of the films of the Competition was, on the other hand, strongly criticized. Alexander Kluge formulated a resolution which demanded that the Senator retract this decision. Rudolph Ganz, in another resolution, found fault with the reason cited by the jury for its resignation. It was not »because of time pressure that it had discontinued its activities, but because the jurors had violated the statutes and proved themselves incompetent«.

De facto, the Competition had come to an end, even though Senator Stein did modify his decision on Monday and allow showings of Competition films. Those films, which had been affected by the premature announcement of the discontinuation, were either withdrawn for good, (Borsalino by Jacques Deray, El extraño caso del Doctor Fausto [The Strange Case of Dr. Faust] by Gonzalo Suárez and La ragazza di nome Giulio [The Girl Called Giulio] by Tonio Valerii, as well as the two short films De baby in de boom and Rembrandt vogelfrij), or were merely shown in the Info-Show (Black Out by Jean-Louis Roy, Baltutlämningen and the short film Rotocalco by Manfredo Manfredi).

Prizes were not awarded. The jury of the FIPRESCI only gave out a high commendation for Latin American cinema as a whole, INTERFILM and the OCIC each gave out individual commendations, and a non-affiliated group of film critics from Belgium, Denmark, the Federal Republic, Netherlands, and Switzerland awarded prizes on their own initiative to three films, which in their opinion were »highly artistic and entertaining«.

Accusations and »the boys from the other side«

The reaction in the press to all of these incidents – sparked off by the screening of the film o.k. and yet which in subsequent discussions digressed further and further from the film, concerning itself in the end primarily with the Festival – was vehement. The same mechanisms were dominant in the press as had been in the course of events: there were insinuations, accusations, half-truths, lack of information, indiscretion. The number of well-informed journalists who had done their homework was few. Depending on their respective interests and position, a guilty party was searched for and found. These included: the selection commission, the jury (especially the members Stevens, Makavejev, Hebecker and Durniok), Alfred Bauer and Walther Schmieding and – an unknown number of unknown persons, also those ominous 400 persons who according to the opinion of the jury president had been egged on by Walther Schmieding in order to disrupt the Festival; in addition there were »the boys from the other side« (Stevens) and, of course, the film-makers and journalists themselves. At a reception at City Hall in Schöneberg on Monday, jury member Manfred Durniok confessed to having been an instigator in the sentiments against o.k. And a particularly blatant case of conspiracy was alluded to by the vice-president of the jury, Klaus Hebecker, in the »Film-Telegramm«, of which he was editor. In an article entitled »Berlin's Debacle«, he wrote: »That which the French member of the jury (Véra Volmane) had heard in Paris long before the Festival had even begun, that is namely, that in one way or another the Berlin Film Festival was to be broken up, found bitter, and for the time being, obscure corroboration.« He did not, of course, provide any details on this French connection.

It is quite difficult to throw light upon the whole affair. The individual versions are too contradictory. Political and economic interests played a role, as did true commitment to film in some instances. Perhaps it was only a momentary irritation, intensified by a lack of communication, which made Dušan Makavejev come to the conviction that o.k. should be excluded. Or maybe the jury really did not realize that in sending o.k. back to the selection commission for reconsideration, they had overstepped their jurisdiction. Perhaps it was merely the awkward treatment of a disastrous situation by the Festival management and the business administration. A conflict had in any case been inevitable; sooner or later, the Film Festival would have been hit. Such a conflict had social and political reasons and these had been caused by the critical circumstances of the past years.

Difficulties in getting Carlos Saura's EL JARDIN DE LAS DELICIAS released

The conflict over O.K. was, however, not the only controversy. On July 1st, the sixth day of the Festival, the selection commission announced to the press that the negotiations – which were still in progress even after the opening of the Festival – for the release of the film EL JARDIN DE LAS DELICIAS [The Garden of Delights] by Carlos Saura had come to nothing, because of objections from the Spanish authorities. It had, however, been this film which had been accepted unanimously by the selection commission for the Competition, whereas the official Spanish entry EL EXTRAÑO CASO DEL DOCTOR FAUSTO by Gonzalo Suárez, had, in reality, been rejected and was being shown only to accomodate the FIAPF requirements. On the same day, a working group of film journalists also issued a resolution, declaring the incident the »submission of the Festival management to the Spanish censors«.

The reaction from Spanish quarters was not long in coming. Four days later, the director of the Uniespaña and at the same time head of the Spanish delegation, Fernando Blanco, who was staying in Berlin, declared that the »Junta de Manifestaciones Cinematograficas« (the commission for film events) had proposed Suárez' film in order to give a young and unknown director an opportunity to show his film to an international audience. Furthermore, »The film EL JARDIN DE LAS DELICIAS directed by Carlos Saura, can – now that the provisions of the administration have been fulfilled to which by law all films made in Spain are subject – be shown in Spain and abroad as of June 25th. The distributors ›Omnia Deutsche Film‹, which have the rights for the film in West Germany, are allowed to show the film, under private arrangement, in public movie houses. Thus, if the film is not presented, it is purely for commercial reasons.« It should be noted here, that in the next to last sentence, the following list had come after »are allowed to show the film«: »in the programs of the Festival, the Film Fair, the Info-Show«; this list was then omitted in the final version.

Volker Baer gave vent to the general confusion in the »Tagesspiegel«, with irony, »Now it can be seen extremely clearly: the one film had in fact not been prohibited, the other film, although sent to Berlin, had on the other hand a director who stood in poor favor. The one film had indeed been accepted by the selection commission, the other in fact rejected and yet just the same, it was the one to be entered in the Competition.« (July 8, 1970.)

This case was also a burden to public – and printed – opinion as it existed towards the Festival management and naturally – with reason – towards the Franco-regime, even though it did not attract the amount of attention which Verhoeven's film had. In the end, Suarez himself withdrew his film, which was to have been shown on July 7th. He did not want to forfeit the opportunity to show his film at other festivals, now that the Competition in Berlin had come to an early end.

An atmosphere of crisis

It was clear to everyone concerned that in 1970 the International Film Festival had become involved in its most serious crisis ever, yet just the same, no one was truly considering closing down this institution. Despite the paralysis which had been caused by the termination of the Competition program, Senator Stein had been able to set a new course when he declared on July 6th, »In contemplating the demand for more artistically valuable films, we are indeed at a new point of departure. Organized events such as the Film Festival shall be held in the future as well.« Yet while Senator Stein was concerning himself with »artistically valuable films«, a member of the Berlin House of Representatives, Heinz Zellermayer, from the opposition, i. e. the Christian Democrats, named the real reasons for a continuance of the IFB. In a

Plans for a new start

motion of urgency made by the Christian Democrats on July 9th 1970, which was also accepted by the SPD, the Senate was petitioned to make proposals by October 1st as to how the damage done to the Film Festival could be repaired. Among other things, Zellermayer stated, »Berlin is more than any other city dependent on its congresses, conferences, as well as a functioning Film Festival; for our viability we need more than just a broad industrial basis: without diversified cultural attractions, we shall not be able to live up to our claim of being a metropolis of world-wide importance. (Stenographic minutes from the 78th session of the House of Representatives, July 9, 1970.)

This motion of urgency made by the House of Representatives was the beginning of all activities having to do with the restructuring of the IFB. In the period which followed, the considerations of the Senator for Science and the Arts were followed up by:

- two hearings of experts at the meetings of the advisory board on September 14th/15th 1970 (9th session) and October 26th/27th (10th session);
- consultations of the board of curators at its 18th, 19th and 20th meetings (July 27th, September 21st and November 9th 1970);
- considerations and memorandums written by different individuals and institutions;
- talks with the various different advisors in the Department of Science and the Arts itself.

A clear turning point in the process of forming opinions within the administration was the 10th session of the advisory board on October 26th/27th, at which the experts of the film industry were consulted: functionaries of the Spio, representatives of diverse companies in Berlin and the managing director of the association of Berlin movies houses. At this meeting, there was a certain feeling of change in the air; the desire to subject the Film Festival to a true structural reform was also existent in the Senate.

Reform proposals

This atmosphere had already been evident at a conference of the advisor in the Department of Science and the Arts on August 6th, 1970, at which time it was agreed to the following fundamental points: besides a part of the program which would take the interests of the film industry into account, there would be a section established for young artistic cinema; the once so desired »A-status« would be relinquished, as would the jury and the awards. The »young artistic cinema« was clearly favored as being the more important event in the program of the new Festival, along with a show of the »most remarkable films of the year«, a film retrospective and a film fair (open to the public).

In the question of the dates for the Festival, one tended towards a rescheduling of the »Berlinale« to late fall. This conference served primarily to define the position of those present, although in addition, it was also in preparation for the two hearings of experts at the extended meetings of the advisory board planned for September and October.

On September 21st, a week after the first hearing of experts, when the board of curators met, they gave preferential treatment to drawing an end – for the time being – to the incidents of the last Festival as they pertained to questions of staff. A decision was made to Walther Schmieding's and Alfred Bauer's letters of resignation. They were accepted, although at the same time, it was decided to propose a new contract to Schmieding for the position of director of the Berliner Festwochen, and Bauer was to be entrusted for the interim with the further management of the IFB.

At the second hearing (Oct. 26th/27th) it was not possible to reach a consensus. The spokesmen for the Spio and the functionaries closely affiliated to it insisted in essence on the conventional structure of the IFB, whereas the faction second in strength, the film journalists, were for a reform.

A modified version of these suggestions for reform were presented by Heinz Rathsack, who supported the idea of establishing a film center, but neither saw the Festivals-Ltd. as the appropriate sponsor, nor the film center as the organizer of the IFB. He was for the jurisdiction of the Department of Science and the Arts. The film industry spokesmen suggested as a compromise the restructuring of the IFB based on the model of the film festival in Cannes, i. e., to divide the program into various events such as »Quinzaine des réalisateurs« (films selected by the association of directors) and the »Semaine de la critique« (films selected by the association of film journalists). (Minutes taken by Senatorial Supervisor Reinhard Wilke, Nov. 3, 1970.)

The International Forum of Young Cinema is born.

The following day this initial eagerness for reform was noticeably checked by the spokesmen from the film industry. After careful consultation, the following conclusions were reached which at the same time were seen as the final resolution (it can also be seen as the hour of birth of the »Forum of Young Cinema«): The »A-status« was to be retained for the main part of the program, so that the participation of the film industry would remain guaranteed. Yet one wanted the FIAPF to accept that »the right to presentation of the large film nations (...) was dependent on the approval of the selection commission«. Along side the Competition, there was to be a »parallel event of equal status«, the »International Forum of Young Cinema (...) and young and progressive cinema was to be the main component of its program«. A board of three persons was to take over the selection and presentation of this event, the organizational responsibility was to fall »to the film center (in planning)«. One also intended to award prizes; grants to the amounts of DM 30 000, DM 20 000, and

Dionysus in 69

DM 10 000 or of DM 20 000 each were to be awarded by a commission of experts. The continuation of the Retrospective was also guaranteed. These were the most significant proposals.

In addition, there was a »special-cycle« suggested by the working group of journalists, which was to show German productions of the last twelve months; in it can be seen the beginnings of todays section »Neue deutsche Filme« (New German Cinema). And for 1971 at least, the dates of the IFB would remain in the summer months; for 1972, one wanted to check the possibility of a rescheduling.

The board of curators drafts a resolution.

The board of curators approved of these suggestions at its meetings on November 9th and December 21st 1970. According to the motion of urgency made in the House of Representatives on July 9th, the Senate should have, however, reacted by October 1st. Yet since there had been delays in the process of negotiations, the Senator had, in an »interim report«, postponed this deadline, moving it from October 1st until after the next meeting of the board of curators. Based on the considerations of the advisory board and the decisions of the board of curators, the Senator for Science and the Arts was then able to write up a draft for a senatorial decree (Dec. 28, 1970) – this decree was to be put up for a vote at the next session of the House of Representatives on January 19th, 1971. It contained the political quintessence of that which had crystallized out of the many considerations. Yet when these audacious plans for the future are measured against the past debacle, it becomes evident how slight the actual leeway was for an institution like the »Berlinale«, which was interlinked to a variety of others and kept on tenderhooks. The only true innovation was the establishment of the »International Forum of Young Cinema«. The decree closes with the lapidary statement, »We ask herewith that the motion of urgency made by the House of Representatives on July 9th 1970 – Document No. 1241 – be regarded as resolved.«

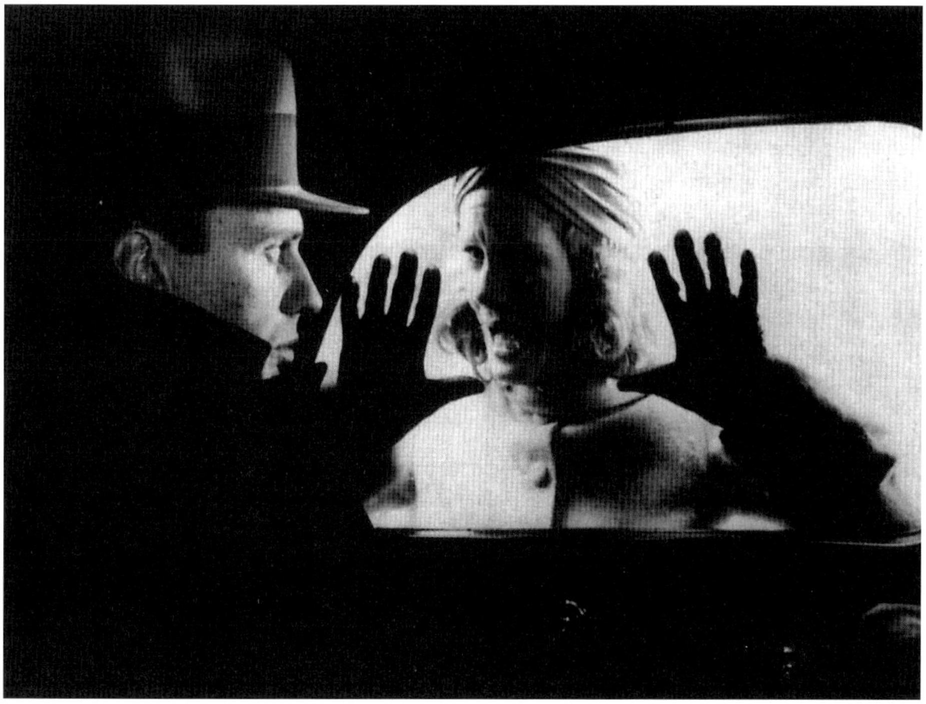

IL CONFORMISTA
[THE CONFORMIST]:
Jean-Louis Trintignant,
Dominique Sanda

International Jury
George Stevens
(USA, president)
Klaus Hebecker
(FRG, vice-president)
David Neves (Brazil)
Véra Volmane (France)
Billie Whitelaw
(Great Britain)
Alberto Lattuada (Italy)
Dušan Makavejev
(Yugoslavia)
Gunnar Oldin (Sweden)
Manfred Durniok (FRG)

The International Jury did not award any prizes in 1970; it resigned on July 5th 1970.

Surprisingly this request turned out to be superfluous; the House of Representatives took no notice of the decree – a fact which is documented in the most wonderful of German officialese and reads something like: »The senatorial decree submitted for approval at the session of the House of Representatives on the 19th of January 1971, pertaining to the enforcement of the resolution of the House of Representatives on the 9th of July, 1970, for the induction of the senatorial resolution to the decree, had to be withdrawn owing to previous arrangements.« (Noted by the Senator for Science and the Arts, Jan. 29, 1971.)

The »previous arrangements« meant were the end of the legislative period and according to § 97 of the standing orders of the House of Representatives, unsettled matters still on the agenda at the end of a term of office were to be deemed settled.

O. K.: Short chronicle of a scandal

By Michael Verhoeven

Christmas 1969. I am spending the Christmas vacation in the countryside of Lower Bavaria. In the »Spiegel« there is a report about US soldiers who raped and killed a South Vietnamese girl out of boredom. I put down the magazine and begin to write a play for the theater in which a girl who is riding her bike to buy milk at a neighboring farm is stopped and raped by five GIs. My piece is set in Bavaria (not Lower Bavaria, since I have no mastery of that dialect); the US soldiers wear American uniforms, but they think and talk Bavarian.

The main figure's name is Hans Abtretter.

Why this alienation?

My interest was not directed toward distant America, but toward the FRG, which is much nearer, and toward Bavaria, which is very close. During walks along the Dammersbach, and in the rustic room with a Christmas-tree, a Bavarian folk play on the Vietnam War emerges. I am convinced from the very first line that it will be an unmistakable piece of contemporary history, regardless of how its quality is judged by critics.

I call the play »Alles okay« [Everything Okay].

When I leave my vacation site in the first days of January 1970, I have the completed work in my pocket. It has not been produced to the present day.

January 1970. Munich. The Dutch film producer Rob Houwer, who engaged me as director for four years, wants me to direct another film comedy for him. However, the script is so reactionary and uninteresting that I must decline.

Houwer insists. It is impossible to reach agreement. I give him my piece to read. He wants to obtain the film rights. I agree. My condition: our contract should end with the completion of this film. His condition: he wants to more or less begin shooting right away. This is fine with me, so I immediately start work on the screenplay.

March 1970. Munich.

We start shooting. From casting photos of 300 young girls I select a schoolgirl who will be playing her first role. She is 16 years old and her name is Eva Mattes.

For the 90-minute film the producer gives me 11 days of shooting. In order to make do with this extreme situation, I practice shooting with the actors for a week in a riding hall in Grünwald. On the last days of practice the cameraman Igor Luther joins us. The riding hall is an ideal place to practice because of the soft ground. The film is set almost exclusively in a forest clearing.

Shortly before we begin shooting a report and a book comes out about the authentic case, from which I learn the real names and the outcome of the trial of the US court martial. I am happy about this knowledge of further developments and unfortunately decide to replace the beautiful Southern German names with genuine US names. The intended dialectic between Bavarian language and home on the one side, and the theater of war in Vietnam, to which the world looks, on the other side remains intact. (It later transpires that an American journalist had invented the names in order to secure the copyright on the true story for himself. Unsuspectingly, I had caused the downfall of a Columbia project with my film. Columbia wanted to film the report of the journalist.)

May 1970. Berlin.

I land at Tempelhof. In my carry-on luggage I have the first copy of my completed film. It is called O. K. *I am alone and carry the copy to the office of the Berlinale, where a selection jury will be shown the film. During the showing I take a walk on the Ku-Damm. After a couple of hours I receive word that the film has been accepted and I fly back to Munich.*

June 30, 1970, 11:00 p.m. Berlin.

I stand with my actors (Eva Mattes, Hartmut Becker, Friedrich von Thun, Wolfgang Fischer) on the stage of the Zoo-Palast. The film has been shown. The audience cheers, we wave to them and are happy. We have given a sign against this war, against our accessory guilt, against our indifference.

In the best of spirits, as if the war were over, we inspect the Ku-Damm and its watering holes.

2 o'clock in the morning.

I am not allowed to enter the bar/restaurant of a Berlin film producer. »Not you!«, says the bouncer. »You are mistaken!«, I say and wave at an acquaintance who is employed by the film producer. The acquaintance says with lowered head: »I can't talk to you now«.

The film producer who owns the bar is a member of the jury. Something is going on here, I simply don't know what. From a telephone booth I call Rob Houwer at the hotel and wake him up.

We decide to drop the invitation to a steamboat ride on the Wannsee the next day and to try to find out what is going on.

July 1, 1970.

Rob Houwer is informed by the Yugoslavian filmmaker Dušan Makavejev, who is a member of the jury, that my film has been excluded from the Competition. Houwer and I find the director of the Festival Dr. Bauer and demand an explanation. Dr. Bauer says, it is all nonsense, where had we heard such a thing? He was always present, nothing at all had happened, naturally the film had not been excluded, that was not even possible, the Berlinale as an A-festival could not do such a thing.

We are not completely mollified and soon receive new information. The acquaintance who works for the film-juror and gastronome asks me to call her back. There are notes for me to call other people. After diverse calls I know more.

*The jury president, the American director George Stevens (*GIANT*), a notorious hawk, applied pressure on the management of the Festival after the showing of my film to the* *jury: »Either O.K. is publicly banned or I leave!« Not all the jury members wanted to yield to the president. But even reminders of the regulations of an A-festival did nothing to change George Stevens' mind. Rob Houwer informs the press of the situation.*

July 2/3, 1970.

At a quickly convened press conference Dr. Bauer denies that there was even a demand by the jury president that O.K. be banned. (»I was there!«). Makavejev, as a member of the jury, is not allowed to go public with internal jury matters. Rob Houwer and I cannot prove our allegations.

There is unrest. Is it thinkable that the direction of the Festival is not telling the truth? Who in the jury has broken the silence? Will it be possible to continue the Festival? In the meantime, two camps have emerged. The one praises the film, the other condemns it. The one see in it a metaphor for an immoral war in which the soldiers necessarily lose their moral bearings, as has already the government which wants to fight such a war. The other camp sees in it an immoral film which insults our ally. The one finds the movie good, the other bad. Only a few people can see the film objectively in the overheated atmosphere of the Festival.

Still, there were some differentiated reviews, for and against, and there were some people in the jury who said, maybe we don't think that much of the film, but we are not going to be party to burning a film.

The scandal is not that Stevens wanted to prevent O.K. from getting a prize. He only needed to vote against it. The scandal is that the US director was able to act like the long arm of his government in Berlin and could force the direction of the Berlin Festival to mislead the assembled critics, journalists and the public.

By this time more was at stake than merely the film itself.

I was accused of anti-Americanism. (For my 1969 documentary film on Vietnam TISCHE I was accused respectively of anti-Americanism and anti-Communism by the two camps in the then still heated Cold War). That O.K. can really not be regarded as anti-American was proven just a few months later at the festival in San Francisco. Albert Johnson had invited me there and the American public understood the film immediately. There the film was viewed overwhelmingly by young people who - in contrast to most people in Berlin - were directly affected by the Vietnam War. They were against this war, and they were Americans. And nobody had even suggested that they might have anti-American sentiments.

In Berlin, 1970, I had to listen to the accusations of anti-Americanism.

In Berlin, 1970, the 1950s were not yet over. And the war in Vietnam was to continue for another five years.

Makavejev wants to show his solidarity to the Berlinale, which is at risk, but he also wants to maintain solidarity with the jury, which had been made a fool of, and uphold the principle of freedom of expression.

July 4/5, 1970.

Makavejev permits Rob Houwer and me to have a Berlin notary take down in writing what had happened with the jury behind closed doors.

The affidavit also contains Makavejev's name.

With this document in our hand, we once face the press again. The atmosphere at this event cannot be described. The hall is full to overflowing, hundreds of people press about the podium at which Rob Houwer and I (backed up by Eva and Hartmut and Wolfi, and my wife) sit across from the official representatives of the Festival. The business director of Festivals-Ltd., Walther Schmieding, fights with his back to the wall. The journalists finally want to know the truth. Had the rape taken place or not? Schmieding says no. It was all made up. A journalist says: take a look at the affidavit which lies in front of you. Are you saying that Verhoeven made all that up? Schmieding says yes, it was all made up.

Evil tongues call: »It is all a publicity stunt created by the producers. Verhoeven is lying.«

Outrage. Dissatisfaction. Somebody yells »Communist«. I yell back, I am already hoarse. Eva brings me a liter bottle of Fachingen mineral water.

People point fingers at each other, hold their fists under each other's faces. One no longer understands even his own words.

Suddenly a messenger appears. A blue postman's cap floats through the crowd.

Then he is on the podium. A Berlin postman with a telegram in his hand. It is like in the theatre when the deus ex machina appears. The telegram is read. Tense silence.

Dušan Makavejev declares telegraphically his resignation from the jury and confirms point by point the sudden take over of the 20th Berlin Film Festival by the American president of a not so independent jury.

Crippling dismay among the officals who had hoped to carry through the hard line of lies.

How could they believe that? How sure could somebody be in Berlin in 1970 that the brutal suppression of a critical film could happen without hindrance because it criticized the military engagement of the USA? How could somebody think that such a scandal could be covered up over the long run?

People embrace each other. The pressure on me disappears. A silencing majority had not been succesful in getting rid of me. Schmieding, pale, covered with sweat, offers me his hand: »It was not meant personally«. I am unable to talk. People laugh, scream, cry.

The majority of the directors want to show their solidarity with me and withdraw their films.

I cannot be happy about this. The scandal deepens the trenches. The Festival is over.

The Senator for Cultural Affairs Stein announces at a press conference, to which I am not admitted, the premature closing of the 20th Berlin Film Festival.

The Vietnam War will last for five more years. Millions of American and Vietnamese people will lose their lives.

Only gradually, cautiously, will the media and public opinion develop a critical distance to the holy war of the Americans in Vietnam. After 20 years almost nobody will remember.

Berlinale in upheaval

By Ulrich Gregor

The shockwaves which broke over the Berlin Film Festival in June/July 1970 and led to hot debates over principles, to ever more vitriolic disputes, and finally to the closing of the entire event, were at that moment a surprise for the participants at the Berlinale. They were, however, as a whole the consequence of contradictions which in earlier times had become increasingly pronounced; thus these events possessed a certain logic and were in a basic sense already overdue.

The Cannes Festival had already experienced its rebellion in May 1968 (from 1969 on the »Quinzaine des réalisateurs« was instituted there). In Venice a process of on-going discussion and the challenging of the statutes of this festival from the time of fascism led to the institution of a parallel festival »Giornate del cinema italiano«, which, however, could never really achieve a profile as a counter-festival.

Only in Berlin did it remain relatively »peaceful« until the summer of 1970. And yet considerable counterforces had already gathered in the Berlin and West German film scene. Since the emergence of the »New American Cinema«, since the foundation of a film cooperative in Hamburg (it organized the legendary »Hamburger Filmschau« in 1968) and the initiation of the »Hofer Filmtage«, indeed since the movement of renewal in German film from the late sixties, more than just a change in generation had taken place; there emerged a utopia of a new cinema with completely changed characteristics and functions in the sense of a comprehensive emancipatory politics and cultural politics. There was a growing interest in the film movements of the Third World (the landmark film was LA HORA DE LOS HORNOS *by Fernando Solanas), in the political documentary, in the »Zielgruppenfilm« (film for targeted audiences). The movement of communal cinemas was born which was concerned with new relationships between film and viewer, new program structures and, in contrast to the purely commercial boulevard cinemas, sought to establish a new culture of film.*

Through its work in the Academy of Arts and other Berlin cinemas, the »Freunde der Deutschen Kinemathek« (Friends of the German Cinémathèque), already founded in 1963, had instigated this movement and also reflected it.

There were constant discussions about the renewal of the film medium in form and content, which was supposed to contribute to a change of society and consciousness. Such a film culture was supposed to have its basis and its productive center in cooperatives of filmmakers and its basis for distribution in the communal cinemas; the film academies were supposed to constantly channel new talent into it; this system, so one thought at the time, could even develop a kind of economic autonomy. Naturally, the student movement, the protests against the Vietnam war, played a strong role in this connection.

All of these ideas were in a »virulent« state during the summer of 1970. However, nobody had prepared, planned or directed the overthrow of the Berlinale. Rather, as has been stated, everyone was downright surprised at the events which suddenly took place. Actually, however, the Festival had in practice removed itself rather far from contemporary and future-oriented currents of renewal of German film. For these, functioning models for festivals had already been drafted.

Already in 1969, the Freunde der Deutschen Kinemathek, then in the Academy of Arts, had in private initiative, and without any subsidies, shown a supplementary program to the Berlinale; short films from Borowczyk, final-exam works from the Berlin Academy of Film and Television, films from Kenneth Anger and Werner Schroeter as well as a night of American experimental films were on the program of this event of several days. Andrei Tarkovsky's Andrei Rublev *was on the program, but the copy which had already been lent to the »Freunde« was then withdrawn at the last moment by the Soviet Embassy in East-Berlin. Because of the events surrounding* Andrei Rublev, *but also because of the night of Amercian experimental film and accompanying circumstances, this »underground festival«, as it was called at the time by the Berlin press, found its way into the history of film in Berlin.*

*In 1970 there then followed in the newly founded »Arsenal« (it had existed since January 1970) a program »on the occasion of the Berlin Film Festival«, which included, among other films, the first Fassbinder-retrospective ever shown (with five films); in addition were shown films by Rosa von Praunheim, Cuban documentary films, films from Japan (*Eros + gyakusatsu *by Yoshishige Yoshida), films by Jonas Mekas and Robert Kramer, as well as two classics of silent film by Feuillade (*Tih Minh *and* Judex*); in this way the »Freunde« expressed the connection between old and new cinema, which has been practiced to the present day in the Forum and in the Arsenal. The program also documented the many-sides and many-layers of new film styles among avantgarde film, narrative film and documentary film. In contrast to the »official« Festival, this program was able to be completed in 1970 as planned.*

These new impulses had, however, not yet really broken through at the Festival, the Berlinale was still a monument to antiquated conceptions of film, or at least so it seemed to many people - even though there had already, at an earlier time, been »Young Cinema a Days« with programs from Yugoslavia and Canada, as well as individual cases of pioneer works e. g., by Jean-Luc Godard, in the Competition. But these attempts to allow the renewal of film to become visible at the Berlin Film Festival seemed to be rather isolated special cases.

*All of these latent forces of alternative reflection in Festival matters combined in a sudden eruption. Cracks appeared in the apparently solid foundations of the Berlinale, when suddenly a rumor circulated that a film would retroactively be removed from the Competition because it contained criticism of the way the USA was waging war in Vietnam (*o.k. *by Michael Verhoeven). This was, at that time, political dynamite of the highest order. It was surprising at the time - and actually still is - that the responsible authorities did not recognize this in time and did not immediately and decisively deny the rumor; especially since the retroactive »removal« of a film from the Competition, in particular as a result, as was reported as an objection by the jury or some of its members, constituted a complete violation of the rules.*

There thus unfolded an ever intensifying cycle of meetings, press conferences and public discussions which came into being in the style of that time, at which Berlinale participants, representatives of the film scene, intellectuals and cultural figures from all areas proclaimed their notions of what actually needed reforming at the Berlinale. There was an altercation between press conferences of the jury or its members (active at the forefront: Dušan Makavejev) and general meetings at which there was much discussion and argument about the goals and new orientation of the Berlinale. Above all there was a focus on the orientation of the Berlinale towards the economic aspects of film, towards commerce and the cinema of Hollywood, which was a matter of earnest criticism for many observers; there was also a focus on the exclusion of and insufficient attention to all forms of alternative cinema, which had scarcely been able to find a real place at the Berlinale in previous years. The principles of film selection, the absence of films from the countries of the Eastern bloc were also criticized. The mood was irritable, the trend of the proposed alternatives was radical. The awarding of prizes was subjected to especially sharp criticism, since this was perceived as a symptom of the orientation of the Festival towards film-capitalism. The meetings and the discussions became increasingly hectic, they forced themselves more and more towards the forefront of the Festival, so that the screenings finally seemed to completely fade into the background.

Certainly nobody back then prepared a chronicle of the incidents and meetings, the positions and counter-positions, from which an exact record of the events which made the Berlinale stagger could be reconstructed. The most important incidents: in light of the general tumult in which the structures of the Festival seemed to be disintegrating, the director of the Festival, Dr. Bauer, and the director of the sponsoring Festivals-Ltd. (Berliner Festspiele GmbH), Walther Schmieding, finally declared their resignations (Bauer came back, but Schmieding did not); the Senator for Cultural Affairs, Stein, declared at that point that the Festival was being prematurely called off.

In the course of the second half of the year 1970, after emotions had cooled a bit, various hearings were held for the purpose of finding out what reforms were called for in the area of the Film Festival. Two views stood in opposition of each other: either the Festival should be reformed from the ground up and pointed in a new direction, whereby, however, in case the Competition was abolished, as many demanded, the threat of the loss of »A-status« was written on the wall; or a new institution which would run parallel to the old structures should be created as a catch-all for everything dangerous, subversive or in any way unruly. The Berliner Festspiele GmbH decided in favor of the second alternative (as did the festival in Cannes), which surely offered the advantage that the old-style festival could be continued for the time being without substantial change. The offer of being able to put on a parallel festival under their own direction was made to the »Freunde der Deutschen Kinemathek« and this came as very much a surprise to its representatives (shortly before Christmas of 1970 the offer was made public - thus resembling a Christmas present). The opportunity was wrapped in sufficient liberties and guarantees - there was only one condition: the parallel festival would be obliged to support the idea of friendship among peoples.

At first, nobody really believed that the newly created »International Forum of Young Cinema« would have a long future. The new values and conceptions for which the Forum stood, however, proved to be solid. They immediately received the full support of a broad spectrum of filmmakers, film writers and viewers; so that the Forum was able, also due to the persistence and engagement of its employees, to develop a continuity and to build up a reputation.

Initially it was quite easy to put together a trend-setting Forum program - numerous films which corresponded to the new ideals were available or were in the process of being shot, were - so to speak - lying by the roadside; the interest of the public in such films was enormous. The Forum began at the same time to concern itself with films from the past (in 1971, at the first Forum, A SIXTH OF THE EARTH *by Dziga Vertov and* L'ÂGE D'OR *by Buñuel were shown) and to place these excavations into relationship with contemporary films. Important principles of the Forum continued to be public discussion and carefully produced program sheets, as well as a concern with the films and their distribution after the Festival was over. These were the foundations and principles upon which the work of the Forum was built and has been continued until the present day.*

The hectic and tumultuous events of the year 1970 appear in hindsight to be almost a curiosity, since in the meantime so much has regressed and so many basic assumptions have been reversed. Nevertheless, the Berlinale days of the summer of 1970 were an historical hour, in which suddenly - with momentum, emotion and far-reaching consequences - conceptions of a cinematography, completely different from that which had previously existed, finally gathered steam and erupted, clearing away the obstacles in their path. Perhaps such days will return sometime, although they are not in sight at the moment. But the ideas which were discussed at the time, the excitement, the impetus, the radical soaring of thought, also the criticism of the existing which was articulated back then, are a form of capital, from which we can still benefit today, a model with which we should compare ourselves from time to time in order to draw a balance on that which we have achieved and since brought about.

Quatre nuits d'un rêveur:
Isabelle Weingarten

A new forum

1971

June 25th-July 6th, 1971 (Competition)
June 27th-July 4th, 1971 (Forum)

»The 20th International Film Festival 1970 in Berlin was not held. The jubilee celebration turned out to be a great nothing. Maybe this is our big chance; I wonder how we will mess it up.« Alf Brustellin in: Süddeutsche Zeitung, July 7, 1970

At the end there was lots of fun. Jaques Tati accepted – on behalf of Jean Gabin – the award for best actor and turned the stage of the Zoo-Palast into a playground. He shook each and every hand as the proud winner, posed modestly, gushingly thanked everyone, rejoiced, was embarrassed, and played the arrogant dandy. Valiantly, Ida Ehre, who had awarded the »Bears« for the jury, tried to keep ceremonial dignity in tact. Yet when Shirley MacLaine stepped on stage, to receive her »Bear« as best actress, Tati had found his partner: she joined right in. For a few minutes the Zoo-Palast was a music-hall and variety-stage. Tati and MacLaine danced, and both the audience and the Festival were at their mercy. Many were amused and laughed, others were puzzled, and some did not find it funny at all. The Film Festival had never before ended on such an unserious note. Yet the films of the Competition in this year had also not been taken seriously by their audiences. Confidence in the quality of the program of the Competition had not yet been won back; scepticism prevailed.

In this first year after the great disruption, the selection commission – its members included among others the journalists Dora Fehling, Kurt Habernoll and Klaus Hebecker – had primarily chosen films by well-known directors. However the films had not lived up to expectations. In addition, the curiosity of the Festival guests lay mainly in the International Forum of Young Cinema, which was being held for the first time. With its clear and unconventionally conceived program, it did in fact immediately offer a counterpole to the Competition. As a result Bergman's THE TOUCH, Bresson's QUATRE NUITS D'UN RÊVEUR (»Four Nights of a Dreamer«), Fassbinder's WHITY, Ichikawa's AI FUTATABI (»To Love Again«), Pasolini's IL DECAMERONE, and De Sicas' IL GIARDINO DEI FINZI CONTINI (»The Garden of the Finzi Contini«) were not the main attractions. Friedrich Luft: »The most important cinema was to be found in the sideshow. The so-called relevant films could no longer disturb the main Festival. All that was left for the grand rooms of the official Competition was to reel off a bunch of bluntly commercial films. It was an intimate party.« (Die Welt, July 8, 1971.) And yet the Festival had survived, the Competition which had met with so much hostility was being held again, and – which most critics tended to overlook – attendance was higher than in the year before: the number of viewers for the Competition alone had risen by 30 percent. This fact could not be explained by mere curiosity in another scandal or in a renewed collapse of the Festival. And the Forum was attracting a new kind of audience. Yes, the International Film Festival Berlin was a remarkable success. The patient had made it.

Rivalries

Internally, there were rivalries. Alfred Bauer saw the Forum as a competitor, and it was only with difficulty that he could get accustomed to the idea of a Festival in two parts. In his final report on the IFB, he wrote that »all tendencies found in film – towards art, commercialism, documentation, ideology and agitation« were shown in the Forum. Especially the choice of the last two words shows the reservation and critical distance which Alfred Bauer felt towards the International Forum of Young Cinema. That the Forum as an independent event in the program of the IFB was not yet accepted, could – during this early period – also be felt in the everyday management of the Festival.

In their first report of their experiences, the organizers of the Forum complained of a lack of personnel and technical cooperation received from the management of the Competition. Technical assistance had been agreed upon in advance. A note by

A bear of a show:
Shirley MacLaine,
Jacques Tati,
Frank D. Gilroy

Dominique Sanda,
Vittorio De Sica,
Helmut Berger

Fritz Lang, Lily Latté

Fernando Arrabal, author and director of the French-Tunisian opening film, VIVA LA MUERTE

the Senator for Science and the Arts (Jan. 12, 1971) states, that in the resolution of the House of Representatives on the restructuring of the IFB, a passage was included stating, »that the offices of the company active for all festival events« must give »organizational as well as technical assistance« to the Forum. In view of the low budget of the Forum of Young Cinema, this was not an insignificant point. The board of curators had decided to grant DM 220 800 from the Berlin Festivals-Ltd. to the »Friends of the German Cinémateque« who were the sponsors of the Forum. In addition, the Berlin Festivals-Ltd. would cover costs for rent and advertising. The total budget of the first Forum, must have therefore run at around a meagre DM 300 000. Interestingly enough, the budget itself and the actual form of the technical cooperation between the Forum and the Festival were only added to the resolution of the House of Representatives after the intervention of Senator for Finance Heinz Striek (letter to the Senator for Science and the Arts, Jan. 8, 1971).

Conception and structure of the Forum

The International Forum of Young Cinema was held from June 27th until July 4th, it was two days shorter than the program of the Competition. The films were shown at the Atelier am Zoo and the Arsenal, as well as at the movie house of the Friends of the German Cinémathèque. Its staff was also responsible for the conception and program of the Forum. They included: Ulrich Gregor, Erika Gregor, Gero Gandert, Heiner Roß and Manfred Salzgeber. As laid down in Item 2 of the regulations, the goals of the Forum were, »to give information on the avant-garde and progressive development of film in all countries, and to support these developments«, as well as to assure »the appropriate reception of the films through discussions and by making informational material available«. Furthermore, in Item 8 it was explicitly noted that the Forum saw »as questionable, the attempt to set up a hierarchy of quality or of merit for individual films which, with their varying intentions and forms, are not comparable«; thus there were to be neither competition nor awards. Each film chosen, however, would receive a »Certificate of Participation«. Important for the image promoted by those responsible for the Forum were the discussions after the film screenings, which were to »deepen the reception of each individual film, and to make sure that the relationship, similarities and differences of the individual films of the ›Forum‹ were perceived« (Item 9 of the regulations). In these conceptual ideas are to be found many of the proposals made in the discussions of the year before. Expectations were, as a result, high, and premature praise was abundant. Christa Maerker, for example, saw the Forum as an event »which achieves more for film than other festivals: not via an old and exhausted glamour, but via solid information and its intention to be a place of work« (Spandauer Volksblatt, Jan. 15, 1971).

Ula Stöckl,
Dušan Makavejev,
Rosa von Praunheim,
Alain Tanner,
Nagisa Oshima and others

The program of the Forum concentrated on: new German feature films (GESCHICHTEN VOM KÜBELKIND/Stories of the Dustbin Child) by Ula Stöckl and Edgar Reitz, DER GROSSE VERHAU/»The Big Mess« by Alexander Kluge, ICH LIEBE DICH – ICH TÖTE DICH/»I Love You, I Kill You« by Uwe Brandner); politically committed and sociocritical feature and documentary films (THE MURDER OF FRED HAMPTON by Mike Gray, W. R. – MISTERIJE ORGANIZMA / »W. R. – Mysteries of the Organism« by Dušan Makavejev); films made for specific target groups (NICHT DER HOMOSEXUELLE IST PERVERS, SONDERN DIE SITUATION, IN DER ER LEBT/»Not the Homosexual is Perverse, but rather the Situation in which He Lives« by Rosa von Praunheim); and films from the Third World, in particular Africa. In addition, experimental films were shown, and directors were introduced that were unknown in West Germany (e. g., Alain Tanner with LA SALAMANDRE, Nagisa Oshima with GISHIKI / »The Ceremony«, or Theo Angelopoulos with ANAPARASTASSI / »The Reconstruction«. A series of modern classics, films by Dziga Vertov, Luis Buñuel, Luchino Visconti, André Malraux and Jean Renoir were also presented. And there was a relationship between these different points of focus: Wilhelm Roth, in his report on the Festival, saw a correlation in theme between the French documentary film NO PINCHA by Tobias Engel, about the fight for independence in Guinea-Bissau, and the American investigation of the murder of the Black Panther leader Fred Hamptom by American policemen, THE MURDER OF FRED HAMPTON by Mike Gray (Frankfurter Neue Presse, July 8, 1971). An interesting attempt was made by the selection commission in asking three European film magazines to put together their own program. The editors of »Cahiers du Cinéma« chose Oshima's GISHIKI, Rome's »Cinema & Film« showed Mario Schiafano's UMANO NON UMANO [Human Not Human] and Adriano Aprà's OLIMPIA AGLI AMICI [Olimpia to her Friends]; the »Filmkritik« from Munich presented Gerhard Theuring's experimental film LEAVE ME ALONE, which Alf Brustellin strongly criticized: »Sensorial material for worthless hours, these are images of no reason, intention and meaning. Popular dream music makes itself heard; there are redundancies, distances, tensions and yet still nothing for one to go by. LEAVE ME ALONE is free of all ideologies, pointless, arbitrarily manipulable, and not pertinent for anything or anyone.« (Süddeutsche Zeitung, July 8, 1971.)

Three European film magazines show films of their choice.

Anaparastassi

Ulrich Gregor commented in an interview with the »Frankfurter Rundschau« on the program of the film magazines, whose reception had correlated least of all to the »perspectives intended«: »The films had too little to do with the stance of the respective magazines; the discussions became bogged down from the outset. This probably had to do with the fact that it is more difficult to carry on a discussion about basic theoretical questions than about individual films.« (July 24, 1971.)

Makavejev's polemic collage, W. R. – Misterije organizma, about the thesis of the Marxist psychoanalyst Wilhelm Reich, who believed a sexual revolution had to take place before socialism could, was discussed with much controversy. Documentary material, interviews with friends of Reich, photos, and scenes of contemporary America were contrasted and dispersed between fictitions sequences, parable-like scenes and excerpts from sex films: »A bit of a more relaxing and relaxed utopia: at the end the smile on a young girl's head (which has been cut off by an adrett socialist sport hero in a fit of sexual frenzy – that which builds up over a long period, becomes destructive) turns into the smile of Wilhelm Reich, and one must, unfortunately, allow this image to take effect for a long time, before one understands that it is too early to write a correct, or rather, uninhibited word about this film.« (Alf Brustellin, Süddeutsche Zeitung, July 2, 1971.)

The sexual revolution

Makavejev's film captured a basic mood at the beginning of the seventies: that society could only become politicized by the student movement if there were first a »sexual revolution«. Rosa von Praunheim's Nicht der Homosexuelle ist pervers … was also evidence of this fact. The film was not solely Praunheim's coming out, for after the screening in the Forum other men also proclaimed their homosexuality. The discussion after the film was angry and abusive; many misunderstood it, believing this feature film to be a documentation. »The satirical elements, and the ironic play of bourgeois-romantic love between men were found

JAIDER – DER EINSAME JÄGER [Jaider – the Lonely Hunter], West German Competition entry by Volker Vogeler: Gottfried John

inappropriate for this theme. But in fact this style of staging the film was an exact expression of Praunheim's thesis, that homosexuals imitate ›normal‹ middle-class life, instead of emancipating and organizing themselves, instead of becoming politically active.« (Wilhelm Roth, Frankfurter Neue Presse, July 8, 1971.)

The Forum, which its critics had seen as a »counter-festival«, had become an important complementary event for the Berlin Festival right from the start; if the Competition was the »standing leg«, then it was the Forum which was the free leg – with which much could be accomplished. Yet the program-makers of the International Forum also received their share of criticism. Critics found fault with the enormous number of films included in the program. »The feeling of having maybe missed something – which could have been of significance – becomes a nightmare. Feverish hallucinations were not rare, confused thoughts, blurred images, and over-strained senses. We are familiar with such turbulent effects of saturation from the Frankfurt Book Fair. At a film event in Germany, it is a new experience«, protests Wolfram Schütte (Frankfurter Rundschau, July 6, 1971).

The International Forum of Young Cinema can be continued.

No one questioned that the International Forum was to be continued; the trial run had proved successful. And so it was merely a matter of form, when Senator Stein at the meeting of the board of curators of Berlin Festivals-Ltd. on October 4th, called for a vote as to whether the IFB 1972 should be continued with this structure. Noone had any objections. More difficult were the negotiations on the future financing of the Forum. In the fiscal plan for 1972, a subsidy of DM 245 000 was planned; yet the amount – already a compromise – which those responsible for the Forum estimated, was DM 296 000. A large part of the financing was intended for the realization of a central concept in the policy of the Forum: it was planned to set up a distributor with films from the program of the Forum, in order to be able to continue to work with these films on a political level after the Festival was over. For this reason, the

Le Chat: Simone Signoret, Jean Gabin

Ulrich Gregor was born in Hamburg in 1932. He studied philosophy, Romance languages and literature, and journalism in Hamburg, Paris and Berlin. From 1955 on, he worked as a journalist and film critic for magazines in Germany and abroad, as well as for radio and television. In 1963 he was one of the founders of the society »Freunde der Deutschen Kinemathek« (Friends of the German Cinémathèque).
Since then he has been its chairman. From 1966 to 1971, he was lecturer for film history and film theory at the German Film and Television Academy. His publications include: »Geschichte des Films« co-authored with Enno Patalas, and »Geschichte des Films ab 1960«.

Forum insisted on funds for the subtitling of copies and for the purchasing of films in the first place. And, naturally, questions of staff were also relevant. The calculation of the Forum included a few new positions: »in particular a spokesman (a kind of artistic director) earning DM 30 000 a year, as well as a managing director and a secretary for the whole year« (minutes of the meeting). Ulrich Gregor and Heiner Roß – who had been asked to explain their ideas to the members of the board – pointed out the necessity of having three members of staff working continuously for the Forum. Especially after pressure from Ministerial Supervisor Dr. Hanns Hieronymus, spokesman for the Federal Minister of the Interior, the board decided on a compromise: the funds for the 1972 Forum were to be raised by DM 50 000 (excluding rent and advertising), in addition, the managing director of Festivals-Ltd. would be allowed some leeway in negotiations: between DM 10 000 and DM 20 000. The drafting of a contract of employment between Ulrich Gregor and Festivals-Ltd. was rejected at this point »for the basic reason that with such a contract the necessary direct responsiblity and independence of the Forum could not be ensured«.

The board of curators were cautious on all questions of contracts. Consultations were also held pertaining to Alfred Bauer's contract as Film Festival director. The advisory board recommended that Bauer's contract »be renewed indefinitely (with a clause for giving notice of termination)«. And it had been Bauer's wish to receive a contract for at least five years. The board of curators however rejected both of these proposals, as it did not want to commit itself »to any particular form for the Film Festival after the year of 1972«. Everyone involved was still recovering from the shock experienced a year earlier. The success of the 1971 Forum, as well as the fact that the Competition had been able to make it did not in themselves seem, at this point, to guarantee the future existence of the IFB. Secretly though, everyone did hope that with the establishment of the Forum, the IFB had survived its structural crisis.

Nicht der Homosexuelle ist pervers, sondern die Situation, in der er lebt

Film - my life

By Rosa von Praunheim

I have never had an entry in the international Competition; my temper boiled whenever Herzog or Fassbinder showed their films there and I ran indignantly out of the cinema - although I would have liked all too well to receive the Golden Bear as did Werner Schroeter, for example.

Yet despite my very poor memory, I remember putting on a counter-festival in 1968 or 1969 in a Kreuzberg apartment. We showed double 8 films. I showed Rosa Arbeiter auf goldener Strasse *(Part 2) and Werner - I don't know any more. The place was packed full and Donloya Luna, the famous model, had come. I will never forget this beautiful woman who died all too early.*

In 1971 I submitted my film Nicht der Homosexuelle ist pervers, sondern die Situation in der er lebt *(»Not the Homosexual is Perverse, but rather the Situation in which He Lives«) to the selection committee of the Forum. It was actually supposed to be called »Das Glück in der Toilette« [Happiness in the Toilet], but this title was rejected by WDR, which had commissioned the film. - I still remember how Erika Gregor, after she had experienced my temper tantrum over conservative and unpolitical gays, said that she knew gays who had actually lived together happily for a long time. I had a lot to say to her about that, and in retrospect I have to be thankful for the courage and far-sightedness of the Forum, especially of Manfred Salzgeber, who showed the film and thereby gave the starting signal for the German gay movement.*

I love film festivals, especially the many receptions, to which I often was not admitted and in which I imagined one could meet particularly important producers. Back then, the Festival was usually held in June so the weather was fine; now one carries a cold and hoarse-throat from one cinema to the other, while choosing among hundreds of films.

International Jury
Bjørn Rasmussen (Denmark, president)
Ida Ehre (FRG, vice-president)
Walter Albuquerque Mello (Brazil)
Paul Claudon (France)
Kenneth Harper (Great Britain)
Mani Kaul (India)
Charlotte Kerr-Sokal (FRG)
Rex Reed (USA)
Giancarlo Zagni (Italy)

The Awards of the International Jury

Feature Films
Grand Prix of the 21st IFB
Golden Berlin Bear
IL GIARDINO DEI FINZI CONTINI
Italy, directed by
Vittorio De Sica

Special Prize of the Jury
Silver Berlin Bear
IL DECAMERONE
Italy, directed by
Pier Paolo Pasolini

Silver Berliner Bear
for the best actress
ex aequo
Shirley MacLaine
in DESPERATE CHARACTERS
USA

Simone Signoret
in LE CHAT
France

Silver Berlin Bear
for the best actor
Jean Gabin
in LE CHAT
France

Silver Berlin Bear
for the best screenplay and dialogue
Frank D. Gilroy
for DESPERATE CHARACTERS
USA

Silver Berlin Bear
for the best camera work
Ragnar Lasse-Henriksen
for LOVE IS WAR
Norway

Mostly very bad films, I think - I am definitely for whipping the makers of bad films, for erecting stocks in front of the Zoo-Palast, even at the risk of someday becoming a victim of my own anger. Otherwise, I love the Festival café, asking foreign guests about their sex-life, but I don't like going to the movies which usually cannot be appreciated under such hectic circumstances. I especially like to get upset anew at each awards ceremony, which is so badly organized, so ugly, that one is amazed that it has to do with serious films rather than a convention of small animal breeders. Why doesn't Mr. de Hadeln hire me to make a big and glamorous spectacle out of it?
Along these lines,
Rosa v. P.

Friends

By Theo Angelopoulos

The screening of ANAPARASTASSI (»Reconstruction«) was over. The lights in the small movie theater were switched back on. Ulrich Gregor and Heiner Ross turned to me. Their eyes smiled. That was 1971, in the first year of the Forum. I had managed to smuggle a copy of the film out of the Greece of the generals in my luggage. It was my first film. I was worried, uneasy, full of doubt. And suddenly I found in Berlin friends, accomplices.

Since then I have returned with my films to Berlin several times. Despite the time which has gone by, despite the changes in the Forum, I believe that it's one of the most open events in Europe for everyone who is young, daring and nonconformist.

Long live the Forum of Young Cinema in Berlin!

When I am eighty…

By Mani Kaul

For all these days I could not phrase my message, but here is how I feel: I saw the birth of the Forum, paradoxically, from the ›other‹ side: as a juror for the Competition in the Berlin International Festival. That was when I was twenty-eight, things have radically changed since that year. Along with Ulrich, Erika and Sylvia I am older now. The Forum is younger, its youth has remained the breath of world cinema. When (and if) I am eighty, I will love to find myself sitting in a café close to the Arsenal.

Can films change the world?

By Christian Ziewer

Ever more film festivals intrigue the world these days. Not few of them are original, informative, animating. Which one deserves the prize?

As the Forum began its work twenty years ago, its initiators were moved by the same question which so concerned us filmmakers: »Can films change the world?« With their program, the Forum-people gave their answer, without pathos: yes. This answer has determined selection decisions, presentations and commitment. It was also the basis on which my own films began their life in the public sphere of the Forum.

Since then we've come of age, and that »yes« is no longer so self-evident. Modestly, we draw back; »Instead of changing«, so it is said, »films can at best interpret the world.« To intervene in the course of events - that can no longer reasonably be demanded of the Forum.

But let's take the name by its word for a moment: the Roman Forum was not only a market, it wasn't only a place where goods were sold, where one stood around and looked, but also where one met, for private and public purposes, one got upset and took a position, conducted meetings, passed judgements, drew conclusions, intervened. Why should a forum of film be less? If we critically appraise people and events, things can begin to move; if we do the thoughts and deeds of cinema justice, they will challenge reality. The »pleasant pasttime« can have an effect.

The Forum continues to trust in the permeability of film and reality. It rejects the spirit of the times, which locks films into the ghetto of screen-experiences and wishes to judge and enjoy only in the frame of the resultant cinema-cosmos. Even as it has aged, it has continued to be for the Festival more than just a place for screening films. The way the Forum perceives the world through films and how it passes this perception on makes it an initiator: it creates private experience and public consciousness.

No, laurels are not appropriate for this celebrant, they imply too much pomp and stateliness. It is better to say that the Forum bears, if not the flag, then the torch which it ignited twenty years ago. Then it will also be able to confront the danger which threatens our film culture: that the glittering lights of the Festival veil the progressing ruin of the cinema landscape. If - with everyone blinded by sporadic major events - there are soon none left who support cinemas in the cities and the countryside, leveling and loss will leave a desert behind into which not even the Forum will be capable of bringing life. It would then have the mere role of a luxury good or a talebearer for the media industry.

In order that this not occur, that instead the Forum continue to be measure, corrective, stimulator, pathbreaker: best of wishes for the next twenty years!

NACHTSCHATTEN:
John van Dreelen

Next time in October?

1972

June 23rd–July 4th, 1972
(Competition)
June 25th–July 2nd, 1972
(Forum)

This year, curiosity was by and large directed at Germany's secret capital: in Munich the Olympic Summer Games were being held.

And what about Berlin? Two newspapers had ceased publication: the »Telegraf« and the »nachtdepesche«, both SPD affiliated, were last issued in June. Berlin's press landscape was quite impoverished; not much was left of the one-time newspaper metropolis. A Berliner – Willy Brandt – had become Federal Chancellor; there were high hopes based on his policy towards the East. Fear was also prevalent, as a result of the activities of the »Rote Armee Fraktion« (RAF). The writer Heinrich Böll was defamed as a RAF-sympathizer – because of an article in which he had carefully weighed the pros and cons in »Spiegel« magazine. The political climate in the Federal Republic of Germany was unstable; fronts were forming.

An unstable political climate in West Germany

The preparations for the »22nd Berlinale« were registered rather marginally. The Festival was still around, and expectations were directed at the Forum. Each of the Festival's visitors had to ask himself the same question: Should he go to the Zoo-Palast or to the Atelier? Did one belong to the older generation or was one progressive? Wolf Donner labelled the alternatives: »plush« or »politics«. Yes, fronts had formed at the Film Festival as well, or at least lines of demarcation. »The difference is actually quite éclatant: at the Competition there is red plush, announcements in three languages, stars with bouquets of flowers, elegance and efforts at ceremonialism (a revolutional reform: no more gong!) – at the Forum, there are more beards and long hair, the hippie-look, an informal atmosphere, discussions.« (Die Zeit, July 7, 1972.)

Plush or politics, Zoo-Palast or Atelier?

At the beginning of 1972, the budget of the Forum was once again on the agenda of the meetings of the advisory board and the board of curators. A contract was to be drawn up between the Festivals-Ltd. and the Friends of the German Cinémathèque; there were, however, to be no subsidies included as had been the case in the first year. Both establishments were understood as being »subject to private law«, and subsidies were only possible in a relationship governed by public law. There was more at stake here then the mere wording of a contract; it was a question of securing the existence of the Forum and at the same time integrating it culturally and politically, that is to say: »binding it to duty«.

In this contract – according to the advisory board at least – there was to be a passage included on the »basic tenets of international understanding« and these tenets were to be imperative. This recommendation of the advisory committee aimed, on the one hand, at a correspondence between the guidelines of the Forum and the FIAPF regulations; at the same time a certain wariness was evident on the part of the members of this board, who wanted to play it safe in light of the political commitment of the Forum – even though the very first item in the guidelines of the Forum defined its goals in relationship to »international understanding«. And yet at this point in time, a binding contract was not signed between the Forum and the Berlin Festivals-Ltd. It was not until the end of the seventies that the relationship between the two institutions was set down on paper. For the meantime, one made do with yearly agreements on the amount of subsidies to be received. As a result, the Forum went into debt for some years, without knowing for sure what sum would be approved of in the end. For the Forum in these early years, much was dependent on how much risk those responsible were personally willing to take.

No contract

Alfred Bauer, Ulrich Gregor

The power of the documentary

»There are films about class and race conflict in both Americas. From the North American Newsreel-Group, the films are about self-determination among Puerto Ricans in New York, about the dynasty of the Dupont family in the state of Delaware, about squatters in the slums of Harlem, about the successful emancipation of a young housewife. WINTER SOLDIER is a film resulting from the confessions of Vietnam veterans. From Latin America there are films about the genocide of the Indians of Columbia, about imperialism and monopolism in Bolivia. It is militant cinema, showing reality as it is not to be seen on television.« Enno Patalas asked: »Have we anything analogous in Europe?« (Süddeutsche Zeitung, July 5, 1972.)

The Forum was showing films which took the straightest route to an object, not side-tracking for reasons of entertainment. These were either documentary films or films whose fiction lived from the power of the documentary. There was, for example: FAMILY LIFE by Ken Loach, about a young girl who is forced by her parents to have an abortion, and who is destroyed by these problems at home; or LIEBE MUTTER, MIR GEHT ES GUT [Dear Mother, I'm Doing Fine], Christian Ziewer's first film, showing the everyday life and politics of a Berlin worker during the period of economic recession in 1966/67. REED – MEXICO INSURGENTE (»Reed: Insurgent Mexico«) by Paul Leduc, EMITAI [The Gods] by Ousmane Sembène, SAO BERNARDO by Leon Hirszman and LES CAMISARDS [The French Calvinists] by René Allio, an episode about the religious struggle of peasants in France during the 18th century after the annulment of the Proclamation of Nantes, all belonged to the politically and socially committed productions of the program of the Forum. At the same time the organizers expanded the program to include historical material. Several films were put in contrast to films from the twenties, thirties and forties. Other films dealt with similar themes, yet approached their subject using different cinematographic means. LES CAMISARDS ran opposite Visconti's LA TERRA TREMA, Ziewer's film was juxtaposed to HUNGER IN WALDENBURG by Piel Jutzi, and Ken Loach's FAMILY LIFE to

Pier Paolo Pasolini, Laura Betti

Abram Room's Tretya meshchanskaya (»Bed and Sofa«). The classic, Salt of the Earth, complemented Marin Karmitz' Coup pour coup [Blow for Blow] which was about a wild strike by women workers in a French textile factory – it was this film which was discussed the most vehemently in West German papers. Enno Patalas compares Karmitz' film with Salt of the Earth, and discovers so many points of contact, »that one could assume, that Karmitz had copied Biberman and Wilson. But if so, then he missed the most essential point: that in the American film, the process of the development of a class consciousness in the oppressed workers has been shown as a subjective, often painful and contradictory process. Karmitz only shows the eruption of these wretched beings.« (Süddeutsche Zeitung, July 5, 1972.)

It was difficult for films which were not politically oriented. Although there was a film – again from Munich, and much like Gerhard Theuring's Leave Me Alone in the year before – which did attract attention: Nachtschatten [Night Shadows], the first full length film by Niklaus Schilling, a seductively aesthetic and ironic film; horror between the images, reminding one of Murnau's Nosferatu and Dreyer's L'Etrange aventure de Allan Grey/Vampyr: »the closing shot: the sun becoming the moon, becomes a star which dissolves. Nature screeches when the lens is slowly shut.« (Frieda Grafe, Forum Info-Sheet No. 14.)

Hotly debated viewpoints

Officially Alfred Bauer had come to terms with the Forum, or at least he did speak out in support of maintaining both the Competition and the Forum, »also as then peace could be kept within the Festival« (minutes of the 14th meeting of the advisory board, Sept. 19, 1972). Yet unofficially, he revealed his scepticism. He could not adjust to the division of the Festival in two major events. In addition, he felt that he was treated particularly badly by West German critics: »The extreme critics, who only think in fixed patterns, merely want to lower the esteem of the Competition by their one-sided support of the Forum. Yet these critics cannot possibly have seen all of the films of the Competition, as they were supposed to write about the films of the

Liebe Mutter, mir geht es gut: Nikolaus Dutsch, Claus Eberth

Forum. It should be indisputable that such a forum of young cinema can in itself not be of international consequence; it has only local significance as a political seminar with the exclusive goal of raising consciousness.« (Letter to the journalist Kurt Joachim Fischer, July 18, 1972.) This riff was the same which had characterized the social conflicts at the end of the sixties and the beginning of the seventies: the mistrust of the older generation in the revolutionary tendencies of the younger. Bauer was able to appeal to the Senate by using attendance statistics: the Competition in 1972 had had 33 000 paying visitors, whereas the Forum only had 8200. To Fischer, Bauer had gone even one step further in stating: »The large majority of the population, which is however a silent majority, has backed the A-Festival since its beginnings.«

The films of the Competition – according to Bauer – also dealt with social themes, but they were »films showing both sides, films in which the commercial character was compensated for by the artistic (and vice-versa), middle class films, and this also means for a middle class audience« (Peter W. Jansen, Frankfurter Rundschau, July 6, 1972). Peter Ustinov's Hammersmith is Out - a movie of the stars, with Richard Burton and Elizabeth Taylor – was not more than a high-strung persiflage: a lunatic, who had escpaed from an insane asylum by making a pact with one of his nurses, maneuvers criminally and becomes a rich and influential man. Marco Ferreri interprets in L'Udienza [The Audience] Kafka's novel »The Castle« – a man wants an audience with the Pope himself, but his attempts are all in vain. Another film with big names was La Vieille fille [The Old Maid] by Jean-Pierre Blanc, a strained comedy with Annie Girardot as a shy thirty-year-old and Philippe Noiret as a greying bachelor who, after some initial complications, find their way to each other. Trivial cinema as well was I racconti di Canterbury [Canterbury Tales], the second part of Pasolini's »Trilogy of Sensuality«, this time based on the tales of Geoffrey Chaucer.

I racconti di Canterbury

Pasolini had enacted eight tales with technical perfection – and with a raw passion for story-telling. »Yet that which puzzles most, is the object to which he devoted so much effort. One could almost believe that Pasolini wants to confront the educated, but in no way emancipated bourgeoisie, which enjoys pornography only on the sly, with the fundamentals of its culture. But by (apparently) rationalizing the pornographic craze, he makes himself one of its commercial advocates«, writes Peter W. Jansen (op. cit.). That Pasolini received the Golden Bear was rationalized by the jury's general perplexitiy in view of the dull program of the Competition: the jury had evidently awarded the Grand Prix to the most internationally famous director.

I racconti di Canterbury: a controversial Golden Bear

Karena Niehoff comments, »Friedrich Luft, an irreproachable judge, who is surely neither an anemic elitist nor a barricade climbing would-be revolutionary, pleads publicly and with anger for the complete abolishment – financially as well – of this Competition which has become so sluggish and senseless. One thing is certain: if we are going to award prizes, then the Forum as a whole – although here too it is true that there is not a pearl in every oyster – deserves, even more clearly than at its première last year, a prize. It is in fact the winner.« (Süddeutsche Zeitung, July 7, 1972.)

There remains an ultimatum which should be mentioned here post scriptum. On June 29th a delegation of German film exporters lodged a complaint with Alfred Bauer and demanded that he arrange that the 1973 IFB be rescheduled for October – a decision which had been made by the assembly of film exporters. The reason given for the rescheduling was – as had always been the case – Cannes, the competitor: it would be easier to invite good films to Berlin in October – or at least such was the claim. However, the decisive element here had rather to do with the promotion of films for export at the Film Fair. There was the hope that with these new dates, one would be able to make the Film Fair more attractive. For the first time –

German film exporters deliver an ultimatum.

International Jury
Eleanor Perry
(USA, president)
Fritz Drobilitsch-Walden
(Austria, vice-president)
Francis Cosne (France)
Rita Tushingham
(Great Britain)
Tinto Brass (Italy)
Yukichi Shinada (Japan)
Julio Coll (Spain)
Hans Hellmut Kirst (FRG)
Herbert Obschernigkat
(FRG)

The Awards of the
International Jury

Feature Films
Grand Prix of the 22nd IFB
Golden Berlin Bear
I RACCONTI DI CANTERBURY
Italy, directed by
Pier Paolo Pasolini

Special Prize of the Jury
Silver Berlin Bear
THE HOSPITAL
USA, directed by
Arthur Miller

Silver Berlin Bear
for the best director
Jean-Pierre Blanc
for LA VIEILLE FILLE
France

Special Prize
for the artistic originality
of his works
Silver Berlin Bear
Peter Ustinov
HAMMERSMITH IS OUT
USA

Silver Berlin Bear
for the best actress
Elizabeth Taylor
in HAMMERSMITH IS OUT
USA

Silver Berlin Bear
for the best actor
Alberto Sordi
in DETENUTO IN ATTESA DI GIUDIZIO
Italy

and with moderate success – under the supervision of the Exhibition, Fair and Congress Association (AMK), the »International Trade Fair for Film, Tele- and Audiovision« (IFTA) had taken place on the fair grounds at the Funkturm. This new fair was an outgrowth of the old Film Fair which had been, up till then, co-organized by the IFB. Ambitiously, one wanted to compete with the Film Market in Cannes. And the German exporters were of the opinion that the Film Festival should see its wishes as secondary to their economic considerations. Once again, a tiresome debate over the dates of the Festival broke out. Whereas Alfred Bauer was quite willing to discuss a rescheduling, the Forum advocated for a continuation in summer – and such was the decision of the advisory board and the board of curators. Bauer had however also put forward another alternative date for the Festival, for he too felt that a rescheduling to October would not bring many advantages. But how about a Film Festival in March or April? Here he could see advantages: »Berlin [would have], then before Cannes, had a better chance of selecting films.« (Minutes of the advisory board, Sept. 19, 1972.) It was to take some time before others were to join Bauer in his considerations. For the time being, one would see each other again next summer.

Congratulations

By Annelies Ruoss and Martin E. Girod

Ever since we discovered the International Forum of Young Cinema in 1972 with one year delay, we have rejoiced at it each year anew. Even though this event has lost the small and family-like character of the early years because of the rising popularity of the Festival in general and has been shoved together with the Berlinale from the relaxed summer-mood into the cold of February, the Forum has maintained two qualities which appear to us to be essential.

Through its specialization on »young« film, which fortunately does not exclude old masters who have held on to their youth, the Forum mediates each year a highly stimulating impression of that which is occupying the most alert minds in the whole world, both at the level of form and at the level of content. In retrospect, it can be determined that the Forum has generally succeeded in avoiding purely fashionable trends and to an amazing extent has presented those works which maintain their value for more than a day.

The other achievement of the Forum, which is not less valuable in our eyes, is that it has made a good portion of the selected films available after each Festival. The showing of culturally valuable films in Basel (and beyond in other cities of German-speaking Switzerland) would scarcely have been possible without the copies from the Forum with their German subtitles.

For both: its yearly insight into the »state of the world« and its friendly cooperation which has always followed, we would like to extend our heartfelt thanks to the organizers of the Forum.

A struggle for money

1973

June 22nd-July 3rd, 1973 (Competition)
June 24th-July 1st, 1973 (Forum)

There had been a fire – a few weeks before the opening of the Film Festival – in an additional wing of the showrooms in the Budapester Straße. Even the floor on which the Cine-Center was to be built had suffered damages. This space could only be partially repaired before the opening. It was necessary to improvise.

Urgently warning letters

Improvisation was needed elsewhere as well. Insufficient funding for the Film Festival also made improvisation mandatory, or to be explicit, costs had to be cut. Both Alfred Bauer and Ulrich Gregor sent urgently warning letters. It was possible to scrape by and hold both the Competition and the Forum on the stagnating budget of 1.2 million marks, but as both agreed, it was difficult to imagine how they would be able to continue on with such a situation. The Film Festival was suffering from under-budgeting: there was too little money to be able to invite special guests, too little to promote the Film Festival for Berlin and on an international scale; the budget for the Forum was even more limited – it was not until February that the board of curators extended the limit and set the budget of the Forum at DM 295 000 (31st meeting, Feb. 26, 1973). And the situation became even more precarious in 1973, as the expected returns did not come in: it had been a very hot summer, and for many Berliners the routes to the beaches at the Wannsee were shorter than to the Film Festival's movie houses. Moreover, inadequate advertising had made itself felt in low attendance; the budget was so tight that it had not even been possible to publish the complete program in the Berlin daily papers. As a result, the total returns only amounted to approximately DM 160 000; DM 140 000 had been brought in by the Competition, the rest by the Forum. These returns were not enough to cover the gaps in the budget.

Financial tight spots

The Festival management was in agreement that the total budget had to be increased. Alfred Bauer formulated the situation for the Competition in retrospect of the

Satyajit Ray with his producer N. Bhattacharya and the actresses Babita and Sandhya Roy

Video-show at the Arsenal

year 1973: »The constant cuts in the budget of the A-Festival on the one hand, and the increase in costs on the other has brought the Berlin A-Festival to the limits of its capacity.« Actually this was an opportune moment to make financial demands on the Bonn Government and the Berlin Senate. With the signing of the Quadripartite Agreement and the Basis of Relations Treaty the »mediating function« of Berlin – especially in cultural affairs – had once again been given emphasis. Yet although the Federal Government and the Senate set much store in the Film Festival, they were not willing to raise the budget accordingly. Bauer stressed in his report that Berlin »needs more than ever to be a supraregional attraction. (...) If – as appears the case at the moment – the Festival were not held back by countercyclical measures to save money, and given little leeway by bureaucratic and purely regional institutions, it would be able to re-establish itself as a Festival having international significance.« (Aug. 30, 1973.) Ulrich Gregor also saw an urgent need for funds: »When the Forum was established three years ago, the total budget was not raised. Instead money designated for other activities was redirected.« (Der Abend, July 20, 1973.)

In their individual estimations, it was only the size of the amounts needed which varied. As a precautionary measure, the board of curators provided an additional DM 100 000 – little more than a drop in a bucket. Bauer argued that even then the amount »would lie DM 130 000 lower than in 1966 (...) not taking inflation into account«. And Ulrich Gregor pointed out that the increase would hardly be sufficient to enable the Forum to maintain the standard of its Info-Sheets, and to top it off, money was lacking to invite guests, for interpreting equipment and for several of the scheduled events. (Report from the 33rd meeting of the board of curators, Nov. 26, 1973.) In addition, Bauer believed that the budget raise should be distributed in a 3 to 1 proportion, in favor of the Competition; there was no way that Ulrich Gregor could agree to such a proposal. The board of curators did not see itself able to endorse more than an increase of DM 100 000, and made as a consequence the following decision for the fiscal budget of 1974: »DM 42 000 would be allotted to the Forum, in consideration of its backlog needs, for equipment for simultaneous translations and to allow for the continuation of its Info-Sheets; DM 54 000 would go to the Competition.« (Minutes of the board of curators, Nov. 26, 1973.) Considering inflation, these amounts were not even a Solomonic judgment; and in comparison to the markedly higher budgets of the rival festivals in Cannes and particularly Venice, the International Film Festival Berlin was left to come in last.

Some of the critics felt that there had finally been a turn of the tide: several of the films of the Competition could be rated »worthy of discussion«, and in the program of the Forum, a decline in purely politically committed films was registered. »In this sphere as well, attempts can be found which cautiously try to discover something completely new in film: fellow man, beauty, personal fears and maybe even something called ›society‹ – but no longer so exclusively as seen through Karl Marx' eyes.« (Die Welt, June 29, 1973.) Friedrich Luft was one to walk the line. Although he was critically faithful to the Competition in the Zoo-Palast, he did not conceal his sympathy for the films of the Forum.

Hors concours in the Competition program, Robert Aldrich presented his new film: EMPEROR OF THE NORTH – showing the struggle of two men, a train engineman and a hobo against the background of the Depression in Amercia. It was an action film with Lee Marvin and Ernest Borgnine, who were also the most greatly admired stars of the Film Festival. André Cayatte and leading actress Annie Girardot had come to Berlin to present IL N'Y A PAS DE FUMÉE SANS FEU (»Where There's Smoke«), Elio Petri and Ugo Tognazzi were the director and star respectively of the Italian entry in the Competition LA PROPRIETÀ NON È PIÙ UN FURTO [Property is No Longer a Theft]. Claude Chabrol's LES NOCES ROUGES (»Wedding in Blood«) received the best reviews: the film was about a criminal case set in the French countryside, making reference to the political situation in France, which was also the reason why the film had not received permission to be released until after the 1973 elections for Parliament. The Japanese entry by Eiichi Yamamoto, KNASHIMINO BELLADONNA [Belladonna], put off some of its viewers. Many had allowed themselves to be mislead by the fact that it was an animated film and had looked much forward to a »Japanese Disney«. Some had even brought their kids along. Friedrich Luft reports: »The young dears were in for quite a shock. (...) Through song and pictures, a hymn praising a totally emancipated sexuality is sung. (...) Lust and pleasure are rampant here. Horniness displays itself again and again. (...) The movie-goer trembles. He is repulsed. He is fascinated. He learns what animated pictures can be (my, when they let loose!). A cartoon can – if left be – do everything, and at that, each time round something quite to the contrary.« (Die Welt, June 29, 1973). Many got up and left the Zoo-Palast; yet it was not enough to cause a real scandal. Times had truly changed.

LES NOCES ROUGES
»This film is like velvet, blood, sirup and silk. It is a delectable colportage – served on a silver platter. Chabrol has effortlessly given this blatantly entertaining and nerve-racking film a quality of art. This revolutionary of form returns to the commercial cinema of cheap entertainment, triumphantly, his head carried high.«
Friedrich Luft in: Die Welt, June 29, 1973

A Golden Bear for Satyajit Ray

The Grand Prix of the Festival, the Golden Berlin Bear, went to the Indian film ASHANI SANKET [Distant Thunder] by Satyajit Ray: the film tells of a teacher and a doctor who set up a school in a village. War breaks out, a famine ensues. Order in the village disintegrates, social and moral categories fail. All is determined by absolute neediness. The fight for survival begins. The film is set during the war and famine in Bengal in 1942/43. Despite the uncompromising portrayal of suffering, death, and the insanity of a man-made catastrophy, Ray keeps distance: pictures of untouched nature and – the film's main motif – shots of butterflies that do not fly. It is an elegiac rather than a plaintive film.

DUEL by Steven Spielberg (hors concours in the program of the Competition): Dennis Weaver

Le Grand blond avec une chaussure noire: Pierre Richard, Mireille Darc

The program of the International Forum of Young Cinema had become more comprehensive. A pluralism could be felt in the selection of films: there were films from Africa and Latin America, from Japan, the USA and Europe; new points of emphasis were a videoprogram shown mornings at the Arsenal movie house and a program of new German films, which had been selected specially for foreign viewers and were run at the late shows at the Arsenal as well. And this pluralism was also evident along thematic lines: Chris. Marker's and Alain Resnais' Les Statues meurent aussi, a documentary about the colonial exploitation of African culture - which had been prohibited by the censors in Cannes in May, 1953 after its première there - correlated to films from Africa; Peter Lilienthal's La Victoria was the link to films from Latin America; other films dealt with the rise of fascism in their own countries - in Japan, Greece and Italy. Georges qui? [Georges Who?] by Michèle Rosier and Year of the Woman by Sandra Hochman were both - in their own way - concerned with women's liberation. Three films from France, however, were the focal point of the program. Jean Eustache's La Maman et la putain (»The Mother and the Whore«), »a film of Proustian dimensions«, had won the Grand Prix in Cannes: »The story tells of a triangular relationship between a young man who spends his time at the cafés on the Saint-Germain-des-Prés reading Proust's ›Remembrance of Things Past‹, a somewhat older woman with whom he lives, and a young nurse who reminds him of his ex-girlfriend. (...) The film is comic and sad, tender and direct. The story flows, begins to falter and widens out like a pond. Love is a last resort here, sex is a weapon to fight the times.« (Michael Stone, Deutsche Zeitung/Christ und Welt, July 6, 1973.) And then there was Out One Spectre by Jacques Rivette, which after a single showing in its original twelve hour form, was shown in a »short« four-and-one-half hour version. It is a film having no continuity of events or episodes; it sidetracks in a labyrinth-like, dramatically entangled play which has a beginning that does not end - »the spectrum of performances and free-improvisation, fixed conceptions and

Il n'y a pas de fumée sans feu: Annie Girardot

Out One Spectre: Jean-Pierre Léaud

Year of the Woman

spontaneous ideas is given a range which Rivette finds worth striving for in order to diagram the relationships of a number of individuals to each other, their encounters, dialogues, and events which are determined primarily by coincidence and a few variables, which in turn merely create more of the ›coincidental‹.« (Christa Maerker, Die Weltwoche, July 7, 1973.) And lastly, there was also Tout va bien (»Just Great«) by Jean-Luc Godard and Jean-Pierre Gorin with Yves Montand and Jane Fonda: a political film in which not only politics are discussed, the bourgeoisie and communism, but which is also politically composed - each movement of the camera marks a viewpoint, and makes reference to the relationship between production and consumption.

The positions found in the French films entered in the Competition, as well as those shown in the Forum were typical of those found in the films of 1973. Godard's and Gorin's polemically attacking film was juxtaposed in the Competition by André Cayatte's politically biased and entertaining film, just as Rivette's essay-like film was countered by Yves Robert's comedy Le Grand blond avec une chaussure noire (»The Tall Blond Man with One Black Shoe«), an endearingly witty persiflage about the life of a secret agent, which was in fact found so amusing, that it won a Silver Bear. And taking a monolithic position in between was the radical film La Maman et la putain - both the epitome of the »Nouvelle Vague« and its culmination.

The Competition awarded prizes; the Forum received one: the Berlin Art Prize in the field of »film, radio and television« for 1973. The jury justified its decision in the following statement: »The International Forum of Young Cinema has shown itself to be a true alternative to the official Berlin Film Festival with its damaged conception of itself. The prize has been awarded in honor of the collective efforts of each member of its team.«

A courageous festival

By Wilhelm and Birgit Hein

The International Forum of Young Cinema is the best-known and most important festival in the world for artistically demanding films.

That is not only our personal opinion; in 1987, for example, at the première of a ›young‹ film in Calcutta, a critic stated: »One sees already, that the film is made for the International Forum.«

Our own history is closely connected to that of the Forum. In 1973 we received the first invitation. This signified, finally, official recognition of our work. Ten years later it was of even much greater significance for us to be represented at the International Forum with Love stinks, *because the point was no longer merely to receive recognition for our work, but the existential struggle against steadily increasing censorship.*

No other festival dared to show Love stinks *and* Verbotene Bilder *[Forbidden Pictures]. By being presented in the Forum, both of these films were protected against defamation.*

For us the Forum is not only the most important and best-known festival, but also the most courageous one.

International Jury
David Robinson
(Great Britain, president)
Freddy Buache (Switzerland, vice-president)
Hiram Garcia Borja
(Mexico)
Eberhard Hauff (FRG)
Harish Khanna (India)
Paul Moor (USA)
Walter Müller-Bringmann
(FRG)
René Thévenet (France)
Paolo Valmarana (Italy)

The Awards of the International Jury

Feature Films
Grand Prix of the 23rd IFB
Golden Berlin Bear
Ashani sanket
India, directed by
Satyajit Ray

Special Prize of the Jury
Silver Berlin Bear
Il n'y pas de fumée sans feu
France, directed by
André Cayatte

Silver Berlin Bear
Los siete locos
Argentina, directed by
Leopoldo Torre Nilsson

Silver Berlin Bear
Le Grand blond avec une chaussure noire
France, directed by
Yves Robert

Silver Berlin Bear
Die Sachverständigen
FRG, directed by
Norbert Kückelmann

Silver Berlin Bear
Toda nudez sera castigada
Brazil, directed by
Arnaldo Jabor

Silver Berlin Bear
The 14
Great Britain, directed by
David Hemmings

FONTANE EFFI BRIEST: Wolfgang Schenck, Hanna Schygulla, Andrea Schober

The ice is broken

1974

June 21st-July 2nd, 1974
(Competition)
June 23rd-July 1st, 1974
(Forum)

The film is a love story about Fyodor, a farmer, and Stepanida, a hired hand. It is the time of the first Soviet collective farms, and some farmers have a difficult time joining up. Stepanida knows which path she wants to take, and Fyodor also comes to realize in which direction their mutual future lies. S TOBOI I BEZ TEBYA is the first work of the actor Rodion Nakhapetov. And although hors concours, it is the first Soviet film to be shown at the International Film Festival. The title of this film, »With You and Without You« can be read as a commentary to the long controversy which had ensued over the participation of films from socialist nations.

It had taken 24 years for one of the countries with the greatest of traditions in film in the world to be able to present itself at one of the most significant festivals in the world. Up until this time, there had been only three years in which a socialist nation – other than Yugoslavia – had participated: in 1969 Rumania and Czechoslovakia had taken part in the Film Fair and sent a delegation of observers; 1972 was the first year in which delegates from the USSR, Czechoslovakia and East Germany, as well as Poland took part; in 1973 Rumania presented short films at the Film Fair and the USSR and Czechoslovakia sent observers.

A study on politics and cultural affairs in East and West

The history of the abstinence of the socialist nations from the »Berlinale« can be seen as a study on politics and culture; it is an extensive chapter on the tension between East and West, a tragic comedy of the cold war, a play with set roles and alternating protagonists.

For the first three years after the founding of the Film Festival nothing whatsever happened. It appears as if no one at this time was even thinking about a participation of the Soviet Union in the Film Festival – neither on this side of the iron curtain, nor on the other. And such was the case, even though it was the participation of the Soviet Union which was the key to the participation of other socialist nations. The only inquiries made were by German companies which had been commissioned to find out if the Berlin authorities were interested in films from »Eastern bloc states« – as they were called in the fifties and sixties. Wishes of this nature were persistently declined.

A letter from the Sovexportfilm

In December 1955, the Sovexportfilm, representative of Soviet cinema in the GDR, caused quite some havoc in the Berlin Department of Education by asking for a copy of the statutes of the 6th International Film Festival (letter, Dec. 12, 1955). The recent establishment of diplomatic relations between the Federal Republic of Germany and the USSR made it more difficult to give the customary categorical refusal. As a result, the Senator for Education at this time, Professor Joachim Tiburtius, turned to the Office of Foreign Affairs in Bonn. The responsible authority, Ministerial Assistant Secretary Dr. Trützschler von Falkenstein from the Section for Cultural Affairs, referred to the matter »as at this point in the affair it was not formally a question of foreign policy (...)« to the Office of the Chancellor (letter, Feb. 6, 1956, AZ 605/452 – 15E/ 01855/56II). The Office advised Bauer to send the following response: »Independently of the question of whether the Sovexportfilm intends to participate in the 6th International Film Festival in Berlin or whether other factors are involved, I herewith enclose a copy of the requested guidelines.« (Cited from a note written by Senior Executive Officer Dr. Herbert Antoine, Department of Education, Feb. 10, 1956.) So that no doubts could arise as to the firmness felt in this basic issue, the Berlin Senate formulated the following decree (No. 1662/56) on March 5th 1956,

Jules Dassin,
Melina Mercouri,
Mikis Theodorakis

which states inequivocally, »The Senate hereby notes that the ›advisory board of the International Film Festival in Berlin‹ has decided not to request any films from Eastern bloc states.«

At the 3rd meeting of the advisory board on March 23rd 1956, a total of 26 persons took part. At this meeting, the participation of the Soviet Union and other socialist nations was discussed. »The Senator«, according to the minutes of the agenda, »once more wanted to know if the advisory board of the Film Festival had appealed for a change in the position taken (by the Berlin Senate and the Federal Government – to not send out an invitation). As this was not the case, all earlier decrees were to be seen as having received explicit confirmation.«

The Federal Government's behaviour is restrictive, the Berlin Senate's shows initiative.

Two attitudes become evident here which are characteristic of the course of events in the years to follow. For one, the restrictive attitude of the Federal Government in the point at hand; and for the other, the not yet clearly articulated, but later stubbornly pursued interest of the Berlin Section for Cultural Affairs (and of the director of the IFB) to include film productions from Eastern bloc countries. At the same time it can be seen that the initiative for easing tension, even if it had come via roundabout routes, had its roots in the East. This was, however, not to remain the case. East and West switched roles at a later date.

For the time being though, such was the status quo. A year later, a renewed inquiry was addressed to the Section of Cultural Affairs in the Office of Foreign Affairs by the Senator of Education. He wanted to know if – in light of the fact that the Federal Republic of Germany and the Soviet Union now maintained diplomatic relations – there would be a continued adherence to the policy of not inviting the Soviet Union (letter, April 4, 1957). Professor Tiburtius' letter was endorsed by a corresponding resolution made by the advisory board (2nd meeting, March 29, 1957).

Senator Tiburtius and the Office of Foreign Affairs

The response of the Office of Foreign Affairs – as it applies to the role of the IFB in these early years – is as plain as it is telling. After consultations »with other in-

Sohrab Shahid Saless

Karena Niehoff,
Alfred Bauer

Forum press conference for MADE IN GERMANY UND USA: Rudolf Thome, Wilhelm Roth

terested authorities«, the conclusion had been drawn »that the Office of Foreign Affairs, as well as all other government ministries involved, regard the main purpose of the Berlin Film Festival to be in a documentation of the free world vis à vis the East. Consequently, the Office of Foreign Affairs does not find it appropriate to alter the original provisions of the Film Festival by inviting the Soviet Union. Instead, it is of the opinion that the Film Festival will only be able to fulfill its actual purpose by remaining faithful to its original tenets, which in turn means restricting the participants to the nations of the free world. The events of the recent past give no reason to revise this position.« (Letter, May 6, 1957, AZ 605/452 - 15E/4269/57.) This closing remark definitely refers to the uprisings in Hungary and the political thaw in Poland in 1956. This self-imposed restriction, limiting participation to the »free world«, and mentioned in this correspondence, was no secret. Up until 1953, item 3 of the IFB guidelines read to the following effect: »The Film Festival shall document the further development of cinematographic art in all democratic nations.« And Alfred Bauer wrote in his final report to the first Film Festival, in complete agreement to the guidelines, that the IFB »represented a peaceful demonstration of the Western cultural world through the entertaining medium of film«.

Nevertheless, the advisory board was gradually becoming convinced - particularly its Social Democratic members - that they could no longer go along with the attitude taken by the Office of Foreign Affairs. The Senator himself was also not one to let things be. Five months later, on October 20th 1957, his advisor in film-affairs, Senior Executive Officer Dr. Herbert Antoine, met in Bonn with Senior Executive Officer Dr. Simon from the Ministry of the Interior and spokesman of the Section Film in the Office of Foreign Affairs, Dr. Rowas, and urged for a rapid reconsideration of these matters. At the beginning of December, Dr. Simon recommended that Antoine first seek a decision from the Berlin Senate and then to submit this decision to the Office of Foreign Affairs. Antoine had Bauer equip him with additional arguments and press commentaries in favor of a participation of the Soviet Union in the Film Festival. (For example, Friedrich Luft, posed the question in »Die Welt« on June 25, 1957, of »whether the extraordinary and interesting intermediate position which the city has gained as a result of damned world politics, should not be cunningly used to open up a gate to the East«.) In a senatorial decree (No. 4018/58) all arguments converged in support of contributions from socialist nations: both of the other two international film events in the Federal Republic of Germany, the Mannheim Festival of Documentary Films, and the West German Festival of Short Films in Oberhausen were officially allowed to show Soviet films – a similar policy would therefore be logical; the recently received recognition of the »Berlinale« as an »A-festival« brought an obligation of inviting the USSR with it; a continued refusal would automatically result in upgrading the rival festival in Karlovy Vary (or the planned festival in Leningard); and lastly, it was the general policy of the Office of Foreign Affairs (responsible for sending out invitations to the IFB at this time) to address all nations which maintained diplomatic relations with the Federal Republic – so why should the Soviet Union remain the exception?

The Berlin Senate had already rejected two such motions, as can be read in the decisions of the Senate, No. 1662/56 from March 5th 1956 and No. 1832/56 from April 12th 1956; yet this time it decided differently: »It is recommended that the Office of Foreign Affairs invite the Union of Soviet Socialist Republics to participate in the 8th International Film Festival 1958. An inlcusion of Poland should also be considered.« (Senatorial decree, No. 4018/58, Jan. 7, 1958.)

A turn in the tide and a mishap

How had it come to this courageous and surprising decision? Attitudes in the Senate on this issue had certainly changed. More over, the decree had in substance already received the okay from Bonn, or at least the impulse for this procedure – first a decision by the Berlin Senate, then one from the Office of Foreign Affairs – had come from Bonn itself. Shortly before the 4th meeting of the advisory board on December 13th 1957, a small circle met at the Ratskeller of the City Hall in Schöneberg; present were Tiburtius, Antoine and Bauer, as well as Messieurs Simon from the Ministry of the Interior, Betz from the Federal Press and Information Services Office and Schwarz from the Export Union of the German film industry. They quickly came to an agreement: an invitation to the Soviet Union should not become a topic of discussion on the advisory board, for tactical reasons – if possible, a public discussion of this touchy matter was to be avoided. And when the uninitiated Senatorial Supervisor Wallner-Basté passed a note concerning this question to Antoine at the next advisory board meeting, it was ignored. In this manner, a possible obstacle en route to a senatorial decision was to be circumvented; and the Senate was now able to presume that it would not come into serious conflict with the Office of Foreign Affairs on this item.

And yet, as could be expected, things did not proceed so smoothly. One mishap even led to the Senator of Education having to apologize to the Minister of Foreign Affairs, Dr. Heinrich von Brentano. Before the decision of the Senate could be made available to the Office of Foreign Affairs, as had been agreed upon, there was a leak to the press; it had been forgotten to put a news ban on the decision. As a result, the outcome of this debate had gone the usual channels – to the public. Especially awkward was that the arguments involved in this decision were also released; as a consequence, exactly that occured which had not been intended: a public discussion of this issue.

Professor Tiburtius apologized to the Minister of Foreign Affairs von Brentano for this »formal slip« (letter, Feb. 1, 1958), but there were hard-feelings. Just the same, at the meeting of the Finance Cabinet in Bonn on February 5th 1958 and one day later at a meeting of the complete Cabinet, it was decided to ask the Soviet Union to take part in the 8th International Film Festival; the participation of Poland, on the other hand, was not deemed opportune at this point. The SPD faction in the Bundestag supported this decision by making the following motion: »The Bundestag should endorse the following resolution: In accordance to the agreement made with the Berlin Senate, the Federal Government is requested to present the Soviet Union with an invitation as soon as possible for the 8th International Film Festival from June 27th to July 8th.« (Document of the Bundestag, No. 271, March 11, 1958.)

The first invitation to the USSR

At long last the time had come: on April 14th 1958, the German ambassador presented the Ministry of Foreign Affairs in Moscow with a note of invitation. Never before had a participation of the Soviet Union in the Film Festival Berlin been so near.

For the next two months, a reaction from Moscow was awaited, but to no avail. It came to rumors: the German embassy had not handed over the invitation; East Germany was against the invitation and had intervened. Finally on June 11th, a good week before the opening of the Festival, the spokesman for the Sovexportfilm in West Berlin, Sergei Gambaroff, notified the director of the Film Festival, that the Soviet Union would not take part in the Festival. He spoke of an »error in form«, and gave no further explanations. Furthermore, he declared that there would be an announcement made by TASS at the beginning of the Festival. A year earlier, TASS had sharply criticized the absence of an invitation; this time the news agency did not comment on the matter at all. The promised announcement was not published and no further statements came from Moscow. The invitation, with which the West German and West Berlin authorities, as well as the public, had been preoccupied for months – no, for years – proved inconsequential. Once again, the International Film Festival Berlin took place without the participation of the Soviets and other socialist nations.

Rejection

And such remained the situation for the next years to come. In 1959, as in the year before, no explanation was given for declining the invitation. It was in 1960 that the Soviet Union finally offered an argument which from then on would dominate the question of participation. The invitation could not be accepted, according to a note from the Soviet Ministry of Foreign Affairs dated January 27th 1960, because West Berlin had never been a part of the national territory of the Federal Republic of Germany, and could neither be administered by the West German authorities, nor did it lie in their jurisdiction.

In response, the Office of Foreign Affairs prepared a note, which was sent on March 28th to the West German embassy for deliverance to the Soviet Ministry of Foreign Affairs. It shall be quoted in full here, as it is of significance for the understanding of the basic positions involved:

A note from the Office of Foreign Affairs

»The Federal Government has noted with astonishment and indignation the contents of the statement dated January 19th 1960 from the Ministry of Foreign Affairs, in which the invitation of the Federal Government and the Berlin Senate for a participation in the 10th International Film Festival in Berlin is rejected and returned. The explanation given herein by the Ministry of Foreign Affairs cannot be recognized by the Federal Government as applicable. The legitimation of the Federal Govern-

Made in Germany und USA: Eberhard Klasse, Karin Thome

ment to send out invitations to the annual International Film Festival in Berlin in collaboration with the Berlin Senate has never before been questioned by any nation. In 1959, 48 nations, as well as representatives of the United Nations, took part in the Berlin Film Festival - from which can be inferred that the Berlin Film Festival is of world-wide interest. The Federal Government is all the more astonished, as the Soviet government confirmed the receipt of similar invitations in both 1958 and 1959, in the notes of June 18th 1958 and April 18th 1959 respectively, and the legitimacy of these invitations was in no way questioned. In these notes, the Soviet government informed the Federal Government that it could not accept an invitation, because the responsible Soviet organizations had no intention of participating in these events in Berlin. The Federal Government knows of no circumstance which could have now prompted the Soviet government - contrary to their treatment of the invitations in 1958 and 1959 - to totally reject the invitation of the Federal Government for participation in the International Film Festival in Berlin. Under the circumstances, the Federal Government regrets sincerely that the Soviet government - whose statements normally attribute a particularly great significance to German-Soviet relations in cultural matters - has rejected, in such an unusual form and for such unjustifiable reasons, a participation of the Soviet Union in this year's Berlin Film Festival.«

Diplomacy

Insight can be gained into this diplomatic paper by noting that the Office of Foreign Affairs had in no way made reference to the legal standpoint of the Federal Government; it was evidently desirable to put off a discussion of the status of West Berlin until the approaching East/West conference. Just the same, a correspondence had begun, in which each side repeated its own interpretation of the Berlin-issue.

Once again, the Senator for Education wanted to set things in motion, this time with a telex. On April 6th 1961, he asked - via the Berlin Senator for Federal Affairs (at this time Dr. Günter Klein) - the Federal Office of Foreign Affairs to send the

L'HORLOGER DE SAINT-PAUL (»The Clockmaker«): Jean Rochefort, Philippe Noiret

Soviet film industry an invitation immediately. Yet the telex was not forwarded; instead, a meeting took place between a spokesman for the Senator for Federal Affairs and a representative of the Office of Foreign Affairs. They made it perfectly clear that, as matters stood, the Office of Foreign Affairs would not send any more invitations to the Soviet Union. With this declaration, things had come full circle.

It was not until two years later that there was a change in the tide. Once again, it was Senator Tiburtius – he had never given up on the matter – who started a new initiative. On December 5th 1962, he informed the Office of the Senate that he intended in the next session of the Senate to force a vote on the question of an invitation of the Soviet Union and other socialist states for the 13th IFB in 1963. This vote took place on December 11th. The Senate decided to authorize the Senator for Federal Affairs to clarify the matter with the Office of Foreign Affairs. (Senatorial decree No. 4248/62). It is worth noting that in this decree both Poland and Hungary were included.

The officials in Bonn remained, however, unyielding. The Senator for Federal Affairs was forced to inform Tiburtius that the Office of Foreign Affairs »had decided against inviting the USSR, Poland and Hungary to participate in the International Film Festival Berlin 1963« (telex to Tiburtius, Jan. 30, 1963). This response was so resolute that Tiburtius gave up all further efforts. And it was exactly at this point that something very remarkable occured. In answer to an inquiry made by Dr. Wolkwitz from the Department of Federal Affairs (Feb. 8, 1963), Dr. Rowas answered »that the Office of Foreign Affairs is at present still considering the possibility of a participation of the Soviet Union, Poland and Hungary in the Film Festival in Berlin« (Feb. 21, 1963). He mentioned »new considerations« which had come up and promised a binding answer soon. The tone here was quite in contrast to the harsh tone used up till then. And in fact: on March 26th 1963, a note arrived at the Office of the Senator for Federal Affairs from the Office of Foreign Affairs, which not only confirmed the intention of inviting the Soviet Union, but even announced that an invitiation had already been made; invitations to Poland and Hungary would not be sent – policy was to remain unaltered here.

Once again, it was the Soviet Union's move; and it repeated its earlier statement. No agreement could be reached; the West renewed its efforts and sent new invitations; the Soviet Union adhered to its position that the political status of West Berlin did not allow for participation – which in turn blocked contributions from other socialist nations. The political climate left the diplomats little leeway.

Until the early seventies the situation did not change. There were invitations, refusals or just plain silence. Some informal talks did, however, take place. In 1967, for example, Bauer met with the Soviet Ambassador Pyotr Abrassimov in Cannes for an informal talk, at which Bauer was told »that so long as the GDR is not officially recognized, it will not be possible to establish normal relations between the Federal Republic of Germany or West Berlin, and the Soviet Union, or in turn to participate in the Festival« (Bauer in a letter to Senatorial Director Harald Ingensand, May 2, 1967).

Brandt's cabinet eases tension.

And then new trends in politics set things in motion, and contacts on a cultural level become lively. Brandt's cabinet brings about an easing of tensions between East and West. In August 1970, the »Treaty between the USSR and the FRG« is signed, in December 1970, the »Treaty between Poland and the FRG«; with these a normalization of relations with the Soviet Union and Poland evolves. On May 17th 1972 the Bundestag ratifies these treaties with the Eastern bloc states; a year later, on June 21st 1973, the Basis of Relations Treaty between the Federal Republic of Germany and East Germany comes into effect – possible in light of the Quadripartite Agreement on Berlin signed on June 3rd 1972. Such is the political context in which negotiations are resumed for the participation of socialist nations in the Berlin Film Festival. And these talks finally take on substance after the signing of the German-Soviet Cultural Agreement on May 19th 1973. In Article 7 this agreement regulates collaboration in the field of film: »The contracting parties shall encourage cooperation in the field of film. For this purpose, the organization of film shows and premières, the exchange of feature, documentary and newsreel films, co-production of feature and documentary films, as well as a reciprocated participation in international film festivals shall be promoted (...).« And in Article 16 of this same paper, provision is made for the inclusion of West Berlin.

Alfred Bauer meets the Soviet ambassador to West Germany at the film festival in Cannes.

As soon as the treaties with the Eastern bloc were signed, hopes for the participation of the Soviet Union in the Film Festival rekindled. Bauer wrote Senator Stein (May 23, 1972), that he had once again met with Abrassimov and that he – after the acceptance of the treaties by the Bundestag – »no longer had any objections (...) to Soviet films taking part in the events in Berlin«. Bauer also held talks with Hungarian officials. Yet all these hopes were premature. On June 14th, Bauer had to inform Stein that the Soviet Union would not send any films to Berlin, »for technical reasons« and »because the period of time between the signing of the Quadripartite Agreeement and the Berlin Film Festival was too short to be able to prepare proper participation«. Bauer was told to wait until 1973. In August 1972 he met several times with representatives of Czechoslovakia, Poland, Bulgaria and the GDR – informally,

Variations in Festival policy: an invitation for the Defa?

at the festival in Karlovy Vary. Yet the attempt of the Senate, prompted by Bauer, to allow for the participation of the Defa – in connection with the signing of the Basis of Relation Treaty between East and West Germany – was unsuccessful.

In 1973, there was renewed irritation. A letter from Bauer containing an invitation to the »Berlinale« and the guidelines of the Festival was returned by the Soviet embassy in Bonn without comment – except that item 2 of the guidelines was encircled. The conclusion made was that the Soviets found the Berlin-Festivals-Ltd. as sponsor and organizer objectionable. This incident took place in February. In May the German-Soviet Cultural Agreement was signed. And yet even then not all difficulties had been resolved. The Soviet Consulate General protested to a letter Bauer had written – on advice of the Ministry of Finances and the Office of Foreign Affairs – in which he invited the Soviet Union »in consent with the Federal Government of Germany and the Berlin Senate« to participate in the »Berlinale« (June 12, 1973). Once again there was hectic activity behind the scenes, until finally the Soviet Consul Kossobrodov sought out Alfred Bauer on June 25th and announced »that his side found the sending out of a new invitation using invitational forms adapted from the Quadripartite Agreement a form of bribery. The managing director of the Festivals-Ltd., Dr. Eckhardt, had promised to hold talks – in advance of a participation of the Soviet Union – on transforming the Festivals-Ltd. (in order to alter the role of the Federal Government)«. (Cited from a letter to the Office of the Senate, June 25, 1973.)

The German-Soviet Cultural Agreement

At long last, a true cause of reservations on the part of the Soviets had been revealed. It took three more rounds of talks to dispel these reservations. The Soviet Consul General Zharkov and his Vice Consul Nikotin met three times with Senate Director Dr. Herz and Government Director Dr. Schröder: on February 25th, on March 6th, and on March 21st 1974. Objections to the Federal Film Prize – awarded during the Film Festival, to a reception of the Federal President, and to the structure of the Festivals-Ltd. (in particular to the presence of representatives of the Federal Government) had to be clarified. Herz and Schröder were quite persuasive – and effective. On June 3rd 1974, Whitmonday, Alfred Bauer received a call from Nikotin, who informed him that the USSR would participate in the »Berlinale« with one film hors concours and with a delegation of observers. Two days later, Mayor Klaus Schütz released a statement: »I am pleased to announce that the Soviet Union will for the first time take part in the Berlin Film Festival. Herewith, the Soviet Union adheres in letter and spirit to both the German-Soviet Cultural Agreement of May 1973, and the Quadripartite Agreement as they pertain to Berlin.« The ice was broken.

Final questions of detail

The Soviet Union consents to participation in the International Film Festival.

Although the participation of the Soviet Union was greeted warmly, the first Soviet film was received rather coolly. Typical was Friedrich Luft's reaction: he called Nakhapetov's film a »socialist-realistic bonbon film« (Die Welt, July 4, 1974). A year earlier the Americans had noticeably held back – they had entered no big productions in the Competition. Festival guests and reviewers conjectured that the Americans feared the at times rigorous Festival reviews and their detrimental effect on box office returns. But now with the participation of the Soviet Union in the »Berlinale«, it was felt certain that prestigious US films would once again be offered to the Festival.

It was a Film Festival which gave rise to new hopes. »It was a quite homogenous Festival« as Peter W. Jansen put it in the »Frankfurter Rundschau«: »The most noticeable development is that the best films of the official program are this time closer in theme to the works shown in this fourth year of the Forum's program: in these films – clad as historical films, comedies, or parables – concrete matters are dealt with more or less directly, especially those particular circumstances of social reality in which an individual must exist.« (July 4, 1974.)

Tabejade Bijan: Zadour Bonyadi (Competition)

Two films by Sohrab Shadid Saless

The thematic proximity noted in the films of the Competition and the Forum could be seen most clearly in two films by the Persian director Sohrab Shahid Saless. His debut film, Yek ettefaghe sadeh [A Simple Event] was run in the Forum, Tabejade Bijan [Still Life] in the Competition. The former tells of a schoolboy, of his daily routines and of the death of his mother; the latter tells of an old gatekeeper and the drudgery of his life. They are both stories of simple people, whose lives are ruled by monotony: they are frugal and almost wordless, and in contrast the landscape shots are of an alluring yet also unsettling calmness. »This perspective would be quite depressing and paralyzing in its complete fatalism, if it were not for the fact that the immense beauty of these films nourishes at the same time new hope, of course, it must be asked here, hope for what?« (Peter W. Jansen, Frankfurter Rundschau, July 4, 1974.)

The Forum makes a go for a Hungarian film.

Another political issue must be mentioned here post scriptum. After the Forum had heard that the Soviets would enter a film, it made efforts to attain the Hungarian film Harmadik nekifutas [The Third Start] by Péter Bascó. Budapest asked for two days to think over the matter. At the same time the organizers of the Forum negotiated with the Berlin Festivals-Ltd. as to the possiblity of extending the Forum for one more day, so as to have time to show the Hungarian film. The Forum received the extension, from Budapest the okay was given. Yet less than a week later, a telegram arrived from the Hungarians withdrawing the film. No explanations were given. Checking for further particulars by phone brought no results. In his final report for the Forum, Ulrich Gregor speculated »that the very enthusiastic articles in the Berlin press commenting on the participation of Hungary, as the second Eastern bloc state in the IFB (heralding in particular the ›liberality‹ of the Hungarian cultural policy), played a role in the withdrawal of the original consent«.

Nevertheless, there is no doubt; the 24th International Film Festival was a success. Notwithstanding that the prize winner was quite a surprise to all: The Appren-

Yek ettefaghe sadeh:
Ane Mohamad Tarikhi
(Forum)

ticeship of Duddy Kravitz by Ted Kotcheff from Canada. It had been expected that the Golden Berlin Bear would go to Rainer Werner Fassbinder's Fontane Effi Briest (»Effi Briest«). There was talk of the blindness of the jurors; it seemed incomprehensible that Fassbinder's film had been left out. And as is so often true in such situations, information leaked out about the procedure leading up to the decision. One of the German jurors was said to have uttered that although he personally liked Fassbinder's film, the regulations stated that a film could only be awarded a prize if it appealed to a wide audience - and he had had his doubts.

No comment is necessary here. It could not be undone.

An act of good will

By Mikhail Shkalikov

Forty years is a good long time for a festival. So many things can happen in that period, that such a risky undertaking as an international film festival can either achieve perfection or fail miserably, despite the efforts of the organizers.

My impression (I use this expression to underline the deeply personal character of my judgement, which does not presume to claim infallibility) is that the West Berlin Festival spent the first 25 years of its existence in well-travelled tracks. It did its job conscientiously. Without flops, but also without particular distinction. This is not to say that its founder, Alfred Bauer, was without ambition or appropriate organizational abilities. On the contrary: he had a feel for the new and an understanding of the complexities of the festival mechanism, and he naturally aspired to make this Festival a really special event of world culture. Yet, although the West Berlin Festival labelled itself »international«, it remained until 1975 rather a local event: the socialist countries did not take part and the Americans were rather cool and reserved, the French had Cannes, the Italians Venice. Apparently Alfred Bauer sensed this, since his persistence finally achieved the participation of Soviet films. However, this question was decided in those days less on cultural than on political levels.

In June 1972, the Quadripartite Agreement on West Berlin went into effect. The central provision of this agreement specifies that the Western Sectors of Berlin »as previously, are not a part of the Federal Republic of Germany and also in the future cannot be administered by her«. Participation of Soviet films in the West Berlin Film Festival was debated under this aspect. The Soviet side insisted on strict adherence to all agreements concerning the status of West Berlin. Apparently the Senate of this city was inclined to adhere to the provisions of the Quadripartite Agreement with respect to the Festival.

However - as is often the case in practice - the first steps toward such a result were taken slowly and with great caution. The opposition accused the government of the FRG and the West Berlin city administration of giving in to the Soviets. At that time, numerous West Berlin and West German press organizations asserted that the Soviet Union wanted to isolate West Berlin from international cultural contact. Of course, the press is free to develop fantastic speculations - prognoses are, after all, part of its business. But in my opinion the Soviet side did everything possible so that the Quadripartite Agreement could create a better political climate around West Berlin and lay the basis for participation of Soviet films in the Festival.

It is also appropriate to recall the not unimportant circumstance, that the »old world«, having grown tired of tension, was moving slowly but surely toward Helsinki, where in August 1975, the Final Act of the Conference on Security and Cooperation in Europe was signed. In this connection I will allow myself to qualify the participation of Soviet films in the 25th International Film Festival in West Berlin as a notable victory of the good sense and good will of all who were involved in finding a solution to this problem.

Since then, fifteen years have gone by. Today the West Berlin Film Festival is recognized and admired by experts and critics from most countries. I hope that this is not a unanimity with ulterior motives but a just tribute to the efforts of this Festival to support international cinematic cooperation. I have the impression that this Festival not only has its »patented« audience, but also a normal audience »from the street«, who find here what they need. And when one considers the precision with which this Festival program is

International Jury
Rodolfo Kuhn (Argentina, president)
Margaret Hinxman (Great Britain, vice president)
Pietro Bianchi (Italy)
Gérard Ducaux-Rupp (France)
Kurt Heinz (FRG)
Akira Iwasaki (Japan)
Arthur Knight (USA)
Manfred Purzer (FRG)
Piet Ruivenkamp (Netherlands)

assembled, in contrast to other international film-forums, then there only remains one difficulty for the audience - the agony of choice.

In these fifteen years, more than a few Soviet films have been shown in the cinemas of the West Berlin Festival, and many Soviet directors have attended as Festival participants.

Has everything always gone smoothly? Not at all. Everything possible has happened: misunderstandings, discussions between the Festival-organizers and the Goskino of the USSR, the search for optimal solutions and general pleasure over a precise selection. In the final analysis that was the key to better mutual understanding in the past - as it still is today. And isn't this exactly the most important task of a festival?

The Awards of the International Jury

Feature Films
Grand Prix of the 24th IFB
Golden Berlin Bear
THE APPRENTICESHIP OF DUDDY KRAVITZ
Canada, directed by Ted Kotcheff

Special Prize of the Jury
Silver Berlin Bear
L'HORLOGER DE SAINT-PAUL
France, directed by Bertrand Tavernier

Silver Berlin Bear
LA PATAGONIA REBELDE
Argentina, directed by Héctor Olivera

Silver Berlin Bear
IM NAMEN DES VOLKES
FRG, directed by Ottokar Runze

Silver Berlin Bear
LITTLE MALCOLM
Great Britain, directed by Stuart Cooper

Silver Berlin Bear
TABEJADE BIJAN
Iran, directed by Sohrab Shahid Saless

Silver Berlin Bear
PANE E CIOCCOLATA
Italy, directed by Franco Brusati

Hanna Schygulla in FONTANE EFFI BRIEST

Örökbefogadás: Kati Berek

Silver anniversary: the Berlinale alive and thriving

1975

June 27th-July 8th, 1975 (Competition)
June 29th-July 6th, 1975 (Forum)

»Oh Léon! Don't ever ask me for a photo of myself. I couldn't stand the idea of being closed up in a drawer. I wouldn't be able to breathe. I just couldn't stand it.« Ninotchka is speaking to Earl Léon d'Algout – Greta Garbo to Melvyn Douglas – in Ernst Lubitsch's NINOTCHKA. And yet this film is not to be found in the Greta Garbo Retrospective of the 25th »Berlinale«. A fact which can be explained by certain considerations, considerations which were also taken years later when the Retrospectives were dedicated to Billy Wilder and to Ernst Lubitsch. It has been a long time since the letters were black from the marks of the censor. We do want to see and hear Ninotchka nowadays.

The German Democratic Republic participates in the »Berlinale«.

There were films from all socialist nations of Europe – with the exception of Albania – at this 25th International Film Festival; even the Peoples' Republic of China was showing two films in the Competition program, hors concours. Yet most significant of all was the German Democratic Republic was partaking in the Competition. It was showing JAKOB DER LÜGNER (»Jacob the Liar«) by Frank Beyer, a film adaptation of the novel by Jurek Becker, who had also written the screenplay. It is a story about a Polish ghetto at the end of 1944. Jakob Heym, a Jew, tells the despairing inhabitants of the ghetto that the Russians are on their way to liberate them – he had heard so on the radio. A compassionate lie, for he did not have a radio and had made up the news. This lie becomes a means of survival.

Little has been mentioned here about the contacts which had been made to the official authorities in the GDR and to those responsible there for matters concerning film. The participation of East German films in the Film Festival had in fact been dependent on the efforts made to invite films from the USSR, yet there had also been additional complications in the negotiations with the GDR.

The first verifiable steps made towards inviting Defa films turn up in 1969. On February 25th 1969, a committee for establishing contacts in matters concerning all German affairs meets in Bonn and holds consultations on the possibility of inviting the GDR to the IFB. The committee comes out against an invitation, as Bauer reports with regret at the next meeting of the board of curators (14th meeting of the board of curators, March 3, 1969). Yet despite this decision from Bonn, neither the Festival management, nor the Senate show signs of discouragement. Bauer draws up drafts for letters to Fred Müller, secretary of the association for film and television in the GDR, and to the board of directors of Defa-Film Productions (March 4, 1969). In support, Senator Stein encloses Bauer's drafts in a letter to Foreign Minister Willy Brandt asking him »to look into the question of an invitation on behalf of Berlin«. Stein personally doubts that East Germany will accept an invitation, because so far it has declined all invitations to the Berlin Theatertreffen – yet he does hope for an »easing of tension«; and it does seem »as if one or the other Eastern bloc countries will be able to act upon its inclination to take part in the Film Festival« (March 5, 1969). This statement signalizes the first attempt to achieve participation of socialist nations independently of an invitation to the Soviet Union; direct negotiations with the GDR are desired in order to gradually end this series of repeated refusals. Furthermore, it was decided that, in the future, the Berlin Senator for Federal Affairs was to support an invitation of the GDR in his function as a member of this committee set up to establish contact in matters concerning all German affairs (talk between Senator Stein and the head of the Office of the Senate, Senatorial Executive Horst

Opening at the Zoo-Palast: Yuri Mikhailovich Zharkov, Soviet Consul General in West Berlin, and actress Tatyana Drubich

Press conference with Erwin Geschonnek, Jurek Becker, Frank Beyer

Reinhard Kolldehoff, Kirk Douglas

Amos Vogel talking to Erika Gregor. In the background (middle) Alberto Grifi

Grabert, April 8, 1969). Such a tactic pointed to a clear change in policy by the Berlin Senate. Almost simultaneously, Stein tried to establish contact with Federal Minister Benda in order to attain his agreement on this matter (talks on April 11 and 21, 1969). Yet time was running short, and although Benda gave his approval to inviting the GDR, it was »not possible, due to the shortness of time, to come to a formal resolution« (Stein at the 15th meeting of the board of curators, May 12, 1969).

In 1970 and 1971, invitations are sent to East Germany and the other socialist countries - which are however not accepted. Early on in 1972 as well, Bauer sends an invitation to the Deputy Minister for Cultural Affairs in the GDR, Günther Klein: »The Festival management would welcome if the GDR were represented at the Festival Berlin with exceptional new films, as well as with a delegation of renowned film artists.« (Jan. 10, 1972.) On June 16th, a week before the opening of the Film Festival, a telegram is received by the Festival management from Günther Neumann, head of the Section for Cultural Relations in the Department of Film, in which Neumann expresses his thanks for the invitation, but adds: »Unfortunately the time left to prepare a contribution is too short.« If one takes into account that invitations had been sent to East Germany in the previous years as well, this statement cannot be seen as much more than a polite but empty phrase. Despite the negotiations between East and West, and the talks which had been held between the Federal Republic of Germany and the German Democratic Republic - initiated by the Socialist-Liberal coalition - the negotiating party in the GDR remains cautious and reserved. And, of course, the special political status of Berlin also played a role. It takes another two years until the GDR decides to send films to the »Berlinale«. It is in 1974 that a first step is made. On June 17th, Bauer receives a call from Berlin/GDR from the director of Defa-export, Diller, who informs Bauer that Dr. Erhard Kranz, the departmental head of the Ministry for Cultural Affairs in the GDR, will attend the 24th IFB as an observer. »In response to my question of why the GDR was not going to participate with a film contribution, Mr. Diller replied, ›one did not want to rush matters. Maybe next year.‹« (Bauer to Senator Stein, June 17, 1974.) And in fact, the GDR did send a film for the Competition in this anniversary year of 1975.

The stars: Kirk Douglas, Claudia Cardinale, Gina Lollobrigida

Yes, and the »Berlinale« jubilee was a real hit. Attendance was high once again. Kirk Douglas, who was showing his political-Western POSSE in the Competition, and Claudia Cardinale, who presented the Golden and Silver Bears, were the stars of the Film Festival. Not that we want to forget: »Gina nazionale«, for years a regular guest of the Film Festival. Yet this time, Gina Lollobrigida had not come as an actress, but as a photographer, to show her most recent works in a gallery on Jebensstraße, right behind Zoo Station; in the show were photos from her first book, »Italia mia«. A small retrospective show was also presenting debut films which had been premièred in Berlin. A book was published telling the history of the Film Festival over the past 25 years – by Hans Borgelt, one-time press spokesman of the IFB – called »Stars and Stories«. And Alfred Bauer was awarded the Highly Distinguished Service Cross of the Federal Republic of Germany: in honor and recognition of his efforts in the field of international film and for Berlin as a film metropolis. The crisis and collapse of 1970 was past and buried. The »Berlinale« – divided up into the Competition, the Forum, the Film Fair and the Retrospective – was alive and thriving. Heinz Klunker called it a »Balance à la Berlinale« (Deutsches Allgemeines Sonntagsblatt, July 13, 1975).

Films by women

There were a remarkable number of films by women running in the Competition and especially in the Forum. Wolf Donner proclaimed it »Woman's Year« (Die Zeit, July 11, 1975). In the Competition, Márta Mészáros presented ÖRÖKBEFOGADÁS [The Adoption]. A woman worker wishes to have a child, but she is not understood by her married lover; she adopts a young girl from a welfare home. »The traditional relationships between people, which are institutionalized and hopelessly bogged down, can only be worked out on a voluntary basis, allowing each person his individual conception of happiness and self-determination. This is indeed not a new idea, certainly also not in socialist countries, but Márta Mészáros understands how to make something like a case study out of it, in which small reactions become more important than larger constructions.« (Peter Buchka, Süddeutsche Zeitung, July 10, 1975.) For the jury, this film was worthy of a Golden Bear. Also from Hungary was the film ISTENMEZEJEN 1972-73-BAN [A Hungarian Village 1972-73] by Judit Elek, which was run in the Forum. It was a documentary about some young women who resisted the traditions of their village. Other examples of the abundant number of »women's films« are: Ingemo Engström's KAMPF UM EIN KIND [Battle over a Child], Yvonne Rainer's FILM ABOUT A WOMAN WHO ..., an experimental montage about ambivalence, and the Danish comedy TA' DET SOM EN MAND, FRUE [Take It Like a Man, Madame] by the production-collective »Red Sisters«. Chantal Akerman's film JEANNE DIELMAN, 23, QUAI DU COMMERCE – 1080 BRUXELLES with Delphine Seyrig as Jeanne Dielman, a widow of 40 and mother, documents everyday monotony. For almost four full hours the film observes a woman – three days of her life: the terror of the treadmill of cleaning and cooking, the pedantic, manic rituals of cleanliness, her attempts to escape – prostitution and murder. A calculating film whose assessment is realistic.

JEANNE DIELMAN, 23, QUAI DU COMMERCE – 1080 BRUXELLES
»Delphine Seyrig plays this robot-like being, its compulsive pedantry, its torturous automatic cleanliness and orderliness with such perplexing ease, mask-like, with traumatic devotion and patient resignation.«
Wolf Donner in: Die Zeit, July 11, 1975

»It is not so much the clinch at home or the battle of the sexes which is the focal point of these new women's films, but women themselves, both those in front of and behind the camera: for men an often hard to understand, female perspective, a new

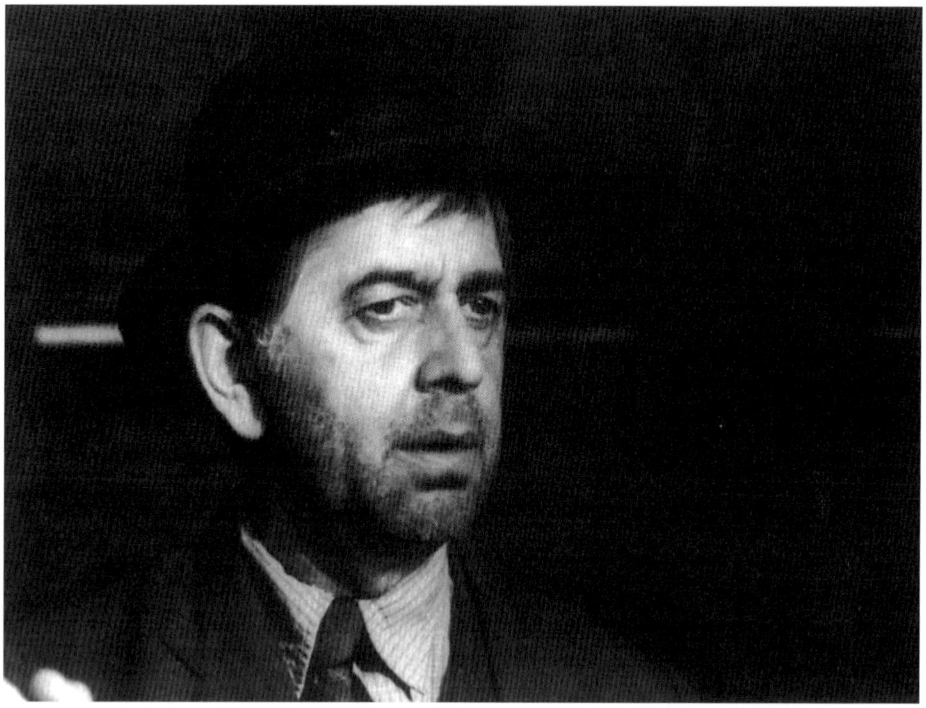

Jakob der Lügner:
Vlastimil Brodsky

feminine self-image.« (Wolf Donner, July 11, 1975.) And Donner also quotes a leaflet which was passed out during the Film Festival: »We demand equal representation of the sexes in all of the selection committees ..., films which reveal the materialistic and sexual exploitation of women and which support their fight for liberation ..., [and clarification] of the sexist image of women to be found in so-called leftist or progressive cinema.«

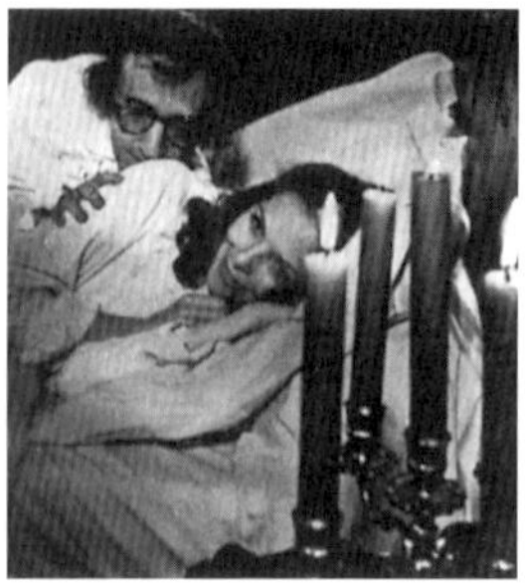

Love and Death:
Woody Allen, Diane Keaton

In Love and Death, Woody Allen makes the most caustic of jokes and undermines nearly everything: from religion to militarism – and sex too, of course. It is the »last night of Boris Grushenko«. In a prison, sometime during the year of 1812, Boris Grushenko – who had wanted to liberate his country by assasinating Napoleon – waits to be executed. It is irrelevant that everything had actually happened quite differently. All that he wants to know is: »What is life after death like? Will there at least be some girls around?«

A difficult situation

By Mrinal Sen

My memory, they say, is unusually sharp. I think they are right in large measure. But, to confess, I confuse which incident took place in which part of the world. And, true, I travel a lot, three times or more in a year, never for more than a week or two, or even less, never failing to multiply both enemies and friends in such sojourns, always remaining youthful irrespective of my age and worries, and then rushing back to Calcutta, my El Dorado, to plan new productions or just to refuel myself. Yes, indeed, I need frequent refueling to keep my body and soul together. Calcutta, for me, acts both as a stimulant and as an irritant.

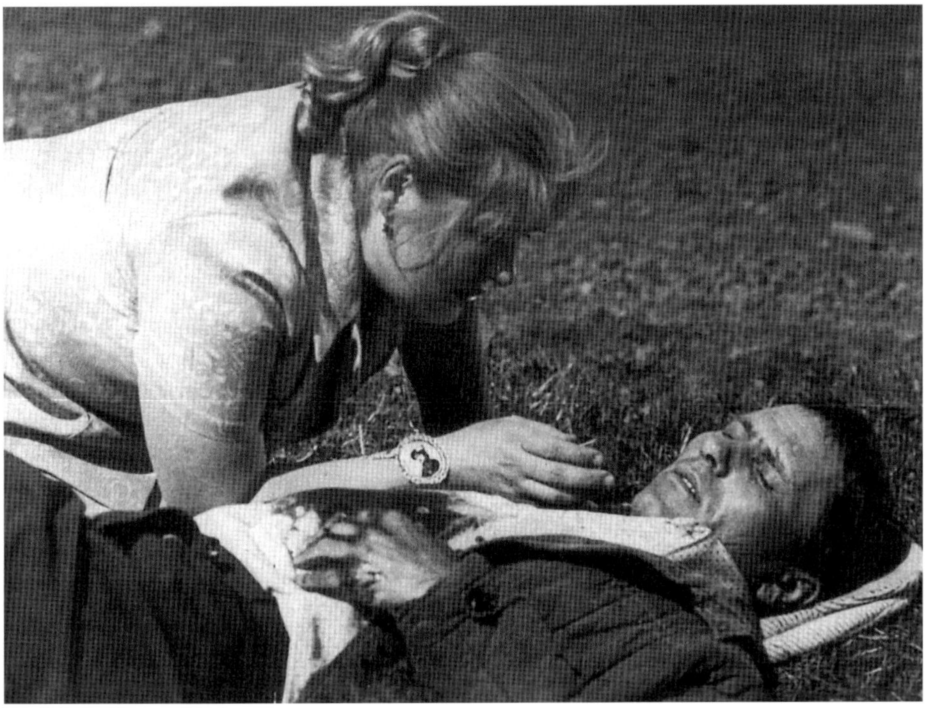

KALINA KRASNAYA by Vassili Shukshin (Forum): Lidia Fedosseyeva, Vassili Shukshin

I remember having been invited to Berlin for the first time by that indefatigable Berliner Ulrich Gregor and his sweet wife Erika. We had met earlier in Venice in a quiet and small get-together, and in a few minutes of that Venetian session I liked the couple. So, I believe, did they like me. As a result I was invited to Berlin the next year. That was the beginning of my romantic association with the »balkanized« city which, immediately after the Second Great War, was completely laid waste, with gas, electricity and water severely cut off, hospitals without medicine, shops without provisions, transport at a standstill, and which, now, is busy, luxurious, modern, vibrant. My relationship with the city and its people and also with the ebullient visitors continued to grow steadily from strength to strength since then until, just five years ago, it came to an abrupt halt, terribly unpleasant, beyond my control and perhaps beyond Moritz de Hadeln's too. That, however, is a different story.

Looking back, I can recall at least a dozen stories worth storing in memory, worth talking about, worth listening to.

The most difficult and funny situation I encountered in Berlin was in 1975 when, just a week after the state of Emergency was imposed in India and a large number of opposition leaders and their ardent followers were arrested overnight by Indira Gandhi's government, my film CHORUS *was presented in a big theatre.*

The theatre was packed, and not one single person left after the 2-hour-long show. Afterwards, the after-show question-answer session started in a minute, with Gregor as the compère.

The first question came from a young woman, bubbling with ultra-revolutionary enthusiasm. In her exuberence, she stood up on her seat and shouted at the top of her voice - a voice which I instantly fell in love with.

»Mr. Sen«, she said in her immaculate English, »I've just seen your film and have loved it. I'll call it a »poster film«, and I ask you to take it as a compliment. Now, in the context

International Jury
Sylvia Syms
(Great Britain, president)
Ottokar Runze
(FRG, vice-president)
Henry Chapier (France)
Else Goelz (FRG)
Albert J. Johnson (USA)
Rostislav Yurenev (USSR)
Carlo Martins (Brazil)
Sandhu Sukhdev (India)

The Awards of the
International Jury

Feature Films
Grand Prix of the
25th IFB
Golden Berlin Bear
ÖRÖKBEFOGADÁS
Hungary, directed by
Márta Mészáros

Special Prize of the Jury
Silver Berlin Bear
OVERLORD
Great Britain, directed by
Stuart Cooper

Special Prize of the Jury
Silver Berlin Bear
DUPONT LAJOIE
France, directed by
Yves Boisset

Silver Berlin Bear
for the best director
Sergei Solovyov
for STO DNEY POSSLE DETSTVA
USSR

Silver Berlin Bear
for the best actress
Kinuyo Tanaka
in SANDAKAN
HACHIBANSHOKAN, BOHKYO
Japan

Silver Berlin Bear
for the best actor
Vlastimil Brodsky
in JAKOB DER LÜGNER
GDR

Silver Berlin Bear
Woody Allen
for his complete works

of your angry film with a positive call to action, will you comment on the state of Emergency imposed in your country a week ago?«

Understandably, I felt nervous. So did Gregor. He felt nervous and embarrassed. Comfortably for me, he took a little time to translate the question into German.

I looked around and located the members of the Indian Mission sitting in the crowd. I looked into myself, did not know how to answer the question. I tried to collect myself during the time Gregor was translating.

I thought Gregor would take some more time to switch over to French. No, he did not. He looked at me. I gave a little cough and cleared my throat. Then slowly but not quite spontaneously I said:

»I come from a country where to be critical of the dominant faction, i.e. the ruling party, is absolutely within my constitutional rights. But, to make a clean confession, I am not aware of the legality of the newly imposed Emergency. So, I do not know at what point I cross the boundary of law. In a situation like this I would, therefore, prefer to keep mum. »Discretion«, I added, »is the better part of valour.« To my surprise, there were wild clappings. Instantly I thanked myself for being so »clever«. I could see it was a big success. My answer, I mean.

The rest of the questions were innocent, and not provocative at all. I think I was reasonably good at all that.

At the end of the session I was mobbed. A little later, the Consul General of the Indian Consulate took me aside and said, »I am happy you have tackled the questions so efficiently. But I would have been happier had you said Mrs. Gandhi was your leader.«

I was taken aback. In a moment I felt amused. I said quietly and confidently, »Admittedly she is our Prime Minister. But in a democratic set-up as ours, is it obligatory that she has to be my leader and political mentor?« And that was all between him and me.

Years later, with my continuing love affair with Berlin under the stewardship of Moritz de Hadeln, I was once a member of the International Jury. One day, between a screening of a competitive film and a secret meeting where votes for or against the films were to be cast secretly, we, the members of the Jury, were waiting in a foyer. I moved up to Joan Fontaine, the President of the Jury, and said, »The more I watch you the more I see you remain as young as in the forties.«

She beamed and exclaimed, »Ah, Mrinal, you are such a delicious liar!« She embraced me and yelled, »Hey, you are hot!« »Yes, I am«, I admitted, without feeling embarrassed. True, I was running a temperature.

Three days later, on my return to Calcutta, the doctor said I had contracted jaundice and advised me bed-rest for three weeks. I wonder if I got it in Berlin, or I smuggled the disease from India, and, being an incorrigible Indian, brought it back to the country of origin.

It was the district attorney's turn

1976

June 25th-July 6th, 1976 (Competition)
June 27th-July 4th, 1976 (Forum)

A news item released shortly after the opening of the 26th Film Festival caught journalists by surprise: »The short film FILMFESTSPIELE BERLIN [Film Festival Berlin], produced with public funds and then shown at the opening of the Film Festival, has forgotten to mention the historic fact that there had been a film festival in Berlin before World War II.« That was news. Arthur Rosenblüth, artistic director in the twenties of the Kamera movie house, Unter den Linden, complained publicly that neither the Festival management, nor the Senate wanted to acknowledge that the producer and director of the Ufa movie house, Hans Neumann, had organized a film festival within the program of the Kunstwochen (an art festival) in as early as 1927 – at the Capitol, Berlin's famous première movie house across from the Memorial Church, as well as at the aforementioned Camera.

A film about the history of the Film Festival causes annoyance.

Bengt von zur Mühlen's short film also raised objections from Ulrich Gregor. As director of the International Forum of Young Cinema, he protested to the opening film of the »Berlinale«, because »this film, subsidized with DM 75 000 from public funds, [contains] photo and sound montages which are the equivalent of a deliberate defamation of a part of the Berlin Film Festival, namely, of the International Forum of Young Cinema« (statement to the press, June 26, 1976).

American films in the limelight

Things were not getting off to a very good start. And there would be even greater worries towards the end of the Festival. Yet for the time being, the »Berlinale« was underway. Five American films were the focus of attention. AMERICA AT THE MOVIES was the name of a documentation by George Stevens jr., presented at a ceremonious matinee in the Zoo-Palast theater – on July 3rd, the day before the bicentennial anniversary of the United States of America's Declaration of Independence. If in Stevens' film a legend was substantiated, then in Robert Altman's

The Retrospective at the Astor-Filmtheater

Buffalo Bill and the Indians or Sitting Bull's History Lesson: Paul Newman

Buffalo Bill and the Indians or Sitting Bull's History Lesson an American legend, from the times of the glorious Wild West, was destroyed. Buffalo Bill, played with a humorous undertone of irony by Paul Newman, glorifies himself. He performs in a Western show, playing the noble and tough American ruffian. Sioux Indian Chief Sitting Bull gives him a lesson in history; he unmasks the hollow pretentiousness with which a whole nation identifies. Robert Altman received the Golden Bear; yet in protest he declared that he did not want it. He did not approve of the version which his producer, Dino de Laurentiis, wanted to show in Europe (excluding France and England): the version to be distributed had been shortened without authorization and went against the intentions of the director. Siding with Altman, the Berlin jury added a sentence to their statement of the reasons for their selection: »It is a masterly staged, self-critical, to-the-point slice of American history.« And yet: »This prize has been awarded solely to the unabridged original version shown in Berlin.«

Two reporters had revealed the largest political scandal in years in the USA: Bob Woodward and Carl Bernstein had investigated the Watergate Affair. Alan J. Pakula's film All the President's Men, in which Robert Redford and Dustin Hoffman play the two »Washington Post« journalists, reconstructs the investigation: »It builds up like a mystery. Via air shots swinging over the streets at right-angles, he maps out the landscape of Washington: ›Such nice little houses and such nice little streets. Strange that with some something is wrong‹.« (Brigitte Jeremias, Frankfurter Allgemeine Zeitung, June 28, 1976.) Facades conceal corruption. It is another film about the ugly side of America, even if based on good faith. All the President's Men was shown hors concours.

Another case from American history was taken up in an entry in the Forum, The Unquiet Death of Julius and Ethel Rosenberg by Alvin H. Goldstein. In the early fifties Ethel and Julius Rosenberg and Morton Sobell were charged with having disclosed secret atomic information to the Soviet Union. The court had found the accused guilty; Sobell was sent to prison for years, Ethel and Julius were given the death penalty. After more than twenty appeals and petitions for a pardon had been rejected, they were executed on the electric chair on June 19th 1953. Ethel and Julius Rosenberg are the only Americans who have ever been sentenced to death by civil law for espionage. Painstakingly, the film attempts to reconstruct the trial, the evidence, which has been questioned from time to time, and gives Morton Sobell, the Rosenberg's sons, former jurors, FBI-agents and other witnesses of this period a chance to speak. This film depicts an era – America in the fifties.

Charlie Chaplin's A King in New York also draws a critical portrait of America; it is a bitter, mockingly comic retaliation on the McCarthy era. A king in exile falls prey to the American way of life. When he helps a young boy, whose parents were communists, he is put on the notorious »black list«, suspected of anti-American activities. Here the film shows its autobiographical character; as an emigrant, Chaplin had had to leave the USA in the forties – as king in New York, he makes his »peace« with America.

After several years of cautious reservation, the presence of Americans in Berlin could once again be felt. Some critics were astonished that such self-critical films were to be seen coming from the USA, and especially to find them entered in the program of the Competition. In general, this trend was judged to be a good omen.

And then – right before the Film Festival was over – something sensational happened. On order of the Tiergarten District Court, a chief inspector confiscated a copy of

A copy of Nagisa Oshima's Ai no corrida is confiscated.

Nagisa Oshima's Ai no corrida (»In the Realm of Senses«). The confiscation took place during a screening of the film by the International Forum of Young Cinema. The police offered no explanations. This incident was unprecedented in film festival history. Never before had the judicial authorities of a country intervened so rigorously and on such questionable grounds. The confiscation had been induced by catchpenny preliminary reviews on Oshima's film in the yellow press; these reviews had caused the authorities to feel obliged to take action against the film. Oshima tells the story of a couple who are possessed with each other sexually to the point of self-abandonment: at the end of the film the man allows the woman to

A King in New York: Joan Ingram, Charlie Chaplin

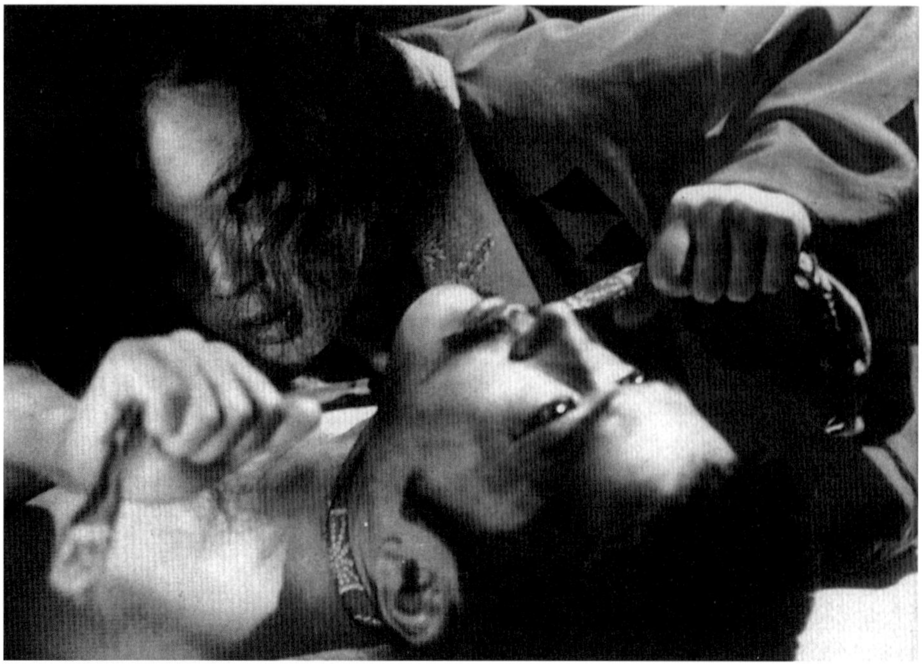

Ai no corrida: Eiko Matsuda, Tatsuya Fuji

mutilate him. In Cannes the film had been presented at the opening of the »Quinzaine des réalisateurs«; there had also been cries of protest, but in all, the film was shown thirteen times. The international critics were unanimous in their judgement, and attested to the »high artistic quality, and important political and aesthetic insights« of the film – as was also stated in a letter protesting to the confiscation, submitted by the association of film journalists. Tiergarten's Office of the District Attorney held a viewing of the film at the Landesbildstelle Berlin; and afterwards the 17th Division of the Berlin Superior Court rejected the complaint which had been lodged by the International Forum against the confiscation. This decision was

The Man who Fell to Earth: Candy Clark, David Bowie

reached on the last day of the Film Festival, which meant that a showing of the film had been conclusively hindered. (Although, at the last minute, the Forum was able to organize a ›secret‹ showing. Equipped with an innocuous title, French producer Anatole Dauman had sent a second copy to Berlin, which was then screened, quasi conspiratorially but publicly, for Festival participants.)

In its justification of the legality of the confiscation, the Office of the District Attorney quoted § 184, paragraph 3, in which a prison sentence of up to one year or a fine is threatened for those who hold a public screening of a pornographic film in which acts of violence occur. The counter-argument, that the Basic Constitutional Law of the Federal Republic of Germany guarantees the freedom of art, was not recognized as applicable in this case by the Office of the District Attorney – which meant that from this moment on, the district attorney had begun its investigation against those responsible for the Forum. Protest had come from the Forum immediately after the confiscation of the copy. It had demanded »the immediate reversal of the confiscation and the return of the copy of the film« and »a confirmation by the responsible authorities of the principle that at an international festival, all films chosen and accepted by the selection committee (or a section of it) can be shown without restriction and judicial intervention. The principle of the unlimited sovereignty of the program and freedom from measures of censorship seems to us to be constitutional to the organization of a festival.« (Statement to the press, Forum, undated.) Journalists, film-makers and guests joined in to support the Forum. Many even extended the protest further, because they saw the action of the district attorney as another sign of restriction of free press and film work in the Federal Republic of Germany.

Without a doubt, the reputation of the Festival – as well as of the judicial authorities – had suffered from this official intervention. In a press conference, the Berlin Senator for Legal Affairs Hermann Oxfort tried rectifying that which was beyond rectification. Ulrich Gregor called the confiscation an »absurd and arbitrary act«, and the Berlin Festivals-Ltd. felt that »the legal right to an appropriacy of means had been violated«.

In the »Deutsches Allgemeines Sonntagsblatt«, Heinz Klunker summed up the mood as follows: »In Berlin the reactions range from resignation to resolutions; everyone is as dopey as if after a heatstroke. And yet this obviously well-planned action is in no way a natural occurence; these official actions intended to harm the Forum not only injured the Festival, but also the City and the Federal Republic of Germany of which Berlin feels a part.« (July 11, 1976.)

The investigation dragged on. It was not until November that it was dropped. Berlin Senator for Science and the Arts Gerd Löffler wrote to Ulrich Gregor: »I regret extremely that such a judgement, which caused the International Film Festival Berlin as a whole, and the International Forum of Young Cinema in particular, such negative publicity was made at all.« (Letter, Nov. 15, 1976.)

The search for a successor

Alfred Bauer

Having reached the age of retirement, Alfred Bauer's term of office was coming to an end; on November 30th 1976 his contract would run out. If his retirement was not to be delayed, then a successor would have to be found quickly.

Alfred Bauer's position as director of the International Film Festival had not always been uncontested. The first considerations concerning his successor turned up in mid-1964; in 1966 specific candidates were even contemplated; and the 1970 crisis also triggered a debate over Bauer's position. But it was not until May 1975, that the board of curators of Festivals-Ltd. decided to officially advertise a vacancy.

In a talk between Parliamentary Undersecretary from the Ministry of the Interior Dr. Gerhart Baum, and Berlin Senator Professor Werner Stein (Dec. 16, 1974), it was agreed to ask for applications to the position of the director of the Film Festival. Senator Stein informed Alfred Bauer of this intention (Jan. 3, 1975). Bauer objected to the early timing of the advertisement, as he was afraid that it would cause disquiet in the preparations of the approaching »Berlinale Jubilee«.

His objection was not taken into account; the Senator for Science and the Arts and the business manager of the Berlin Festival-Ltd., Dr. Ulrich Eckhardt, agreed to bring up the question of advertising the position at the 36th meeting of the board of curators (May 23, 1975). After a controversial discussion, it was unanimously decided to fill the position by December 1st, 1976, and so that the person could familiarize himself with the job, he would begin as of April 1st. The application deadline was set for September 30th 1976. An advertisement appeared in the »Zeit«, »Tagesspiegel«, the »Frankfurter Allgemeine Zeitung«, the »Süddeutsche Zeitung« and the »Film-echo/Filmwoche«. A personality was desired »with comprehensive knowledge in the field of international film on artistic and commercial levels« and with the »ability to convincingly organize and develop the Berlin Film Festival«.

... with his sucessor Wolf Donner (on the left)

It was through these ads in the newspapers that Bauer found out that his request had not been respected. He protested to the newly elected Senator for Science and the Arts, Gerd Löffler, who however pointed out that this step had been necessary because one of the Berlin papers had announced prematurely on April 10th 1975, that Alfred Bauer was planning to retire.

The Senator was making reference here to the so-called »exclusive« news item in the »BZ«, in which it was claimed that Bauer would withdraw from office »sometime this year«. The headline read: »A Man with Loads of Money to be New Berlinale Boss«; the person meant here was the business manager of the Berlin Chronos-Film GmbH, Bengt von zur Mühlen, who even at this early date was being treated as if he were the future director of the Film Festival.

By September 30th, the deadline for applications, fifteen interested parties had responded. Here are the names of those who were well-known to the public at this time:

Nine candidates

- Dr. Rainer Antoine, at the time film director and head dramatic advisor of the Staatstheater Wiesbaden; responsible for the program and director of the festivals: Maifestspiele Wiesbaden, the Industriefestspiele in Wetzlar, and the festival in Bad Hersfeld;
- Hans C(hristoph) Blumenberg, at the time free-lance contributor responsible for the film section of the »Kölner Stadt-Anzeiger«, and film critic for »Die Zeit«, for which he had been writing since 1971;
- Dr. Hans Borgelt, free lance writer, and former long-time press spokesman of the Berlin Film Festival (1953-1968);
- Ulrich Gregor, chairman of the »Freunde der Deutschen Kinemathek eV« (Friends of the German Cinémathèque), and director of the International Forum of Young Cinema;
- Kurt Habernoll, free-lance journalist and affiliated to the IFB for years through his activities in the selection commissions and as of 1972 in documentary work;
- Joe Hembus, free-lance journalist, worked for Tobis-Filmkunst, television and book author (»Der deutsche Film kann gar nicht besser sein«, 1961);
- Bengt von zur Mühlen, business manager of Chronos-Film Productions;
- Steffen Wolf, associate of Miekus Filmverleih (distributor) and owner of the company Lernsysteme; director of the Filmothek der Jugend des Landes Nordrhein-Westfalen;
- Ulrich Schamoni, film director (e. g., Es [It], Alle Jahre wieder [Every Year Again], Chapeau Claque).

These nine were the favored candidates of the board of curators, which also set up a commission to find the most qualified among the candidates. This commission was to narrow the selection down to four or five persons who would then be invited to Berlin for interviews. In this commission were Parliamentary Undersecretary Baum, Senator Löffler and head business director of the Spio Ulrich Pöschke.

The fact that a representative of the film industry was, along with prominent representatives of the Senate and the Federal Government, to search and find the right person was not in itself criticized – yet still the question did arise as to whether the Spio was the most competent of parties for such negotiations. Contemporary film-makers who had won international recognition as representatives of German cinema – Fassbinder, Herzog, Kluge, Lilienthal, Schaaf, Schamoni, Schlöndorff, Syberberg, Wenders (to name only a few) – were not affiliated with the Spio, but with the »Arbeitsgemeinschaft neuer deutscher Spielfilmproduzenten« (founded in 1962), the »Syndikat der Filmemacher – Verband deutscher Film- und Fernsehregisseure« (1970) or the »Filmverlag der Autoren« (1971). All initiatives attempting to take this altered situation into account, i. e. by placing an additional spokesman from the film industry at the side of the delegate from the Spio, were to no avail.

Positions taken by the commission in their search for candidates

The commission first designed a questionnaire asking for opinions on the structure of the IFB and on the responsibilities of the future director; this questionnaire was sent to six experts, who were asked to return it by the end of the year. These experts were:

- Dr. R. F. Goldschmidt, delegate of the board of the Export-Union of the German film industry;
- Dr. Heinz Rathsack, director of the Deutsche Film- and Fernsehakademie Berlin (German Film and Television Academy) and chairman of the Stiftung Deutsche Kinemathek (German Cinémateque Foundation);
- Dr. Horst von Hartlieb, president of the Spio and member of the board of directors of the Verband der Filmverleiher (association of film distributors);
- Dr. Kurt Joachim Fischer, journalist;
- Dr. Alexander Kluge, film director and author;
- Dr. Wolf Donner, television and film editor for the weekly paper »Die Zeit«.

It should be noted here, that for Alexander Kluge, who was working on a film at the time, Florian Hopf answered, speaking at the same time on behalf of the board of directors of the Arbeitsgemeinschaft der Filmjournalisten (working group of film journalists) and the Arbeitsgemeinschaft neuer deutscher Spielfilmproduzenten (working group of new German feature film producers).

It cannot be claimed here that the responses received to the questionnaire – for the most part carefully formulated and with an attempt at objectivity based on their individual positions – brought in many new ideas for the conception of the Film

Press conference for CARO MICHELE with Mario Monicelli and Mariangela Melato

Festival and the profile of the future director. And yet, there was a surprising number of points of agreement. All six experts spoke out for a continued division of the Festival in Competition (with the Film Retrospective and the Film Fair) and Forum; for the continuation of the Competition as a prerequisite for »A-status«; and for the necessity of cooperation, based on a vote of confidence, with the film industry. If one thinks back to the irreconcilable fronts during the crisis in 1970, one finds that the willingness to compromise on basic issues had become greater. The limitations set by the form of the events themselves and the abundancy of international regulations made drastic reorganization and reform unrealistic.

Internal changes

The commission convened in Berlin and Bonn six times; the sixth meeting preceded closely the board of curators' meeting for making the final selection, set for February 18th 1976. Five candidates had made it into this last round: Antoine, Blumenberg, Borgelt, Gregor and Schamoni. Nonetheless, interviews were not held with them alone: two others - who had made strong impressions - received letters of invitation: Wolf Donner and Hellmuth P. Gattinger. Yet it was rather remarkable, that when the Senator for Science and the Arts informed the members of the Berlin Senate how matters stood in the selection process on February 9th, he did not mention Wolf Donner in the list of remaining candidates; instead the name Gattinger was included, who at this time was public relations manager, later becoming business manager and general director of 20th Century-Fox of Germany. Gattinger had not, however, submitted an expertise, or at least not in writing; he had been - after several talks with Ulrich Pöschke from the Spio - asked to come to an interview to introduce himself to the commission on January 15th. (Contact was also made with a third additional candidate, Ottokar Runze, director and producer, who - independently of the application process for Alfred Bauer's position - had written an exposé on the situation of the German film industry, and sent it to the Office of the Senate at the end of November 1974.) Remarkable as well is that in a letter, Löffler does not name Donner and Gattinger as being among the candidates, yet does mention that preliminary interviews were being held with Ulrich Schamoni, as well as with Ulrich Eckhardt and Alfred Bauer. And yet, there is no doubt that after the meeting on January 21st, at which the applicants were interviewed, a preliminary decision in favor of Wolf Donner was reached. It was right before the next-to-last meeting of the commission on February 9th 1976 that Wolf Donner handed in his official application.

Wolf Donner was born in 1939 in Vienna. He studied German, philosophy and theater studies, graduating with a doctorate. Subsequently he worked as a journalist and editor, e. g. for »Die Zeit«. From 1977-79 he was director of the International Film Festival Berlin. Afterwards he was editor of the cultural section of the »Spiegel«. Wolf Donner lives as a free-lance publicist in Berlin.

It was no secret that up until this point Hans Borgelt had been the favored choice of the film industry, at the cost of Ulrich Gregor whom it decisively opposed. With the candidacy of Wolf Donner, the situation changed. Even Ulrich Pöschke was impressed by the arguments of his two political partners in the commission and by Donner's specific qualifications; moreover Borgelt's age - he was over 60 - had already caused moments of hesitation. Pöschke decided to invite Donner for a talk, which then took place on February 13th in Wiesbaden. It was certainly on this day that the course was set.

At the 38th meeting of the board of curators, on February 18th 1976, Wolf Donner was unanimously elected to be Bauer's successor. His contract was to begin on June 1st, allowing him time to familiarize himself with the work until Bauer retired on November 30th.

Such was the route the search had taken. In the media and internally, there had been moments of irritation, complications and power struggles, which considering the importance of this change in personnel for the IFB is not astonishing, yet it did seem excessive at times. Particularly in the campaign against Ulrich Gregor, the threshold of fairness was often overstepped. An especially foolish campaign was launched by the »Bild-Zeitung«: »Gregor is said to be a leftist. He loves communist cinema and signed a statement for Holger Meins.« (Jan. 24, 1976.) This announcement had its consequences; the board of curators decided to investigate the matter. It was unclear what was meant by this »statement for Holger Meins«, an especially dreadful attack, and it did place Gregor in the vicinity of a group which seemed born to ruin reputations.

A campaign against Ulrich Gregor and protest in solidarity

On March 29th 1975, on the third channel of the ARD broadcasting station, a film adaption of Schönberg's opera »Moses and Aron« by Jean-Marie Straub and Danièle Huillet had been shown. Although the viewers certainly did not notice, two cuts had been made in the credits at the beginning of the film: Straub/Huillet had not originally mentioned the ARD as co-producer, but instead had added: »including the Broadcasting Station West Berlin«. The actual cause of controversy however was a handwritten dedication reading: »For Holger Meins, J. M. S. and D. H.« Both passages had been cut out after an internal dispute at the ARD, in which also the program directors took part. As a consequence, numerous European film-makers and institutions published a resolution, in which – among other things – they proclaimed: »We vehemently protest to the impertinence of German and Austrian television, as well as to the German publisher, and the American spokesman for Arnold Schönberg's heirs, to the unconstitutionality of this censorship imposed by the German film industry, demanding that a handwritten dedication to a young man be removed – a young man who died after two and a half years of imprisonment, without having had a trial, that is, an innocent man. No democratic institution can challenge Danièle Huillet's and Jean-Marie Straub's right to dedicate a film of which they are the authors (even if this film is an adaption of the opera ›Moses and Aron‹ by Arnold Schönberg) to Holger Meins, a colleague and a friend.«

The »statement for Holger Meins«, with which the »Bild-Zeitung« had started rumors, and which had in turn weakened Gregor's position as candidate for the office of director of the IFB, was then this resolution directed against an unauthorized cut in the film credits. It is true that Gregor's name appears among those who signed – as a member of the board of the film journalists' association. It should be mentioned here that the signature of one of the experts who had been asked for his opinions by the commission in search of a candidate was also to be found on the resolution. Still another fact, more than just a technicality, should be remarked on here in connection with the debate surrounding Gregor. It has to do with the »innocence« of Holger Meins who died in prison before being tried: according to the constitution of Berlin (Article 65, 2) a person is defined »as not guilty«, that »has not been convicted by a court«.

If the minutes, letters and other documents are examined and other press commentary read, then this »chronique scandaleuse« could be extended to cover several more or less odd as well as disgusting details; squabbling is probably the norm when it comes to filling an attractive position, and usually things tend to smooth over once it has become a fait accompli. Reputable observers protested above all to the long-windedness of the procedure, which had been unnecessarily delayed by the fact that the commission had sought expert advice at a wrong and belated time. There were also complaints that the procedure had taken place behind closed doors. The Berlin

International Jury
Jerzy Kawalerowicz (Poland, president)
Hannes Schmidt (FRG, vice-president)
Marjorie Bilbow (Great Britain)
Michel Ciment (France)
Guido Cincotti (Italy)
Georgi Daniela (USSR)
Wolf Hart (FRG)
Bernard R. Kantor (USA)
Fernando Macotela (Mexico)
Márta Mészáros (Hungary)
Shuji Terayama (Japan)

The Awards of the International Jury

Feature Films
Grand Prix of the 26th IFB
Golden Berlin Bear
BUFFALO BILL AND THE INDIANS OR SITTING BULL'S HISTORY LESSON
USA, directed by Robert Altman

Special Prize of the Jury
Silver Berlin Bear
CANOA
Mexico, directed by Felipe Cazals

Silver Berlin Bear
for the best director
Mario Monicelli
for CARO MICHELE
Italy

Silver Berlin Bear
for the best actress
Jadwiga Baranska
in NOCE I DNIE
Poland

Silver Berlin Bear
for the best actor
Gerd Olschewski
in VERLORENES LEBEN
FRG

Silver Berlin Bear
for his first work as a director
László Lugossy
for AZONOSITÁS
Hungary

Silver Berlin Bear
BAGHÉ SANGUI
Iran, directed by Parviz Kimiavi

Gerd Olschewski

Cultural Council released a statement which criticized the selection of Donner, because it is »unadmissable« to »put someone – who has been an advisor for the selection – on the list of the possible candidates after the list has been deemed closed, and then in the aftermath to nominate him director« (Feb. 17, 1976). It is, however, of relevance to know that the Cultural Council had endorsed Gregor for the position of IFB director.

By and large, Donner's nomination was judged to be a compromise. There could be no doubt that he was in all ways competent for the job. And it was in the end the journal »Filmecho/Filmwoche«, as the voice of the film industry, which signalized a certain willingness towards tolerance. Truly pertinent and fair commentaries were, however, seldom. Volker Baer wrote in the »Tagesspiegel«: »The decision has hardly fallen and there are cries of protest. Shortly before the nomination, both the Berlin FDP and the Berlin Cultural Council came out for Gregor. And right after the nomination, the CDU/CSU factions in Bonn had their objections ready. Now, since the man has been selected, he should at least be given an honest chance. He will notice soon enough, that it is not all that easy to change over from the métier of a critic to that of a Festival director.« (Feb. 19, 1976.)

An era had come to an end; a new stage in the history of the Festival was beginning.

Ulrich Gregor, the dinosaur

By Med Hondo

One sees him everywhere, discreet and attentive, no film eludes him, at any important festival anywhere. He loves a certain type of film, the so-called author's film, as if other types had no author; (but it is the film dealers who create outsiders with words).

In Berlin the movie theaters of the Forum are full and the debates lively – an ideal audience, which one would like to see in other movie houses as well – but alas! only a few of the films of the Forum come into normal distribution for the »general public« or to television – I am talking, of course, about African films – the world's greatest outsiders.

Despite everything, I wish the Forum and its organizers a long life.

The Berlin Sandwich

1977

June 24th-July 5th, 1977 (Competition)
June 26th-July 3rd, 1977 (Forum)

A roll with a black strip of film in it; in one corner a bite of roll, film strip and all, is missing. Such was the appetizer served to arouse curiosity in the 27th Film Festival. Amused and with a bit of mockery, Berliners spoke of this year's »Berlin Sandwich« Festival.

Large crowds gathered round in front of the Zoo-Palast. Yet not everyone there, on this June evening, wanted to go to the opening of the Film Festival. Many had come to marvel at the stunts performed by several tight-rope artists in front of the Zoo-Palast. While the visitors outside held their breaths, the »Berlinale« guests inside were leaning back and enjoying Ryan O'Neal and Burt Reynolds in Peter Bodganovich's NICKELODEON: an amusing film for an opener, telling a nostalgic, cheery story about the early days of film.

Changes in the concept of the Festival

The International Film Festival Berlin had taken on new contours. Wolf Donner had succeeded in putting through a new concept for the Festival. It included advertising more intensively and offensively, in order to arouse enthusiasm for the »Berlinale« in new sections of the population. This plan worked; the motif on the Festival poster was soon quite popular – the »Berlin Sandwich« was literally the food for much talk. Yet decisive for this success were the changes made in the side-events. The Film Fair, which till then had mainly been restricted to the film branch itself, was opened for the general public; the Info-Show was enlarged. Numerous films from socialist countries were shown within its framework. Thematically, they often complemented films in the Competition from Eastern Europe. In addition, a series of films about the »image of Lenin and the Revolution in Soviet cinema«, and a small show of works – six films – by Konrad Wolf from East Germany were presented. A retrospective of films by Ula Stöckl was also included to complete the selection of

Jeanine Meerapfel, François Truffaut, Sabine Glaser

new German films in the Info-Show. It is here that another point of focus in Donner's concept became clear. In addition to the four West German entries, one of which was the special screening of the controversial documentary film by Joachim C. Fest and Christian Herrendoerfer HITLER – EINE KARRIERE [Hitler – a Career], and the films in the Info-Show, there was a series »German Films« as part of the Film Fair; it was an outgrowth of the program originally initiated by the International Forum of Young Cinema, yet which was now subject to both the Competition and the Forum and included many more films. Cooperation between the two parts of the Festival did bring results, but was also somewhat problematic. Tension, that is, the rivalry between these two parts of the Festival, had not yet been resolved. Although this time roles were reversed: if it had been the Competition which had felt threatened by the Forum up till then, it was now those responsible for the Forum who watched the extension and restructuring of the Competition and its side-events critically this year. Wolf Donner's conception of the program, his cinematographic and aesthetic interests clearly differed from Alfred Bauer's; the realm of competence of the selection committee had been extended; it now previewed films at an earlier date than had been customary up till then, making more often direct contact with producers and directors on location in the different countries – all these changes seemed to be at the expense of the Forum. The Competition and the Info-Show were more open for committed and aesthetically experimental films. Rudolph Ganz, one of the most openly critical voices against the Competition in its old form and concerned advocate of the Forum, recognized the dangers and demanded that »The Festival be turned into a forum« (Deutsches Allgemeines Sonntagsblatt, July 10, 1977). Donner and Gregor did however declare that they wanted to intensify their collaboration. At best, it might turn into a productive kind of tension – in no way harmful for a festival.

Other changes made in the Competition proved to be worthwhile as well. Participants and guests no longer needed tickets for afternoon screenings; their Festival passes were enough. Informational material, modeled after the Info-Sheets of the Forum, was made more comprehensive – press commentaries, excerpts from interviews, biographical and filmographical information about the directors, and sometimes also about the actors, actresses and authors were added to the synopses. As of 1981, these loose sheets were bound in a brochure – today's »Documentation«.

It had been possible – despite less time than usual to make arrangements – to give the Festival a new allure. In the reviews, the relaxed atmosphere was celebrated, and when the final balance was drawn, it showed that attendance and returns had been increased by 20%.

The Stiftung Deutsche Kinemathek takes over the planning of the Retrospectives.

The Retrospective – which film-historically interested Alfred Bauer had often called his »favorite child« – also underwent changes. For the first time it fell under the supervision of the Stiftung Deutsche Kinemathek, which took over all matters concerning content, although still in cooperation with the Film Festival, which remained the financer of this part of the program, also retaining the right to propose themes. Retrospectives had been held since 1951. The first ones were organized in collaboration with the Film Club of the British Centre. The program had included silent films, German ones at first, later also films from England and France, and many from Russia. It was a classical canon. Gradually there was a development toward monographical series: e. g. in 1960 the Retrospective was dedicated to the American comedian Harold Lloyd. Contemporary directors who were little known in Germany were also presented from time to time: in 1961 Akira Kurosawa, in 1964 Yasujiro Ozu. For both of these directors, these Retrospectives meant the beginning of the reception of their films in West Germany. A series of films by the Brazilian Cinema Nôvo in 1966 was also a point of emphasis. Some of the Retrospectives were organized in connection with the »Deutsches Institut für Filmkunde« (German Institute for Film Studies) in Wiesbaden. Documentations were compiled by Walter Kaul, Gero Gandert, Ulrich Gregor, Hans Borgelt, Peter Spiegel, among others; Werner Schwier was responsible for the coordination several times; and from the mid-sixties on, Peter B. Schumann was in charge of the program.

A large Marlene Dietrich retrospective, in two parts to be shown in two years, was begun in 1977 - and it took up a thread which had already been loosely spun: the treatment of films made by Germans in exile. Since then there have been Retrospectives on Billy Wilder, Kurt (Curtis) Bernhardt, Fred Zinnemann, Erich Pommer and six actors and actresses who had to leave Nazi-Germany. One of the most successful Retrospectives was in 1984, and dedicated to Ernst Lubitsch; two years later, there was an homage of the actress Henny Porten. In addition, technical themes - 3-D film, special effects, color-film - have attracted a broader spectrum of younger viewers. To accompany each theme of these Retrospectives, a book was published.

The continuation of this tradition has been endangered from time to time. Just where the lobby is presumably the weakest, financial constraints are often easily realized. It does, however, sometimes take more than just a bit of luck to survive.

Running in the Competition of 1977 were films by François Truffaut, Robert Bresson, Robert Benton, Joan Micklin Silver, Niklaus Schilling and Bernhard Wicki, to name only a few. The GDR had entered a film by Konrad Wolf, MAMA, ICH LEBE [Mama, I'm Alive]. The script had been written by Wolfgang Kohlhaase. Four German prisoners of war in the Soviet Union join the Red Army; when they encounter German soldiers for the first time again, they cannot bring themselves to shoot.

Bernhard Wicki, Konrad Wolf

Peter Bogdanovich

Ousmane Sembène and his wife

Some critics found the film immaterial, others praised the stringent narrative style, its »sincerity«. Henning Harmssen wrote: »The greatness of this film lies in its declared scepticism, and the unwavering refusal of the film-makers Wolf and Wolfgang Kohlhaase to evolve a cheap, apodictic thesis. The film, addressed to the viewer, takes on the question of moral conduct in extreme situations.« (Rheinischer Merkur, July 8, 1977.)

Objections from the Jewish Community to Rainer Werner Fassbinder as member of the international jury

The jury included more celebrities than it had in years: actresses Ellen Burstyn and Senta Berger, producer Hélène Vager, critic Derek Malcolm and directors Andrei Mikhalkov-Konchalovsky, Ousmane Sembène, Humberto Solas, Basilio Martin Patino and Rainer Werner Fassbinder. To the appointment of Fassbinder there had been objections. The Jewish Community in Berlin accused his play »Der Müll, die Stadt und der Tod« of anti-semitism. Among other things, the statement of the Jewish Community proclaimed: »Criticism has not brought Fassbinder to the insight that he is on the wrong track. To appoint such a man to a position which is so significant to the cultural life of the City of Berlin not only offends the feelings of the Jewish Community. If Fassbinder had even a bit of sensitivity for the situation, he would resign from this body of his own accord.« On June 1st 1976, Mayor Dietrich Stobbe talked with representatives of the Catholic Church and the Jewish Community. Heinz Galinski, head of the Jewish Community, once again presented the objections to Fassbinder. Nonetheless, the Senate had no desire to take action against Fassbinder's appointment. Instead the responsible senator, Dr. Dieter Sauberzweig, was instructed to talk to Galinski again. Senatorial Supervisor Peter Nestler wrote the Mayor: »In this affair I am of the opinion that the film (!) by Fassbinder, referred to by Mr. Galinski, ›Der Müll, die Stadt und der Tod‹ is not anti-semitic. Rather, he touches on the problem of real-estate speculation in our modern big cities.« (Letter, June 15, 1976.) Fassbinder's appointment was not contested any further.

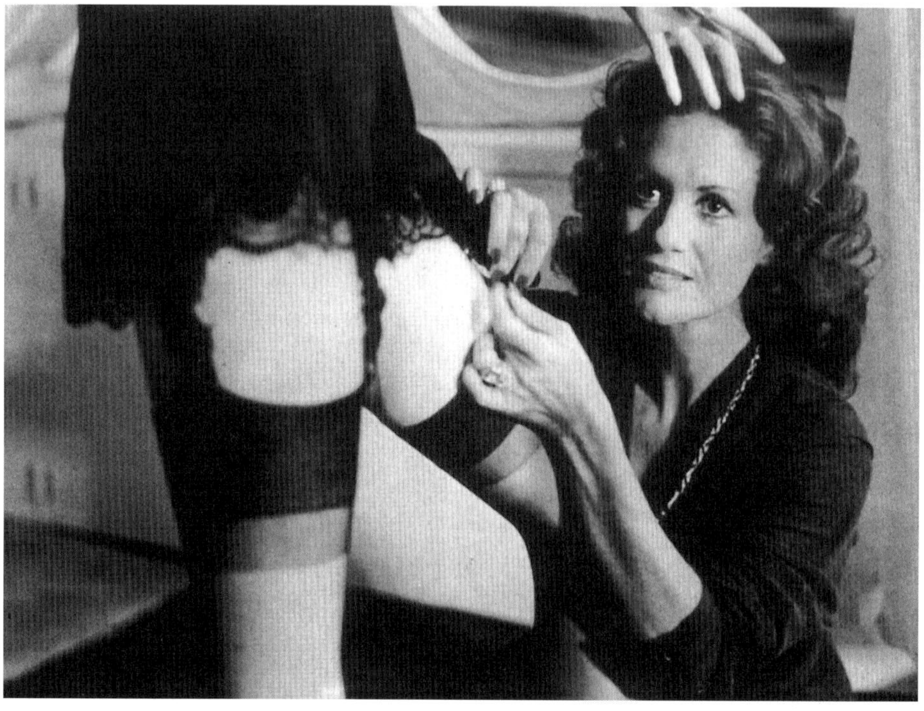

L'Homme qui aimait les femmes: Brigitte Fossey

The jury's job this year was a hard one. The films were in too great contrast. Alongside politically committed films such as the East German entry, there were elegant essayistic films such as Truffaut's L'Homme qui aimait les femmes (»The Man who Loved Women«), a radical and pessimistic late work like Bresson's Le Diable probablement [The Devil, Probably] or Joan Micklin Silver's Between the Lines about a group of young people involved in making a newspaper. To the surprise of many critics, who on the most part favored Truffaut and Silver, the Golden Berlin Bear went to the Soviet film Voshozhdeniye [The Ascent] directed by Larissa Shepitko. Just the same, they could not deny that it had been a good choice. »At first one thinks, one will have to bear through another one of those war and partisan films typical for this country. It's the Second World War, winter, the steppe, there's the rat-a-tat-tat of machine guns. And it does indeed evolve into a film about partisans – yet in a totally different way. Things are not sorted out into Good and Evil, or nationalities. A religious fervor and beauty – of a kind usually not permitted in Soviet films – are communicated. The film argues in an insistent and credulous manner. At the end there is a veritable ascension to heaven by all suffering beings. The skies open. The film transcends, breaking with all clichés. It expresses a realistic holiness. One watches, wonders, and realizes that one is devastated.« Such was the praise given by Friedrich Luft in »Die Welt« (July 7, 1977).

Between the Lines: Jeff Goldblum

One film shown in the Forum, Aus einem deutschen Leben [From a Very German Life] particularly offsets a film entered as a special screening in the »official« program, Fest's Hitler-film: in adapting the novel »La Mort est mon métier« by Robert Merle, Theodor Kotulla creates a cool psychograph – a study of a concentration camp commander. His name in the film is Franz Lang, however, in him the life of the Auschwitz commander, Rudolf Höß, can be easily discerned. As Kotulla comments, »I am (...) interested most of all in the man who helped invent and supervise

Le Diable probablement: Antoine Monnier

Mababangong Bangungot:
Kidlat Tahimik

Ceddo
by Ousmane Sembène

industrialized killing. I try to observe how such a person functions.« Götz George plays this concentration camp commander in a pervertedly conscientious manner.

The FIPRESCI, the International Federation of Film Journalists, awarded their prize to the imprisoned Turkish director Yilmaz Güney for the entirety of his works up to date. Two of his films were presented in the program of the Forum: UMUT [Hope], about the hard life of a coachman, whose horse is killed in an accident, destroying his livelihood; and ENDISE [Unrest], realized together with Şerif Gören as co-director, about the life of an oppressed cotton picker. There was also a film from the Philippines, which almost became a cult in itself: Kidlat Tahimik's MABABANGONG BANGUNGOT (»The Perfumed Nightmare«). A taxidriver, a young Philippino, dreams of America, the promised land of modern technology in which nothing is impossible. A rich American takes him along with him to Europe; in Paris he has to refill the man's chewing gum machines. The candy-like colors of his dream fade; life is black and white.

While everyone is in the theater watching the screen – hooting, clapping or booing when the picture is out of focus for a second or the sound distorted – film director Wim Wenders goes into the projection room of the Zoo-Palast and encounters there, a person who is in love with his job, a craftsman by passion: Arnold Ladwig, the projectionist. Wenders watches him, listens to him, and hears: »We up here don't reap our rewards until we hear ›Lights on! Curtain down! Mikes off! All's okay!‹« (berlinale-tip, No. 11, July 4, 1977.) An homage to a projectionist, a sign of the times in this Berlin Film Festival of 1977.

HITLER – EINE KARRIERE and AUS EINEM DEUTSCHEN LEBEN
»This film is so fascinated by its subject, by its significance, in which it plays a part, that the subject takes possession of the film again and again; it becomes its secret narrator. (›In it, the saying that history so far has loved to concentrate itself in *one* person, proves true‹.)
Here a man believed, arrogantly and with utter carelessness, that his language – successfully tested in a bestseller – is superior to a language of demagogic images; he believed that via well-thought out commentary he could cut everything down to size, like a Lord God from heaven. (...)
I guess, in a way, I'm just doing some promotion here too. The only recommendation which can really be made is to *not* go see this film. Or, if you absolutely must see it with your own eyes, and above all – with your own ears – then only to verify this fascination of which this film reports, victimized itself.
One will have to wait for the film by Theo Kotulla, AUS EINEM DEUTSCHEN LEBEN, which is able to say more about this fascination by refusing it. I hope that this film will be shown soon, as a rectification. But even if there were more film-makers with such a presence of mind, the setback which the film by Fest and Herrendoerfer has caused German cinema cannot be compensated for easily.«
Wim Wenders in: Die Zeit, Aug. 5, 1977

THE LAST MOVIE: Dennis Hopper, also director of the film

Larissa

By Wolf Donner

Two or three things that I know about Larissa. During a short, intensive period, over two years, we met on many occasions in Berlin and in Moscow, we visited, we sat together with friends through the night. Anybody who knew her even casually will never be able to forget Larissa Shepitko. She was particularly pretty and warm, a very unusual person and an ingenious artist. Encounters with Larissa.

There she stands suddenly, tall, thin, amazingly beautiful. An appearance which does not at all fit into this shabby restaurant of a Moscow hotel in the style of the 1950s. It is dark, smoky, the usual band plays the usual music for dancing, the customers yell without inhibition in order to communicate above the din. Ron and I stand up, stutter like schoolboys and stare at Larissa. She struggles with a couple of English sentences, smiles disbelievingly, shakes her head. Berlin, the Festival, my film? No, no, impossible. They will never give it to you.

Preface. I had travelled to Moscow for the selection of films with Ron Holloway, member of the new Festival committee and expert for the socialist countries. Winter 1976/77. At the official welcoming dinner, I was obliged constantly to drink toasts to the friendship of peoples, art, cinema: pure vodka, down the hatch. Towards the end, when I didn't quite know what was going on anymore, they got me to confess that the Berlin delegation would naturally need its own flag when it visited the Moscow Festival. After this triumphant victory of the tripartite-theory, I was allowed to eat something.

Now we are sitting in the Goskino viewing room, still with a heavy head, looking at one film after the other, almost all of it boring, party-line stuff. Usually we cut it off. The apparachiks are angry: The new people from Berlin are impolite, special flag for Berlin or not. We ask time and time again about particular titles from Ron's secret list, we always receive the same stupid excuses: sorry, not here right now, copy underway, not done yet, not at Goskino.

We remain stubborn, and finally see two or three better films on the third day. And Larissa Shepitko's »Ascent«. We know immediately, this one or none of them. Since all the »delegatsi« rooms are said to be bugged, we discuss our further tactics in the hotel toilet, whereby one of us constantly flushes. At a dinner with Minister of Film Yermash, I declare emotionally, it is time not to once again show the German public a typical partisan film with the usual clichés, but to show a film which goes deeper, further, which tells more about the Russians. »Ascent« would certainly have a chance for a prize. Not a word about the clearly religious symbolism, the recognizable personages of the passion story, the more than double-meaning of the title (Ascent? Rise? Resurrection?). We get the film. In the Festival program. Ron will later write very clearly about the Christ figure and the many biblical allusions of the film. The leader of the Soviet delegation is very angry. But it is too late. We cannot believe that nobody in Moscow knew what sort of film they had let us have.

Berlinale 1977. Larissa moves insecurely through the foreign terrain, happy that she can be here. The competition among films is fierce: Truffaut (»L'Homme qui aimait les femmes«), Wicki (»Die Eroberung der Zitadelle«), Konrad Wolf (»Mama, ich lebe«), Bogdanovich (»Nickelodeon«), Joan M. Silver (»Between the Lines«), Terry Gilliam (»Jabberwocky«), dos Santos (»Tenda dos milagres«). The struggle in the jury is bitter. The final debate revolves around the alternative »Le Diable probablement« by Robert Bresson or »Ascent«. Ellen Burstyn finally decides the issue for Larissa. Fassbinder and Hélène Vager

International Jury
Senta Berger (Austria)
Ellen Burstyn (USA)
Hélène Vager (France)
Rainer Werner Fassbinder (FRG)
Derek Malcolm (Great Britain)
Andrei Mikhalkov-Konchalovsky (USSR)
Ousmane Sembène (Senegal)
Humberto Solas (Cuba)
Basilio Martin Patino (Spain)

from Paris are outvoted and insist on a declaration at the awards ceremony that the decision was 5 to 4. Bresson receives the Special Prize of the Jury, Larissa the Golden Bear and the FIPRESCI Prize.

A few weeks later we meet again at the Moscow Festival. In the small, modern apartment of Larissa Shepitko and Elem Klimov. She works on a tiny balcony with plants, Elem tells of a Rasputin-film, »Agoniya«, which the censor is holding under lock and key. In the evening the crowded living-room is reduced to a single giant festive table, suitcases and beds on top of the wardrobes. Numerous friends of the two are present, directors, actors. People laugh, sing, talk about films and festivals in the usual tangle of languages and constantly drink toasts with emphatic speeches. Always down the hatch. Larissa is the warm-hearted center of the round.

The next day Larissa, Elem, Jeanine Meerapfel and I drive outside of Moscow (which is forbidden). The little old car sputters and moans frighteningly. Larissa has prepared a typical Russian picnic, naturally too much of everything. She and Elem talk with such enthusiasm and, in a postive sense, with such patriotism about beautiful old Russia, as they will later celebrate it in »Farewell to Matyora«. They show us the historical location Susdal, the famous old wooden churches, the area in which Tarkovsky shot »Andrei Rublev«. The church is closed, the barkeeper crabby. But with a few words Larissa achieves everything. Her charm, her magical radiance have their effect here as elsewhere. The drive back is at night in the rain, the car stalls now and then, we are all freezing, we miss an appointment in Moscow. Larissa sings old Russian songs.

Thereafter for months we receive only sporadic news. Grand USA tour, Larissa on the East and West Coast, at all imaginable festivals, in Telluride; Larissa in a convertible with Werner Herzog and Tom Luddy in the Rocky Mountains. She radiates in the photos, looks genuinely happy. She is celebrated, the Amercians love this clever, attractive, self-confident Russian woman. The West shines.

At the Berlinale 1978 she is in the jury along with Patricia Highsmith, Frieda Grafe, the Mexican actress A. C. Soares, Angelopoulos, Konrad Wolf, Sergio Leone, Jacques

The Awards of the International Jury

Feature Films
Grand Prix of the 27th IFB
Golden Berlin Bear
VOSHOZHDENIYE
USSR, directed by
Larissa Shepitko

Special Prize of the Jury
Silver Berlin Bear
LE DIABLE PROBABLEMENT
France, directed by
Robert Bresson

Silver Berlin Bear
for the best director
Manuel Gutiérrez Aragón
for CAMADA NEGRA
Spain

Silver Berlin Bear
for the best actress
Lily Tomlin
in THE LATE SHOW
USA

Silver Berlin Bear
for the best actor
Fernando Fernán Gómez
in EL ANACORETA
Spain

Silver Berlin Bear
LOS ALBAÑILES
Mexico, directed by
Jorge Fons

Silver Berlin Bear
HERKULESFÜRDÖI EMLÉK
Hungary, directed by
Pál Sándor

Adrienne Mancia from the Museum of Modern Art, Ron Holloway, Larissa Shepitko

Rozier, the Spaniard A. Sansinenea. Too many complicated celebrities in one compulsory family. Leone often stands with his overcoat in the doorway, wanting to leave, Angelopoulos always pulls him back again. Patricia Highsmith does not like Larissa, who walks through the Festival like a queen, and on the last day hurls the accusation at me: I had shoved Larissa to the center of the awards ceremony, thereby relegating her, Highsmith, the elected jury president, to the sidelines. In a Highsmith text for the »Jahrbuch Film« this later came indirectly to expression: »A woman in the jury, the Russian woman Larissa Shepitko, did not vote for me (good), and excused herself the next day, because she had taken me for someone else«.

Hardened by a jury experience in Mannheim, Larissa takes the office very seriously, confers with Konrad Wolf, constantly obtains information. She sleeps too little, sits up late at night with the jury or with the always mistrustful Soviet delegation in the bar of the Palace Hotel, or better, with friends in the Terzo Mondo, the meeting place of the socialist countries and the Latin Americans. Costas raves and makes eyes, Conny Wolf is relaxed as never before, Larissa exuberant. Twice she collapses.

The last time I meet Larissa is in Moscow in the winter of 1978, once again together with Ron. The grand party at her home, the old and new friends. Elem is down in the dumps, cannot work, cannot get »Agonia« released. Nothing is happening. Larissa also has problems, the preparations for her »Matyora« project are being obstructed. Four of us are together in the grand-bourgeois house of one of the »Agonia« actresses, who is married to a famous Moscow cancer specialist. A dinner fit for a prince. The Russian hospitality and warmheartedness, the high-spirited tales and toasts pull us in their wake, as always. But Larissa is hidden within herself, melancholy, speaks for the first time about her intimations of death. Our hostess will shortly thereafter lose her life in a fire on a set.

Two evenings later once again at Elem's and Larissa's place. We discuss how we can avoid the narrow-minded functionaries of Goskino so that we can obtain better films from their friends and perhaps even secure the release of »Agoniya« for the West. We are not in a good mood. The words »glasnost« and »perestroyka« still slumber in Russian dictionaries. In the doorway Larissa ties a thick red shawl around my neck: I should protect myself better in this cold land.

In the summer of 1979 Larissa Shepitko died in an automobile accident while returning to Moscow. She was 40 years old. Four young colleagues who had inspected a site for »Matyora« died with her.

Years later Elem Klimov completed the film. »Farewell to Matyora« was shown in the 1987 Berlinale program.

Auguri e saluti!

By Clemens Klopfenstein

Whether I'm pleased and happy that the Forum exists?! For twenty years now?! Indeed!

In 1977 was my first Berlinale, as spectator; it was in the summertime in those days, and I remember how my painter friends and I, after the last screening, collected in the slow, soft dawn of Berlin the first Bolex-pictures for GESCHICHTE DER NACHT *[Night Story]. Now, there is no longer that summertime-easiness, on the contrary! Now, in winter in the jam-packed Delphi – the smoke, beer- and smog-vapors justify its name and nearly transport me; as a free-breathing Umbrian – I often feel wedged into a mammoth culture-machine.*

Nonetheless, without the Gregors and their friends my films wouldn't exist! (Wouldn't that be awful?) As Jura-southside filmer, I grew up in Bielersee, not known to be particularly supportive of film, and after two starting phases, first underground, then serious, engaged film school, both damned by commissions and critics, I wouldn't have made it with this background to phase three ... if it hadn't been for my Berlin friends and those of the »Kleines Fernsehspiel« in Mainz. The Gregors are authorities recognized even in Switzerland. (When »Night Story« was selected for the Forum, the »Zürcher Fähnchen«, which had, as a member of the Filmmakers' Guild, found the submitted trial film »atrocious«, did an about-face and wrote wonderful texts, for which I am today still grateful.)

The Forum strengthened my backbone, gave me the courage to stand by my radical film forms which would otherwise, in the daily struggle with commissions, critics and editors, have been eroded or subdued.

I wish for you, dear friends, another hundred years of pulling obstinate filmmakers out of the swamp: the Forum is an SOS-helicopter!

The new and the old

By Hans Helmut Prinzler

All eyes are directed straight ahead: the public at a film festival is primarily interested in new films, it wants to be part of a première, to help form the first critical opinions, to be included in the direct immediacy. Where is there room for films from yesterday and the day before?

A critical view of films from the present is defined by the presence of films from the past. New films are always - in the most various ways - results of older films, even if they consciously negate a tradition or newly define aesthetics. A view backwards relativizes things. In the excitement of the current competition for prizes and general recognition, a retrospective provides calm and an overview.

Therefore, a section »Retrospective« was a component of the Berlinale from the very beginning. The thematic goals and the form of the presentation have changed. To show only a dozen »masterworks of international filmmaking« - as was done in 1958 - would be neither original nor sensible today. The German need to catch-up on the basic »masterworks« has been satisfied, and the communal cinemas have the most famous »100« or »150« films in their repertory. For a festival retrospective, the classics must be placed in a new context, must be combined with the unknown.

Das Cabinet des Dr. Caligari was shown at the Berlinale of 1951 in the series »Silent Films«; a fragment was shown. The screening was apparently very successful, it was shown once again in the very next year. In 1954 it was to be seen in the »Show of Famous Films«. Then one granted this film a pause. In 1975 it naturally belonged to a Conrad-Veidt-Retrospective. In 1988 a reconstructed, tinted copy was used to open a program on the history of color film, and in 1989 it was an illustration of the creative role of the film producer Erich Pommer. There has not yet been a Robert-Wiene-Retrospective at the Berlinale. The respective context changes and expands the view of the individual film, shifts the accents of perception. There is, in the case of many films, a joy in repeated viewing.

We will not be left without themes for Retrospectives. There is a broad field of interconnections. And external occasions also require appropriate attention. The 100th birth-

day commemorations of great directors and actors are becoming more frequent. The European cinema will be 100 years old in 1995.

However, the audiences of the Retrospectives, in contrast, are becoming younger. They have little interest in a sentimental rendezvous with once admired stars. They discover for themselves the tradition of some genres, the work of some not very well known directors and the technical processes of the medium. The public is growing in sophistication.

Thus the showing of old films in the cinema must always prove itself anew. It competes with the many television stations which offer one feature film after (or parallel to) another. It competes with the small and large collectors of videos, who, to an extent previously inconceivable, have nearly the entire history of sound-film available to them at all times. The large movie screen is still superior to the small television screen, but available copies of the films are often scratched, cut or faded. And the standardized projectors at the cinemas, with which current films are shown throughout the year, are scarcely equal to the individual specifications and requirements of a film-historical retrospective. The day will come when film history can only be presented in special archival cinemas (and the daily need for movies will then be taken care of electronically in any case).

Publications are produced in connection with the Retrospectives. That is the annual opportunity to add a title to German film literature, to write a new chapter for German film history. The first German-language books about Billy Wilder, Ernst Lubitsch, and Fred Zinnemann are attributable to the Berlinale. This aspect is also a motive for putting on Retrospectives and it sometimes determines the choice of a theme.

The idea for a retrospective is o n e *thing. It may be farfetched or obvious, esoteric or popular, boring or original, laughed at or praised. To have an idea, to check it out, to make it concrete, to vary it - all this is a playful and exceptionally amusing matter. Planning, preparation and organization of a retrospective are something else, hard work which takes place in silence for months on end. Searches must be undertaken, copies located, rights clarified, authors reminded, programs finalized. Sometimes the ideal realization of the idea is achieved. This would never come about without the help of the various film archives in the world, without the advice of friends and the action of colleagues who then sometimes finally sit in the cinemas and themselves enjoy the very Retrospective to whose existence they have made their invisible contribution.*

The most important things for a festival are good new films. However, a consciousness for old films also belongs to its cultural ambience. They do not receive prizes, but they have survived.

Knit caps

1978

Feb. 22nd-March 5th, 1978 (Competition)
Feb. 24th-March 3rd, 1978 (Forum)

A Dixieland band played the opening bars: first in front of the Zoo-Palast, then on the Kurfürstendamm. Before the opening of the Festival 1978, a publicity campaign was in full swing. Donner and his helpers distributed programs and knit caps, conceived to draw crowds to this first »Berlinale«, to take place in late winter instead of summer. The »berlinale-tip« reported that all of Berlin's knitwear-makers were producing to full capacity, and that the popular colorful caps had now to be brought in from West Germany. Despite the cold and constant drizzle - for which visitors could purchase a fire-engine red »Berlinale«-umbrella - the showings at the Zoo-Palast were sold out such as they had not been in years. Donner described the Film Festival as »a chameleon oscillating between a congress, fair, workshop, and supermarket, a glamorous ambience, cultural barometer of public opinion, and uninhibited cinema gluttony« (berlinale-tip, No. 1, Feb. 22, 1978). The Berlin Film Festival was in fashion again, and the wrangling over the change in dates which had preceded it was quickly forgotten.

The first »Berlinale« in winter

Thoughts of giving up the IFB's summer dates had been around every now and again. The film industry had for the most part advocated for a rescheduling to fall, Alfred Bauer had tended more and more towards choosing a time in spring. Yet the rescheduling of the »Berlinale« was not seriously pursued for years. Those responsible were reluctant to come into conflict with the FIAPF. Unease, however, persisted over the fact that the Festival in Berlin was scheduled for so soon after the festival in Cannes.

With the establishment of the International Forum of Young Cinema, the discussion of a rescheduling became even more complex; the Forum organizers were for keeping the Film Festival in summer, as they were often able to find significant films in Cannes, which were then premièred in Germany in the Forum.

Controversy over the dates

In 1974, Alfred Bauer came out strongly for a rescheduling of the Film Festival to March. In the 34th meeting of the board of curators (May 13, 1974), he explained his reasons; his most important, even if not new, argument was that all new films produced in winter would then also be up for selection and there would be a better chance of contrasting to the film festival in Cannes. This reflection was motivated by concern over the rivalry between Cannes and Berlin. Surprisingly, Alfred Bauer was backed by Ulrich Pöschke, spokesman for the film industry. Nevertheless, the representatives of Berlin Festivals-Ltd., the Berlin Senate and the Federal Government regarded a rescheduling as »risky«, »speculative«, or even »harmful and an existential threat«, and saw no »guarantee of success«. Bauer's proposal was rejected by five to two votes.

Donner revived this plan in 1976. His reasoning however was orientated differently. In a letter to the chairman of the board of curators, Senator Löffler, Donner lists his arguments for arranging earlier dates for the IFB - in March. He even states that he would like the »Berlinale« 1977 to take place at this new time. An important line of argumentation concerned expanding the Film Fair: in Donner's opinion, importers and exporters would have in late winter - a »period of meager trade and few festivals« - yet before Cannes and the fair in Milan (MIFED), in Berlin the best possibilities. His reasoning took the film industry into account and gained even more weight with the explanation that distributors could then take advantage of Festival films immediately after the end of the Festival; in summer the films had always had to be

Children's Film Festival at the Ufa-Pavillon

Berlin versus Cannes? An old (and false) comparison

shelved until the end of the holidays. Furthermore, as Donner wrote: »The dualism – Cannes = commercialism and Venice = art – is in the process of being destroyed by the disintegration of the festival on the Lido. The international film world needs the great turbulent fair in Cannes, but dreams of an ambitious festival dedicated to artistic cinema such as Berlin and Venice once were.« (Aug. 3, 1976.) Such a statement was aiming at a redetermination of the »Berlinale's« artistic standpoint – and this was indeed the decisive point. Donner's hopes lay in contrasting Cannes and Berlin.

For DEUTSCHLAND IM HERBST: Bernhard Sinkel, Rainer Werner Fassbinder, Alexander Kluge, Volker Schlöndorff, Edgar Reitz

Press conference with Margarethe von Trotta and Ulrich Gregor for DAS ZWEITE ERWACHEN DER CHRISTA KLAGES

Patricia Highsmith, Wolf Donner, Sergio Leone

At the Zoo-Palast: Ilse Stobbe, Dietrich Stobbe, John Cassavetes, Gena Rowlands

»Cannes desires in the future, as well as in every part of its festival, at all costs, novelties, the spectacular, prestige-objects, celebrities in front of and behind the cameras, well-established cinema and the jet set. Berlin is committed to young cinema, and uses the Festival as an international showcase for contemporary German films; in Berlin alongside the Competition, there are such significant events as the International Forum of Young Cinema, the historical Retrospectives, or the Info-Show. Cannes/Berlin, that means contrast, not rivalry. (Donner in: Jahrbuch Film 78/79, Munich, Vienna, 1978.)

The Senate called for an examination of the arguments. Donner was supported by the advisory board of the Festival, which unanimously recommended that the board of curators reschedule the Festival to March. Donner also elucidated on his concept to Mayor Stobbe. And he summarized his position once again for the press, »I am convinced that the present dates are the most unfortunate that a festival in Berlin could possibly have. It is a contradiction in itself to hold a festival at a time when almost the whole of political, cultural and public life is at a standstill and every second person is on holiday. It is quite common nowadays for Berliners not to even know that the ›Berlinale‹ exists.« (Der Abend, Aug. 19, 1976.) Even though organizational and administrative problems hindered an IFB 1977 in March, the board of curators did endorse a rescheduling of the Festival for the year of 1978.

The FIAPF sets the terms.

It was at this point that complications on an international level began. The FIAPF accepted Berlin's decision, yet required the IFB to adhere to a time before March 15th 1978 – which made Berlin pressed for time; and there was indeed reason to presume that the festival management in Cannes had used its influence to protect its festival. Furthermore, there were covert threats of a boycott from France, e. g., to not permit any more German films in Cannes in the case of a realization of Donner's plan to reschedule the Berlin Festival. These were clearly obstacles, even if it would

The End of the World in Our Usual Bed in a Night Full of Rain: Giancarlo Giannini, Candice Bergen

be possible to remove them. Donner had at any rate to fulfill the demands of the FIAPF and fixed the dates of the 28th Film Festival for February 22nd to March 5th, which meant accepting a change in the scheme regarding which days of the week the festival fell: the opening of the Festival would now fall on a Wednesday. Donner was, however, able to avoid an overlap of the IFB with the »Internationale Tourismus Börse« (ITB), which was to take place from March 4th to March 12th.

For the Competition the new dates were not all that advantageous. Critics found that »quality fluctuates here more than in the Forum, which does not have to worry about international participation. Even though the standpoint of wanting to present films from as many countries as possible in the Competition has not led to completely unjustifiable choices – i. e., choices which could have only been smoothed over by diplomacy – there have been many films which were (at least for the critics) disappointing. Plenty of craftsmanship, but nothing new.« (Wolfram Schütte, Frankfurter Rundschau, March 6, 1978.)

The Film Festival's program opened and closed with two American films. It began with John Cassavetes' Opening Night with Gena Rowlands, playing a Broadway star who has a physical and mental breakdown on opening night: a somtimes exalted, but continuously exciting study. And it ended with Close Encounters of the Third Kind, Steven Spielberg's fairytale-like utopia, secretly an homage to the humanitarian François Truffaut.

There was a thread running through both the Competition program and the films of the Forum. An attempt had been made to try to coordinate (as far as possible) the two parts of the Festival, the Competition being the »primus inter pares«. There were films presenting melodramatically exaggerated conflicts with a touch of irony: for example, in the Competition, Lina Wertmüller's high-strung love story The End of the World in Our Usual Bed in a Night Full of Rain was shown, in which

Opening Night:
Gena Rowlands

Candice Bergen plays an American journalist and Giancarlo Giannini an Italian intellectual - emancipation versus machismo, a love war as Italo-Western. In the Forum, on the other hand, Das andere Lächeln [The Other Smile] by Robert van Ackeren was presented - a spiteful and stylized melodrama about a triangular relationship: a woman shuts herself off from the world, rejecting her husband's advancement in society, enthrones her own successor, and becomes a better wife at her husband's side. And then in the Competition, there was Niklaus Schilling's Rheingold - which was not understood by the audiences of the Festival and was torn apart in most reviews: a calculated and formally precise film, a journey of exaggerated emotions.

Films by women:
Helke Sander,
Margarethe von Trotta,
Gisela Tuchtenhagen,
Jutta Brückner,
Elfi Mikesch

A point of focus in the Forum program were films by women. There was Helke Sander's Die allseitig reduzierte Persönlichkeit - Redupers [The All-Round Reduced Personality - Outtakes], »a relatively comic contribution to the question of why women so rarely amount to much« (Sander); and Margarethe von Trotta had succeeded in producing a hit with her debut film, Das zweite Erwachen der Christa Klages (»The Second Awakening of Christa Klages«). In writing about the film Joe and Maxi by Maxi Cohen and Joel Gold from the USA, Brigitte Jeremias called it »a new and unique form of Cinéma Vérité«. The film is a portrait of her father who has cancer. »The changes in the relationships between the film director and her brothers and sisters to their father are made visible; through them, the kindness, strength and originality of this old man - features which his children had not earlier perceived in him - take on expression; suddenly they have a notion of what it is all about: death.« (Frankfurter Allgemeine Zeitung, March 8, 1978.) From France came a filmic reconstruction of a life, A. Constant by Christine Laurent, from Norway Vibeke Lökkeberg's Apenbaringen [Revelation], an almost documentary portrait of a housewife. Three documentary films from West Germany formed a complex of

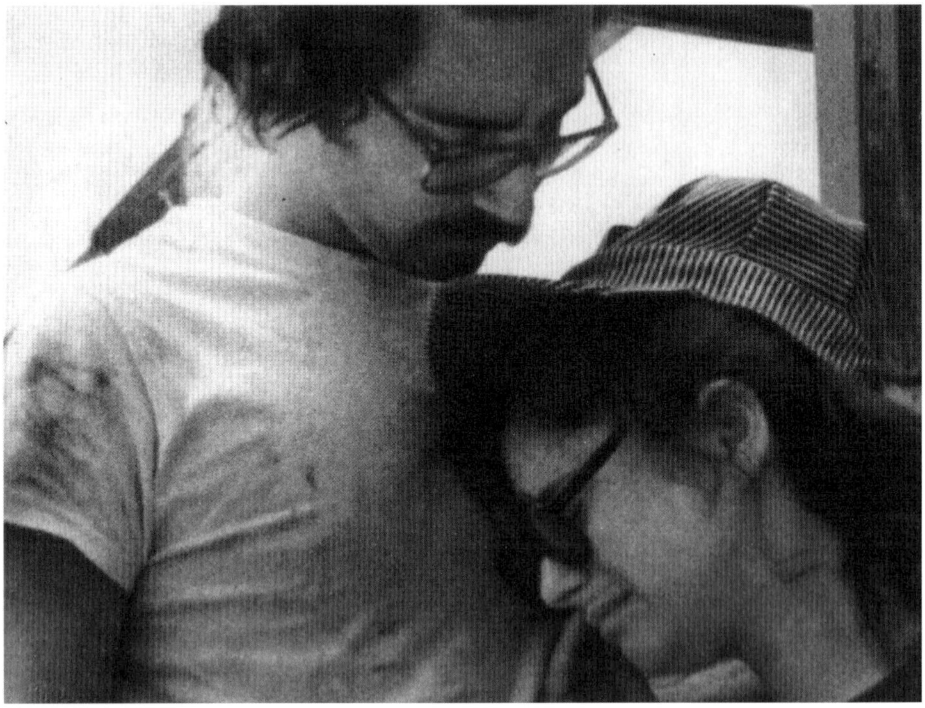

JOE AND MAXI:
Joel Gold, Maxi Cohen

their own in this part of the program: Monika Held's and Gisela Tuchtenhagen's SING, IRIS – SING, Jutta Brückner's EIN GANZ UND GAR VERWAHRLOSTES MÄDCHEN [A Totally Wild Girl] and ICH DENKE OFT AN HAWAII [I Often Think of Hawaii] by Elfi Mikesch. As Brigitte Jeremias stated: »Women – as this Berlinale has made evident – are winning self-confidence in film, they are on the forward march.« (op. cit.)

Politically topical:
DEUTSCHLAND IM HERBST

Festival guests had awaited with eagerness a film which was the group work of West German directors: DEUTSCHLAND IM HERBST [Germany in Autumn]. Eleven filmmakers reacted – with methodic variation – to the political events of fall 1977 in the Federal Republic of Germany: the abduction and murder of Hanns Martin Schleyer, president of the employers' association, and the suicides in Stammheim prison. The film is to be seen as a kaleidoscope of viewpoints, of intense reflection, and alert self-violation: in addition to other historical material, the red thread running throughout the individual episodes are the documentary shots of Schleyer's funeral and of the four members of the »Rote Armee Fraktion« (RAF), who committed suicide in Stammheim. »The depth of focus of DEUTSCHLAND IM HERBST in these segments brings, almost exclusively, atmospheric and factual details to light, capturing the grotesque and the absurd, the threatening and the intimidating, the surrealistic reality of these days and weeks.« The most intense episode came from Rainer Werner Fassbinder, and was an autobiographical record: »A strong, vehement, and radically open piece of self-disclosure, in which anger and desperation, fear and aggression, self-repulsion and a search for love are oppressively concentrated as in a magnifying glass.« (Wolfram Schütte, Frankfurter Rundschau, March 8, 1978.) Donner's decision to show this film had been a risky one. The political climate was tense, discussions on terrorism were not free from accusations. The word »Sympathisanten« (sympathizers) had taken on new meaning. Almost ten years later, at the Film Festival in 1989, there was to be a near scandal: over Reinhard Hauff's film STAMMHEIM.

Die allseitig reduzierte Persönlichkeit – Redupers: Helke Sander

When the prizes were distributed, the international jury, with Patricia Highsmith as its president, awarded Deutschland im Herbst a special commendation, a novum indeed. The Grand Prix of the Film Festival was however a surprise, the Golden Berlin Bear went to the Spanish entries as a whole, i. e., to Las truchas [Trout] by José Luis García Sánchez, Las palabras de Max [What Max Said] by Emilio Martinez Lázaro and the short film Ascensor [Elevator] by Tomas Muñoz. This decision was to be taken as a political award – a bow of the jury and the Festival to the still young Spanish democracy.

The Children's Film Festival

»Movies for people from six years and up« was the motto of a new film series included in the Film Festival. At Donner's instigation, film events for children were organized – in cooperation with the Landesbildstelle Berlin. »Children, unencumbered and spontaneous, are ideal viewers«, wrote Wolf Donner. In the Ufa-Pavillon, in the Kino im Märkischen Viertel and in the movie theater of the Landesbildstelle, ten films were presented – to an enthusiastic audience. 12 000 visitors, large and small saw children's films from round the world – from Australia, Czechoslovakia, the USSR, East Germany, Great Britain, West Germany and India. It was in fact not a totally new idea: as early as in 1957, film events for young people had been held as a part of the Film Festival, organized by the Department of Education and the Department of Family, Youth and Sport. In 1966, a jury of young people awarded one film a prize; however, since interest was low and the films could hardly find distributors, these film events for young people were dropped from the program. It was in this year of 1978, that films – not only for »old fogeys« – were once again offered in the program.

Seen as a whole, 1978 was a successful year for the »Berlinale«. The rescheduling of the Film Festival had paid off; public interest had grown, the movie houses were often sold out and – of particular importance – the film industry was playing a more

International Jury
Patricia Highsmith (USA, president)
Sergio Leone (Italy)
Theo Angelopoulos (Greece)
Jacques Rozier (France)
Konrad Wolf (GDR)
Frieda Grafe (FRG)
Antonio Eceiza Sansinenea (Spain)
Ana Carolina Teixeira Soares (Brazil)
Larissa Shepitko (USSR)

The Awards of the International Jury

Feature Films
Grand Prix of the 28th IFB
Golden Berlin Bear
for all of the Spanish entries
LAS TRUCHAS, directed by
José Luis García Sánchez
LAS PALABRAS DE MAX
directed by
Emilio Martinez Lázaro
ASCENSOR (short film)
directed by Tomas Muñoz

Special Prize of the Jury
Silver Berlin Bear
A QUEDA
Brazil, directed by
Ruy Guerra, Nelson Xavier

Silver Berlin Bear
for the best director
Georgi Dyulgerov
for AVANTAGE
Bulgaria

Silver Berlin Bear
for the best actress
Gena Rowlands
in OPENING NIGHT
USA

Silver Berlin Bear
for the best actor
Craig Russell
in OUTRAGEOUS
Canada

Silver Berlin Bear
for his first work
Octavio Cortázar
for EL BRIGADISTA
Cuba

Silver Berlin Bear
Jerzy Kawalerowicz
for SMIERC PREZYDENTA
as well as for the rest
of his works
Poland

active role in Berlin. And it was for this reason that Donner wanted to enlarge the Film Fair. In a report to the board of curators, he points out: »More film industry means also a greater willingness to take part in one or another part of the Festival. (...) Most festivals having an adjoining film fair suffer from an underrepresentation of buyers. Berlin in 1978 was in the fortunate situation of having an oversupply of interested buyers and too few products, that is, too few films.« (Sept. 4, 1978.) The Berlin Film Fair had become economically attractive. In 1976, 28 countries had taken part in the Fair, the next year, 34, and in 1978 there were 36. There was a definite upward trend. Donner's arguments for enlarging the Film Fair were persuasive. On September 11th 1978, the Berlin Festivals-Ltd's advisory board for film decided to »expand the Film Fair Berlin for politico-cultural and film-related economic reasons«. Consequently, the conversion of the so-called »Luftetage« in the Budapester Straße into a Film Fair-Center with diverse rooms for screening films was begun. The Film Fair was turning into a more and more important economic factor for the IFB.

These developments could only be realized with additional funds. The Federal Government decided – on the initiative of Chancellor Helmut Schmidt – to raise the subsidies for Berlin in cultural-domains. Yes, substantially more federal funds went to Berlin; for the »Berlinale« this meant an increase in its budget of approximately DM 500 000.

Recognition

By Jerzy Kawalerowicz

The forty-year-old Berlin Film Festival makes an eternally young impression. The merit and the recognition which it has achieved are based on the climate which is particularly favorable here for an international artistic competition of performance, and on its particular prestige among the film festivals of the world. It has developed a program structure which supports and encourages the art of film. As a Polish director, I owe the Berlin International Film Festival high recognition for all that has been done for the Polish art of filmmaking and for my own work. I had the honor to participate in this festival in 1976 as a juror and received a Silver Bear in 1978 for my film SMIERC PREZYDENTA *[The Death of the President]. In this anniversary year I wish the Berlin Film Festival a further blossoming and I wish its organizers a consistent perpetuation of their creative shaping of the program, which contributes very significantly to the distribution of the best and most original works of the international art of film.*

A scene from a film presented in the Forum, Drevo Zhelaniya [The Miracle Tree] by the Georgian director Tengis Abuladze

The Deer Hunter:
Robert de Niro, John Savage

Change in mid-flight

1979

Feb. 20th-March 3rd 1979, (Competition)
Feb. 22nd-March 3rd 1979, (Forum)

The 1979 Film Festival was not born under a particularly good sign. Snow and ice – and no end in sight. An exceptionally cold winter wore the Berliners down. Quite a few Festival guests shivered too. This year the posters for the Festival were missing from many of the outdoor advertising pillars: they hadn't been hung because some felt that nobody would pay attention to them in such extremely cold weather. Instead the programs of the Festival were mailed out. However, not every Berliner received a copy. This provoked ironic remarks in the press.

Three important events paved the way for the opening of the Film Festival on February 20th: the retirement of Wolf Donner as the director of the International Film Festival Berlin, a power struggle with the FIAPF over the dates for the »Berlinale«, and the appointment of Moritz de Hadeln as the new director of the Festival.

Wolf Donner's resignation

When on November 2nd 1978, Wolf Donner's resignation as director of the Film Festival was announced by the »Tagesspiegel«, rumors of his leaving were confirmed. He had accepted an offer by the news magazine »Der Spiegel« for the post of editor of the cultural section. At the press conference, Dr. Dieter Sauberzweig, then Senator for Cultural Affairs, stated, alongside words of gratitude, »The director of the Berlin Film Festival does not have to be appointed for life.«

By and large, Donner's work was assessed positively in the press, even though bringing forward the dates of the IFB (which had been planned during the Bauer »era«) – which was accomplished during his period in office – had almost always been accompanied by problems (which was also due to the fact that the occasional journalist reduced the switch in dates to the argument that Berlin simply wanted to start earlier than Cannes, period!).

Balance

At a press conference held on November 15th, Donner himself gave a review of his work. Summing it up in ten points he stated:

- Rescheduling the Festival proved to be the right decision and both good and useful for Berlin, in spite of critical utterances in Cannes and from the FIAPF.
- The Cine-Center in the Kunsthalle was an attraction.
- The Film Fair had been expanded under his guidance.
- Initiatives had been undertaken with respect to program events: the German Cinema Series, the Children's Film Festival, the Info-Show.
- The budget of the Film Festival had been enlarged.
- By working on the image of the Film Festival, it now had a more youthful and lively appearance. »The Berlin-oriented Festival« had been given the right of way.
- A new, different, younger, and more sophisticated audience had been won over for the »Berlinale«.
- Cooperation with other Berlin cultural institutions had been taken up anew and intensified.
- The programs, publications, and brochures had met with a very positive response.
- Finally, the internal organization of the Festival had been changed and improved.

By way of summary: »The basis has been established, it exists, and it works.« Even if it was a bit squeeky on occasions...

At first there were problems with the dates, which had been set for March 14th-25th, 1979. That this should prove to be a disaster became apparent when the FIAPF

Federal President Walter Scheel, Regina Ziegler, Ulrich Schamoni

Jeanne Moreau

Wolfgang Staudte

Astrid Henning-Jensen

expressed its disapproval of these dates at its meeting of November 10th. Formally, this was in fact justifiable, since moving forward the International Film Festival Berlin in principle had only been agreed to on the proviso that the »Berlinale« would finish - at the latest - two months before Cannes. That would have been March 15th - and the opening date for the Festival fixed by the Festival management was March 14th. Donner based his arguments in favor of the shift on two points: first, the elections to the House of Representatives on March 18th, and, second, the International Tourism Fair from March 3rd to 11th, which would make hotel beds scarce.

At the beginning both stuck to their respective positions. Rumors circulated that Berlin was in danger of losing its »A-status«, if the dispute continued to escalate, and if the president of the FIAPF continued to make use of his right, as laid down in the statutes, »to withdraw the recognition accorded, if he deemed this necessary.« (FIAPF regulation.)

Although for a time it looked as if Donner was preparing himself for a power struggle with the FIAPF, and had even declared that the status had ceased to matter, the board of curators of the Festivals-Ltd. had already decided to take the line of retreat and agreed, on December 10th, not to jeopardize cooperation with the FIAPF by insisting on the dates already settled. Instead the International Film Festival was to be held from February 20th to March 3rd 1979. At the same time, and to avoid further trouble, the 1980 »Berlinale« was set for a non-controverisal time extending from the middle to the end of February.

The merry-go-round with the candidates

At around the same time the organizers gave greater thought to the question of a successor to Donner. There was agreement on one issue, more importance should be attached to the person and function of Ulrich Gregor and thus of the Forum. Furthermore, the most diverse candidates were the subject of speculation and rumors.

This was partly deliberate, in order to pursue specific personal interests, in part it was due to a genuine interest in finding a suitable person for this key position.

»Die Zeit« and the »Süddeutsche Zeitung« favored the Munich film reviewer Florian Hopf: Peter Buchka argued that he had »excellent connections in France (and elsewhere), he has advised the festival in Cannes on the selection of German entries, and he is on friendly terms with Gilles Jacob, the director of Cannes« (Süddeutsche Zeitung, Nov. 25, 1978). Wolfram Schütte, writing in the »Frankfurter Rundschau«, proposed Ulrich Gregor for the overall management of the Festival, with the following reservations, »He would at least have to make a greater number of, and more painful compromises than has been the case in his field of activity so far. He would also have to adopt more problematic positions than he has cared to do in the past. (...) The question Gregor has to be asked is: does he want to do this, and does he have - as the Berliners say - ›the gumption to do it‹« (Nov. 4, 1978). Brigitte Jeremias also pleaded in favor of Ulrich Gregor as Festival director: »He has more international contacts than anyone else, even with problematic film countries, such as - at the moment - France, which is piqued about Berlin as far as film is concerned. Above all, however, he has sound knowledge of the industry, both artistically and in economic terms. Ulrich Gregor is the right man for the Berlinale. Even the coat and tails would suit the forty-six year old.« (Frankfurter Allgemeine Zeitung, Nov. 11, 1978.)

The board of curators appoints a selection commission.

The board of curators of the Film Festivals-Ltd. took a different approach to that adopted three years before, when it had been a question of finding a successor to Alfred Bauer. At that time a selection commission was instructed to look for applicants by inviting tenders. Furthermore, a number of well informed and competent persons were called in as assessors to give advice. If we recall, not one of the 15 applicants found mercy in the eyes of the commission so that in the end it was one of the assessors who made the running - i. e. Wolf Donner.

This time the board of curators approached people who it considered suitable. Its members included - by virtue of their political office - Dr. Pfeiffer, for the Federal Ministry of Finance, Mr. Baum, the Federal Minister of the Interior, Assistant Secretary Dr. Koppenhöfer from the Federal Foreign Office, and Kreutzer, Assistant Undersecretary of State representing the Federal Ministry for Intra-German Relations. On behalf of Berlin there were Cultural Senator Sauberzweig, Senator of Finance Riebschläger, and Professor Heimann as head of the Office of the Berlin Senate. The film industry was represented by the managing director of the Spio, Ulrich Pöschke.

The board of curators set up a selection commission which was not only to find a new Festival director but also to work out a new Festival structure. It was made up of Senator Sauberzweig, Ministerial Supervisor Dr. von Köckritz from the Federal Ministry of the Interior, and Ulrich Pöschke; Ulrich Eckhardt and the then Senatorial commissioner for Film, Dr. Günter Struve, acted in an advisory capacity.

While arrangements were being made, speculation continued in the press. Volker Baer discussed, in the »Tagesspiegel« (Nov. 15, 1978), a list of names which gives some idea of the broad conception of how the new director was to be: Heinz Ungureit, Dr. Peter W. Jansen, Dr. Günter Rohrbach, Ulrich Schamoni, Dr. Günter Struve, and of course, Florian Hopf and Ulrich Gregor. More names were added by other newspapers: Bernd Plagemann, the artistic director of the Nordische Filmtage (Nordic Film Festival) Lübeck, Kurt Habernoll, Joe Hembus, Michael Lentz, Gerhard

Die Ehe der Maria Braun (»The Marriage of Maria Braun«): Hanna Schygulla

Moritz de Hadeln was born in 1940 in Exeter, Great Britain. He spent his childhood in Switzerland. First he studied natural science, then film in Paris. As of 1961 he made photoreportages, in 1963 his first documentary about a pilgrimage to Chartres (Le Pélé), in 1967 another about youths on the eve of May '68 in Paris, Ombres et mirages.
From 1964 on he was assistant film editor and cameraman for Ernest Artaria and Yves Allegret among others, in 1967 assistant director for an Artur Brauner production in Berlin. In 1969 he established the Documentary Film Festival in Nyon, remaining its director until 1979. From 1972 till 1977 he was also director of the International Film Festival in Locarno.

Schoenberner, all journalists, and Peter Schamoni. Moritz de Hadeln's name was also mentioned.

Four sessions of the selection commission were held with a total of eleven hearings. Not everyone appeared in front of the commission. Those invited in the end were: Ulrich Gregor, Heinz Badewitz (director of the Hofer Filmtage - the Hof Film Festival), Bernd Plagemann, Wolfgang Ruf (director of the West German Short Film Festival in Oberhausen), Moritz de Hadeln, Peter Konlechner (director of the Vienna Film Musem), the film economist Dr. Hubert Ortkemper, managing director of the Polytel in Hamburg, and Heinz Falk, sales manager of Telepool in Munich, as well as the film critics Klaus Hebecker (Hamburg), Joe Hembus, and Florian Hopf (both from Munich).

While the newspapers gave out the first film titles for the 29th International Film Festival Berlin news began to leak out about Moritz de Hadeln's position as favorite. »The man from Switzerland is very likely to follow in Donner's footsteps on May 1st.« (Volker Baer, Der Tagesspiegel, Jan. 27, 1979). Admittedly, the »Berliner Morgenpost« had spread this news a few days before - which provided grounds for speculation. Volker Baer suspected a »well-organized leak«. Behind this supposition was the fact that Bernd Lubowski, film critic of the »Morgenpost« - and now the new PR man of the Berlin Festivals-Ltd. - continued to write for his old newspaper. (Subsequently Lubowski cancelled his contract with the company and returned as a journalist to the »Berliner Morgenpost«.)

On January 31st the decision was finally made. At a press conference of the board of curators held in the Akademie der Künste, Senator Sauberzweig - in his capacity as deputy chairman of the board of curators - announced that Moritz de Hadeln would assume the position of new director of the »Berlinale« when the contract with Wolf Donner expired on May 1st, or June 1st. Furthermore, he pointed out that the board of curators and all those involved wanted to preserve »thematic controversy«

Messidor:
Clémentine Amouroux,
Catherine Rétoré

which had been a »positive feature« of the Film Festival so far. The Competition and the Forum were now, for this very reason, placed under separate directors with distinct responsibilities. However, in contrast to the previous regulation, the status of the Forum - and of Ulrich Gregor - was assured by the fact that the Berlin Festivals-Ltd. would initially commission the Freunde der Deutschen Kinemathek (Friends of the German Cinémathèque) with the running of the Forum within the framework of the Berlin Film Festival for a period of five years.

This solved the problem of Wolf Donner's successor just three weeks before the last »Berlinale«, under his supervision, was due to open. On the whole the approach adopted by the board of curators was well received. This attested to its having made a good choice in selecting de Hadeln. The nomination of the new director was received happily and optimistically. The Film Festival could now begin.

Yet the Film Festival was not able to enjoy the conciliatory, or even light-hearted and relaxed atmosphere, with which it had begun, for long. A mere four films had been shown in the Competition, when, on February 23rd, Michael Cimino's The Deer Hunter raised a storm. Nine years after the scandal surrounding Michael Verhoeven's o. k., it was once again a Vietnam film which caused a furor at the »Berlinale«. Once again the (political) opinions were divided as to whether this film was suitable for »promoting understanding among nations« as the regulations demanded.

The film tells the story of three men drafted into the military and sent to Vietnam. One returns as a cripple, another survives without any - external - injuries; the third remains in Saigon, psychologically disturbed, having succumbed to the deadly game of »Russian roulette« in which one bullet is loaded into the magazine of a revolver, and the »player«, without knowing which chamber contains the bullet, directs the weapon against himself. This is a film which »does not try to depict the authentic experiences of the American trauma from a liberal, intellectual standpoint, but

GESCHICHTE DER NACHT

through the unpolitical eyes of three steel workers from a small industrial town in Pennsylvania, decendants of Russian immigrants, who experience the war as a perverse orgy of total destruction. The deadly game of Russian roulette - which the Americans first come across in a prison camp in North Vietnam, and not only practised by sadistic Vietcong officers but also by Americans, French, and South Vietnamese - becomes the dominant metaphor of this bleak, but grandiose film« (Hans C. Blumenberg, Die Zeit, March 2, 1979).

Protest from the socialist countries to Cimino's Vietnam film, THE DEER HUNTER

On the eve of its screening the delegation from the USSR published a declaration expressing its »resolute objection« against the showing of the film, arguing that the film contravened the regulations calling for »better mutual understanding among nations«. Among other things they stated: »In a number of episodes of the film the heroic people of Vietnam are insulted, something which is particularly impermissible now at a time when the Socialist Republic of Vietnam is being subjected to barbaric aggression from China, and is fighting a just battle for its freedom and independence.« The declaration continued: »The Soviet delegation had in good time repeatedly warned the Film Festival management, basing its arguments on the protests against this film lodged at the film festival in Belgrade.« As a consequence, the Soviet delegation left the Festival and withdrew their films from the program, yet not before laying the blame for the incident with the Festival management.

That very evening, the Cuban delegation followed suit and the GDR, Hungary, Poland, Bulgaria, and Czechoslovakia joined in the protest. Rumania, on the other hand, left its films in the program, while the USSR and the GDR blocked the screening of their films in the Fair. Two jury members, Pál Gábor from Hungary, and Vera Chytilova from Czechoslovakia, resigned from their posts.

My Way Home: a scene with Stephen Archibald (on the left)

On February 23rd participants from the Third World submitted a declaration protesting against the screening of the film and expressing their solidarity with the delegation from the socialist countries, without, however, taking the same step of leaving the Festival.

The Festival committee (i. e. the selection committee) – which, in 1979, included Stefan Lukschy, Christa Maerker, Jeanine Meerapfel, Michael Weinert, Kraft Wetzel, and Regina Ziegler – speedily followed up the exodus with a press statement. All forms of interference in the program planning were dismissed »irrespective of the party involved« and regret was expressed that some delegations considered it necessary to pull out of the Berlin Festival because of The Deer Hunter. The selection committee was unanimous in its support of the decision to screen the film at the Film Festival since it was »a serious and important artistic contribution attempting to come to terms not only with recent American history, but, above all, with the phenomena of war and violence«. It continued: »No matter how we may judge the film for its contents and aesthetic style, we feel that it promotes discussion, something which no international festival such as ours should ever shy away from.«

The remaining members of the international jury – Ingrid Caven, Liliana Cavani, Julie Christie, Georg Alexander, Paul Bartel, Jörn Donner (as president) and Romain Gary – expressed their views, regretting the developments, but at the same time giving their assurance that they would continue their work »in order to support the freedom of thought which we believe should be independent of tactical considerations.« However at the end of the Festival, Julie Christie gave a personal statement in which she gave her support for the jury's declaration. Having now seen the film she felt that it encouraged that kind of racism which ultimately made a war such as that in Vietnam possible in the first place: »I do not think that one can present an entire nation as sadistic, and then claim that one is only doing so for dramatic effect.« With this she was undoubtedly referring to a sentence uttered by Cimino made just before he flew back to London (prior to the film's screening) in which he had stressed the fact that his film did not have any political leanings, but simply described an exemplary war situation which could have been depicted equally well with any other war.

In some ways the Film Festival now found itself – over night – in the kind of tense political situation which recalled those years in which the socialist countries had kept away from the Film Festival. In order to minimize the damage, the Festival management endeavoured to bring forward specific films; at least we know of a screening of Andrzej Wajda's Czlowiek z marmuru (»Man of Marble«). Nevertheless, in the Competition, four feature films and five short films suffered as a result of the exodus of the socialist countries; in the Info-Show this number was four, and in the Children's Film Festival it was five. Only two films were withdrawn from the Forum: one Soviet and one Hungarian contribution.

In spite of it being depleted of films in this manner and despite the resignation of two jury members, the Festival continued. This was due to the fact that these developments had, to a certain degree, been predictable, so that the Festival management had had time to organize emergency plans. On the other hand, however, it was due to the steadfest attitude of Wolf Donner and the political backing given him by the Senate. »The Berlinale«, Donner wrote, »is free and tolerant enough to engage in debates over difficult films and controversial topics. There are good reasons why our statutes preclude the possibility of censorship – the Festival does not withdraw nominated entries because of objections.« And Mayor Dietrich Stobbe, who had to stand for election just two weeks after the IFB, gave him flank protection: »The Senate has no sympathy for such measures, even if the Soviet representatives declare that they are not directed against Berlin or its Festival. I regret this burden on the Film Festival and on all those involved in it.«

The Soviet protest had, however, been formulated rather moderately. Rumor circulated that they had suggested switching the showing of The Deer Hunter with the closing film Superman, in order to avoid a scandal on the third day; yet the Americans were said to have rejected this proposal. There was even talk about the Soviet delegation being upset about the move, and yet considering it unavoidable given the political constellation. At the same time it indicated that no final withdrawal from the »Berlinale« was connected with this step. Whatever truth there was in these rumors, and no matter how energetically work went on behind the scenes to minimize the damage, the delegations left Berlin and the show went on – peacefully.

Films from Spain and a Panorama of Indian cinema

The Forum screened films from Spain, where the film industry was booming following the end of the Franco dictatorship. There was a panorama of Indian films – including three films by Mrinal Sen – showing a different Indian cinema, with independently produced films, made outside the commercial film sector. One of Sen's films Parashuram [The Man with the Axe], was screened in the Competition, supplementing the Forum program and giving a small presentation of the Indian director's work.

Conspicuous, in turn, was the common subject matter of the Forum and the Competition films: travel films, not only geographical journeys, but also autobiographical journeys. Askndrie... lie? (»Alexandria... Why?«) by directed Youssef

Chahine, the portrait of this Egyptian town, was shown in the Competition. It depicted the dream of a boy in America, containing »documentary shots and fictitious material [revealing] a panorama of the bustling town in all its contradictions, with its people and political as well as cultural movements.« (Wolfram Schütte, Frankfurter Rundschau, March 6, 1979.) In the Forum there was MY WAY HOME by Bill Douglas, the story of a young man in a Scottish village who had to do military service in Egypt. Or there was MESSIDOR by Alain Tanner (in the Competition), an unplanned journey, with no definite goal, through Switzerland by two women. Improvised, they hitch around, increasingly desperate, because the final goal of their aimless journey is a murder. The dream of freedom and an absence of ties turns out to be a nightmare for a friendship which is just beginning. And – in the Forum – Clemens Klopfenstein's GESCHICHTE DER NACHT [Night Story] was of »peaceful images unaccompanied by words, showing dark streets and squares devoid of people all over Europe. (...) filmed in a coarse-grained black and white, with phantoms, shadows, the supernatural play of light between Belfast and Basel, Stockholm and Warsaw.« (Hans C. Blumenberg, Die Zeit, March 9, 1979.) Rudolf Thome's and Cynthia Beatt's BESCHREIBUNG EINER INSEL [Description of an Island] – somewhere between a documentary and a feature film, between comprehension and distance – was among the filmic journeys of this year's Festival.

Many reviews spoke of a Festival of quiet films. There was no opposition when the Golden Bear was awarded to Peter Lilienthal's DAVID. This was seen as a signal by the jury, a move to contrast the gentle humanism of this film to the nihilism of DEER HUNTER.

As producer at the Berlinale

By Joachim von Vietinghoff

In the fifties, I participated in the glamour of the »Berlinale« only via the weekly newsreels in the cinema. My heart beat faster when stars, from Lollo to Gary Cooper, had a rendezvous.

After I, by way of journalism and photography, advanced in the sixties to a »young producer« of New German Cinema, Dr. Bauer brought me with my first production – Roland Gall's WIE ICH EIN NEGER WURDE – to the Berlinale in 1970. However, before the curtain rose for the première, we joined a boycott by all German producers and directors of the Festival. Jury president George Stevens had protested against another German contribution, Michael Verhoeven's O.K.! That was the end of my first international appearance.

Nonetheless, that Festival encounter was not to be my last. After my apprenticeship with Heinz Angermeyer in Munich, experience in production with Klick, Sinkel and Brustellin, Kückelmann, Perakis and others, the new head of the Festival Wolf Donner invited me to the International Competition with the Lilienthal film DAVID in 1979. Our films had, up until then, attained recognition above all in foreign countries, at Cannes and Venice; DAVID was able, for the first time in 24 years (Siodmak's DIE RATTEN), to win the Golden Bear for a German production.

The 1979 Festival was a highlight for me personally, as well. I made the acquaintance of the actress Mareike Carrière; we have been married since 1981, we live and work in Berlin.

International Jury
Jörn Donner
(Finland, president)
Julie Christie
(Great Britain)
Romain Gary (France)
Ingrid Caven (FRG)
Georg Alexander (FRG)
Liliana Cavani (Italy)
Vera Chytilova (departed early – Czechoslovakia)
Pál Gábor
(departed early – Hungary)
Paul Bartel (USA)

The Awards of the
International Jury

Feature Films
Grand Prix of the 29th IFB
Golden Berlin Bear
DAVID
FRG, directed by
Peter Lilienthal

Special Prize of the Jury
Silver Berlin Bear
ASKNDRIE... LIE?
Egypt, directed by
Youssef Chahine

Silver Berlin Bear
for the best director
Astrid Henning-Jensen
for VINTERBØRN
Denmark

Silver Berlin Bear
for the best actress
Hanna Schygulla
in DIE EHE DER
MARIA BRAUN
FRG

Silver Berlin Bear
for the best actor
Michele Placido
in ERNESTO
Italy

Silver Berlin Bear
for the entire film crew of
DIE EHE DER MARIA BRAUN
FRG, directed by
Rainer Werner Fassbinder

Silver Berlin Bear
Sten Holmberg
for his camera work
in KEJSAREN
Sweden

Silver Berlin Bear
Henning von Gierke
for his scenic work in
NOSFERATU - PHANTOM
DER NACHT
FRG/France

The Film Festival became a perennial integral component of my wor, a promotion for my own work, and a meeting point for all branches of the business, co-production discussions, castings, resumées and perspectives. Most difficult work, but also constant partying and the possibility of closeness once again to those things one often misses during the rest of the year.

I continued supplying the Festival with films: Luc Bondy's DIE ORTLIEBSCHEN FRAUEN *ran in the Forum in 1980; Hellmuth Costard's* ECHTZEIT/REALTIME *ran in 1983 in a night special in the Zoo-Palast which was sold out days in advance; Matthias Zschokke's* EDVIGE SCIMITT *was awarded the German Film Critics' Prize at the Delphi during the 1986 Festival.*

In the meanwhile, Moritz the Hadeln has become director of the »Berlinale«, perhaps not the easiest of bosses - his program is not always identical with the wishes of the official contingent - but one who has courage to take risks and provides for the necessary internationality, and who has developed the »Berlinale« into a place of East-West encounter (as demonstrated by the 1987 »summit meeting« between Jack Valenti and Elem Klimov). He has made use of the generation-change introduced by Wolf Donner and has continued to develop and mold the Festival history of the eighties.

Since 1983 I have been a member of the selection committee for Competition films of the »Berlinale«. This honorable but sometimes thankless office is a great challenge and a continual learning process. Just as I have, over the years, become a part of this city, I feel personally closely committed to the »Berlinale«. The annual Festival is like this city - a formidable melting pot: alive, open and hearty, unruly, headstrong and insatiable. A comparison with Cannes and Venice appears to me to be superfluous. The elements are too different. Time, place and the audience of each festival speak for themselves, and I don't find it important, which of the three be named number one. I think each one should preserve its individual image.

Berlin does so.

DAVID: Mario Fischel

Palermo oder Wolfsburg:
Nicola Zarbo, Brigitte Tilg

And then there were two

1980

Feb. 18th-Feb. 29th, 1980 (Competition)
Feb. 19th-Feb. 29th, 1980 (Forum)

A festive opening at the Zoo-Palast. Guest of honor is Mayor Stobbe. The lights go out, the projection begins, and the first pictures appear. Curiosity mounts. Suddenly the picture flickers, someone can be heard cursing loudly in the projection room. Contemptible commercials fill the screen – the film is in a tangle. There is uneasiness and grumbling in the parquet. From the projection room noises can be heard like those preceding a fight. Then an announcement is made to calm everybody: »The police are on their way. The projection room has been stormed. Scandal, scandal! Stobbe remains calm, his bodyguards do too. Gradually it dawns on everyone. It's all just a gag – a theatrical trick in the movie house. Rod Gröth [Red Berry Jelly] is the title of the short film by Jörg Moser-Metius.

The Film Festival is celebrating its 30th birthday, the Forum is now ten years old. For the first time, there are two directors with equal status; Moritz de Hadeln is director of the Competition, the Info-Show, the Retrospective, the Children's Film Festival, and the Film Fair since May 1st, and Ulrich Gregor has remained in his old post – yet now as an equal partner – of director of the International Forum of Young Cinema.

The Forum program is extended, and a cooperation agreement reached between the Competition and the Forum.

The program of the Forum was extended to ten days. Up till then films had only been shown in the Forum for eight days. This was the most important agreement covering cooperation with the Competition. In the future it was hoped that organizational problems would be solved jointly – both with respect to questions of dates and the accrediting of journalists and guests. However, the management also wanted to be more precise about the contents of the Festival sections. The »tension« between the Competition and the Forum was to be preserved, for: »It is certainly a positive feature of the Berlinale that it makes available two quite different situations for presenting films, both as far as the venue and the expectations of the audiences are concerned.« (Ulrich Gregor, final report, 1980.) The Forum was also quite open in its own conception of its role: it was not the entertainment value of a film, nor simply its »artistic value« that were decisive, but – according to Ulrich Gregor – film as a »medium for investigating reality, for communicating, and for reflection«.

Altogether there were 158 events with 94 films at the 1980 Forum. New directions in documentaries were presented, a number of Brazilian films, independent productions from the USA, and seven West German films, more than ever before – as well as the Forum's own block of programs with experimental films.

Conspicuous was the degree to which the West German contributions shared the same subject matter, stories of the war and the postwar period, of mothers and daughters, private images which also passed over into political views. There were autobiographical reminiscences too. Recha Jungmann recalled her own life, her childhood, and her family, as well as the place she grew up in. She visited the house – long since dilapidated – in which she was born, in a small village in the Rhön. A work which fluctuates between documentary and poetic sketches, subjective alienation of reality, risky at times because it containes memories which are all too personal: that was Etwas tut weh [Something Hurts]. Recha Jungmann's film, which was part of the Forum program, was not only linked to Deutschland bleiche Mutter (»Germany, Pale Mother«) by Helma Sanders-Brahms (one of the three West German films in the Competition) by virtue of its subject matter, but also methodologically. Helma Sanders-Brahms also related her own story and that of her

DEUTSCHLAND BLEICHE MUTTER
»A few faces stay in mind: the wide strong face of Eva Mattes in the film DEUTSCHLAND BLEICHE MUTTER by Helma Sanders-Brahms, a most fascinating attempt, a piece of radical-subjectivist recollection (not without its embarassing moments, like anytime someone strips off) linked to a collective myth of history. Helma Sanders describes her relationship – broken at so many instances – to her mother and her country, under the Nazis and shortly afterwards: unrelentingly gentle; sentimental research, but not a historical reconstruction.«
Hans C. Blumenberg in Die Zeit, Feb. 29, 1980

mother as a war marriage, the woman and her daughter fight for their survival, while her husband has to go to the front, and the woman becomes alienated from her husband. The war is over, and with it their love and their lives. The director supplements the fiction with autobiographic details. There are breaks where the connections do not always work: a war ensues between fiction and reality. A third film – Jutta Brückner's HUNGERJAHRE [Hunger Years], about the economic miracle, political restoration – was screened in the Forum. It shows a hate-love relationship between a mother and a daugther: the cold, prudish look, the gentle yearning: for what though? As with Helma Sanders-Brahms, Jutta Brückner intervenes from the outside as author, commenting on »her« story, polemically, as well as distancing herself from it. Documentary shots are also blended in (e. g. from June 17th), as well as speeches, and sweet-talk, by politicians and by others. The demure and unbalanced nature of the film, both aurally and visually, with a narrative rhythm that is rough in places, and a refusal to adapt itself just as the girl refuses to adapt herself to life, breathes life and vitality into the film.

A different trend which was revealed in the films of the Forum and the Competition was that of films about youths, with their insistent contrariness, their hopes, and those which adults would like them to cherish; a utopian closeness and a mythological distance. In the Competition, Marco Ferreri's CHIEDO ASILO [My Asylum] was screened. This was a film about a teacher who founders on his own educational demands, and rejects society. He applies for asylum at the very place where he does not belong, both owing to his sex and his status: with a cushion stuffed up his pullover he states that he is pregnant. This is a surreal projection, a myth, which takes up the dream of an unblemished childhood. Two other films served as a counter-balance: Hark Bohm's IM HERZEN DES HURRICAN [In the Heart of the Hurricane], the adventure of two boys who chase after an elk that is lost, and

Moritz de Hadeln, Alfred Bauer

Ingrid Thulin, Moritz de Hadeln, Ulrich Gregor, Dietrich Stobbe, Peter Kern

Press conference for LA MORT EN DIRECT (»Death Watch«) with Romy Schneider and Harvey Keitel

Peter Stein, Andrzej Wajda

who have to learn the value of solidarity in their actions, and Jack Hazan's RUDE BOY, a film about a roadie in the punk rock group »The Clash«. He is an outsider who never establishes any social contacts. Both films deal with expectations and make a clear distinction between good and evil. They are biased and show no respect for the utopia of their protagonists. As a counter-example, András Jeles' film, A KIS VALENTINO [The Little Valentino], tells of a twenty-year old from Budapest, who – in one day – spends all the money with which his boss has entrusted him. »The depressing and radical thing about this film, so deliberately arranged in black and white, is that it summarizes in one day something which, for most people, would serve as a program for the whole of their lives: i. e. the illusion that possessing money enables one to have a better life. On one single day the boy tests out the thing which is always held up as a career goal worth striving for: consumption. But he doesn't like it, and his face remains sad up to the end. In one day he has understood more than most people do in a lifetime.« (Gertrud Koch, Frankfurter Rundschau, March 8, 1980.) Jeles' hero does not apply for asylum – he doesn't lose sight of utopia.

AMOR DE PERDIÇÃO [Love of Perdition] by the Portuguese director Manoel de Oliveira was almost monolithic in the Forum program. It was a love story set at the end of the 18th century, a love affair like »Romeo and Juliet«. The film was the first step towards the discovery of the works of Oliveira in the Federal Republic of Germany, works which cannot deny their inspiration from art history. The film was superbly arranged, with allusions and omissions, staged with infinite patience, shifting between decor and decoration, with a tension and contradiction between the imagery and the commentary, the narration and the reading of the original novel.

Manoel de Oliveira

Ekkehard Pluta gave a »well-considered evaluation« of the Forum films. He found »the selection of films most attractive, even the questionable works failed in an interesting manner«. However, the Forum had, in the meantime, become established, and »if the principle ambition of its initiators is to obtain better films than the official Competition – one could not always clearly tell which films belonged where – then a time is foreseeable when both of the alternative Festival sections will once again merge to form a joint event«. (Stuttgarter Zeitung, March 7, 1980.) For the time being, however, it could be said that the Forum and the Competition had entered into an »entente cordiale« with one another.

Moritz de Hadeln's initiation as director of the Competition had not been easy. Particularly troublesome was the fact that the socialist countries had withdrawn from the Festival only a year before. Their confidence had to be regained, even if the 1979 retreat had been backed up by relatively moderate arguments. The situation was very delicate and politically encumbered by the sending of Russian troops to Afghanistan, and by the discussion surrounding the western countries' plans to withdraw from the Olympics in Moscow. Finally, de Hadeln succeeded in inducing renewed participation of films from the socialist countries in the »Berlinale«. A factor which certainly helped was the involvement shown by the Deputy Minister for Culture in the GDR, Horst Pehnert, who was responsible for film. The tenseness of the situation was revealed by three marginal events. Firstly, after it had been announced in a press release that the South African production MARIGOLDS IN AUGUST by Ross Devenish – based on a script by apartheid opponent Athol Fugard – was to be screened in the Competition, the USSR ordered the participation of the socialist countries in the Festival to be stopped. The Soviets referred to a UN resolution which opposed cooperation with South Africa. All objections raised by the manage-

Typical marginal incidents surround MARIGOLDS IN AUGUST; ONE, TWO, THREE; and WUNDERBARE JAHRE

ment in Berlin to the effect that the film was against radical segregation and pointing out that Fugard's plays were also shown – without any objections – in socialist countries – remained ineffective at first. Finally, a special showing was organized in West Berlin for the Soviet delegation. Since the objections to the film, inasmuch as they contained any real basis in fact, could not be upheld, a compromise was reached. The USSR declared that it would agree to the screening of the film and lift the »temporary« boycott; at the same time the film was listed in the program and in the Festival documentation without any indication of the country of origin. Thus the first obstacle was removed.

The second concerned the Retrospective. Films by Billy Wilder were to be shown. First thoughts turned to NINOTCHKA, for which Wilder had written the script, and to his Berlin film ONE, TWO, THREE. When this became known there were again objections on the part of the Soviets. NINOTCHKA was said to be a dangerous ideological comedy, and there were reservations about ONE, TWO, THREE as well. In some scenes the Russians do not seem to come off so well. Consequently the films were not shown in the Retrospective.

The third problem revolved around the film by the East German dissident Reiner Kunze, WUNDERBARE JAHRE [The Wonderful Years], which had been rejected for the Competition program for reasons of quality. However, some journalists refused to accept this. They insinuated that it was due to false considerations vis-à-vis East Germany. A polemical commentary appeared in »Die Welt«: »Berliners have kept their hands clean« (Feb. 2, 1980). And the working group of the Young Liberals, politically close to the FDP (the Free Democrats), adopted the slogan »Festival of fear«, talked of »self-censorship« and distributed pamphlets at the opening stating »We are ashamed of this cowardice«. Karena Niehoff commented: »This is pretty stupid of the Young Liberals when one considers that even Springer's ›Welt‹ and the local CDU

AMOR DE PERDIÇÃO:
António Sequeira Lopes

have roared only very quietly as far as this matter is concerned. The prospect of all of the Eastern bloc countries withdrawing their films from Berlin yet again, or not sending them here at all (which would most certainly mean for a number of years) is one which not even the CDU would want to assume the responsibility for in Berlin.« (Süddeutsche Zeitung, Feb. 20, 1980.) So much for politics - it can be extremely touchy sometimes.

Jerzy Bossak

At the beginning, de Hadeln added new features to the organization. He continued to extend the Film Fair, following the lines laid down by Wolf Donner, entrusting Aina Bellis with its management. He appointed Manfred Salzgeber - who later gave the Panorama its image and its present form - head of the Info-Show. It was the first time that these sub-sections were no longer co-managed but were given independent control over their own programs.

The adjustment period was difficult, and there were some misunderstandings at first. The advisory board was reconstituted with new members, and with a greater representation of film experts. It now included, among others, the film-maker Charlotte Kerr, the director Heidi Genée, the producers Dr. Alexander Grüter, Regina Ziegler, and Renée Gundelach, and the critic Florian Hopf. It was chaired by Ministerial Supervisor Manfred Hohnstock. De Hadeln also set up a working group for the selection of films, seeing this group as a partner of the Festival director, which, however, did not receive the right to invite films. These steps were all taken to consolidate the organizational structure of the Festival.

What about the program itself? The press could not come to agreement. Some critics found that the films in the Competition lacked something, others mentioned the impressive list of names of the directors participating. Listed were films by Marco Ferreri, Miguel Littin, Zeki Ökten, Werner Schroeter, Helma Sanders-Brahms, István Szabó, Bertrand Tavernier, Andrzej Wajda, and Konrad Wolf.

A KIS VALENTINO: János Opozki

Attention was drawn to the amusing moments provided by films from the USSR and the GDR. Three women were the main characters in Vladimir Menshov's MOSKVA SLESAM NE VERIT [Moscow Does Not Believe in Tears], who settle down in Moscow at the end of the fifties, and look back soberly, sentimentally, and sadly on their lives twenty years later. Peter Buchka wrote about Menshov's film that »The past protects the sarcasm with which it turbulently describes the way in which three girls try to organize and indeed determine their private lives in the face of difficult circumstances. The occasional disrespectful word slips out about conditions in Russia. However, in the second part of the film, which shows what has become of these restless, disrespectful girls, the power of detailed observation wanes quite noticeably. Menshov seems to be more cautious here, more ›balanced‹, and perhaps even more resigned.« (Süddeutsche Zeitung, Feb. 23, 1980.) SOLO SUNNY by Konrad Wolf tells the story of a popular singer in East Germany, the ups and downs of her life. This is an actor's film, with which Renate Krößner – sassy and with the Berliner's gift of gab – cheerfully conquers all hearts, winning a Silver Bear as best actress in the process.

Andrzej Wajda's DYRYGENT and an amazing award

»The best film came from Poland« according to Hans-Christoph Blumenberg: DYRYGENT (»The Orchestra Conductor«) by Andrzej Wajda – on the surface, the story of a famous conductor who returns to Poland from the West only to send a younger colleague into an artistic and personal crisis. Identity problems, the dialectic of phantasy and control. »However, the film's fascination doesn't end there: the play of symbols, documentary film (...) and, not least, a meditation on professionalism and amateurism.« (Die Zeit, March 7, 1980.) The fact that a supporting actor in the film, Andrzej Seweryn was awarded the Festival prize for best actor and not the composed John Gielgud, who played the part of the conductor, not only amazed people but even led to reactions of anger. This decision was to remain a jury secret. It was also

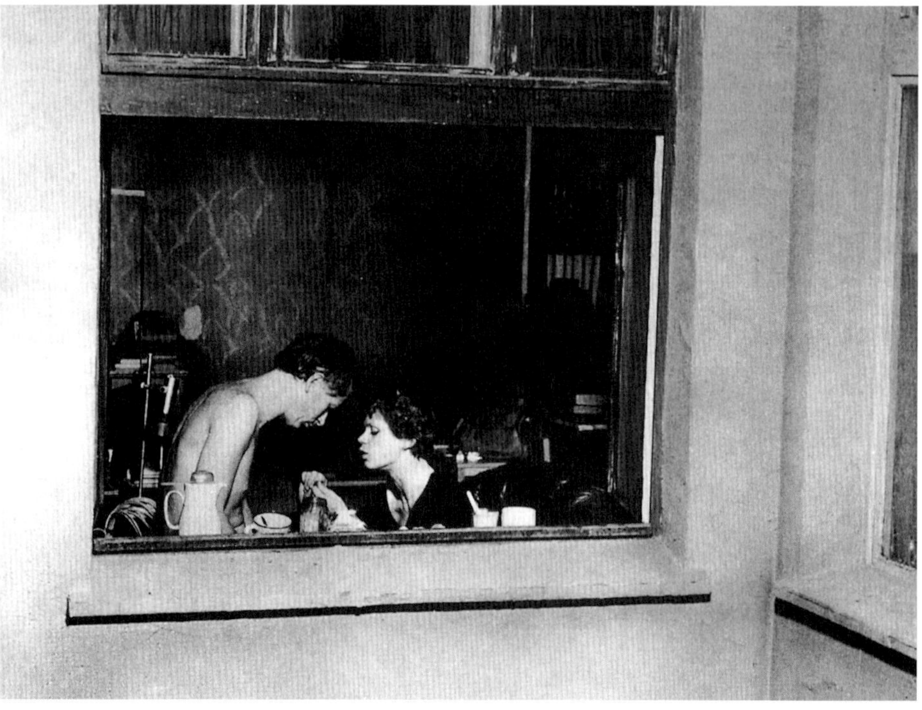

SOLO SUNNY: Alexander Lang, Renate Krößner

noted, with some suspicion, that the Grand Prix of the 30th Festival was awarded ex aequo to the American film HEARTLAND by Richard Pearce, and PALERMO ODER WOLFSBURG [Palermo - Wolfsburg] by Werner Schroeter. Rumors circulated that the decision had been manipulated in favor of the American. Journalists and guests only agreed on one thing: that the Golden Bear award for Schroeter's film had been a courageous and unconventional decision. »A three hour story of a young Sicilian ›guest worker‹ who stabs to death two men was the most outstanding of all the German entries« wrote Wolfram Schütte. »Germany – as difficult a place to enliven as the moon, a nightmare. This was the only daring and correct decision made by the international jury.« (Frankfurter Rundschau, March 8, 1980.)

Two debates also deserve mention here: one flared up over William Friedkin's CRUISING. A detective is instructed to solve a series of murders in New York's gay scene. A controversial discussion ensued about the superficial and sensationalist exploitation of the »scene«. The screening of the Italian-American co-production CALIGULA by Tinto Brass, which was dismissed as a pure pornography spectacle, was considered to have been a mistake. Karena Niehoff commented: »This art isn't begging, it's trading in flesh.« (Süddeutsche Zeitung, March 1, 1980.)

The Retrospectives were by no means marginal phenomena. One covered Billy Wilder, the other dealt with a technical subject for the first time. Revealing a passion for cinema, as well as expertise and inventiveness, Peter A. Hagemann put together a program of 3-D films for the Kinemathek. Three-dimensional cinema – that meant cinema with glasses. Long queues formed in front of the Kurfürstendamm movie house Astor-Filmtheater. It was a technical subject with a great fascination, to which were added nostalgic memories and wonderful films: the audience was spell-bound by Rita Hayworth in Curtis Bernhardt's MISS SADIE THOMPSON - and at that in 3-D. What more can be said?

International Jury
Ingrid Thulin (Sweden, President)
Betsy Blair (Great Britain)
Mathieu Carrière (France)
Alberto Isaac (Mexico)
Peter Kern (FRG)
Karel Makk (Hungary)
Aleksandr Mitta (USSR)
Alexander Trauner (France)
Angel Wagenstein (Bulgaria)

RATATAPLAN, a film in the Info-Show: author, director and leading actor Maurizio Nichetti

The Awards of the International Jury

Feature films
Grand Prix of the 30th IFB
Golden Berlin Bear
ex aequo
HEARTLAND
USA, directed by
Richard Pearce

PALERMO ODER WOLFSBURG
FRG, directed by
Werner Schroeter

Special Prize of the Jury
Silver Berlin Bear
CHIEDO ASILO
Italy/France, directed by
Marco Ferreri

Silver Berlin Bear
for the best director
István Szabó
for BIZALOM
Hungary

Silver Berlin Bear
for the best actress
Renate Krößner
in SOLO SUNNY
GDR

Silver Berlin Bear
for the best actor
Andrzej Seweryn
in DYRYGENT
Poland

Jubilee Prize
Berlin Bear
Athol Fugard
on the occasion of the screening of
MARIGOLDS IN AUGUST

Special Mention
for the script of the film
DÜŞMAN
Turkey

Special Mention
KORPINPOLSKA
Finland/Sweden, directed by
Markku Lehmuskallio

Special Mention
RUDE BOY
Great Britain, directed by
Jack Hazan, David Mingay

The »real« première

By Stefan Jarl

Sweden is a small country, only eight million people live here and speak Swedish. This means that we are isolated, we are a minority in the world. When I first was invited to Berlin I didn't understand that a film festival can change this cultural isolation. For me, the Forum, during the years, has become very important: as an independent film-maker Berlin is the opportunity to tell the audience that I have made a new film. I look upon the Forum as the »real« première for my films, because in Berlin I meet and discuss with the audience; I can meet the distributors of non-commercial films and sell my films and I can get a chance to see good films that I have no possibility to see in my country. But perhaps first of all it's important for a film-maker to have his new film discussed with the audience - after the screenings in Berlin I've always known if I have made an international film or just a Swedish film. And that is a good lesson to learn. In that respect the Forum has for me become an important »institution«. I clearly understood this last year when my film of that year wasn't selected for the programme. Then I really felt homeless and disappointed …

Boycott! Boycott?

1981

Feb. 13th-24th, 1981 (Competition)
Feb. 14th-24th, 1981 (Forum)

A press conference. Nothing exceptional really. Jean-Luc Godard talked, and not only about SAUVE QUI PEUT (LA VIE) (»Every Man for Himself«) which was shown in the Forum. Godard spoke about film history: the history one could read about, and the history he hoped to be able to show. He spoke about his work, film-making, and about control over film-making which was being made increasingly difficult for film directors. He talked of the intervention of others, the producers and the editors, in his own work. A director lets off steam; this was not a press conference but a workshop and a lesson. Norbert Jochum wrote in the »Zeit«, »During the talk a man imparted an impression of what this could still be, cinema, and what it had once been. What it means to be aware of the work of a director, handling images and sound. And of the relationship of the two to one another. Films had become increasingly adapted to television production where the rhythm of the spoken word dominated the rhythm of the images to such an extent that a feeling for the pace of movements had thus been lost completely.« (Feb. 27, 1981.)

Press conference with Jean-Luc Godard

The IFB 1981 was born under a bad sign. The Working Group of New German Film Producers and the Federation of Television and Film Directors threatened to boycott the IFB in the future following a unanimous resolution. This protest was published on February 19th with the second half of the Festival already under way. The resolution included the comment that the Berlin Film Festival was »in a deep crisis (...) In our opinion, the reason for this is to be found in the dilettantism and the inability of the Festival management to make contacts.« The management had failed to give the IFB »a new image« and for this reason the protesters would no longer participate in the Film Festival »if decisive steps were not taken to ensure that a representative Festival was taking place in Berlin under a new management«. In this manner, the »majority« of West German directors declared that they had no con-

West German directors threaten to boycott Moritz de Hadeln.

Jean-Luc Godard

fidence in the Festival management. However, one thing had apparently been overlooked in formulating the protest: Moritz de Hadeln and Ulrich Gregor were jointly responsible for the Festival. The general reproach was modified. When asked, it was said that it was not Ulrich Gregor who had been meant, since they had expressedly wanted to exclude the Forum; protest was directed solely against Moritz de Hadeln and his Festival policy. What was behind this threatened boycott? Quite specifically, only one West German film was represented in the Competition, Herbert Achternbusch's DER NEGER ERWIN [»Black Erwin«]. De Hadeln had backed his decision not to invite any other West German films with the argument that the entries examined were of mediocre quality and spoke of a »crisis in German film«. The directors, for their part, accused de Hadeln of adopting undiplomatic tactics. Alexander Kluge spoke of »an inability to establish contacts« adding that de Hadeln cared more about the desires of American major companies and neglected the necessary and constant contact with West German film-makers. All this took place at a press conference for which, incidentally, no room was made available by the Festival management. The discussion had long since taken on an emotional character, and the directors, as well as their spokesman, Alexander Kluge, had still not managed to make their general accusations more specific. For example, what had been meant by a »representative Festival«? »One director after another evaded the issue by promising to present a paper on a new conception for the Film Festival in the near future. What was left was a vacuum«, wrote Peter Buchka (Süddeutsche Zeitung, Feb. 26, 1981). The film-makers' interests evidently differed too greatly, and their ideas of a »representative Film Festival« – a formulation which had incidentally been favored by Spio in the fifties and sixties – were too divergent. It certainly became apparent that the relationship between the Festival director, de Hadeln, and the West German film-makers was completely unsatisfactory. This was primarily due

Mrinal Sen, Markus Imhoof

Moritz and Erika de Hadeln

Nicole Garcia

Martin Scorsese

to the fact that de Hadeln knew little about the West German film scene, having worked up to this time in Locarno. Furthermore, he knew hardly any of the directors personally. Thus each waited for the other to make the first move, which also meant that time was lost, while disappointment and resentments grew. The fact that the threatened boycott, which initially also meant a refusal to talk, could also restrict de Hadeln's room to maneuver at an international level, had not been taken into consideration by anybody. How was a Festival director, who did not even have the support of the nation's film-directors, supposed to operate in the international arena? Wolfram Schütte assured polemical clarity: a representative Festival - »for whom, with what, and why? We lack compelling answers. They are to be submitted later, again, in an extensive paper: to the pertinent committees, and the authorities. Typical German bullshit - one is tempted to say. Didn't you have any time or place to discuss this earlier? To clear up the contradictions, or at least to formulate them? I am only asking questions. In this case, there would really have been something to talk about. As things stand, there only remains the dilettantish film policy of organizations which act as if they have been insulted. They talk about their emotions without being able to present a conception worthy of discussion. Sensations in public - followed by secret cabinet policy? I am not at all happy about this.« (Frankfurter Rundschau, Feb. 23, 1981.) Undisputable mistakes on the one hand and an ill-considered overreaction on the other. What was left was the shattered remains of a film policy, a badly shaken Festival director, and, despite everything, the offer of dialogue, which de Hadeln and Gregor had made together in response to the boycott resolution. Not every »difference of opinion«, they retorted, should automatically be stylized into a »crisis of the Festival«. »Sometimes one wishes that there was more solidarity in this country; after all, it is a matter of course in other countries among the institutions which are working towards the same goals.« (Feb. 19, 1981.)

Moritz de Hadeln reacts.

However, this did not mean the end of the confrontation. In March, at a general assembly (March 23, 1981), the Berlin Working Group Film (BAF) called on de Hadeln to resign and, at the same time, criticized the state of film policy in West Berlin, accusing the Senator for Cultural Affairs, Dieter Sauberzweig, of pursuing a misguided film policy. At the 30th advisory board meeting on June 23rd 1981, the producers Renée Gundelach and Regina Ziegler submitted a joint declaration supporting the resolution of the Working Group of New German Film Producers and the Federation of Television and Film Directors of February 19th »because of the national affront provoked by the director of the Berlin Festival and the damage he has done to German film«. Once again, the familiar accusations against de Hadeln were repeated together with the demand for his replacement and a »fundamentally new conception«. »We need a festival which reflects the specific situation of German film, the special situation of Berlin, and of the International Film Festival in competition with the other international festivals as well as with new forms of communication and presentation: a Festival of the eighties!« At the same time, Renée Gundelach and Regina Ziegler offered to resign their posts on the advisory board.

Leo Hurwitz, director of DIALOGUE WITH A WOMAN DEPARTED

However, the rejection of de Hadeln as Festival director was not unanimous. Some directors and producers submitted statements in his favor, indicating a willingness to talk about matters. The discord gradually cleared up behind the scenes. Munich was set as the center of the opposition. De Hadeln reacted offensively and skillfully, by extending the spheres of competence of Heinz Badewitz, director of the Hof film festival, who had also been responsible for the series of New German Cinema in

Berlin and made him into the contact man between the IFB and the West German directors. Badewitz enjoyed their confidence. Finally, a political development worked in de Hadeln's favor: the Senate elections were approaching, and there were signs that the Christian Democrats would make up the new Berlin Senate. It was not possible at this time to estimate what their conceptions of film policy would be; thus it did not seem opportune to continue risking the position of the Festival director.

A discussion over the future of the »Berlinale« – organized by the Film Commissioners of both churches, Dr. Gerd Albrecht and Dr. Reinhold Jacobi – which was to have taken place on September 22nd and September 23rd in Bonn-Bad Godesberg – did not come about because the Working Group of New German Film Producers declined to participate at short notice. It is interesting to note that not one representative of the Berlin Senate was invited to this discussion, although it had a 50% participation in the Film Festival through the Berlin Festivals-Ltd. In the »Volksblatt Berlin«, Heiner Roß, co-organizer of the International Forum from 1971 to 1979, formulated heretic proposals extending from dropping the »A-Status« and terminating Spio cooperation in the board of curators to giving up the spring dates, and the cancellation, without any replacement, of the Information Show. He also argued in favor of extending the series of New German Cinema to make a »National Film Festival«.

Yet it was not only West German films which failed to measure up to the selection criteria this year; not one film from East Germany had received an invitation to the Competition. The GDR declined the offer to show four Defa films in the Info-Show and withdrew its films from the other sections too, because it was not represented in the main program. A copy was even refused for the Peter Pewas Retrospective. Nevertheless, a delegation of the GDR did participate in the Film Festival, and five Defa films were shown in the Film Fair. Thus, in 1981 the quality of the films was – at least from the standpoint of those responsible for the Festival – an »all-German« problem.

Deprisa, Deprisa! [Hurry, Hurry!]: Berta Socuellamos Zarco, José Antonio Valdelomar

In spite of the disputes and discord, the organization of the Festival was praised by all participants, and the IFB was able to register a new record number of visitors for 1981. Approximately 15% more spectators saw the films in all parts of the »Berlinale« program. Another positive feature was the fact that, apart from independent US productions, major film companies once again participated in the »Berlinale« after being absent in the previous years. Martin Scorsese's Raging Bull opened the Festival, and the first piece of directing by the actor Robert Redford, Ordinary People, provided the final act. Furthermore, Scorsese gave a lecture on »color fading«, which dealt with the fading of colors in color films and the problems of color preservation. The continued internationalization of the Festival became apparent in greater participation by Southeast Asian countries.

American major and independent companies are heavily represented.

The films from Switzerland in the Competition, and in the Forum, were films full of memories, as well as films about the homeland and films about homelessness. Kurt Gloor's Der Erfinder [The Inventor] tells of a farmer who refuses to fight in the first World War and, living alone on his farm, works on an invention to prevent carts and other vehicles from getting stuck in the mud and in impassible terrains: the pacifist invents the principle of the tank track. In his film Das Boot ist voll (»The Boat is Full«) the direktor Markus Imhoof makes use of historical facts. A group of Jews risks their lives to escape from Nazi Germany into Switzerland, however, the Swiss bureaucracy sends the people back across the border – to certain death. Es ist kalt in Brandenburg (Hitler töten) [It's Cold in Brandenburg (Kill Hitler)] by Villi Herrmann, Hans Stürm, and Niklaus Meienberg is a documentation about Maurice Bavaud, who tried to assassinate Hitler and was executed in Plötzensee in Berlin in 1941. Züri brännt [Zurich is Burning] produced by Videoladen Zürich was a documentary statement, an angry film about youth unrest in the summer of 1980. It presents reflections on a country and descriptions of its conditions which grasp history at the present, linking it with human destinies. Immense energy and the

Films from Switzerland

Das Boot ist voll: a scene with Tina Engel, Curt Bois

greatest mournfulness is shown by Curt Bois; an immigrant plays an immigrant, however, the boat is full.

Agnieszka Holland's GORACZKA [Fever] tells the story of a failed attempt made by a Polish socialist to assassinate a Czarist governor while using the medium of the farce, and tracing the present in history. Meanwhile, Christo Christov's KAMIONAT [Truck] shows a merciless picture of Bulgaria. »The lungs of the quarry workers are ruined together with their marriages and their hopes; the party behaves in a shabby manner; four people on a calamitous journey through the winter wilderness and with a coffin - of all things - on board, more or less tear one another to pieces; en route they encounter nothing but arrogant hotel managers, the lame, the sick, the unkind, and the insane. Even the dogs bite them without respite; and when they finally want to deliver the corpse which they rescue from the burning truck, in the village they come from, they find the village uncannily deserted, destroyed, a realm of the dead on earth.« (Karena Niehoff, Süddeutsche Zeitung, Feb. 25, 1981.)

STALKER:
Aleksandr Kaidanovsky

Alongside Godard's SAUVE QUI PEUT (LA VIE), Andrei Tarkovsky's STALKER was the outstanding film of the Forum. This year the Festival movie theater for the Forum was the Delphi, a large old movie house on Kantstrasse next to the Theater des Westens. Unfortunately, however, like so many movie houses in Berlin, the Delphi was in a sorry condition, and there were protests during screenings. The quality of the projection left much to be desired, and there were no facilities for interpreters. As much as those responsible for the Forum were delighted at the new location in which a greater number of viewers could be accommodated, so they also complained that the available funds made it impossible to provide the Delphi movie theater with adequate technical facilities.

Wolfram Schütte entitled his closing report in the »Frankfurter Rundschau« (Feb. 25, 1981) »In Search of Buried History«. He wrote about the Iranian documentary DJOSTEDJU [Search] by Amir Naderi, which documented a massacre by the army and the secret service Savak at the beginning of the Iranian revolution. »His film, which

DIALOGUE WITH A WOMAN DEPARTED: Peggy Lawson

International Jury
Jutta Brückner (FRG)
Denis Héroux (Canada)
Astrid Henning-Jensen (Denmark)
Irina Petrovna Kupchenko (USSR)
Peter Bichsel (Switzerland)
Antonio Isasi (Spain)
Prince Chatrichalerm Yukol (Thailand)
Jerzy Plazewski (Poland)
Italo Zingarelli (Italy)

uses imagery and sound documentation and imagination in a highly artistic manner, is a requiem, an evocation, an epitaph, and an appeal in one. (...) Since Alain Resnais' NUIT ET BROUILLARD [Night and Fog] - about German concentration camp atrocities - I have not seen one comparable film about comparable atrocities.«

The films by the Turkish director Yilmaz Güney, who was in jail in Turkey in 1981 as a policital prisoner on the charge of murder, are also historical in contents. The Info-Show also dedicated a retrospective to him. Hans Stempel and Martin Ripkens had visited Güney in prison two years earlier and made a film about him: BESUCH AUF IMRALI - EINE BEGEGNUNG MIT YILMAZ GÜNEY [Visit to Imrali - Meeting Yilmaz Güney]. After fleeing the country to live in exile in France, Güney received an invitation in 1982 to participate on the jury of the International Film Festival Berlin. Since, however, the Turkish authorities were searching für Güney via Interpol he was unable to travel. The West German authorities were unable to promise the safe conduct which Güney requested, i.e. to guarantee that he would not be arrested. Thus, Güney was prevented from attending the »Berlinale«.

Insiders

By Herbert Achternbusch

Dear Moritz de Hadeln, the fact that you invite me to write something on the occasion of the 40th anniversary of the International Film Festival Berlin is an honor, but that I, the most honored Mr. Achternbusch, am supposed to be among the most important guests at our event - that is painful. And this for three reasons: because it is not true; because Berlin was for me the only peephole to the outside world; because I cannot offer you another film.

As you are the only person I know in such a high position in the cinematic world, I can easily say that you are the only person who is not biased against me and my films since Lotte Eisner with her incorruptible one eye died, and I will come later to Heinz Badewitz with his all-encompassing eyes. 1981 you invited my film DER NEGER ERWIN *(»Black Erwin«). You were being boycotted then by German producers. There were weighty insider-discussions, which did not interest me. Many of my colleagues of that time postured as leftist, but because they were never liberal, they have become socially acceptable in very different circles, where money is to be had. You gave me and my friends a small reception, and one sensed that you were not stingy with the whiskey bottle. After that I received an invitation to Berlin every fall, and every fall I had a film. When the jury once rejected a film on the grounds that the first half of the film was ingenious, the second half was weaker in comparison, but that one would have accepted the film if the relationship between the halves had been reversed - well, this rejection did not hurt much of anything. For I received compensation: when the illiberal forces began to publicly fight me, even wanting to ban one of my films, you showed the film in question out of competition. That was courageous. I have also heard that whenever one of my films ran at the Berlin Film Festival, you received two to four calls from Bonn, and certain State Secretaries wanted to know whether the Minister of the Interior was insulted in the respective film. And when in my film* WOHIN? *[What direction?] I made fun of the Cerberus of Bavarian politics, you answered correctly: No. Now precisely this film, as I have heard, nearly received a Golden Bear. But when some members threatened to leave the jury in protest, the matter was dropped. A prize from an A-festival is connected to a flow of money from the Filmförderungsanstalt, and thus certain channels will have been activated in order to keep me small. In any case I have kept the forces which would like to shove me and my work out of the film business busy. However, I must say that it was helpful not to know this insider-clique - only the one or the other by sight. I must confess that I slowly became ashamed of the yearly invitation to Berlin, because I never won anything and other people don't know any shame. But what seems to have been most important: in my films you always had an unamerican film. And after* HEILT HITLER! *[Heal Hitler!] you confessed to me that you now understood the Bavarian dialect better. What festival director had ever looked at one of my films, and if so, when had one ever attempted to understand anything at all?! I will come to Heinz Badewitz directly.*

I know of a young policeman in Ulm who gave up his uniform after seeing my film DIE FÖHNFORSCHER *[Föhn Researchers]. Somebody from Bremen wrote me that he would already have emigrated if not for my films. Now, I don't like fans, because they have the status of insiders and carry on dumb conversations which only they understand, whether they are the »Autonome« from Kreuzberg who beat up policemen, or the nobility from the Vienna Opera Ball who are protected by policemen, or policemen who for whatever reason always vote for right-wing radicals. Insiders, nothing but insiders and no overview. Like destructive gold prospectors in the Amazon, and, as if I were an Indian, they call me an ape. Others recommend that I enroll in a basic course at a film academy. I think more along the lines of an old-people's home, or let's say, a residence for my old age, and for this purpose I study the real-estate ads in my local newspaper. An up-market 3-room apartment in Unterhaching for DM 370 000 is too expensive for me. If I don't make a film this year, and cannot reckon with any public subsidy at all, then I may limit my interest to a 1-room-apartment, 27.5 square meters, ground floor, balcony, including garage for DM 135 000 in Unterhaching, because I cannot come up with a larger sum privately for a film each year. But courage deserts me before I make my 20th film, even though something pulls at my heartstrings, dear Mr. de Hadeln, when I think that in the fall your invitation will once again lie on my table. There are no other invitations. For the Bavarian Film Prize I am the last negro. Who calls a real-estate agent to check whether the offer in the Bavarian Woods with one brook-crossing for DM 260 000 or two brook-crossings for DM 290 000 means that the second brook-crossing could be had alone for DM 30 000 - naturally not!*

Now I do have to correct one thing, Heinz Badewitz, a staff-member of the International Film Festival Berlin, has invited me as a pars pro toto of his film festival in Hof, has invited me with such fervor and warmth that I do not intend to go there anymore. He takes care of every person from early to late. In Cannes he grabs a copy from under Samuel Fuller's arm so that Fuller must follow him to Hof; I will see to it that this busybody experiences defeat: I will no longer travel to Hof, and yet I have a dark foreboding that when we meet at the tiny film days in Bozen and he makes his offer, that we will not see the Latemar because it is behind clouds, you know, and the street is wet because it has rained, you know? You know, it was nice in Hof. And without Hof, Herbert, you never would have got the Golden Bear in Berlin, you know? I protest. And Heinz says, well you almost got one, you know that, it's nice anyway and so on - I have this dark foreboding that I had better not make another film. But I must still know, he says on the way to Welschenofen, that this is the highest forested mountain in Europe, because it is so high, or did I misunderstand because he talks as much out the window as to the passengers, this perpetual mobile! Dear Mr. de Hadeln, please excuse this little tangent,

The Awards of the International Jury

Feature Films
Grand Prix of the 31st IFB
Golden Berlin Bear
DEPRISA, DEPRISA!
Spain, directed by
Carlos Saura

Special Prize of the Jury
Silver Berlin Bear
AKALER SANDHANE
India, directed by
Mrinal Sen

Silver Berlin Bear
for the best actress
Barbara Grabowska
in GORACZKA
Poland

Silver Berlin Bear
for the best actor
ex aequo
Jack Lemmon
in TRIBUTE
USA

Anatoli Solonitsyn
in DVADZAT SHEST DNEY IS ZHISNI DOSTOYEVSKOGO
USSR

Silver Berlin Bear
for script and directing
of actors Markus Imhoof
DAS BOOT IST VOLL
Switzerland

Special Mention
for ZIGEUNERWEISEN
Japan, directed by
Seijun Suzuki

Special Mention
for LE GRAND PAYSAGE D'ALEXIS DROEVEN
Belgium, directed by
Jean-Jacques Andrien

and be accompanied by my good wishes, and give my greetings to the small, dark lady photographer who ages considerably less than the likes of me.
Herbert Achternbusch

Raging Bull:
Robert de Niro

Head wind

1982

Feb. 12th-23rd, 1982 (Competition)
Feb. 13th-23rd, 1982 (Forum)

Berliners greeted her at Gatow Airport with cries of jubilation. Then she drove in an automobile covered in flowers via the Kurfürstendamm to Rathaus Schöneberg (the city hall), where Mayor Ernst Reuter awaited her. Journalists wrote about her »golden-blond hair« and the »brilliant red evening dress« which she wore to the Film Ball. »A turn-out organized as if she were Truman – just that she's prettier!«. This was the comment Berliners made about the appearance of Joan Fontaine who had been the star of the first »Berlinale« in 1951. In 1982 Joan Fontaine returned to Berlin: she had the prominent position of president on the international jury of the International Film Festival Berlin. And director Helma Sander-Brahms, who was also on the jury, wrote after the Festival was over: »As far as the question of its being interesting for international business the Berlinale has one glaring disadvantage at the moment: there is no sparkle, it is not attractive, it lacks glamor and show, it is too petty, staid and simple. Joan Fontaine, for example, and Brigitte Fossey do not appear in their most glamorous outfits, because ... well, where are you supposed to put your coat, do yourself up, leave your make-up and things, find a mirror? Are these things unimportant? Not at all. This is turning Berlin into a pullover festival – and business is not interested in that sort of thing. The Americans, who avoided Cannes last year, will still prefer Cannes, because they take such things into account there.« (Closing report IFB, 1982.)

Joan Fontaine presides over the jury.

It seemed as if the Film Festival wanted to regain some of its old aura. In front of the entrance to the Zoo-Palast incandescent lamps glowed under a baldachin. It had been a long time since so many directors and actors had presented themselves to the public and the press: Lino Ventura, Claudia Cardinale, Franco Nero, Jeanne Moreau, Brigitte Fossey, Ingrid Thulin, Sally Field, Michel Piccoli, Lilli Palmer, and – as guest of honor – James Stewart, who was paid homage to by the screening of twelve of his best films. At the Zoo-Palast the spectators gave him a standing ovation. Hollywood in Berlin. It was like going back thirty years!

New glamour

During the preparation time, however, there had been disputes and trouble. And as in 1980 with Reiner Kunze's Die wunderbaren Jahre [The Wonderful Years], controversy was caused by a film with a German-German subject.

In 1979 two families had flown from East to West Germany in a hot-air balloon. It was not long before interest was shown in filming this spectacular escape. Finally Disney productions carried out the project. Delbert Mann directed the film and John Hurt, Beau Bridges, and Klaus Löwitsch took the leading roles. Night Crossing tells the story of an adventure, in which the facts are given somewhat free treatment. This film was offered to the Berlin Film Festival in the fall of 1981 as the opening film by the general director of 20th Century-Fox in Germany, Hellmuth P. Gattinger. »Of course, hors concours« wrote Gattinger, who characterized the film as being »completely free of values for both East and West« (letter to de Hadeln, Oct. 29, 1981). Moritz de Hadeln replied a few days later; he had not seen the film but he referred – as a precautionary step – to the FIAPF guidelines which did not permit the screening of films »which are directed against other countries participating in the Festival«. He emphasized the important role of the Film Festival in an international cultural exchange and admitted that he was extremely worried about the contents of this film, »which was certain to create ill-feeling in the GDR« (letter to Gattinger, Nov. 5, 1981). So far this was not a rejection but a careful act of distancing himself

Controversy surrounds Night Crossing, the film of an escape from East Germany

from the film. Following the incidents surrounding the American film THE DEER HUNTER, the withdrawal of the socialist countries, and in view of the fact that contacts to the Soviet Union and the GDR had only just been reestablished, de Hadeln did not want to risk the position of the Film Festival as an intersection in East-West cultural exchange by adopting a flippant attitude. After seeing the film in January, he finally rejected it: »Having consulted my advisors, I do not think, unfortunately, that this film is really suitable as a Festival film even though it undoubtedly has some great qualities. As you know, a Festival film must be an outstanding film.« (Letter to Gattinger, Jan. 5, 1982.)

Gattinger resorted to public relations tactics. In particular, Berlin's Springer press, »Bild«, »BZ«, »Berliner Morgenpost« and »Die Welt« took up the subject of the film's rejection, talking of »obsequiousness« towards East Germany and of »cowardess« among the Festival's management. Was Gattinger a good public relations strategist who wanted to exploit the rejection of the film to attract the public, or did nationalist feelings move him to push the issue? What is conspicuous, in any case, is the fact that the press was well-informed and cited passages from the exchange of letters between de Hadeln and Gattinger. One is also forced to suspect that some commentators also threw their political rancor into the debate. Moritz de Hadeln's position was not unchallenged, the political landscape in Berlin had changed, the parliamentary elections had given the CDU a majority while de Hadeln had been appointed under a Social Democrat Senate. Thus, the discussion about a film developed into a settling of accounts with the director of the Film Festival; and although it was not mentioned at first, behind this was the desire to restructure the Festival. Film policy was being debated.

Under the heading »A Hymn to the Freedom Which Does Not Resound in Berlin« Will Tremper, for example, wrote polemically in »Welt am Sonntag«: »The Berlinale,

Joan Fontaine, James Stewart

Japanese hospitality: Kashiko Kawakita, Toyoji Kuroda, Moritz de Hadeln, Michiko Tanaka

Bertrand Tavernier

Corinne and Arthur Cantrill

which used to be a genuine people's festival, has deteriorated into a dull meeting place for ideologies in the shadows of détente.« (Jan. 17, 1982.) Berlin CDU politicians joined into the discussion; Heinrich Lummer thought that the film would have been a good opening film, and the deputy chairman of the CDU faction in the Berlin House of Representatives and head of the Jugendfilmverleih, Jürgen Wohlrabe, published an article in »Bild« calling for »a dazzling Festival which impresses both national and international audiences« – it was »not enough« for the International Film Festival Berlin to be »the link between East and West«. For this reason »reorganization of the Film Festival« was necessary. »It is necessary to carry out measures which tighten up the organization and give its staff a more disciplined approach, which revise the Festival regulations and the selection procedure for the films.« (Jan. 23,1982.) This attack on Festival policy was a public relations exercise which finally turned the debate into a political issue. The decisions of those responsible were put in question, as were – indirectly – the fields of competence of the Berlin Festivals-Ltd., which bears an obligation towards the cultural policy of the city, yet remains independent with respect to film selection and the drawing up of the program. Furthermore, there was the issue of years of effort to bring about a cultural rapprochement between West and East.

Festival director under attack

De Hadeln was given support, be it for tactical reasons, by the Senator for Science and Cultural Affairs, Professor Dr. Wilhelm A. Kewenig, who made it clear in a letter to de Hadeln that he »did not identify with the campaign in favor of the film«, but pointed out »that the film has to be shown outside the Competition in Berlin«. (Jan. 20, 1982.) The standpoint of the board of curators and its chairman, the Undersecretary at the Federal Ministry of the Interior, Andreas von Schoeler, was unequivocal. In a press declaration, he dismissed the criticisms which CDU politicians had made of the Film Festival and of de Hadeln's decision; they represented »a vehement attack on the freedom of art and culture as protected in Article 5 of the constitution«. The Federal Government would »not allow the Film Festival, which was jointly born by the Federal Republic and the city state of Berlin, to be turned into the plaything of commercial interests«. This clarified positions. As did the fact that Gattinger placed a full-paged advertisement in the trade journal »Filmecho/Filmwoche« (No. 7/8, Feb. 6, 1982), which stated, among other things: »Mr de Hadeln is not turning up his nose at anything but the cries for help by the persecuted – because this is what the film is about – the escape, by balloon, of two families from one part of Germany to the other.« This was quite in line with the tenor of the Springer commentaries; for the publisher himself, Axel Cäsar Springer, was meanwhile sponsoring the Berlin première which was to take place on the opening day of the IFB, February 12th, as a kind of counter-event.

Political backing

The new Mayor, Dr. Richard von Weizsäcker, adopted a diplomatic attitude. Without actually naming the conflict, he stated: »When it is a question of films from all parts and areas of the world – i. e. in the geographical, political, and cultural sense – the management will constantly be faced with ever new and big problems. The management will master these problems if it is capable and willing to be independent, and if its independence is also respected. I, for my part, am willing to show this respect.« De Hadeln had asserted himself by making a politico-cultural decision which was correct.

Manfred Salzgeber

The extent to which a Film Festival director was dependent on the decision of producers revealed itself in two other cases. For example, the co-producer Gaumont prevented Hans W. Geißendörfer's Zauberberg [The Magic Mountain] from being shown as the closing film of the »Berlinale«, although German producers had agreed to its screening. Controversey also surrounded the première of Carlos Saura's new film Dulces horas (»Sweet Hours«). The film was withdrawn from the Film Festival program at short notice, likewise owing to pressure by the French co-producer Jacques Roitfeld, because the French preferred to show the film during a homage for Saura in Cannes. This also took place in opposition to the veto of the Spanish producer Elias Querejeto who, acting together with the Office for Film at the Madrid Ministry of Culture, had entered the film in the »Berlinale«. There were growing attempts by multinationals, producers and distributors, to influence the film program of the Festival.

New dialogue between the »Berlinale« and the Working Group of New German Film Producers

The 1982 Film Festival was clearly marked by the presence of West German films. The dialogue between the Festival management and the Working Group of New German Film Producers had got under way, with Heinz Badewitz mediating between the parties. He had at his disposal an independent budget for extending invitations, and had the right to vote in the selection commission. Five films were shown in the Competition of which three, however, did not have competitive status. A total of almost ninety West German films were in the programs of the various sections of the Festival. The Golden Berlin Bear went to Rainer Werner Fassbinder's Die Sehnsucht der Veronika Voss (»Veronika Voss«) which was considered by journalists and guests in general to be a kind of redress for Fassbinder; for twice in the past when it was expected that he would receive a prize, i.e. for Fontane Effi Briest (»Effi Briest«) and Die Ehe der Maria Braun (»The Marriage of Maria Braun«) he had gone away empty handed. Although Fassbinder's new film was considered to be less of a success, the award was not criticized. The Polish entry in the Competition Dreszcze (»Shivers«) by Wojciech Marczewski was well received. This film was a family history and an attempt to come to terms with the Stalin era. »Timid attempts

Requiem by Zoltán Fábri: Edit Frajt

to settle accounts with Stalinism are not so rare. In this case, however, this system of terror is not considered an accident of history; here the question is raised about what we are to think of an order which allows such a rule of force and such inhumanity to exist. The critique is directed at the structure and not at the temporal event.« (Michael Schwarze, Frankfurter Allgemeine Zeitung, Feb. 25, 1982.)

»Years of emotional apprenticeship«: films en vogue

Two films were exemplary for a trend which could be discerned both in the films of the Competition as well as the Forum: Michel Soutter's L'AMOUR DES FEMMES, the story of four men and their relationship to women, a sobering role play with exquisite imagery; and – in the Forum – Claire Clouzot's L'HOMME FRAGILE [The Fragile Man], a film about a man who is searching and running away, about a »married ideologist of the seventies« who has become »a fragile father« (Clouzot). »A generation communicates with itself (those in their mid-thirties to mid-forties). Frequently, it is a bourgeois Left which has entered its hard years, and is at odds with itself; a loss of identity as mal de siècle, the first signs of aging. In this political vacuum, the years of emotional apprenticeship make themselves felt at this late stage.« (Wolfram Schütte, Frankfurter Rundschau, Feb. 25, 1982.) In the Forum, the independent radical films had become rare. An exception to this, in 1982, was the Irish film TRAVELLERS by Joe Comerford. Michael and Angela, both under the age of twenty and without any fixed abode, are forced to marry by their parents. Gradually, they get to know one another. They travel across the country. A robbery takes place, and later – following an argument – a murder. The aimless journey turns into a flight which tears them apart again. Comerford does not stage scenes. He lets his actors speak as they might speak for themselves, curtly and harshly in their attempts to come together. Desperation, a story as one might find it in reality.

The Info-Show contains films from Southeast Asia.

In the Info-Show, Manfred Salzgeber continued to focus intensively on films from Southeast Asia. A series containing Indonesian films presented Berlin with completely unknown film territory. The Korean film MANDALA by Im Kwon-Taek and

DIE SEHNSUCHT DER VERONIKA VOSS: Rosel Zech, Hilmar Thate

Rosel Zech, Rainer Werner Fassbinder

International Jury
Joan Fontaine (USA, president)
Vladimir Baskakov (USSR)
Brigitte Fossey (France)
Joe Hembus (FRG)
László Lugossy (Hungary)
Gian Luigi Rondi (Italy)
Helma Sanders-Brahms (FRG)
Mrinal Sen (India)
David J. Stratton (Australia)

Zai sheng ren [Life after Life] by Peter Wai-Chuen Yung from Hong Kong made famous two independent young film-makers who represented a newly found confidence in Asian cinema. Films from the People's Republic of China supplemented this program block. A retrospective of the critic and film-maker Alf Brustellin, who had met with a fatal accident, was also shown. The performances were introduced by Bernhard Sinkel and Ula Stöckl, friends and colleagues of Brustellin.

The »Berlinale« was changing. Although Moritz de Hadeln appeared outwardly to some observers as an ill-fated Festival director, inwardly he had given the Festival a new organizational structure, and had won over colleagues who were to work together with him for years. There was an official Festival bulletin again, the »FilmFest Journal«. The Festival broke with the »berlinale-tip« and its editor, Klaus Stemmler, who, however, continued to run »tip« under its editor Florian Hopf. Thus, two magazines on the Film Festival appeared each day – the official yet independent voice of the Festival, and a polemical counterbalance. This had also been the case in the sixties when there had even been three competing »Berlinale« magazines. The Times They Are Changing...

Showing the flag

By Arthur and Corinne Cantrill

Our participation in the Internationales Forum des Jungen Films (1982, 1984 and 1985) has been very helpful in reinforcing our confidence in our own film work. Experimental film is generally not regarded very highly in Australia (even though it has always been the experimental filmmakers who have ›shown the flag‹ during periods when the

La Femme de l'aviateur [The Aviator's Wife] by Eric Rohmer in the Forum: Marie Rivière

Pastorale by Otar Yoseliani: a scene with Lia Tokkadze-Dyoegueli, Marina Kartsewadze, Tamara Goeabarachvili (in the Forum)

mainstream film production has declined!) and the kind support we have received from the dedicated Forum staff was a significant factor in our continuing with our work. The 1982 experience, in particular, remains strongly in our memory. This was the year when an image from our film The Second Journey (To Uluru) *was used on the Forum poster and program book. It was one of the high points in our life when we walked out of the hotel on the first day and were confronted with the image enlarged to massive proportions on the Delphi Filmpalast!*

Homage

By Ingo Kratisch and Jutta Sartory

In the Forum what we think,
see, hear becomes public,
in the presence of the others
then light dark reality.

If only the Forum were a land
and we could live in it.

The Awards of the International Jury

Feature Films
Grand Prix of the 32rd IFB
Golden Berlin Bear
Die Sehnsucht der Veronika Voss
FRG, directed by
Rainer Werner Fassbinder

Special Prize of the Jury
for originality
Silver Berlin Bear
Dreszcze
Poland, directed by
Wojciech Marczewski

Silver Berlin Bear
for the best director
Mario Monicelli
for Il Marchese del Grillo
Italy

Silver Berlin Bear
for the best actress
Katrin Sass
in Bürgschaft für ein Jahr
GDR

Silver Berlin Bear
for the best actor
ex aequo
Michel Piccoli
in Une Etrange affaire
France

Stellan Skarsgård
in Den enfaldige mördaren
Sweden

Silver Berlin Bear
for an outstanding
individual performance
Zoltán Fábri
for the script to the film
Requiem, Hungary

Special Mention
Absence of Malice
USA, directed by
Sydney Pollack

Special Mention
The Killing of Angel Street
Australia, directed by
Donald Crombie

Special Mention
Muzhiki
USSR, directed by
Iskra Babitch

TOOTSIE: Dustin Hoffman

Heading for success

1983

Feb. 18th-March 1st, 1983 (Competition)
Feb. 19th-March 1st, 1983 (Forum)

A woman in a wide, black dress takes the stage: Jeanne Moreau. She sings a song – her song from QUERELLE. She sings it alone, simply, and for someone who has passed away. She sings it for Rainer Werner Fassbinder, who died in June. The music is from films by the director, a suite composed by Peer Raben. A quiet and moving homage and memorial. A subdued start to the 1983 International Film Festival Berlin.

Exile – six German actors and actresses

A raid. A traveller does not have any identity papers, he flees and wants to hide in the crowds at the market. There is a shot and he falls. In his hand, the police find pamphlets with the demand »Free France«. A scene from CASABLANCA. The refugee is played by Wolfgang Zilzer. A minor role for which he is not even mentioned in the credits. The fate of an emigrant. In memory of those actors who had to flee Germany following the seizure of power by the National Socialists: »Exile – Six Actors from Germany« was the title of the Retrospective, shown by the Stiftung Deutsche Kinemathek at the Festival. Films were screened showing Elisabeth Bergner, Curt Bois, Dolly Haas, Franz (Frances) Lederer, Hertha Thiele, and Wolfgang Zilzer, who named himself Paul Andor subsequent to his emigration. There were films from Germany before 1933 and films made in exile, including many anti-Nazi-films from the USA in which the emigrants – owing to their German accents – had to play Nazis. And all of them, with the exception of Elisabeth Bergner, who was ill, attended the Festival.

There were queues at the box offices, and performances were sold out. More than 4500 accredited participants arrived, the Film Fair was booked out – 537 screenings with 394 films from 43 countries; the number of visitors had risen constantly in the past few years: more than 110 000 spectators saw the films in the Competition, in the Info-Show, the Retrospective, and the Children's Festival. (The Info-Show registered the greatest increase in the number of visitors.) On top of all that, 63 000 attended the International Forum. The »Berlinale« was heading for success.

The Competition program was more comprehensive than it had been in previous years, a fact rendered possible by a change in the FIAPF guidelines. The major US companies participated, and France was very well-represented. This created main areas of interest. Alongside the great entertainment films – e. g. Sydney Pollack's TOOTSIE - which opened the Festival, there were films with politically explosive subjects: IN THE KING OF PRUSSIA by Emile de Antonio, the reconstruction in film of legal procedures instituted against a group of militant Catholics who had broken into the technology center of General Electric in the Pennsylvanian town King of Prussia, and destroyed a number of nuclear warheads in 1980. Or there was Chris. Marker's narratory »ciné-poème« SANS SOLEIL alongside the entertaining narratory cinema of Eric Rohmer's PAULINE À LA PLAGE (»Pauline at the Beach«). Films from the People's Republic of China, Hungary, the CSSR, and the USSR represented the socialist countries. East Germany, however, had withdrawn Frank Beyer's film DER AUFENTHALT [Turning Point] at short notice, although it had already been entered. No official reason was given for this move, but it was suspected that the East Germans were complying with a wish expressed by Poland. »For all that, its withdrawal seems rather absurd. Not only that they would have given themselves the opportunity to compete for the Golden Bear with certain prospects of success with this film, which clearly surpassed the level of the other Defa films; it is not really easy to understand how this work by Frank Beyer – which depicts the difficult times of

SANS SOLEIL

Alain Tanner

Press conference for the French-Belgian entry in the Competition CAP CANAILLE: director Jean-Henri Roger, co-director and leading actress Juliet Berto

Mayor's reception: Wolfgang Zilzer, Richard von Weizsäcker, Dolly Haas, Walter Reisch (in the background), Franz Lederer, Hertha Thiele

Jeanne Moreau, Erden Kiral, Moritz de Hadeln

East Germany withdraws a film.

a young man who has unjustly been suspected of murdering a Polish child - could do much to nourish anti-Polish sentiment. (...) Thus, one can only consider Warsaw's move as hysterical and the submissiveness of East Germany as servile.« (Michael Schwarze, Frankfurter Allgemeine Zeitung, March 3, 1983.) It was, incidentally, not the only film which was withdrawn during the preliminary stages of the International Film Festival: Alan Pakula's SOPHIE'S CHOICE was blocked by the producers and Mrinal Sen's KHARJI was removed from the program because Sen's producers chose to show the film in Cannes instead.

Margarethe von Trotta's film HELLER WAHN (»Sheer Madness«) was a failure. Some of the spectators reacted with boos and whistling, and many critics, especially Wolfram Schütte in the »Frankfurter Rundschau« (Feb. 26, 1983), wrote scathing critiques. Once again, the »Berlinale« confirmed that films from the Federal Republic of Germany were given particularly critical receptions. Many film-makers felt that the Festival audiences were unfair; and some of them no longer entered films in the Berlin Competition because of this.

Another film from the Federal Republic of Germany, ECHTZEIT/REALTIME by Hellmuth Costard and Jürgen Ebert, dealt with the measurement of the earth for military purposes. »Realtime« is a concept taken from computer science, a method of time-coding in which analysis, computation, and control of a process occur simultaneously. The computer is as fast as the event which it is intended to compute and to control; the computer can simulate life. »A disquieting, fragmented film, a combination of documentary, quotations, and feature film, which is frequently left unresolved in a honeycombed computer picture that reduces the outlines and colors of people into so many minute fields just as they would appear behind checkered frosted glass. Disturbing, difficult to understand, speculative and ironic: isn't this a strange journey into our common future which has been measured out, fixed, stored, and simulated by IBM, Sony, BKA, NASA, and NATO?« (Wolfram Schütte, Frank-

Squatters protest in the Zoo-Palast before the première of Margarethe von Trotta's HELLER WAHN (»Sheer Madness«). Moritz de Hadeln is successful in mediating between them and the police called by the movie house management - a confrontation is averted

furter Rundschau, March 12, 1983.) A film by Heinrich Böll, Alexander Kluge, Volker Schlöndorff, Stefan Aust, and Axel Engstfeld appeared to have a closer relationship to the present. Their film dealt with the NATO decision to build up its stock of arms by pushing ahead with the deployment of nuclear weapons in the FRG. KRIEG UND FRIEDEN (»War and Peace«) was a discussion that contributed to an explosive, current political subject. At the »Berlinale«, more than 300 participants from 40 countries signed the »Berlin Appeal for Peace«, which the International Forum of Young Cinema had initiated together with the Working Group of Film Journalists.

Political films and the »Berlin Appeal for Peace«

The Grand Prix of the 33rd International Film Festival Berlin was awarded ex aequo to the Spanish film LA COLMENA [The Beehive] by Mario Camús, about life in Madrid after the civil war, and to the English debut of Edward Bennett with ASCENDANCY, »which, even if in a somewhat strained manner, portrays the psychological impoverishment of a young woman and the moral impoverishment of her father - an entrepreneur - in Ireland at the beginning of the civil war.« (Manfred Delling, Deutsches Allgemeines Sonntagsblatt, March 6, 1983.) The awarding of a special prize by the Jury for HÂKKARI'DE BIR MEVSIM [A Season in Hâkkari] by Erden Kiral was met with acclamation; a film with imagery which was almost archaic, full of an involved calmness, and sparing in its use of theatrical gestures.

The 1983 International Forum suffered from cutbacks in the budget. Above all it was necessary to save on advertising and invitations of guests. As a result, the films of the 1983 Forum were given less press exposure than before. Nevertheless, Peter Greenaway's intriguing film THE DRAUGHTSMAN'S CONTRACT was real hit material for the Forum program. In the judgement of the critic writing for the »Neue Zürcher Zeitung«: »The structure of the film music, the artistic dialogue, the over-emphasis placed on fashionable utensils from the time made the film, notwithstanding the ›reality‹ of its subject matter, into an enchanting visual score on the problem of perception« (Erwin Schaar, March 17, 1983). While Greenaway's film was a suc-

THE DRAUGHTSMAN'S CONTRACT: Anthony Higgins

Experimental films in the Forum

cessful attempt at combining forms from avant-gardist experimentation with narrative film, other film-makers such as Michael Snow in SO IS THIS and Ernie Gehr in LISA & SUZANNE, SHIFT, UNTITLED, EUREKA persevered with experimental imagery in order to explode the dimensions of perception with purely avant-gardist forms. For years the characteristic feature of the Forum program had been its focus on experimental films, especially the American scene. (Alf Bold was, as a rule, responsible for selecting the films.)

Independent films from the USA

Independent American films were heavily represented; the Forum and the Info-Show – in which Arthur J. Bressan's ABUSE and Michael Oblowitz's KING BLANK were screened – increasingly supplemented one another in this respect. The Forum ran Lizzie Borden's feminist utopia BORN IN FLAMES, VORTEX by Scott and Beth B., and a »New Wave«-underground film, Wayne Wang's CHAN IS MISSING, a detective story with an amusing plot which takes place in San Francisco's China Town, and Haile Gerima's ASHES AND EMBERS, the story of a black G.I. Vietnam veteran. Ulrich Gregor wrote: »In ASHES AND EMBERS the protagonist runs out of a church service; on his flight he is accompanied by the gospel music being sung in the church; Gerima makes the rebellion and the desperation of his hero evident by adding ever new images of his mindless flight in an accelerating rhythm. This is a sequence which literally takes your breath away.« (FilmFest Journal extra, 1983.)

When the Film Festival came to an end, with the awarding of the prizes on March 1st, it was uncertain who would be the director of the next Competition. Moritz de Hadeln's and Ulrich Gregor's contracts had expired; nobody doubted that Ulrich Gregor would be confirmed in his post. However, in spite of the consolidation which had taken place in 1982/83, de Hadeln's position was disputed. There was opposition, especially in Bonn. The screening of Herbert Achternbusch's film DAS GESPENST [The Ghost], which had been given a special showing in the Competition, and which the Federal Minister of the Interior, Dr. Friedrich Zimmermann had

La Colmena

vehemently opposed, had resulted in considerable ill-feeling, although it did not become a public issue, towards the International Film Festival and its director de Hadeln. The controversy surrounding Herbert Achternbusch's film, which reached its climax in the temporary refusal by the Commission for the Voluntary Control of Standards (FSK) to release the film in 1983 was the first sign of a turnabout in film policy under the CSU Minister of the Interior Mr. Zimmermann. The inclusion of Krieg und Frieden in the program also met with reservations from the Ministry of the Interior. The independence which de Hadeln had maintained when making specific decisions had not secured his position vis-à-vis the authorities. The press speculated on who would be de Hadeln's successor. The name mentioned most was that of Theo Hinz, who had taken his leave of the Filmverlag der Autoren. An article appeared in »tip« by Hans-Ulrich Pönack, who put forward Hinz as the most likely successor. (Feb. 16, 1983; at this time Pönack was also a member of the advisory board and some observers suspected that there had been a clash of interests in his case.) Theo Hinz, commenting on this article, found it showed »a good imagination« and disclaimed it. In a written statement (Feb. 17), which he sent to »tip« and to Moritz de Hadeln, he declared that he would continue to be active in the film industry and would not be available for the position of director of the Film Festival for this reason. De Hadeln also found similar solidarity in the Working Group of the New German Film Producers, the Federation of TV and Film Directors in Germany, and the Association of European Directors, whose board, Dr. Norbert Kückelmann, Eberhard Hauff, and Peter Fleischmann, had sent off congratulations with the same wording to Erika and Moritz de Hadeln, and to the managing director of the Berlin Festivals-Ltd., in which they noted »that the International Film Festival Berlin, as it is now developing, is on the right road«. They added to this their hope that »the new start which had been made on this basis would be continued in a manner useful to German film as a whole and to Berlin« (telex – not dated).

Contracts at stake

International Jury
Jeanne Moreau
(France, president)
Alex Bänninger
(Switzerland)
Franco Brusati (Italy)
Elem Klimov (USSR)
Ursula Ludwig (FRG)
Kurt Maetzig (GDR)
Josef L. Mankiewicz (USA)
Franz Seitz (FRG)
Huang Zongjiang
(PR China)

In the Info-Show:
Arvottomat [The Worthless]
by Mika Kaurismäki,
Finland: Matti Pellonpää,
Pirkko Hämäläinen

Diva by Jean Jacques
Beineix, France:
Frédéric Andrei
(on the right)

At the 61st session of the board of curators on June 13th 1983, the decision was made. Shortly before there had been a political change in the Berlin Senate. Wilhelm A. Kewenig had given up the office of Senator for Science and Cultural Affairs and had become Senator of the Interior, while Dr. Volker Hassemer, previously Senator for City Development and the Environment had taken over the responsibility of Senator for Cultural Affairs. Moritz de Hadeln and Ulrich Gregor were confirmed in office at this meeting of the board of curators. The decision was unanimous. The extension of the contracts was only valid now for three instead of the previous five years. The cooperation agreement between the Competition and the Forum was also renewed. However, Item 6 of the agreement was re-written. Not only was coordination laid down between the Festival directors in »structural and program matters«, but also in »questions of cinemas« on request of the Forum, which had always felt at a disadvantage in this part of the organization. Reducing the term of the agreement may have been due, on the one hand, to the political change in the Senator responsible, or perhaps in the reservations of the Spio to de Hadeln, which were announced at the board of curators' meeting. Dissatisfaction was expressed at the fact that exporters, distributors, and producers were not adequately taken into consideration in the selection commission of the Film Festival. Nonetheless, Ulrich Eckhardt did defend the independence of the Festival director on this question, something which de Hadeln considered to be vital. The new Senator declared officially that the three year period, on the one hand, rendered continuous work possible, but that it, on the other hand, prevented »the Festival directors from becoming too complacent«, although neither de Hadeln nor Gregor had yet shown any such tendencies.

No vacuity

By Emile de Antonio

First there is Berlin itself with its historically uneasy brash mockery and wit, sitting between two troubled worlds. For me, ironic and fruitful. Ironic, in that I bumped into Americans I always avoid. I also saw a few I always enjoy. Martin Sheen and I both enjoyed the audience at the screening of IN THE KING OF PRUSSIA. *It was cycnical, tough, witty, the questions were alive. No lollipops, no vacuity. Seriousness and critical views. I loved going into the zoo on my way to the Festival. Cities that are alive for 24 hours a day are for me. Sleep is not the stuff of festivals.*

I made sales at Berlin, and, of course, they were important but what matters most is films, talk, ideas. Berlin is a central point in international film and culture.

The Awards of the International Jury

Feature Films
Grand Prix of the 33rd IFB
Golden Berlin Bear
ex aequo
ASCENDANCY
Great Britain, directed by Edward Bennett

LA COLMENA
Spain, directed by Mario Camús

Special Prize
Silver Berlin Bear
HÂKKARI'DE BIR MEVSIM
Turkey, directed by Erden Kiral

Silver Berlin Bear
for the best director
Eric Rohmer
for PAULINE À LA PLAGE
France

Silver Berlin Bear
for the best actress
Yevgeniya Glushenko
in VLYUBLYON PO SOBSTVENNOMU ZHELANIYU
USSR

Silver Berlin Bear
for the best actor
Bruce Dern in
THAT CHAMPIONSHIP SEASON
USA

Siver Berlin Bear
Xaver Schwarzenberger
for DER STILLE OZEAN
Austria

Honorable Mention
MO SHENG DE PENG YOU
PR China, directed by Xu Lei

Honorable Mention
DER ER ET YNDIGT LAND
Denmark, directed by Morten Arnfred

Honorable Mention
DIES RIGOROSE LEBEN
FRG, directed by Vadim Glowna

The City Girl:
Laura Harrington

Politicians speak

1984

Feb. 17th - 28th, 1984
(Competition)
Feb. 18th - 28th, 1984
(Forum)

In the White Hall at Schloß Charlottenburg, Berlin's Mayor holds a reception for Great Britain's Prince Philip, who will subsequently be awarded the »Golden Camera '84« at the Axel Springer Publishing House. It is Thursday, February 16th; the following day there is yet another event planned at Schloß Charlottenburg: the Senator for Cultural Affairs, Volker Hassemer, and Prince Louis Ferdinand of Prussia sign an agreement for the purchase, by the state of Berlin, of Jean Antoine Watteau's painting »The Embarkation for Cythère«. Noblesse oblige.

Politics also means obligations, cordial speeches on ceremonial occasions. On the evening the »Berlinale« opened, Mayor Eberhard Diepgen, who had only been elected to office a week earlier (after Richard von Weizsäcker had submitted his resignation in order to stand as candidate for the position of Federal President), held a speech. Diepgen gave his assurance that the independence of the Festival and of the selection commission would not be interfered with since independence was »the air which artistic competition needed in order to live«. And he added that »the Berlin film sponsorship served the freedom of cinema, freedom of production, and freedom of content«. These words were directed at the controversy surrounding the new guidelines on film sponsorship put forward by Minister Zimmermann, which were to come into effect as of March 1st. Zimmermann's film policy was at the center of the debate; his rigid refusal to grant funds for two films had caused public outcry. It also became known that there had been behind-the-scene attempts to influence the invitation procedure for which Festival director de Hadeln and the selection commission alone were responsible. In 1983, this problem had arisen in connection with the films KRIEG UND FRIEDEN and Herbert Achternbusch's GESPENST, which had also been refused grants. In 1984, worried questions were asked about the participation of Achternbusch's new film WANDERKREBS which included the role of a minister president and led some to suspect that this was a caricature of the Bavarian Minister President, Franz-Josef Strauß: »Life is just so remote.« (Achternbusch.)

A politicial statement

Comments from the Federal Ministry of the Interior on films by Herbert Achternbusch, and Rüdiger Neumann

Yet another film of this Festival was affected by the Minister of the Interior intervening in film policy. This time it was a film in the program of the Forum, Rüdiger Neumann's MERIDIAN ODER THEATER VOR DEM REGEN [Meridian or Theater Before the Rains]. As in the case of Achternbusch, the Ministry of the Interior refused to pay the final grant premium arguing that given to the script, the film now had »a version which was different to that presented to the commission responsible for selecting films for sponsorship«. Payment of the premium was made dependent on whether or not the film adhered to the planned version. The passage which was incriminated by the Minister of the Interior formed part of the credits and was worded as follows: »During the filming of MERIDIAN, American President Ronald Reagan expressed the view that the use of ›Theater Nuclear Forces‹ made a nuclear war – limited to Europe – against the Soviet Union conceivable. Let us take a look at the place where this nuclear theater is to be staged. Work is proceeding at quite a pace.« Both films, MERIDIAN and WANDERKREBS were run at the Festival. Nonetheless, an attempt by the Ministry of the Interior to exert influence on the content of a film or on the program of the Festival were signs of political censorship. In his foreward to the Festival documentation de Hadeln wrote: »that changes had indeed taken place within the past year«. He described the confrontation of opposing interests and conceptions and that with Zimmermann's film policy, »The outcome of this duel could

Ida di Benedetto, Ula Stöckl

Jack Nicholson and Debra Winger with their director James L. Brooks (Terms of Endearment)

Melina Mercouri, Jules Dassin, Volker Hassemer

Agnieszka Holland, Henri Storck

be dangerous for German film if it did not have that irreplaceable, non-alienable capital, its talent.« In a report about a public discussion organized by the Forum on the »Future of the German ›Autorenfilm‹« Wolfram Schütte took the argument further in the »Frankfurter Rundschau«: »The future of German author-made films will (...) be decided by their artistic creativity, imagination, social experience, and attentiveness: where it possesses these qualities they will be mobilized ›in the face of danger and peril‹ to take up the challenge presented by Zimmermann and put up resistance to this ›compromising course‹. If this doesn't help, the grave-diggers have already dug the grave.« (Feb. 28, 1984.) In both sections of the IFB a total of twelve new German films were screened.

Moritz de Hadeln, James Stewart

The opening film of the »Berlinale« was a stroke of luck, Ettore Scola's Le Bal. This was a dance sequence without words, relying solely on gestures and mime to show forty years of revue: the thirties, occupation and collaboration in France, the sixties – May in Paris. Pop songs, fashion, dances, film stars: Jean Gabin, the anarchist hero of the Parisian underworld, and Gabin the just policeman and inspector. Actually, a completeley different film was supposed to have opened the »Berlinale«. However, Elem Klimov's Proshchaniye (»Farewell to Matyora«) was not released for export by the Soviet Film Association. It was only three years later, when a change in the political climate was brought about by the politics of Gorbachev, that Klimov's film was shown in Berlin.

An expanding program

Complaints could be heard about the continued growth in the program. As Karena Niehoff wrote: »Nearly every night there are Competition films on at the Zoo-Palast, the main movie house of the Competition. There are also films which are not competing.« At the same time, however, because they are »chosen with particular care, they must not be confused with those ›special screenings‹ in the other movie theaters (which are thus apparently not to be taken so seriously). Yet, on the other hand, as de Hadeln points out, the latter are part of his ›overall program‹ to which – and this is something new – the ›Mediterranean program‹ belongs as a very special series. This does not apply ›directly‹ but indirectly to the Info-Show.« (Süddeutsche Zeitung, Feb. 27, 1984.) In the Competition, the Info-Show, the Children's Film Festival, the New German Cinema Series, the Retrospective, and the Film Fair, a total of 556 films were screened. The Forum also had extended its program, or at least established new series, such as a »Homage to the ›Kleines Fernsehspiel‹ of the ZDF (German television Channel Two)« and – in addition to the series of New German Cinema – a program focusing on debut films and works by film students entitled »Perspectives«.

A jury composed of eleven members (instead of the previous nine) now made the decision on as to who would receive the Golden and Silver Bears. The president was Liv Ullmann, vice-president was Jules Dassin. When, on the last day – before the last film was shown: Love Streams by John Cassavetes – the Bears were awarded, the decision to award the Grand Prix to Love Streams was met with joyous acclaim. But then, after the showing there was booing and whistling. Part of the audience revised its initial positive reaction and support for Cassavetes' film, perhaps because Cassavetes seem to avoid any staging in his film. It was the story of a brother and sister who run into ever new difficulties: compulsive and helpless gestures, outbreaks of anger, and a quiet sinking into despair. Every-day chaos, erratic and restless. Since life cannot be staged, the chaos *is* the staging. Love Streams is a concentrated moment of all that happens in Cassavetes' films: »a radical, desperate, eccentric, and yet occasionally comforting film, which distinguished itself from the Hollywood smoothness which characterized films such as Terms of Endearment by James L. Brooks (the author); and it was thus justified to have received the Golden Bear.« (Ulrich Greiner, Die Zeit, March 9, 1989.) Applause also greeted the award of the jury's Special Prize to the Argentinean film No habra mas penas ni olvido [Funny Dirty Little War], a farce about the Peronist civil war struggles in Argentina. However, there was disapproval over the fact that Jean-Marie Straub's and Danièle Huillet's Kafka adaptation Klassenverhältnisse [Class Relations] did not receive a prize but merely an honorable mention. Hans-Dieter Seidel noted in the »Frankfurter Allgemeine Zeitung« that, »The film swears in the spectator, who has no choice but to become a listener here, to the typical Kafka situations and tone by maintaining the dialogue, which has been gained partly from the literary text and is strictly divided up with breaks, at a specific level. The actors do not speak but articulate. The black and white framing fixes the imagery in an equally rigid manner, with very little tracking except for outside takes. Hardly any panning is used to accompany the movements of the actors. This strict use of artistic means as a stylistic principle, preserved over a period of two hours may seem strange at first, but as time progresses one comes increasingly under its spell.« (Feb. 23, 1984.) Some critics noted with regret that Peter Lilienthal's Das Autogramm [The Autograph] did not receive a prize. Otherwise, the general reaction to the jury was one of satisfaction.

A Golden Bear for John Cassavetes

Samuel Fuller, director of Les Voleurs de la nuit [Thieves After Dark], in the Competition

Jules Dassin and his wife Melina Mercouri – Greek Minister of Culture – came to Berlin to attend the »Berlinale« as guests. A retrospective of eleven films was dedicated to them. On February 20th Melina Mercouri visited her fellow countryman Minas Kontos, who was imprisoned on remand in Moabit prison, having been charged by the district attorney of being guilty of grievous bodily injury, severe civil rioting, and contravening the law regulating public meetings during the visit of

Melina Mercouri criticizes the Berlin judiciary.

Love Streams: John Cassavetes, Gena Rowlands

the US President Ronald Reagan during the summer of 1982. Melina Mercouri lodged a protest with the Mayor against the fact that Kontos had been detained in custody for twenty months. She criticized this for being unreasonable in view of the charges, which had not, moreover, been proven up to this point in time. At a joint press conference with the Senator for Legal Affairs, Hermann Oxfort, she severely criticized the Berlin judiciary. Oxfort dismissed the accusation that Kontos was being kept in prison for political reasons. In a resolution, directors, actors, and journalists at the Festival declared their solidarity with the demand to release Kontos.

Two other political guests received less attention in the headlines. Head of the delegation of the GDR Horst Pehnert, also deputy to the GDR Minister for Culture and head of the Central Administration Film, stayed in West Berlin for a few days. The official character of this visit was not evident since a cultural agreement between the two German states had hitherto foundered on the Berlin question. For this reason Horst Seeman's film Ärztinnen [Lady Doctors], after the play of the same name by Rolf Hochhuth, was screened at the Competition as the sole contribution from the GDR, although it was a co-production in which the West Berlin producer Manfred Durniok, among others, had participated. New York Mayor, Edward Koch, also visited Berlin for two days; he became involved in political discussions, and was a guest of the »Berlinale«.

Thematic focal point in the Forum: music

Tango films; Humberto Rios traced the connection betwen tango music and the political history of Argentina in his documentary El tango es una historia [The Tango is History], in which the musicians Osvaldo Pugliese, Astor Piazzolla, and Susana Rinaldi supplied the music. Films with Carlos Gardel, the tango king of the thirties, who is still a legend and a popular hero in Argentina, and the re-screening of the German silent movie Die Tango-Königin [Tango Queen] by Max Mack from 1913 constituted the thematic focal point in the Forum. In general, the theme of music was reflected in variations in many Forum films: e. g. in Mani Kaul's Dhrupad

Le Bal

On page 314
Der Schlaf der Vernunft: Ida di Benedetto

from India, a documentary about a traditional line in classical Indian music, in the Canadian film Au pays de Zom, [In the Land of Zom] by Gilles Groulx, which formally resembled an opera, the musical thread caricaturing the hero, or Sally Potter's The Gold Diggers, in which waltzes structure the drama and which the director herself referred to as a musical.

Alongside Ulrike Ottinger's Dorian Gray im Spiegel der Boulevardpresse [The Image of Dorian Gray in the Yellow Press], which also featured musical elements of production, Ula Stöckl's Der Schlaf der Vernunft [The Sleep of Reason] was the West German film which received the most attention. »Her paraphrase of the Medea myth, which she has transposed into the present, begins as a social melodrama, only to allow itself to be drawn into the sway of expressionist melodrama, a dream piece, whose aesthetic approach calls to mind the Bergman of Gyklarnas afton (›The Naked Night‹). (...) Without any shadow of a doubt, Der Schlaf der Vernunft is a veritable piece of cinema which deals profoundly with controversial experiences in the consciously lived lives of women.« (Wolfram Schütte, Frankfurter Rundschau, Feb. 24, 1984.)

New Austrian films, a series with independent American films, and US non-majors were screened, including Henry Jaglom's Can She Bake a Cherry Pie?, an affectionate, hilarious succession of episodes about a New York couple, told in a manner which is spontaneous and full of improvisation. Martha Coolidge's The City Girl, the carefree filming of a rocking love affair and films from the Mediterranean countries also provided subject matter for the Info-Show. Because the showing of Raafat El-Mihi's Al avocat [The Advocate] – a farce about a shrewd lawyer who takes the side of the little man and fights against the corruption of the authorities – was prohibited in some Egyptian cities as a result of protests by the local law firms, some Arab critics sent a letter of protest to Egyptian President Hosni Mubarak after the film had been screened in Berlin. «Tracing the tracks in one's own country, often

International Jury
Liv Ullmann (Sweden, president)
Jules Dassin (France)
Edward Bennett (Great Britain)
Manuela Cernat-Gheorghiu (Bulgaria)
Lana Gogoberidze (USSR)
Tullio Kezich (Italy)
Steffen Kuchenreuther (FRG)
Jeanine Meerapfel (FRG)
Kevin Thomas (USA)
Mario Vargas Llosa (Peru)
Adolphe Viezzi (France)

The Awards of the International Jury

Feature Films
Grand Prix of the 34th IFB
Golden Berlin Bear
Love Streams
USA, directed by
John Cassavetes

Special Prize of the Jury
Silver Berlin Bear
No habras mas penas ni olvido
Argentina, directed by
Héctor Olivera

Silver Berlin Bear
Ettore Scola
for Le Bal
France/Italy/Algeria

Silver Berlin Bear
Monica Vitti
for Flirt
Italy

Silver Berlin Bear
for the best actress
Inna Churikova in
Voenno-polevoi roman
USSR

Silver Berlin Bear
for the best actor
Albert Finney
in The Dresser
Great Britain

Silver Berlin Bear
Morgen in Alabama
FRG, directed by
Norbert Kückelmann

Silver Berlin Bear
Rembetico
Greece, directed by
Costas Ferris

Special Mention
Jean-Maria Straub and
Danièle Huillet
for Klassenverhältnisse
FRG

in rural areas for things unknown, forgotten or left unspoken, constituted the background of many films« wrote Ursula Ahrens (Der Tagesspiegel, March 4, 1984).

Music again. At a joint showing organized by the Film Festival together with the Stiftung Deutsche Kinemathek, a restored and color copy of Friedrich Wilhelm Murnau's Nosferatu. Eine Symphonie des Grauens was presented with the original music for a ›salon orchestra‹ at the Zoo-Palast. This screening was dedicated to the film historian Lotte H. Eisner who had supervised the restoration and had died in 1983. »You were with us from the very start on our journey to the ›original Nosferatu‹, with the things you wrote and in the many conversations we had. Without you this screening would have been inconceivable« wrote Enno Patalas in a fictitious letter to and for Lotte Eisner in January, 1984 (IFB Documentation, p. 309).

The Retrospective told a different story: of Siegmund Lachmann and Sally Pinkus, of Ossi Quaker and Prince Nuki, of Madame Dubarry and Anna Boleyn. This was a true love story, between the film characters, the director and the cinema, as well as the audience and the director. So this is Lubitsch!

King Kong and the Bears

1985

Feb. 15th-26th, 1985 (Competition)
Feb. 16th-26th, 1985 (Forum)

On the roof of the Europa Center, in the city center, King Kong reaches for the star. The »king of a forgotten world« above the roofs of Berlin. This is how it should have been during the 1985 »Berlinale«. However, the lack of funds put the dampers on the spectacle with the gigantic figure of the gorilla. The Senator for Cultural Affairs refused to finance it, the budget of the Film Festival was too small, and there were no private sponsors to be found.

Special effects: the Retrospective and an exhibition

Nonetheless, the wonder-world of monsters, mutations and tiny folk, of sophisticated horror and fantastic rogues dominated the Film Festival. The »never-ending story« of special effects was presented by an exhibition, conceived by Rolf Giesen, which the Stiftung Deutsche Kinemathek had set up on one floor of a department store. Models from all over the world, running through all aspects of film history, as well as sketches and written documents imparted an impression of that obsessive innovative power which makes dreams come true: »King Kong, Orphée, and the Journey to the Moon«. This year's Retrospective showed rarities, phantastic inventions and experiments made by the pioneers of film, as well as fairy tales, fables and lavish American science fiction films, e. g. from THE WAR OF THE WORLDS and STAR WARS; in fact there were so many films altogether that an exception was made and the Retrospective started a week before the Film Festival.

The Retrospective »Special Effects« must be considered at least in part, as Moritz de Hadeln's tireless efforts to boost the presence of American films in Berlin. »King Kong has a US passport« de Hadeln wrote in an interim report for the members of the board of curators on the preparation of the 1985 IFB (Sept. 14, 1984). In this paper de Hadeln also expressed his desire to extend the Festival's »function as a link with Eastern Europe«. Following the success of the Mediterranean Panorama in 1984, there was a Baltic Panorama in 1985 in which films from the USSR, Poland, GDR, Scandinavia – Sweden, Denmark, and Finland – as well as the Federal Republic of Germany participated.

Above all, however, de Hadeln had tried in the past few years to ease tension in the relationship between the film festivals of Berlin and Cannes. A visible sign of this, in 1985, was the visit of Berlin Cultural Senator Hassemer to the festival in Cannes. The nomination of the actor Jean Marais as jury president was a gesture to the French. And, at a small, informal ceremony, Moritz de Hadeln was awarded the order of »Commandeur dans l'ordre des arts et lettres« by the French government, handed over to him by the general director of the Centre National de la Cinématographie, Jérôme Clément. Détente between festivals...

LES ENFANTS by Marguerite Duras: confusion over the credits

Three French films were shown at the Festival. A lascivious detective film by Michel Deville, PÉRIL EN LA DEMEURE (»Peril«) starring Nicole Garcia and Michel Piccoli; it was a fascinating elliptical game of love and death. Rather more inaccessible was the second film from France, Marguerite Duras' LES ENFANTS [The Children], which was the cause for some irritation prior to the Festival. For while Marguerite Duras insisted on naming Jean Marc Turine and Jean Mascolo as co-directors and, in fact, informed the Festival of this by telegram on February 19th, the producer of the film, Frédéric Vieille, amended this wish and ordered that the credits be cut so that only Marguerite Duras was named as director. While the Festival management sought a fair decision, a representative of the French producer managed to obtain the copy and change the credits. Finally, de Hadeln, after consulting Unifrance, saw to it that the credits were re-inserted as desired by the director. In her film, Marguerite Duras plays with the metaphor of the »school of life«. Young Ernesto refuses to go to school any more, because he doesn't want to learn things he doesn't know. All attempts to explain things simply do not get through to him, and there is no room for positive statements in his system of thinking, »Dieu n'existe pas«. Thus, Ernesto, the grown-up child, takes the Socratic statement »I know that I do not know anything« and combines it with his new philosophical system. Foolish and wise at the same time, »this is a small and maliciously insistent film, which runs counter to everything now en vogue. A film with rigid framing, precise acting, and exploding ideas. It performs, in a natural manner, which Alexander Kluge referred to as the most noble task of the responsible director in the age of excessive exposure of the senses: the annihiliation of images.« (Peter Buchka, Süddeutsche Zeitung, Feb. 28, 1984.)

Once again questions are raised at the Federal Ministry of the Interior: this time the film concerned is Jean-Luc Godard's Je vous salue, Marie.

There were apprehensive questions from the Bonn Ministry of the Interior concerning the invitation for Jean-Luc Godard's Je vous salue, Marie (»Hail Mary«), a reflection on the images which men and women have of one another, a Protestant discourse on the biblical myth of Joseph and Mary. De Hadeln had invited Godard's film to the »Berlinale« as early as November 1984. The film hit the headlines because of vehement protests from broad Catholic circles, and in particular from the supporters of the traditionalist Bishop Lefebvre, who accused Godard's film of blasphemy. They went to court in an attempt to prevent a public screening. At the end of January/beginning of February – in the meantime the West German press had carried reports on the controversy surrounding the film in France – there were calls from the Federal Ministry of the Interior to the Festival organization asking whether the film would really be shown in the Competition, and whether it would be possible to receive informational material or to see the film in advance. Also there were fears that the Catholic Church might feel that it had been portrayed in a bad light (Notes on talks, IFB, Jan. 29–Feb. 1, 1985). De Hadeln, who was presented with the

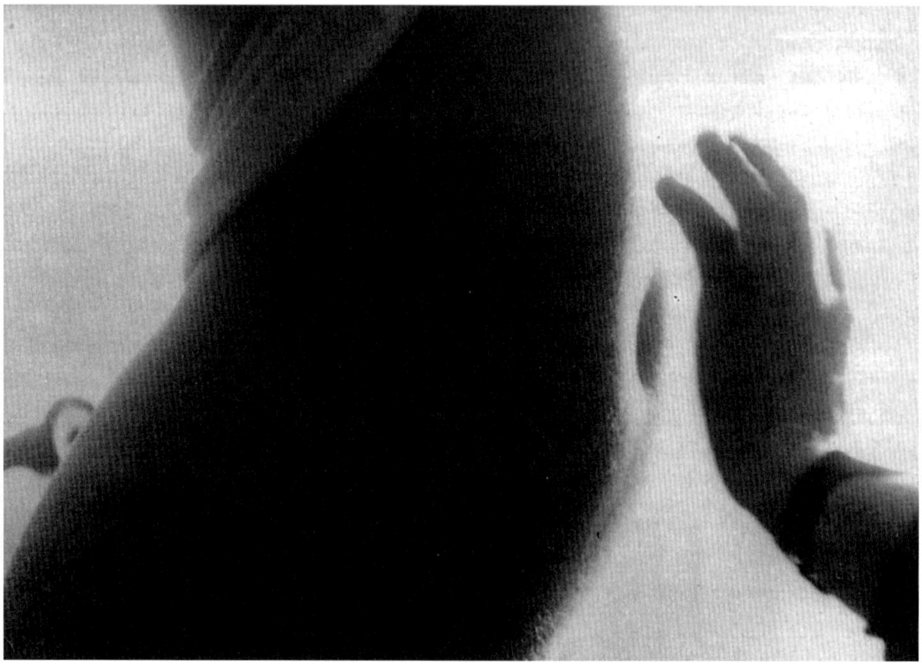

Je vous salue, Marie

questions raised by the Ministry of the Interior, gave a curt reply. Thanks to the political solicitude of the Federal Ministry of the Interior under Friedrich Zimmermann, he once again found himself in a somewhat precarious situation, one which concerned the independence of the Festival in artistic questions. For all that, the accusation of blasphemy directed at Jean-Luc Godard's film was a grotesque misunderstanding. For Godard's film is more of an obsessive and utopian blueprint of love. The film's critics need only have solved the anagram in the title; Marie means »aimer« - i. e. love.

The Festival Grand Prix was awarded. Ex aequo the Golden Bear went to DIE FRAU UND DER FREMDE [The Woman and the Stranger] by Rainer Simon from East Germany - a sensitive filming of a novel by Leonard Frank, of a love affair between three individuals during the First World War - as well as to the debut film of the British playwright David Hare. WETHERBY is a psychological teaser told at a number of different dramatic levels: »As far as cause and effect are concerned it was certainly overdone, especially as Hare refers to and underlines each motif at least twice: his film (...) makes you think, and not just feel for the characters: because he presents real people with all their faults.« (Hans-Dieter Seidel, Frankfurter Allgemeine Zeitung, Feb. 20, 1985.) Basically, both Bears were also awarded in recognition of the exceptional acting performances of both leading ladies: for Kathrin Waligura as Anna in Simon's film, and for Vanessa Redgrave as Jean Travers in Hare's debut as director.

Films on the situation of homosexuals

San Francisco, 1978. City Councilman Dan White shoots dead Mayor George Moscone and Councilman Harvey Milk, a prominent spokesman of the civil rights movement for gays and lesbians. The documentary, THE TIMES OF HARVEY MILK, reconstructs the life of the civil rights' activist, a resolute opponent of the diverse legal initiatives undertaken by Californian Governor John Briggs aimed at restricting the rights of homosexuals. In the Info-Show, films dealt with the legal and psychological situation of homosexuals. A further example was BEFORE STONEWALL

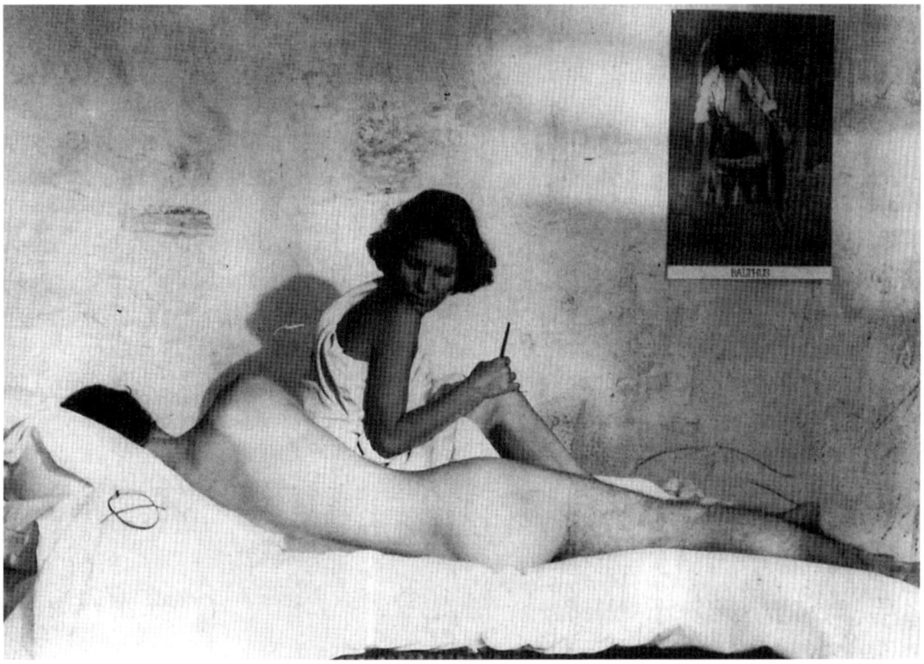

PÉRIL EN LA DEMEURE by Michel Deville: Nicole Garcia, Richard Bohringer

by Greta Schiller and Robert Rosenberg on the invisible face of the American gay movement.

Cities and subcultures: independent productions from the USA

Cities and subcultures (focusing on New York) provided the subject matter for other contributions to the Info-Show: GRINGO by Lech Kowalski, images of New York's tough Lower East Side junkie scene; PAUL CADMUS – ENFANT TERRIBLE AT EIGHTY by David Sutherland, a portrait of the painter and designer, who became famous primarily for his male nudes; AMERICA AND LEWIS HINE by Nina Rosenblum, a close-up on the work of Lewis Wickes Hine, the pioneer of social photography in the USA. There were also independently produced documentaries about the history of the USA and its present. Feature films, showing the works of the American »independent film-makers« which treat the set pieces of Hollywood cinema in an ironic manner, were also screened. SCREAMPLAY, by Rufus Butler Seder, is a black comedy about »scriptwriter Edgar Allen who works on ›murder movies‹ in the shadows of the Hollywood hills in a dismal welcome-apartment, and who actually does experience the crimes he invents. Nothing seems to be serious in this apparently naive studio production which lightheartedly, and with a youthful and satirical bite, pokes fun at the financially powerful industry.« (Wolfgang Würker, Frankfurter Allgemeine Zeitung, Feb. 27, 1985.) Or IT DON'T PAY TO BE AN HONEST CITIZEN by Jacob Burckhardt, an ironic New York thriller in which the guest roles are played by the novelist William Burroughs as a mafioso and Allen Ginsberg as a restless, witty lawyer. There were exciting moments of friction created by the independent productions shown in the Info-Show and the big films of the American major studios which were run in the Competition. The entire diversity of the American film landscape was present at the »Berlinale«.

Furthermore, the International Forum of Young Cinema showed US films with a critical involvement. In 1985, the oustanding example of this was Robert Altman's SECRET HONOR. This was a fictitious historical reconstruction of the politics of

LES FAVORIS DE LA LUNE by Otar Yoseliani: Bernard Eisenschitz, Katja Rupé

Films about war crimes

Richard M. Nixon and an indictment of the moral corruptibility of a politician and of politics in general. With his film WUNDKANAL: HINRICHTUNG FÜR VIER STIMMEN [Wundkanal: Execution for Four Voices], Thomas Harlan attempted to reconstruct history and to confront his own. Thomas Harlan, son of director Veit Harlan, the often criticized representative of Nazi cinema, takes a close look at the biography of a mass murderer. »Speechless one watches (...) at the way in which this Filbert, who is subtly and slyly manipulated by his trainer Harlan, begins to place himself in the clutches of the inquisition and, in so doing, increasingly forgets who he is and slips into the role of the old, experienced policeman and interrogation specialist with ever greater satisfaction« wrote Karena Niehoff (Süddeutsche Zeitung, Feb. 25, 1985). NOTRE NAZI [Our Nazi] filmed by Robert Kramer and produced by Thomas Harlan is a documentary on the film work for WUNDKANAL and an unsparing document about the emotions between fathers and sons. »The film constantly questions the courage, the motives, the methods, the apparently fatal trauma of this avenging angel who, enraged, kills his father, or rather all fathers and brutally exposes them« (Niehoff). Eberhard Fechner's three-part documentary DER PROZESS [The Trial] records the »Majdanek Trial« in Düsseldorf in 1975-81 at which members of the guards from the concentration camp Lublin/Majdanek were called to account for mass murder. What is the judgement of a West German court thirty years after the war? How does it expiate mass murder by Nazi executioners? How does a German society, saturated yet again, react to the confrontation with the Nazi period? Impressively and unerringly, Fechner captures the events surrounding this concentration camp trial: history lessons of a lasting quality. Masaki Kobayashi's documentary TOKYO SAIBAN [The Tokyo Trial] is an attempt to come to terms with the atrocities and the responsible politicians and generals who determined Japanese politics during the Second World War. It reports on the »International Military Tribunal for the Far East« which was constituted on the initiative of the Commander of the Allied Forces,

THE TIMES OF HARVEY MILK

General Douglas McArthur, in Tokyo on May 3rd 1945. »Forty years later« was the title of a special series of films on the Nazi period, and the presentation of the Second World War in films, which were screened as part of the official program outside the Competition. The International Film Festival Berlin saw itself, more than ever before, as a festival of political films.

Art and entertainment: at the Forum these were primarily provided for by two films in 1985. The Japanese farce, GYKUFUNSHA-KAZOKU (»The Crazy Family«) by Sogo Ishii, an eccentric satire about the institution of the family, and LES FAVORIS DE LA LUNE (»The Favorites of the Moon«) by the Georgian director Otar Yoseliani: a painting, the valuable portrait of a lady, is stolen and crudely removed from its frame with the aid of a razor blade. The painting constantly changes hands, becoming smaller and smaller in the process, since the frame is abandoned each time it is stolen and only the canvas is passed on. Images and recollections return to their point of departure while changing in the process. Only a piece of the magnificent painting is left, the head of the lady, en face and en détail.

West-Berlin round trip

By Rainer Simon

One ticket to West Berlin, round-trip. This man is too young, the glance of the German Reichsbahn civil servant behind the ticket counter says, he doesn't yet walk with a cane, why should he be allowed to go?

The dirty S-Bahn car jogs along from one world into the other. The minutes between Friedrichstraße and Lehrter Station pass so slowly, as though one were flying to Vanuatu. Perhaps one could travel there more easily. My gaze is drawn to the police barricades. Seen from above, at such close proximity, this collection of barriers we call the Wall is,

Helma Sanders-Brahms, Brigitte Fossey, László Lugossy

David Hare, Rainer Simon

Hildegard Westbeld, Elfi Mikesch, Monika Treut, Mechthild Grossmann on the occasion of the screening of VERFÜHRUNG: DIE GRAUSAME FRAU [Seduction: The Cruel Woman] in the Forum

Lotti Huber, Rosa von Praunheim, Heinz Badewitz

foremost, ugly. An ugly monument of a post-war politics of division in East and West. But monuments often fulfill their purposes for centuries, one recalls undeserving emperors. More recently, however, young people have come to understand that one can also achieve immortality by pulling monuments down.

The GDR filmmaker, who on »official business« - namely to prepare a film on the German explorer and naturalist Alexander von Humboldt - is allowed, in 1983, to pass this way a few times, uses the daily expense account in order to catch up on what was for years off limits. In art cinemas he finds old and new films by Pasolini, Fassbinder, Wajda, Kluge, Bresson, Bergman, Allen - in the Arsenal they are screening Parajanov's »Color of the Pomegranate«.

The filmmaker is allowed, today, to cross this border, for official business, having officially said to have become more permeable - the film on Alexander von Humboldt titled Die Besteigung des Chimborazo *was produced as a German-German co-production in 1988 and will be premièred in September 1989 -, he only very rarely feels drawn to the cinemas. The interchangeability of the titles is in itself a sign of the commercial trash which is flooding the world from North America. In the meanwhile it has become easier to find a good film in GDR-Berlin. But it is frightening to see, at the box offices (in West and East), what the broad mass of spectators is interested in. The appeals and declarations of those working for a European film culture seem halfhearted, as though one knows, they will be dashed against the wall protecting the money - this wall, too, is hard to tear down. The European Film Prize, awarded courageously in 1988, will be forced into the tasteless garments of Hollywood glamour.*

Once a year, the GDR-filmmaker still goes to the movies around the clock in West Berlin. In contrast to many of his western colleagues, the no longer so very young director still looks at films himself, without the stress of fearing he will miss some reception at which he might shake hands with a producer. Since he was able to present his film Die Frau und der Fremde *in 1985, he has belonged to the privileged and envied who are allowed to go every February.*

Let us protect the festivals, where one now and again still sees good films, for these oases, too, are threatened.

Moritz de Hadeln receiving a French orden

We'll talk again

By Wolfgang Kohlhaase

My view of world cinema, every year between winter and spring, is always fixed on a small diner on the direct route from the Festival office to the Zoo-Palast. In the flow of faces and handshakes combined with the sentence »we'll talk again«, it offers a bit of comfort. A few people at least manage to meet there.

The waiter speaks German with an accent like Moritz de Hadeln, although with a Slavic coloration, this man, like that one, serves the Film Festival. Good and bad films would be difficult to take, were they not separated by a pause, during which social life takes place with the possibility of ignoring the films.

Add a coffee, a beer and something little from the grill. You pay with the fork still in your mouth and drink the last swallow while standing, happy expectation or tired duty rushes by in front of the window.

Sometimes one just continues to sit there. Somebody comes in who has seen the film and strongly advises against it. And we elevate him to a person of our trust - the more so, the

International Jury
Jean Marais
(France, president)
Max von Sydow
(Sweden, vice-president)
Alberto Sordi
(Italy, vice-president)
Regimantas Adomaitis
(USSR)
Sheila Benson (USA)
Wolfgang Kohlhaase (GDR)
Onat Kutlar (Turkey)
Luis Megino (Spain)
Ingrid Scheib-Rothbart
(FRG/USA)
Chris Sievernich (FRG)
István Szabó (Hungary)

WETHERBY:
Vanessa Redgrave

longer the Festival lasts. Of course somebody always comes around later to call your attention to what you have missed. It is in our nature to miss a lot.

Nights, after the last showing, nobody looks for solace in that diner. More distant spots come into play. An invisible jury decides where it is good to be or where one no longer goes, although it was still nice to go there last year. Pubs also get failing marks, one doesn't always know why.

When the Berlinale is over, Berlin is, as one notices with amazement, still there. At least on the day after, however, one avoids the scenes of such recent collegial sociability. More or less already departed, one wanders in and out alone. In the Zoo-Palast, RAMBO *VII is being shown.*

Viva el Forum de Berlin!

A good place for lizards and other independent artists
By Jeanine Meerapfel

Surely it sounds too direct, even childish, for my films to participate in the Forum means to belong to the people I most admire in the film world. It means to be accepted into the »family« of Erika and Ulrich Gregor, whom I respect and love. And to be part of their grand mishpocha; and to gain, as relatives, fighters for film like Sylvia Andresen, Alf Bold, Peter Schumann and the many others who make up the Forum, the Arsenal, the Freunde der Deutschen Kinemathek. To show one's films in the Forum is, for me, like being at home. It means showing one's films at home. Not at home because we live in the same place, in Berlin, but because the intellectual home of the Gregors is my home, a place in which one will always fight fascism, in which resistance to forgetting, to colonialism and the loss of identity is practiced by narrating, by reminding. A place, too, in which one loves film. Not only utilizes it, but loves it. And that is how the filmmakers feel who participate in the Forum: I have always felt loved and respected.

My films IM LAND MEINER ELTERN *(»In my Parent's Country«, 1982),* DIE KÜMMELTÜRKIN GEHT *(»Melek Leaves«, 1985),* DESEMBARCOS – ES GIBT KEIN VERGESSEN *(»Desembarcos - When memory speaks«, 1989) became, through the Forum, internationally known, were discussed, often invited to other festivals, often even (because of the positive reaction of the public and the press as well) purchased by TV or taken up by a distributor.*

Does this all sound too positive? It is positive. I have the most wonderful memories of every Forum of which I have been part.

And in spite of the sad experience I had at the Film Festival with DIE VERLIEBTEN *(»Days to Remember«) in 1987, I am very fond of this whole Berlin Festival.*

The Awards of the International Jury

Feature Films
Grand Prix of the 35th IFB
Golden Berlin Bear
ex aequo
WETHERBY, Great Britain, directed by David Hare

DIE FRAU UND DER FREMDE
GDR, directed by Rainer Simon

Silver Berlin Bear
Special Prize of the Jury
SZIRMOK, VIRÁGOK, KOSZORÚK
Hungary, directed by Lásló Lugossy

Silver Berlin Bear
for the best director
Robert Benton
PLACES IN THE HEART, USA

Silver Berlin Bear
for the best actress
Jo Kennedy
WRONG WORLD, Australia

Silver Berlin Bear
for the best actor
Fernando Fernán Gómez
STICO, Spain

Silver Berlin Bear
for an outstanding individual achievement
Tolomush Okeyev for the artistic work on his film
POTOMOK BELOGO BARSA
USSR

Silver Berlin Bear
for a highly imaginative film
RONJA RÖVARDOTTER
Sweden/Norway, directed by Tage Danielsson

Special Mention
LES ENFANTS
France, directed by Marguerite Duras

Tarik Akan
for the part he played in
PEHLIVAN
Turkey

Damiano Damiani
for his film
PIZZA CONNECTION, Italy

Ginger e Fred:
Marcello Mastroianni

One voice

1986

Feb. 14th-25th, 1986 (Competition)
Feb. 15th-25th, 1986 (Forum)

A housing councilor was being remanded in custody and the head of a construction company was arrested; corruption in the Berlin housing sector. The Senate also came under political pressure, leading to hefty debates in the House of Representatives. Politicians were surrounded by suspicion. A vote of no-confidence in Mayor Diepgen, demanded by the Social Democrats and the Alternative List was defeated by the majority vote of the Christian and the Free Democrats. This was fourteen days before the International Film Festival Berlin opened. Such was the gray and dreary world of every-day politics.

An article in the »Zeit« and its consequences

At the beginning, things did not look too rosy for the IFB either. At least this was what Siegfried Schober, film editor for the »Zeit« claimed (Jan. 17, 1986). He polemically wrote that West German film-makers were in agreement that the »Berlinale« was »not good for German films«, basing his argument primarily on the strong and vehement rejection of Margarethe von Trotta's HELLER WAHN (»Sheer Madness«) at the 1983 Film Festival, which finally would lead to the director giving her latest film ROSA LUXEMBURG to the »rival festival in Cannes, which always took the wind out of the Berlin Festival's sails in any case«. He insinuated that Moritz de Hadeln »was not really interested in German films at all« and that »German film-makers, with their stubborn spirit of resistance and tendency to play the eternally offended party ... [were] ... not free from blame for this miserable state of affairs«. This was an old conflict, and one which had appeared to be long since dead and buried. Nor was there any acute reason for raking up old stories again. Nevertheless, Schober's »Never again Berlin« polemics did scare the Berlin FDP Senate member Dietrich Pawlowski, who raised a question (No. 1442, Feb. 6, 1986) directed at the Senator for Science and Cultural Affairs, to find out among other things, the extent to which the claims made in the »Zeit« applied, and what the Senate intended to undertake so that German films would not have their first screenings in Cannes, but in Berlin. In his reply (March 3, 1986) the Senator, Volker Hassemer, stood up for his Festival director and dismissed the reproaches of the »Zeit« as unfounded. He also remarked laconically that it did not »go against Berlin's interest if an occasional German film had its première in Cannes. Incidentally, the première of the film to which the ›Zeit‹ article devotes most of its attention is due to have its first screening in Berlin at the beginning of April; so the film won't be given its première in Cannes.« The real conflict and the dynamite in the »Zeit« article was contained in the closing remarks, i. e. that Munich would »sooner or later« ... »profit« from the Festival policy pursued by Berlin vis-à-vis German film-makers. »And if that means never again in Berlin, everyone will be most sincerely upset. But Munich has such wonderful beer gardens.« Indeed, the establishment of the Munich Film Festival, to which Eberhard Hauff had been appointed director, had been a repeated reason for speculation: might it even rival the »Berlinale«? Moreover, assurance that the Munich Film Festival would not stage any competitions were not taken very seriously at first. (In Berlin this was rubbing salt into old wounds; as early as 1954 proposals made by the Munich journalist Kaesbach to move the location of the Film Festival to Munich had caused quite an uproar.)

Great cinema: GINGER E FRED and OUT OF AFRICA

However, this drama was soon forgotten, for the »Berlinale« opened spectacularly with the new Fellini film, GINGER E FRED (»Ginger & Fred«), a dancing duo meet again thirty years later at a TV show. Their gentle, awkward, shy, and melancholic attempt

STAMMHEIM: Ulrich Tukur, Sabine Wegner, Hans Kremer, Therese Affolter

to be like they were thirty years before (and like Fred Astaire and Ginger Rogers) disperses the traces of time (and superficial and flashy TV can no longer show its face). Amelia and Pippo, Giulietta Masina and Marcello Mastroianni triumph, and with them the great European cinema regains its former glory. Opulent American cinema followed. OUT OF AFRICA, by Sydney Pollack, traced the life of the Danish poet Tania Blixen, a love affair in black Africa during the First World War. This was a film of stars: Meryl Streep, Klaus Maria Brandauer, and Robert Redford.

Stammheim – a word which arouses very intense and mixed feelings in the Federal Republic. In Stuttgart-Stammheim there is a prison with a maximum security wing and a provisional courtroom. It was here that members of the »Red Army Faction« were tried, and where Andreas Baader, Ulrike Meinhof, Gudrun Ensslin, and Jan Carl Raspe were imprisoned; it was also here that they later committed suicide. They were arrested in 1972 and accused of forming a terrorist organization and of carrying out a number of acts of violence. After being remanded in custody for three years, they were tried at Stammheim. STAMMHEIM, the film by Reinhard Hauff, based on a book by the journalist Stefan Aust, reconstructs the history of this trial, taking its information from authentic texts and actual events; the film traces the debates and communication among the prisoners from letters and cell circulars. No side emerges unscathed, neither the representatives of the militant group nor the district attorney.

Continuing concern at the Federal Ministry of the Interior

When it became known that Reinhard Hauff's film was to be shown in the Competition of the IFB there were once again questions from the Ministry of the Interior in Bonn. This time they were also directed at another film, which had not, however, been entered in the Competition: Herbert Achternbusch's HEILT HITLER! [Heal Hitler!]. Moritz de Hadeln replied to the Federal Minister of the Interior in a letter, in which he pointed out the difficulties involved in selecting German films, since »the contents and the form of some films could give reason for concern, especially considering the fact that nobody should be hurt in any way«. He continued, »As,

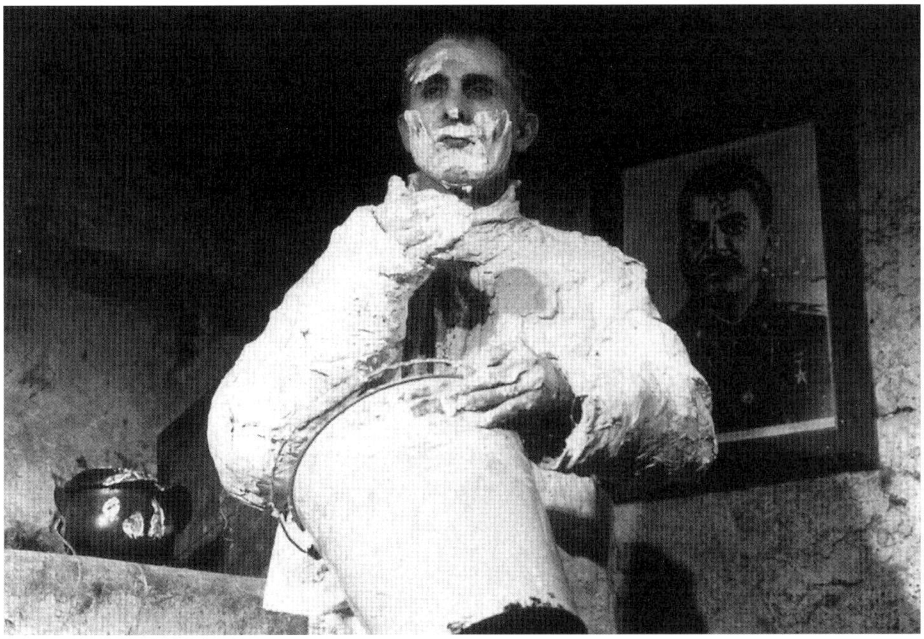

Heilt Hitler!:
Herbert Achternbusch

however, art and talent always require freedom and innovation, I feel that, within the scope of the artistic mandate given me by the Festivals-Ltd, there would be a contradiction if I were to start imposing restrictions on my judgment of art by introducing considerations of possibility and necessitiy.« (Jan. 24, 1986.) De Hadeln insisted on his responsibility (and that of the selection commission) for inviting the films Stammheim and Heilt Hitler!

Reinhard Hauff's and Stefan Aust's attempt to come to terms with Stammheim

Hauff's film had been given its première in Hamburg and had been screened in other West German cities before its initial showing in Berlin. The screening of the film in Hamburg had to be stopped after firecrackers had been let off while the film was running and former Government Spokesman Klaus Bölling was assaulted. The fact that Stammheim could be shown at all in the Festival Competition, in spite of its having been screened in other cinemas was made possible by a change in the guidelines which now stated that German films could be shown previously in the Federal Republic, although not at other festivals. This gave West German productions the same status as foreign films; it was also the same procedure adopted in Cannes with respect to French films. This amendment was to be beneficial to German films as a whole and was not a special regulation introduced for Stammheim as some observers suspected.

Screenings of Stammheim at the IFB were accompanied by special security precautions. There had been anonymous threats, indications of intended disruptions, as well as threats to kill members of the jury. The Festival management attempted to coordinate security precautions with the police; director Reinhard Hauff also participated in the talks. Police presence was very strong, and there was one incident. A photographer working for the FilmFest Journal was not only obstructed by the police, she was also arrested. Nonetheless, the screening of the film took place without any disturbances, and the only unpleasantry was the smell of butyric acid which hung in the air at the Zoo-Palast. The film was given a cool reception. »The applause at the end of the film was short and, at best, polite, being more like an

Half Life
by Dennis O'Rourke

embarrassing silence.« (Hans-Dieter Seidel, Frankfurter Allgemeine Zeitung, Feb. 20, 1986.)

Gina Lollobrigida distances herself from the Golden Bear for Stammheim.

There was an éclat when the prize was awarded. The international jury had awarded the Golden Bear to Stammheim. Gina Lollobrigida, the jury president, and Rudi Fehr, the vice-president, awarded the prizes. Even before the actual award it became known that the decision in favor of Hauff's film had been close. Thus it was not so surprising at first that Gina Lollobrigida, clearly annoyed, should announce the winner with the sentence that »the majority on the international jury had reached this decision after a controversial discussion«. However, she also added a personal remark: »I was against this film« and insisted on Rudi Fehr translating this sentence into German. This was an unprecedented act; the jury president had thus broken the pledge of secrecy of the jury and snubbed the other jurors. The final vote had initially ended in a stalemate, with five for and five against Stammheim. (Incidentally, August Coppola, was the chief spokesman for the film's opponents, who argued that the film was an inner-German problem.) Rudi Fehr, Werner Grassmann, Norbert Kückelmann, Françoise Maupin, and Jerzy Toeplitz voted for the film; votes against were cast by August Coppola, Otar Yoseliani, Gina Lollobrigida, Rosaura Revueltas, and Naoki Togawa. It should also be mentioned that the opponents of Stammheim were unable to raise a majority for another film. Three votes were cast for Nanni Moretti's La messa è finita [The Mass is Ended] – including Gina Lollobrigida's; the Brazilian film A hora da estrela [The Hour of the Star] by Suzana Amaral, and the Japanese film Yari no Gonza (»Gonza, the Spearman«) by Masahiro Shinoda received one vote each. Nobody seemed to have won. Faced with this situation, Lindsay Anderson, who had abstained up to this point, cast his vote, for Stammheim.

After the Film Festival was over, Gina Lollobrigida gave an interview for the »Spiegel« (No. 10, March 3, 1986) in which she attacked the jury members claiming that the decision in favor of Stammheim had been »pre-arranged«. In response to this, Moritz de Hadeln released the jury members from the pledge of secrecy in order that

Shoah

they could defend themselves against Gina Lollobrigida's reproaches. It also became known that at the jury meeting, Gina Lollobrigida had threatened to resign, only allowing herself to be persuaded otherwise to prevent the film from being given even greater attention. In her opinion the film was merely »banal, vacuous, and unimaginative reporting, which is suitable for reading but not for making a film«.

Yet this was not the only ill-feeling of a political nature in this particular year. A protest made by the Soviet Union against the French film Rouge baiser [Red Kiss], by Véra Belmont, which told the story of a young girl in Paris in the fifties, a convinced communist whose impassioned ideals were disappointed by Stalin, caused vexation for a while, as did an attempt by Romaniafilm – the state-owned Rumanian production company – to intervene against the film and to withdraw the Rumanian films. However, these protests had no effect.

Shoah: Claude Lanzmann's documentary about the murder of European Jews

The focal point of the Forum was the 9 1/2 hours long documentary, Shoah, by Claude Lanzmann. »Shoah« is Hebrew for »abyss«, and »extermination«. Lanzmann's film is a document about the merciless murder-machinery of the Nazis and the extermination of the European Jews. In the film, Lanzmann makes no use of archive material, utilizing solely interviews and images from the present. »At the beginning one of the survivors does, to be sure, state that ›Nobody can really imagine what happened here‹ and later adds, ›You are only human, and want to live, and that's why you have to forget.‹ But then, when victims, murderers, Nazi-members, and witnesses allow the past to come to life again at the green, overgrown fields of death, it is as if the places themselves speak of the million-fold horrors which – as recent examples show – are still, or are once again, being repressed here.« (Roland Keller, Stuttgarter Zeitung, Feb. 25, 1986.) A number of times the director met with spectators to talk about his film, so that the holocaust would not be repressed or forgotten. (It was all the more difficult to understand – in view of this outstanding film and its German subject matter – that, after the Film Festival, voices could be heard in the advisory board complaining that by screening Shoah the

An award for STAMMHEIM: Gina Lollobrigida, Moritz de Hadeln, Reinhard Hauff, Stefan Aust, Rudi Fehr

Forum had provided TV with publicity, since broadcasting time had been set aside on West German TV (WDR) and the latter had co-financed the film. Ulrich Gregor rightly pointed out that the film was »an important event, and one whose significance should by no means be underestimated«. Fortunately, most of the other members of the advisory board shared this opinion. (Minutes of the 40th session, March 10, 1986.)

The subject matter of some of the other films was closely related to that of SHOAH: e. g. Josh Waletzky's PARTISANS OF VILNA which told the story of Jewish youths who organized resistance in the Vilna ghetto; WE WERE SO BELOVED, about Jewish emigrants from Nazi Germany who lived in the New York district of Washington Heights; and two documentary films by Lea Rosh: EIN NAZI PROZESS [A Nazi Trial], and VERNICHTUNG DURCH ARBEIT [Extermination through Labor].

Latin America: documentary and feature films in the Forum and in the Panorama

The new Argentine cinema provided the second focal point of the Forum program. These films dealt first and foremost with the search for a national identity, for lost political traditions, for the democratic Argentina behind the brutal and murderous facade of the military regime, e. g. LA HISTORIA OFFICIAL (»The Official Story«) by Luis Puenzo, in which an adoptive mother begins to ask herself whether the daughter she has taken on is not the child of abducted parents. Werner Schroeter's documentary DE L'ARGENTINE [Concerning Argentina] also formed a part of this series. A many-sided picture of contemporary Argentina is allowed to come out in interviews. Relatives of »missing persons« talk about what is happening, the »Mothers of Plaza de Mayo« accuse, politicians and church representatives give their view of events.

Latin American films were also shown in the Panorama, which had now been given a new structure and a new name (changed from the previous title of Info-Show). LOS MOTIVOS DE LUZ [Luz' Reasons] by Felipe Cazals from Mexico tells of a tragedy in the slums of Mexico City: a mother kills her four children. A Columbian-Cuban co-production TIEMPO DE MORIR [A Time to Die], based on a script by Gabriel García Márquez deals – in the style of a cowboy film – with Latin American machismo.

Fred Zinnemann, Giulietta Masina, Federico Fellini

Sydney Pollack, having received the »Berlinale Camera«

Following the Mediterranean and Baltic Panorama, this year's program turned its attention to films from the countries around the Black Sea including Bulgaria, Rumania, Turkey, and the USSR (the Ukranian, Moldavian, and Georgian Soviet Republics, and the Soviet Federated Socialist Republic). The program was put together by Hans-Joachim Schlegel, who maintained contacts with the socialist states on behalf of the »Berlinale«, and especially with the USSR. The film which attracted most attention came from Georgia: Eldar Shengelaya's satire GOLUBYE GORY ILI NEPRAVDOPODOBNAYA ISTORIYA (»Blue Mountains«); here a house literally collapses around the bewildered bureaucrats who are in it. (Incidentally, this film also showed that Soviet film policy was opening up.)

New juries

In spite of all the excitement surrounding the awarding of the Bears, the Film Festival ended on a happy note. It had also revealed its political character.

Although the increase in the number of juries and prizes at the »Berlinale« was not received warmly among all those responsible, two new features deserve mention here. The »Berlinale Camera«, which was endowed in honor of outstanding personalities, connected with the International Film Festival. The first to receive the prize were Giulietta Masina and Fred Zinnemann, to whom a Retrospective was also dedicated, as well as Gina Lollobrigida and Sydney Pollack. In addition, the Children's Film Festival had, for the first time, a jury composed solely of children. This series for children had established itself alongside the »senior« program sections and was a unique phenomenon for a film festival.

A resumée by one of the critics: »All things considered, the 36th Berlinale was one of the best in recent years. The Berlin public accepted the privilege of being able to participate enthusiastically in this encounter of international cinema. Yet which of these films will make their way into our movie theaters, or into the TV film programs? Where in the provinces - which one can understand not only as a place but also as a time: the every-day life of cinema outside the big cities - where in the provinces does the longing to participate in the Film Festival find the ways and means to be able to enjoy the luxury of the Berlin events? What happens to the Forum program, and who pays attention to it?« (Frankfurter Rundschau, Feb. 27, 1986.) Ques-

International Jury
Gina Lollobrigida (Italy, president)
Rudi Fehr (USA, vice-president)
Lindsay Anderson (Great Britain)
August Coppola (USA)
Werner Grassmann (FRG)
Otar Yoseliani (USSR)
Norbert Kückelmann (FRG)
Françoise Maupin (France)
Rosaura Revueltas (Mexico)
Naoki Togawa (Japan)
Jerzy Toeplitz (Poland)

tions were left open, and not only those which Wolfram Schütte posed concerning the film and cinema culture of a country. There were also practical problems, both internal to the Festival and of a broader nature. Once again the prolongation of Moritz de Hadeln's and Ulrich Gregor's contracts was on the agenda. Once again there were discrepancies and indiscretions.

In May the board of curators of the Berlin Festivals-Ltd. reached an agreement with Moritz de Hadeln and Ulrich Gregor to extend the so-called reply-time for prolonging or annulling the contracts by two months. A decision should have been made by March 31st. Greater leeway for negotiations was felt desirable, because the chairman of the board of curators, Parliamentary Undersecretary at the Federal Ministry of the Interior Horst Waffenschmidt, and deputy chairman, Berlin Cultural Senator Volker Hassemer had been instructed by the members of the board of curators to negotiate with other candidates on an equal footing with Moritz de Hadeln. (As in the case of the first impending extension of the contract three years before, it was only de Hadeln's contract that was contested; Ulrich Gregor's confirmation as director of the International Forum was, by way of contrast, unquestioned.) The fact that de Hadeln's position as director of the Festival was once again the subject of negotiation was primarily due to political reasons. In particular, it was his insistence on standing by critical films - for the »Berlinale«, which had just closed, this meant, first and foremost, STAMMHEIM, HEILT HITLER!, and the filming of Walraff's GANZ UNTEN [Right at the Bottom] by Jörg Gfrörer, the latter having run in the Panorama - which provoked opposition to him. Prolongation of his contract foundered, above all, due to objections by the Spio, which - at the board of curators' meeting of April 21st - had pleaded for the contract to be left open, even though negotiations with de Hadeln had already taken place and some compromises had been reached. Under consideration as rival candidate were the director of the Munich Film Festival, Eberhard Hauff, as well as the head of the Frankfurt Department of culture, Hilmar Hoffmann, with whom negotiations as a possible successor were also conducted for a time, he had however declined candidacy at a very early stage.

The West German press followed the Berlin decision-making process very attentively, analyzing the background to the distrust and the reservations in Bonn. The »Tagesspiegel« published a long report on July 6th, and on the following day a polemic article on the question of de Hadeln's successor appeared in the Social Democratic paper »Vorwärts«, headed »They are quietly hacking away«: »Are Munich's film circles working to put the worm in the Berlin Film Festival and boost Munich? Is the film distributor Wohlrabe ([translator's note: Wohlrabe = good raven] who Herbert Wehner once referred to as Übelkrähe [= ›Evil-crow‹]) the one pulling the strings in the background? One is entitled to ask such things, because Moritz de Hadeln is most certainly not one of those versatile and eloquent PR men, a jack-of-all-trades courting the media.« (No. 23, June 7, 1986.) The author of this declaration in support of de Hadeln was the former Bundestag deputy of the SPD, now appointed Senator for Culture, Anke Martiny. In Berlin the director of the Festivals-Ltd, Ulrich Eckhardt, as well as the Berlin Working Group Film (BAF), and the department for film and media at the Akademie der Künste (Academy of Arts) spoke out in favor of his contract being renewed. The Working Group of New German Film Producers and the Working Group for Documentary Films also voted for de Hadeln, i. e. precisely those associations which had opposed him a few years previously. The Spio was increasingly isolated with its objections even if its chairman, Horst von Hartlieb, once again emphasized, in a talk with the German Press Agency on June 12th 1986, that the IFB needed a new director, both owing to its international standing and its importance for the domestic film market. (Tagesspiegel, June 13, 1986.) In this desolate situation, in which it appeared that the reputation of the Film Festival and its future director were at stake, the board of curators decided to renew the contracts of both de Hadeln and Gregor. There was once more a detailed round of talks between the Berlin Senator for Culture and the Federal Ministry of the Interior in order to persuade the latter to agree to de Hadeln's appointment. Thus, at the end of June, it was announced that the contracts were to be extended for five years. A period of irritating uncertainty seemed to be over. However, the fruitless discussions surrounding the contracts were not finished yet. Bonn continued to exert pressure on Berlin. The five year extension, which the Berlin Senate wanted to carry through, was not accepted; the Federal Ministry of the Interior declared that it was willing to consent to an extension of three years at the most. Only two weeks before the 1987 Film Festival was due to start, the contracts had not yet been extended; it was not until February 7th that the contracts were signed, for a further three years. Berlin had not been able to get its way on this political question entirely. However, this trial of political strength, which had been to the detriment of the Festival, had now finally come to an end. It was not the Festival, but the politicians who were at the touchstone.

Concerning the moral rights of authors

By Fred Zinnemann

While celebrating the 40-year jubilee of the Berlin Film Festival and the enormous contribution it has made to the art of film making, it is perhaps important to consider the future which is awaiting the masters of tomorrow: the young writers, designers, cameramen, editors and musicians.

What began as a new art-form is being reduced by a flood of mass-produced industrial garbage, corrupting everything it touches. Great masterpieces are being mutilated in the name of bigger profits, chopped to pieces, colorized, reduced to caricatures and lost to future generations. If nothing is done to stop this infamous abuse, the standards of excellence set by great directors will have disappeared.

People may be the legal owners of copyrights, but it is the entire world which truly owns the music of Beethoven, the paintings of El Greco, the writing of Goethe, as well as the films of Chaplin, Griffith, Murnau, Pabst and so many other film-makers.

Tampering with their work means paving the way for barbarism and for the new dark ages. This must be forbidden by law in every country, as it is in France, as a cultural crime against the world's heritage; the moral rights of authors must be protected against the mercantile mutilation of their work.

A yearly event dedicated to protecting moral rights at the Berlin Film Festival could play an important role in such an initiative.

The Awards of the International Jury

Feature Films
Grand Prix of the 36th IFB
Golden Berlin Bear
Stammheim
FRG, directed by
Reinhard Hauff
The majoritiy of the International Jury arrived at this decision after a controversial discussion.

Silver Berlin Bear
Special Prize of the Jury
La messa è finita
Italy, directed by
Nanni Moretti

Silver Berlin Bear
for the best director
Georgi Shengelaya
Achalgasrda kompositoris mogsauroba/Puteshestviye molodogo kompositora
USSR

Silver Berlin Bear
for his harmonic composition
Yari no Gonza
Japan, directed by
Masahiro Shinoda

Silver Berlin Bear
for the best actress
Charlotte Valandrey
in Rouge baiser
FRG/France

and ex aequo

Marcelia Cartaxo
in A hora da estrela
Brazil

Silver Berlin Bear
for the best actor
Tuncel Kurtiz
in Hiuh hagdi
Israel

Silver Berlin Bear
for his visual presentation
Caravaggio
Great Britain, directed by
Derek Jarman

Special Mention
Pas în doi
Rumania, directed by
Dana Piţa

PROSHCHANIYE:
Stefania Stanjuta
(sitting in the middle)

Farewell to the past

1987

Feb. 20th - March 3rd, 1987 (Competition)
Feb. 21st - March 3rd, 1987 (Forum)

A decade of the Children's Film Festival

»Everything was great!« and, »Actually I thought the film was good, especially the bit with the spaghetti« and, »The rainbow and the way the sun's rays fell so purely in the forest.« These were letters from children to films in the Children's Film Festival, which took place for the tenth time in 1987. »What was initially rather timidly presented under the title ›Movies for people of six and upwards‹ had long since turned into an essential part of the Festival, loved not only by the very youngest, but also by the older children and their parents« wrote Carla Rhode (Der Tagesspiegel, Feb. 22, 1987). UNICEF, the United Nations Children's Fund, had meanwhile become the patron of the Children's Film Festival, and three juries – which, since 1986, included one which consisted solely of children – distributed the prizes. »The Children's Film Festival is an integral part of the International Film Festival Berlin and is open to all Festival participants and visitors. Thus the children's film has been released from its outsider position for enthusiasts and placed on an equal footing with all other sections of the Festival. This is an opening in two directions: for those interested in the Children's Film Festival, it extends their horizon to tendencies in international film-making which go way beyond children's films; and for all the other participants at the Festival, this presentation clearly shows the significance of the children's film for the future of cinema.« (Moritz de Hadeln, Dokumentation 10 Jahre Kinderfilmfest 1978-1987 [Documentation of 10 Years of the Children's Film Festival].) One girl had the following to say about a film, »I liked it best of all when the house burned down.« That had nearly happened during the 1987 Film Festival; it was pure chance that a fire, which had broken out in a store above one of the offices of the Film Festival in January, had been discovered. However, there was little damage; the »Berlinale« was not endangered.

A thaw in the political and cultural climate

A thaw in relations. The world is changing, and the Film Festival Berlin benefits from it. In a manner hitherto unprecedented, a link was established from the West to the East. This shift was made possible by the social and political changes under Mikhail Gorbachev in the Soviet Union. »Glasnost«, »perestroyka« and »demokratsia« marked a new phase in Soviet politics. Especially in the domain of film, these new ideas began to make major breakthroughs. At the 5th meeting of the Soviet association of film-makers in May 1986 it was decided on a new policy, which was to function as a public signal. The old leading cadres were voted out, and a start was made in reforming the production and distribution structures. Goskino chairman Yermash was replaced by pro-reformer Aleksandr Kamshalov. Director Elem Klimov, whose films had been subject to an export-ban for some time, was elected chairman of the association. A special committee, which included – among others – the »Pravda« film critic Andrei Plakhov, selected the films which had been banned from screening up to this time. For the first time, feature films and documentaries which had been locked away in the safes of the censors were shown to the Soviet public. Directors and their works were rehabilitated. Films by Andrei Tarkovsky, who had died in exile in 1986, were run in a Moscow movie theater. Above all, the export-ban had been lifted so that old and new Russian films could also become known internationally, including films by Elem Klimov, Gleb Panfilov, Aleksandr Sokurov, Kira Muratova, Sergei Parajanov, and many more besides.

The first forum for these banned films of Soviet cinema was the Film Festival in Berlin. Three films were shown in the Competition program alone or hors concours.

Jürgen Böttcher, Ulrich Gregor

A sign of change: Elem Klimov, Jack Valenti, Volker Hassemer, Moritz de Hadeln

Carmen Maura, Pedro Almodovar

Lina Wertmüller, Claude Chabrol

In the Panorama, feature films and documentaries were screened, and two other films from the censor's strong-box were run in the International Forum of Young Cinema.

Elem Klimov, Gleb Panfilov, Aleksandr Sokurov, and others: new films from the Soviet Union

Elem Klimov's PROSHCHANIYE (»Farewell to Matyora«) - which was to have opened the 1984 »Berlinale« and was prevented from doing so because the Soviet authorities refused to release it - was run by the IFB hors concours. The construction of a dam meant that the inhabitants of a Siberian village had to evacuate their homes and villages. They were compulsorily resettled and only a few old women remained, unwilling to give up their homes. The river is flooded... Matyora, the village disappears. »Elem Klimov focuses on the faces of the people, picking out each one in turn; but he also puts them all - peasants and workers - together in groups; the choreography is very tight: they often stand there like a choir from antiquity, yet silent, aware of the magnitude of the catastrophe, but unable to comprehend the destruction of their world.« (Volker Baer, Der Tagesspiegel, March 5, 1987.) Before the peasants leave their village they set fire to their houses. The flames of offerings rise into the heavens; an old woman cleans her house, and decorates it with flowers. It is like an open grave; she will stay behind, to die in the floods. The story stands still again and again, waiting; pictures freeze, as symbols which become fixed, until the flow of the story surges forward again. This concentration of images, which plead to be read as metaphors, was also peculiar to other Soviet films. Gleb Panfilov's TEMA [The Theme] arose as early as 1979. In one scene this film gives an explosive account of the alienation of a successful writer from society and from himself. The hero of the film meets a young author who has to work as a grave-digger. The author expresses his desire to emigrate to Israel but is resigned and has no opportunity to publish in his own country, preferring to »die of loneliness in a foreign country, than of hatred towards his own country at home«. This breaking with taboos demonstrates »the degree of self-confidence which the Soviet Union is now capable

The movie house in the Bundesallee: cinema for the films of the Panorama

of ›showing‹, by even allowing self-critique at an international festival« (Karena Niehoff, Süddeutsche Zeitung, March 3, 1987). The international jury of the Film Festival awarded the Grand Prix of the IFB, the Golden Berlin Bear, to TEMA. This honor was not questioned artistically, but was viewed, above all, as a political gesture, as a sign of respect for the reform policies of the Soviet Union and its cultural »transparency«. Aleksandr Sokurov, whose films had found the support, in particular, of Andrei Tarkovski, was represented with a new film, SKORBNOYE BEZCHUVSTVIYE [Heartless Grief], a fantasia based on George Bernard Shaw's play »Heartbreak House«, which Shaw himself had referred to as »a fantasia in Russian style about English topics«. This was, then, the metamorphosis of a metamorphosis, an experimental piece of nonsense: alienation and stylization, a collage of images which uplifts its documentary character in the fiction, a concocted dream, bold and selfless. A villa, like a kind of »Noah's Arc« in which a society gathers, infatuated with itself, and hopelessly lost, while »outside« the First World War rages. Karsten Witte criticized the excessively polyphonic structure of the imagery and the text, »The evidence, which is compounded in the gesture of the all-too-apparent, is lacking in the humor which it claims to possess. This is demonstrated in the sound track. Chopin and tank-tracks, a musical clock and machine guns, war outside and the absence of peace internally, there is no inter-relationship, but talking at cross-purposes.« (Frankfurter Rundschau, Feb. 24, 1987.) At the »Berlinale,« a new Soviet cinema presented itself with a creativity which had hitherto merely been divined in the West; a passion for the fabulous and for imagery which also had something disturbing about it – for both parties. The arc explodes, farewell to yesterday.

In the Forum, Agasi Aivasan's ZAZHONY FONAR [The Lit Lantern] was screened. This was an Armenian feature film about the painter Vano Khodzhabenko, a contemporary of the Georgian artist Niko Pirosmani. There was also Sergei Parajanov's LEGENDA O SURAMSKOI KREPOSTI [The Legend of Suram Fortress] which tells the story of a fortress on which a spell has been cast. In the Panorama, both feature films and documentaries dealing with problems of environmental destruction were shown. Above all it was a documentary about the reactor accident at Chernobyl which people awaited with great interest. However, for some time it remained unclear whether the film would actually be run. A number of times the date of screening had to be postponed because the copy had not arrived in Berlin. Nor was it possible to obtain any reliable information about why the film was being withheld. It was suspected that the documentary was too explosive for the Russians and that political interests were blocking its release. Finally, on March 1st, the copy of the film KOLOKOLA CHERNOBYLYA (»The Bells of Chernobyl«) by Rolan Sergeyenko arrived. It was now in Berlin, after all, and was screened for the first time in a foreign country one day before the end of the Festival at a late showing in the Zoo-Palast. The audience was hoping for something more than the TV pictures, which had already been shown throughout the world. »Conventionally put together from interviews with inhabitants from the area around Chernobyl, as well as with experts and with detailed shots of the reactor site, the film surprised the audience, above all, by its tone. It was steeped in a respectful sadness, and certainly free from vacuous pathos. Even the obligatory reverence to the government, which would come to grips with all the problems, was kept to a minimum.« (Thomas Rothschild, Frankfurter Allgemeine Zeitung, March 7, 1987.) Yet the film did make one thing particularly clear – establishing, almost by chance, a link to Elem Klimov's PROSHCHANIYE – just how dif-

A documentary film about the nuclear reactor accident in Chernobyl

Mélo by Alain Resnais (in the Forum): Fanny Ardant

ficult it is for people to accept an invisible danger, and to leave their houses, their villages, and their towns. Those interviewed constantly repeated their desire to return, »and the film encouraged them to do so. Courage is better than panic, was the film's watchword. However, the images told a different story. Again and again the zoom caught the ruins of Reactor IV. The zoom is, so to speak, the film's Geiger-counter, revealing the extent to which the contents of this film are contaminated. The town has moved. It has migrated as a chip in the respiratory system of Europe«. (Karsten Witte, Frankfurter Rundschau, March 5, 1987.) These were no longer pictures bidding farewell to yesterday; but bidding farewell to today. The cinematographic and political accents of the 1987 Film Festival were set by the films from the Soviet Union. Viktor Dyomin, secretary of the Soviet film association, head of the critic section, and member of the jury in Berlin, criticized a situation in which »films used to be sent to foreign festivals even though they did not have any real chance of becoming a competitive threat. (...) At the same time, however, films by Aleksei Gherman and Gleb Panfilov, and the outstanding works of Georgian directors, were not released for the festivals. Fortunately, the International Film Festival Berlin is presenting a completely new approach by showing something of the new climate in our country.« (Talk with Hans-Joachim Schlegel in FilmFest Journal No. 8, Feb. 27, 1987.)

»A film-makers' Reykjavik«: Elem Klimov and Jack Valenti meet for talks at the »Berlinale«.

The most visible sign of this opening in Soviet policy was the moment when Elem Klimov shook hands with Jack Valenti, president of the Movie Producers' Association of America. The fact that they met one another in Berlin for a talk received great acclaim, a »Reykjavik of film-makers«. The Film Festival underlined the importance of this dialogue by awarding the »Berlinale Camera« to both representatives.

The Journey was more than 14 hours long, taking its audience through five continents and twelve countries. It was made in eight languages; this was a cinema trip

Mon cas [My Case] by Manoel de Oliveira (in the Forum): Bulle Ogier, Axel Bougousslavski

filmed by Peter Watkins, and an expedition through war and peace. People were spoken to all over the world on the subject of the global nuclear threat. »Watkins not only engaged in a globe-embracing dialogue with an overabundance of information dealing with the madness of a very real prospect: war. He also shows that he conceived of making the film itself as a journey of agitation, as a tool of dialogue. This is what makes The Journey into an adventure of insights, and, at the same time, into a remarkably ›elevating‹ experience, about how useless knowledge is, if one does not know the price of not-knowing.« (Michael Kötz, Deutsches Allgemeines Sonntagsblatt, April 12, 1987.) The Journey was like a political clip holding together the past - pictures of the memorial park in Hiroshima, where the ashes of uncountable thousands of victims of the atom bomb are kept - with the present in a journey on a train - loaded with nuclear warheads - right across the USA, and with the future in a vision of a world free of nuclear bombs. This film also touches on questions of glasnost, perestroyka, and democratsia.

An »Alfred-Bauer-Prize« in honor of the first Film Festival director

At a special performance - the screening of Michelangelo Antonioni's La notte (»The Night«)-homage was paid to Alfred Bauer, who had died in October 1986. The Film Festival donated a prize in his honor, bearing his name, to be presented each year to »a full-length feature film, thus opening up new perspectives in the art of film-making«. The first winner was the French director Léos Carax, who was awarded it for his film Mauvais sang [Bad Blood].

After the Festival, it became apparent how deep the rift had become as a result of the delayed contractual negotiations within the Festival commissions and between the co-workers. Moreover, in the board of curators there were again discussions about the influence of the board itself. When the Festival was over de Hadeln also parted company with Aina Bellis, who had so far been head of the Film Fair. For 1988, Beki Probst assumed responsibility for this area. However, Berlin had at that moment other cares and joys. The city was celebrating its 750th Jubilee!

International Jury
Klaus Maria Brandauer (Austria, president)
Juliet Berto (France)
Kathleen Carroll (USA)
Callisto Cosulich (Italy)
Viktor P. Dyomin (USSR)
Reinhard Hauff (FRG)
Edmund Luft (FRG)
Jiří Menzel (Czechoslovakia)
Dana Piţa (Rumania)
Paul Schrader (USA)
Antonio Skármeta (Chile)

THE COLOR OF MONEY by Martin Scorsese (in the Competition): Helen Skaver, Paul Newman

MAUVAIS SANG [Bad Blood] by Léos Carax (in the Competition): Denis Lavant, Julie Delpy

Klimov and Valenti

By Volker Hassemer

The most important part of the Film Festival for me was always meeting the artists, film people from around the world. The pleasure of coming together with everyone was a strong stimulant for my personal interest in the Film Festival.

One of these encounters was exceptional and therefore had a special significance: the one with Elem Klimov and Jack Valenti at the Film Festival of the year 1987.

It demonstrated first of all that the Film Festival had solved two of its most pressing problems. On the one hand, the politically motivated hesitancy of the Soviet Union and,

The Awards of the International Jury

Feature Films
Grand Prix of the 37th IFB
Golden Berlin Bear
Tema
USSR, directed by
Gleb Panfilov

Silver Berlin Bear
for the best director
Oliver Stone
Platoon
USA

Silver Berlin Bear
for the best actress
Ana Beatriz Nogueira
in Vera
Brazil

Silver Berlin Bear
for the best actor
Gian Maria Volonté
in Il caso Moro
Italy

Silver Berlin Bear
Special Prize of the Jury
Umi to dokuyaku
Japan, directed by
Kei Kumai

Silver Berlin Bear
for an exceptional individual achievement
El año de las luces
Spain, directed by
Fernando Trueba

and ex aequo

Naplo szerelmeimnek
Hungary, directed by
Márta Mészáros

Silver Berlin Bear
for a film dealing sensitively and in a popular manner with an uncommon subject
Children of a Lesser God
USA, directed by
Randa Haines

Alfred-Bauer-Prize
Mauvais sang
France, directed by
Léos Carax

on the other, the economically motivated caution of the American majors with regard to Berlin.

While in the person of Jack Valenti the most important representative of the American film industry was once again present, at the same time in the person of Elem Klimov the new Soviet reality presented itself for the first time. Berlin had thus become the place where both great powers - yes, also in the realm of film - demonstrated their willingness to cooperate.

I can remember very well a lunch that I gave for them, Klimov on the one side, Valenti on the other. With Klimov I sensed that the Soviet artists who had been kept so far away by the division of Europe had suddenly moved quite close to us. I felt the neighborliness which had been hidden for so long by the drawing of political barriers. On the other side with Jack Valenti, the American, whose films we knew much better despite the enormous distances, I sensed the interest in sharing with us the possibilities which the new openings promise.

This was a real event which took place on the terrain of the Berlin Film Festival but which reached far beyond it. It bore witness to the strength, the solidity and the significance of the Film Festival in Berlin and also that it is more than merely an opportunity to look at and give awards to films. It is a place to come together, to make plans, to make and renew friendships.

Building stones for the »European House«

By Jiří Menzel

In spite of its greatness, Berlin impressed me as friendly, pleasant and forthright, with a family milieu. I met there with many excellent people, I especially like to remember my participation in the International Festival jury in 1987, where there was especially joyful work for me in a friendly atmosphere. But it may not be so important. What the Berlin Festival especially is to me - is its aim. A long time before the evolvement of the »European House«, it beats down the little paths from East and West and it created the first building stones for the »European House«.

Professional experience

By Peter Watkins

I have attended many festivals in the past 20 years, and I have found some of them good, some of them rather superficial. But most of them lack the spirit - and the actual means - of the direct participation and inter-action with the audience that can occur at the Forum, and the way in which this occured in 1987 with THE JOURNEY *was very valuable for all of us, as well as for the process of the film.*

It has been rather seldom that I have been to a festival where I felt that there was a genuine understanding of what my work individually stood for - all too often ones films are part of a factory line-up of products only seen as faceless screening material. The Forum is completely different in this respect - in fact, I think it is unique in the serious and individual attention it pays to its films - and I am certain that I am only one of many who has already told you this.

The showing of THE JOURNEY *at the Forum in February 1987 was the single most important professional experience that has occurred to the film in its career thus far, and it has been our profound regret that we have not been able to find similar experiences in the years that have followed - another indication of the uniqueness of your Festival.*

Seven hundred and fifty one

1988

Feb. 12th-23rd, 1988 (Competition)
Feb. 13th-23rd, 1988 (Forum)

»Verrücktbleiben« [= stand back + stay crazy] shouts a passer-by on the subway platform of Line 1. Sunnie, a girl from the provinces, looking for the great love of her life - between the subway stations of Schlesisches Tor in Berlin's Kreuzberg district and Zoo Station. Sunnie and the punks from the »scene«, Sunnie and the Wilmersdorf widows. Big city adventures, Berlin community life as a musical. There were also protests against LINIE 1, a film by Reinhard Hauff, the opener to the 1988 »Berlinale«. The wreckage of a burning car is left in front of the Zoo-Palast. The »Bureau for Unusual Measures«, from the politico-cultural scene of Berlin carried out disruptive actions and organized a happening against the »authorities« on the opening night because Hauff's film, it was argued, lived off the »cultural feelings of the scene«, at a time when the Senate was destroying local community culture. »Verrücktbleiben« was the slogan of all those who thought differently at this year's Berlin Film Festival. Following the 750th Jubilee in 1987, Berlin was the »Cultural City of Europe« in 1988«. It was also against this concentrated succession of festivities that youth protest was directed, and not only in the city district of Kreuzberg.

Demonstrations in front of the Zoo-Palast

The spectacle at the Zoo-Palast was not the only demonstration this year. Prior to the screening of Richard Attenborough's CRY FREEDOM, gays and lesbians gathered to protest against the anti-homosexual »clause 28« of the British Thatcher government. The protests found support among directors and actors. Derek Jarman, Julian Cole, Peter Wollen, and James McCay showed their solidarity, and the president of the international jury, Guiglielmo Biraghi, and Tilda Swinton, a member of the jury, supported the demands of the demonstrators against »clause 28«.

Searching for a new jury president

However, the first headline of the »Berlinale« was addressed at the jury. The actor Gert Fröbe, one of West German film's few internationally known personalities, and known to Berliners as the lean Otto Normalverbraucher (Otto Average-Consumer) in Robert A. Stemmle's post-war film BERLINER BALLADE (»The Berliner«) had surprisingly requested that he be released from his acceptance to chair the international jury. For health reasons, Fröbe was unable to participate in the »Berlinale«. Thus it appeared as if the jury would remain without a president. Finding an international star for this post was next to impossible at such short notice. Moritz de Hadeln arrived at a Solomonic solution: he nominated Guiglielmo Biraghi, film critic and director of the film festival in Venice, »Berlinale« jury president. The 1988 jury was also to give people something to talk about with an unusual award.

Gigantomania?

The number of films shown in the various sections of the Festival continued to grow. Critics complained about »gigantomania«. It was more or less impossible to even begin to take in the diversity of the programs of the »Berlinale«. Above all, retrospectives and works reviews made their way into the programs. The Forum put on a series »Film in India« and of films by the Italian comedian Totò and the Panorama presented a retrospective of new Australian cinema, as well as a comprehensive program with feature films and documentaries from the Baltic Soviet Republics, which had been put together in cooperation with the documentary film festival in Nyon. Furthermore, Moritz de Hadeln had to put up with some critical remarks concerning the strong presence of American studios. Wolfram Schütte wrote that he was creating a »Cape Canaveral for the major US companies who were launching their spring rockets here« (Frankfurter Rundschau, Feb. 15, 1988). Yet which Festival director would have rejected films by Woody Allen - SEPTEMBER - and Steven

Heavy American participation

Spielberg – EMPIRE OF THE SUN? Also screened in the Competition or hors concours were: Alex Cox' film WALKER, a controversial film, which drew parallels between the historically authentic career of an adventurer and the present politics of the USA in Nicaragua; James L. Brooks' comedy BROADCAST NEWS; Taylor Hackford's rock'n roll homage CHUCK BERRY: HAIL! HAIL! ROCK'N ROLL; Norman Jewison's delightful love story MOONSTRUCK, starring Cher and Nicholas Cage (which, however, suffered disastrously from the equipment used at the Zoo-Palast, a technical failure which made the Festival the target of much criticism); Godfrey Reggio's POWAQQATSI, and Martin Ritt's courtroom story NUTS, with a tremendous Barbara Streisand. De Hadeln's intensive efforts to increase participation in the »Berlinale« by American production companies had been successful. The fact that the IFB thus offered the American majors the chance to display their products internationally before launching them in the movie theaters was the unavoidable consequence of this policy. This was counteracted by the enormous efforts made by the Panorama and the Forum where independent American film-makers showed more films than ever before. The fact that the Americans vehemently pursued their own interests is demonstrated by a conflict between the IFB and the American Film Market (AFM), whose rescheduling meant that the Berlin Film Festival was moved forward a week. Consequently, some members of the board of curators began to consider, after the Film Festival was over, whether to hold the IFB in the summer period again. To start with, however, Moritz de Hadeln and Beki Probst expanded the Film Fair in order to create a counterbalance to the AFM. They extended the Fair to establish a »European Film Market« and introduced national days on which the individual countries could present their latest productions. This gave the Berlin Film Fair a new profile.

The role the International Film Festival Berlin had now come to play as a result of the new politics of the Soviet Union also become apparent in 1988. It was, above all,

International jury, almost in full: Anna-Lena Wibom, Ellen Burstyn, Guiglielmo Biraghi, Tilda Swinton (sitting), Heinz Rathsack, Daniel Schmid, Heiner Carow, Eberhard Junkersdorf, Tom Luddy, Pavlos Zannas (standing)

Aleksandr Sokurov, Ruth Malez (interpreter), Andrei Plakhov, Ulrich Gregor

Laura Betti, on the occasion of a Totò-symposium, guest in the Akademie der Künste

Alec Guinness, being asked about LITTLE DORRIT by Christine Edzard

Aleksandr Askoldov's film KOMISSAR [The Commissar] which raised furore in Berlin and was awarded many prizes, including the Special Prize of the Jury, a Silver Bear. Askoldov's film deals with a woman commissar, a convinced communist, in the Russia of the twenties, at the time of the civil war between the »Reds« and the »Whites«. A deserter is shot at her command. She gives birth to a child, when lodging with a Jewish craftsman's family, in the midst of the confusion of war. Out of the shared fear of pogroms and terror grows friendship and solidarity between the commissar and the Jewish family. Askoldov's film was made in 1967, and was his debut as director. However, the film was banned for »slandering the revolution« and for being »Zionist propaganda«. Askoldov was unable to make any more films. The censor's decision meant that he was put on the black-list of directors. It was not until July 15th 1987, that KOMISSAR had its première at the 15th Moscow Film Festival. The fact that the Soviet authorities then released this film for the Berlin Film Festival was a further sign of »glasnost« and »perestroyka« in the field of cultural policy. It also showed how good relations had meanwhile become between the IFB and the filmmakers in the USSR. In the »Frankfurter Rundschau« Wolfram Schütte wrote the following about Askoldov's film, »The KOMISSAR is unique in the history of Soviet cinema. Its subject and aesthetics recall Isaac Babel's stories about ›Budyonny's Red Cavalry‹ in their creative and physical intensity and the way in which Askoldov is able to give a loving and humorous description of Jewish life in the shadows of everpresent dangers. Insofar the film is also the historical reconstruction of a mode of life which has been destroyed, thus rendering it a work mourning a remembered past, as well as the utopia, recalling that past which recollects the human promise contained in the early days of Bolshevism« (Feb. 17, 1988).

Aleksandr Askoldov's film KOMISSAR and the political repercussions in the Berlin House of Representatives

It was annoying that not all political parties in Berlin were able to acknowledge the link-function which the Film Festival had between East and West and respect Askoldov's exceptional film. The screening of KOMISSAR during the IFB had political

Jane Birkin, Agnès Varda

Chuck Berry

repercussions. On February 25th 1988, the CDU member of the Senate Dr. Roman Legien raised a question (No. 4412) directed at the Senator for Culture asking whether Askoldov's film had also been shown outside the Film Festival in Moscow in the Soviet Union, or whether performances were planned. Behind this question was the fact that Askoldov's film had not gone round Moscow's movie houses first, so that the »Berlinale« was accused of pursuing an opportunistic policy diverting attention away from the real situation in the Soviet Union, by showing so-called »films from the safe«. Attentive observers of the Soviet Union could not have failed to notice that it was precisely film which was playing such a pioneering role in cultural policy. Volker Hassemer's reply was correspondingly sober (March 14, 1988); on June 6, after he supplemented his first reply, having made enquiries at the Embassy of the Federal Republic of Germany in Moscow, that the distribution of the film in the Soviet Union was »not to be expected before September of that year, as the required number of copies had not yet been made. Those interested could, for the time being, only see the film in Moscow in private sessions after having previously made an appointment with Mr. Askoldov.«

»Films from the safe« from Poland and the GDR

Alongside Askoldov's film, Andrei Mikhalkov Konchalovsky's Asino stshastye [Asja's Happiness] – also made in 1967 – was entered in the Competition. (Konchalovsky had been working exclusively in the USA since the early eighties.) From Poland came Matka Królów [Mother Król and Her Sons], by Janusz Zaorski, about two dramatic decades of Polish history, war and Nazi occupation, and the Stalinist period of the fifties. The extent to which a coming-to-terms with their own history was being carried out in the Socialist countries could also be seen in the documentary film Bolshe sveta! [More Light!] by the Russian director Marina Babak, a reappraisal of Russian history from the October Revolution to the present. The fact that Heiner Carow's film Die Russen kommen [The Russians are Coming], made in 1968, could be shown at the IFB, and that Lothar Warneke's Einer trage des anderen

The Last of England by Derek Jarman (in the Forum)

Last... [Bare Ye One Another's Burdens...], which represented the GDR in the Competition and dealt with the early years of the German Democratic Republic could be presented in the Competition, suggested a change in political emphasis.

A surprising decision: the Golden Berlin Bear goes to a film from the People's Republic of China.

The jury of the Film Festival came up with a decision which surprised everybody. For the first time at an international film festival a film from the People's Republic of China was awarded a prize. The Grand Prix of the IFB went to Hong gaoliang [Red Sorghum] by Zhang Yimou. A blood-red ballad from the China of the thirties: a woman is sold to a liquor dealer as his bride, she is kidnapped and raped and then becomes head of the distillers after the death of her bridegroom. Only her son manages to escape the terror of local gangs and the war atrocities perpetrated by the Japanese occupying army. With this prize the jury not only wanted to present an award to a film which was a superb work of cinematography as well as being shocking in contents, but also to support the cultural liberalization of China. This was a courageous and politically calculated decision for February 1988. Just how little room there really was to maneuver both politically and culturally in the People's Republic of China was revealed most clearly by blood-red pictures at Tiananmen Square just over a year later.

Asian films in the Forum

There was an »Asian Context« at the Film Festival; at the Forum, films from Korea, China, Hong Kong, Japan, the Philippines, and Vietnam were screened. »International Forum of Reborn Cinema« was the solution to the riddle for the Chinese characters in a photo from Ann Hui's Shu jian en chou lu [The Romance of Book and Sword] on the Forum poster. This was a co-production from Hong Kong and the People's Republic of China; a historical epic from the 18th century; the »definitive Kung Fu film« in Wilhelm Roth's words. He added, »After only five minutes, there is the first spectacular fighting scene which comes up again and again until the end of the three hours' long epic; swords flash, karate fighters do flying somersaults through the air, huge armies of horsemen approach, there are battles,

Family Viewing: David Hemblen, Gabrielle Rose

massacres, all brilliantly choreographed, performed, photographed, and cut.« (Frankfurter Rundschau, Feb. 25, 1988.) Another highlight of Asian cinema at the Forum was PABO SUNON [The Fool's Manifesto] by Lee Chang-Ho from Korea. A child's voice tells the story of Dong-chil, a man with a limp, and the girl Hae-yong. This is a love story and at the same time it isn't a love story, yet it is also a dream, with the craziness of slapstick, a piece of cinematographic fury, and the manifesto of an unknown direction in film. It had been a long time since the Forum had shown an opening film which was so rigorous and so radical.

Those responsible for the International Forum expressed criticism over the ever greater presence of the Panorama, which sometimes seemed to be a rival feature. Initially the Panorama was conceived of as a supplement to the Competition, to the so-called main program. Whereas in the early years (as Info-Show) it had been a kind of catch basin for films rejected to the Competition or for those which simply did not fit into the program structure, the organizers of the Panorama, especially Manfred Salzgeber, had worked out a conception which could be seen both as a supplement to the Competition and to the Forum. The selection criteria no longer differed as greatly from those of the Forum as had once been the case. In 1988, the Panorama screened a number of films from the new Greek cinema, alongside the Baltic films which the Forum had also endeavored to obtain. But there were also individual films which people had previously tended to expect in the Forum program, and were now screened in the Panorama program, such as Jean-Luc Godard's SOIGNE TA DROITE [Watch Your Right]. »A confusing title, because Godard has long since learned how to safeguard his rights. He takes the duties of cinema more seriously. And the most important duty is not to stand still, not to give up, not to stagnate. His vitality undiminished, Godard continues to fight for a cinema of the future.« (Claudius Seidl, Süddeutsche Zeitung, Feb. 25, 1988.) Thus arose a productive, and in some cases disruptive, rivalry, at least from the point of view of the Forum. This opinion was

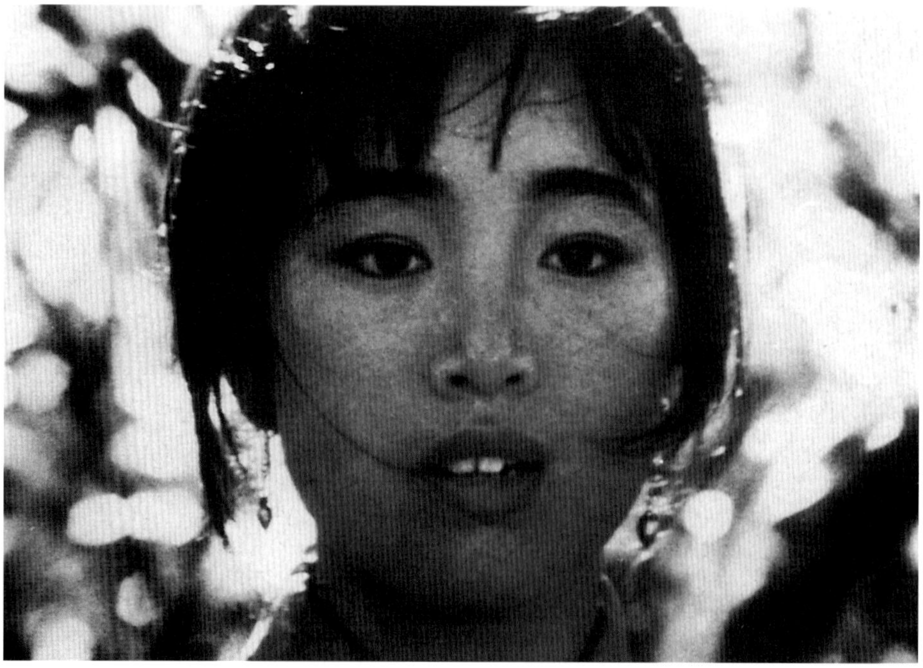

HONG GAOLIANG: Gong Li

also shared by the members of the board of curators, who debated this issue after the Festival was over and called on the Panorama to develop a »more modest« program in the future.

»Color – Die Farben des Films«, a history of color film, was the subject of the Retrospective. Having already taken on three-dimensional film and special effects, the Stiftung Deutsche Kinemathek was dealing with technical problems for the third time. One of the finest copies was an old John Ford film, SHE WORE A YELLOW RIBBON, starring John Wayne, and, above all, Maureen O'Hara. Frieda Grafe, who made up her own program, wrote the following about her own favorite color films, »I can see something you can't feel«. And it is via color that we recall two films in the Competition, Agnès Varda's KUNG FU MASTER and the documentary film JANE B. PAR AGNÈS V. is a poetic and hallucinatory declaration of love to the actress Jane Birkin. It is angular and beautiful.

My second city of birth

By Aleksandr Askoldov

The West-Berlin Festival of 1988 is probably the most important date of my life. Berlin became, so to speak, my second city of birth. The impressions which I gathered there will never be forgotten. They were also not overshadowed by the fact that thereafter I was able to travel over three-quarters of the globe. I remember the streets of this city, the movie theater in which KOMISSAR *(»The Commissar«) was shown – and above all the audience. I had indeed hoped that people here would understand and accept my film, but I was still very excited since I did not know this audience. I first re-entered the hall near the end of the film and experienced then the pause of silence before the applause. I sensed then that the film had been accepted. By various types of people, because not only intellectuals were*

KOMISSAR:
Nonna Mordyukova

International Jury
Guiglielmo Biraghi
(Italy, president)
Ellen Burstyn
(USA, vice-president)
Heiner Carow (GDR)
Eberhard Junkersdorf (FRG)
Tom Luddy (USA)
Heinz Rathsack (FRG)
Daniel Schmid (Switzerland)
Andrei S. Smirnov (USSR)
Tilda Swinton
(Great Britain)
Anna-Lena Wibom (Sweden)
Pavlos Zannas (Greece)

Reefer and the Model
by Joe Comerford (in the Panorama): Carol Scanlan

seated there, but also the so-called »normal« movie-goers. And that the film was able to bring together these various persons, this is an experience which I will never forget.

Family Viewing at the Delphi
By Atom Egoyan

The screening of Family Viewing at the Forum in 1988 was a revelatory event in my career.

Having made a film which tried to find a new language for telling a very private story, I expected to be appreciated by a few people, tolerated by some others, and ignored by the vast majority.

At 7 p.m. on Thursday, February 18, 1988, something very important happened to me. I was in a huge theatre full of people all appreciating my efforts. I was completely overwhelmed by that evening at the Delphi, and I am grateful to the Forum for having nurtured such a demanding, curious and progressive audience.

The Awards of the International Jury

Feature Films
Grand Prix of the 38th IFB
Golden Berlin Bear
Hong Gaoliang
People's Republic of China, directed by Zhang Yimou

Silver Berlin Bear
Special Prize of the Jury
Komissar
USSR, directed by Aleksandr Askoldov

Silver Berlin Bear
for its outstanding artistic quality
La deuda interna
Argentina, directed by Miguel Pereira

Silver Berlin Bear
for the best director
Norman Jewison
Moonstruck
USA

Silver Berlin Bear
for the best actress
Holly Hunter
in Broadcast News
USA

Silver Berlin Bear
for the best actor
ex aequo
Jörg Pose
Manfred Möck
in Einer trage des anderen Last
GDR

Silver Berlin Bear for an outstanding individual performance
Janusz Zaorski
Matka Królów
Poland

ARIEL by Aki Kaurismäki
(in the Forum): Turo Pajala

Dustin, Isabelle, and little Vera

1989

Feb. 10th - 21st, 1989 (Competition)
Feb. 11th - 21st, 1989 (Forum)

The surprise came at the end. Nobody had been expecting it. The prize was awarded on the stage of the Zoo-Palast. The Silver Bear for the best actress went to Isabelle Adjani. And then she stood there, on stage, amidst the dazzle of the photographers' flashes, protected by a pair of sun-glasses. She said thank you in German, explaining that she hadn't really wanted to come, but that she was now glad to be in Berlin. This was a prize for an actress who had taken her chance with a major European film project, and a part that was tailor-made for her: CAMILLE CLAUDEL. And when the awards had all been given, it was Barry Levinson's RAIN MAN which took the Grand Prix of the Festival. Dustin Hoffman stood next to Isabelle Adjani. The »Berlinale« had a special award for him: a Golden Bear of Honor for all his acting performances to date. So far only James Stewart and Alec Guinness had received this award before. At the Zoo-Palast there was a standing ovation for Dustin Hoffman and a kiss from Isabelle Adjani. Some time had passed since the »Berlinale« had witnessed such excitement and so much jubilation over an actor.

Two international stars in Berlin

There were also touches of bitterness. For some visitors felt that Jodie Foster, by playing a part in Jonathan Kaplan's THE ACCUSED, had done more to deserve the prize for best actress than Isabelle Adjani. And although the Golden Bear for an American major production seemed long overdue this year, many regretted the fact that Oliver Stone's TALK RADIO, a politically explosive film dealing with the murder of a Jewish radio moderator, had not received an award. The Silver Bear for Eric Bogosian, who had both written the script and played the leading role, was considered by many to be a sort of »consolation prize«. What did seem fully incomprehensible, however, was the fact that the jury only came up with a Special Mention for Jacques Rivette's LA BANDE DES QUATRE (»The Band of Four«), »for the charm, the witty use of language and the imaginative script«. For Rivette's film about theater and the art of acting, which was a trial run of Marivaux' »La double inconstance« – an attempt to stage it as one of the constants in staging, starring Bulle Ogier as the acting instructor Constance Dumas – was considered by almost all critics as the favorite for the Golden Bear. »LA BANDE DES QUATRE is the critique of many other films shown in Berlin. Rivette opposes the heavy march of cultural content with the art of improvisation, and the well-intended preoccupation of the camera with the perfection of artistic expression. (...) For Rivette it is not the form which imparts the meaning of life, but life which imparts the meaning of form. (...) The ›Band of Four‹ knocks a window in the screen, a window through which one can breathe at last.« (Andreas Kilb, Die Zeit, Feb. 24, 1989.)

Objections to the distribution of the prizes

The neglected film of the Festival: LA BANDE DES QUATRE by Jacques Rivette

At the beginning of the year a political change had taken place in Berlin. The elections to the House of Representatives had brought about a Red-Green majority; the Social Democrats now nominated the Mayor. A shock, which could have repercussions in the Federal Republic, was the election of a party of the far right into the House of Representatives. This resulted in a spontaneous demonstration against the discriminatory attitude towards foreigners held by that particular party.

Past and contemporary history were a main topic of the Forum, containing documentary films on questions of German history and the Nazi past. The focal point of this complex of issues was Marcel Ophul's documentary film HOTEL TERMINUS dealing with Klaus Barbie, who had been head of the Gestapo in occupied Lyon from 1942 to 1944. The interrogation rooms of the Gestapo were located in

Documentary films concerning questions of German history and the Nazi past

Marcel Ophuls

Jodie Foster

Aki Kaurismäki

Dušan Hanák

Hotel Terminus; it was here that Barbie, the »Lyon Executioner« sent people to their deaths. Barbie himself was able to hide for decades and thus avoid being tried for the mass murder for which he was responsible. »The cautiously assembled wealth of statements and descriptions, extenuations and accusations, which have long since ceased to concern one man alone, but deal with a historical rupture, after which history can never be written the same way again; together, these things constitute a film of quite epic proportions. The documentary-maker has approached his subject with sarcasm and the cold fury of the researcher; sifting through facts, asking people questions, finding witnesses and chance acquaintances, revealing details and entire structures of actions and consciousness.« (Gertrud Koch, Frankfurter Rundschau, Feb. 21, 1989.) LODZ GHETTO, by the American documentary directors Alan Adelson and Kathryn Taverna, documents the history of the very last ghetto established by the Nazis in occupied Poland; and VOICES FROM THE ATTIC by Debbie Goldstein and JACOBA by Joram ten Brink follow the tracks of Nazi terror, reconstructing Jewish family history in the process. VIENNA IS DIFFERENT: 50 YEARS AFTER THE ANSCHLUSS, a documentary film by Susan Korda and David Leitner dealt with Austrian identity. 1988 was the year of the discussion about Austrian President Kurt Waldheim's share of responsibilitiy in the Third Reich. The West German documentary GESUCHT: MONIKA ERTL [Wanted: Monika Ertl] presented a portrait of a woman involved socially and politically, a fellow comrade of Che Guevara, who was shot in 1973 in an attempt to kidnap her »uncle« Klaus Barbie. History and contemporary history – the circle closes. The actuality of the topics, and the necessity of not forgetting what happened, was revealed in the election results in Berlin in 1989.

The fact that the »Berlinale« was now the most important film festival for films coming from Eastern Europe became quite apparent this year. In the Forum program, films were screened by the Tarkovsky student Aleksandr Sokurov. In the Competi-

Press conference for Johanna d'Arc of Mongolia by Ulrike Ottinger with Delphine Seyrig and Xu Re Huar

Gila Almagor, Wolfgang Kohlhaase

Receiving the »Berlinale Camera« from Moritz de Hadeln (on the left):Mikhail Shkalikov, Marc M. Spiegel, Horst Pehnert

Rolf Liebermann, Gila Almagor, Leslie Caron, Dustin Hoffman, Isabelle Adjani

tion one of the first films of the Gorbachev period was shown, Vadim Abdrashitov's Sluga [The Servant], the puzzling and allegorical relationship between »master« and »slave«, and the documentary by Marina Goldovskaya about the hitherto taboo topic of the »gulags«, the camps for political prisoners, Solovetskaya vlast [The Power of Solovki]. Two films by the Czechoslovakian director Dušan Hanák were screened in the Competition and in the Panorama: Ja milujem, ty milujes [I Love, You Love] made in 1980, and Obrazy stareho sveta [Pictures of the Old World] which had been banned up to this time and covered the forgotten traditions of peasants and shepherds. Bulgaria presented three films in the Forum, the most unconventional and most loaded with political allusions being Binka Zhelyazkova's Privarzaniyat balon [The Captive Balloon] made in 1967, which, on the face of it, was a burlesque story about a dispute between two village communities. Ivan Nitchev's film Ivan i Aleksandra [Ivan and Alexandra] attempted to come to terms with episodes from the Stalin era. Probably the most exciting film of this Festival was shown at the Forum, Malenkaya Vera [Little Vera], by Vassili Pichul. This was a love story in a dreary provincial town with a stifling, philistine atmosphere. The only reason for Vera's birth is to enable the family to get a bigger apartment from the state. Heavy drinking, the tensions of daily life and a romance are all presented in an unpretentious manner, a love story of the Soviet »lost generation«. »Pichul tells his love story – which is perverted by Soviet daily life – about a relationship between the pretty Vera and her lady-killing Romeo with a sarcastic sense of humor. The so-called ›lost generation‹ of youth in the Soviet Union on the one hand, the disaster of the average family on the other, one is gripped by sympathy for Gorbachev, for wanting to achieve anything at all with such a basis. ›Good health and not down the hatch, that's not right‹, says the father, a bestial vandal alongside a wife who is always nagging. ›Has the vocational school written yet?‹ is the running joke in this

Czechoslovakian and Bulgarian films which had been withheld up to now

»Little Vera«

Krotki film o milosci: Olaf Lubaszenko

film. It is a metaphor for the relationship to the state, which is still permeated by an attitude of desperation and sarcasm.« (Michael Kötz, Frankfurter Rundschau, Feb. 22, 1989.)

By 1989, Moritz de Hadeln had been directing the International Film Festival Berlin for ten years. For ten years there had been a coordination agreement with the Forum. Now there was a small internal jubilee to celebrate. Three »Berlinale Cameras« were awarded to men, who had made »Berlinale« history. For Moritz de Hadeln, these were »three people who had made a contribution in everything they had done, in order to reestablish a climate of trust and thus make it possible for an ever greater number of films from East and West to participate in the Film Festival«. He referred specifically to the affair surrounding The Deer Hunter in 1979, which had disrupted the cooperation of the Festival with the socialist countries and the USA. The award was given to Horst Pehnert, chairman of the central administration for film in the GDR and Deputy Minister for Culture, Mikhail Shkalikov, deputy chairman of the state committee for cinematography of the USSR for foreign affairs, and Marc M. Spiegel, Senior Vice President of the Motion Pictures Association of America. The awards for Pehnert and Shkalikov were not undisputed in some quarters. Some felt that these awards were out of place in the age of »glasnost« and »perestroyka«.

»Berlinale Cameras« to politicians responsible for films

After the »Berlinale« had drawn to a close there were but minor uncertainties. These primarily concerned the finances, for the Film Festival budget had not been altered, and cuts were necessary. In 1989, there was a danger that the Retrospectives – European films from the year 1939, and films by the producer Eric Pommer – would be struck off the list. It was very late in the day, and preparations for the Retrospectives were being undertaken without any certainty that they would actually take place, when the decision was made to keep them in. Both Festival directors had to

La Bande des quatre: Bulle Ogier

fight for their budget requirements. However, the contracts of both Moritz de Hadeln and Ulrich Gregor were renewed once again for a period of three years.

A personal recollection of Chantal Akermann's summer-night film Histoires d'Amérique in which Jewish emigrants, somewhere in Manhattan, are telling jokes. »How's it going Finkelstein? – My shoes are pinching me. – Why don't you take them off? – I have no money, both my daughters are ugly, they'll never find a husband; my son is dumb and my wife never stops nagging. When I think of them the thing I'd like to do most is kill them. But then comes that moment when I sit down and ease off my shoes. That's the moment that makes life worth while.«
Looking forward to the 1990 jubilee …

How I felt at the Forum

By Aki Kaurismäki

I don't especially like the Berlin Film Festival, but the Forum is something else; the audience understood the jokes and »the deeper meanings« (if there were any, which I doubt) of my films. They have to be some kind of masochists to see the films anyway. The beer in Berlin is not especially good and it takes a lifetime to get one. Luckily they have other drinks in the city too. Summary: the Film Forum Berlin is one of my mental homes.

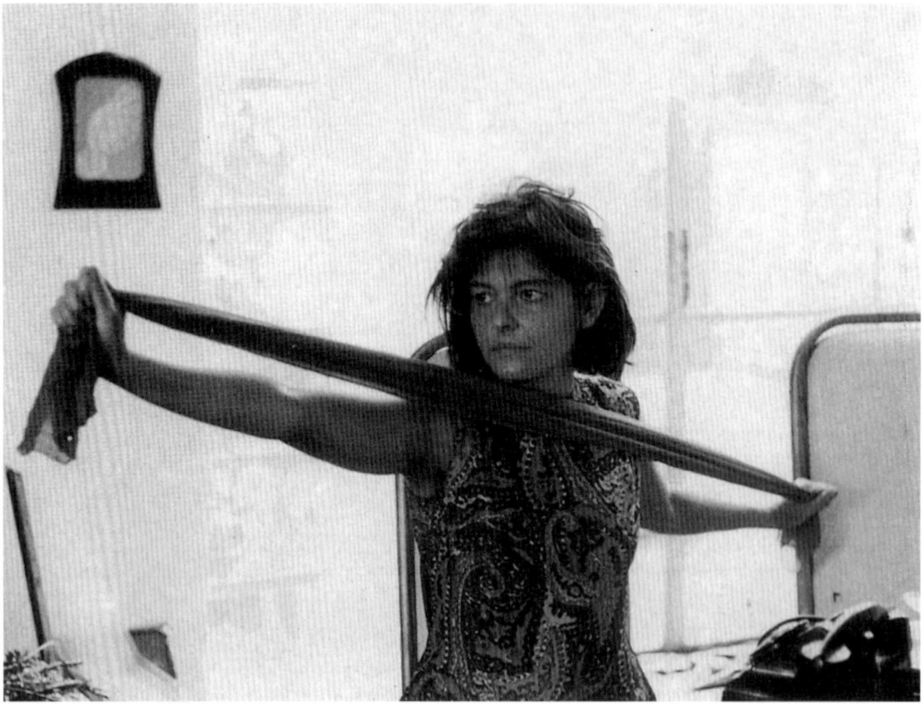

Romance by Sergio Bianchi (in the Panorama): Imara Reis

Lodz Ghetto

By Kathryn Taverna and Alain Adelson

We came to Berlin with a highly sensitive Holocaust-related film, Lodz Ghetto. The film is based entirely on diaries and documents which were left behind when this second largest Jewish community in the world was progressively destroyed. The film depicts life within the ghetto, and involves a considerable degree of Jewish self-criticism. It is made in a unique way, utterly authentic in its use of the diary and photographic materials, but artistic and dramatic in its presentation. It is an understatement to say we were apprehensive. We had never stepped foot in Germany. The sight of smokestacks, the similarity of the industrial signs, Hiller, with »Hitler«, railroads, all gave us grim memories in our first hours.

But we found with the Forum audience the most responsive and assertive people, willing to debate issues and to delve deeply, thrashing out conflicts sometimes late into the night. Our screening at the Arsenal left us with some 25 young Germans who earnestly wanted (till 2 a.m.!) to examine the causes of the Nazi Holocaust. And after the screening at the Akademie der Künste, several hundred people gathered around us pursuing more background on the film, treating a survivor of the ghetto who stood up as if he were a precious relic.

This was an incredible experience for all of us. Something revelatory was happening among us, we were learning together, with the film as a context for discussion, but so much energy and intellect was functioning, reaching for understanding and coming forward as earnest and intelligent expression. We remained in a state of excitement for days afterwards and remember the experience as one of the most enriching and inspiring contacts we have had as filmmakers with an audience. A few weeks later we received a letter from one woman who had actively participated in the Akademie der Künste discussion.

Malenkaya Vera: Natalia Negoda

On page 360
Rain Man: Dustin Hoffman, Tom Cruise

To show this bridge between filmmakers and audience, we would like to take the liberty to quote from the message from Melissa Vogelsang:

»Thank you both once again for Lodz Ghetto *and particularly for the evening of discussion it sparked at the Akademie der Künste ... That was one of the most honest and emotionally/factually productive exchanges I've witnessed on the Holocaust (for lack of a more satisfying term) in either country. In part that may reflect that the time is ripe, but to a large measure the discussion grew obviously out of the framework established by your film. With respect and compassion, you made it possible for people, who had been silenced, to speak. My respect to both of you!«*

Mr. Gregor, I would extend that recognition to you, as the prime mover in that event. Ms. Vogelsang's reference to the framework for discussion is justly an acknowledgement of the Forum's fortuitous and salutary contribution to Berlin's intellectual, social and cultural life. We hold your work in the greatest respect and appreciation.

International Jury
Rolf Liebermann (Switzerland, president)
Leslie Caron (France, vice-president)
Chen Kaige (People's Republic of China)
Vadim Glowna (FRG)
Randa Haines (USA)
Vladimir Ignatovski (Bulgaria)
Adrian Kutter (FRG)
Francisco Rabal (Spain)
Cliff Robertson (USA)
Zdenek Sverak (Czechoslovakia)
Boris Vassilyev (USSR)

The Awards of the International Jury

Feature Films
Grand Prix of the 39th IFB
Golden Berlin Bear
RAIN MAN
USA, directed by
Barry Levinson

Silver Berlin Bear
Special Prize of the Jury
WAN ZHONG
People's Republic of China,
directed by Wù Ziniu

Silver Berlin Bear
for the best director
Dŭsan Hanák
JA MILUJEM, TY MILUJES
Czechoslovakia

Silver Berlin Bear
for the best actress
Isabelle Adjani
in CAMILLE CLAUDEL
France

Silver Berlin Bear
for the best actor
Gene Hackman
in MISSISSIPPI BURNING
USA

Silver Berlin Bear
for an outstanding
individual performance
Eric Bogosian
TALK RADIO
USA

Silver Berlin Bear
for a moving film with
outstanding acting
performances by Kaipo
Cohen and Gila Almagor,
whose stories are told
HAKAYITZ SHEL AVIYA
Israel, directed by Eli Cohen

Special Mention
for Jacques Rivette for a
script full of charm, witty
language, and imagination
LA BANDE DES QUATRE
France/Switzerland

Alfred Bauer Prize
SLUGA
USSR, directed by
Vadim Abdrashitov

Don't change the Festival!

By Krzysztof Kieślowski

The International Forum of Young Cinema has always been a very important festival for me. I didn't realize the extent at first since I was too young and inexperienced. Later, however, I realized that this was the place where I encountered a real audience - those who go to movies because they love them and who can articulate their responses and feelings. So many people came to see KROTKI FILM O MILOSCI *[A Short Film About Love] during my last visit, and I found that I could have a real understanding with them; and since I make films in order to be understood, I was deeply gratified. Another important thing is that I get to meet really young viewers, and from their reactions I can feel what my next steps should be. So don't change the Festival!*

Look back without anger

Flashback
1975–1989

Its founding fathers intended the Berlin International Film Festival to be »a showcase of the free world«. Yet politically, the Berlinale was also an instrument of the Cold War, even though the Berlinale management had made repeated attempts to open the Festival to Eastern Europe. Nevertheless, due to the general political situation, these hopes could not be realized for years. It was not until after the »Basic Treaties« which the Federal Republic of Germany negotiated with its Eastern neighbors, that the participation of films from nations behind the »Iron Curtain« became possible. The isolating barrier to the East was now less stable and more pervious: in 1974, a film from the Soviet Union participated in the Festival for the very first time; the German Democratic Republic followed a year later.

When Mayor Walter Momper, former Senator for Cultural Affairs Volker Hassemer and GDR Deputy Minister for Culture Horst Pehnert – three Berlin politicians of differing complexions and political convictions – met at the Berlinale's closing night reception in 1989, none of them foresaw the political changes which would occur in the coming year. They also had no idea of the immediate impact these would have on the Film Festival: both the Berlinale's structures and its profile would change. The era of the Cold War was over for good. A new phase of Berlinale history was beginning. Let us now take a look at the past.

With respect to film, politico-cultural relations with East Germany had recurrently been the focus of debates concerning the Festival's politico-cultural orientation in film matters. Today, access to the files allows us to make the first cautious additions to what was known about the film-political context of internal GDR policies and the relationship of GDR cultural policies to the Berlinale. These additions explain the pressures and restrictions existing at the time. Beyond the official political course, functioning, semi-official and personal contacts between those involved over the years had also existed. The days of absolute silence were few, instead there was a quiet dialogue at irregular intervals.

Politburo minutes

No entries are to be found about the Berlinale in the minutes of the SED Central Committee Politburo from the fifties. However, the newly established »World Youth Festival« in summer 1951 was a topic, and the West saw it as a counter-event to the Berlinale. Obviously, in the first years after the founding of the GDR, other questions and problems had priority for the Politburo. Just the same, it is interesting to observe how themes, which were initially very pragmatic – providing the population with basic supplies, for instance – became ever more ideological and abstract. Beginning in 1974, the minutes also include notes on the state of negotiations concerning cultural matters with West Germany. Minutes No. 49 from the SED Central Committee (ZK) office on April 28th, 1975, contains the first entries on film policies: about the participation of GDR films at the Oberhausen International Short Film Festival, and at the festival in Cannes. (Bundesarchiv, Department GDR, file number (AZ SED J IV 2/3–2304) A month later, GDR leaders dealt with GDR participation at the »25th IFB Berlin (West)«. In enclosure 5 of minutes No. 57 from May 20th, 1975, item 2 succinctly states: »The film JAKOB DER LÜGNER (›Jacob the Liar‹) will be suggested to the Festival organizers for entry.« Item 3 went on to add who would be able to attend the Berlinale screening: Gunter Schröder, artistic director for feature films at VEB Defa studios, director Frank Beyer and the actors Erwin Geschonneck and Blanche Kommerell. The minutes were signed personally by

GDR's first participation at the Berlinale

Erich Honecker as Secretary-General of the ZK. (AZ SED J IV 2/3–2312) No further notes are to be found in the file on this so significant event for the Berlinale; there were also no reports on the participants' visits or other remarks about the course of events at the GDR's first Berlinale.

Bulletin on the Berlinale '82

Yet the attention which the Film Festival attracted, the kind of marginal observations recorded, and above all the notice given to films from other socialist nations and their reception at the Berlinale are all illustrated by an »information« about the Film Festival in 1982. Presumably, it was addressed to the ZK Politburo of the SED. The name of the author was not given. It begins by stating: »The organizers did due honor to the GDR as a nation and its film authorities (flag, press material). Conduct toward the participating delegation was objective and correct. There was no provocation of any kind.« These are stereotype, empty formulations and observations, and similar ones are to be found in other reports. In the run-up to the Festival in 1982, there was a debate about the American film NIGHT CROSSING: de Hadeln rejected it primarily so as not to jeopardize the Soviet Union's and the GDR's participation. This caused quite a stir in Berlin's conservative press, and a number of conservative politicians felt obliged to express their opinions. According to the author of the »information«, the rejection of the film had been discussed by Helmut Diller, director of Defa-Export and head of the GDR delegation, and de Hadeln. The author went on to describe de Hadeln's position, who had again emphasized that »he stood by his decision not to show the film NIGHT CROSSING in the Competition«. The author went on to say that for de Hadeln, »political reasons [had] priority«. Yet of even greater interest was how the films from other socialist nations were evaluated. In the subtext, it became evident how great the pressure was for GDR film politicians to justify their decisions, what considerations they had to keep in mind and in what overall politico-cultural context they were forced to take a stance. »Before screenings of films from the USSR and the People's Republic of Poland, groups of demonstrators ›protested‹ outside the cinema with banners, posters and leaflets against imprisonment in Soviet camps (...), for the termination of martial law in Poland and for freedom of activity for Solidarity.« Opinions fluctuated between a feeling of solidarity and the desire for disassociation from these »brother states«. The tendency toward disassociation was directed primarily against the attempts toward reform in Poland and Hungary. An entry on Zoltán Fábri's film REQUIEM stated that it was an attempt »to present a reappraisal of history in the fifties based on the case of a ›victim of the Hungarian Stalin era‹«. What is most revealing about these two remarks are the inverted commas, which serve to relativize the formulations, giving them a note of irony, and questioning political convictions. Critical reservations are conspicuous in the author's reports on events related to the Polish film DRESZCZE (»Shivers«) by Wojciech Marczewski, a film which also dealt with the Stalin era. »Contrary to custom, the Polish director of the film addressed the audience before the screening, conveying his delight in being able to present the film ›Shivers‹ personally. He wished the audience a good time but did not hide the fact that it had not been made merely to do that.« After this speech, members of the audience declared their support for Solidarity, a banner was unrolled, and when the Festival staff intervened, some of the Zoo Palast audience booed. Both of these films received awards: the Polish film was honored with the Special Prize of the Jury, the Hungarian entry with a Silver Bear for best script. The résumé given by the author in his report left little unsaid with regard to political clarity. »Even if assessments of the Polish and

GDR's stance to the film NIGHT CROSSING

Considerations of GDR politicians

Skepticism toward the signs of reform

Hungarian films varied« – and it was presumably the Polish film which was received more negatively – »the value of political representation of films from these countries is to be seen as detrimental«. (AZ DY 30 J IV 2/9.06–24)

Frank Beyer's film DER AUFENTHALT

A year later, in 1983, the GDR, at short notice, withdrew its entry after it had already been submitted: DER AUFENTHALT (»The Turning Point«) by Frank Beyer. No official reason was given for this move, but it was suspected that the East Germans were complying with a request from Poland. The film was based on episodes from Hermann Kant's novel of the same name, and had been adapted into a script by Wolfgang Kohlhaase. It dealt with the issue of guilt and all those who went along with fascism. In the film, a young German war prisoner is unjustly accused of being a member of the SS and of murdering a child. Confronted with the disapproval of the Polish investigating authorities, on the one hand, and the views of his fellow German prisoners – who have committed war crimes – on the other, he comes to realize that he cannot absolve himself of responsibility for the crimes of Germans.

Polish objections

The extent of the pressure on GDR film officials to cancel the film's participation at the Berlinale – due to foreign policy, and further kindled by controversial political standpoints in Poland – can be reconstructed in detail with the aid of the documents to be found in the files of the Office of ZK Secretary Kurt Hager in the Bundesarchiv under the signature SED 35491. The Polish actors were not even allowed to attend the film's opening on January 20th, 1983 in Berlin (GDR). All efforts to prevent a scandal by the film associations of both countries were in vain. Due to the political circumstances in Poland, the powerful reform movement and people's solidarity with it, relations with the GDR had been strained since 1981, and this included the politico-cultural sphere. Not to mention the Poles' great sensitivity to the anti-Polish sentiments of Germans.

Pehnert and de Hadeln

On January 11th, 1983, in other words before the film's premiere, Horst Pehnert and Moritz de Hadeln held a talk at which Pehnert firmly promised that Beyer's film could participate in the Berlinale Competition. Filmmaker Kurt Maetzig was to represent the GDR as a member of the International Jury. Three days later, de Hadeln confirmed the arrangements; the date for the screening was scheduled for February 23rd, invitations were sent out to the director and the scriptwriter. Yet there were already indications that the film's participation would encounter political opposition. Pehnert internally warned that a withdrawal of the film would be of »grave political consequences« and also result in a loss of credibility, for after all, the invitation had been accepted by a deputy minister. There were also those who feared that the »Western media« might play up a cancellation, causing a scandal that could be »misused for a campaign against the GDR«. After all, what reasons might be given for withdrawal? »If foreign policy were to be cited as the reason for the film's withdrawal, then all other GDR activities abroad would have to be canceled as well.« Pehnert also feared inner-cultural problems, for »tensions would be expected to increase again between Frank Beyer and the authorities«. This assessment of the situation was based on the fact that Beyer's film SPUR DER STEINE (»Traces of Stone«) had been forbidden during the campaign against critical authors and film people at the notorious 11th ZK plenary session of the SED in December 1965. Beyer was subsequently forced to take up a position as a theater director at a provincial East German theater, and it was not until ten years later, with JAKOB DER LÜGNER, that he was able to make a film for the Defa. On January 17th, Stanislaw Stefanski, Undersecretary of the Polish Ministry of Culture and Art, sent a telex in which he

Der Aufenthalt: Sylvester Groth (right)

asked that the line »supported by Žespoly Filmowe« be removed from the opening credits, and went on to say that Polish actors would not attend the premiere. The participation of the film at the Berlinale was viewed with reservation, because »wide-distribution of the film would not be conducive to developing the desired cooperation between the Polish people and the people of the GDR, and especially not to strengthening relations between the People's Army of the GDR and the People's Army of Poland«. On January 21st, one day after the film premiered in Berlin (GDR), Pehnert asked Stefanski to revise his negative opinion, given the success of the film. In the meantime, GDR Foreign Minister Oskar Fischer had become involved in the discussion, and in a note to Hager on January 19th, he outlined a talk held between Polish Ambassador Wirowski and GDR Deputy Foreign Minister Gerd König: from the Polish standpoint, objections to the script had already been expressed a year earlier, moreover, these had been supported by ZK member Werner Krolikowski.

Telex from Warsaw

GDR Foreign Minister intervenes

The debate took on ever greater dimensions, it was no longer merely a matter of cultural, but also of foreign policy. In a telegram dated January 24th, the GDR ambassador to Poland, Neubauer, informed Hermann Axen, member of the Politburo and ZK secretary of the SED, Günter Sieber, former GDR ambassador to Poland and head of the Department of International Relations for the ZK, Hans Joachim Hoffmann, Minister of Culture and others, that Poland was adamantly opposed to the film's participation at the Berlinale. Word had it that the film contained historical inaccuracies that might be »exploited by enemies«. At this point, they were also disappointed by the GDR's reaction, but they would hold those who had promoted the project in Poland answerable for their decisions. A day later, in an internal communication, Kurt Hager informed Erich Honecker about the state of affairs. On the same day, on January 25th, Axen sent a telegram to Neubauer in which he stated that the ZK had examined the objections of the Polish ZK Secretary Waldemar Swirgon: although they could not find any anti-Polish sentiments in the film, they would still withdraw the film from the Berlinale.

ZK of the SED becomes involved

At this point Hans Dieter Mäde, general director of the Defa, intervened. In an »internal SED communication« on January 26th to Honecker, he gave the original reasons for submitting Der Aufenthalt to the Film Festival, namely because of »its anti-fascist position, its artistic quality and its inherent ›alliance-forming‹ effect on current political debate in the FRG«. Since in substance this statement contains little more than a catalogue of propagandist platitudes, it is difficult to assess whether it displayed a true commitment to the film, or was merely a dutiful response from an official in charge. The ›blocs‹ within the GDR hierarchy were, in this case, not clear. On the one hand, there was Horst Pehnert, who as Deputy Minister and the functionary responsible for film, used clever tactics, wheeling and dealing between internal fronts and the Berlinale. He saw his own personal credibility with his Western partners staked on the question of the film's participation at the International Film Festival. On the other hand, there was Kurt Hager, who represented all those who were more concerned about the GDR's image abroad, and this did not necessarily involve politico-cultural credibility. In this context, Mäde's further reasoning to Honecker was marked by a strange balancing of correct and relevant arguments for the film, and ideological embellishment: »Aside from forgoing the opportunity to have the anticipated offensive impact on the Festival's international audience, such a withdrawal would be bound to involve complications and a public stir. It must be

Hans Dieter Mäde to Honecker

feared that Western media would blow up such a move into a scandal and misuse it in a campaign against the GDR. This would provoke speculations, especially with regard to the differences in opinion which exist between us and our Polish partners.« Fear is the driving force behind these arguments, although without reason, as politico-cultural commentary in the West had been as yet rather scant. Ultimately, the film's withdrawal caused wide-spread incomprehension: it was believed that a film like DER AUFENTHALT – convincing in both content and artistic quality – would have had a good chance of winning a Berlinale Competition award. No one could understand the foreign policy behind the GDR's decision not to allow the film to take part in the Competition. Mäde's cautiously supportive arguments for Honecker seemed somewhat forced. On the one hand, in the hope of ensuring the film's participation, he wrote: »It is the duty of the GDR delegation to respond to all inquiries and objections at the Festival with great decisiveness, in keeping with the basic anti-fascist position of our country and its well-known internationalist attitude to the Polish people and its working class.« Erich Honecker's response is not known, although Axen's telegram to Neubauer suggests that the decision to withdraw the film from the Berlinale was made at top ZK levels. And so on January 28th, Neubauer sent telegrams from Warsaw to Honecker, Axen, Hager, Fischer and Sieber, confirming the withdrawal. Just the same, he decisively repudiated that the film contained »anti-Polish sentiments« and »anti-Polish propaganda«. Swirgon was grateful for this decision and considered it an »expression of the SED leadership's great understanding and internationalist attitude«. Above all, he saw it »as support for the PUWP«. This last slant might conceal the reason why the Poles were so vehement and unyielding toward the film: namely, the fear that the film's rather critical and liberal viewpoint of historical fact might undermine the authority of the Polish state and party leadership even more: an argument of inner-political importance for a government that was exposed to constant critique from its citizens through the ›Solidarity‹ movement.

ZK decision

Pehnert's fear that a decision against the film might have repercussions, both culturally and film politically, was indeed in part well-founded. For instance, in a letter to Kurt Hager dated January 28th, scriptwriter Wolfgang Kohlhaase protested that: »The request to withdraw the film from the West Berlin Film Festival would discredit our position completely. As Kant says, you can't be just a bit pregnant. We cannot confirm this film's political and artistic qualities inside the GDR and then not credit it with them outside the country. (...) A withdrawal would ultimately lead to completely abandoning the film's distribution abroad.« Kohlhaase's formulations suggest that at this point, no one who had worked on the film knew that the ZK had long decided to withdraw the film from the Berlinale. Even Hermann Kant had not been officially informed, as can be seen on January 29th, when he wrote on this subject to Erich Honecker and stated that he had heard from Hager »what has been said against the film, and the stance you have all taken«. He is referring here to the ZK's assessment, that the film was not anti-Polish. »I have already thanked Kurt Hager for the party leaders' position, but I would like to repeat here that it does one good to receive such support. I express my warm gratitude, especially to you.« Yet beyond this, Kant suspected that in the end they would comply with the Poles' request against participation. »If my suspicions are correct, then I want to have at least spoken my mind: either the objections to the film are right, and then everyone who is more or less responsible for the film (which applies in particular to me) belongs behind bars,

Wolfgang Kohlhaase to Kurt Hager

Hermann Kant to Honecker

or they are not right, then there is no reason not to show the film anywhere. If it is not allowed to participate in the Festival, because the accusations are true, then it is self-evident that it should also not be shown on the Karl-Marx Allee or be sent to Karl Marx Stadt or Moscow or Budapest or Hollywood. The film would be dead.« In his plea for the film, Kant used the same vocabulary as Mäde had used in his. »Politically, I see no one on our side who can benefit from our dissociating ourselves in one way or the other from a film which testifies so magnificently to our internationlist and humanist convictions.« He goes on to state that he realizes »that in politics, amongst friends, concessions have to be made sometimes, but a concession in this case would mean to acknowledge a blemish. A blemish with which I could not work, or be politically active, or live. My view of the leadership of my party and the leadership of my country includes the belief that they will try to protect me and my work from political disparagement.« Kant closes with an appeal to Honecker: »Dear Comrade Secretary-General, this film was in many ways a victory, and because I do not want it to turn into a defeat, I have written you all this.« Yet when he wrote the letter, Kant could certainly already deduce from other sources that the film could no longer be saved from withdrawal from the Berlinale, as can be seen from another letter he wrote on the same day. It was addressed to Kurt Hager and in it he refers to a talk he had with an official from GDR television, after he had found out that coverage of Beyer's film had been deleted from a »Kulturmagazin« report. The person he talked to told him the reason behind this was that the authorities had first wanted to see how the film was received. Kant commented: »Since such orders do not come from the doorkeeper, I can no longer believe in the promise that the film will run under ›normal‹ conditions. I am practised at reading such signs.« This pessimistic interpretation of the situation did in fact prove correct: a last attempt by the Department of Film, in other words by Pehnert, to argue the case fell on deaf ears. The letter to Hager on January 21st stated that the Berlinale had been »striving for years, despite certain open hostilities, to secure the participation of socialist countries without any kind of discriminating circumstances«. Hager informed Wolfgang Kohlhaase on February 1st, that absolutely no objections to the film existed, and he regretted to have to »emphasize once more what I already told Hermann [Kant]: there is no way for us to repudiate the objections raised by Poland and so we have to follow through and withdraw the film from the West Berlin Festival«. The decision had been finalized.

An appeal

Withdrawal unchanged

Yet behind the scenes in the GDR, discussion about the film continued along bureaucratic routes. Even after the Berlinale began on February 18th and long after the end of the Festival, the case preoccupied ministries and other bodies. Foreign Minister Oskar Fischer, for instance, informed Hager on February 22nd, that the Polish ambassador, Maciej Wirowski had come forward and expressed his amazement that Beyer, Kohlhaase and Kant had asked him to illuminate Poland's negative attitude. Moreover, the fact that Beyer and Kant had stated in an ARD report on West German television that the withdrawal of the film was due to Polish objections had caused irritations. Fischer kept a low profile in his response and pointed out that this was more of a »personal affair« between those involved; the official GDR position was known.

Polish sensitivities

There has been much speculation as to why exactly Poland disapproved of the film. Today, the complicated and contradictory mechanisms behind the Polish position are gradually coming to light. In a report from March 30th which Peter Ulbrich,

Reasons for the rejection

first secretary of the GDR Association of Television and Filmmakers (VFF), wrote to Ursula Ragwitz, head of the Department of Culture for the Central Committee of the SED, and which was then passed on to Kurt Hager, Ulbrich explained the contact his association had on such matters with the honorary president of the Polish association, director Jerzy Kawalerowicz. Mediation had been sought at this level. Although in this context, it must be mentioned that Kawalerowicz had been elected honorary president of the association in competition with Andrzej Wajda, who had held the office of honorary president till then. And Kawalerowicz was not one to have put »this sharp ideological and political rivalry« to Wajda last. Wajda, on the other hand, planned to establish a new association for those interested, in order to exclude all communist intervention, yet this would have led to alienation from the associations in the other socialist countries. After the VFF had made contact with Kawalerowicz, he agreed to mediate, promising to view the film DER AUFENTHALT. For no leading filmmaker is acquainted with the film, no one knows why there are objections and negative feelings harbored against the film. Yet due to the time-consuming conflict with Wajda, Kawalerowicz did not get to see the film until he visited the GDR at the end of March. The Festival was long over. After seeing it, Kawalerowicz backed »the film without any reservations«, and according to Ulbrich, spoke of a »tragic shortsightedness« in rejecting the film, for there was »not even a hint of anything anti-Polish«. For the first time, Kawalerowicz also indicated the reason for disapproval. Ulbrich noted that Kawalerowicz »had meanwhile found out that it was the fact that the prison officers in the film wore Polish army uniforms that had scandalized some of the film's critics in Poland, indeed, it had led to their absolute rejection of the film«. Kawalerowicz saw such argumentation as politically limited. »First of all, this depiction corresponds to historical reality. He [Kawalerowicz] had lived through the period and he knew what he was talking about. Secondly, those wearing the uniforms in the concrete historical situation were upholders of justice, both then and now, as shown in the film. Exactly this fact is of eminent political and emotional significance in the present situation in Poland, and for this reason deserves the highest regard, elevating this film to the height of the epoch. It was illegitimate – historically, politically, aesthetically and emotionally – to base one's arguments against the film on this.« Actually, few people in Poland had seen the film – members of the Polish ZK, the army and those responsible in the Ministry of Culture. There had been no unequivocal and unanimous rejection of the film, viewpoints had just differed. In the end, however, it was the faction which saw Poland's reputation discredited that won out: they believed, since no Nazi crimes were shown, that the film wronged Poles who had fallen or been murdered in the war. Kawalerowicz, Ulbrich went on to say, had spoken in this context of »noticeable tendencies of a new chauvinism«. But Kawalerowicz was also not free of ideological reservations, comparing the withdrawal of DER AUFENTHALT with Andrzej Wajda's new film DANTON. »What especially angers him«, Ulbrich writes, »is that the GDR was made to withdraw its announcement for the West Berlin Festival, while Wajda with his film DANTON, was ›able to sell‹ his ideological platform as ›Polish‹.« Which was not true as such, since Wajda's film was not presented at the Festival.

Kawalerowicz vs. Wajda

Kawalerowicz speaks out for the film

»A new chauvinism«

Admittedly, the dispute about DER AUFENTHALT is an isolated case, but it illustrates the intricate web of political views and sensitivities in which film-political decisions in the GDR – also with regard to the Berlinale – were entangled. Practical

Der Aufenthalt: Sylvester Groth (left)

approaches to discussing these matters could be undermined and counteracted by considerations dependent on foreign or domestic political events. And this was, incidentally, also true for films from other socialist countries.

New sources – a look back

Sources are gradually becoming available that make it possible to uncover the conditions shaping the backdrop for relations between former socialist nations and the Berlinale. These sources enable new historical and political insights. They go beyond the Berlinale and are of general politico-cultural significance, as in the case of the film Der Aufenthalt. The fact that the Berlinale, as of the mid-seventies, was a focal point of intersection for conflicting interests between the West and East is well-known. A look back at these entanglements is a look back without anger – albeit sometimes with great wonder.

Recollections of the Berlinale

By Michael Williams-Jones

The Lufthansa flight to Frankfurt from New York was uneventful. The solitude of long distance journeys always enables me to catch up on my backlog of mail, read a couple of scripts and just occasionally, indulge in a little writing of my own. It was February 22nd, 1979, and in my capacity as President of United Artists International, I was on my way to Berlin for the presentation of our film, THE DEER HUNTER, *at the Berlin International Film Festival.*

From Frankfurt, I caught a connecting flight to Berlin. As I gazed out of the window, over the bleak, snow-swept landscape, I wondered if we had crossed the Iron Curtain into GDR airspace.

During the short flight, I dozed off but was abruptly awakened by the stewardess announcing over the intercom that we were about to land at Tempelhof Airport. Tempelhof! My thoughts went back to those indelible, black and white newsreel images of planeloads of life-giving supplies being airlifted to the same field during the Berlin blockade. Other images of the beleaguered city flooded my imagination. The ghostly, pock-marked skeleton of a dead city, in the immediate aftermath of total war. The broken body of a young man, his life extinguished on the barb-wire barricades of a divided city, as he made his bid for freedom. The checkpoints, the sentry towers and above all the Wall.

Postwar West Berlin had evolved into an ersatz pressure pot of stressed out, guilt-stricken citizens, hell bent on an ever spiralling, hedonistic lifestyle. The city had been the focal point of so much evil and over the last thirty-four years, was the defiant symbol of a fragile peace held together by the nightmare scenario of nuclear war.

My excitement mounted as I drew my Burberry over my shoulders, collected my briefcase and hurried up the exit gangway to the frantic arrival hall. There, I was met by Fred Sorg, the chief executive of United Artists Germany, his marketing director, Werner Rochau and representatives of the Berlin Film Festival. Although I was bone weary from the long journey, it was impossible not to notice the sense of gloom that hung, like a thick fog, over my welcome committee. We exchanged pleasantries and made our way to the awaiting cars. As we exited the arrival hall, the numbing chill of a howling February wind, gusting snow and sleet in sheets, hit me like a sledge hammer. I sucked air in through my teeth desperately trying to adjust to the near arctic conditions. Finally, the door of the black Mercedes slammed shut and we were on our way to the Intercontinental hotel near the Kurfürstendamm.

Fred Sorg broke the silence first.

»Michael, we have a little problem.« He wasn't kidding.

He informed me that the delegation from the USSR had published a declaration expressing »resolute objection to the showing of THE DEER HUNTER *in the Festival«. It went on to argue that the film contravened the Festival's lofty regulations that called for »better mutual understanding among nations«. It claimed that the film was an insult to the Socialist Republic of Vietnam besieged by naked aggression from the USA and China. The declaration also observed, pointedly, that a Soviet protest denouncing the film had already been made earlier in the year, at the Belgrade Film Festival and by implication, warned that it should have been heeded when making the selection of films for the Berlin Film Festival.*

Without any further ado, the Soviet delegation in a fit of arrogant self-righteous-

ness, threatened to withdraw all their films from the program unless THE DEER HUNTER *was formally withdrawn.*

I wiped the misted window of the Mercedes and gazed out at the grey, soulless post-war architecture of what was now West Berlin. The snow had done its best to soften its harsher edges but all the same, the bleak cold-war atmosphere of that most isolated of cities, patrolled by Americans, Russians, French and British, was rapidly closing in on us.

Fred went on. »Michael, Wolf Donner needs to talk to you. He's getting pressure from all sides and the press is going mad.«

I asked if Michael Cimino, and our stars, Robert de Niro and Christopher Walker had arrived. They had. Cimino apparently refused to talk to or see anyone, including the Festival director, and was holed up in his hotel suite in a fit of understandable pique.

As we pulled into the Intercontinental hotel forecourt, I noticed a gaggle of journalists approach our car. One shoved a microphone into my face and demanded to know if United Artists would withdraw the film. Fred and the others cleared a path through the throng and as I was led through, I looked at the earnest young woman who had asked the question, shook my head and silently mouthed the word no.

The vast lobby was plastered with an insane mosaic of posters representing all manner of films from soft core pornography to Hollywood blockbusters to ones with much higher pretensions. Every bar, restaurant and available corner seemed to be buzzing with delegates, journalists, starlets, groupies, wannabes and spies all touting their special interests, or so it seemed to me. The atmosphere was surreal.

Installed in my suite with a cup of life sustaining expresso in my hands, I called a worried Wolf Donner, who informed me nervously that the political views in both Berlin and Bonn were divided on the issue of THE DEER HUNTER. *Surrounded by a vast Russian army with thousands of troops and tanks a few kilometers away, one could quite reasonably understand their concern.*

To his eternal credit, Wolf at no time pressured me into withdrawing the film. Nevertheless, he deftly manipulated the conversation and articulated what he saw as the considerable risks of keeping the film in the Festival, cautioning me that any decision would have to be mine alone. Someone in the room suggested the possibility of a terrorist attack and I overheard whispered mention of the need for more security. The relative sanctuary of New York was beginning to fade into a distant memory and I had only just arrived in Berlin!

Wolf added that he had just learned that the Cuban delegation had joined together with the GDR, Hungary and Czechoslovakia in pulling their delegations out. Two Eastern bloc jury members, Pál Gábor and Vera Chytilova had also dutifully lined up behind their masters and resigned in »protest«.

As I listened to Wolf, I looked around at the tight, anxious faces seated around me in the suite. In the incestuous, confined atmosphere of divided Berlin, rumors seemed to take on distorted proportions, way beyond their substance. The dark shadow of recent history, the ever present army of occupation and a brooding, implacable enemy just over the Wall magnified and twisted reality.

The snow was getting heavier outside.

»Wolf, I am not going to withdraw the film from Berlin under any circumstances. Hell, it's only a damn movie! They can go fuck themselves!! If we are to leave Berlin, it will be because you've thrown us out.«

I urged Wolf to consider the implications of this. The integrity of the Festival would be forever tainted and I informed him frankly, that, were we to be thrown out, as long as I still had influence, I would never again return to the Berlin Festival with a film.

Wolf was left in no doubt about my views and generously assured me that he shared my sense of outrage adding that he had secured the support of Mayor Dietrich Stobbe who just happened to be standing for re-election in a couple of weeks' time. In closing, he informed me that given my unyielding position, he felt certain that he could secure all the necessary political support to keep the film in the Festival.

I called Cimino and briefed him on the conversation. He was moody and felt cornered and handed the phone over to his producing partner Joann Carelli, who informed me that they were leaving Berlin that day. I protested, arguing that they had an obligation to stay, at least until after the screening, if for no other reason than to defend their right to express their vision freely. I recall telling Joann that there would be no better platform than Berlin to make the point.

That night, I took a few friends through Checkpoint Charlie into East Berlin for dinner. As we cruised the empty snow-clad streets, passing the occasional Trabant in our sleek, purring Mercedes, I became aware of an acrid smell that began to filter through into the plush leather interior. I looked enquiringly at Fred.

»Young brown coal ...«

He paused, then added softly:

»For the fires you know.«

I thought about his words late into that night. One city, one people torn apart by history and conflicting ideologies, one part straining at the seams with vitality and renewed expectation, the other, searing their lungs on the smoke of young brown coal, just to keep warm.

A sense of the surreal continued to dominate the few days I remained in Berlin. Back at the Intercontinental, I received word from Wolf that all the participants from the Third World countries had submitted their own declaration protesting the presence of the film. At least they didn't leave en masse, but they had struck yet another blow against that fundamental human right, the right of freedom of expression.

The depleted Festival ran its course and of course The Deer Hunter *was screened to a rapturous reception in the vast Zoo Palast theater. Sadly, at that moment, to the best of my recollection, the talented director and producer were somewhere over the Atlantic, flying home to the USA.*

Huge and very vocal protests on both sides of the argument flanked the soaked red carpet like a gauntlet as we left the theater. Wearily we wandered through the slush and snow, back to our hotel and to another endless night of restless, disturbed sleep.

I recall seeing Moritz de Hadeln. Wolf Donner's successor, in the lobby of the Intercontinental the next morning, as I was about to depart for the airport. I wandered over and wished him well. He smiled enigmatically and asked if I would be returning to Berlin. At the time, I must admit that I was more than ready to leave the claustrophobic, hemmed-in city. I needed to breathe some fresh, freer air and I left the question hanging for several years.

Of course I returned to Berlin and to the Festival! It's irresistible!

Ten years later actually, almost to the day and incredibly, with yet another film, whose story was deeply rooted in the Vietnam War. It was Born on the Fourth of July.

On this occasion, Oliver Stone and I were presented with hammers and chisels and together with thousands of others, we proceeded to use them, violently, against that graffitied bastion of the cold war, the »Wall«, now tumbling before our very eyes into the trash heap of history.

Berlin was no longer divided and I recall feeling a wild sense of elation tinged with odd, troubling doubts.

Nine years later, I returned once again, with my wife Eve, this time as a member of the Jury for the 48th Berlin International Film Festival.

A glorious, unpretentious Brazilian film, CENTRAL DO BRAZIL, *won the Golden Bear. It was a triumphant symphony to the enduring resilience of the human spirit.*

A thin February sun shone through the city, illuminating a stunning landscape of giant construction cranes, scaffolding and building sites.

Potsdamer Platz had become the largest urban development in the world and the Wall was now a fading memory, but most heartening of all was the flowering of a small, but vigorous Jewish community, whose enriching presence was once again contributing to the life of an extraordinary city.

Berlin was being reborn, setting the stage for the new millennium and the next fifty years of its compelling, essential Berlinale.

Motives behind the Soviets' reaction

By Mikhail Shkalikov

The following text presents a very personal account from the point of view of the former deputy chairman of the department of foreign affairs of Goskino in the USSR on the events accompanying the showing of THE DEER HUNTER *at the International Film Festival in West Berlin in February 1979. In the republics of the former USSR and elsewhere, there may, of course, be different views on these events, and different explanations of this or other moves. These views and explanations have a right to exist as does, I hope, what is presented here.*

In my opinion, some aspects of the international situation then prevailing should be taken into account in order to clarify the motives behind the Soviets' reaction.

In 1979, seven years after the Quadripartite Agreement on West Berlin had come into effect, the Soviet leadership was still devoting special attention to the city of West Berlin. The Soviets carefully followed the way the agreement, which had been signed by all sides, was observed. In addition, every report containing any mention of the city was analyzed with truly pedantic meticulousness and, depending on the importance attached to the information contained therein, submitted to the Politburo members of the Central Committee of the CPSU and to the USSR Foreign Minister A. A. Gromyko.

In the East, developments in Vietnam were also followed attentively. And although it was quite evident that the problem of West Berlin had primarily become the concern of a relatively small circle of politicians in the meantime, and not so much that of the average Soviet citizen, the situation was very different with respect to Vietnam. As the most important scene of war in Southeast Asia, Vietnam not only engaged the interest of diplomats and the military establishment. In the sixties and seventies, the colonial war of 1946–54 and the US bombardment of North Korea had engendered feelings of solidarity with Vietnam among broad sections of the

Soviet public not familiar with the subtleties of international politics. People were aware that Vietnam had been in a state of war for decades. And many in the Soviet Union still knew all too well what war meant. Incidentally, this sympathy was felt for both North and South Vietnam.

At the time, thousands of Vietnamese students were studying in the Soviet Union, and voluntary collections of donations of food, clothes and medical supplies took place throughout the country, independently of the very considerable amounts of state aid, to support Vietnam in its struggle.

There was a third factor, too: the division of the world into military-political blocs, whose relations with one another were anything but idyllic. And there was the phenomena of bloc solidarity, which grew as tensions increased in one region or another.

In July 1999, Michael Cimino's THE DEER HUNTER *– like hundreds of other films – was shown on Soviet television. It was simply presented as an Academy Award-winner and no longer evoked memories of the incident in West Berlin in 1979, when a completely different mood prevailed.*

In early February 1979, a Soviet film delegation saw Michael Cimino's THE DEER HUNTER *at the »Fest 79«, the international film festival in Belgrade. At a press conference, the delegation described the film as a »crude distortion of the struggle for liberation of the Vietnamese people against the American invaders« and as a justification of US intervention in Vietnam. The delegation condemned the festival in Belgrade for including the film in its program. It later transpired that there had been a heated debate among the festival organizers over the film, too. Initially, the selection commission had rejected its inclusion by thirteen votes to two. The film was only included in the program following the intervention of the Yugoslav Ministry of Foreign Affairs. What is noteworthy is that the Soviet delegation, allowing for the possibility of further incidents accompanying the showing of the film at the »Fest«, had not felt the need to leave Belgrade before the end of the festival.*

On its return to Moscow, the delegation submitted a report on the film. It became known that THE DEER HUNTER *was programmed to be shown at the West Berlin Film Festival. The film authorities in the socialist countries were notified accordingly and, as was to be expected, informed their respective political leaderships. Critical commentaries about the film appeared in a number of Soviet newspapers. Even so, the film representatives did not initially plan any diplomatic moves to oppose the intended showing of* THE DEER HUNTER *in West Berlin. The model adopted in Belgrade seemed to be the right approach for West Berlin, too. The USSR Consulate General in West Berlin began negotiating with both the Festival management and the Senate Office to have* THE DEER HUNTER *excluded from the Festival program. Yet Festival director W. Donner, who had invited Michael Cimino's film, stood by his decision.*

On February 20, the Soviet film delegation arrived in West Berlin. However, in the meantime it had decided not to adhere to the »Belgrade model« and instead to adopt a tough, resolute approach. Between the end of the Belgrade »Fest« and the opening of the West Berlin Festival, an incident had occurred which, in my opinion, radically brought to a head both the controversy surrounding THE DEER HUNTER, *and the worsening international military and political situation. On February 17, 1979, an armed conflict began between China and Vietnam, resulting in countless civilian victims on the Vietnamese side and considerably damaging the country's economy.*

Under the impact of certain factors, developments now assumed a completely political character. The Soviets maintained that showing a film which presented the

Vietnamese in such a bad light was not only tantamount to justifying US aggression in Vietnam, but also to approval and toleration – by the Festival organizers and thus of the West in general, too – of the armed Chinese invasion of Vietnam. In everything they said, the critics completely ignored the overall anti-war stance of both the film and its American director.

On top of all this, accusations, similar to those expressed by the Soviets, were leveled against the Festival organizers, by some of the German mass media and in statements issued by Western artists for including this film in the program. Thus, one could read, for instance in Berlin's daily papers, that Berlin's profile, which was not yet fully developed as a city and place of international encounters, had been seriously damaged. Responsibility for this lay in the hands of Senator for Culture Sauberzweig who should have prevented the Festival director at the time, Dr. Donner, from combining his premature retirement with the ›thunderous commotion‹ caused by a totally superfluous act of provocation against the USSR and the other Eastern bloc countries, thus leaving behind a pile of wreckage in Berlin. After all, the Russians' response had been predictable. Those responsible had had sufficient advance warning.

Julie Christie, a member of the International Jury, declared that a film which presented the people of a small country waging a successful partisan war against an overpowering aggressor as a mob without any human dignity, without any human qualities whatsoever, encouraged that very form of racism which played a decisive part in unleashing wars of this nature.

In my view, however, the parties involved in the controversy surrounding THE DEER HUNTER, were pursuing quite different goals. The Soviet side and the socialist countries were demonstrating their support for Vietnam at a time which was very critical indeed for that country, whilst the Festival management and Berlin's political leadership were defending their right to an independent Festival program. If the dispute had taken place in a more peaceful international situation, it would have probably been fought out with less vehemence and in a calmer tone. To my way of thinking, this is confirmed by the Soviet delegation's decision not to leave the Belgrade »Fest 79« prematurely, despite all the attention Cimino's film received. In reality, it was the Chinese-Vietnamese conflict that had acted as the catalyst triggering the »West Berlin incident«.

Incidentally, counselor E. Lindemann from the Federal Republic of Germany's embassy in Moscow also added fuel to the flames. She phoned me on February 22, 1979, expressing her desire to see me and discuss the Soviet delegation's protest against the inclusion of a certain American film in the West Berlin Festival. After consulting the management of the Third West European Department of the Soviet Ministry of Foreign Affairs, I informed Mrs. E. Lindemann, a half an hour later, that the West Berlin Festival management would be able to negotiate all questions related to Soviet participation in the Festival with the Soviet delegation itself, or with the Consulate General of the USSR in West Berlin. There were well-known reasons why these questions concerning West Berlin were not to be discussed with the Embassy of the Federal Republic of Germany (note what was said about West Berlin at the beginning of this essay).

On February 23, the Soviet delegation left the Festival, followed by the delegations from Bulgaria, Hungary, the GDR, Cuba, Poland and Czechoslovakia. Furthermore, the Hungarian and Czech members of the International Jury were recalled. The Rumanian delegation continued to participate in the Festival, a decision reflecting political relations then prevailing among the socialist countries: the general »moral and political unity« and the special path taken by Rumania.

For the Soviets, the relations between Goskino in the USSR and the International Film Festival in West Berlin not only effected Goskino's festival policy, but also the special situation of a »political entity, situated in the middle of the territory of the German Democratic Republic, with special status under international law«, which West Berlin had had, from the standpoint of the USSR, since the end of the Second World War.

In March 1969, the Soviet Ministry of Culture, then responsible for film-related questions, approached the Central Committee of the CPSU and proposed changing the procedure for selecting Soviet films for international festivals. From that time on, the Soviet Minister of Culture (later the Goskino of the USSR) made the final decision on the film lists submitted to organizers of international film festivals, along with the organizational committee of the film workers' association (later the association of filmmakers of the USSR) in agreement with the Department of Culture of the Central Committee of the CPSU. However, this did not apply to the festivals in Moscow, Karlový Vary, Cannes and Venice. When considering films for these festivals, the Ministry of Culture had to turn directly to the Central Committee of the CPSU, which then decided which film was to be sent to which festival. Soviet participation in the West Berlin Festival had, of course, received special attention from the very start.

When the Soviet Union first participated in the West Berlin Festival it was, of course, under the sign of a political decision made at the time. In June 1972, the Quadripartite Agreement on West Berlin came into effect, under which the Western Sectors of Berlin ceased to be a part of the Federal Republic of Germany and were thereby no longer subject to the administration of the latter. Soviet participation in the West Berlin Festival thus took place in consideration of this fact.

I do not believe that there was ever any discrimination whatsoever by Goskino in the USSR against the West Berlin Festival. In the early days, of course, priority was given to selecting films for the older festivals in Cannes and Venice, as well as for those in Moscow and Karlový Vary. However, if a film was »banned from leaving the country«, the ban generally applied equally to all festivals abroad.

There were, however, occasions when the West Berlin Festival organizers did not obtain a film they would have liked, only to see it then be shown at a different festival later. This was due to the simple fact that the Soviet film industry did not follow any rigid patterns. As a rule, however, those selecting films for the West Berlin Festival were able to view virtually the entire annual production of Soviet films. At the same time, they would apparently hear rumors of a masterpiece, which was not going to be released, lying somewhere on shelves behind locked doors at Goskino. Then negotiations would be held, after which those selecting films generally returned home empty-handed. After their departure, lively discussions would begin over the desired film. Its directors would go to the management, there would be semi-secret showings, and the film's reputation would grow. The Goskino management would then discreetly approach the higher authorities and those which were less closely linked to the Party, arguing quite convincingly that a single showing at some festival or other would, after all, not really shake the Soviet Union's position of power, but might, instead, subdue much dissatisfaction in artists' circles. Sometimes this approach worked, and the film in question would then be sent to one of the international festivals.

Generally, however, the film continued to lead a lonely existence out of sight of cinema audiences.

From the early eighties on, Party supervision of festival affairs was relaxed somewhat. I certainly cannot remember having to submit to the Central Committee of the CPSU any Goskino project outlines at the time, concerning the participation of this or that film at, let's say, the Venice Festival. Now and again, I would receive a weary call from one of the Party authorities: »Why do you want to send director X to San Sebastian (Cannes, Montreal, etc.) when he's just got married for the fifth time?« – »He has made a good film and, after all, he is legally married!« – »OK, never mind ...«

Of course, the Party leaders' neglect of the Soviet film industry met with incomprehension among the political leaderships of the other socialist countries. At the end of the eighties, some followed developments in the Soviet Union with sympathetic interest, others issued warnings and responded negatively. The noisiest objections came from the German Democratic Republic, which saw itself as the outpost of socialism. However, there is reason to believe that the ban imposed in the GDR on Soviet films shown at the West Berlin Film Festival had not been issued by the GDR Central Department of Film.

The Soviet Union's sensitive reaction to »incorrect« films such as Lubitsch's NINOTCHKA, shown at the West Berlin Film Festival, or the »James Bond« films, which were shown throughout the world, was most certainly due to ideological inflexibility and indignation based less on rational consideration than on a lack of humor. However, one should not ignore people's deeply rooted fears. »What is that supposed to mean? They are screening a satire about the Soviet Union. The bourgeoisie is laughing at us – and we just sit back and let them? What are we in for?« As painful as it may sound, such fears did exist, and they were by no means unfounded. Over the course of time, and with the emergence of new generations, these fears slowly subsided, of course, – but it was a very slow process indeed.

Then came perestroika and glasnost. People and, of course, filmmakers in the Soviet Union became more courageous. So courageous, in fact, that they tore Soviet cinema to pieces with fierce criticisms, throwing out the baby with the bathwater in the process, as a wise friend once remarked. Today, people are paying due credit to Soviet cinema from past epochs – while they are doing everything they can to criticize contemporary cinema.

Defa at the Berlinale

By Horst Pehnert

Just why it took so long for Defa to present a film in the Competition of the International Film Festival is a long story. Wolfgang Jacobsen documented this extensively in his history of the Berlinale, on the occasion of its 40th anniversary. Bonn (and to some extent, the West Berlin Senate) was against it, and the GDR did not want it. According to Jacobsen, many feared that »an invitation to the GDR could be interpreted as the first step towards recognition of the East German state«. The »other side«, as the GDR was often referred to, feared that their participation in an event that was linked in a number of ways to the West German government, despite being international, could undermine their firm policy that West Berlin was not part of the

First call by the GDR delegation in 1982 on Moritz de Hadeln: Helmut Diller, Horst Pehnert, Moritz de Hadeln, Eberhard Ugowski

Federal Republic of Germany. But not only Defa was conspicuous in its absence: indeed there were no films at all from the socialist countries of the time, which was increasingly seen as a deficiency. Repeated attempts to correct this by the long-term director of the Berlinale, Alfred Bauer, were thwarted regularly by Bonn's Foreign Ministry, via which invitations were sent or not sent, as the case may be. It was not until 1967, when the Film Festival was able to issue invitations itself, that film authorities in the so-called Eastern bloc were asked to the Berlinale, although at the behest of the Senate, the GDR was explicitly overlooked (Senate Director Ingensand: »We will not be inviting the other side.«). The only result of this invitation policy was that it resulted in nothing. Cold war basically, on all fronts.

It was not until the era of Willy Brandt's »Ostpolitik« and the signing of the subsequent political agreements that the framework changed, albeit slowly. From 1970 on, the GDR also received an invitation to the Berlinale, which it nonetheless failed to respond to. At this point I was not yet involved, but one can safely assume that the GDR must have closed ranks with the Soviet Union, which ignored the Berlinale until 1973. But in 1974, Soviet film was represented for the first time in the Competition section of the Berlinale and the GDR sent an official »observer«. In the following year, the 25th anniversary of the Berlinale, all were present, with the exception of Albania. Defa entered the Competition with Frank Beyer's and Jurek Becker's film Jakob der Lügner *(»Jacob the Liar«). The Golden Bear promptly went to Hungary and both the Soviet Union and the GDR received Silver Bears.*

So much to the background history. I feel compelled to recall it here, as it shows just how deep and wide the gulf was that needed to be bridged before cooperation was actually possible, even before the Wall went up – and just how vulnerable the bridge was in the early days. It simply wasn't entirely clear whether a point had been reached where East and West could meet at the Berlinale and calmly work together, despite the existence of a border separating the two opposing social systems.

In 1979, earlier sensitivities were reawakened with the withdrawal of all contributions from socialist countries – apart from Rumania – due to the planned screening of the American film by Michael Cimino, The Deer Hunter. *I was not there at the time, so the Foreign Ministry informed me of the protest and ensuing departure of the Soviet delegation, along with the Cubans, and that the other brother nations were planning to leave too. I consulted the Minister of Culture and we agreed that our delegation could not remain alone on the battlefield, although we did still want to participate in the Film Market. With a heavy heart, I withdrew our delegation. We were not familiar with Cimino's film and had been hoping audiences would applaud our Competition contribution* Anton der Zauberer *(»Anton the Magician«) by Günther Reisch, and that it would possibly even win a prize. The sacrifice was painful, not only for the film's makers. But given the state of affairs – after all, there was a kind of loyalty between allies which in the past had actually worked in our favor – we had no option but to participate in the withdrawal. The fact that Jury member Julie Christie distanced herself from Cimino's film in a personal statement at the end of the Berlinale was viewed by us as a confirmation of our position and attitude.*

But what next? Had the bridge to Eastern Europe – as Moritz de Hadeln, one of the two new Berlinale directors appointed after the controversy, was often to describe the Berlinale – already collapsed under the first signs of pressure? The ball was now in our court. In the executive bodies of socialist film it was necessary to grasp the sit-

uation and reach an agreement. I sought the support of my fellow officials for unrestricted participation in the Berlinale, at both our annual meeting and in individual talks. My argument, in short, was that the politics of reason which had visibly begun to alter the relationship between the two competing systems had to be followed by the same for cultural policies. Moreover, I had an entirely personal agenda. I believed that it was not particularly exciting – even for state film – to crouch comfortably in its nest when it had the possibility of »taking off« right outside and flying routes into a world that had been off bounds for so many years. I for one was interested in drawing attention to Defa film in the Western hemisphere, on the one hand, for reasons of personal ambition and, on the other hand, because of the impact it would have at home. It was quite simple: were a film to be well-received at the Berlinale, audience ratings at home would also increase. It wasn't difficult to persuade my colleagues, since most of them shared my view a priori anyway. Even the director of the Soviet film organization Goskino put up no resistance, although as I remember, he gave no explicit approval. In any case, Goskino was not in a position to exert pressure on the film authorities of allied countries, in the form of instructions. At our meeting, the matter was not subject to any actual decision. No one had anything against the Berlinale and it was implicitly clear that earlier disputes as well as any to come were begun in the foreign ministries and blown up by the ambassadors, rather than in the film organizations themselves.

Individual stances toward the Berlinale were now up to the film authorities themselves.

SOLO SUNNY, a film by Konrad Wolf and Wolfgang Kohlhaase, was the 1985 Defa entry in the Competition of the Berlinale. Henceforth, everything ran smoothly, almost too smoothly, as if we had always belonged or because we had not belonged for so long. We were present in all sections of the Festival, primarily, of course, with documentaries in the International Forum of Young Cinema, but also in the Panorama, the Children's Film Festival and the Film Market. The films were proposed by the studios and then confirmed by the Department of Film. This was not so difficult, since the number of films completed in a limited period of time which promised to be of thematic interest and quality was not large. In contrast to the Forum, which was regularly able to make a selection from a number of offers, we often had just one single film to submit to the Competition. No one tried to influence us in any way. Not even when it came to selecting and sending the delegation. I still use this term today – which even at the time was undoubtedly an unusual one in the West – because the situation then meant that not just anyone who wished to was allowed to travel to the Berlinale. A travel permit was required, a little pocket money, free accommodations and food vouchers issued by the Berlinale. We settled all this for the Berlinale participants delegated by the Department. The delegation met before the Festival began in order to be briefed on the current state of play in the tussle over West Berlin as well as to have a few organizational points explained to them by the director of the Department for West Berlin Affairs in the Foreign Ministry. I am not aware of any objections from the Ministry for State Security against certain members of the delegation, and I believe it would most certainly not have escaped me had there been any. I supplied both the Minister of Culture and the Department for Cultural Affairs of the Central Committee of the SED with information on the films and the delegation, and these were always accepted without objection. It should be also pointed out that the Secretariat of the Central Committee of the SED kept an eye on our festival policy by requesting a statement from us each calendar year that indicated at which international film festivals Defa intended to participate, without necessarily naming particular films. These statements were then approved – often as circulars – and I believe they were what gave us the freedom of action that allowed us to proceed from case to case.

In 1983, however, an unfortunate incident occurred: we were reluctantly obliged to withdraw our entry, Der Aufenthalt *(»The Turning Point«), for which we had high hopes, from the Competition section of the Berlinale after the Polish ambassador to the GDR protested against the screening of the film. We felt this was completely unfounded. Our decision was met with a certain incomprehension and the GDR was accused of servile obedience to Warsaw. Clearly, those (including the »FAZ«) who said or wrote that they had never actually thought about the fragility of the relationship between the GDR and Poland as neighbors – for Poland had suffered acutely under Germany in the past – had no intention of thinking about it now either. But, the relationship between Defa and the Berlinale was not seriously damaged. Professor Kurt Mätzig remained on the Jury. And in 1986, the bond between the Berlinale and its erstwhile problem children in the East proved so resilient that a Rumanian-backed Soviet protest against the screening of the French film* Rouge Baiser *(»Red Kiss«) had no impact.*

From 1982 on, I was allowed to attend the Berlinale, with permission from the Secretary for Culture on the Central Committee of the SED, Professor Hager. This went largely unnoticed. Only the memorable Karena Niehoff writing in »Der Tagesspiegel« observed a new quality to GDR participation and described the lodging of the GDR's Deputy Minister for Culture at the (also former) »Schweizer Hof« a »small sensation«. A first visit with Moritz de Hadeln and his wife Erika was comfortably low-keyed and henceforth we cultivated a stable working relationship that allowed us to communicate well and to work out both trivial and delicate problems at all times.

We were also able to develop a relationship based primarily on mutual respect with Hassemer who was Senator for Cultural Affairs at the time. This began with the request, handed over to the GDR by the Senate, for a meeting between myself and Hassemer. This took place during the 1983 Berlinale at the Hotel Steigenberger. The meeting was refreshingly relaxed. This young Senator, not yet jaded by politics, was surprisingly loquacious, to such an extent that the head of the Office of the Senate, who was also present, had to intervene occasionally and restrain him. At least, this was my impression. What was significant about the meeting was not so much its actual content, but the fact that it took place at all, representing as it did another step towards rapprochement. This was clearly desired from both sides and its preparation and evaluation in the GDR was on the political agenda at the top echelons. The working relationship between myself and Hassemer, which began at the Berlinale, then developed such an effortless momentum and continuity – also in the context of his plan to create a European film prize – that when he lost his office after the CDU defeat at the elections he sent me a good-bye letter saying he hoped we would keep in touch.

By this time I always attended at least half of the Berlinale every year, where I was able to make many contacts for both myself and Defa, as well as strengthen already existing contacts, in particular with producers, directors, actors and also politicians. In these years the cooperation between Defa and producers in West Berlin and the Federal Republic on concrete film projects developed rapidly. In successive years I invited Sydney Pollack, Cliff Robertson and Jack Valenti over to that part of the city behind the Wall. We took them to the Pergamon Altar, the Schauspielhaus at the Gendarmenmarkt and to Brecht's flat where they were allowed to sit in his chair in front of his typewriter – and look out onto the cemetery where he was buried. All three of them particularly enjoyed the occasion. We had many meaningful conversations, also over dinner, and Jack Valenti casually said he would never have expected to find so much beauty behind the Iron Curtain in Berlin. This was also part of the Berlinale for us.

In early 1989, before anyone had any idea how the year was going to turn out, Moritz de Hadeln proposed showing the Competition films in East Berlin cinemas as well as in the West. This meant including that part of Berlin known as the capital of the GDR in the Berlinale. A bold proposal, with little hope of success. But at least it was now up for discussion. And I personally felt it was not as hopeless as it seemed. For I had seen how rapidly and easily I had been granted permission from Erich Honecker to implement Loriot's request to premiere his film ÖDIPUSSI *in East Berlin (at 5 p.m.) and in West Berlin (8 p.m.) on the same day, which no one else had thought possible. And our success at the Berlinale, a Golden Bear ex aequo and four Silver Bears, had done much to boost the reputation of the GDR. But things only really speeded up after Honecker's resignation – he had clearly had other things on his mind at the time – and the fall of the Wall. After the government was reshuffled by Hans Modrow, a wonderful but virtually utopian idea was turned into real life.*

We discussed arrangements in-depth when de Hadeln and his wife Erika visited the Leipzig Documentary Film Week in November. Dr. Dietmar Keller, Minister for Culture in Modrow's cabinet, participated in a first round of talks. Parallel to this, Ulrich Gregor and his wife were conducting talks to the same end in Leipzig. Previously, in a letter to me, de Hadeln had described concrete plans to bring about the Berlinale's move into the GDR capital. In it he said: »The Berlin Film Festival was the first cultural event to bring about open and constructive cooperation with the GDR, and perhaps it is for this reason that it is now in the position to take this new step together with the GDR.«

He was right.

The GDR was interested and soon signaled its approval. On December 7, a joint press release announced that films from the Competition, the Forum and the Children's Film Program of the 40th International Film Festival would also be shown in the eastern part of the city.

We were all set. The atmosphere in the premiere cinema, the »Kosmos« on Karl-Marx-Allee, was electric when I introduced the Senator for Cultural Affairs under Mayor Momper, Dr. Anke Martiny, who then presented the director of the Berlinale Moritz de Hadeln and – drum roll – the US stars Michael Douglas and Danny DeVito, there to promote their film THE WAR OF THE ROSES*. This represented both a new departure and the beginning of an end. Soon afterwards the GDR ceased to exist and both Defa and the story of its relationship to the Berlinale were relegated to the history books.*

During the 1989 Berlinale I was honored, along with an American and a Soviet colleague, with the Golden Berlinale Camera. I was extremely proud and still am. I believe that all of us at Defa did everything in our power to make the Berlinale bridge the gulf caused by the Cold War and its consequences. To me, the Berlinale Camera represents a lasting memory of exciting years and wonderful people.

The fuss about the prize

By Winfried Junge

The lengthy chronicle LEBENSLÄUFE – DIE KINDER VON GOLZOW *(»Personal Records – The Golzow Children«) was projected to continue until the year 2000. Which is where we've now arrived. Our innovative work outlived the GDR even if not as a Defa project. And to a large extent, the reputation it has established has been thanks to our sixfold participation in the International Forum program at the Berlinale.*

The attempt to accompany a first grade class from Golzow, as they progress through life, with a camera for as long as possible began on August 28, 1961 – two weeks after a border of barbed wired went up across Berlin.

On that thirteenth day in August, I had gone to the Brandenburg Gate and asked the officer on duty not to carry out the measures with such haste. I wanted time to fetch my cameraman. He had already been assigned to me for Golzow; actually, at that very moment I should have been there in the kindergarten and begun work. Yes …

As a Berliner by birth who had spent time all round the city till the age of 26, it was painful only to be able to move about in the eastern third for »a while«, as we thought at the time. Until then, the movie theaters in the west of the city had also been part of my »universities«. As a disciple and student, I had hardly missed a noteworthy film. By carefully juggling my schedule, it was possible for me to run or bike to as many as four theaters a day. To my delight, as a resident of the East, I could often do so for less than 5 West marks, which were either slipped to me by my uncle or aunt or, if necessary, exchanged at a rate of 1 to 5. And this amount also included a sausage or a large portion of ice cream.

The last film I saw at the Delphi was MY FAIR LADY. *Of course at the time I had no idea that one day something I would make would be shown on its huge screen.*

Over the years and decades, »a while« turned into what seemed like »for ever and ever«. Nevertheless, I was able to make films behind the Wall. The Defa colleagues who lived in the West were no longer around – a chance for the first graduates of the Babelsberg Film Academy.

My first film about the school class in Golzow was followed by a second one in 1962 and a third in 1966. Prizes received at the Leipzig Documentary Film Week enhanced the project's reputation internationally. Between 1969 and 1979, I made three short films and one long one, which reviewed the first 18 years in Golzow: ANMUT SPARET NICHT NOCH MÜHE, *named after Brecht and Eisler's »Children's Songbook«.*

Our work was not up for consideration for the festivals in Mannheim and Oberhausen, but instead drew the attention of the Gregors. Yet due to its text, they ultimately decided not to take the film. But then our eighth one, which had followed in 1980/81, LEBENSLÄUFE – DIE GESCHICHTE DER KINDER VON GOLZOW IN EINZELNEN PORTRÄTS *(»Personal Records – the History of the Golzow Children in Individual Portraits«), was accepted. In Leipzig in 1981, the film's 4 hours and 17 minutes exceeded the number of minutes allowed in the GDR for films in the competition. But no such regulation existed for the Forum and so it was welcome to participate in its main program. Nevertheless, due to the unmistakable response which this unusual film received in Leipzig at its 9 a. m. screening,* LEBENSLÄUFE *was awarded a »Golden Dove for honor's sake« (or for »decency's sake« as cameraman Leupold's younger daughter later told her class).*

In Berlin, on the other hand, it immediately won two »real« prizes. The FIPRESCI award – also honorary in nature – and that of the church (ex aequo with a French film). This prize came with a purse. To be more specific: the Otto Dibelius Film Prize of the International Protestant Film Jury with a 2500 (two-thousand-five-hundred) mark purse, which – so the statutes – »is intended for directors of films of high artistic quality that in a special way express an attitude in accordance with the Gospel or stimulate a discussion of it«.

A prize from the church of all institutions and then one named after Otto Dibelius? Wasn't he that »cold warrior« who had drawn up that pastoral military contract with Adenauer and looked, unfortunately, like Walter Ulbricht? God be with us, what had we done wrong that our film could please the class enemy to such a degree? Off the cuff, Leupold and I guessed that it was because in the seventh of the nine »Personal Records« a Marieluise was to be seen, who unlike the others in her class, did not take part in the impious »Jugendweihe«, the ceremony in the GDR at which 14 year-olds were given adult social status, because her father – a devote Christian – planned her confirmation. We had had no desire to comment negatively on this and did not find our behavior in any way courageous. For us, this was just another aspect of the reality of »real socialism«. Recognition of this fact could indeed be called »an attitude in correspondence with the Gospel«. And for this we were getting money. A bit embarrassing, but lovely.

Contrary to our expectations, we were immediately consoled among our own ranks: be it as it may – it was booked as a success for the GDR. We were merely advised never to mention the award as the Otto Dibelius Prize at home, but instead to call it the Interfilm Prize, although this was in fact the abbreviation for the International Protestant Film Jury itself. But then who would know. All right then. And according to the motto: »You know what is allowed to be said«, we were then permitted – without having to cross ourselves – to meet the »enemy« media for questioning.

This Berlinale of 1982 was indeed a success for the GDR. In the run-up, the organizers had had to find a way to exclude the Hollywood film NIGHT CROSSING, *which had tried to force its way into the program. The film told the legendary story of how some GDR citizens had risked escape by a hot-air balloon. If the Berlinale had decided in favor of this film, the GDR would not have participated and in solidarity, the other socialist countries would have withdrawn as well. For it was not yet the period of Gorbachev's perestroika. We of course went to see this cinematic spectacle in dolby stereo.*

Now to conclude my tale of the fuss about the prize:

The day »after«, the telephone woke Leupold and me out of our deep sleep in the double bed at the Savoy Hotel. The GDR Deputy Minister for Culture and head of the Central Department for Film, comrade Horst Pehnert, expected us in his office at 11 for a report. We should bring the money with us, too.

Had we perhaps been expected not to accept the award? Or had the rather nonsensical suspicion arisen that we regarded the money which had come our way as starting capital for fleeing to the West?

We negotiated an hour's more time so we could wash, get dressed, pack and eat breakfast. I went without the latter, and instead ran out and around the Gedächtniskirche so I could find something to bring back with me for Barbara and our daughter.

Totally exhausted, we sat down opposite Horst Pehnert: it was thanks to him that the film had been officially recognized and submitted to the Berlinale. He congratulated us on the prize (thank God!), but then asked us to understand that we would have to turn over the money for the time being. We would get it back: 60% in East marks – for that's how these things were done, apparently – and 40% in West marks. Although the latter would not be in cash, but on a »valuta entitlement account« which we would be permitted to open. For shopping in a GDR Intershop, we could use so called forum checks. And for private trips in »non-socialist countries«, we would be able to draw the legally permitted daily rate. Although for me, private trips were out of the question; for I had not mentioned my uncles and aunts in the West in my official personal file.

»So you handed over the money«, our team asked us later. And I think it was Volker Koepp who remarked: »You should have said: What money? – Oh, the money from the prize, hic? Well we blew the whole wad that same night with a big crowd who were so pleased about the GDR's success. If only the Minister had ordered us phoned earlier …«

Der Aufenthalt:
Sylvester Groth
(in the middle)

Music Box: Jessica Lange

All quiet on the western front?

1990

Feb. 9th-20th, 1990 (Competition)
Feb. 10th-20th, 1990 (Forum)

A parade of stars at the Brandenburg Gate: Darryl Hannah and Sally Field, Michael Douglas and Oliver Stone – no one wanted to miss the chance of posing in front of Berlin's famous landmark or in front of remnants of the Wall. This year everything in Berlin was different. The sight of a former GDR Politburo chairman giving autographs at the opening reception in the hotel foyer had to be seen to be believed, but this is exactly what Egon Krenz was doing. Was it a farewell? Many guests wondered, especially those from the GDR who were invited to the reception at Bellevue Palace given by Federal President Richard von Weizsäcker, who attempted to calm spirits by remarking that when the commotion about the mark was over, everything would take a turn for the better. Prognoses in a time when everything was changing. »Children, when you write the word GDR, do it reverently, for it will be the last time.« Erika Gregor's words to her staff before the Festival were already a bit closer to reality. And the Berlinale '90 was not just taking place in movie theaters. As Karena Niehoff wrote in the »Süddeutsche Zeitung« on February 22th, 1990, this was primarily due to »that gigantic open-air show which is on everyday, day after day, between the Potsdamer Platz and the Brandenburg Gate: here's looking at you, border guard kid.« Not surprisingly, the fact that it was the Berlinale's fortieth anniversary was not foremost in people's minds: although it too was reason to celebrate.

Political reform processes

Political reform in the GDR was also felt by the Berlinale. The impact events were to have on the planning of the Festival can be seen by briefly recalling the historical developments in 1989 – and relating them to Berlinale interests. As early as February 1989, in a talk with Horst Pehnert, GDR Deputy Minister for Culture and head of the Central Department of Film, Moritz de Hadeln had expressed the desire to present the Competition program of the Film Festival in Berlin (GDR). This was an idea that the first director of the Film Festival, Alfred Bauer, had also persistently pursued. But as in Bauer's time, de Hadeln's suggestion was still utopian in February 1989. Nobody really believed it would happen in the near future. German-German reality was still very different: on February 14th – the Berlinale '89 was just four days into its program – two young construction workers broke through GDR border barriers along the Spree River with a truck, and then swam across to reach the west bank: however, one of the men fleeing was pulled back out of the water by GDR border guards, which the Western powers labeled a »flagrant violation of human rights«.

Mikhail Gorbachev and Helmut Kohl

Whenever West German politicians had visited East German leaders, the question of border traffic and restrictions had been on the agenda. It still was, but GDR politicians recurrently explained that these matters were an internal issue, pertaining to the GDR alone and forbade any kind of interference from West Germany. But then international political developments gained a momentum of their own. In June, Soviet President Mikhail Gorbachev and West German Chancellor Kohl signed a »Joint Declaration«, in which both nations affirmed their determination to work toward overcoming Europe's division. Gorbachev explained at a press conference that the Wall had been erected under special political circumstances, and did not constitute the only obstacle in building a »European house«, he could indeed imagine it being opened, given the right circumstances. Gorbachev's openness to democratization created a new basis for political discussion in the GDR.

Resistance in the GDR

Public unrest in East Germany grew, partially ignited by people's distrust of the last communal election results. The Politburo called these activities acts of provocation. But the civil rights movements did not budge in their criticisms. Opposition to the government was growing, and the wave of those leaving the country swelled. Hungary's Foreign Minister Gyula Horn discussed the flood of East German refugees with his GDR colleague Oskar Fischer at the end of August, when Fischer pointed out that all attempts by East German citizens »to force exit by staying at diplomatic missions (...) are unacceptable«. Only a few days later, the GDR government urged all their citizens attempting to flee via Hungary, CSSR and Poland to return. On the night of September 10th to 11th 1989, the Hungarian government finally allowed several thousand GDR citizens to leave for the Federal Republic of Germany via Austria. In West Berlin, Mayor Momper welcomed Hungary's humanitarian conduct and advocated supporting the growing reform initiatives in the GDR; yet he emphasized that »present exercises in reunification rhetoric« were doing little to promote democratization in the GDR.

Hungary opens its borders

Calls for reforms

Calls for reforms in the GDR – internally and externally – became stronger, and opposition increasingly emphatic. The GDR's massive propaganda and extravagant celebrations for its 40th anniversary between October 5th and 7th were hardly more than a spooky invocation of the past. When asked by reporters about the situation in the GDR, Mikhail Gorbachev, guest of honor at the celebration, replied that he was certain, »that each nation must determine itself what it becomes«. And he added that his German friends were capable »of learning from life and making the appropriate corrections in policy if necessary«. After his meeting with Honecker, spokesman of the Soviet Foreign Ministry Gerassimov stated that Gorbachev had warned his discussion partner that »he who comes too late, is punished by history«.

Meanwhile, cries for freedom were becoming louder: »Gorbi, help us!« Simultaneously, however, the security forces began reacting to the protesters with increas-

CONTE DE PRINTEMPS: Hugues Quester, Eloise Bennet, Florence Darel, Anne Teysèdre

ing brutality. In Leipzig, thousands demonstrated peacefully each week against the GDR government. On October 18th, the Central Committee of the SED dismissed Erich Honecker »at his own request« from all offices and elected Egon Krenz as new Secretary-General.

Erich Honecker and Egon Krenz

Demonstrations continued, and the government leaders cautiously attempted to correct their course, but the civil rights movement persisted in their protests. On November 4th, the largest rally since the end of World War II was held in Berlin. Initiated by East Berlin artists and intellectuals, over a half a million people gathered at the Alexanderplatz and in the neighboring streets. At the SED Central Committee's 10th conference from November 8th to 10th, the Committee – for the first time in its history – resigned en bloc and a new one was formed. On November 9th, SED Politburo member Günter Schabowski announced, almost casually, that the Council of Ministers of the GDR had approved a new travel law, which permitted East German citizens to travel abroad for private reasons without needing to meet specific requirements, and that all border crossings »to the FRG or to Berlin (West)« would be opened. In the course of the evening, people poured into the West from the East. An important step had been taken toward tearing down the Wall and reunifying Germany.

The GDR opens its borders

On November 9th, 1989, in a letter to Horst Pehnert, Moritz de Hadeln renewed his proposal for holding the Film Festival in East Berlin as well, and put his ideas in concrete form. His plans were also backed by the director of the Berlin Festivals Ltd., Ulrich Eckhardt. De Hadeln offered the GDR the opportunity to screen the complete Competition program, and also formulated terms for realizing the event, such as uncomplicated procedures at border crossings for Berlinale guests and staff, and the possibility of free admission to screenings for GDR audiences. »The Berlin International Film Festival was the first cultural event«, de Hadeln wrote to Pehnert, »to achieve an open and constructive cooperation with the GDR, and thus, perhaps

De Hadeln to Pehnert

SKŘIVÁNCI NA NITÍCH: Jaroslav Satoranský, Jitka Zelenohorská (both on the left)

Sally Field, Julia Roberts, Olympia Dukakis

Anlage 1

MORITZ DE HADELN
LEITER DER INTERNATIONALEN
FILMFESTSPIELE BERLIN

BERLINER FESTSPIELE GMBH
BUDAPESTER STRASSE 50
D-1000 BERLIN 30
TELEFON (030) 254 89 225

Herrn Horst Pehnert
Stellvertretender Minister für Kultur
Vorsitzender der Hauptverwaltung Film der DDR

Berlin (West), den 09. November 1989

Sehr geehrter Herr Minister,
Lieber Herr Pehnert,

bei den Internationalen Filmfestspielen Berlin 1989 hatte ich Ihnen in einem persönlichen Gespräch spontan und ohne vorherige Rücksprache mit anderen den Vorschlag gemacht, das offizielle Programm der Filmfestspiele in Berlin (Ost) ganz aktuell, ja fast zeitgleich, zu wiederholen. Ihre Reaktion darauf hinterließ bei mir den Eindruck, daß Sie von der Idee sehr angetan waren, mir aber antworteten, daß wir beide diesen Moment mit großer Wahrscheinlichkeit nicht mehr erleben würden.

Die Entwicklung nimmt jedoch manchmal einen schnelleren Lauf als man sich vorstellen kann. Deshalb erlaube ich mir, Ihnen diesen Vorschlag jetzt noch einmal in einer präziseren Form zu unterbreiten. Bisher habe ich nur meine engsten Mitarbeiter bezüglich dieser Initiative ins Vertrauen gezogen. Sollten Sie diesem Projekt zustimmen, bin ich zuversichtlich, daß ich bei allen Beteiligten volle Unterstützung finde.

Die Internationalen Filmfestspiele Berlin sind die erste kulturelle Veranstaltung, die eine offene und konstruktive Zusammenarbeit mit der DDR realisiert hat, und sie sind vielleicht gerade deshalb in der Lage, diesen neuen Schritt gemeinsam mit der DDR zu tun.

Falls Sie diesem Vorschlag zustimmen, könnte ich Ihnen das vollständige offizielle Programm der Berlinale (Wettbewerbsfilme und Filme, die außer Konkurrenz im Zoo-Palast laufen) mit je einer Vorführung anbieten. Um dieses Projekt erfolgreich durchführen zu können, müßten folgende Punkte in Erwägung gezogen werden:

- Ein möglichst zentral gelegenes geeignetes Großkino mit der notwendigen technischen Einrichtung sollte zur Verfügung stehen. Es ist unser Wunsch, daß, wie bei allen anderen Vorführungen der Filmfestspiele, die entsprechende Werbung und Öffentlichkeit ermöglicht werden.

- Das Zoo-Palast-Programm (Spiel- und Kurzfilme) sollte komplett, seiner Programmstruktur entsprechend, wiederholt werden.

- Die praktische Durchführung dieses Projektes bedarf einer unkomplizierten Regelung bezüglich der Teilnahme von beauftragten Mitarbeitern der Internationalen Filmfestspiele Berlin.

./2

Letter from Moritz de Hadeln to Horst Pehnert

Julia Roberts, Sally Field

-2-

- Es sollte des weiteren gewährleistet sein, daß alle mit den Filmen verbundenen Personen, wie Regisseure, Verleiher, Produzenten, Schauspieler etc., die Gelegenheit haben, der Vorführung ihres Films beizuwohnen.

Falls Sie uns Ihre Zustimmung bis spätestens Anfang Januar geben, könnte ich Ihnen zusichern, alle notwendigen Genehmigungen seitens der Rechteinhaber, wie auch der FIAPF (Fédération Internationale des Associations de Producteurs de Films) einzuholen.

Die IFB würden alle mit diesem Projekt verbundenen Kosten tragen.

Da die Filmfestspiele strengen Regeln hinsichtlich des Copyrights unterliegen, die unter anderem von der FIAPF kontrolliert werden, gehe ich davon aus, daß man auch seitens der DDR Sorge tragen wird, daß diese Regeln respektiert werden.

Diese Idee ist seinerzeit spontan entstanden und es wäre bedauerlich, den besonderen Anlaß des 40. Jubiläums der Filmfestspiele nicht für dieses Projekt zu nutzen, weil wir glauben, ein Angebot an Filmen zu haben, das auch für die Bürger der DDR von Interesse sein wird.

Ich wäre Ihnen dankbar, wenn Sie unter anderem auch den Verband der Filmschaffenden der DDR über den Inhalt dieses Briefes informieren würden.

Ich hoffe, daß trotz der relativ kurzen Zeit eine positive Entscheidung erreicht werden kann. Selbstverständlich stehe ich Ihnen jederzeit für technische oder inhaltliche Fragen zur Verfügung und freue mich schon jetzt auf ein persönliches Gespräch in Leipzig.

Mit freundlichen Grüßen

Moritz de Hadeln

for exactly this reason, it is now in the position to take this new step together with the GDR«.

Meeting in Leipzig

At the opening of the Documentary Film Week in Leipzig on November 24th, de Hadeln met for exploratory talks with Horst Pehnert and the new Minister for Culture of the GDR, Dr. Dietmar Keller. They both expressed interest in his offer. Two days later – still in Leipzig – talks were held between Moritz and Erika de Hadeln, Horst Pehnert, his deputy Dr. Eberhard Ugowski as well as the official in charge of international relations from the GDR Central Department of Film. Proceeding from the assumption that the GDR would decide in favor of the proposal, the Kosmos movie theater was mooted as a possible venue. The problem of consent from the FIAPF was given particular consideration, as according to their regulations for film festivals »within the framework or on occasion of a festival, no film from any festival section at festivals with non-specialized competition sectors may be shown in more than a total of four screenings and only within the city district or city in which the festival is being held and during the festival's official dates.« (§ 15 of the FIAPF regulations) All parties present agreed that Berlin (West) and Berlin (GDR) were parts of the same city. They also discussed the collaboration of the Film Festival and the Association of Television and Filmmakers in the GDR with respect to accreditation.

On November 28th, de Hadeln informed Mayor Walter Momper of his activities in a letter, and asked him to discuss with the federal government if it would cover the additional financial burden which would result from such a cooperation, for »at this historic moment, it would be difficult for people to understand that controversies between the Federal Government and the Land of Berlin might result in Berlin not being able to meet these new expectations properly«. Yet talks between the Festival and GDR representatives had long since taken on a momentum of their own; the process initiated for cooperation was for the moment ahead of all politico-cultural considerations.

Nastassja Kinski

Volker Schlöndorff

Jean-Luc Godard

Isabelle Huppert

Berlinale in Berlin (GDR)

Finally on December 4th, the East German authorities gave their consent by phone to screen Berlinale films in Berlin (GDR). Written confirmation from Horst Pehnert was to follow. On the same day, the Festival director and the two organizers of the Children's Film Festival, Renate Zylla and Martina Hey, met with Beate Hansbach, director of the Children's and Youth Film Center of the GDR, and agreed to repeat the Children's Film Festival's program in the eastern part of the city as well. One day later, de Hadeln flew to Prague. On the next day, December 6th, the GDR negotiators announced that their joint project would be announced in »Neues Deutschland« on the following day. Word had it that news of the cooperation had already been reported in the »Daily Variety« in Los Angeles. Moritz de Hadeln, on his flight home, ran into West Berlin Mayor Walter Momper at Frankfurt Airport, and informed him of the GDR's decision and the forthcoming press release, which would be made before written confirmation had been received from the GDR Ministry of Culture. Back in Berlin, de Hadeln negotiated with GDR officials on the wording of a joint press statement which was to be released simultaneously by both sides. On December 7th, de Hadeln informed Senator for Cultural Affairs Dr. Anke Martiny of the course which negotiations were taking. On the same day, the announcement of cooperation between the Film Festival and the GDR was published in the daily papers in both parts of the city. In talks between Anke Martiny and Dietmar Keller on December 8th, at which general questions of cooperation were discussed, the decision to show the films of the 40th Berlin International Film Festival for the first time in East Berlin was commended and substantiated. The International Forum of Young Cinema – as could be concluded from the papers that day – would also show parts of its program in East Berlin. The negotiations which Ulrich Gregor had meanwhile held with GDR partners had also been crowned with success.

In a letter from December 12th to the members of the board of trustees of the Berlin Festivals Ltd., director Ulrich Eckhardt requested the board's official approval

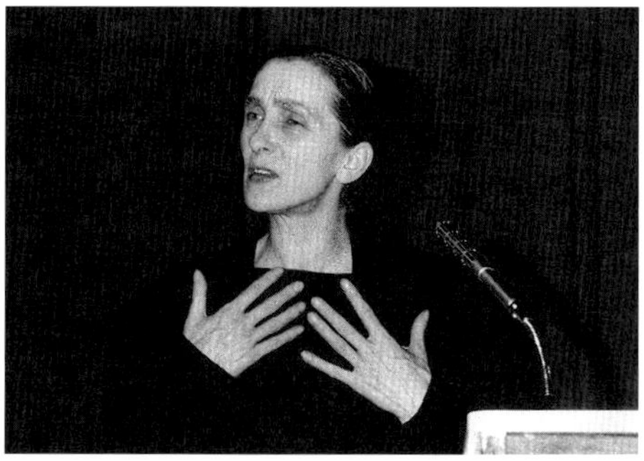

Wim and Lia van Leer

Michael Snow

Pina Bausch

Jürgen Böttcher,
Naum Kleiman

Senator for Cultural Affairs Anke Martiny and Ulrich Eckhardt, director of the Berlin Festivals Ltd.

for these plans. He also subtly pointed out the greater financial expenses that would result from this decision – a wise move, as de Hadeln's efforts in this direction had not been a numerical success. Eckhardt wrote that the Film Festival was »the first large cultural event in Berlin« to be faced with problems that »emerged unexpectedly after the opening of the border and for which we were unprepared«. He himself was »whole-heartedly in favor of Mr. de Hadeln's ideas, also shared by Mr. Gregor«. Hard work set in on a daily basis. Meetings, phone calls, telexes – the West and the East at one table. History, and Festival history, was being made.

Joint talks

The number of factors which needed to be considered at the eight meetings which de Hadeln and his team held with GDR representatives – headed by Rainer Otto from the Ministry of Culture and Bernd Rüdiger Mann from the District Film Direction Berlin – can hardly be described for the profusion of details. But the very fact that a Film Festival accreditation card was to be recognized as a valid document for crossing the border to Berlin (GDR), and there would be no so-called transit card or mandatory currency exchange was indicative of the difficult and touchy political terrain with which the parties were dealing and which was ultimately successfully negotiated. Bureaucratic and organizational obstacles had to be surmounted; moreover decisions were delayed by the GDR's need to reclarify responsibilities. GDR officials also confessed that they had initially not reckoned with questions concerning border-crossing being solved before the new passport laws were passed. An agreement was reached that the entire Competition program, all Children's Film Festival films and parts of the Panorama program would be repeated in the Kosmos and Colosseum movie theaters. Parallel to this, in negotiations with the GDR National Film Archives and its director Wolfgang Klaue, the Forum arranged for a large portion of its program to be rerun at the International movie theater. All these cinemas would be made available to the Berlinale without charge and the District Film Direction Berlin would also cover the costs for advertising in the east of the city. In return, the proceeds from the respective screenings would go to the District Film Direction. The proceeds from advance ticket sales for all screenings not repeated in Berlin (GDR) would be transferred to an extra »foreigner currency account« opened for this purpose at the East German National Bank. The account had to be applied for from the Ministry of Finance, and would be placed at the disposal of Berlin Festivals Ltd. for future projects. Permission to transport film prints and advertising material at no cost was attained from both the GDR and the FRG customs authorities. The diplomatic lane at the checkpoint at Invalidenstraße was opened for Berlinale guests. And not least, questions of postal sovereignty had to be solved so that Film Festival staff would be able to use six portable radio telephones on GDR terrritory. Filmmaker Ula Stöckl, as representative of the Berlinale, was put in charge of Festival events in the east of the city. A multitude of organizational details had to be considered. For example, a representative framework was required for international guests at the Kosmos. A red carpet was to be unrolled – like at the Zoo Palast. But where could one get such a carpet? Then the Berlinale's GDR partners hit upon the idea of using the red carpet kept at Schönefeld Airport for greeting official visitors to East Germany. And – in a flash – it was rolled out in front of the Kosmos movie theater.

Agreements

A bad start

Now nothing stood in the way of a happy and successful Berlinale jubilee. The fact that it got off to a bad start and the American opening film STEEL MAGNOLIAS did not go over well with the audience and critics was seen simply as »artistic mis-

Born on the 4th of July:
Tom Cruise

fortune«. In the run-up to the Festival, there had been grumblings of disagreement in the advisory selection committee. Filmmaker Helma Sanders-Brahms had even publicly announced her resignation from her advisory position and complained that Hollywood's dominance in the Festival program was constantly growing. In an interview with the Italian paper »Corriere della Sera«, which, as a member of the selection committee, she should not have authorized for publication, she stated her criticisms: she deplored the »insipid compromises« and questioned the opening film. Above all, she expressed her regret that the Berlinale was not responding adequately to the events of November '89. This was disputable, since films from the GDR as well as from the other East European countries were strongly represented in all sections of the program.

Banned GDR films

In the Forum, seven films were participating from the GDR, the so-called »shelved films«, forbidden since 1965/66, films by Kurt Maetzig, Frank Vogel, Gerhard Klein, Günther Stahnke, Herrmann Zschoche, Jürgen Böttcher and Egon Günther. In the Competition, Frank Beyer's film SPUR DER STEINE (»Traces of Stones«), also a film banned in the GDR, ran hors concours. As official GDR entry, the Competition screened Heiner Carow's film COMING OUT, and the Forum presented numerous documentaries about autumn '89. Yet, thematically, the Russian contributions were the most explosive. Aleksandr Rogozhkin's austere documentary parable KARAUL (»The Guard«) in the Competition, for example, revealed the nightmarish conditions in the Russian army: the story of a soldier, who in his indignation and anger at the injustice of the hierarchical system shoots six of his comrades; a true story. How Russian directors dealt with the crushing realities in their country, which aesthetic forms they adapted, which traditions of narrative techniques they continued or broke with, was impressively illustrated by these diverse films. Sergei Ovcharov's film ONO (»It«) is an ironic take on everyday life in Russia; Valeri Ogorodnikov, in his film BUMAZHNYE GLAZA PRISHVINA (»Prishvin's Paper Eyes«), develops a phantasmagoria

Russian presence

DAS SCHRECKLICHE MÄDCHEN: Lena Stolze

of fiction and historical reality, while Sergei Bodrov uses moving, rigorous but pragmatic images to show a son visiting his father in prison in his film S. E. R. – SVOBODA ETO RAI (»Freedom's Paradise«). All these films ran in the Forum. Many considered Kira Muratova's film ASTENICHESKIJ SINDROM (»The Asthenic Syndrome«/ »The Weakness Syndrome«), which was shown in the Competition, the most outstanding of these powerful cinematographic films from the former Soviet Union: the film depicts »a sarcastic and depressing picture of Soviet society, in which spongers, rank outsiders, boozers and slackers are locked up together like mangy dogs in the cage of their no future«. (Ruprecht Skasa-Weiß, Stuttgarter Zeitung, Feb. 21, 1990) Films from Poland, from Czechoslovakia and Hungary completed this panorama from Eastern Europe. They took stock of societies in upheaval, radical and uncertain in form, but alive in their images and insistently close to the present. To the shrewd observer it was possible to see how the Berlinale had compellingly fulfilled its commitment in the different sections as a showcase for the East.

Fragile social relationships from France and Spain

For the most part, West European cinema presented stylized depictions of fragile social relationships, such as those in Jacques Doillon's filmic battle of words between Isabelle Huppert and Béatrice Dalle LA VENGEANCE D'UNE FEMME (»A Woman's Revenge«), or in Pedro Almodóvar's Spanish entry ATAME! (»Tie Me Up! Tie Me Down!«), a quick look at an erotic obsession featuring Victoria Abril and Antonio Banderas. But the presence of films from the West remained remarkably diffuse and unreal, perhaps partly because of the political circumstances that outweighed everything else, and the keen perception of the East.

America at the Berlinale

From America, there were new films by Danny DeVito (THE WAR OF THE ROSES), Roland Joffe (SHADOW MAKERS), Bruce Beresford (DRIVING MISS DAISY), Woody Allen (CRIMES AND MISDEMEANORS) and Oliver Stone (BORN ON THE 4TH OF JULY), all big major productions but none truly sensational. Even the political explosiveness of Oliver Stone's film was relativized against the backdrop of daily political events, at this point in time it was just

SPUR DER STEINE: Manfred Krug, Eberhard Esche

history. For most observers, this year's most interesting American films at the Festival were Gus van Sant's story of a junkie (DRUGSTORE COWBOY) in the Forum, and Kathryn Bigelow's controversially brutal BLUE STEEL in the Panorama, »a whodunit in which a monster film lurks, and the worst thing about the monsters in it is that they not only look exactly like us but are exactly like you and me«. (Claudius Seidl, Süddeutsche Zeitung, Feb. 14, 1990)

Golden Bears

The International Jury decided to award the Golden Bear ex aequo to Jiří Menzel's poetic-anarchistic SKŘIVÁNCI NA NITÍCH (»Larks on a String«) from 1969, a film which had also been banned for years, and to Costa-Gavras' political fable MUSIC BOX. A decision balanced between the East and West, which some called wise, while others would have preferred to see Menzel's Czech film win the award alone. And so applause was divided somewhat unequally at the award ceremony: intense for Menzel and rather reserved for Costa-Gavras. This Jury seemed to have a tendency to seek balanced decisions, also awarding two Silver Bears to two German films, one for Heiner Carow's GDR entry COMING OUT, and one – for best director – to Michael Verhoeven for his FRG film DAS SCHRECKLICHE MÄDCHEN (»The Nasty Girl«). A special prize, also a Golden Bear, was awarded by Moritz de Hadeln for Oliver Stone's film to Ron Kovic, the author of the film and a war invalid confined to a wheelchair. This was a surprise, and seemed to contradict the Jury's decision, as was noted by some journalists, encouraging speculations that it had only been possible to show the film in Berlin because it had been promised an award in advance. While in fact the award was meant as a token of a festival director's esteem for a filmmaker who had given his most important films to the Berlin Film Festival over the years. »De Hadeln must go« was the headline in the »tageszeitung« on February 21st, and this polemic title was explained by the strong presence of the Americans. But the assertion – in this rather meager film year – that this had been a determining factor for selection did not hold up if one looked at the entire program. Rather, the

LENINGRAD COWBOYS GO AMERICA by Aki Kaurismäki (in the Forum)

Competition lacked a strong West European counterweight, and this impression could not be dispelled by the disparate and abundant program offered by the Panorama.

Experiences and disappointments

It had been a year of new experiences. Especially surprising were the disappointingly small crowds attending screenings in the east of the city. Above all, it was noted, the American films had done well, while films from Eastern Europe had attracted far fewer viewers. Over 38 000 moviegoers were counted at the Berlinale screenings in the east of the city, approximately half of them went to Competition films at the Kosmos; the Forum registered 10 000 visitors; the Panorama recorded about 5200; and another 3400 saw the films repeated from the Children's Film Festival's program. GDR citizens clearly had other worries. Daily political events still held them captive, and there were more urgent everyday issues than catching a glimpse of the glamorous or not so glamorous movie world which had so suddenly and openly presented itself.

And so ultimately, the Festival management was able to review the events critically but positively: politically, time had been taken by the forelock and the Berlinale's 40th anniversary had come out ahead. Finally, the Festival had outlived its usefulness as an instrument of the Cold War. Now people nourished new hopes. For example, at talks held after the Berlinale, Rainer Otto advised against using the Palast der Republik as a venue for future joint events, as was de Hadeln's wish. Instead, he proposed erecting a new festival center near the Friedrichstraße, which he envisaged completed in time for the 100th anniversary of film in 1995. These were grand ideas that were not, however, to be become reality. First other questions had to be answered. Unresolved, for instance, was the presence of the Retrospective program in the east of the city. True, Hans Helmut Prinzler, director of the Stiftung Deutsche Kinemathek, had discussed prospects for cooperation with representatives of the GDR National Film Archives, but there had been discord with the Festival director, who expressed organizational qualms, which ultimately caused the project to fail.

Questions open

Tulitikkutehtaan tyttö: Kati Outinen in the middle (in the Forum)

Erika and Moritz de Hadeln

Erika de Hadeln, director of the Lyon Documentary Film Festival and co-responsible for selecting French films for the Competition in Berlin, is honored at a parallel event with the »Chevalier dans L'Ordre des arts et lettres de la République Française«.

And then, when Manfred Lichtenstein sent a telex on January 31st 1990 on behalf of the National Film Archive to Moritz de Hadeln in which he remonstrated – in a very forceful tone – that nothing from the program of the Retrospective should be presented »on GDR territory«, a new ice age began. De Hadeln could hardly do otherwise than to »object quite energetically (...) to this astonishing protest and especially the tone«; although he went on to suggest repeating the Retrospectives in the east of the city in the future. (Telex de Hadeln to Lichtenstein, Feb. 2, 1990)

Issues concerning the mutual future of the two Germanies were also affected by these talks. Wolfgang Klaue, director of the GDR National Film Archives, wrote to Ulrich Gregor in a letter dated February 26th: »The Berlinale is over, we have returned to our daily routines. Nevertheless, we do not want just to check this off as merely another program item, for we believe it can, indeed, be counted as good and useful experience. A cooperation of new dimensions has been initiated by the screenings of the International Forum of Young Cinema in our part of the city.« And although this was directly addressed to the Forum, this résumé can be seen to apply to the entire 1990 Berlinale. Just the same, the statement had a subtext which reflected substantial political sensibilities. Indeed, both sides, the Berlinale management and its GDR partner as well as the politicians were proceeding from the same assumption: there would continue to be two Germanies. »All in all, I think our venture has been worth the effort«, Klaue added, »we even had fun, and from our point of view it is viable and worth developing further, despite the many uncertainties inherent in the rapidity of external developments«. Yet outside, the so-called »Wallpeckers« were hammering away. Never again would there be new films from the GDR. The jubilee had turned out to be a farewell, too.

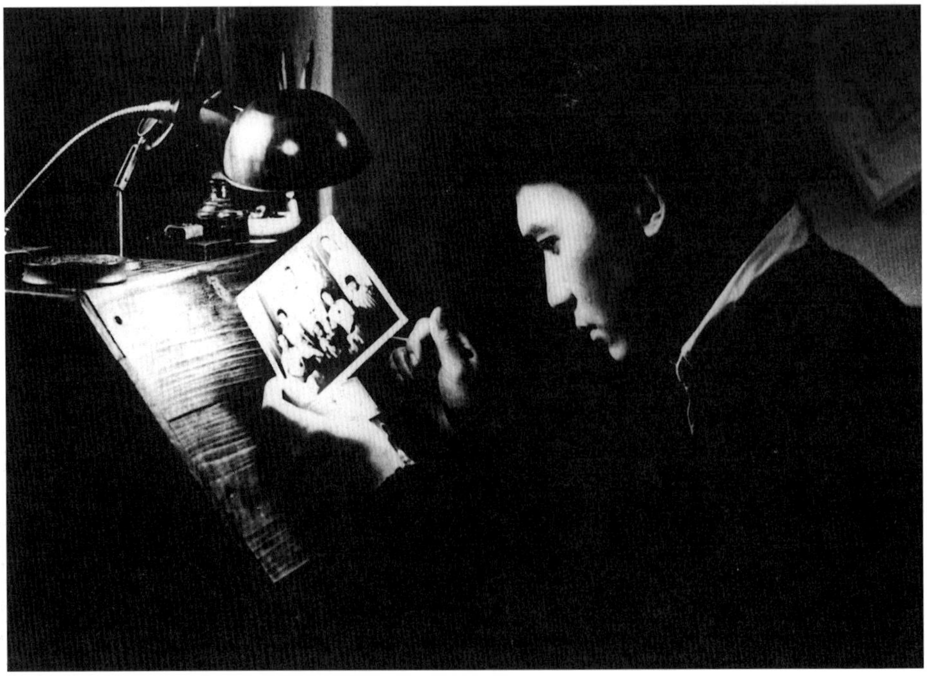

Beiqing chengshi
by Hou Hsia-hsien
(in the Forum)

International Jury
Michael Ballhaus (FRG, president)
Margaret Menegoz (France, vice-president)
Vadim Abdrashitov (USSR)
Suzana Amaral (Brazil)
Steven Bach (USA)
Roberto Benigni (Italy)
Livia Gyarmathy (Hungary)
Helke Misselwitz (GDR)
Otto Sander (FRG)
Stephen Silverman (USA)
Rita Tushingham (Great Britain)

The Awards of the International Jury

Feature Films
Grand Prix of the 40th IFB
Golden Berlin Bear
Music Box
USA
directed by Costa-Gavras
ex aequo
Skřivánci na nitích
CSSR
directed by Jiří Menzel

Silver Berlin Bear
Special Prize of the Jury
Astenicheskij sindrom
USSR
directed by Kira Muratova

Silver Berlin Bear
for the best director
Michael Verhoeven
Das schreckliche Mädchen
FRG

Silver Berlin Bear
for the best joint dramatic performance
Jessica Tandy and Morgan Freeman
in Driving Miss Daisy
USA

Crimes and Misdemeanors by Woody Allen (in the Competition): Martin Landau

Silver Berlin Bear
for the best individual
achievement as an actor
Iain Glen
in SILENT SCREAM
Great Britain

Silver Berlin Bear
for an outstanding individual
achievement
Xie Fei
BEN MIN NIAM
People's Republic of China

Silver Berlin Bear
for dealing sensitively with
the dilemma in which
minorities – all minorities –
find themselves and for
bringing to expression a
profound regard for human
rights, humanity and
tolerance
COMING OUT
GDR
directed by Heiner Carow

Alfred Bauer Prize
KARAUL
USSR
directed by Aleksandr
Rogozhkin

Short Films
Golden Berlin Bear
MISTERTAO
Italy
directed by Bruno Bozzetto

Silver Berlin Bear
ILHA DAS FLORES
Brazil
directed by Jorge Furtado

Special Mentions
KOROVA
USSR
directed by Aleksandr
Petrov

TMA, SVĚTLO, TMA
CSSR
directed by Jan Švankmajer

DIE PANNE
GDR
directed by Klaus Georgi,
Lutz Stützner

ATAME!: Victoria Abril

Berlinale: what next?

1991

Feb. 15th-26th, 1991
(Competition)
Feb. 16th-26th, 1991
(Forum)

Hopes were high for the Berlinale in the first year after Germany's reunification. Would the Festival be able to reclaim its former position as pivotal point between the East and West? Would it have the innovative strength to extend the dialogue with Eastern Europe as well as to instill this dialogue with new life? Many critics believed that the Berlinale's claim to be the cultural mediator between the political blocs had primarily been mere assertion.

Hopes and expectations

The Festival's two directors, Moritz de Hadeln and Ulrich Gregor, were aware that politicians, the press and the public had high expectations; they also realized that structures for altering the profile of the Berlinale had to be reconsidered – and that such a process of change would not occur without irritations and opposition. Questions had arisen about the future, and answers were being worked on. Amongst the organizers there was a general feeling of breaking new ground. Demands and projections that had caught on and stimulated expectations and ideas after the last Berlinale now had to hold up in face of unanticipated realities. Confronted with the disillusioning austerity of daily life, the initial euphoria had died down. The news had been bringing alarming reports from the Middle East during the first two weeks of 1991, and on January 16th, two days after the selection process for the Competition had been completed, the Gulf War broke out. Immediately people began speculating whether the Film Festival would be affected by the military conflict and these international political events, especially after the ceremony for the Bavarian Film Awards and other cultural film events were canceled. Rumor had it that the festivals in Cannes and Venice would not be held. American and Israeli commentators advocated canceling the Berlinale. In Berlin, the decision of whether it was acceptable to hold a festival in view of the war was not taken lightly. What if it were to escalate, and ground troops were to be sent into Kuwait, as political observers were predicting? It might even occur during the Berlinale (which is exactly what did happen, on February 24th, two days before the Festival was over). Karena Niehoff, for years a politically astute and critical observer of the Festival, wrote in the »Süddeutsche Zeitung« that »the moment is not one for decorum but truth, a truth which officially, of course, wide-eyed functionaries do not want to examine as it would make all their cool pros and cons fall out of their mouths like rotten teeth; the moment of truth would be this: a poisonous gas attack on Israel. Tears and anger of hate and pain would then, indeed, spoil more in this country than just the Berlinale.« (Feb. 15, 1991)

The outbreak of the Gulf War

Cancellation – pros and cons

In the end, the opinion prevailed that the Film Festival should not be canceled, despite the critical situation: preparations for the program were too advanced and too many participants had already been notified. Politicians in the city backed the Festival organizers' decision. In the run-up, there were some cancellations: guests, primarily from Japan and the USA, decided at short notice not to participate (for instance, Robert Mitchum, to whom the Homage was dedicated along with Jane Russell, did not come to Berlin). A planned conference of the FIAPF, the International Federation of Producers' Associations, could not be held, and Israel withdrew its stand from the CineCenter. Nevertheless, at 8342, the number of accredited participants reached an all-time high, and amongst these were also journalists from Israel as well as Yoram Golan, director of the Israeli film center. The general internal situation certainly seemed to speak in favor of holding the Festival.

Protests and security precautions

Within the context of these tensions, between political reality and cultural efforts, the 41st International Film Festival finally opened on February 15th, 1991. Security precautions were – perceptibly and imperceptibly – intensified; a private service hired by the Festival was to support the provisions made by the police (although not in all instances successfully). Demonstrators gathered in front of the Zoo Palast movie theater in protest against the Gulf War, carrying posters with the American and Iraqi flags, and performing provocative acts such as carrying the »dead« off on biers, wiping up »pools of blood«, or sarcastically demanding a Golden Berlin Bear for CNN. And only a few meters away, other Berliners protested loudly against a speed limit on the Avus Expressway. Mayor Eberhard Diepgen asked the opening-night audience to rise for a minute of silence in memory of those who had died in the Gulf War. Volker Schlöndorff, as president of the International Jury, vigilantly and with an awareness for the paradoxical nature of the situation, introduced his colleagues as a »rather nameless war jury«, who could also be viewed as »soldiers in action«. Not all guests understood his bitter undertone as they might have.

The Festival's central focus was European cinema, and its presence was felt more strongly in all sections of the Berlinale than it had been in ages. Particularly French and Italian films determined the Festival's program, and the fact that Italy had four films in the Competition surprised many.

Difficulties in selecting Eastern Europe films

Selecting Eastern European films had been problematic. For instance, there had only been one Polish film available that the Festival would have wanted for the

Satana by Viktor Aristov (in the Competition)

Competition. But this film was suddenly considered a favorite for Cannes and in the end, it was shown in their »Un certain regard« section: a first sign of warning for Berlinale organizers that now that the Iron Curtain was gone, rivalry between their festival and those in Cannes and Venice was growing. Berlin's position as the traditional venue for films from Eastern Europe was no longer uncontested. Consequently, only a Slovakian film was included in the Competition program, Dušan Trančík's KED HVIEDZDY BOLI CERVENE (»When the Stars Were Still Red«). Incidentally, this was the first film financed by the special fund established by French Minister of Cultural Affairs Jack Lang for saving and promoting Eastern European cinema. And although selecting films was extraordinarily difficult in the Soviet Union – due to economic and administrative restructuring and, above all, the decentralization of film production – it was at least possible to invite one film to the Competition, Viktor Aristov's SATANA (»Satan«). Yet here, too, the choice was accompanied by unfortunate incidents. At the last moment, films that had already been promised to the Panorama were retracted by their American co-producers. One of these was PUTESESTUL TOVARISCASTA STALINA V AFRIKU (»Comrade Stalin Goes to Africa«) by Georgian director Irakli Kvirikadze, a blend of private footage of Stalin and dramatic reconstructions with his doubles.

Just the same, in both the Panorama and the International Forum of Young Cinema, there was ultimately a considerable number of feature and documentary films from Eastern Europe that examined their countries' histories critically, adjusting to the new situation with an astonishing range of filmic vocabularies. For example, Miklós Jancsó's viciously satirical and labyrinthine film ISTEN HÁTRAFELÉ MEGY (»God Walks Backwards«) caused quite a sensation in the Panorama thanks to one scene: communists and nationalists are seen excitedly debating controversial matters when they are interrupted and told that Gorbachev has just been executed as an enemy of the people. In the Forum, there was Aleksandr Sokurov's personal and poetic study of death KRUG VTOROY (»The Second Circle«) and the Polish entry GLUCHY TELEFON (»Crossed Lines«) by Piotr Mikucki, first attempts to develop a new post-communist cinematic language. Especially a retrospective of Rumanian documentaries from 1898 to 1990 attracted particular attention, for however different the individual films from over ninety years were, they all evoked the feeling »that Ceaucescu's 25 year-long ›golden époque‹ was the angle of view of even those films made long before his rise to power«, as Dieter Bertz wrote. »In view of the later personality cult, even the group of silent films from the twenties, mostly short reports about royal pomp and splendor, seem like a prologue to the vain filmic showmanship of the Ceaucescu clan. The absence of a middle-class democratic tradition as well as the sharp contrast between those ruling and ordinary citizens may explain the self-affirmation of power immortalized on celluloid such as exists throughout the entire program.« (Freitag, March 29, 1991)

Rumanian documentaries

The German films participating in the Festival were rather unconvincing. A new film by Wim Wenders had not been finished in time, and Werner Schroeter's MALINA was released in movie theaters right before the Festival: the producers had displayed no interest in changing their distribution arrangements in favor of the Berlinale. Franz Seitz' Competition entry ERFOLG (»Success«), an adaptation of the novel of the same name by Lion Feuchtwanger was certainly brilliantly cast, but turned out to be another example of narrative cinema past its prime. The film had been hotly debated in the selection commission, as was also the case with Roland Gräf's Compe-

History in Germany

Die Mauer by Jürgen Böttcher (in the Forum)

tition entry Der Tangospieler (»The Tango Player«). This film is based on a story by Christoph Hein and is set in the GDR in 1968: a man tells the story of his life, which has oscillated between adaptation and resignation. Seitz' film, on the other hand, tends toward the picturesque despite being set against the background of rising National Socialism in Germany. It does little more than nostalgically depict historical fact. In contrast, Gräf recounts his tale with a »soft irony that consistently just scrapes by along the edge of desperation«, as Michael Althen wrote in the »Süddeutsche Zeitung,« and although Gräf's »coming to grips with the past« does not work by his »acting like a know-it-all but by remembering with precision«, the impression persists that »his images rarely go beyond television format« (Feb. 22, 1991).

The German-German unification found stronger expression in the Forum films. In the »Süddeutsche Zeitung« (Feb. 16, 1991), Klaus Dermutz entitled the program's focus »Ceremonies of Parting«. It was true that this series – which included films by Jürgen Böttcher (Die Mauer/»The Wall«), Andreas Voigt (Letztes Jahr Titanic/»Last Year Titanic«), Sibylle Schoenemann (Verriegelte Zeit/»Locked-up Time«), Lew Hohlmann, Joachim Tschirner and Klaus Salge (Ein schmales Stück Deutschland/»A Narrow Piece of Germany«), Lily Grote and Ulrike Herdin (Berlin – Bahnhof Friedrichstrasse/»Berlin – Friedrichstrasse Station«), Marcel Ophuls (November Days) and Ulrike Ottinger (Countdown) – resembled a farewell to the GDR as a film nation. In some ways it represented a secretly nostalgic retrospection, while in others it involved sharp analyses of a country paralyzed before its downfall. These films were searching for clues, especially Jürgen Böttcher's tightly-knit impressions of when the Wall fell and the period afterwards: pessimistic images that fused into a document of the times. He ironically cuts back and forth from the overwhelming joy in the center of town on New Year's Eve 1989 to later observations on the ensuing commercial and tourist boom as well as historical reflections. Ulrike Ottinger's film, on the other hand, documents the last ten days be-

Jürgen Böttcher and Ulrike Ottinger

COUNTDOWN by Ulrike Ottinger (in the Forum)

fore the monetary union, a film which not only takes an exact and compelling look, but also listens. According to Karsten Witte, »COUNTDOWN takes stock not so much of the gaps in the Wall but of those in our awareness of history. This is a journey into a lost past, beginning at the Einstein tower in Potsdam, built by architect Mendelsohn, which moves on and invites us to linger at the Jewish cemetery in Weißensee, as if the signs that would lead to the countdown in our historical awareness were already readable there. This seemingly silent film – which in fact makes intense use of sounds from the streets and the surroundings, the camera aimed mostly at moving cars, boats and cable cars – counts down those ten days before the monetary union in June 1990.« (Frankfurter Rundschau, March 7, 1991)

A European focus

Not all the critics were happy with the Festival's focus on Europe, especially in the Competition. Claude Berri's opening film URANUS, about French collaboration with the German occupying forces, considered by many a well-intended but ponderous film, was described by Volker Baer in »Der Tagesspiegel« (Feb. 16, 1991) as »an actors' film on the one hand, a melancholy yet also rather gentle view of the times on the other, in any case too gentle in its dealings with all those who went along with everything«. THE MIRACLE, an Irish-British co-production by Neil Jordan, attracted more attention. This was the moving account – spun like a fairy-tale and staged with great visual wit – of two adolescents who uncover a secret. Simon Callow's wicked BALLAD OF THE SAD CAFE was also well-received. Aki Kaurismäki's I HIRED A CONTRACT KILLER ran in the Forum and aroused particular interest: it had not been submitted to the Competition – the director's decision and one that was to hold for all his films. Overlooked by both the public and critics was the Greek entry for the Competition ISICHES MERES TOU AVGOUSTOU (»Quiet Days of August«) by Pantelis Voulgaris, a panorama of small stories, isolated encounters in the hot days and nights of a summer, lyrically dense and with a wistful undertone. Once more, it became evident that intimate films in the Competition were easily overlooked in the com-

Francis Ford Coppola

Marco Ferreri

Bruce Beresford

Anthony Hopkins

motion of the Festival, especially if they were from a more minor film nation. Films screened in the Forum or Panorama were later often treated as if they would have belonged in the Competition; whereas interest in quiet, unspectacular but cinematically stimulating films in the Competition was fading.

Mexican feature films

Given these circumstances, the success of CABEZA DE VACA, Mexican director Nicolás Echevarría's debut film, was all the more gratifying. It follows the fate of a Spanish conquistador stranded in Florida in the 16th century, who survives by working as a shaman's apprentice: »In the historical figure of the Spaniard, an ethnologist avant la lettre, the film reveals a rare deviation from the prototype of the modern individual. A person, all on his own, at the limits of existence and the known world, where all commitment to obey the Crown dissolves. This film portrays the basic figure of an individual attempting to reestablish order in a world once guaranteed by God and his earthly representatives, the feudal powers of the church and the state.« (Peter Körte, Frankfurter Rundschau, Feb. 25, 1991) The shock suffered when two cultural identities clash, mystically inspired reason and shamanism, was also the topic of other Mexican films running in a special series in the Forum.

Erika de Hadeln and Beki Probst, director of the European Film Market

The different sections of the Festival were shrewdly linked in this year's program: the Swedish feature film in the Competition GOD AFTON, HERR WALLENBERG (»Good Evening, Mr. Wallenberg«) by Kjell Grede (about the fate of the Swedish diplomat who saved thousands of Jews from Nazi persecutors in Hungary) corresponded well with the Russian documentary in the Panorama MISSIJA RAOULJA WALLENBERG (»Raul Wallenberg's Mission«) by Alexander Rodnyansky. Asian, and especially Chinese cinema was represented in the Festival by a variety of films; in the Forum, for instance, by a series of Hong Kong productions by King Hu, Tsui Hark and others: in the »Süddeutsche Zeitung«, Fritz Göttler raved about »a furious burst of sword and karate fights in which bodies not only dance but fly«, and went on to state: »Here too we have experimental cinema that flaunts its special effects,

Sion Sono

Maggie Cheung

Peter Cohen

Jean-Pierre Léaud

presenting a spectacle, while simultaneously exposing how it all works.« (Feb. 20, 1991) Equally sensational in its sets and costumes, historical accuracy and the sophistication of its story was the Competition entry DA TAIJIAN LI LIANYING (»Li Lianying, the Imperial Eunuch«) by Tian Zhuangzhuang, a co-production between the People's Republic of China and Hong Kong. In the run-up to the Festival, a controversy had arisen related to the new film by Wu Ziniu, who had received a Silver Bear for his film WAN ZHONG (»Evening Bell«) in 1989. His film DO MO FANG (»The Big Mill«) had been invited to participate in the Competition by the Festival. The selection commission had been impressed by the seriousness with which he dealt with a difficult topic – a communist is outraged by the power structures in his village in China during the thirties – and its intense visual realization. The film was initially confirmed for participation by Beijing, but withdrawn again two days later. After protest from the Festival management to the Chinese authorities and intervention by the co-producer from Hong Kong, who assured that the film could also be shown as an exclusively Hong Kong production, the film was reconfirmed. A few days later the decision was reversed once again and the film's participation at the Berlinale hindered this time by Hong Kong. In Berlin, one could only speculate: the reasons were most likely political, since previous films by this director had been banned and his new film also had a critical subtext that would provoke censorship.

China withdraws

And American cinema, whose strong presence had met with repeated vehement criticism? Kevin Costner's neo-Western DANCES WITH WOLVES in the Competition was considered a sure candidate for one of the top awards. Francis Ford Coppola presented the third part of his trilogy THE GODFATHER hors concours, a melange of grand opera and Mafia legend. Yet Jonathan Demme's thriller THE SILENCE OF THE LAMBS with Anthony Hopkins and Jodie Foster was considered the most unnerving and brilliant film, »a masterpiece, cruel, cynical, cold. (...) Like in Fritz Lang's best films, the world is hell, and only those who have descended to its depths are able to

Susanne Lothar

STATE OF GRACE by Phil Joanou (in the Panorama): Robin Wright, Sean Penn

escape. Demme's film has no moral, only a metaphor: stripped skin. Underneath are the viewers' nerves, and the film subtly plays with these like only a nineties action film can. There's absolutely no way out.« (Andreas Kilb, Die Zeit, March 1, 1991) Stephen Frears' American film noir THE GRIFTERS, Phil Joanou's STATE OF GRACE, both in the Panorama, and Amos Poe's tribute to the black Hollywood series TRIPLE BOGEY ON A PAR FIVE HOLE in the Forum all reinforced the impression made by American cinema.

Italy wins

Nevertheless, in retrospect, most critics spoke of a weak festival and to everyone's astonishment, Italy dominated the Competition. The main prize went to Ferreri's LA CASA DEL SORRISO (»House of Smiles«), a playful anarchistic attack on the elderly and sex in old age. For want of a better solution, the Golden Bear was awarded to a film which a year earlier had been rejected for competition in Cannes. That the Jury had also had a hard time arriving at a decision could be gathered from a joint declaration: this Golden Bear was also to be seen as honoring Marco Ferreri's complete oeuvre. In awarding the other prizes, Volker Schlöndorff added that the Jury had felt committed to »standards of common sense«. Their decisions – given the backdrop of the political events in the Near East – had not been guided by whether the films actually mirrored the real world. And so there were boos, not only for the award that went to Ferreri, but above all for the Special Prize of the Jury which went to Marco Bellocchio's LA CONDANNA (»The Condemnation«) (ex aequo with Viktor Aristov's SATANA), and because Jonathan Demme was made to share a Silver Bear with Ricky Tognazzi for his film ULTRÀ. Writing in the »Frankfurter Allgemeine Zeitung«, Verena Lueken summed it up by remarking that »the strong presence of European cinema in the Competition was supposed to be a signal against the dominance of the Americans, an effort which the Jury's decisions backed. Yet it is no more than a statement of demarcation; of all the films officially honored, only the Soviet film SATANA can be viewed as an uncompromising artistic effort to translate

THE GRIFTERS by Stephen Frears (in the Panorama): Anjelica Huston

contemporary experiences into a modern new form of narration based on national, cinematic and literary traditions.« (Feb. 28, 1991)

The new press center

The 1991 Berlinale had not brought about the desired breakthrough, expectations were not fulfilled, disillusionment and disappointment were widespread. The Festival had also undergone organizational changes. The House of World Cultures in the Tiergarten District was added as a new decentralized venue for press screenings, which was received negatively by many journalists. They felt excluded, forced into a ghetto, isolated from Festival events, and neither a shuttle service nor improved technical working conditions were able to compensate for the feeling that the Festival management was willfully disregarding the press. Yet spatially and above all financially, Moritz de Hadeln and Ulrich Gregor had had no alternative for the recurrent and long-standing request for a press center. For years now, the CineCenter had been increasingly unable to accommodate the growing number of journalists. Yet this first attempt to make a virtue of necessity had not succeeded, and this was particularly conspicuous because the quality of this year's screenings had also left much to be desired.

Efforts to establish the Festival in the eastern part of the city were also rather unsuccessful. Despite great engagement and a large advertising campaign, the Kino International – where a program of films from the Competition, Panorama and the Retrospective (with the problematic topic »Cold War«) was presented – was filled to only 25% of its capacity: which meant a mere 9426 viewers attended a total of 70 screenings. Anger about these deficiencies was again directed primarily at Moritz de Hadeln. Criticism concentrated on him, polemical or not. Only the Forum, that island for cineastes, was spared criticism, while rivalry between the Forum and the Panorama continued behind the scenes.

No matter: what resounded in the ears of Festival visitors was the »till we meet again« which guest of honor Jane Russel had whispered huskily into the microphone

International Jury
Volker Schlöndorff
(Germany, president)
Chantal Akerman (Belgium)
Laurie Anderson (USA)
José Luis Borau (Spain)
Judith Godreche (France)
Yuri Klepikov (USSR)
Renate Krössner (Germany)
Gillo Pontecorvo (Italy)
Simon Relph (Great Britain)
Catharina Stackelberg
(Sweden)
Mircea Veroiu (Rumania)

The Awards of the
International Jury

Feature Films
Grand Prix of the 41st IFB
Golden Berlin Bear
La casa del sorriso
Italy, directed by
Marco Ferreri

Silver Berlin Bear
Special Prize of the Jury
La condanna
Italy, directed by
Marco Bellocchio
ex aequo
Satana
USSR, directed by
Viktor Aristov

Silver Berlin Bear
for the best director
to two directors whose films
reflect opposing directions
of fiction and realism
Ricky Tognazzi
Ultra
Italy
ex aequo
Jonathan Demme
The Silence of the Lambs
USA

The Godfather. Part III:
Al Pacino

The Miracle: Mikkel Gaup, Lorrain Pilkington

at the closing ceremony – a glimmer of hope for the year to come. The Berlinale, once again declared dead, was still alive.

Silver Berlin Bear
for an outstanding individual achievement
as actor, producer and director
Kevin Costner
Dances with Wolves
USA

Silver Berlin Bear
for the best actress
Victoria Abril
in Amantes
Spain

Silver Berlin Bear
for the best actor
Maynard Eziashi
in Mr. Johnson
Great Britain

Special Mentions
Le Petit criminel
directed by Jacques Doillon
France

Dandan-e mar
directed by Masud Kimiai
Iran

Da Taijian Li Lianying
directed by Tian Zhuangzhuang
Hong Kong/People's Republic of China

Short Films
Golden Berlin Bear
Six Point Nine
directed by Dan Bootzin
USA

Silver Berlin Bear
Posledních 100 let Marx-Leninismu v Čechách
directed by Pavel Koútský
CSFR

La casa del sorriso:
Ingrid Thulin, Dada Ruspoli

Right from the start

By Katsue Tomiyama

I was invited to the International Forum of Young Cinema and thus participated in the Berlin Film Festival for the first time in 1983. The year before, Mr. Gregor, the program director, had come to see us at our office at Image Forum to view the experimental films we were distributing uncommercially. That was when the two of us met for the first time. Since our activities for distributing films started in the same year as the International Forum of Young Cinema was established (both in 1971), I remember the enthusiastic discussions we had on how cinema had developed in Japan and Germany respectively over those last ten years. It was as if unseen walls had broken down between us.

Seventeen years have passed since then. Ever since I've been a guest at the Festival every year, and the program of Image Forum and the films we are distributing have been invited to the Festival. So our intimate relationship has continued in various ways. Also we have been taught many things by the Forum. We were able to see broadening ways of expression, ranging from purely experimental films of the kind we had been introducing to features and documentaries with experimental aspects. Every film organization and filmmaker has its or his own color. We, however, are convinced that this festival, the International Forum of Young Cinema, is the most precious place for learning about the range of styles at this point in time when ideologies are breaking down, and when we are faced with a chaos of different genres.

I respect the International Forum of Young Cinema for continuing their activities towards discovering the new, and for keeping their ideas as fresh and alive as they were right from the start.

Édes Emma, drága Böbe:
Eniko Börcsök, Johanna ter Steege

Delusions and disappointments

1992

Feb. 13th-24th, 1992 (Competition)
Feb. 14th-24th, 1992 (Forum)

Infinitive Diversity in Infinitive Combinations – in short, IDIC – is the Starfleet philosophy. Its members all gathered one evening during the Berlinale in front of the Zoo Palast movie theater: Trekies in colorful uniforms and costumes – Mr. Spock, Vulcans and Yetis. A whole lineup of beauties put in an appearance and then beamed themselves into their seats inside the theater for the gala to celebrate the sixth part of the cult film STAR TREK, entitled THE UNDISCOVERED COUNTRY. Whilst the fan community's delight was tremendous, the professional critics viewed this event with a certain uneasiness, in a not very IDIC manner.

Beam me up, Scotty

The fact that American films have had a tendency to dominate the Berlinale is a standard critique, especially from German film journalists reporting on the Film Festival. For many, the presence of the American major studios in the Competition and also the wide range of American films in the other sections is a continuous annoyance. The main objection, which the Festival has heard with reliable regularity, is that the selection is one-sided and makes too many concessions to commercial interests. Although how differently this emphasis on American cinema is seen abroad came to attention in November 1991. It had been predicted for some time that the rivalry between the three large European festivals – Cannes, Venice and Berlin – would intensify. Nevertheless, people were still surprised when the festival management in Cannes set out to challenge the position of its two rivals, after noting how many important American films were premiered Europe and world-wide in Berlin. Wolf Donner's previous coup, namely his rescheduling of the Berlinale from summer to February, and de Hadeln's skill – although accompanied by much criticism – in enticing major studios to come to Berlin, had rekindled the controversy and the fierce rivalry between the competitors behind the scenes: Cannes launched an offensive against Berlin and Venice, and announced that it would move its traditional May festival dates either back, to Berlin's disadvantage, or forward to autumn, to Venice's disadvantage. French Minister of Cultural Affairs Jack Lang was cited as having said that nothing was eternal and chiseled in marble. This impressive and threatening gesture from Cannes certainly had the desired effect. The International Federation of Film Producers' Associations (FIAPF), which was ascribed an interest in maintaining the status quo, dealt with the topic at a meeting in December, and Berlin asked for assistance from Minister of Foreign Affairs Hans-Dietrich Genscher, who contacted his French and Italian colleagues. Even Minister of the Interior Wolfgang Schäuble was asked to intervene. Yet it was exactly those whose favor was being so manipulatively courted who took it most calmly. For the Europeans it might be an existential matter of film policy, but for the Americans it was simply a financial consideration. They would send their films to the location which had the better conditions for launching and marketing a film. For the USA it was merely all a matter of business. De Hadeln summed it up: »The Americans couldn't care less, they just want to hold on to the market. Although, if one side were just to settle matters, things might suddenly look grim for Berlin.« (Berliner Morgenpost, Nov. 15, 1991) Ultimately nothing changed, and Berlin was left with a topic that was to be debated for years to come.

Cannes mobilizes itself

In the run-up to the Berlinale, the »tageszeitung« (Jan. 25, 1992) addressed another aspect of the situation. In an article entitled »Preferably Cannes« it was reported that Italy – which had been so successful the year before – would not send any films to

Italy cancels

Berlin. The paper played up this decision as an outcome of de Hadeln's failure to pay due attention to European films. Gianni Amelio's LADRO DI BAMBINI (»The Stolen Children«) and Mario Martone's MORTE DI UN MATEMATICO NAPOLETANO (»Death of a Neapolitan Mathematician«) had been invited to the Competition, and Aurelio Grimaldi's LA DISCESA DI ACLA A FLORISTELLA (»Acla's Descent into Floristella«) and Fiorella Infascelli's ZUPPA DI PESCE (»Fish Soup«) to the Panorama. Whereas the latter was simply not made available to the Festival, it was said that Martone's and Grimaldi's films would not be completed in time, an argument that could hardly be disputed. The real snub to the Berlinale was that Amelio's film was to participate in the competition at Cannes (where it went on to receive the special prize of the jury). Producer Angelo Rizzoli explained that the reason for this decision was that after being selected for the Berlinale, the Festival had not attempted to reach an agreement with him about its presentation. It seems more likely, however, that Rizzoli had withdrawn his consent due to pressure from his French co-producers, who had persuaded him to show it in Cannes. Calisto Cosulich, Italy's Berlinale delegate, spoke of Rizzoli's »non-existent reasons« and of the damage to the reputation of Italian cinema. It nonetheless seems fair to suspect another reason, one that was to reemerge from time to time in years to come. Some producers considered an invitation to the Berlinale a trial run, which could then be used to exert pressure on Cannes as well as to promote a film. The tighter the market became, the more susceptible festivals were to such influences.

On February 13th, the International Film Festival – which after the depressing international conflicts of the previous year, was now colored by Germany's political normalization – was opened not by the Mayor of Berlin as had been the custom, but by Minister of the Interior Rudolf Seiters. The traditional function of the Berlinale as a bridge between the East and West was in jeopardy, as had already been experienced in 1991. In the preface to the Berlinale catalogue, Moritz de Hadeln wrote that

David Cronenberg

Carmen Maura

Jiří Menzel

Lily Tomlin

while the Festival had once been »a bridge between different ideological systems«, it now constituted »a bridge between cultures in a new Europe whose focus has shifted eastwards«. Consequently, many films were screened under the motto »history and identity«. The Festival's controversial opening film, Andrei Konchalovsky's BLIZHNIJ KRUG (»The Inner Circle«), an Italian-Russian co-production, centered on these issues. It told the true story of Stalin's projectionist at the Kremlin, Alexander Sanshin, who also attended the Berlin premiere of »his« film in person. But what might have been a parable of totalitarianism fizzled out in striking but overly melodramatic private episodes. Similarly, the German Competition entry GUDRUN by Hans W. Geissendörfer told its story of everyday life in Nazi Germany with unnecessary sentimentality; and the Spanish Competition entry EL LLARG HIVERN/EL LARGO INVIERNO (»The Long Winter«) by Jaime Camino, failed to provide images that convincingly conveyed the ruin of a family wavering between conformism and betrayal in Francoist Spain. In the »Süddeutsche Zeitung«, Michael Althen asked, »why does cinema recurrently turn to such periods, when it has to search for ever more devious access to them? Is history truly the final adventure of our times? Or are the films just feigning a relevance which they would lack without a historic backdrop? Unthinkingly, an interest in the figures is sacrificed to the course of history, as if the impotence of the individual still required verification.« (Feb. 18, 1992)

Bridge between cultures

»History and identity« and the breaking of a national taboo – these were also the basic themes of Bertrand Tavernier's four-hour documentary about the Algerian war, which ran hors concours in the Competition program. LA GUERRE SANS NOM (»The Undeclared War«) is a montage of 50 hours of original material: Tavernier meticulously interviews eyewitnesses, soldiers and politicians, while attempting to search for clues to the truth. Yet he does not insist on illuminating the politics behind the war or on relating them to the end of French colonial rule in southern Asia. The film remains a panorama of oppressive individual interviews and impressions of a

Documentaries deal with historical taboos

David Cronenberg, Peter Weller

Alexander and Alexandra Kluge

Annie Girardot, president of the International Jury, and Berlin's Senator for Cultural Affairs Ulrich Roloff-Momin

Producer Hal Roach, 100 years old, is awarded the »Golden Berlinale Camera« by Moritz de Hadeln

Naked Lunch: Peter Weller

dirty war. It also stresses that we recognize the importance of breaking the silence. Helke Sander's documentary screened in the Panorama, Be-Freier und Befreite (»Liberators Take Liberties«), also breaks a silence. The director talks with women raped during World War II, with German and Russian soldiers, with offenders and victims on both sides: German victims of the Red Army, and Russian victims of the German campaign on Russia. For Helke Sander, it is not a matter of graphic clarity, but instead of unraveling interwoven stories, painful stories. Anke Sterneborg wrote in the »Tagesspiegel« that by »always integrating herself into the film, the camera panning quite consciously from her interview partner to her and back again, and then staying there for a long time, she sabotages the documentary quality of the film and makes herself not only the prosecutor, but also someone directly affected«. (Feb. 26, 1992)

Patterns of Jewish life

Historical images were also to be found in the Forum, for instance in the »Patterns of Jewish Life« series, supported by the National Center for Jewish Film in Waltham, Massachusetts. Features and documentaries, films and documentations in Yiddish were shown, among which was a first film by Leningrad's theater director Dimitry Astrakhan. In his film Izydi! (»Get Thee Out«), he sombrely depicts the development of a pogrom in Russia at the beginning of the century: a reflection also on anti-Semitism in modern Russia, a parable set against the rampant nationalist conflicts in the former Soviet Union.

Highlights from Russia and Hungary

Cinematically, two Eastern European films at this year's Festival were especially remarkable. The Competition's unspoken highlight – shamelessly overlooked by the Jury in awarding the prizes, receiving only the Alfred Bauer Prize – was Marlen Khutsiyev's Infinitas (»Infinity«). It describes a journey into a man's past, his encounter with himself and with 20th century history; a film of elegiac calm, an inner examination and affirmation of personal identity. The fact that what was right yesterday can be wrong today is portrayed by István Szabó in his tempestuous and si-

Dead Again: Emma Thompson

multaneously touchingly enacted Édes Emma, drága Böbe (»Sweet Emma, Dear Böbe«): after the Iron Curtain disappears, two Russian teachers are retrained so that they can teach English. An intimate story, yet pointedly realistic and astute; of all the films at the Festival, this film gave the most powerful impression of this period of political upheaval and so, with good reason, Szabó received the Special Prize of the Jury for his ›little big‹ film from Hungary.

Infinitas by Marlen Khutsiyev (in the Competition)

Just the same, America came out on top once again. Contrary to expectations, the Golden Berlin Bear went to Lawrence Kasdan's film Grand Canyon, about »the disparate lives of eight main figures which intersect coincidentally in one single, immensely alarming but amusing and even funny story of turbulence«. The film, set in Los Angeles, is »staged in the multiple levels of the mega-city with its street-gangs and melting pot of violence«. (Ruprecht Skasa-Weiß, Stuttgarter Zeitung, Feb. 24, 1992) Frauke Döhring remarked sarcastically that she felt she had been »duped by a snazzy soap opera« and wondered who was actually deluding whom, »the director the jury, the jury the audience, or the audience itself«. (Deutsches Allgemeines Sonntagsblatt, Feb. 28, 1992) Violence was the theme of the American films: Martin Scorsese's remake of Cape Fear, Paul Schrader's Light Sleeper; Barry Levinson's Bugsy, Kenneth Branagh's Dead Again, all in the Competition; as well as Lizzie Borden's Love Crimes in the Panorama. Whether brash or restrained, by ironic citation or broken distance, they were all dominated by images of brutality. The shock of reality and the impact of fictionalization were closely related. In the »tageszeitung«, Christiane Peitz compared – pars pro toto – Scorsese's and Borden's films, which tell »of violence to women and female fantasies of violence. Lizzie Borden fails because she ignores the difference between fantasy and reality: a female district attorney wants to put an end to a photographer's game of abusing women. By a hair's breadth, she herself escapes succumbing to him. Borden wants to make us believe that it is not so much the man's violent acts that are a danger to the heroine but their

Violence as portrayed in American films

Les Amants du Pont-Neuf: Denis Lavant, Juliette Binoche (in the Forum)

fascination (yet she does not even take five minutes to draw the viewer into the photographer's spell: he remains just an average guy). On the other hand, Cape Fear is a masterpiece, because it makes the moment of seduction itself the film's focal point. The scene of seduction between Robert de Niro and Juliette Lewis mercilessly reveals how fear can switch to desire, how the victim exposes herself to the other person's will and extinguishes difference; moreover, Scorsese seduces us too: whoever claims that he can resist the fascination of this scene is either lying or blind.« (Feb. 25, 1992) In David Cronenberg's British-Canadian production Naked Lunch, a drug-laced cinematic odyssey based on the novel by William Burroughs, the nightmarish fantasies make our hearts miss a beat, turning inwards, they shake all forms of psychological confidence, exploring the fine line between reason and insanity.

Two comedies from the USA

In a special screening, the comic unmasking of horror was taken to an extreme by Woody Allen's film Shadows and Fog, a tribute to a deeply black genre. Allison Anders demonstrated in her film Gas Food Lodging that American cinema can portray reality without showing violence, and more realistically than the artificiality of a genre film does or can ever profess to do. It tells of a mother and her daughter in a shabby small town in New Mexico: an outsider film which the commission had selected to counterpoint major productions, and which some journalists would have liked to have seen receive a Silver Bear.

Europe on the defensive

It seemed as if European cinema was on the defensive at this year's Berlinale. Aside from a few films – Szabó's film, and the controversially disputed Swedish-Finnish-Danish-German entry Il Capitano (»A Swedish Requiem«) by Jan Troell, as well as Eric Rohmer's brilliantly light and French view of reality, Conte d'hiver (»A Winter's Tale«) – the European entries in the Competition and other sections did not produce anything particularly remarkable. The Russian-French entry in the Competition, Samostoyatelnaya shizn (»An Independent Life«) by Vitali Kanevsky was withdrawn from the program by Moritz de Hadeln a day before its premiere.

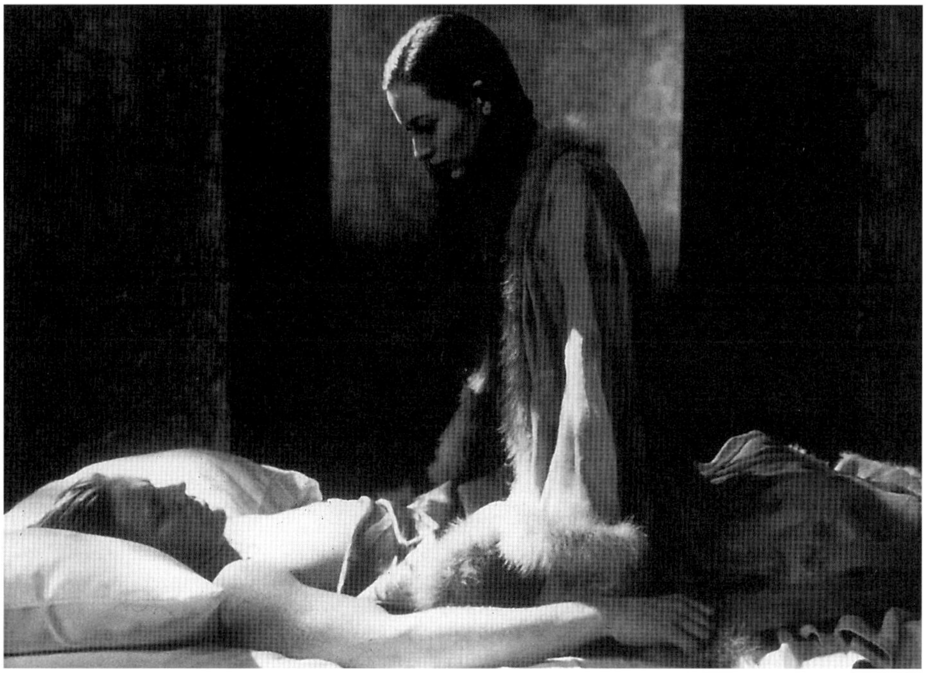

EDWARD II: Steven Waddington, Tilda Swinton (in the Forum)

The Festival director had not been able to mediate a quarrel between the director and its producers, and so it was replaced by Alain Corneau's film TOUS LES MATINS DU MONDE (»All the Mornings of the World«).

An air of indifference

The Berlinale's entire program had an air of remarkable indifference, with too many diverse points of interests and special series for visitors to be able to attain an overview (in the Panorama, for instance, there was also a retrospective called »Sorbian Cinema Landscapes«, and in the Forum, alongside the »Patterns of Jewish Life« program, there was a retrospective of »Mexican Melodramas«). The impression was one of conformity within diversity, not necessarily a reproach applicable to the Berlinale alone, but still an expression of an ever-growing economic pressure in the world of film production that permitted no risks. This year's Berlinale had not succeeded in spotlighting the alternatives in this jungle of uniformity. It was business as usual, even if the intentions were good; yet the promised new image had not materialized, and a readiness to restructure the program was not identifiable. The Panorama and the Forum were obstinately entangled in an unyielding rivalry, and conceptual boundaries were blurred. As a consequence, it was a year of delusions and disappointments, marked more by small cinematic treats than by a persuasive overall concept.

Contract renewals and polemics

In March, when the Festival was over, Berlin's Senator for Cultural Affairs Ulrich Roloff-Momin approved the renewal of Moritz de Hadeln's and Ulrich Gregor's contracts for another five years – for the period from May 1st, 1993 to April 30th, 1998. There were voices, especially in Berlin, which criticized the renewal of their contracts at a time when it was too early to draw any conclusions about the concept of the Berlinale '92. Moreover, these critics once again raised objections against de Hadeln personally, not least with the argument that he had ›sold out‹ to the Americans. That structural problems were to be answered for and solved by both Festival directors was often nonchalantly ignored. In Berlin, alliances had formed that were

Mahapritivi by Mrinal Sen (in the Forum)

perhaps understandable but not always reasonable. Personalizing the Festival's conceptual crisis was an oversimplification of the situation; and so, for the time being, the chance to debate the matter properly was lost.

The Berlinale of 1992 was soon history, and forgotten. The Retrospective had been devoted to the history of German cinema: its theme was Babelsberg Studios: 1912–1992. Reminiscences played a role, but also the prospects of Berlin-Brandenburg as a media location and thus, indirectly, the Berlinale as an international film event. This was a topic which would remain on the agenda for the next years. The Homage was to centenarian producer Hal Roach, who had ›made‹ Laurel and Hardy. At a reception, when he was presented with a golden pin with portraits of the two comedians, he commented that the two looked somehow familiar (as did the Festival's recurrent daily problems and polemics). In his final report in the »Süddeutsche Zeitung« on February 26, Michael Althen dryly commented: »A hundred years old, like cinema itself. In comparison, a festival is a nothing.«

International Jury
Annie Girardot (France, president)
Charles Champlin (USA)
Sylvia Chang (Hong Kong)
Ildiko Enyedi (Hungary)
Irving N. Ivers (Canada)
Wolfgang Klaue (Germany)
Fernando Lara (Spain)
Eldar Schengelaja (Georgia)
Dahlia Shapira (Israel)
Susannah York (Great Britain)

The Awards of the International Jury

Feature Films
Grand Prix of the 42nd IFB
Golden Berlin Bear
Grand Canyon
USA
directed by Lawrence Kasdan

Silver Berlin Bear
Special Prize of the Jury
Édes Emma, drága Böbe
Hungary
directed by István Szabó

Silver Berlin Bear
for the best director
Jan Troell
Il Capitano
Sweden/Finland/Denmark/Germany

Silver Berlin Bear
for its cinematic quality
Beltenebros
Spain
directed by Pilar Miró

Silver Berlin Bear
for the outstanding
debut film
La frontera
Chile/Spain
directed by Ricardo Larrain

Silver Berlin Bear
for the best actress
Maggie Cheung
in Ruan Ling-yu
Hong Kong/Taiwan

Silver Berlin Bear
for the best actor
Armin Mueller-Stahl
in Utz
Great Britain/
Germany/Italy

Special Mention
for her outstanding
performance
Barbara Thumet
in Gudrun
Germany

Alfred Bauer Prize
for a film opening up new
perspectives in film art
Infinitas
Russia
directed by Marlen Khutsiyev

Short Films
To preserve the high level of esteem associated with the Golden and Silver Bears for past and future winners, the Jury decided not to award any prizes in this category. Moreover, the Jury recommended that the process for selection of short films be reviewed by the Festival. The Jury believed it would be ideal in the future for a short film of Festival quality to be presented before each feature film in the Competition program.

Gas Food Lodging by Allison Anders (in the Competition): Ione Skye

A place of friendship

By David Streiff

From the start, the »International Forum of Young Cinema« was an important address and a point of reference for me in the coordinate system of my filmic expeditions. From the start means since 1973, the year I became director of the Swiss Film Center which was teeny at the time. Swiss cinema was much sought after at many of the more avant-garde international festivals. The Forum was presenting some Swiss films that year too, which has also been the case almost every year since. I remember one of the films in that distant year of 1973, LO STAGIONALE *by Alvaro Bizzari, a Super-8 film by an Italian »guest worker« who worked in Switzerland. With his small feature film, that used the stylistic means of neo-realistic cinema, he had taken up the political fight against the statute on seasonal workers in Switzerland.*

For me, 1973 also signifies when I first began working for the Locarno Film Festival (of which I was director from 1981 to 1991). Within the framework of the »Tribune libre« program section, This Brunner, Theres Scherer and I, during de Hadeln's era, were free to show the films of our choice, those which we found especially important or to which we had taken a particularly fond liking at other festivals. I think that there was hardly a »Tribune libre« at which we did not show films that we had discovered in the Forum. The first film from the Forum program that I can recall presenting was YEK ETEFAGH SADEH *(»A Simple Event«) by Sohrab Shahid Saless, a film that is still considered one of the best Iranian films ever, as a survey by the leading Iranian film journal just recently revealed. That was in 1974.*

The Forum gradually changed from a point of reference to a place of friendship: the hospitality I encountered each time in Berlin, I was able to reciprocate in Locarno (as my precursor had done and my successor does today), and we helped each other out with information and addresses. We were insiders in a profession that like migratory birds travel with unflagging energy the entire year over from film festival to festival, from country to country to discover new films. We met regularly or by accident and were happy to do so.

When I stopped working in Locarno and before I began a new and fully engrossing job in Bern, I was kindly offered a position on the Forum's selection committee. Hence I had the opportunity to experience the last phase of the selection process in the winter months before the program took on its final form three times: in 1991, 1992, and 1993.

It was a lovely time during an exciting period of Berlin's history (which I saw little of – how could it have been otherwise: there were hundreds of films to be viewed and they were what counted then).

I am extraordinarily grateful to Erika, Ulrich and Milena Gregor, to Silvia Andresen and the memorable Alf Bold as well as everyone else for everything they have done and are doing for film. For over thirty years now, I have been an admirer of their endurance, their never-ending faith in a cinema which is valuable, politically involved and formally sophisticated, and their demand that films be not consumed but understood. It is from this desire that Ulrich Gregor's book on the history of film evolved as well as with consistency the Forum's exceptionally precise and detailed information sheets.

To me it seems particularly admirable – and this sets it apart from almost all other festival-like events – that the Forum is embedded in the activities of the »Freunde der Deutschen Kinemathek«, with its parallel concept and organization on an all-year-round basis and a program with all that film history has to offer. Over the past thirty years the Forum's inventory of films has continually grown and provided the program with nourishment. The daily work at the Arsenal theater as well as all distribution activities have furthered the knowledge and experience of the organizers and the German public. Due to the program and distribution work of the »Freunde«, more than a generation of cineastes and avid movie-goers have been able to become versed in film at the Arsenal or at other affiliated communal cinemas in many German cities. For this – also for this – I extend my jubilee thanks!

Remembering the »Forum«

By Barbara Hammer

The celebratory screenings in four huge theaters in the Forum section of the International Berlin Film Festival of my two experimental documentaries, NITRATE KISSES (1992) and TENDER FICTIONS (1995) were thrills of a lifetime. First, the theaters are always packed with an enthusiastic audience that prefers the unconventional; second, the projections are superb with brilliant screen illumination and clear sound; and, third, the discussion on stage following the screening with the director of the Forum, Ulrich Gregor, and the filmmaker stimulates audience members to ask provocative and challenging questions.

I was so elated after seeing NITRATE KISSES at the Delphi theater with an audience of 1200 that afterwards when a photographer wanted to take a press photo I couldn't stop dancing and whirling my black cape in circles in an outside courtyard. I love the Berlin Film Festival, the stimulation of an international and critical movie-going audience in one of my favorite cities, plus the inclusion in one of the most experimental curatorial programs of the long film form in the world is a true incentive to continue making avant-garde and independent cinema. I hope to be invited to return with the third 16 mm film of this trilogy of lost and recovered lesbian and gay histories, »Culture Doctor« (working title), when it is completed in the year 2000!

Hsi yen by Ang Lee
(in the Competition)

Action

1993

Feb. 11th-22nd, 1993
(Competition)
Feb. 12th-22nd, 1993
(Forum)

A monster was advertising the Berlinale, and an American one at that. A larger-than-life figure of King Kong had been installed on the canopy of the Zoo Palast. Bavaria Studios had constructed a friendly styrofoam beast for the Berlinale. It was a gift from the Festival's sponsor SAT 1 television network, which had also helped finance the restoration of Ernest B. Schoedsack's classic KING KONG, which was to be shown in a special screening. After all, it was this cinema creature's 60th birthday, and the Zoo Palast was sold out for the festivities.

Yet despite groans in the run-up and this invocation of an American movie myth, this year's Berlinale would not be dominated by the USA. The Film Festival was to bear testimony to the fact that it was indeed possible to do otherwise. Berlin as a city, however, was having a harder time proving itself: in Lausanne on January 27th, it had officially applied to the International Olympic Committee to be the venue for the Summer Olympic Games. And on February 15th, it presented its candidacy to the German press at the Grand Hotel Esplanade. Still, not everyone was as convinced as Mayor Eberhard Diepgen of the city's validity as a genius loci.

Gregory Peck and
Billy Wilder

Europe, Africa and Asia – in 1993 the films that attracted attention in Berlin came from these continents. And this fact was in no way affected by the Golden Berlin Bear that went to the wildly celebrated Gregory Peck for his lifetime achievements. Another honorary Golden Berlin Bear went to Billy Wilder, who roguishly accepted the laurels for his lifework, for bridging the gulf between the Old and New World with his wit, irony and charm. Indeed, this year's Berlinale – as it turned out – had a lucky hand in awarding its prizes. And the correction of course was registered with interest both before and after the Festival. The number of European films in the Competition was increasing; Scandinavian countries (like Denmark and Norway), who had not been represented in the Competition for some years, were showing films in Berlin again; and Frank Beyer, a renowned eastern German director, was the president of the Jury. These factors paved the way for a more relaxed attitude in the media. Even Harald Martenstein, Volker Baer's successor as new film editor of Berlin's »Tagesspiegel«, and critic of Moritz de Hadeln's alleged »Hollywoodophilia« and of the Festival's gigantism, displayed leniency and understanding, saying: »The Festival is more European and more manageable: there is absolutely nothing to be said against that.« (Feb. 3, 1993) And while relations between the Festival and its critics remained somewhat reserved, the ice appeared to have been broken. A contributing factor was also that the Panorama – now under the direction of Wieland Speck, who had taken over for Manfred Salzgeber who was seriously ill – had reduced its program. Speck took first steps toward conceptually revising the selection process: for one, establishing a closer and more distinct connection to the Competition, and for the other, reinforcing the Panorama's own program interests. And although the Berlinale was forced to cope with cuts of about one million marks, they did not play a role in these decisions: money was saved elsewhere. A distinctive touch regarding conceptual matters became apparent, a long-outstanding response to criticisms of the past years, and a move toward finally ending institutional ossification. That certain changes were not radical enough for some people was not surprising: however, such critics overlooked the fact that the politico-cultural climate had changed. The kind of radicalism that had led to the establishment of the International Forum of Young Cinema in the seventies would now – twenty years later – have en-

Hollywoodophilia, ade!?

Wieland Speck,
the Panorama's new director

Billy Wilder

Gregory Peck

Spike Lee

Emir Kusturica

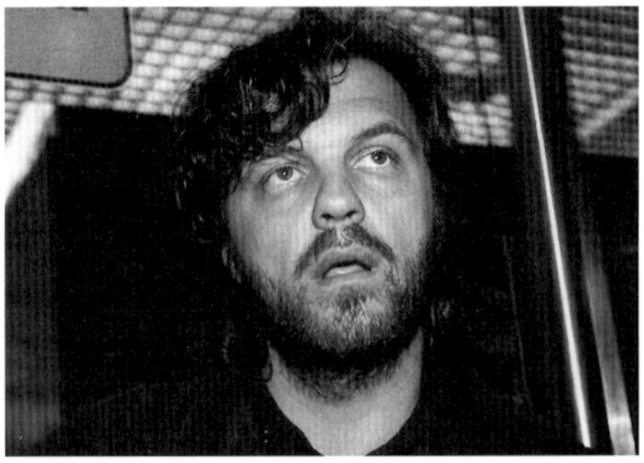

dangered the existence of the entire Festival. It was time for changes, but they had to be carefully laid out. »The time of the ideology of quantity is over«, Harald Martenstein commented. »In the worldwide flood of images, priorities have to be established, truly important events sought and spotlighted.« (Der Tagesspiegel, Feb. 3, 1993) That it was now the Forum's turn to rethink its program structures and react to the challenge provided by the Panorama, as well as to redefine its boundaries did not become a topic of discussion during this year's Festival. Or was this because the impression had arisen that such a rivalry should better not be mentioned? At least discussion was under way and considering Berlin's obstinacy, this could be booked as a success: it was a time of action for the Festival.

Nevertheless, as luck would have it, the Berlinale once again began against a backdrop of unfortunate political events. Federal Minister of the Interior Rudolf Seiters could not attend the Festival and his wife had to open it on his behalf. A Lufthansa plane had been hijacked, and Seiters had been called at short notice to head a committee to manage the crisis from Bonn. An additional strain on the Festival's atmosphere – and for Germany's international reputation in general – was the growing number of right-wing extremist attacks and unrest. Fortunately, people gathered in protest in front of the Zoo Palast, and some guests at the opening reception spontaneously joined in. The armed conflicts in former Yugoslavia, between Bosnians, Croats and Serbs, also triggered protest and a controversy with regard to the director of the opening film. Emir Kusturica was accused of pro-Serb conduct, an idea which he and the Festival direction immediately and indignantly repudiated.

Danny DeVito, Gong Li, Zhang Yimou

However, afterwards inside the movie house, the audience burst into spontaneous applause during Kusturica's film ARIZONA DREAM. His eccentric individualism and brilliant editing demanded candor, and the premiere audience was more than willing to accept his cineastic invitation. And although some viewers believed that the film lost itself in a filmic patchwork, it had been a long time since a first night film at the

Haile Gerima

Graham Weinbren

Volker Koepp

Nick Gomez

A splendid opening film

Berlinale had met with such resounding approval. Kusturica had evidently succeeded in blending American narrative forms with European style. Wolfram Schütte noted in the »Frankfurter Rundschau«, the film is »also a dream of ›America‹ – like Kafka's ›Der Verschollene‹ which is carried by slapstick. In this tale told from the USA by the thirty-seven-year-old melancholiac [Kusturica] – who lives in exile (and fortunately not in arms) – Hitchcock's and Wilder's films but also (...) the WIZARD OF OZ shimmer through.« (Feb. 13, 1993) In his film, Kusturica depicts European ideals in an American fairytale land, and Johnny Depp, Faye Dunaway and Jerry Lewis are his dramatic dream dancers.

Focal point Yugoslavia: »No More War«

The Berlinale had gotten off to a good start – and the Festival went on to balance artistic, aesthetic and political expectations. Under the title »No More War«, a special event was held in protest against the war in former Yugoslavia. The documentary film, UN JOUR DANS LA MORT DE SARAJEVO («A Day in the Death of Sarajevo«), prompted by an idea from French philosopher Bernard-Henri Levy, was shown. It is a film that aims to set an example, yet it is partial and occasionally »borders on the unbearable« in the unchecked pathos of its commentary, as Fritz Göttler wrote in the »Süddeutsche Zeitung«, »but for exactly this reason [it gives rise to] a longing in the viewer for silence, a silence which would not clutter images with words. A persuasive silence, such as prevailed at the outset of cinema, when images spoke for themselves, when nothing was conceived and arranged, contrived or consciously designed. When films themselves had impact by simply placing one image next to the other.« (Feb. 19, 1993) In complete contrast to this emotional narrative approach was Romuald Karmakar's documentary WARHEADS in the Forum. In this film, a nineteen-year-old from Munich tells how he set off to Croatia as a volunteer, a mercenary soldier fascinated and bedazzled by a political idea. With cool detachment, this film turns emotionality into dismay, and reveals the stupidity of the killing which lies behind these perpetrators' striking but desperate masks.

Patul conjugal by Mircea Daneliuc (in the Competition): Gheorghe Dinica

Testimony of the times: films from Rumania

Characteristic for many European contributions at the Berlinale was this quality of being a testimony to contemporary times. American cinema, on the other hand, focused on the past, staging opulent reconstructions of its own history – such as Danny DeVito's union melodrama Hoffa or Spike Lee's epic film Malcolm X. The Rumanian film Patul conjugal (»The Conjugal Bed«) by Mircea Daneliuc, for instance, took an angry but despondent, ghastly and grueling look at his country, a corrupt nation, hell on earth. According to Josef Schnelle, this was a film that »momentarily banishes the profusion of images at a festival, because it so despairingly tells of the death of all emotions and the imperialism of hard currencies«. (Frankfurter Rundschau, Feb. 16, 1993) A similar absence of sentimentality was to be found in a Rumanian film shown in the Forum, Bose Ovidiu Pastina's documentary Timisora – Decembrie 1989 (»Timisora – December 1989«), in which the director seeks the seeds of the Rumanian revolution and the man who gave the command to shoot at the demonstrators in his hometown: initially, a business-like search for clues, over which »a mysterious gray zone of suspicions and rumors spreads«, leaving scope for »other attempts at clarification, but also for the viewer's straying fantasy«. (Jan Ross, Frankfurter Allgemeine Zeitung, Feb. 23, 1993) A feature film shown in the Panorama, Der Fuchs der Jäger/Vulpe - Vanator (»Fox: Hunter«), was a German-Rumanian co-production directed by Stere Gulea and based on a script by author Herta Müller. It tackled the issues of a post-revolutionary society, such as guilt and atonement, and the latent fear that former conditions might return.

Precisely this mixture of document and fiction was the distinguishing feature of many Berlinale films. Sometimes in quite willfully stylistic forms, they depicted what happens when ideologies sell out and did not shy away from presenting chaos as chaos (as in the Rumanian films), or a farce as a farce. The latter quality could be found, for instance, in Temur Babluani's Georgian film Udzinarta mse (»The Sun of the Wakeful«), Israeli director Assi Dayan's entry Ha chayim alpy Agfa (»Life

Udzinarta mse by Temur Babluani (in the Competition): David Kazishvili (on the left)

According to Agfa«) or in Costa-Gavras' work, the closing film of the Competition, La Petite Apocalypse (»The Minor Apocalypse«). In the latter, »Czech filmmaker Jiří Menzel plays a Pole in exile in Paris, who is to be turned into a best-seller author, his success heralded by a beacon at St. Peter's Square«. (Michael Althen, Süddeutsche Zeitung, Feb. 23, 1993). Dramatic reconstructions of realities were to be discovered in these films; an unconditional confidence in the power of the authentic was no longer existent. This quality displayed itself in diverse forms also in many of the films screened in the Forum, which played its ›American trump card‹ at this year's Festival by showing independent productions. These included Jon Jost's films The Bed You Sleep In and Frame Up, both very personal analyses of American society. Or Nick Gomez' Laws of Gravity, »fiction, close to reality, that evokes the impression of authenticity, not least through the actors' inexperience. A chain reaction of recklessness and violence unfolds within a group of adolescents. The most interesting figure is a stupid young man, a general menace to society. Not only does Jon not have himself in control but he drifts almost unconsciously from one confrontation to the next. In the end, he is shot dead. Ill will is not a must for a catastrophe. It can suffice to overtax someone intellectually.« (Jan Ross, Frankfurter Allgemeine Zeitung, Feb. 23, 1993)

The USA in the Forum

African films also offered diagnoses of the times. Their large number had surprised many when announced, and this was the case even though the Forum had repeatedly demonstrated over the years that Africa was no longer an underdeveloped film continent. Burkina Faso in particular has evolved a lively cinema culture and was represented by two films: Nissi Joanny Traoré's Sababu (»The Cause«) in the Forum, and Idrissa Ouédraogo's Samba Traoré (co-produced with France and Switzerland) in the Competition. Neither one was an exotic marginal film; they were both stylistically confident examples of a different – i. e. African narrative – style, of a light and casual thrift that compensated for the deficits in the sets and costumes with ac-

African films

curate observation. Particularly Ouédraogo's film – which tells of a man who returns to his village with a fortune, and how he then lies, telling everyone he came by his wealth honestly although he hadn't – is persuasive in its dramaturgy and staging. The second Competition entry from Africa, SANKOFA by Haile Gerima, a co-production between the USA, Germany, Ghana and again Burkina Faso, was clearly more committed in its style to American and European cinema. It is a mythical ballad about a shaman who conjures up the spirits of African slaves, and for whom »an adherence to non-violence [means] merely a prolongation of inhumanity«. The film is »a wise combination of African myths of liberation and American narrative cinema« and »lives from a forceful symbolic language which works primarily by juxtaposing sound and images«. (Eugen L. Ribnitzer, Berliner Zeitung, Feb. 20, 1993) The impression left by this film was more direct in its orientation to ancient myths as well as more aesthetic than the Hollywoodesque invocation of African culture found in Spike Lee's MALCOLM X, which seemed to be mere citation and a senseless appeal. And to round off the Festival's focus on Africa, GUELWAAR, a Senegalese production by Ousmane Sembène, was presented in the Forum. Here again we have a director who is also an African storyteller. He successfully demonstrates that he is a master at accentuating the tragic in this farce about the burial of a politician whose corpse has been accidentally switched with someone else's: a parable about life in contemporary Africa, between tradition, belief and bureaucracy.

Winners from Asia

Asian films also made a big impression. The Forum presented, amongst other events, a series of new films from China; in addition to a Japanese film, the Competition once again featured a film from the People's Republic of China. Xie Fei's XIAN HUNNÜ (»The Women of the Lake of Scented Souls«) was also meant to signalize politically that the dispute resulting from the previous year's Berlinale entry had had no political consequence and had not triggered a new ice age in relations to the Berlinale. And from Taiwan (China), Ang Lee's film HSI YEN (»The Wedding Ban-

SANKOFA by Haile Gerima (in the Competition): Alexandra Duah, Oyafunmike Ogunlano

quet«) was screened. Two Chinese films that could not have been more different: Xie Fei's film was an artistically staged reckoning with antiquated village manners and customs, and a plea for the self-determination of women; Ang Lee, on the other hand, tells us with humorous verve of a young Taiwanese man in New York who is living in a gay relationship, but has to feign a wedding and marriage for the benefit of his parents. Taboos are broken here, too, but those of another world. That the Golden Berlin Bear went ex aequo to these two films could be understood as a gesture towards political balance; a clever decision that paid tribute to both cineastic achievements and popular issues.

And so this Berlinale turned into a triumph for two ›hostile brothers‹. Simultaneously, African and European program entries also received recognition in the prizes. For the first time, »The Blue Angel« was awarded, donated by the Académie Européenne du Cinéma et de la Télévision in Brussels, a statue with a purse of 50 000 marks: it went to Jacques Doillon for his film LE JEUNE WERTHER (»Young Werther«). Detlev Buck received a honorable mention for his comedy WIR KÖNNEN AUCH ANDERS (»No More Mr. Nice Guy«), »a lush road movie peppered with situation comedy and topical-satirical elements«. (Brigitte Desalm, Kölner Stadt-Anzeiger, Feb. 20, 1993) At least this could be interpreted as a good omen for German cinema, which had been represented by three films in the Competition. The other two films – by Wolfgang Kohlhaase and Thomas Mitscherlich – had met with little response. Furthermore, a special event was dedicated to a showing of Edgar Reitz' DIE ZWEITE HEIMAT (»Home away from Home«). And then there was a dispute related to another German film, although since the problems and irritations had been primarily with regard to the Forum, it had lost significance by the time the prizes were awarded: director Christoph Schlingensief had submitted TERROR 2000 in the New German Films program. This meant that two commissions had to view it, one for the Competition, headed by Heinz Badewitz, the other for the Forum, headed by Ulrich

A new prize: »The Blue Angel«

German films: praise and problems

GUELWAAR by Ousmane Sembène (in the Forum)

Arizona Dream:
Johnny Depp

International Jury
Frank Beyer (Germany, president)
Juan Antonio Bardem (Spain)
Michel Boujut (France)
François Duplat (France)
Katinka Faragó (Sweden)
Krystyna Janda (Poland)
Naum I. Kleiman (Russia)
Brock Peters (USA)
Susan Strasberg (USA)
Johanna ter Steege (Netherlands)
Zhang Yimou (People's Republic of China)

The Awards of the International Jury

Feature Films
Grand Prix of the 43rd IFB
Golden Berlin Bear
Xian hunnü
People's Republic of China
directed by Xie Fei
ex aequo
Hsi yen
Taiwan (China)
directed by Ang Lee

Silver Berlin Bear
Special Prize of the Jury
Arizona Dream
France
directed by Emir Kusturica

Silver Berlin Bear
for the best director
Andrew Birkin
The Cement Garden
Germany/Great Britain/France

Gregor. The idea of having two commissions was to guarantee proportional representation at the Festival, and in the last years the commissions' existence had seemed quite justified by their cleverly complementary selections. Schlingensief's film got caught between the two selection commissions. It had already caused strife at the festival in Hof: it is an intentionally provocative film in its wildness and ›bad taste‹, as well as in its tale about a place called Rassau where hatred of everything foreign or unknown reigns. Nevertheless, it illustrates a possible reaction to events in Germany today. The film was rejected by the Competition commission, yet it was unclear whether this was for reasons of taste (which is probable), or political censorship (rather unlikely), or a misunderstanding between the commissions (which was certainly the case): whereas the Forum's explanation for its refusal appeared to have solely to do with formalities – they claimed to have not attained a copy –, the Competition's explanation – they were dealing with a film designated for the Forum – seemed rather evasive. Yet both commissions had in fact viewed the film. It turned out that Badewitz and his team had passed the film on to the Forum due to its ›experimental‹ nature, and the Forum's commission just did not like the film. Just the same, the manner in which the film had been rejected was unfortunate, giving rise to needless speculation and rumors, which were then cultivated with delight – always a potential danger with German films at the Berlinale.

To sum up the Berlinale of 1993: a step had been taken in the right direction, the course had been corrected and there was a temporary truce between the Festival and the critics. One memorable image is of the five actresses who were awarded the »Berlinale Camera« for their close bonds to the Festival: Victoria Abril, Gong Li, Corinna Harfouch, Johanna ter Steege and Juliette Binoche. And Gregory Peck joyfully applauded his young female colleagues at the award ceremony. Moritz de Hadeln also appeared on stage with a smile, and holding a kalashnikov with a white lily stuck in its muzzle – cunningly presented to him by Detlev Buck – another no-

LOVE FIELD:
Michelle Pfeiffer

table moment at this Berlinale. And still a third one lingered on from a film, perhaps from the most beautiful one presented at this Festival, a zany movie by Dušan Makavejev: GORILLA BATHES AT NOON. A film about Berlin, about the fall of the Wall, about a Russian soldier who has missed leaving Germany with his unit, and who now roams through the city with the Soviet flag. Lost in time, he – whose father had once placed the flag on top of the destroyed Reichstag – then hoists his own flag above Berlin's paint-splattered monument of Lenin, which has already been cleared for demolition. Bizarre and accidental commentary on the final report made by a committee set up by the Berlin Senate to discuss and make proposals for the future of »socialist« monuments in the eastern half of the city. On February 15th, Senator for Cultural Affairs Roloff-Momin had presented the final report of the committee to the public as an essential contribution to the culture of political debate. Everything had overtones of a farewell – as well as of a grotesque and skeptical welcoming-in of a new era.

Silver Berlin Bear
for the humanistic and
hopeful interpretation of
societal and private crises
UDZINARTA MSE
Georgia
directed by Temur Babluani

Silver Berlin Bear
for the sincere portrayal of
daily life in Burkina Faso
SAMBA TRAORÉ
Burkina Faso/
France/Switzerland
directed by Idrissa
Ouédraogo

Silver Berlin Bear
for the best actress
Michelle Pfeiffer
in LOVE FIELD

Silver Berlin Bear
for the best actor
Denzel Washington
in MALCOLM X

The Blue Angel
LE JEUNE WERTHER
France
directed by Jacques Doillon

Special Mention
for its humor and brashness
in dealing with contemporary
German reality
WIR KÖNNEN AUCH ANDERS
Germany
directed by Detlev Buck

Special Mention
Assi Dayan
for his sincere and
courageous work in
HA CHAYIM ALPY AGFA
Israel

Short Films
Golden Berlin Bear
BOLERO
Russia
directed by Ivan Maximov

Silver Berlin Bear
AŤ ŽIJE MYŠ
CSFR
directed by Pavel Koutský

Malcolm X by Spike Lee (in the Competition): Denzel Washington

Breathing room

By Jon Jost

In a world where commerce and art mix in a rather ungainly manner – not to mention in the world of film, where the scale tilts drastically to commerce with precious little and increasingly less space left for the utterances of art – the Berlin Forum has stuck it out, insisting on a bit of breathing room for the artistic side, and backing it up with tangibles. Not only has its over-worked crew carved out a platform next to (and perhaps even more-than-equal to) the »official« space of one of the world's truly major film festivals, it has also thought past the glitz of festivals, and established a distribution system to work in tandem with the utility of a festival. A lot of work, but of a lot of value for those who work in, or are interested in (especially in Germany though not only), the artistic side of film. Were it not for the Forum and the FdK, a lot of work would simply not be available in Germany (or for others in Europe as well). That would most definitely include my work, which surely would otherwise have gone unnoticed by the commercially-minded business people of distribution.

I first went to Berlin in 1977, flown in to show Ulrich and friends, as a kind of preview, Angel City, *and was invited then to the Forum in '78. Since then I've been back I forget how many times, and also found myself living in Berlin a fair while, in no small part thanks to the help of the Forum and Arsenal. I think it is fair to say that thanks to the efforts of the Forum, experimental-avant-garde-artistic or whatever-label-one-wishes-to-stick-on-it cinema grew and lasted a bit longer than it might otherwise have done. It certainly had a very real and tangible impact on my modest career, for which, along with a handful of others in this world, I must say, profoundly, thanks. And likewise for many others who I know are similarly indebted.*

The Wedding March by Erich von Stroheim (in the Retrospective): ZaSu Pitts, Erich von Stroheim

Beyond Hollywood

1994

Feb. 10th-21st, 1994 (Competition)
Feb. 11th-21st, 1994 (Forum)

What a hustle and bustle at the airport! As if the clock has been put back and the Berlinale returned to the fifties. Not quite, but almost: frantic excitement about a star. Sophia Loren, to whom this year's Homage is dedicated, is about to arrive. There are journalists, autograph hunters, and curious bystanders who don't even know who they are waiting for. An excited as well as amused Moritz de Hadeln tries to calm everyone down: »We wouldn't want her to take fright, now would we!« Then the first camera's flash – and a slightly flustered Lothar de Maizière, last Minister President of East Germany, passes through the crowd. He is asked for autographs and cannot quite fathom what is happening to him. And then finally: the star herself. Cheers, autographs, photographs, until she vanishes into the limousine. Yet it is time enough for her to reach the hearts of Berliners and of critical and ill-humored journalists. She does it again at the press conference, where her entrance is greeted with applause, and then draws even more when she exits. Hardly any other star guest had been so open, inquisitive and willing to meet the public – for instance, during a spontaneous excursion amongst the people after visiting the red »Infobox« at Potsdamer Platz where she took a look at the construction site at Berlin's new center; or during a short outing to the Children's Film Festival. Last not least, she is presented with her Golden Berlin Bear for her lifetime achievements: she is welcomed with lengthy standing ovations at the gala in the Zoo Palast and even a few tears are shed. She graciously accepts the bouquets and Golden Bear, posing splendidly and expressing words of gratitude. Finally the film of the evening, »her« film, is shown, LA CIOCIARA (»Two Women«) by Vittorio de Sica, and it, too, receives spontaneous bursts of applause.

Sophia Loren

It was to be a happy year for the Berlinale. Last year's pleasant atmosphere was still in the air; the program came up to expectations; the press center in the Congress Hall in the Tiergarten district, which had been so criticized, was perhaps not fully accepted but at least its infrastructure had been improved. Great efforts had been made to organize everything so it would run more smoothly and more agreeably for the public – especially with regard to protocol, ticket sales and the Festival magazine. The Berlinale was now collaborating with the English journal »Moving Pictures« and although this first year was not an editorial success, it constituted a financial saving, and as such bore fruits. The Festival management had had great financial worries in preparing for this Berlinale. It was not until the end of November 1993 that the Festival was informed of 500 000 marks in cutbacks – about 6 % of the total budget. And these were to be made despite considerable commitments – for example, rents for movie theaters and higher personnel costs. For the Competition and the Panorama, the Berlinale had always had to make do with a very small permanent staff of eight, and then to hire temporary personnel during the Festival. And although some of the cuts could be compensated for by increasing sponsoring (considering the importance of the Berlinale, still disappointingly low in international terms), it was not possible to avoid cuts in the budgets for advertising and invitational policies. In public statements, Moritz de Hadeln tried to avoid a feeling of doom, but these financial developments definitely represented a threat to the entire Festival. Especially in comparison with its rivals, the festivals in Cannes and Venice, Berlin's position seemed to have weakened. And this at a time when a survey among the members of the International Federation of Producers' Associations to determine the most

Financial cuts

Isabella Rossellini

Sabrina Ferilli

important and outstanding film festivals had ranked the Berlinale second to Cannes and above Venice. Hence, in this situation, it made sense to concentrate on the Berlinale not as a local cultural event but one of international repute. Nonetheless, it was no surprise that the Film Festival, as part of the Berlin Festivals Ltd., became involved in the increasingly harsh battle for ever tighter cultural funds.

Uncertainty about the Film Market's location

Prospects for the European Film Market's location in the CineCenter in the Budapester Straße were also uncertain. The Film Market had flourished and expanded under Beki Probst's management, as well as adeptly exploited commercial niches in competition with other international film markets. And although official numbers were not available, it was said that in Berlin transactions were made of between 30 and 40 million dollars. Yet the Berlin Senate had decided to shut down the Kunsthalle, the Film Market's previous location. Moreover, AMK fairs' association opted to give up their film studio operations there. As a result, these urgently needed premises were in danger and higher costs for rent were imminent. With the size of its budget, it was unimaginable, for example, for the Film Festival to lease rooms for the entire year when they only needed them for about a month. Yet still another factor spoke against these developments: the Berlin Senate had passed a resolution in November 1992 for the preservation of the historic film center in the area around the Zoo Palast; this venue was also to undergo expansion. However, for financial and political reasons at this point in time, it was neither opportune nor actually feasible to implement these plans. Ultimately matters would take a different turn, as seen in the developments of the next years. At least in agreement with de Hadeln and the head of the Berlin Festivals Ltd., Dr. Ulrich Eckhardt, and his committed initiative, the acute danger was averted for the time being. Once more it became evident – and this was not new for the Berlinale – that the Festival was handicapped in its location in comparison with its rivals: in its more than forty-year history, it had not succeeded in establishing its own independent Festival center.

Nansal Uranchimeg

Morgan Freeman

Krzysztof Kieślowski

Brian de Palma

Tom Hanks

GATT: Jack Valenti is conciliatory

With regard to film policy, this year's Berlinale was influenced by the end of GATT negotiations and concern about European cinema in relation to the USA's leading position on the market. Jack Valenti, president of MPAA, the Motion Picture Association of America, was greeted at the Berlinale with curiosity: he had represented the American film industry at the negotiations, a clever and unyielding lobbyist, who had disregarded European interests. Yet the negotiations had come to an end on December 15th, 1993 without including a passage in the final draft to accommodate American demands for the audiovisual industries. Instead, a regulation had been explicitly excluded, which was considered, internationally, a defeat for Valenti and a victory for the Europeans. Nevertheless, wherever Valenti showed up in Berlin, he was conciliatory and surprisingly pragmatic; he showed respect for the European position and its desire to protect its cinema culture. Wolf Donner, former Berlinale director, carefully commented on Valenti's remarks: »On the one-way road between Hollywood and Europe, traffic is beginning, thank Gatt, to flow cautiously in the other direction for the first time. Within this context, Jack Valenti's new mission – although no one is quite ready to trust it yet – may be the overture to new and completely different calculations. It is time for a global network of future communications superhighways via digital distribution technology, and supranational satellite providers on a grand scale, as well as thousands of feature films accessible via telephone cable. The future of the media is just dawning, and the United States are once again a step ahead. For some time now, Jack Valenti has been preparing himself for new worldwide diplomatic battles.« (Frankfurter Allgemeine Zeitung, Feb. 14, 1994) And on the periphery of the Berlinale, a meeting – organized by the FERA (Féderation Européenne des Réalisateurs de l'Audiovisuel) – was held to save European film. Filmmakers as well as European politicians for culture and the media participated. They settled on a catalogue of 15 items, which included proposals that ranged from providing tax incentives and financing for films by the European Union through

Jonas Mekas

the promotion of a movie theater network, to establishing a high commission for audiovisual media in Europe. All these measures were conceived to counteract the unchecked expansion of American movies. The fact that these proposals were based on a somewhat naive utopia did not seem to bother anyone for the moment: more important was the growing ability to unite disparate European interests. The new French Minister of Cultural Affairs, Jacques Toubon, announced that a chance now existed for a »European protective association« with a »competitive film program, reflecting our identity« – at this point, still just a politician's words.

But first of all, European cinema had to stand the test at this year's Festival – both with the press and the public. 1994 was to include some pleasant surprises. In the Competition, 22 features were presented, six were screened hors concours. There were two special screenings: one in honor of Sophia Loren; the other for Marcel Carné's LES ENFANTS DU PARADIS (»Children of Paradise«), in memory of the actor Jean-Louis Barrault, who had died only shortly before on January 22nd, and to whom the Berlinale had dedicated a Retrospective in 1987. The selection commission had viewed almost 300 films, an extravagant and sometimes counterproductive process: day after day, video material had to be looked at and films evaluated which had also been submitted to the Panorama or the Forum. Criteria, as the commission's experiences revealed, needed to be revised and interpreted more strictly, primarily in order to reduce the deluge of video cassettes. Ultimately, films from 25 countries were accepted for the Competition program – from Europe, the USA, from India, Korea, Hong Kong and the People's Republic of China, from Australia, Brazil and Cuba.

Difficulties in the selection

Within this spectrum of films, the American entries seemed like somewhat coy exceptions. These included: Jonathan Demme's PHILADELPHIA; the first mainstream film about AIDS, with Tom Hanks and Denzel Washington in the leading roles; Peter Weir's FEARLESS with Jeff Bridges and Isabella Rossellini, about a man no longer afraid of anything after surviving a plane crash, who deludes himself he is

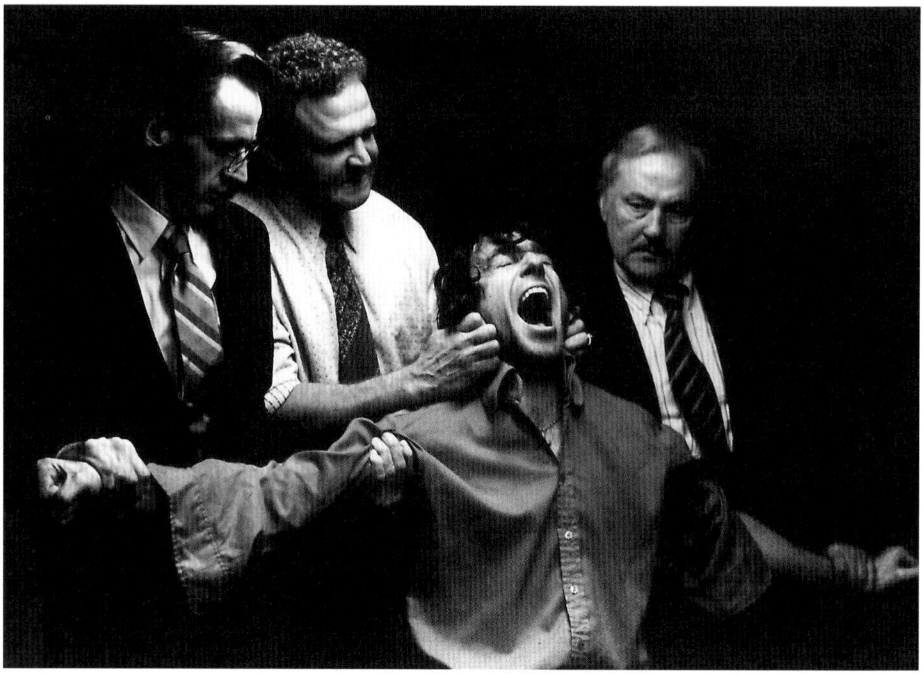

IN THE NAME OF THE FATHER by Jim Sheridan: Daniel Day-Lewis (in the middle)

humanity's savior and apostle of the truth – »the myth of the American hero as a vision of a disturbance«, as Christiane Peitz wrote in »Die Zeit« on February 25th; and lastly, Brian de Palma's underworld drama CARLITO'S WAY, with Al Pacino and Sean Penn, spectacularly and terrifically crafted. The fact that Steven Spielberg's SCHINDLER'S LIST could not be shown in the Competition was regarded as a deficit but despite great engagement, Moritz de Hadeln had not been able to convince the director to present his film in Berlin. Instead Spielberg decided that the German premiere of the film would be in Frankfurt. The decision had to be respected, but the suspicion remained that Spielberg had reservations toward the Berlinale and its audiences because they had failed to unanimously applaud his film THE EMPIRE OF THE SUN in 1988.

Steven Spielberg not in Berlin

The presence of the Americans was balanced out by the big names of European cinema. Alain Resnais presented SMOKING and NO SMOKING, Ken Loach LADYBIRD, LADYBIRD, Jim Sheridan IN THE NAME OF THE FATHER, Krzysztof Kieślowski TRZY KOLORY: BIAŁY (»Three Colors: White«), Márta Mészáros A MAGZAT (»Fetus«) and Bernardo Bertolucci LITTLE BUDDHA. The latter was the opening film of the Festival, yet it was received with reserve.

A look eastward

Unexpected focuses on specific countries emerged across the various sections of the program. A panorama of contemporary Russian films came together in Aleksandr Sokurov's TIKHIYE STRANITSY (»Whispering Pages«), a very free adaptation of motifs from Dostoevsky's novel »Crime and Punishment«, packed into a cinematic puzzle of Russian sensitivity; and, in the Competition as well, Semyon Aranovich's GOD SOBAKI (»The Year of a Dog«), the bitter tragedy of a criminal, another film reporting in cryptic coded images of a society in agony. Yuri Mamin portrayed contemporary Russia in his parodistic work OKNO V PARIŽ – SALADES RUSSES (»Window to Paris – Salades russes«) in the Panorama. Another series in the Panorama's program

GOD SOBAKI by Semyon Aranovich: Inna Churikova, Igor Sklyar

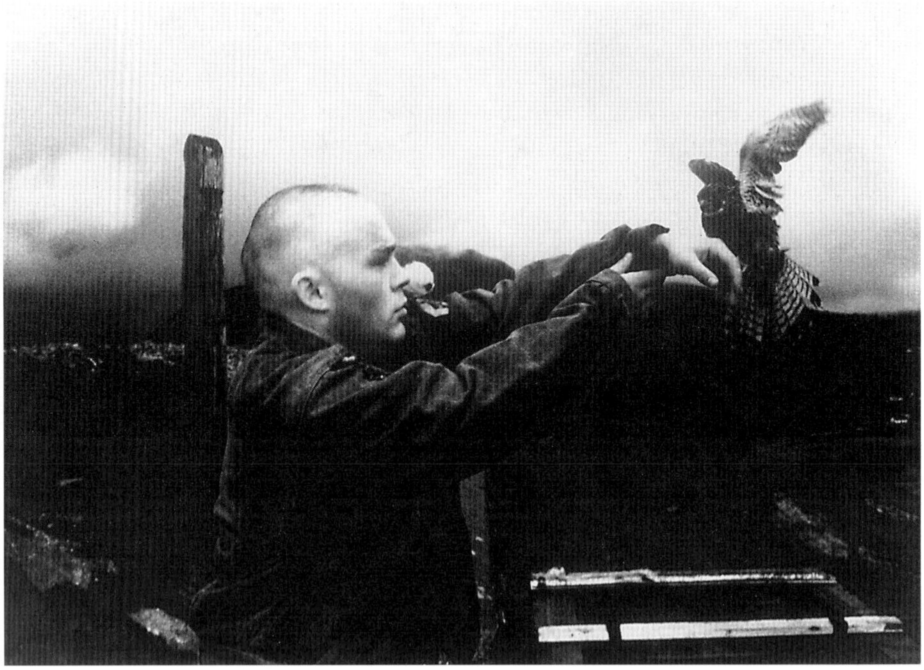

High Boot Benny by Joe Comerford (in the Forum): Marc O'Shea

was entitled »A Look Eastward«, in which Kira Muratova's Uvlecheniya (»Passions«) was presented, a »surreal but light drawing-room comedy« in which Muratova makes »the large oval of a country horse race-course the world stage«. (Angela Schmitt-Gläser, Frankfurter Rundschau, Feb. 22, 1994) In addition, there was Nikita Mikhalkov's first documentary film: Anna: 6–18 (»Anna: from Six to Eighteen«), about his daughter, a long-term study in which changes in Russian society unfold, imperceptibly making this film a chronicle of the times in Mikhalkov's beloved home country, which he nonetheless observes with skepticism. Vitali Kanevsky's documentary in the Forum Nous, les enfants du vingtième siècle (»We, the Children of the 20th Century«) also fits into this series of films which critically take stock of a nation. It is a collage of interviews with »juvenile murderers and drug addicts, with institutionalized children of all ages and with diverse police records«. Peter Körte delivered his opinion of these portraits in the »Frankfurter Rundschau«: »The murderers have no notion of guilt; and the petty thieves who may follow in their footsteps have no understanding of good and evil. Many tell of alcoholic parents and grandparents, of mothers who sell their children to customers for a glass of vodka. Kanevsky asks each interview partner to sing something. And so they sing: about sex, to show off; about love, to console themselves; about waiting and being waited for, to make them feel stronger. In speaking of his deeply moving film, Kanevsky states that the director's task is not to judge but to love.« (Feb. 18, 1994)

The Berlinale was finally able to fulfill its function as a bridge to the East again. In accord with all three Festival sections, a dense, imposing – and due to their pessimistic contents, sometimes oppressive – program of films from Eastern Europe could be presented: from Russia, Hungary, Rumania, Georgia, Kazakstan, Latvia and Estonia. A focus on Mongolian films in the Forum drew attention to a completely unknown film nation with a historical retrospective of older films and a review of newer post-socialist productions. The most outstanding films in the Forum were: the seven-

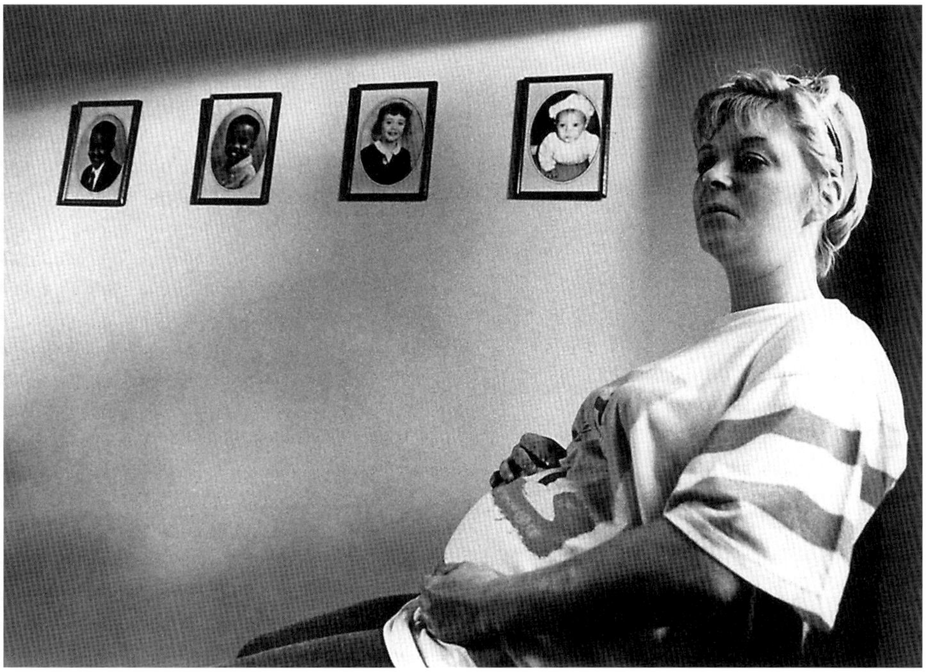

LADYBIRD, LADYBIRD by Ken Loach (in the Competition): Crissy Rock

and-a-quarter-hour film SÁTÁNSTANGÓ (»Satan's Tango«) by Béla Tarr from Hungary, an apocalyptic vision of the end of the world based on the novel of the same name by Lásló Krasznahorkai: »staking off the medium's limits, an acid test for its makers and its viewers« and »a panorama of perfect hopelessness, because it attempts to crush the last bastion of a negative metaphysics. For these Hungarian fatalists an apocalypse no longer exists, because the comfort in the very idea of a dreadful end is too great.« (Peter Körte, Frankfurter Rundschau, Feb. 21, 1994).

SÁTÁNTANGÓ by Béla Tarr (in the Forum)

In a daring montage of documentary and fictional scenes which are simultaneously structurally self-reflective and doubting, Lordan Zafranović's three-and-a-half hour documentary ZALAZAK STOIJECA (TESTAMENT L.Z.) (»The Decline of the Century: Testament L. Z.«) tells of a torn country, of battles and civil war, of fascism and resistance. In the run-up to the Festival, there had been stiff competition between the Forum and the festival in Rotterdam, which had already announced Zafranović's film in the program of its »FilmFree« section. But then the film was suddenly withdrawn from Rotterdam due to strong pressure from the Forum, according to festival director Emile Fallaux. Such a claim to exclusivity was in itself not new for festivals in their conduct with one another. This case drew attention primarily because this film was not one that would have been accepted in an international competition anyway. Instead, in Berlin's Forum, a competitor had emerged on the scene which was pursuing the same interests as those responsible for the »FilmFree« series in Rotterdam.

Quarrels between the Forum and the festival in Rotterdam

Derek Malcolm, president of the FIPRESCI, the international association of film critics, and his colleague Nenad Dukic, who headed the FIPRESCI jury in Amsterdam, decided to address a note of protest to the Forum, in which they criticized the conduct of the Festival organizers in Berlin, because »in the case of the Croatian film, viewers in both Rotterdam and Berlin could have benefited considerably from a screening«.

JEANNE LA PUCELLE by Jacques Rivette (in the Panorama): Sandrine Bonnaire

This was not the only film in this year's program over which the International Forum of Young Cinema and Rotterdam quarreled. The Forum had to make do without Bakhtiyar Khudojnazarov's new film KOSH BA KOSH (»New Game, Fresh Luck«), but with regard to Joe Comerford's Irish film HIGH BOOT BENNY, it prevailed over Rotterdam. After five years of research, Comerford portrayed the life of his father, an IRA activist. This film was meaningfully complemented by Jim Sheridan's feature IN THE NAME OF THE FATHER in the Competition. Sheridan dealt with an authentic judicial scandal during the Irish-British conflict, with the injustice done to a man wrongly convicted as an IRA terrorist, as well as the struggle between a father and his son, and their difficult relationship to their own personal and national identity. »That two so disparate directors such as Sheridan and Comerford ultimately come to the same radical conclusion, sending their heroes off into battle, is characteristic of the mood amongst the country's intellectuals«, Wolf Donner summarized. (Frankfurter Allgemeine Zeitung, Feb. 18, 1994)

Irish films

Along with these two powerful Irish films, English entries set the tone. SHADOWLANDS by Richard Attenborough and THE REMAINS OF THE DAY by James Ivory were brilliantly cast actors' films in which Anthony Hopkins shone. Ken Loach's LADYBIRD, LADYBIRD was an example of realistic and emotionally harrowing cinema: the true story of a housewife from Liverpool who has four children from four different fathers, and who gets caught in the machinery of the social services and loses custody of her children. »As always, Ken Loach sets to work with documentary directness, showing at frightening, upsetting and even nerve-racking proximity, the utter inextricability of this woman's life (...), a life, in which giving birth becomes a Sisyphean task, dismal, fatal. And when we are forced to watch how the idiotic claim for custody made by these well-meaning authorities, who lack all insight, instantaneously destroys the hopes of a family as they are just beginning to stir, we are cut to the quick. A mighty as well as important film.« (Ruprecht Skasa-Weiss, Stuttgarter

Attenborough, Ivory & Loach

Trzy kolory: Biały by Krzysztof Kiéslowski (in the Competition): Julie Delpy

Zeitung, Feb. 21, 1994). Loach had cast an amateur, Crissy Rock, in the leading role; she, too, was a housewife from Liverpool and she interpreted her role with enormous force. And so it was with good reason that she received the Silver Berlin Bear as best actress. At the award celebration she thanked the Jury and the audience for making it possible for her to feel like Princess Diana for a day.

Resnais, Rivette, Rohmer and others

And then there were the French highlights of this Berlinale: Alain Resnais' two-parter Smoking/No Smoking (in the Competition), an artistic and sophisticated situational comedy, naive and shrewd, comic and intellectual. Tonie Marshall's down-to-earth and ironical story about a woman detective Pas très catholique (»Something Fishy«) was the surprise of the Competition. In the Panorama, there was Jacques Rivette's two-parter attempt to approach the myth of Joan of Arc, Jeanne la Pucelle (Les Batailles and Les Prisons) (»Joan the Maid: The Battles and The Prisons«) – about which Fritz Göttler wrote in the »Süddeutsche Zeitung« on February 15th: Jeanne La Pucelle is »the incarnation of anarchy« and in Rivette's work, »each take is like an act of creation, the long scene with the king's coronation in Reims is as vivid as the Corpus Christi festivities in Vienna's St. Stephan's Cathedral« in The Wedding March by Erich von Stroheim (to whom the extensive and extremely successful Retrospective was dedicated). And in the Forum, Eric Rohmer's film L'Arbre, le maire et la médiathèque (»The Tree, the Mayor and the Mediatheque«) was presented, an equally magical film, full of gentle escapism and veracity.

A comedy and the Stasi

The German films, along with Reinhard Münster's cheery comedy Alles auf Anfang (»Back to Square One«), were a succès d'estime and a worthy follow-up to Detlev Buck's funny hit Wir können auch anders (»No More Mr. Nice Guy«) from the preceding year. And the fact that Lienhard Wawrzyn in Der Blaue (»The Blue One«) and Michael Gwisdek in Abschied von Agnes (»Farewell to Agnes«) dealt with very recent German history and the criminal activities of the Stasi in different ways was also registered with respect – although their films met with a luke-

Alain Resnais

Sophia Loren with the Golden Berlin Bear for her lifetime achievements

warm response. Whereas Wawrzyn's film was criticized for trying to tell too much at once, as well as adhering too strictly to the dramaturgy of a mystery, Gwisdek was rebuked for too tenaciously pursuing a psychodrama and losing sight of the political implications of his material.

Two German documentaries in the Forum received more substantial recognition: Barbara and Winfried Junge's DAS LEBEN DES JÜRGEN VON GOLZOW (»Jürgen of Golzow: His Life«) and Volker Koepp's DIE WISMUT (»The Wismut«). Life in the GDR evidently evaded all narrative attempts and could only be adequately captured by documentary.

Prizes, guests and dashed hopes

Before the award ceremony, opinion on who would win was divided between Jim Sheridan's film and Ken Loach's. In the end Sheridan's work received the Golden Bear, while Loach's leading actress – with poetic justice – was awarded a Silver Bear. There were cheers for the Special Prize of the Jury which went to the Cuban film FRESA Y CHOCOLATE (»Strawberry and Chocolate«), a comedy about politics and homosexuality which examines the problems of fear and of taboos in Cuban culture with a light-hearted touch and slight smile. Many regretted that Resnais' film received only a secondary award, while the best director prize that went to Kieślowski was equally controversial.

Tom Hanks' Silver Bear as best actor, on the other hand, was more than just a bow to American cinema. The Berlinale had withstood an important test, with filmic highlights, national focal points, and stars. For in the end, Bernardo Bertolucci and Samuel Fuller, Liv Ullmann and Isabella Rossellini, to mention only a few, and nearly all the directors of the films in the Competition program had come to Berlin.

A star is born

And a new star was discovered: Linda Fiorentino, who played the lead in John Dahl's film noir THE LAST SEDUCTION, a genuine thriller of the nineties. Provocative, cool and yet emotionally deep, a true daughter of Barbara Stanwyck and Lauren

Hsu Feng

Krzysztof Kieślowski

Bacall. The fact that her film was shown in the Panorama and not in the Competition reflected the selection commission's indecision. Just the same, the members must be given credit for selecting this film at all, thereby enabling the discovery of this outstanding actress.

International Jury
Jeremy Thomas
(Great Britain, president)
Chingiz Aitmatov
(Kirghizia)
Maria Luisa Bemberg
(Argentine)
Morgan Freeman (USA)
Francis Girod (France)
Corinna Harfouch
(Germany)
Hsu Feng (Hong Kong)
Carlo Lizzani (Italy)
Wolfram Schütte (Germany)
Susan Seidelman (USA)
Hayao Shibata (Japan)

The Awards of the
International Jury

Feature Films
Grand Prix of the 44th IFB
Golden Berlin Bear
IN THE NAME OF
THE FATHER
Ireland/Great Britain/USA
directed by Jim Sheridan

Silver Berlin Bear
Special Prize of the Jury
FRESA Y CHOCOLATE
Cuba/Mexico/Spain
directed by Tomás Gutiérrez
Alea and Juan Carlos Tabío

Silver Berlin Bear
GOD SOBAKI
Russia/France
directed by Semyon
Aranovich

Silver Berlin Bear
for the best director
Krzysztof Kieślowski
TRZY KOLORY: BIAŁY
Poland/France

The Blue Angel
IL GIUDICE RAGAZZINO
Italy
directed by Alessandro
di Robilant

Silver Berlin Bear
for the best actress
Crissy Rock
in Ladybird, Ladybird
Great Britain

Silver Berlin Bear
for the best actor
Tom Hanks
in Philadelphia
USA

Silver Berlin Bear
for an outstanding individual achievement
Alain Resnais
Smoking/No Smoking
France

Alfred Bauer Prize
for a film opening up new perspectives in film art
Hwaomkyung
Korea
directed by Chang Sun Woo

Special Mention
for his cinematography
Huo hu
Hong Kong/People's Republic of China
directed by Wu Ziniu

Special Mention
for our dear friend Mario Monicelli, who always entertains us so well
Cari fottutissimi amici
Italy
directed by Mario Monicelli

Special Mention
for her outstanding performance to
Rosie Perez
in Fearless
USA

Short Films
Golden Berlin Bear
Hamu
Hungary
directed by Ferenc Cakó

Silver Berlin Bear
Balthazar
Belgium/France
directed by Christophe Fraipont

The Last Seduction
by John Dahl
(in the Panorama):
Linda Fiorentino

Tikhiye stranitsy by
Aleksandr Sokurov
(in the Competition):
Elisaveta Koroljove

Butterfly Kiss:
Amanda Plummer

New Berlin afflictions

1995

Feb. 9th-20th, 1995 (Competition)
Feb. 10th-20th, 1995 (Forum)

There were anniversaries to be celebrated. A wild good time was to be had by all. It was film's 100th birthday, the Berlinale's 45th, and the International Forum of Young Cinema's 25th. Yet as so often the case, the idea for the festivities had failed to arouse much enthusiasm. Critics were already bemoaning one thing or another, or everything in general, as if the changes of the past two years had never happened. Nothing was left unquestioned: neither consolidation plans, future perspectives, nor the Berlinale itself. Although there was no shortage of polemics, malicious glee, good and bad advice, little was actually done. There were few relevant considerations or distinct tips. What had happened?

No stars?

In the run-up to the Festival – during preparations – there had been complications: financial, personnel and organizational problems. And then while the Festival was in process, the atmosphere was disturbed by a number of incidents – for instance, certain guests decided to cancel. One of these was Robert Redford, whose attendance had already been announced and on whom public attention had concentrated. Yet the distributors of Redford's new film QUIZ SHOW, which was in the Competition, failed to take the star's decision to cancel seriously and still counted on him putting in an appearance. By the time the truth dawned, it was too late. Expectations were so high that Redford's cancellation was blamed on the Festival. The overwhelming disappointment distracted from the fact that glitter and glamour had nonetheless most certainly come to Berlin, with Michel Piccoli, Leslie Caron, Harvey Keitel, William Hurt and guest of honor Alain Delon. Goodness knows what would have happened if word had got out that Paul Newman, who was later to receive a Silver Bear as best male actor, had had to cancel coming to the award ceremony at the last minute for personal reasons. Inconceivable what fatal effect this second »No. Sorry!« would have had on public opinion.

Old sores reopened

Yet far worse, old sores were reopened. The press center, which had been lodged off into the House of World Cultures was one point of issue, the general feeling being that it was an affront to the press. Despite organizational improvements, this location was still considered a makeshift solution. The relative calmness of those affected, the journalists who had worked there over the past two years, turned out to be the lull before the storm. It was obvious that another solution had to be found: but where, and on what terms? There were also problems at the Zoo Palast. On January 1st 1994, the management switched hands and it was taken over by UCI, which, according to the company's own information, was investing 20 million marks in remodeling and renovating the entire cinema complex. Unfortunately, however, insufficient arrangements were made with the Festival management, and certain suggestions could not be realized for financial reasons. What was possible to blame on mere »teething troubles« in the first year after redoing the building had turned into a serious problem by the second year. The screen was moved a meter closer to the audience, which reduced space on the already narrow stage, so that it was as crowded as a train station platform at the award ceremony. Furthermore, in many respects, the projection technology was not up to the standards of an international festival. It was no longer possible to accept the incessant work being done to correct these deficiencies. The Festival itself was becoming an object of criticism, despite it having rather limited responsibility for some of these difficulties. Relations between the Festival and Berlin Festivals Ltd. were also often strained. And although the Film

Amanda Plummer

Marcel Ophuls, Youssef Chahine, Claude Lanzmann

Relations with the Berlin Festivals Ltd.

Market's location was no longer in danger – the administration of the former Kunsthalle premises had been taken over by the Festivals Ltd. – cost-cutting measures did not allow for resolving other organizational and personnel problems. And to crown it all, there was an ongoing debate in which the individual program sections of the Berlin Festivals Ltd. were played off against one another, and one of these was the Berlinale. This time, the Film Festival was being maneuvered into opposition against the Berlin Theater Meeting, whose very existence appeared threatened. It was a great time for lobbyists, and any kind of objective discussion was rapidly losing ground.

Between fronts

These conflicts took place against the background of a fundamental debate about Berlin's cultural policies and the influence of the federal government on cultural events in Berlin, which by no means eased the situation. The sensibilities of individual cultural institutions were involved. Existential anxieties caused vulnerability, and at such moments nothing else counted but each institution's own interests. Solidarity, as well as the much-acclaimed sense of mutuality between East and West, turned out to be fragile. It was first and foremost a matter of limiting damages, hardly one of new perspectives. Attempting to maintain at least the status quo was the order of the day.

The Berlinale was not exempt from this general politico-cultural predicament: it obstinately tried to keep all ground won and spoke of the threat to all that existed, painting the future black. As shortcomings arising during the Film Festival were to make evident, this was not without good reason. Admittedly, attempts at structural changes had been made in the past two years, but some matters had been taken only halfway due to daily concerns. In 1995, the Festival ended up paying dearly for its occasional indecision. And there was no denying that the two Festival directors, de Hadeln and Gregor, seemed to be at a loss for words. Instead of making a virtue of necessity and jointly presenting the Berlinale's positions to the public, known and unknown conflicts came to light: especially the indisputable rivalry between the

The Competition and Forum – unclarified relations

Margarethe von Trotta, August Zirner

Wayne Wang, Paul Auster

Ethan Hawke, Julie Delpy

Agnès Varda, Julie Gayet

Festival sections, in particular the direct competition between the Forum and the Panorama in their films and program images. In fact, the Panorama had demonstrated in the past two years that it had become more flexible in its conception and was now held in higher esteem. The Forum did little to relativize its special cineastic and conceptual position, or to back the Competition with its completely different needs. Somewhat overly self-sufficient, the Forum cultivated its own image and righteously pointed out its constant success, which did indeed fantastically affirm its activities. That the Forum had tacitly distanced itself from the dogma of its founding days (as well as in part from current regulations) – for instance, in respect to the prizes – did not become an issue or simply went unnoticed. Closer examination revealed, however, that boundaries had shifted over the years. This was by no means surprising, but a quite natural development. It only became questionable when it was not used as a reason to reexamine the Festival's profile or scrutinize and eliminate rifts. Once again and with alarming clarity, this neglect constituted a danger, especially for the Competition. For the public, opposition to the Panorama became visible in a way that had never been intended nor actually existed internally. As a consequence, films running in the Panorama (and to a certain degree also in the Forum) were seen increasingly often as predestined for the Competition. As a rule, it was impossible to get across the idea that regulations for the Competition and those set by the FIAPF for international festivals limited selection criteria extremely, and many of these subsequently highly-praised films would perhaps have been eligible for the Competition quality-wise, but not based on formal criteria – not to mention that the subjective opinions of the selection commission members also played a part. Ruled out by the regulations are all films that have already been screened at other festivals, and the few exceptions that have been made tend to confirm this rule, particularly in the case of the American Sundance Festival, which also co-produces films. More significant, however, is that by limiting participation to world premieres

Wieland Speck, director of the Panorama

or European and German first runs, the selection of films is restricted to those made between October and January. Very few films presented in the Panorama and Forum are able to meet this requirement.

Pressure on Moritz de Hadeln

Yet this complicated system of international guidelines and internal battles for positions, of local and national cultural interests and of crises in Berlin's cultural institutions, reflected to what extent the reunified city had been affected by a cultural shock and its anxious search for a new identity of its own. This was particularly true of film, anyhow not a ›flourishing landscape‹ within German federal cultural policies, and prone to vanities and showy affectations. In the complexity of the situation, critics from outside had it easy. Moritz de Hadeln was particularly under pressure, more so than Ulrich Gregor. Oddly, the failures at this year's Berlinale were once again seen as related to the renewal of de Hadeln's contract. According to Peter Buchka, de Hadeln »had wanted his own contract renewed (which in the meantime has occurred)« and secondly, he continues, »efforts in Bonn« were evidently being made »to disassociate oneself from the Berlin Festivals Ltd. and hence from the Berlinale«. Buchka goes on to add: »Indeed, this was also the reason why de Hadeln committed himself unusually early to certain films and then had to refuse other offers later.« (Süddeutsche Zeitung, Feb. 22, 1995) This attempt from Munich to analyze Berlinale issues mixed facts and rumors and led to false conclusions. What is correct is that internal exploratory talks had been held between Bonn and Berlin in the direction suggested by Buchka, but no exact details were known. However, exactly what this had to do with film invitations and refusals, and with de Hadeln's (and Gregor's) contract renewal, remained incomprehensible. And so there was discord on all counts. More than ever, the Berlinale had to prove its worth. Yet just the same, the opening of the Festival on February 9th was unusually stately and magnificent.

Federal President Herzog opens the Festival

For the first time in the Festival's history, the Federal President of Germany opened the International Film Festival. Roman Herzog not only announced his commit-

LIVING IN OBLIVION by Tom Di Cillo (in the Forum)

ment to international film culture »which is capable of having an effect across national, linguistic and cultural borders«, but also said that he was personally particularly fond of going to the movies, in fact he had a certain passion for film. Moreover, he was especially pleased that the Berlinale was opening with a German film: Margarethe von Trotta's DAS VERSPRECHEN (»The Promise«). As he stated: »We can only grasp the good fortune of German unification if we constantly force ourselves to keep the tragedy caused by decades of division in this city and our country in mind.« To be exact, the Berlinale began with two German films. The restored version of the first films projected by the Skladanowsky brothers in Berlin's Wintergarten in 1895 was also presented at the Zoo Palast. The Festival's program was to reflect a hundred years of film history. It was also noted with respect that Margarethe von Trotta was finally showing a film again at the Berlinale, the first since her film HELLER WAHN (»Sheer Madness«/»Friends and Husbands«), which had so disastrously flopped at the Festival twelve years ago. It was a significant and politically astute decision to open the Festival with the film DAS VERSPRECHEN as it reflected thirty years of German history, right up to the fall of the Wall. A very worthy prelude. Hans-Dieter Seidel wrote in the »Frankfurter Allgemeine Zeitung«: »life's portrayal [takes on] authenticity through those moments in which personal fates bring into focus the fate of an entire nation«. (Feb. 11, 1995)

Not in the Competition program

The difficulty of selecting films for this year's Competition was already felt in December 1994. Never before had so few films been confirmed for participation as the year drew to an end, and a number of hopes had already been dashed. New films by Robert Altmann (PRÊT-À-PORTER), Wim Wenders (LISBON STORY), Michael Apted (NELL), and Nicholas Hyttner (THE MADNESS OF KING GEORGE) were not available for the Festival. And although the presence of QUIZ SHOW by Robert Redford, NOBODY'S FOOL by Robert Benton and SILENT FALL by Bruce Beresford meant that three US major productions were screened in the Competition, it was ul-

TZEDEK by Marek Halter (in the Forum)

timately a festival of outsiders. Simultaneously, it seemed that almost no one had noticed that the selection commission had consciously tried to break new ground. On the contrary: the very absence of those films expected in Berlin – mentioned here were, for example, Barbet Schroeder's KISS OF DEATH, Mike Newell's AN AWFUL BIG ADVENTURE and Roman Polanski's DEATH AND THE MAIDEN – was booked as the Festival's failure. Meanwhile, the American film THE ADDICTION by Abel Ferrara – a provocative vampire and drug tale with political and theological undertones, whose participation had caused fierce and controversial debate in the selection commission, and which made the Competition by a mere one-vote majority – was listed as just a kind of side-event. Others failed to receive the attention or critical appreciation which the selection commission had anticipated. These included films by: Patricia Rozema from Canada (WHEN NIGHT IS FALLING), a subtly recounted story about a love between two women; Im Kwon Taek from Korea (TAEBAEK SANMAEK/ »Taebaek Mountains«), a historical review of societal conditions in Korea at the end of the forties, after Japanese colonial rule had come to an end and before the civil war broke out between the north and the south; Marius Holst from Norway (TI KNIVER I HJERTET/»Cross My Heart and Hope to Die«), a cleverly orchestrated psychological study about a boy, which blended various genre elements; Jorge Fons from Mexico (EL CALLEJÓN DE LOS MILAGROS/»Midaq Alley«), a melodrama about the big emotions of small people; and Shmuel Hasfari from Israel (SH'CHUR/»Magic«), the story of a Moroccan-Jewish family caught between the worlds of traditional Morocco and modern Israel.

Disregarded outsiders

Three surprises

Nevertheless, there were a few exceptions: Richard Linklater's American-Austrian co-production BEFORE SUNRISE was one. In it, Ethan Hawke and Julie Delpy play a couple who meet and fall in love on a train from Budapest to Vienna. It is the story of a single night full of unbridled conversation and youthful naiveté. And at the other end of the emotional scale was the British film BUTTERFLY KISS by Michael

BEFORE SUNRISE by Richard Linklater (in the Competition): Julie Delpy, Ethan Hawke

Winterbottom, starring Amanda Plummer and Saskia Reeves, a disturbing depiction of a murderous love affair: »Two women – one of whom, Miriam, unconditionally accepts whatever the other, Eunice, might do – become so close by committing murders together, that Eunice ultimately allows Miriam to drown her. And it is in this very act that they both seem to find redemption.« (Hans-Dieter Seidel, Frankfurter Allgemeine Zeitung, Feb. 17, 1995)

Another notable exception was the double feature SMOKE/BLUE IN THE FACE by director Wayne Wang and novelist Paul Auster from the USA, giving the Competition substance after all: SMOKE, »a ballad about Brooklyn, a multi-cultural patchwork«, and BLUE IN THE FACE, an improvised puzzle of allusions to SMOKE, of citations and pure jokes, that »allows the actors complete freedom« (and among these actors were Madonna, Jim Jarmusch, Lou Reed, Roseanne, Lily Tomlin and Michael J. Fox). Peter Körte wrote: »You go into the film like you do into your regular place or favorite bar. You stand at the counter and listen to the buzz of the voices, and shreds of stories float your way. You have reason to be amused, there are snips of gossip, news and jokes circulate, while small and somewhat shady deals are made. You always enjoy going back there again.« (Frankfurter Rundschau, Feb. 18, 1995)

Tavernier and the Jury

And although all three of these films were in the running for a Golden Bear, the French entry L'APPÂT (»The Bait«) by Bertrand Tavernier came in first – which did not, however, please everyone. From the point of view of festival politics, the Jury, presided over by Lia van Leer, had not made a bad choice: the last time the Grand Prix had gone to France was in 1965 (for Jean-Luc Godard's ALPHAVILLE). Yet it was felt that the Jury had passed judgment based on their sense of morals. This appeared to be the reason why they had favored this grim and coldly realistic account of Parisian adolescents, who murder for money so they can live the good life, above formally more daring productions. And the fact that the jurors decided not to award

TAEBAEK SANMAEK by Im Kwon Taek (in the Competition): O Jung-Hae (left)

the Alfred Bauer Prize, which had been established to honor especially new cinematic discoveries, was seen as further indication of this attitude.

History documented in the Forum

The International Forum of Young Cinema was dominated by documentaries that dealt with the conflict »between history and the present, between politics and myth«, as Ulrich Gregor wrote in his program notes. These included such controversial films as ERNESTO »CHE« GUEVARA, DAS BOLIVIANISCHE TAGEBUCH (»Ernesto ›Che‹ Guevara – A Bolivian Diary«) by Swiss director Richard Dindo, and ULRIKE MARIE MEINHOF by French director Timon Koulmasis. Both films chronicle lives, examining and questioning the legends of their ›heroes‹ by exploring their environments: »The rigorous hermetical quality of Dindo's method, which, by repeating images with regularity, adopts the suggestive monotony of a diary, hardly daring commentary, speaks for the scruples, the doubts and the skepticism of contemporary European intellectuals in dealing with this material«, Sabine Horst reasoned. And of Koulmasis' film, she went on to say that the director approaches with »amazing impartiality« the biography of his »lost heroine«. In comparing the two films, she sums up: »Whereas Richard Dindo with ERNESTO ›CHE‹ GUEVARA has failed ambitiously at least, Koulmasis' film barely arouses our interest. (...) In ULRIKE MARIE MEINHOF, ghosts from the past are merely charmed away, while ›Che‹ gazes somewhat at a loss from his poster on a living-room wall in Berlin: not a hero, not even a fallen one – just an old-fashioned piece of décor.« (Frankfurter Rundschau, Feb. 18, 1995)

Lanzmann and Ophuls

Claude Lanzmann's five-hour film about the Israeli army, TSAHAL, fits into this series of films that document the present, but also evoked mixed feelings, because it did not show »even one frame from the six wars that this army had waged, let alone from its missions internally«, as Thomas Rothschild stated in the »Stuttgarter Zeitung« (Feb. 22, 1995). Marcel Ophuls' new film about war correspondents, VEILLES D'ARMES/THE TROUBLES WE'VE SEEN, blended meticulously researched material and essayistic commentary into a montage which sought, with ironic distance,

SH'CHUR by Shmuel Hasfari (in the Competition): Orly Ben-Garti

the truth behind the images: »The film revolves around a hotel, the Holiday Inn in Sarajevo, where the reporters live. Its dominant tone is one of gloomy mirth: an attitude which deflects cheap sentimentality. Ophuls does not accuse the reporters, amongst whom there are, as always, different kinds, adventurous types on the one hand, and those who are willing to risk their lives for the truth, on the other. No, Ophuls supports them, just as the reporters all apparently firmly support the victims in this war.« (Harald Martenstein, Der Tagesspiegel, Feb. 20, 1995) In TZEDEK (»The Righteous«), Marek Halter takes up the most painful era in German history: the murder and extermination of the Jews. Yet he introduces a different angle from previous documentaries about the Holocaust: he seeks the »righteous« rather than the guilty, those who had the courage to save fellow human beings from persecution and death. Halter's film was complemented in the Competition by Herbert Achternbusch's film HADES. »Achternbusch makes the tragedy of the Holocaust accessible to us by using an artificial device, by turning a small Jewish boy's biography into his own«, Carla Rhode wrote in the »Tagesspiegel« on February 14th. »Historical footage from the Warsaw ghetto, in black-and-white and slow motion, becomes the core. Dead bodies lie outside each house, they are then loaded onto wooden wagons and carted off, emaciated bodies sliding down a ramp into a pit. For a piece of bread, the small boy dances in tatters in front of a German cameraman, his smile distorted, his dance steps stirring in their endless spin. The poor little chap pivots round and round to the melody of ›My Hat It Has Three Corners‹, and this frivolous song suddenly sounds tremendously sad. And then, without hesitating even a moment, a German soldier grabs the child and helps him crawl into a box which he carries off.«

Halter and Achternbusch

In the Panorama, many films dealt with themes of homosexuality and AIDS, documentaries and feature films, amongst which were the last films by directors Derek Jarman, GLITTERBUG, and Marlon T. Rigg, BLACK IS ... BLACK AIN'T, who both died in 1994. In connection with these screenings and as an avowal to thematic continu-

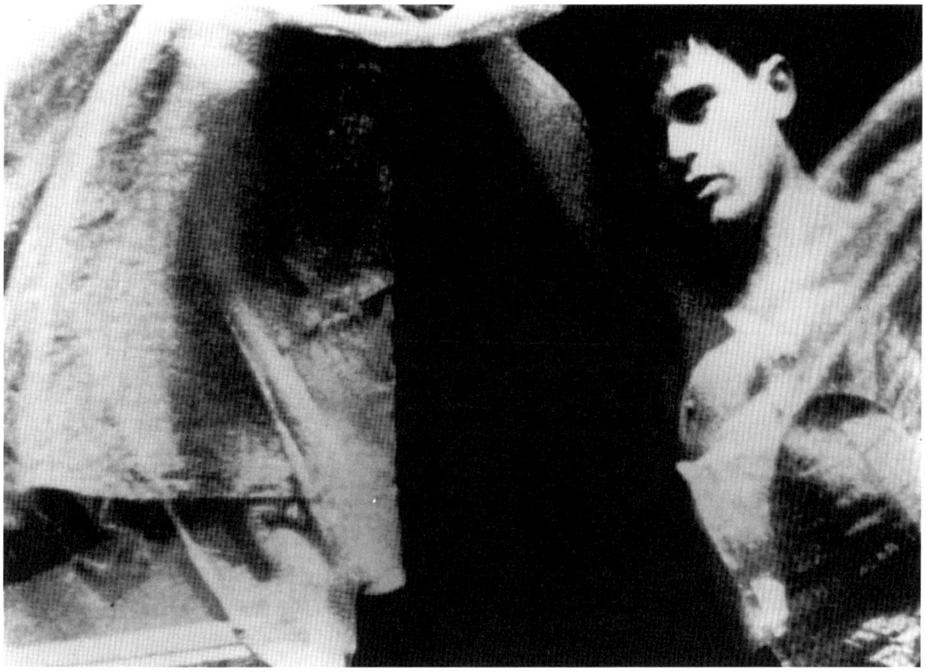

GLITTERBUG by Derek Jarman (in the Panorama)

Manfred Salzgeber, Isaac Julien (at the Berlinale in 1994)

Ingrid Scheib-Rothbart, Wolf Donner (at the Berlinale in 1992)

ity, there was also the final good-bye for Manfred Salzgeber, long-standing director of the Panorama, who had died in August 1994 of AIDS. Salzgeber, a film-lover, took over organizing the so-called Info Show of the Festival in 1980, and at de Hadeln's request, developed it into a reputable Festival program section. In 1986, the Info Show was renamed Panorama and took up position alongside the Forum: complementing the Competition, but also at times counterpointing the Forum. Salzgeber had an extraordinary eye for new talents: and so the Panorama had presented films by Jean-Jacques Beinix, Pedro Almodovár, Detlev Buck, Im Kwon Taek, Alex Cox and Gus van Sant, long before they became widely known. He gave many underground films a chance and established the Panorama as a forum for gay cinema. In honor of Manfred Salzgeber, the Panorama, now under the direction of Wieland Speck, showed Salzgeber's favorite film: MONSIEUR VERDOUX by Charlie Chaplin.

Another special event commemorated the former director of the Berlinale, Wolf Donner, who had died in September 1994. In his last years, he had been a critical companion of the Festival. Donner had headed the Berlinale from 1976 to 1979 and had implemented a number of essential innovations: he rescheduled the Festival from summer to winter, extended and remodeled the CineCenter, established the Children's Film Festival, as well as assigned conceptual and organizational responsibilities for the Retrospectives to the Deutsche Kinemathek. Donner had a passion for the political contradictory, and so it was the film DEUTSCHLAND IM HERBST (»Germany in Autumn«) which the Festival presented in his memory.

What impressions were left of the Berlinale afterwards? Discoveries from America: Richard Linklater and Wayne Wang/Paul Auster, joined by Tom Di Cillo's film LIVING IN OBLIVION, which blurred boundaries between cinema and reality. And discoveries from Great Britain: the films by Michael Winterbottom and – the secret hit of the Festival – the black comedy FUNNY BONES by Peter Chelsom in the Panorama. There were reminiscences on 100 years of film: CITIZEN LANGLOIS by

BLUE IN THE FACE: Harvey Keitel, Jim Jarmusch (in the Competition)

Edgardo Cozarinsky, for example, a documentary about the founder of the Cinémathèque française; and also in the Forum, a film series entitled »Rediscovered«, in which long-lost and forgotten films were brought to public notice. Distinct memories lingered after Agnès Varda's playful homage to the cinema, LES CENT ET UNE NUITS (»One Hundred and One Nights«). It had also been the most successful Retrospective in the Festival's history, »Happy Birthday, Cinema« with films by Buster Keaton (although with a touch of bitterness because the rising costs of the Retrospective were to temporarily jeopardize these events). The final event was equally splendid: the screening of a restored copy of ASPHALT, made in 1929 in Berlin by Joe May, accompanied live to a new musical score by Karl-Ernst Sasse. »The first kiss is a clap of thunder, triumphal fanfare and an ominous tempest of sounds all in one. A masterpiece of German cinema, finally, at long last – too late«, Andreas Conrad commented in the »Tagesspiegel« on February 22nd.

Everyone was aware that things could not continue as they were. And after this Berlinale, many – perhaps too many – thought they knew just where to go from here.

International Jury
Lia van Leer
(Israel, president)
Georgi Diulgerov (Bulgaria)
Alfred Hirschmeier
(Germany)
Christine Hörbiger (Austria)
Vadim Ivanovitch Yusov
(Russia)
David Kehr (USA)
Michael Kutza (USA)
Pilar Miró (Spain)
Siqin Gaowa (People's
Republic of China)
Tsai Ming-Liang
(Taiwan/China)

The Awards of the
International Jury

Feature Films
Grand Prix of the 45th IFB
Golden Berlin Bear
L'APPÂT
France
directed by Bertrand
Tavernier

Silver Berlin Bear
Special Prize of the Jury
SMOKE
USA
directed by Wayne Wang
(on presenting the award, the Jury emphasized Harvey Keitel's outstanding performance)

Silver Berlin Bear
for its special stylistic and
thematic qualities
PYESA DLYA PASSAZHIRA
Russia
directed by Vadim
Abdrashitov

Silver Berlin Bear
to the team for the visual
design of
HONGFEN
People's Republic of
China/Hong Kong
directed by Li Shaohong

FUNNY BONES: Freddie Davies, George Carl, Lee Evans (in the Panorama)

Silver Berlin Bear
for the best director
Richard Linklater
Before Sunrise
USA/Austria

Silver Berlin Bear
for the best actress
Josephine Siao
in Xiatian de xue
Hong Kong

Silver Berlin Bear
for the best actor
Paul Newman
in Nobody's Fool
USA

The Blue Angel
Ti kniver i hjertet
Norway
directed by Marius Holst

Special Mention
for the unique way in which
the story is told
El callejón de los
milagros
Mexico
directed by Jorge Fons

Special Mention
for a special blend of reality
and magic
Sh'chur
Israel
directed by Shmuel Hasfari

Special Mention
for performances in
supporting roles
Colpo di luna
Italy/France
directed by Alberto Simone

Short Films
Golden Berlin Bear
Repete
Czech Republic
directed by Michaela
Pavlátová

Silver Berlin Bear
My Baby Left Me
Hungary
directed by Milorad Krstic

L'Appât by Bertrand
Tavernier (in the Competition): Marie Gillain

The warmth of Berlin

By Ann Hui

The Berlin Festival is associated with some of my best memories. In 1981, as a young filmmaker, I went there for the first time on an invitation from Mr. Moritz de Hadeln to attend a conference. My film ZHUANG DAO ZHENG *(»The Spooky Bunch«) was also screened in the Panorama. It was very cold, there was sleet and slushy streets. The sky was overcast all the time. But people were all very warm. I remember the publicist Ann Head in a long black coat, haggard and worrying about the reception of my film more than I was. Midnight shows, hurrying with the crowd to attend a film by Godard: laughter, hushed expectation, then comments breaking out all over the place after the show. An invitation by the mayor's wife to a tea party at a palatial house, complete with butlers holding trays of sherry. During which I consumed the greatest amount of assorted cakes in my whole life. And then the panoramic survey of international films by an informed, deeply concerned audience ... I was quite electrified ... I just hoped, someday I'd be back with a film which this audience liked ...*

I wasn't back until 14 years later. In 1995. So much had happened. I went back with XIATIAN DE XUE *(»Summer Snow«), a deeply scarred, middle-aged filmmaker, after a lot of ups and downs in her career, with not too many expectations of warmth from humankind. But again, despite the nagging cold, Berlin was as warm as ever. Our film got a best actress prize, and I was launched back into the second spring of my career ... This spring didn't last, however, but the warmth of Berlin is something I treasure and will give me strength in the forthcoming years!*

My best wishes to the Berlinale on its march into its 50th year!

Dead Man Walking:
Susan Sarandon

Stars, stars, stars

1996

Feb. 15th – 26th, 1996 (Competition)
Feb. 16th – 26th, 1996 (Forum)

Even the opening was turbulent and fraught with suspense. The audience had gathered in the movie theater at the Zoo Palast, but the curtain didn't rise. The politicians had taken their seats, and Federal Minister of the Interior Kanther and Mayor Diepgen were ready to make their speeches. But some guests still hadn't arrived. Twenty minutes passed, then cameras flashed and actress Emma Thompson and her director Ang Lee entered. A burst of applause from the audience. The VIPs shook hands and kept smiling, but the show still didn't begin. A few more minutes went by and people started fidgeting again; suddenly a group of photographers rushed forward, stumbling over one another, cameras flashed again and there were cries of »John, John«, then more applause – and a path opened for the star: John Travolta entered. He shook hands with the governing officials, exchanged small talk with the Federal Minster of the Interior and then they posed for a photograph (what an odd couple!) and waved to the audience. Finally the show could begin, behind schedule, but the dramaturgy had been good (thanks to the Berlin police: it had classified the International Film Festival as a private event and then evidently underestimated evening traffic; moreover, the police had felt responsible for clearing the way to the Zoo Palast for the politicians, but not for the Berlinale's international guests, who then got caught in traffic while everyone else was waiting).

Federal Minister of the Interior Manfred Kanther and John Travolta

The opening night film was a true gala event: Sense and Sensibility. It had been years since the Berlinale had gotten off to such a promising start. Afterwards, when Emma Thompson asked the audience in German (and with a charming accent) whether they had cried, she was a resounding success and smiles flitted across people's faces. What did it matter that Berlin's weather was once again proving troublesome and most inhospitable? The rain was torrential and snow was forecast. Skies were gray but the mood was superb. The Berlinale itself was less capricious, showing it had changed. Had people learned their lessons after all? Or was this all just a lucky coincidence? There was also a reunification of a different kind. The journalists, who had been lodged out in the Congress Hall, returned to the Festival Center. A hotel, the »Intercontinental«, took on a central role in everyday Festival life – as the new press center and meeting place. Surprised and with a certain degree of satisfaction, Harald Martenstein noted in the »Tagesspiegel«: »This year, a Berlinale mile connects the Zoo Palast with the Interconti hotel, where the media and the stars meet. Flags are flying. Posters are up. The public is out strolling – as far as the weather in February and the rather austere surroundings allow. Those who have known the Berlin Film Festival only for the last few years are enjoying amazing innovations. Marble floors! A champagne bar! Modern toilets! Berlin has gone all out and spirits are improving.« (Feb. 18, 1996)

New press center in the Intercontinental hotel

Even before the Berlinale, there had been signs that things were in motion, also with respect to criticism of specific individuals. Again it was Harald Martenstein, one of the Berlinale's fiercest critics in previous years, who published a portrait of de Hadeln entitled »Trademark: A Slight Accent« in the »Tagesspiegel« on February 15th. In this article, slight corrections in mood were perceptible, despite the absence of a fundamental rapprochement of positions; yet the tone was definitely more conciliating toward Festival policy. Amongst other things, Martenstein wrote, »that there have recurrently been delays and grumbling about de Hadeln's contract renewal« (Martenstein himself had participated in such grumbling). He went on to add: »It has

Atmospheric corrections?

often been said that Berlin's Festival boss has served American interests too well: a reproach which has quietened down over the last years.« (Opinions may vary on this assessment of the press' response in recent years, but this statement can still be [mis]understood as relativizing former assessments!?) And: »De Hadeln has enabled the ›Panorama‹ to attain its own independent profile as a third section of the Festival. He was the one to appoint young Manfred Salzgeber as head of the ›Panorama‹.« To Festival observers, there was a new friendliness in the air, which would inevitably help improve the public's perception of the Berlinale, even if Martenstein still displayed a certain ironic distance. »He [de Hadeln] seems, all the same, to cultivate a certain aloofness to conceptual matters, and he does not exactly attract attention at parties as an elegant conversationalist. But then is there an executive in Berlin who does?« (Some might scream in protest here ...)

Changes in organization and service

Notwithstanding, this year's organizers had definitely made huge efforts. They created not only the new press center in the Intercontinental hotel and a sort of mile-long walk that linked the »Interconti« to the Zoo Palast and the other venues, but also the entrance area to the Zoo Palast itself had finally been redecorated more

SENSE AND SENSIBILITY: Kate Winslet

festively and the service area in the CineCenter improved. The Royal Palast and the Titania Palast movie theaters were added as new locations for screenings; at the Film Market, the German stands were finally all united under one roof for the first time, which clearly underscored the presence of German cinema. And Festival director de Hadeln now had a representative to help him deal with the press. In many areas, the Festival demonstrated greater efficiency. The organization had been jolted into action after last year's debacle: an upward trend was a must. And the film industry did its part.

Stars, stars, stars

If there had been complaints about the absence of stars the year before, a kind of reparation took place this year – especially from Hollywood. This did not, however, please all critics, who now lamented that the films should be treated as the more important factor, because they were what ultimately constituted a festival's glamour. Nonetheless, both the stars and the films prevailed in 1996. Instead, it was the nuances that were missing, a kind that few had wanted to discern at previous Festivals. Stars were applauded, cheered and criticized: Claudia Cardinale, Danny De Vito, Robert Downey Jr., Sally Field and Jodie Foster (both of whom received a Berlinale

NIXON: Anthony Hopkins

Emma Thompson

Anouk Grinberg

Julia Roberts

Jodie Foster

Camera); Stephen Frears, Terry Gilliam, Ang Lee, Paul Mazursky, Tim Robbins, Julia Roberts (whose press conference was absolute bedlam: almost 150 photographers fought to get the best shot, while she casually stole the show from her director Stephen Frears); Oliver Stone, Emma Thompson, John Travolta and Bruce Willis (who topped everything off by giving a rock concert in the Universal Hall in the Moabit district, accompanied by his band The Accelerators and his wife Demi Moore – which resulted in Andreas Conrad giving him the pretty byname »The Lad with the Harmonica« in the »Tagesspiegel« on February 26th). And then there were the two guests of honor for the Berlinale's Homage, who were greeted with standing ovations at the Zoo Palast and received Golden Bears for their lifetime achievements: Jack Lemmon and Elia Kazan. And as Anke Sterneborg remarked in her Festival report, there were also the three daughters and son of William Wyler, to whom the Retrospective was dedicated, and who could be seen luxuriating »packed tightly into the deep leather couch in the Interconti's Library Bar«. (Süddeutsche Zeitung, Feb. 19, 1996) Yes indeed, this Festival had both its stars and starlets. And the smallest of them were probably to be found at the Children's Film Festival, which Renate Zylla had been in charge of for a decade now.

Lemmon, Kazan and Wyler

Pressure from the majors

And the films? For the Competition, 158 feature films and 200 short films had been viewed. Trips to select films had been intensified – not always successfully, as the rather meager participation of Eastern European, Latin American and African films in the program indicated. What became clear during the selection process was that the Berlinale's position – in competing with Cannes – was strong when it came to courting Hollywood films. This situation increased the pressure put on the Festival by the major studios, and occasionally forced the Festival management to resist their attempts to intervene so as to preserve independence in choosing and putting together the program. Consequently, there was ultimately an exciting juxtaposition of big and popular Hollywood productions – such as Barry Sonnenfeld's Get Shorty

Joan Allen, Oliver Stone

Bruce Willis, Terry Gilliam

Dani Levy, Maria Schrader, Jürgen Vogel, Mark Schlichter

Marika Lagercrantz, Bo Widerberg, Johan Widerberg

and Oliver Stone's NIXON – European and Asian pictures, as well as an African film, Férid Boughedir's UN ÉTÉ À LA GOULETTE/HALK-EL-WAD (»Summer in La Goulette«). Jodie Foster presented her enjoyable family portrait HOME FOR THE HOLIDAYS; Stephen Frears his somewhat different adaptation of the Dr. Jekyll and Mr. Hyde myth, MARY REILLY; Bo Widerberg a dangerous liaison in LUST OCH FÄGRING STOR (»All Things Fair«); Andrzej Wajda his investigation of Polish anti-Semitism WIELKI TYDZIEN (»Holy Week«); and Bertrand Blier a playfully malicious erotic fable, MON HOMME (»My Man«). From Germany, Michael Verhoeven's adaptation of the story by director and author George Tabori of his mother's life MUTTERS COURAGE (»My Mother's Courage«), and Dani Levy's melodrama STILLE NACHT (»Silent Night«) were also successful.

Three American highlights

A highlight – alongside the opening film SENSE AND SENSIBILITY – was certainly Tim Robbins' film DEAD MAN WALKING (with Sean Penn and Susan Sarandon) which tackled the issue of the death penalty: »While DEAD MAN WALKING explicitly avoids all polemics against the death penalty, the subliminal appeal for us to rethink society's demand for punishment becomes all the more urgent. Robbins succeeds in treating the relatives of the victim with respect, even when they no longer know how to cope with their hatred toward the murderer and their bereavement. By resisting the temptation of loading these events with what we supposedly expect of a movie, and instead objectively pursuing, in predominantly static shots, the confrontations and conversations of those concerned, the film develops a high degree of intensity«, Hans-Dieter Seidel wrote in the »Frankfurter Allgemeine Zeitung« on February 24th. Another outstanding film was Terry Gilliam's movie, an astute vision of time and the future: 12 MONKEYS (with Bruce Willis, Brad Pitt and Madeline Stowe) was based on Chris. Marker's LA JETÉE (»The Pier«) and depicted a contemporary apocalypse. Holger Kreitling recapitulated: »Everything we see or seem to be is only a dream within a dream.« (Der Tagesspiegel, Feb. 25, 1996)

MON HOMME by Bertrand Blier (in the Competition): Gérard Lanvin, Anouk Grinberg

Discoveries in the Competition went unnoticed

On the other hand, the more minor films to be found in the Competition had a hard time: this included CSAJOK (»Bitches«) by Ildikó Szabó from Hungary, a »garish Gothic film about the life of three betrayed wives«, as Angela Schmitt-Gläser wrote (Frankfurter Rundschau, Feb. 19, 1996); or MAHJONG by Edward Yang from Taiwan/China, a disturbing picture of urban youths who have no ties; and finally PORTLAND by Niels Arden Oplev from Denmark, a feature debut. Its harsh visual language made many viewers feel uneasy, and some critics found it out of place in the Competition. Others, Daniel Blum from the »Frankfurter Rundschau«, for instance, considered it »by far the boldest film of the Competition (...) a visual and acoustic barrage whose intensity aims at the pit of your stomach, but hits your mind. Without psychologizing, and in the excessive violence and subjugating rituals, one recognizes a desperate attempt to wrest orientation and direction from life.« (Feb. 27, 1996)

Awards: winners and losers

In the Jury's deliberations, three films had an equal chance for the top award: SENSE AND SENSIBILITY by Ang Lee, DEAD MAN WALKING by Tim Robbins, and Bo Widerberg's LUST OCH FÄGRING STOR. That the Golden Bear ultimately went to Ang Lee's film was justifiable, although also a compromise. Sean Penn was honored as best male actor, a well-deserved award, but still a consolation prize for Tim Robbins' film, and rather astonishing, since the actual leading role was played by Susan Sarandon. Otherwise the awards were distributed across the board, although Bo Widerberg with the Special Prize of the Jury and the Blue Angel could be seen as the unspoken winner of this year's Festival. 12 MONKEYS, on the other hand, undeservedly came away empty-handed.

It was difficult for this year's Panorama to assert itself against the Competition. The outstanding films were John Dahl's science-fiction thriller UNFORGETTABLE with Linda Fiorentino, and STREETLIFE, Karl Francis' impressively realistic portrait of a child killer: »A film that takes the side of a child murderer – outrageous, wouldn't you say? No, Jo behaves as she has to – and without great fuss, this film makes us understand her.

Duoluo tianshi by Wong Kar-wai (in the Forum)

The milieu in which she lives seems like a trashy social report, and yet every dialogue, every picture fits.« (Jan Schulz-Ojala, Der Tagesspiegel, Feb. 26, 1996) In addition, the Teddy awards, ›gay/lesbian film prizes‹, were presented for the tenth time: they went to the documentary The Celluloid Closet by Rob Epstein and Jeff Friedman, and the filmic essay I'll Be Your Mirror by Nan Goldin and Edmund Coulthard.

Teddy's 10th anniversary

The Forum also had a more difficult time in 1996. Its program included a number of American independent films, such as the documentary about one of the most spectacular murder cases in the USA's criminal history, Paradise Lost: The Child Murders at Robin Hood Hills by Joe Berlinger and Bruce Sinofsky. The film portrays three underage killers who brutally murdered three eight-year-olds, a »gripping piece of cinéma vérité«, as Peter Körte wrote: »The film does not seek ›the truth‹, but explores what prevents it from emerging. The lack of evidence, does not, however, lead to an acquittal, because the trial is at all times defined by its desire to convict. Even if the defendants are actually the killers, the trial is a declaration of bankruptcy for the US system of justice. Paradise Lost unfolds this tale like a detective story, but without the comfort of a conclusive end.« (Frankfurter Rundschau, Feb. 26, 1996)

US independents and Burma as a film nation

The unknown film nation of Burma was presented, and for starters there was a very personal documentary film by Lindsey Merrison, Our Burmese Days, a portrait of the life of her Anglo-Burmese mother. Egon Humer's Emigration N.Y. offered a different kind of search for clues, a three-hour documentary about twelve Viennese Jews, who fled Nazi terror to New York at the end of the thirties. The »chronicle of an expulsion«, as Stefan Reinecke called the film in the »Frankfurter Rundschau«, »crammed full of odd, sad, bizarre episodes. (...) Egon Humer has no desire to uncover hidden traumas, but rather to illuminate profoundly reflected experience. (...) Aside from sparsely scattered historical shots, Emigration N.Y. is a pictureless film: puristic, curt, monumental.« (Feb. 23, 1996)

Emigrants in New York

Wong Kar-wai

Aleksandr Sokurov

Todd Solondz

A new film by Wong Kar-wai

As the cineastic highlight of this Forum, Wong Kar-wai's new film Duoluo tianshi (»Fallen Angels«) made a lasting impression. It is a bizarre nineties love story, hectic and shrill, a metropolitan film from Hong Kong, with excessive, stylized jungle-images of emotions gone wacky: not a movie to be consumed casually.

Breitscheidplatz or Potsdamer Platz: a question of location

It was a happy, successful Berlinale. Just the same, no one rested on their laurels. New problems were imminent. The issue of the Festival's location resurfaced. Should it remain at its traditional venues around Breitscheidplatz, or should it move to Potsdamer Platz, and be held at Berlin's new center for the first time in 2000? Here was an unexpected alternative and it was suddenly brought into play. Mayor Eberhard Diepgen initiated the idea. Originally, no one had thought of moving the Berlinale to a new location at the debis (Daimler-Benz InterServices) grounds at Potsdamer Platz, or even to the premises planned by Sony. The investors articulated this wish at a late date, because they were looking for additional cultural and international flair for their architectural centers. Clearly, developing an infrastructure now that planning and construction were under way would be problematic. One had the slight impression that difficulties were being invented, in the absence of real problems. Yet the plan represented a real opportunity, and the notion that political resolutions were reversible came as no surprise to all those aware of the city's difficult financial situation. Certainly, a resolution had been passed by the Senate in 1992 for the preservation of the Festival's center at the Zoo and any spatial problems arising were to be resolved by remodeling or adding to existing locations, or constructing new buildings there; yet a lack of funds made this impossible. Just the same, in 1993, it was once again agreed upon to preserve this location at the Zoo in the long term. Now, in 1996, these resolutions were seen as water under the bridge – due to a blend of Berlin brashness and friendly pressure from investors. Moreover and quite fittingly, the Berlin Senator for Financial Affairs, Annette Fugmann-Heesing, announced on February 21st after reviewing the budget that: »a harsh road full of deprivations«

Jack Lemmon, honored with the Golden Berlin Bear for his lifetime achievements

Moritz de Hadeln presents Elia Kazan with a Golden Berlin Bear for his lifetime achievements

Wieland Speck and Chingiz Aitmatov, who was honored with a Berlinale Camera

lay ahead for Berlin. (Der Tagesspiegel, Feb. 22, 1996) The eastern part of the city could also no longer be excluded from cost-cutting measures, because, as Senate Spokesman Michael-Andreas Butz explained, after five years, standards had been attained there that were, in part, higher than in the West. Against this budgetary background, it was easy to understand that if investors' wishes were thought to bring economic relief, they were lent a willing ear. Director of the Berlin Festivals Ltd. Ulrich Eckhardt's initial reaction was hesitant: both locations were desirable. And Festival directors de Hadeln and Gregor were for proceeding cautiously, because the pro and cons had to be carefully weighed first. Besides, the advantages and disadvantages for the competing Festival sections were not completely congruent. These new considerations did not make an internal reform of the Festival structure any easier. And the general state of politics in Berlin (and of cultural policies in particular) was difficult terrain to negotiate. Unanticipated and delayed political decisions had already wasted precious planning time. In 1996, the Festival had once again been fortunate, but it was important to make sure that this success did not turn out to be a mere flash in the pan. Unnoticed by many, a new chapter of Berlinale history had irrevocably begun.

Organizers display reserve

International Jury
Nikita Mikhalkov
(Russia, president)
Gila Almagor (Israel)
Vincenzo Cerami (Italy)
Joan Chen (USA)
Ann Hui (Hong Kong)
Peter Lilienthal (Germany)
Jürgen Prochnow
(Germany)
Claude Rich (France)
Fay Weldon (Great Britain)
Catherine Wyler (USA)
Christian Zeender
(Switzerland)

The Awards of the
International Jury

Feature Films
Grand Prix of the 46th IFB
Golden Berlin Bear
SENSE AND SENSIBILITY
USA
directed by Ang Lee

Silver Berlin Bear
Special Prize of the Jury
LUST OCH FÄGRING STOR
Sweden/Denmark
directed by Bo Widerberg

Silver Berlin Bear
for the best director
Yim Ho
TAI YANG YOU ER
People's Republic of China
ex aequo with
Richard Loncraine
RICHARD III
Great Britain

Silver Berlin Bear
for the best actress
Anouk Grinberg
in MON HOMME
France

Silver Berlin Bear
for the best actor
Sean Penn
in DEAD MAN WALKING
USA

LUST OCH FÄGRING STOR:
Marika Lagercrantz,
Johan Widerberg (in the
Competition)

Silver Berlin Bear
for his originality in depicting childhood
E NO NAKA NO BOKU NO MURA
directed by Yoichi Higashi
Japan

Silver Berlin Bear
for an outstanding contribution to contemporary film art
Andrzej Wajda
WIELKI TYDZIEN
Poland/Germany

The Blue Angel
LUST OCH FÄGRING STOR
directed by Bo Widerberg
Sweden/Denmark

Alfred Bauer Prize
for a film opening up new perspectives in film art
VITE STROZZATE
directed by Ricky Tognazzi
Italy/France

Special Mentions
MAHJONG
directed by Edward Yang
Taiwan/China

RI GUANG XIA GU
directed by He Ping
Hong Kong/People's Republic of China

STILLE NACHT
directed by Dani Levy
Germany/Switzerland

Short Films
Golden Berlin Bear
PRIBYTIE POEZDA
directed by Andrei Zheleznyakov
Russia

Silver Berlin Bear
MAALAISLÄÄKÄRI
directed by Katariina Lillqvist
Finland/Czech Republic

STREETLIFE: Helen McCrory (in the Panorama)

To tell chalk from cheese

By Fay Weldon

I was alarmed to be asked to be a juror on the film panel in 1996. I know films from the working end: I had never before sat in judgement upon the made thing. Books – yes, I am a writer – but films? Simply to get one onto a screen seemed to me achievement enough, forget good or bad, forget rating one amongst others. By the working end I mean I have written numerous film screenplays, commissioned and uncomissioned, and pitched many an idea, and got so far and no further, though once I got as far as the first day of production only to have the director killed in a road accident on her way to the studio. That was terrible. And I did once have a novel of mine adapted for Hollywood, of the starriest kind, of which by the rules of my contract I must speak no ill. And that was all. But I was flattered: I accepted: presumably the committee knew what it was doing or why ask in the first place? It soon became clear that the same principles apply to films as to books: the filmmaker, like the novelist, puts endless work into this single act of the imagination, creating something where there was nothing before: bares their soul, making a stupendous offering to the world, and a little group of people out there in a foreign land shakes their mutual heads and says, sorry, not good enough, so-and-so over there does it much better. And that's after the critics at home have done with you.

The trouble is that as viewer not maker you have so little doubt: this is better than that; and though the criteria you use sounds lofty, as the jury itself struggles for credibility, it is all quite simple. You tell chalk from cheese by measuring how far each soars above the normal in its sphere and mark the difference. And that is all. It is not so much what you ›like‹ as what you are compelled to admire. And the astonishing thing in all judging, books or films, is the extent not how much the jury disagrees, but how much it agrees on what it admires.

So it was a pleasure. Like being a student again and going to five films a week, all the town's cinemas would allow. Only it was four or five films a day. And having to sit still, silhouetted, as the jury is in the front row, forbidden to show by our body language what we thought of the film. Lest others might read too much into it. Not for us to cringe, to shriek, to throw our hands in the air: to fall in the aisle laughing or weeping. No. But it was a small price to pay.

Wyler reunion

By Catherine Wyler

My first experience of the Berlin Film Festival was a heady compilation of delights, as I was both a member of the International Jury in my own right and the daughter of the director whose work was given a major retrospective that same year, 1996. The jury was a memorable experience, due mainly to the lively, smart, funny and fascinating, sometimes wicked, often provocative, thoroughly delightful cohorts, the other jury members. The demands of jury service left few opportunities to visit the Wyler retrospective, but I managed to see a number of his films I'd never seen, and was always surprised by the packed houses for these old movies. Berlin has great audiences.

We had a fine Wyler reunion in Berlin that year: my two sisters, brother, sister-in-

law, husband and daughter all came to see the Wyler pictures we knew we might never see otherwise, because who else would ever do such a comprehensive retrospective!

I've been at every festival since then, and the most memorable moment for me last year was sitting in the audience in the Zoo Palast for the premiere of the documentary, THE LAST DAYS. *I thought about my father, who was born in Alsace when it was part of Germany, whose mother and first language were German … how amazed and pleased he would have been to see that film in that theater in Berlin, playing to another packed house. And then the concise eloquence of the survivor, who was profiled in the film, and who came on stage to say that the main lesson she had learned from the Holocaust was never to generalize about a people …*

Waiting for Claudia, dreaming of the Bear

By Férid Boughedir

My two most lasting memories of the 1996 International Film Festival in Berlin, which presented my film UN ÉTÉ À LA GOULETTE *(»A Summer in La Goulette«) as an official entry in the Competition, are its first public showing and my desire to win a prize – unfulfilled, as it turned out. A comedy,* UN ÉTÉ À LA GOULETTE *depicts the peaceful coexistence of Arabs, Jews and Italian Catholics in Tunisia shortly before the outbreak of the Six Day War in June 1967, which led most religious minorities to leave the country. Once I had explained the state of affairs, Moritz and Erika de Hadeln were generously willing to invite not just one actor or actress as was standard practice, but all three main actors who in reality actually did belong to the three religions depicted coexisting peacefully in the film: Mustapha Adouani (a Muslim Arab), Guy Nataf (a Tunisian Jew) and Ivo Salerno (a Tunisian of Sicilian origin). The three met during the shooting of the film and have been inseparable ever since … just like in the film! Then, miraculously, the other actors all got together and arranged to come to Berlin too, some as guests of WDR and thanks to the generous support of Joachim von Mengershausen, who had co-produced the film. In short, all three families, Moslem, Jewish and Catholic, were present in full number, reunited in Berlin! Now only the film's most famous star was missing: Claudia Cardinale, a Tunisian-born Italian, who had first arrived in Italy at the age of 18. In the film she had played herself: a star, returning to the land of her birth to the cheers of the crowds … While I awaited the arrival of Claudia Cardinale at the airport in Berlin, leafing through German newspapers that showed photos from her last Berlinale visit over twenty years ago, I became aware of the throng of photographers and camera men surrounding the exit, where the Festival's official welcoming committee had already gotten into position. I suddenly understood what the word »star« really meant and I realized that even if it was just for a brief – but therefore even more intense – period, I was no longer a spectator but a participant in the film world, which, as a tireless film enthusiast and avid film magazine reader, I'd constantly dreamt about. I was overcome by the strange feeling that I'd slipped imperceptibly onto the other side of the mirror, home of all my childhood dreams.*

The film's reception and the audience's response that day were completely unusual. Beaming and cheering, the audience gave us veritable standing ovations, and the entire film team, clustered around Claudia Cardinale on the stage of the Zoo Palast, were moved to tears by the never ending storm of applause, laughter and shouts of joy.

The response was all the more surprising since we'd been warned in the run-up to the Festival about the reserved, stern Berlin audiences, who were known to simply get up and leave, loudly banging their seats, if a film wasn't to their liking. Moritz de Hadeln himself told us that he'd seldom experienced such an overwhelming response and when even Claudia Cardinale spoke of a »triumph«, we were in seventh heaven.

It didn't take much to set us dreaming of a Bear! Not of the Golden Bear, mind you, the highest honor awarded by the International Film Festival, but far more modestly, of one of his many smaller brothers in silver, which would guarantee the film's international distribution. As it was, the buyers weren't wasting any time. By the next day they were crowding around the »Flach Pyramide International« stand at the market and Eric Lagesse, who was marketing the film. The previous evening's success with the public meant that our small Tunisian film could be sold almost all across Europe and even in Australia!

But then on the last day of the Festival, when the prizes were awarded, we experienced an emotional roller-coaster. Claudia, who had been completely selfless in her commitment to the film from the beginning to the end, praising it in all her interviews instead of discussing her own career as her interview partners would have liked, had already departed. The Australian buyer joined our group and waited impatiently for the announcement of the winners, along with his Spanish, Scandinavian and Canadian colleagues. Every time the winner of a Silver Bear was announced the German public sitting near the UN ÉTÉ À LA GOULETTE *team smiled at us warmly, giving encouragements such as »All the better – if you're not among the Silver Bears you must be right up at the top!«*

As the award ceremony progressed and the main prizes were due, the more confident and expectant we became. But then we suddenly fell to earth: UN ÉTÉ À LA GOULETTE *was left completely empty-handed! »A shame« said the Australian buyer, visibly disappointed. »I bought the film because after the screening I was one hundred percent sure it would win a Bear.« (Luckily for him and the other buyers,* UN ÉTÉ À LA GOULETTE *proved to be a huge hit at box-offices in Europe, Canada and … Australia).*

Not far from me, a German member of the audience was railing against the Jury: »It's always the same. The Jury never gives the prizes to comedies and feels it's their duty to reward serious and difficult subjects. But your subject is serious and topical, even if the film is light.« But we weren't listening anymore … we were numb. We had naively confused the public's support with the Jury's decisions and dreamt of the completely unattainable Bear, which we would never even have dared hope for when we arrived … Seeing how distraught I was, Moritz de Hadeln, clearly moved by the film's success with the audience, made the gracious offer of including me on the Jury in the following year, 1997 …

For this I was truly thankful, and a whole new adventure began that I will surely tell you about in the next Berlinale anniversary publication.

Note: It's better to sell the Bear before you've won it!

Mary Reilly: Julia Roberts
(in the Competition)

The Island on Bird Street: Jordan Kiziuk

Noli turbare circulos meos

1997

Feb. 13th-24th, 1997
(Competition)
Feb. 14th-24th, 1997
(Forum)

Berlin. Mayor Eberhard Diepgen had an appointment with photographers for a symbolic political gesture: he was to mark off the former course of the Berlin Wall in red paint at »Checkpoint Charlie«. According to Diepgen, this twelve-centimeter-wide stripe would help »keep the memory of the tragic history of this city alive«. Later, the painted red stripe would be replaced by a double row of large cobblestones. Not all Berliners approved of marking off the Wall in this way. The PDS spokesman for cultural matters, for one, believed it counteracted all efforts to »actively remember history«, and the fact that the paint was red made him wonder whether »the line was also meant to suggest: ›the bloody trail of communism‹?« (Der Tagesspiegel, Feb. 21, 1997)

Once again, the political skies were darkening in this period after the Reunification. The climate had turned harsher. And what was bound to happen, came to pass. Or happened as things were inclined to in Berlin. The high spirits of last year's Berlinale dissolved into tears. Misunderstandings, squabbles, and a new wave of polemics overshadowed the Festival. The films with their advocates and adversaries were less the focus of interest than the cultural and cinematic political tug-of-war about the Festival's future. And of course, debate concentrated on individuals, with Festival director de Hadeln becoming the object of much criticism. The Competition and the Forum were played off against one another again. Constructive proposals to improve the Festival's conception and organization were hardly of importance. Whoever joined in these wranglings, was doing cultural politics on his own account: from the Senator for Cultural Affairs to the commenting journalists. What was going on?

Senator for Cultural Affairs considers separating the Competition and Forum

The point of departure for this sometimes grotesque and distorted discussion was the problematic issue of the Festival's envisioned move to Potsdamer Platz, as well as negotiations for renewing the Festival directors' contracts. Furthermore, there were misunderstandings and occasional breakdowns in communication between the Berlinale and the management of the Berlin Festivals Ltd. Last but not least, there was the presentation of a paper up for discussion, entitled: »Information on the cultural program subsidized in Berlin«, which Senator for Science, Research and Culture Peter Radunski published in September 1996. In this paper he introduced his ideas for reorganizing Berlin's cultural landscape. It became known as the ›Paper on Spheres‹, because it divided Berlin's cultural landscape into individual spheres »so as to enable an integrated discussion of structure«. It was a paper that immediately provoked criticism, throwing much into question, forcing misapprehensions and giving rise to protest from those affected – as well as causing helpless and ironic shrugs. To crown it all, the paper resulted in the Senator publicly announcing a proposal to examine whether the International Forum of Young Cinema was central to the Festival's attractiveness, or whether the Competition and the Forum should not in fact be held at separate dates. It was to be examined, »whether this organizational link between the two festivals, between the International Film Festival and the Forum of Young Cinema, with respect to their effective management and a visitor-friendly course of events, is wise; and whether the Festival's variety of programmatic means and the extravagant character of the accompanying events are still essential for the Festival's attractiveness; and whether it is necessary to continue to fill a gap in the program offered by the film metropolis of Berlin. Within this context, reconception is imperative in both contents and organization.«

Kristin Scott Thomas

Juliette Binoche

Arielle Dombasle

Catherine Deneuve

These considerations came at the wrong moment not only because they aggravated existing rivalries but also because they disregarded Festival structures and reputation. For despite all competition, the Festival was an extraordinarily lively – albeit inherently contradictory – organization. It would have been much more constructive to emphasize this vigor while insisting on a reform of structures and a revision of the regulations for the individual sections: for their boundaries had indeed become blurred and the Forum, whose role had changed over the years, could no longer retain its function as cineastic »anti-festival« within the Festival. The rivalry between the Competition and the Forum was anyway a chimera, as their divergent program missions excluded actual competition. On the other hand, there was some conceptual overlap between the Forum and the Panorama from time to time, here certain agreements would make sense. In addition, arrangements between the Forum and the Retrospective might be occasionally advisable so as to achieve a more targeted program conception. The crux of the matter for the Festival was not to be found in the network that had evolved, but in the outgrowths at its edges. Just as the Forum scarcely restricted itself to presenting only avant-garde and new films, the Panorama was hardly a mere supplement to the Competition. Both sections had their enthusiastic followers and communities, as well as their successes. Nonetheless: joint reorientation – which did not mean parting with one of the two sections – might do the Festival good. The Senator's suggestion – which failed to find approval – appeared not to understand the realities of the Festival and its internal difficulties.

Ben Kingsley

When the German press agency (dpa) announced on September 10th, just one day after the »Paper on Spheres« was made public, that Moritz de Hadeln could imagine »the Forum rescheduled to summer, while the Berlinale could take place as always in February«, confusion reigned. In a press statement on September 11th, the Forum protested against such ideas, and Jan Schulz-Ojala commented in the »Tagesspiegel« that Radunski's proposal would split the Berlinale: »If there really is a political demand

Yolande Zauberman

Tata Amaral

to hold the Competition and the Forum at separate dates, it will signal the beginning of the end of the Film Festival. Moving the Forum to summer is – in as far as my modest research possibilities were able to reveal – so far only a topic that has been discussed by Radunski ›in the presence‹ of de Hadeln; the Forum, on the other hand, as well as Festivals Ltd. boss Eckhardt were totally surprised, if not to say perplexed. Which leaves room for hope. Or perhaps – for exactly this reason – does not leave any at all? (Sept. 12, 1996) In this context, how is de Hadeln's statement, such as announced by the German press agency – that he could imagine the Forum separate from the Berlinale's official program – to be evaluated? According to de Hadeln's account, he received a call from the dpa on the evening of September 9th during which he was asked to comment on Radunski's suggestions. The contents of the paper were not known to him at the time. He had then spoken his mind on the problem of moving the Berlinale. In the course of the conversation, he was confronted with the news that the Forum was talking about the possibility of rescheduling to summer. After his initial surprise, he answered that it was not prohibited »to question things or voice ideas« (cited from a letter written by de Hadeln to Ulrich Gregor on Oct. 20, 1996). But at no time had he advocated such a separation, especially given that it was not until September 11th, upon asking the Senator, »that excerpts from the aforementioned Senate paper« became known to the Film Festival. »It is to be emphasized«, de Hadeln stated, »that talks never took place between Senator Radunski and Mr. de Hadeln on this topic« (loc. cit.). De Hadeln's statement was also passed on to the members of the board of the International Film Festival.

In any case, the whole matter caused quite a stir. Somehow everyone felt involved, misunderstood or falsely interpreted. Ulrich Eckhardt described the heated debate as »removed from reality«. »It was not until September 2nd, 1996, that the Festival's board of trustees – which is appointed by the federal and regional government, and

Jack Lang

Jubilee celebration at the Children's Film Festival: Josefin Årling (on the left), Renate Zylla, director of the Children's Film Festival (in the middle), Göran Carmback (on the right) with two young visitors

Christina Schindler, Renate Zylla

Mohammad-Ali Talebi, Renate Zylla

Rosa Vergés, Renate Zylla

which Radunski chaired at the time – confirmed that it wanted to keep the present structure of the Festival. It warned not ›to bring on a crisis that did not exist‹.« (Der Tagesspiegel, Sept. 12, 1996) The controversy had an epilogue during question time in parliament. Alice Ströver, spokeswoman for cultural policy for the Bündnis 90/ Die Grünen, asked Radunski to explain these plans for separation. In his answer, the Senator commented that it had merely been a »proposal up for discussion: the paper explicitly states that in the year 2000 the Film Festival might occur within a different framework as well as alter its contents. This is based on the speculation that by then Berlin will be a true media town, and hence be able to handle two large annual events. Thus we are looking at the question – mind you, for the year 2000 – of whether the Forum as a forum of young cinema, video festivals and the likes, might not constitute a second central event alongside the Film Festival.« Radunski's answer was evasive and simply postponed the issue. In a further, rather barbed and biased question, Alice Ströver somewhat unhelpfully asked »whether Mr. de Hadeln had put ideas« into the Senator's head in order »to get rid of a rival that often has a much better reputation than the Competition«. This question could be seen as an act of sheer political-party positioning as well as of enjoyment in being oppositional despite knowing better – Radunski did not bother to answer this question.

A Berlin melange

And so everything turned into a melange typical of Berlin at the time, a melange that mirrored both Berlin's indecision and political conflicts. The city was searching for a new self-image, one often heard muttered apologetically. Yet the fact that people could be so openly and frequently mistaken, and that self-correction was so difficult to prompt, set many outside observers thinking.

In June 1996, at the request of the Berlin Festivals Ltd., the Film Festival examined the offer made by the debis property management Ltd. to the Berlinale for a move to Potsdamer Platz. The Festival studied the proposal in relation to existing structures and to the urgent need for organizational improvement. The outcome of this analy-

Michael Hausman, Milos Forman, Courtney Love

Mirjam Quinte, Hans Koschnick, Pepe Danquart, Ulrich Gregor

Jürgen Vogel, Wolfgang Becker, Christiane Paul

Helmut Dietl, Veronica Ferres

»A-status« in jeopardy?

sis was the discovery of a large number of deficiencies, of spatial and technical flaws, which did not make unconditional agreement to the proposal seem advisable, that is, unless one was willing to accept a change for the worse. The Festival management, especially Moritz de Hadeln, realized that the Berlinale's assessment of this proposal corresponded to the views of the international associations: i. e., of the International Federation of Producers' Associations (FIAPF) and its secretary-general Alphonse Brisson, as well as of the MPAA, and its president Jack Valenti, who somewhat vaguely pointed out that a move would have to involve improvements for the Festival, if the Berlinale did not want to jeopardize its »A-status«. A risk which neither the Festival nor those who financed the Festival – the federal government and Berlin – could take. Differences in opinion seemed to be non-existent, everyone just wanted the best for the Festival. In practical terms, this meant, for instance, that the offer from debis did not include adequate office space and the offices planned were too scattered around the grounds. Furthermore, there was no provision for a film depot and the question of the Film Market's venue had not been sufficiently clarified, which was also true of the press center, which needed a certain technical infrastructure. In addition, it turned out that the technical specifications at the Stella Musical Theater were not adequate for a Competition premiere movie theater, and opinions differed as to how much it would cost to equip it properly (and who would do the financing): for although the theater had 1680 seats, which meant it was larger than the Zoo Palast – which had about 600 seats less – the 18 meter-wide screen which was to be installed was no larger than the current one in the smaller Zoo Palast, and thus would hardly be acceptable for viewers in the last rows and in the upper balconies. De Hadeln pointed out that the screen in Cannes was 24 meters wide, whereas at the Royal Palast, where the seating capacity was 930, the screen was 30 meters wide. Crucial questions related to projection requirements and above all to the acoustics (films demand ever more sophisticated sound systems) were completely unresolved, especially at this location, a space which had been built for theater performances and thus has quite different reverberation needs from a movie theater.

Sufficient seating capacity?

Another problem was the size of the movie theaters available in the adjacent Flebbe CinemaxX complex (as well as of the movie theaters that were to be situated on the Sony grounds, that might also be used by the Forum – but for which so far no operator had been found – which meant there was no one with whom one might negotiate). After all, at Breitscheidplatz, there were the Zoo Palast, the Royal Palast and the Delphi, three movie theaters with a seating capacity of 1000 each, as well as the smaller studio cinemas; while the »CinemaxX« had a total capacity of only 3500, and its largest theater had only 700 seats, not enough for the Panorama and the Forum. A new endless controversy between these two competing sections was inevitable, particularly since the Forum was not content to sit back while they were being excluded from the cinemas on the debis grounds. On the other hand, de Hadeln, if he wanted to help shape the future of the Festival, could not just obstinately insist on the old center: the Zoo Palast's lease would expire in 2010, moreover, in terms of technology, this theater was not optimally equipped. Yet caution was the order of the day, for although investors painted vivid pictures of how public access from the western part of the city to Potsdamer Platz would improve, it was all still very speculative. Just the same, in the medium-term, there was much to be said for the new location.

Anyone seriously advocating the Film Festival's move to Potsdamer Platz could hardly have been surprised by the need to discuss improvements and basic reconceptions, which made the reactions to the considerations presented all the more baffling. Whereas the board of trustees had responded with caution to the list of insufficiencies, the only word that made its way to the public's ears was the Festival management's »no«. Moritz de Hadeln was soon singled out as the prime adversary

Clubbed to Death by Yolande Zauberman (in the Forum): Elodie Bouchez

of the move; moreover, his preference for Breitscheidplatz, in view of the terms offered, was dramatized as prevention tactics. Yet the problems involved were not about trifling details, but fundamentals. And these were giving Peter Radunski, the official responsible, a hard time. On the level of municipal politics, the move to Potsdamer Platz represented a huge opportunity, yet if improvements were not negotiated, the Festival would move into a makeshift situation for an indefinite amount of time, and sooner or later lose its status. Berlin was in trouble. Politics had pressed ahead, but good political intentions alone were not a sound basis. Contracts had not been drafted yet, and negotiations were almost non-existent. Everything was caught in the initial stage, and no one dared to take the next step. The Berlinale was in a bind. The future was within reach and yet – for the time being – perdu.

An urban political chance or a makeshift solution?

Strained relations

And while this state of affairs was causing enough problems, tension between the Film Festival and the Berlin Festivals Ltd. was mounting. The Film Festival is a part of the Berlin Festivals Ltd. but enjoys a special status: by contract, the Festival director has been granted room for negotiating the Berlinale's conception and organization. Within the scope of the approved financial plan, he is, for example, authorized to carry out legal transactions in areas directly related to the Festival. Moreover, the Berlin Festivals Ltd. must inform the Festival director of all matters concerning the Film Festival and ask him for his opinion. In addition, the Festival director is to participate in drawing up »the annual budget for the Film Festival as well as in all changes as demanded for by the Festivals Ltd. members, the board of trustees or its work group, or the donators«. However, as the years went by, de Hadeln was to see how these items were interpreted more and more restrictively by the Berlin Festivals Ltd.'s management. The inherent structure of the contract led to conflicts of interests, and these were intensified by the overall tight budgetary situation. In 1997, the Berlin Festivals received 11.5 million marks from the Land of Berlin and 7.5 million from the federal government. How these funds were to be distributed was decided

Tri istorii by Kira Muratova (in the Competition)

by the Festivals Ltd. internally. The Film Festival was once again hit by cuts: the majority of official receptions had to be canceled; simultaneous translations of Competition films were reduced to English and French – Spanish and Russian were no longer offered. A general accreditation fee of 50 marks was introduced, which did not go down well, especially not with journalists.

Endless contract negotiations

Against this backdrop, negotiations for the renewal of the Festival directors' contracts – which were supposed to have been completed by October 1996 – were still being waged; and they were still undecided when the Film Festival opened. That the negotiators were gambling was clear to everyone involved. Yet, considering the general state of the Festival, it was only possible to speculate at what price. Public statements made by Axel Wallrabenstein, press spokesman for the Senator for Science, Research and Culture, only increased speculation. In December, at least, it was announced that the idea of separating the Competition and the Forum was no longer on the agenda. On December 5th, this fact was corroborated and confirmed by Berlin Festivals' director Eckhardt and Forum director Ulrich Gregor before the parliamentary media commission. Gregor declared that the Forum was a prerequisite for the Berlinale's attractiveness internationally, and Eckhardt unambiguously added that he had little interest in what was written in the Senator's paper on this topic. Head of the Department for Cultural Affairs Bernd Mehlitz amended that by no means had anyone intended to endanger the Berlinale's future success by forcing changes.

Gregor advocates decentralization

Meanwhile Ulrich Gregor signalized something else: namely, that no one had ever had the intention of completely giving up Breitscheidplatz as the Festival's location, and yet »the city's changed circumstances« called for »decentralization« (Berliner Morgenpost, Dec. 6, 1996). The debate picked up momentum again when Moritz de Hadeln gave an interview, also in December, to the journal »MedienBulletin« stating that he foresaw »a depressive and gloomy atmosphere«. The financial cuts were so great that they could hardly be coped with; just the same, he hoped to be able to

Exil Shanghai by Ulrike Ottinger (in the Forum)

»maneuver« things so »that the Film Festival's core, its spirit« would not »suffer«. Simultaneously, he hoped »that the politicians would give the matter some thought«. This was now a fight with no holds barred and an official denial came from the Senate immediately. Radunski's spokesman Wallrabenstein declared that it was by no means a question of jeopardizing the Festival and that a concept for the Festival existed for beyond the year 2000 – which was news, but it was not elaborated on further. And to claim that the Senator was the one who wanted to move the Film Festival to Potsdamer Platz and de Hadeln the one who was against it did not correlate with the facts. Wallrabenstein proceeded: »The Film Festival will continue. Although, it is uncertain whether this has to be with the present constellation of personnel.« (Berliner Morgenpost and Der Tagesspiegel, Dec. 30, 1996) And so the cat was out of the bag. A risky statement, as clear as it was nebulous. Everyone knew that the pokering for contracts was not over yet, however that the cards would be played so publicly – with an open hand, as it were – put everything in a new light. And so almost in passing, the following question arose: if contracts were not to be made with the two current Festival directors, or at least not with one of them, in which case the remark was clearly aimed at de Hadeln, who would then head the Festival? Where would they get a competent Festival director so quickly, a director who would be able to find his way in the jungle of such a highly complex political and organizational situation? One could discern a certain unheeded rashness in these remarks. Ulrich Eckhardt warned – regarding Wallrabenstein – not to talk the matter to death or to »muzzle« anyone; above all, restructuring the Berlinale »involves the danger of losing all meaning (…) due to false actionism«. (Die Welt, Jan. 3, 1997) Wallrabenstein defended himself by pointing out »it would not do for an influential person in the field of culture, such as Berlinale director de Hadeln, to attack the Senator for Cultural Affairs« and it was »truly nonsense« that the Senator for Cultural Affairs would question the Festival's existence. De Hadeln had warned not to endanger the Film

The Senator's press spokesman's denial

De Hadeln warns

AMSTERDAM, GLOBAL VILLAGE by Johan van der Keuken (in the Forum)

He liu by Tsai Ming-liang (in the Competition)

Festival. And as to the issue of contract renewal, Wallrabenstein explained that this was the business of the Berlin Festivals' board of trustees (as mentioned earlier, Senator Radunski was the board's chairman), »and just like in politics, no one is entitled to a job for life«. Which in fact no one had demanded, and so this remark could be dismissed as a tactical ruse. And with regard to the dangers involved in restructuring the Berlinale, these encountered little understanding from Berlin's Department of Cultural Affairs, for: »Why shouldn't we think about new perspectives? If the Festival moves to Potsdamer Platz, we will have to rethink things in any case.« An answer that was both bold and naive, yet missed the point. During this whole debate, Senator Radunski was in Cannes on holiday. (Die Welt, Jan. 3, 1997)

On January 29th, de Hadeln repudiated the idea that he was against the move, yet pointed out that he did have a number of objections. He went on to say he would not let himself be blackmailed by contract negotiations. His contract would run out in May 1998, and he could not accept a two-year renewal, four years would be the minimum, although he could also imagine resigning at short notice. Shortly before the Festival began, a meeting was held between those responsible for the Film Festival and debis: the different points at issue were discussed and the investors promised to make concessions. Many of these were still rather vague, but nevertheless, on February 13th, the opening day of the Berlinale, the Festival management advised the Festivals Ltd. board of trustees to decide in favor of a move to Potsdamer Platz. It was consequently possible to wrap up the protracted negotiations, even though it by no means meant the end of the chaotic planning situation. On the same day, the board of trustees gave the go-ahead to a contract renewal of five years, although with a modified clause of notice for both parties. The Festival could begin, yet unfortunately it did not develop much spirit.

A solution – but no end in sight

For the Berlinale fell short of its possibilities, and this was the case in all the sections. True, after a long absence, two major studios, Warner Bros. and 20th Century

William Shakespeare's Romeo & Juliette by Baz Luhrmann (in the Competition): Leonardo DiCaprio, Claire Danes

Problems with Italy

Fox, were represented in the Competition, and French participation was strong, but Italy was missing again. Thirty films had been viewed in Rome, 90% of which were television productions, and it seemed preposterous that they had even been offered to the Festival at all. After another viewing in Berlin, an invitation was finally sent to Marco Bellocchio's Kleist adaptation Principe di Homburg (»The Prince of Homburg«), which was then accepted. Yet on the very day when the film was to be announced in a press release, it was unexpectedly withdrawn with the explanation that the director now had other plans. Speculation was directed toward Cannes, Berlin had just been the dry run. The Panorama experienced something similar. One of the two Italian films that had been invited was withdrawn at the last moment.

America, Taiwan/China, Russia and Israel

Another aggravating incident for the Festival was that David Lynch's film Lost Highway, which had been offered to the Festival by its German distributor Senator Film and accepted for participation by the selection commission, was then retracted by its French production company Ciby 2000. America dominated the Competition with new films by Milos Forman (The People vs. Larry Flint), Spike Lee (Get on the Bus), John Singlewood (Rosewood), Nicholas Hytner (The Crucible), Baz Luhrmann (William Shakespeare's Romeo & Juliet), Tim Burton (Mars Attacks!) and Anthony Minghella's melodrama The English Patient. Noteworthy was also the large number of Asian films from Taiwan/China, from the People's Republic of China, from Hong Kong and Japan. Tsai Ming-liang left a cineastic impression on the Competition with the film He liu (»The River«), a bleak and mysterious film, on the surface a story of a family, but »the contaminated water of the river is less an ecological metaphor than one for the human psyche, for as we all know the body consists largely of water. Above all, their relationships are contaminated, contaminated like the rain, the flooded flat, the tea, soup, urine, blood and semen, everything is water and everything is contaminated.« (Jan Schulz-Ojala, Der Tagesspiegel, Feb. 19, 1997) Kira Muratova's Russian Competition entry Tri istorii

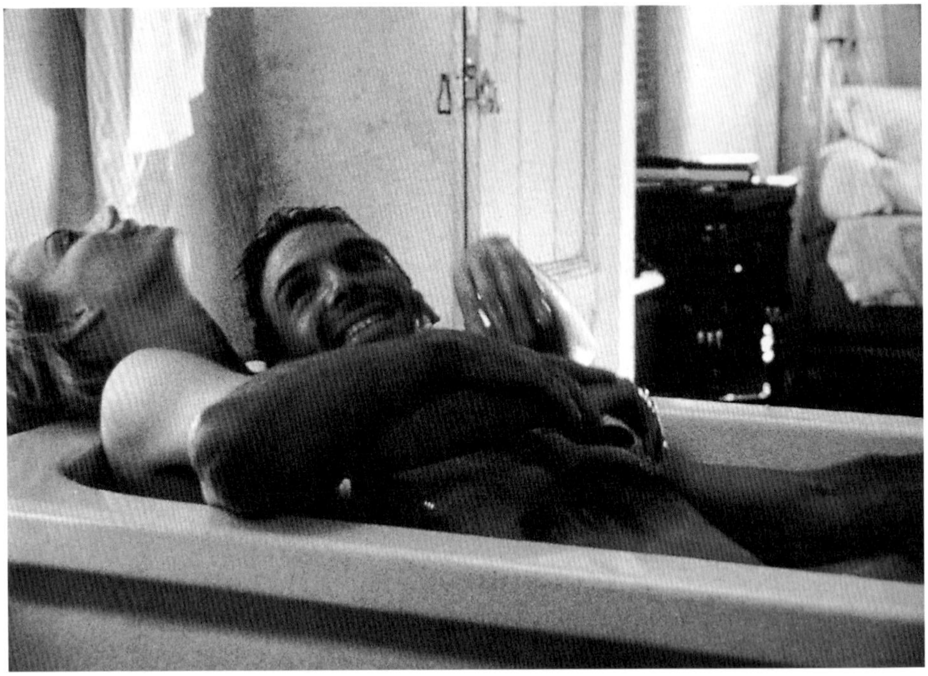

THE ENGLISH PATIENT by Anthony Minghella (in the Competition): Ralph Fiennes, Kristin Scott Thomas

(»Three Stories«) was a film told against the current of time, a film of mystical realism, brimming with allusions, barely decipherable: Muratova seems to be depicting the story of four somewhat coincidental murders. Like Tsai Ming-liang's film, this work also takes time to unfold its tale, and requires viewers who are willing to follow such a picture puzzle. Yet on the whole, the Competition seemed quite disparate, and it was Forman's and Minghella's films that stood out, whereas Tim Burton's MARS ATTACKS! added a loony kick and Joseph Pitchadze's cryptic and elegiac black-and-white film LENEGED ENAYIM MAARAVIOT (»Under Western Eyes«) was a hot tip from Israel.

Even in the Forum, stagnation and disappointment prevailed. Geographical focal points were to be found in a number of film series: with eight films from Brazil, and seven from Asia – of which three were from Korea and four from Japan. Africa and the Arab Near Eastern countries were not represented. Two documentaries in the Forum were outstanding: Ulrike Ottinger's EXIL SHANGHAI (»Exile Shanghai«) and Johan van der Keuken's AMSTERDAM, GLOBAL VILLAGE. Both films approach a big city although from different perspectives: »whereas Ulrike Ottinger seems to seek the homelike, the European, in what is foreign, Johan van der Keuken goes right outside his front door to discover the exotic in the everyday«. (Veronika Rall, Frankfurter Rundschau, Feb. 20, 1997)

Documentaries by Ottinger and van der Keuken

BRASSED OFF by Mark Herman (in the Panorama)

The documentary essay REPRISE (»Resumption«) by Hervé Le Roux was also an exciting work. The starting point of Le Roux's investigation was a ten-minute documentary – one that has in the meantime become quite famous – from May '68 about a labor dispute at a factory in the French provinces. It proceeds from a picture of a young woman who disgustedly refuses to accept the negotiated compromise. What begins like a detective's search for clues – with a streak of a love story between the director and his lost protagonist – turns, almost without us noticing, into a piece of contemporary history.

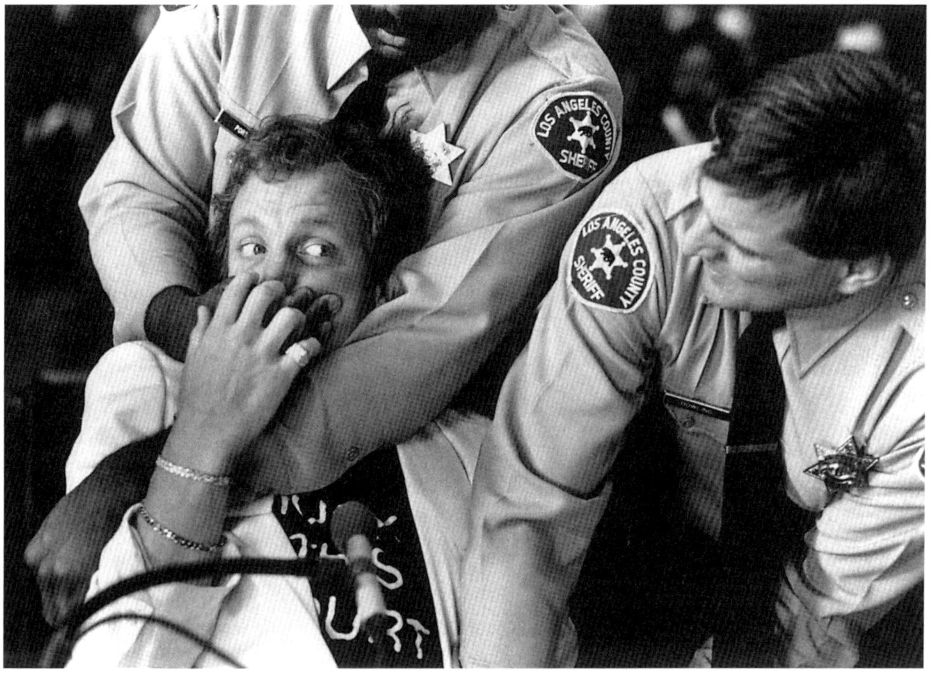

The People vs. Larry Flint by Milos Forman (in the Competition): Woody Harrelson

More than usual, the Panorama alternated between the presentation of large productions and small side events. Here too, there was a focus on Asia that complemented the Competition and the Forum. From England, there was Mark Herman's Brassed Off, a film which charmed audiences and critics alike, reconciling them; then there was the Norwegian film Mendel by Alexander Rösler, a quiet, endearing work, which told of a Jewish boy, a victim of the second generation. The boy learns about the Holocaust – which his grandparents did not survive – in talks with his parents, despite the fact that they would prefer to conceal what happened from him.

Jubilee: the Children's Film Festival

The Children's Film Festival took place for the twentieth time: it showed fourteen features and nine short films. It was a festive event in which the young audience actively took part, and the program satisfied expectations. For those who were not so content, a selection of ten films from the past twenty years was shown, refreshing memories, or – even better – enabling rediscovery.

What more? Catherine Deneuve, Lauren Bacall and Kim Novak, to whom the Homage was dedicated, attended the Festival. There was a commemorative screening of Die Legende von Paul und Paula (»The Legend of Paul and Paula«) for deceased director Heiner Carow. The Retrospective screened G. W. Pabst's complete works, and an exhibition about the director was held to accompany the event in the Literaturhaus Berlin. Pabst's classic Die Büchse der Pandora (»Lulu«/»Pandora's Box«) with newly composed music by Peer Raben was given a splendid show in the final screening of this year's Festival. And then there were the prizes, awarded by the Jury under the presidency of Jack Lang, the former French Minister of Cultural Affairs and one of the superior Jury presidents of the last years. The award-winners met with unanimous approval: Milos Forman's ›bio-pic with message‹ about Larry Flint received the Golden Bear, even if some might have liked to see it go to Minghella's The English Patient. The latter nonetheless received a consolation prize: the award for best actress went to Juliette Binoche. The Special Prize of the

International Jury
Jack Lang (France, president)
Hark Bohm (Germany)
Férid Boughedir (Tunisia)
Maggie Cheung (Hong Kong)
Fred Gronich (Israel)
David Hare (Great Britain)
Per Holst (Denmark)
Boleslaw Michalek (Poland)
Marianne Sägebrecht (Germany)
Humberto Solas (Cuba)
Ning Ying (People's Republic of China)

The Awards of the International Jury

Feature Films
Grand Prix of the 47th IFB
Golden Berlin Bear
THE PEOPLE VS. LARRY FLINT
USA
directed by Milos Forman

Silver Berlin Bear
Special Prize of the Jury
HE LIU
Taiwan/China
directed by Tsai Ming-liang

Silver Berlin Bear
for the best director
Eric Heumann
PORT DJEMA
France

Silver Berlin Bear
for the best actress
Juliette Binoche
in THE ENGLISH PATIENT
USA

Silver Berlin Bear
for the best actor
Leonardo DiCaprio
in WILLIAM SHAKESPEARE'S ROMEO & JULIET
USA

Silver Berlin Bear
for a special individual achievement (music)
Zbigniew Preisner
THE ISLAND ON BIRD STREET
Denmark/Great Britain/Germany

Silver Berlin Bear
for his outstanding contribution to film art
on the occasion of his film
GÉNÉALOGIES D'UN CRIME
to Raoul Ruiz
France

Jury was awarded to Tsai Ming-liang – which was considered a bold and just move. Leonardo DiCaprio was honored as best actor, for his role as an American Romeo. The »Titanic« had not yet set sail.

Overall, this year's Festival was not overwhelming, but nor could one say it had been bad. And at the suggestion of the Jury, a small change was made: in the future, the Festival would begin one day earlier so that it could end on a Sunday. One tiny but easy step had been taken toward reforming the Festival. In any case, this year's event had not turned out to be the big flop some had predicted. The prospects were obvious: the year 2000. A challenge which meant that the Berlinale would require more political support than ever before. Time would tell.

A head full of images

By Jack Lang

The Zoo Palast's majestic theater, Gong Li's radiant face, the countless cranes at Potsdamer Platz, Kim Novak's mythic presence, Bernard-Henri Lévy's tristesse, Milos Forman's delight, the nightly cold, the warming glances, the glittering lights on the Kurfürstendamm, the public's passion for film, the Jury's lively but relaxed discussions, Louise Brooks' mysterious smile, a beautiful Golden Bear, a tasty light beer and films, films, films .... So many images are imprinted on my mind.

In February 1997, I took part in a film festival from beginning to end for the first time. It was not just any festival. It was not just any city. It was not just any function. It was the Berlinale. It was Berlin. It was the Jury presidency. What memories!

The International Film Festival in Berlin is an event with human dimensions. And it is held in pleasant theaters. For more than ten days, cinema is given the undivided attention of the Jury members, who live at a pace of 24-frames per second. Life totally revolves around films. In other words, one literally bathes in images. A strange and at the same time thrilling sensation.

If you are on a jury, you must have endurance, because each member has to watch all the films, the good ones as well as those that are not so good. Yet this task is made less strenuous for those involved by the remarkable organization. Admittedly, I do regret it a bit that the extensive Festival program only allowed me to steal away from screenings and meetings for one afternoon. How I would have liked to have had the opportunity to stroll along Unter den Linden, to wander through the streets of Prenzlauer Berg and become involved in the intoxicating discovery of a metropolis undergoing rapid change, to observe the capital taking shape. Even my one short outing made me realize what an extraordinary cinematic setting Berlin is. Fritz Lang, G. W. Pabst, Billy Wilder and Wim Wenders have all shown us.

The position of the Jury president is an especially privileged one, for he does not only cast a vote like all the other Jury members, but is actually also a kind of moral authority. He can give a discussion direction and steer it in a way that is often decisive, not least with regard to awarding the prizes.

As a Frenchman, I presided over the Jury with undisguised pride and great delight. The relationship of the French to Berlin and the Berlinale has been manifold and intense. The history of film has developed in a brotherly fashion, especially in Berlin. I need only recall the amicable rivalry between those who gave birth to cinema: the Lumière brothers and the Skladanowsky brothers. Later, during the era of silent

The Blue Angel
SECRETOS DEL CORAZÓN
directed by Montxo Armendáriz
Spain/France/Portugal

Alfred Bauer Prize
WILLIAM SHAKESPEARE'S ROMEO & JULIET
directed by Baz Luhrmann
USA

Special Mention
for the humorous and ironic portrayal of change in contemporary Berlin
DAS LEBEN IST EINE BAUSTELLE
Germany
directed by Wolfgang Becker

Special Mention
for the extraordinary interaction of the entire cast
GET ON THE BUS
USA
directed by Spike Lee

Special Mention
for a promising performance to Anna Wielgucka
in PANNA NIKT
Poland

Special Mention
for a promising performance to Jordan Kiziuk
in THE ISLAND ON BIRD STREET
Denmark/Great Britain/Germany

Short Films
Golden Berlin Bear
SENASTE NYTT
Sweden
directed by Per Carleson

Silver Berlin Bear
LATE AT NIGHT
Germany
directed by Stefanie Jordan, Stefanie Saghri, Claudia Zoller

PANNA NIKT by Andrzej Wajda (in the Competition): Anna Wielgucka

films, there were a whole series of French-German co-productions. These were followed by an epoch of versions in both languages from Neubabelsberg, by directing tandem Reinhold Schünzel and Roger Le Bon, and with the successful duo Lilian Harvey and Henri Garat.

The Berlinale has also been extremely fertile for French film. The Golden Bear has been awarded six times to French films; and actors and actresses such as Jean Gabin, Simone Signoret or Jean-Louis Trintignant have been honored with awards. I also recall that it was Willy Brandt, Mayor of West Berlin at the time, who presented the deeply moving film NUIT ET BROUILLARD *(»Night and Fog«) by Alain Resnais in 1956. And not least, it was the Berlinale which consecrated the Nouvelle Vague by awarding the Golden Bear to Claude Chabrol's film* LES COUSINS *(»The Cousins«) in 1959 and by regularly celebrating Jean-Luc Godard.*

*I love the Berlinale because it is a special festival. Established during the Cold War at a time of confrontation between the antagonistic camps, it paradoxically fulfilled a role as a bridge between cultures, above all between East and West. And so in 1997, Asian film was given special attention and presented alongside major Hollywood productions, a special feature of the Berlinale which was also reflected in the distribution of the awards. The Golden Bear went to an American film (*THE PEOPLE VS. LARRY FLINT*), while* HE LIU *(»The River«), the enigmatic work of Tsai Ming-liang, a young Taiwanese director, and* GÉNÉALOGIES D'UNE CRIME *(»Genealogies of a Crime«), the black film farce by Chilean director Raoul Ruiz, were among the prize-winners.*

With the respect for freedom

By Milos Forman

I do not think that in the past century any other city in the world has been chosen more often by Good and Evil as their playground than Berlin.

In 1941, in occupied Czechoslovakia, my father tested Berlin's tolerance for freedom of expression by distributing to his students books by Kafka, Hemingway, Thomas Mann and other literary giants.

He paid for it with his life.

45 years later I brought to Berlin my film THE PEOPLE VS. LARRY FLINT, *which has as its principal theme the necessity for a free and open society to protect its freedom of speech even when the person conducting the battle is a pornographer.*

That this theme was still deemed controversial, even at present, fortified my certainty of the need for our persevering vigilance.

When the film was honored by the Berlin Film Festival with the Golden Bear, the Berliners certainly were not applauding the pornography.

I believe that they were expressing their commitment to enter the 21st century with the respect for freedom in their hearts. Keep it that way. The whole world will benefit.

It all began in Berlin

By Ben Sombogaart

The premiere was fantastic at the Berlin Children's Film Festival in 1989. The whole crew had come, even our 9-year-old leading actress Wenneke with her parents. For the first time we saw the film on a large screen, and in the Urania it was a very big one at that. At least 1000 people were seated in the theater. One could not have wished for a more lovely world premiere. Only our author was missing. He had said he would come. He had wanted to take the train through the GDR and had planned to leave the previous night from Amsterdam.

Midway through the screening, Wenneke's father was overcome by emotions. The film's story, the entire situation, the suspenseful quiet in the theater, the reactions of the children all affected him so strongly that he decided to smoke a cigarette in the lobby. And whom did he find out there but the author, who was smoking a cigarette too, although in his case it was because he believed he had arrived much too early and that the film hadn't started yet.

The end credits went off the screen and the curtain fell. The lights went on. People were moved, there were tears, applause, a great deal of applause. And flowers and cameras and interviews … and a cognac at Café Einstein. My first feature film MIJN VADER WOONT IN RIO *(»My Father Lives in Rio«) was a success.*

Excited, we left for home, back to the Netherlands, where we had not been able to find a distributor who wanted to bring out more than two copies of the film at once. We had struggled hard to raise the money for the film, for we believed that it had to be possible to make good quality films for children in the Netherlands, too. Scandinavia had set a great example.

But without a distributor we would have no audience, without an audience, no premiere.

Then the call came. It was Renate. She asked whether we could make it back to Berlin by tomorrow. We had won the Children's Jury Award. A Bear, a real Berlin Bear!

We drove off from Amsterdam at five in the morning, at one o'clock in the afternoon, we were back in Berlin. I had a stomachache, it was my nerves and much too much coffee. At the press center I had to run for the restrooms and almost missed the award ceremony.

The news was faster than we were. Even the biggest Dutch paper had a photograph of Wenneke on the front page. MIJN VADER WOONT IN RIO *had been discovered. Distributors were enthusiastic and the film journalists full of praise.* MIJN VADER WOONT IN RIO *was a gigantic hit … in the Netherlands. We could continue on with our next projects … with foreign co-producers.*

Two years later, we had our next world premiere, this time in unified Berlin. Again, the whole crew had come with us, the 9-year-old leading actor Olivier with his mother, too. HET ZAKMES *(»The Pocketknife«) was the opening film of the Children's Film Festival. The reactions of the audience and the press surpassed our wildest expectations. We dined at Café Einstein.*

We drove merrily home, full of optimism. Maybe we'd win a prize again. A distributor wanted to release ten copies of the film at once. As a precautionary measure, the author of MIJN VADER WOONT IN RIO*, now the producer of* HET ZAKMES*, reserved tickets for a flight to Berlin and booked hotel rooms for the night of the award ceremony. There were rumors that …*

No call came. No Renate. No prize. Nothing. Bitter tears, disappointment. But not for long. HET ZAKMES *was a huge success, at home and abroad. I think that no other Dutch film had ever received so many festival prizes, even a Grammy! We could continue on with our projects, and with even more foreign co-producers.*

Two years later. This time it was the world premiere of DE JONGEN DIE NIET MEER PRAATTE *(»The Boy Who Stopped Talking«). Guarded optimism.*

The films shown during the Children's Festival were wonderful and of high quality, and DE JONGEN DIE NIET MEER PRAATTE *was a film with a political message. The two 9-year-old leads, Ercan and Louis, enjoyed the commotion at the Festival, the interviews, their success. We dined at Café Einstein.*

It was the last screening. The house was full. The end credits. Emotions. Applause. And then one of the organizers said that there was a call for me. We ran through the immense theater. Passageways, stairs, an office. It was Renate. The jury of film experts had awarded us their prize. Another Bear!

DE JONGEN DIE NIET MEER PRAATTE *began its triumphant advance. Although not in the Netherlands, but in North and South America, and especially in France, movie-goers raved. There were even more awards, and even greater interest in our projects from foreign co-producers.*

ABELTJE. *It took years until the financing for this film was clinched. It was strange that people had more faith in us and our projects abroad than at home. Germany had contributed, too.*

But ABELTJE *was different. More a family film. With two children in the leading roles, but without a clear message. More* INDIANA JONES *and less* ZAKMES, RIO *and* DE JONGEN*… a humorous action film.*

This time the film premiered worldwide in the Netherlands. More than 100 copies were in circulation, and nearly a million viewers saw it within five months. For the Netherlands, a gigantic success. Naturally we wanted to go to Berlin again. I noted the dates in my diary, because I wanted ABELTJE *to set out to conquer the world from there.*

Then a letter arrived. It was from Renate. The film had been rejected. They did not think that ABELTJE *was suited for the Children's Film Festival in Berlin.*

And so there was no Urania. No spoken German translation. And no Bear and no Café Einstein. Our world collapsed.

I have gotten over the disappointment. I am working on new projects, and I'm sure that they will one day have their world premieres in Berlin. Some time at the beginning of the 21st century.

True, it's still sad that ABELTJE *could not be screened at the Children's Film Festival. Maybe I should ask if they would show the film in 2000 hors concours … because in the end it all began in Berlin.*

Lucie Aubrac:
Carol Bouquet
(in the Competition)

THE BIG LEBOWSKI:
Jeff Bridges

Cancellations!?

1998

Feb. 11th-22nd, 1998
(Competition)
Feb. 12th-22nd, 1998
(Forum)

What a year! A glance at the Berlinale's program in all sections boded well. There was certainly no shortage of international stars: Catherine Deneuve, Robert de Niro or Samuel L. Jackson and Toni Colette, Pam Grier, Gwyneth Paltrow, Corinna Harfouch, Rachel Weisz, Jürgen Vogel, Labina Mitevska, Lambert Wilson – all icons of modern cinema. And yet: this year things just didn't seem to want to succeed, the Festival's positive vibes were failing to reach the public, and, in particular, the critics. The atmosphere at the Berlinale was poor. And a delight in disaster was spreading. As so often when the mood had started off strained, there was no escaping this low. Every good moment was negated by bad news or badmouthed. Only one person remained unimpressed by the Festival's difficulties – and went on photographing photographers, giving autographs to fans, attracting attention, as if he were the only cosmopolitan at the Festival – someone whom you could ask anything and everything, and who had lots to tell: Curt Siodmak, science-fiction scriptwriter and guest of honor of the Retrospective which was dedicated to him and his brother, director Robert Siodmak. Curt Siodmak was the secret star of the Festival. Regardless who else came!

Curt Siodmak: the secret star

Curt Siodmak

Why spirits suddenly sank couldn't really be explained. Was this the consequence of last year's turmoil between the Competition, Panorama and Forum? Did it signalize a departure, one burdened by uncertainties and unresolved problems? Or was it a mixture of both, connected with a pleasure in polemics at taking the hated and beloved Berlinale to task before moving on to the year 2000? Was it a delight in the Berlinale's apocalypse, or dissatisfaction with the Festival management? In any case, the great number of cancellations with which the Festival had to come to terms did not improve the mood. There were cancellations that affected the Berlinale before its opening, and cancellations that were received while it was in process. And so it was just a small step to suggest canceling the whole Festival – or at least writing it off. Was the Berlinale over and done for?

The Festival management and the advisory selection commission had viewed 504 feature films for the Competition and the Panorama, more than it had in years. Twenty-nine films were chosen. Commission members had traveled to Beijing, Budapest, Buenos Aires, Gdansk, Hong Kong, Kiev, Copenhagen, Lisbon, London, Los Angeles, Madrid, Milan, Moscow, New York, Oslo, Paris, Prague, Rio de Janeiro, Rome, Shanghai, St. Petersburg, Taipei, Tokyo, Toronto and Vienna. Yet despite the success of being able to present new films, for example, by Joel and Ethan Coen, Gus van Sant, Quentin Tarantino, Barry Levinson, Robert Altman, Jim Sheridan, Neil Jordan, Alain Resnais and Michael Winterbottom, the Competition was regarded as a competition of those films which the members had failed to obtain.

Clint Eastwood cancels

The new film by Clint Eastwood, MIDNIGHT IN THE GARDEN OF GOOD AND EVIL, did not participate in the Competition, although the Festival had announced in a press release that it would. Why Warner Bros. retracted the film at short notice could only be guessed. On December 2nd 1997, Clint Eastwood's agent arrived in Berlin with a copy of the film, which was then viewed immediately and invited to the Competition. Yet Eastwood's agent asked the Festival to wait to announce the film's participation, because he had not received Eastwood's consent yet. But then communication broke down between the Festival and Warner Bros., or rather Eastwood's agent: even on request, no message arrived confirming Eastwood's film. But since the

Robert de Niro, Gwyneth Paltrow, Alfonso Cuarón

Lee Kang-sheng, Lin Cheng-sheng, Chen Shiang-chyi

Lu Lu, Lopsang, Joan Chen

Pam Grier, Samuel L. Jackson

production company had already expressed its interest in the film's participation in the Competition, and Eastwood's consent appeared to be a mere formality, the Festival management ultimately decided, to announce the film's participation in the Competition officially. Warner Bros. protested immediately and notification that the film was no longer available promptly followed. Presumably, the film's cool reception on its release in the States caused them to alter their distribution strategy. More or less with relief, the film was withdrawn from the Berlinale – nevertheless, this did not help the Festival's reputation.

Problems with Scorsese's Tibet film

The complications which arose regarding Martin Scorsese's Tibet film KUNDUN were even more complex. Contact between the Festival management and the German distributor had been established in May of the previous year. The objective was, if possible, to show the film at the Berlinale – provided Scorsese decided not to present the film in Venice. Yet in the course of the year, tensions mounted between the film authorities of the People's Republic of China and three major studios that had films about Tibet in production; Scorsese's film was also affected by their restrictive attitude. It became more and more evident that the tensions related to the politico-cultural situation were going to complicate the film's participation at the Festival, that is, if the contacts that had evolved with the Chinese partners were to be maintained. It was also obvious that it would be unacceptable to bow to the demands from Beijing, whose ultimate aim was the film's rejection by international festivals. The Festival management took a diplomatic course, consulting the German embassy in Beijing and discussing the situation with Deputy Minister for Radio, Film and Television Zhao Shi, and head of the Chinese National Film Office Liu Lianzhong. The impression they gave was that it would indeed be possible – despite politico-cultural pressures – to show the film without the Chinese delegation feeling compelled to withdraw the film in protest from the Festival, as had recently happened in a similar situation in Tokyo. Politically, it was not easy for the Festival management to demonstrate

Nils and Bertrand Tavernier

Johan van der Keuken, Ramon Gieling

Boris Lehman, Dominique Loreau

Yolande Zauberman, Lena Stolze

backbone and avoid succumbing to the censorship measures on the one hand, and on the other, to ensure that China's overall participation at the Berlinale would not be endangered. The fact that everything worked out quite differently was only partially related to this predicament. The Festival's attitude – to wait patiently before confirming Scorsese's film – caused irritation. When the Festival finally asked if they could show the film to the selection commission, Scorsese felt his artistic reputation had been slurred. Yet the request had little to do with actual »selection«, but was rather an occasion to become acquainted with the film; not an unusual request, and one usually complied with. After all the political complications, the film could anyway hardly be rejected, unless the Berlinale was prepared to risk losing face. In a letter addressed to Martin Scorsese, dated December 12th, 1997, de Hadeln tried to correct the wrong impression: Berlin had not asked for a copy so that the film could go through the selection process. Besides, as he pointed out, Scorsese's films RAGING BULL and CAPE FEAR had taken a similar route. He explicitly assured Scorsese that the film's and Scorsese's invitation was a »very special event« for the coming Festival. All these efforts were in vain. Scorsese had his agent inform the Berlinale that he was grateful for the invitation, but would unfortunately have to refuse. This was a major disappointment for the German distributor, who had developed his entire distribution strategy on presenting the film at the Berlinale, which complicated communication behind the scenes even further. No matter: the film KUNDUN was lost for the Berlinale. And the two other films selected in Beijing as Competition candidates could not be shown either, because the Chinese authorities refused to give their consent. Hence, the People's Republic of China was represented by only one short film in the official program.

Closing film: perdu, too

The Festival had to cope with still another loss, namely the film SLIDING DOORS by Peter Howitt, which had been viewed in London and invited as the closing film of the Festival. Everything had seemed finalized; there were no indications that difficulties might also arise with this film. But then suddenly, one day before the first press conference on February 2nd, its world distributors announced that the film was being withdrawn on »technical grounds and for strategic distribution reasons«. And although the Festival management immediately contacted Sydney Pollack, one of the co-producers, it was not successful in reversing this decision. Evidently, distribution strategies had been changed – as with Eastwood's film – and now editing and sound were to be redone; in other words, the version that had been shown at the festival in Sundance was being reexamined. The Festival management could protest against this conduct, but they could not undo the cancellation, which in press reports was interpreted as a weakness of the Festival. And although Francis Ford Coppola's film John Grisham's The Rainmaker was found at short notice as an attractive substitute, Festival critics remained unconciliatory.

In conflict with international festival interests

Indeed, with the withdrawal of this film a basic problem became evident that affected also other independently produced American films. They had been invited to the Panorama and had already been shown at the festival in Sundance; special terms had been agreed upon by the Berlinale and the films' producers, which their distributors then failed to stick to. As a consequence, these films could not be shown in Berlin. The relative importance of the festival in Sundance, as well as of the festivals in Rotterdam and Brussels – all three took place before the Berlinale – had changed:

Central do Brasil by Walter Salles (in the Competition): Fernanda Montenegro, Vinicius de Oliveira

for some time now they were no longer just a refuge for independents. International distributors had recognized what chances such films had on the market, and so went to these festivals to shop for rights. In turn, they often marketed the films without consideration for festival interests. To complicate matters, the Sundance Festival was sometimes also co-producer, as was the case with Walter Salles' CENTRAL DO BRASIL (»Central Station«), which went on to win the Berlinale. This led to the Berlinale being accused of not observing its own guidelines, but of screening films that had already been shown at other festivals. In fact, the film's main producer, Arthur Cohn – despite pressure from Cannes – decided to send the film to Berlin after the selection commission had responded positively to a viewing. At this point in time, the Festival management already knew that the film, which Sundance had co-financed with 150 000 dollars, would be shown in Sundance; yet they reached an agreement that it could be screened only once, and on the last day. And this agreement was kept. The accusation that the Berlinale was dodging its own guidelines was about as wrong as it was right, and as much a question of interpretation as of realistic assessment of the market. A transgression perhaps, that is if one were to commit further transgressions, and assuming that other Festivals would also be willing to play by these new rules. Yet it would certainly not do to ignore these warnings completely.

An absence of stars and directors

Cancellations? There were more. However, what probably carried the most weight was that a number of directors were not in Berlin to present their films in the Competition; they were either prevented by illness, like Alain Resnais; by alleged indisposition, like Robert Altman; or by their contempt of the Festival, like Barry Levinson. Not a single actor from Levinson's film WAG THE DOG put in an appearance, which was a singular incident in the Festival's history and bound to provoke snide comments. For although the film's production company and distributor had known for days about the actors' disinterest and rejection, they had neglected to inform the Festival management. Of course the fact that large sums of money also played a part because stars and star directors receive princely fees to attend festivals was no longer a secret of the trade. Such expenses cannot, however, be covered by a festival, but are as a rule paid by distributors and production companies, or by sponsors who are presumably also sometimes extremely generous. Notwithstanding, the public image of this year's Berlinale had suffered.

In this context, the appearance of Robert de Niro – who had supposedly been detained by an entanglement in Paris, but then finally arrived – was nothing more than a brief media event, a mere side-show, making the absence of the many other stars who had been expected all the more conspicuous. And it was awkward that the attendance of those who did put in an appearance – for after all, some stars had come to Berlin – had so little impact on the Festival. The management needed to ask themselves whether they had always judged glamour's significance correctly, and if they knew how to use it to their advantage.

JACKIE BROWN: Pam Grier

And thank goodness: at this point no one knew there were also problems with Italy. True, Moritz de Hadeln and Italian Minister of Cultural Affairs Walter Veltroni had succeeded in clarifying former misunderstandings. Moreover, with Pupi Avati's IL TESTIMONE DELLO SPOSO (»The Best Man«), Italy was represented in the Competition. There was also an Italian film program, »Italia Cinema«, running in Berlin parallel and supplementary to the Festival. Yet the very film that Berlin might have shown but didn't, did not represent Italy: Roberto Benigni's LA VITA È BELLA (»Life is Beautiful«) was screened in Cannes, even though it had been offered to Berlin.

The Butcher Boy by Neil Jordan (in the Competition): Eamonn Owens, Alan Boyle

It had been among the films which two members of the selection commission had viewed in Rome. The version they saw was not the cut later released to movie theaters. Their feelings were mixed, for and against the film. And so as usual in such situations, they asked Anica, the Italian export union, to send a copy of the film to Berlin. Their efforts to get a video cassette, which would have speeded up the process, were in vain. Back in Berlin they described their impressions and gave their assessment. The other members of the selection commission, however, never got to see the film. There was no cassette and a copy never arrived. No one paid further heed to the matter – and so the film ran in Cannes and was a hit worldwide. One might ask how the film would have done if it had been presented in Berlin. Would it have also received an award from the Berlinale Jury? Would the critics and the audience have reacted as strongly to this film as they did in Cannes? Pure speculation. But beyond mulling over the fact that such a successful movie was not screened at the Berlinale because it had disappeared in the bustle of business as usual, one must ask if this was not in fact a stroke of luck for the film itself.

Europe vs. USA

Just the same, this year's Berlinale could not just be written off, for some films were of excellent quality. European cinema seemed rather stuffy, if not museum-like, yet powerful examples were set by Alain Resnais' delightfully arty comedy On connaît la chanson, Jim Sheridan's political drama about the civil war in North Ireland, The Boxer, and above all, by Neil Jordan's intense and surreal portrait of an outsider, The Butcher Boy. Uwe Schmitt asked in relation to Jordan's film in the »Frankfurter Rundschau«: »What can a youth – from an asocial family with dreams of omnipotence but without a chance – do at the beginning of the sixties in a lonely Irish nest in the province, abandoned by all good spirits, except for the Virgin Mary, besides stealing apples, and riding with John Wayne to fight off aliens, communists and Apaches, and murdering Mrs. Nugent?« (Feb. 16, 1998). Jordan, who superimposes one stylistic level over the other and in doing so achieves a grotesque aesthetic

I WANT YOU by Michael Winterbottom (in the Competition): Luka Petrusic, Rachel Weisz

quality, succeeds in timelessly capturing the moment: »Black humor hallows and heals everything in this great film about despair.« These were films that could hold their own with American cinema, such as presented at the Festival in Gus van Sant's pedagogic effort GOOD WILL HUNTING; in the sometimes frantically obtrusive, sometimes vain and zany THE BIG LEBOWSKI, by Joel & Ethan Coen; and above all in Quentin Tarantino's sophisticated monomaniac art-thriller JACKIE BROWN, filmed in the cool-warm color blue. Barry Levinson's WAG THE DOG constituted the satiric counterpart to these American *auteur* films.

Asian counterweight

Asian cinema was represented by five films in the Competition, and even more strongly in the International Forum of Young Cinema. For instance, there was a series of Korean films, interesting primarily because they portrayed life in a country which was undergoing a transition toward democracy, and in which censorship was beginning to relax. Peter Körte remarked that »the gap between modernization along Western lines and regional traditions« was not only the subject of these Asian films, but shaped »the films' signatures, right down to their form, giving them an independence and a seismographic feel« (Frankfurter Rundschau, Feb. 23, 1998). Above all, the Taiwanese film FANG LANG (»Sweet Degeneration«) by Lin Cheng-sheng conveyed something of this melancholy weightlessness that distinguishes the culture of such a nation: changes, indeed, but in what direction?

Searching for traces in the past and present

In the Forum, the dominant themes were related to Jewish biographies. The six-hour documentary SHIVREI TMUNOT YERUSHALAÏM (»Fragments: Jerusalem«) by Ron Havilio revolved around the Jaffa Gate, the principal entrance to the Old City of Jerusalem, the center where »Arabs and Jews meet, and a place where the Israeli-Palestinian conflict persistently rekindles«. The history of a city, but also a history linked to autobiographical discoveries about the director's own family history. Director Lisa Lewenz also set out to find family traces in her documentary A LETTER WITHOUT WORDS, searching for traces of her grandmother in Berlin, motivated by the experiences of a granddaughter whose parents were forced into exile. In SHALOSH ACHAYOT (»Three Sisters«), Tsipi Reibenbach documents memories »of the Holocaust within a very intimate sphere«, filming the everyday life of her mother and two aunts, »a painful documentation«, which shows »that every shaky step of the three aged sisters through their daily lives is a balancing act. Above an abyss of depressions, of silence: the past.« (Kolja Mensing, Berliner Zeitung, Feb. 18, 1998) This film was complemented by Richard Dindo's documentary DER FALL GRÜNINGER (»The Grüninger Case«) about a Swiss police captain, who gave Austrian Jews false traveling documents in 1938, and as a result lost his job. He was not rehabilitated until over forty years later, after his death. The Israeli films screened in the Panorama could also be seen as supplementing the others: a love story, that had an almost legendary twist, THE DYBBUK OF THE HOLY APPLE FIELD/DYBBUK M'SDE HATAPUCHIM HAKDOSCHIM by Yossi Somer, and Assi Dayan's caustic picture of contemporary Israel THE 92 MINUTES OF MR. BAUM.

The German game

The German films represented in the Competition of 1998 were rather disappointing. The Festival management had tried to get Max Färberböck's film AIMÉE & JAGUAR, but it was still in post-production. Other films, which had been hoped for, were out of the question because they were to be released in December and January, and their distributors were not willing to make allowances for the Berlinale. After an extremely controversial debate, in which it was also discussed whether it was acceptable to show no German films in the Competition, an agreement was reached to screen Michael Gwisdek's film DAS MAMBOSPIEL (»The Big Mambo«), even though some members of the commission clearly objected to this choice. That George Sluizer's film THE COMMISSIONER ran on the ›German ticket‹ in the Competition was further evidence of the desolate state of the films offered this year. Only Rudolf Thome's contribution to the Forum TIGERSTREIFENBABY SUCHT TARZAN (»Tiger-Stripe Woman Waits for Tarzan«) made any impression, a playfully consistent

Jeroen Krabbé

Catherine Deneuve, honored with a Golden Berlin Bear for her lifetime achievements

»present-day science fiction: the story of the intergalactic Frank MacKay, who beams himself into the present from a future time without women, in order to find Laura Luna, the author of the Tiger-Stripe Woman novel. (...) Unique about Thome's little stories of big loves is how each story evolves with self-evidence and stringency on the screen right in front of our eyes.« (Angela Schmitt-Gläser. Frankfurter Rundschau, Feb. 20, 1998)

Winners and a ray of hope

It had been a difficult year for the Berlinale. True, in financial terms, further consolidation had been possible, and a new sponsor had been found in SAT 1 Television Network. Mercedes-Benz had increased its involvement, and the rights-holders relations group AGICOA succeeded Kodak as sponsor of the purse for »The Blue Angel«. There had been important films in all sections. Yet the Berlinale had not been able to live up to the atmosphere expected of an international festival. Even the lucky winners, producer Arthur Cohn, director Walter Salles, and leading actress Fernanda Montenegro of CENTRAL DO BRASIL, were not able to make up for this in the public mind.

Nevertheless: critics who had demanded that the Berlinale be canceled had overshot the mark. Seen as a whole, the Berlinale had not lost: but it had been a draw at best and a close one at that. Berlin's soccer team Hertha BSC had beaten the favorites Bayern München one goal to nil in a championship match: at least a happy ending for one of Berlin's problem children – giving hope for the others.

Berlinale winners: Neil Jordan, Walter Salles, Fernanda Montenegro, Jeroen Krabbé, Gus van Sant, Lawrence Bender

International Jury
Ben Kingsley (Great Britain, president)
Senta Berger (Germany)
Leslie Cheung (China/Canada)
Helmut Dietl (Germany)
Annette Insdorf (USA)
Li Cheuk-to (Hong Kong/China)
Maurizio Nichetti (Italy)
Héctor Olivera (Argentina)
Brigitte Rouan (France)
Maya Turovskaya (Russia)
Michael Williams-Jones (Great Britain)

The Awards of the International Jury

Feature Films
Grand Prix of the 48th IFB
Golden Berlin Bear
CENTRAL DO BRASIL
Brazil/France
directed by Walter Salles

Silver Berlin Bear
Special Prize of the Jury
WAG THE DOG
USA
directed by Barry Levinson

Silver Berlin Bear
for the best director
Neil Jordan
THE BUTCHER BOY
Ireland

Silver Berlin Bear
for the best actress
Fernanda Montenegro
in CENTRAL DO BRASIL
Brazil/France

Silver Berlin Bear
for the best actor
Samuel L. Jackson
in JACKIE BROWN
USA

Silver Berlin Bear
for his outstanding contribution to contemporary film art
Alain Resnais
ON CONNAÎT LA CHANSON
France/Switzerland/Great Britain

SUE by Amos Kollek (in the Panorama): Anna Thomson

A family of smiles

By Lynn Hershman

Fourteen years after turning on my camera, I arrived in Berlin, invited by the Forum at the Film Festival.

I'm not used to this cold. White puffs bite into the air as I speak. The streets are museums of disappearance and survival. I slosh through the evaporating landscapes and see buildings waiting to be reborn.

I'm welcomed by a family of smiles and feel warm.

At the opening reception, flickering lights ignite velvet walls and exotic food. I, along with other sweat soaked bodies squeeze inside this dream.

I see old friends, make new ones. I see new films and then old ones. Honest, courageous films. Honest, courageous people. I think I see Vertov on the other side of the street, but he disappears into an alley.

I revel in the glory of light and breathe in the spirit and power of art in this rare, transcendent and invigorating moment and am grateful to be part of it.

Spaghetti alla Berlinale

By Maurizio Nichetti

An image which has stuck in my mind and which pleasantly reminds me of my adventure in Berlin is how Moritz de Hadeln and his wife were sitting off on their own one evening, at around eleven, in a hotel restaurant, while the Festival was in full swing all around them, and eating spaghetti with tomato sauce.

It seems to me that if a festival director can leisurely and quietly treat himself to the luxury of a plate of spaghetti during a film festival, then this means that the organization is working well and the official protocol is absolutely humane. These are the two huge merits of the Festival as I experienced it in Berlin in 1998. With Ben Kingsley presiding expertly over the Jury, I was able to live through what it means to be a jury member at a large international film festival. I had never met Moritz de Hadeln personally before, and I must admit that upon my arrival in Berlin, I had felt a certain apprehension, not least due to all the senseless polemic statements that have always accompanied announcements of the entries to the Competition each year.

The man I got to know is a very likable one who is downright proud of his achievements and lifework. And since I also was able to see my old friend Annette Insdorf again, who was also on the Jury, I immediately felt right at home.

I was among people who loved cinema and were willing to discuss films night after night.

I saw beautiful films on many evenings, and little that was mundane. The Film Market was interesting, and the long walks from the hotel to the Festival venues were just right for stretching your legs after one, two or even three screenings. There was the euphoria to find yourself in a babel of languages this and that side of the screen again: Chinese films with German subtitles, French coming from the earphones into your left ear; and at the touch of a button, you were at all times ready to switch over to the English translation, while the right ear remained free for the original track, for the unspoiled emotional effect.

Silver Berlin Bear
for an outstanding
individual achievement
(script and acting)
Matt Damon
GOOD WILL HUNTING
USA

The Blue Angel
LEFT LUGGAGE
directed by Jeroen Krabbé
Netherlands/Belgium/USA

Alfred Bauer Prize
YUE KUAI LE, YUE DUO LUO
directed by Stanley Kwan
Hong Kong/China

Special Mention
for her extraordinary
performance as
»Mrs. Kalman«
Isabella Rossellini
in LEFT LUGGAGE
Netherlands/Belgium/USA

Special Mention
for his amazing performance
as the young leading actor
Eamonn Owens
THE BUTCHER BOY
Ireland

Special Mention
for his forceful images
Slavomir Idziak
I WANT YOU
Great Britain

Short Films
Golden Berlin Bear
I MOVE SO I AM
Netherlands
directed by Gerrit van Dijk

Silver Berlin Bear
CINEMA ALCAZAR
Nicaragua
directed by Florence Jaugey

And there were new friends: Senta, Brigitte, Maya, Michael, Hector, Helmut, Leslie, Li, a jury capable of deciding quickly, thanks also to the mathematical voting procedure under the supervision of an extremely precise president. A prize-winning film which drew applause from everyone, from viewers and journalists. A Brazilian film of the emotions: the Jury had to remain open, even after viewing almost thirty Competition entries, to allow itself to be moved by an emotional story, by feelings that are as immortal as cinema itself.

I would have liked to have given Moritz one bit of advice that evening, while he was eating his spaghetti, but I didn't dare. I had no desire to disturb the intimacy which was so precious to him. The Italians – and I know them well – are quite straight forward and they make an effort to understand and speak every language, and it does not take much to win their friendship. Sometimes, even a single word is enough. To throw in a benvenuto *now and then between a* bienvenido *and a* bienvenue *surely does not do much to further deeper understanding. Just the same, it would make those Italians also feel at home who had not been so lucky to be a member of the Jury like I had or to become acquainted with that exquisite German hospitality – or, above all, to have the opportunity to experience how de Hadeln and his wife leaned over a plate of spaghetti just like two real Italians.*

An attempt to rediscover the face of Brazil

By Walter Salles

Jean-Luc Godard once said that television manufactures oblivion. Conversely, cinema brings with it the possibility of permanence. Our film memory is filled with unforgettable moments – for me Chaplin's CITY LIGHTS, *Eisenstein's* STAROYE I NOVOYE *(»Old and New«), Dreyer's* LA PASSION DE JEANNE D'ARC *(»The Passion of Joan of Arc«), the discovery of Pereira dos Santos'* VIDAS SECAS *(»Barren Lives«) and the radical aesthetics of Cinema Nôvo,* LIMITE, *an experimental film made in 1931 by a 21 year-old Brazilian director, Mário Peixoto … the list could go on indefinitely. I could also mention* ROCCO E I SUOI FRATELLI *(»Rocco and His Brothers«) by Visconti,* PROFESSIONE: REPORTER *(»The Passenger«) by Antonioni, all the films which made me want to make films, to become a director.*

It seems to me that today, surprisingly, the weeks spent on the set are no longer the most complex part of film-making. There is a moment when a film breaks away from you and starts acquiring a life of its own – this in a scenario where distribution is ever-increasingly congested by the North American industry. »The moment I speak of is already far from me«, Borges said. Indeed: in order for all the effort and passion devoted to bringing a film to life to have been worthwhile, the moment in which it encounters audiences for the first time, its birthplace, must be chosen very carefully.

In the case of CENTRAL DO BRASSIL *(»Central Station«), we were just emerging from an atypical moment in Brazilian cinema. Brazil was one of the first countries to adopt the Lumière brothers' invention, in 1896. In 1909, over 100 films, both documentaries and fictional films, were made in the country. Since then, local production has only stopped twice: during the Great War, due to a shortage of film stock, and in 1990, during President Collor's (mis)government, due to a shortage of scruples. Film production fell from 70 films a year during the 1980s to zero in 1991. That situation persisted until 1994.*

A country without images is like a country which stops creating or examining its own reflection. A country without a face and without a voice. CENTRAL DO BRASIL *was just that, an attempt to rediscover the face of Brazil, and listen to a nationwide hush. It was such an intrinsically Brazilian project that I wondered whether the film would manage to speak to audiences beyond our borders.*

Then we decided to submit the film to the Berlin Festival, following a suggestion by producer Arthur Cohn and José Carlos Avellar, the director of Riofilme – the production and distribution institute created by Rio de Janeiro City to make possible the revival of Brazilian cinema. Modern Brazilian cinema has largely been discovered in Berlin, where it has won six Silver Bears (four for features, two for actresses) in just over 30 years. In 1966, Berlin also organized an important Cinema Nôvo retrospective, which helped crystallize the movement in Europe.

I'll never forget the day CENTRAL DO BRASIL *was chosen for Berlin, and the warm letter from Berlinale director Moritz de Hadeln. Nor will I ever forget, naturally, the day the film won the Golden Bear, as well as the best actress Silver Bear for Fernanda Montenegro. But one moment transcends both these events: the day the film encountered the Berlin public for the first time, in the Zoo Palast. I've been to dozens of film festivals and I doubt very much whether there are audiences as sharp and attentive as those in Berlin. A cosmopolitan public, thirsty for differentness, interested in understanding others. The opposite of those audiences made up of what Godard (there he goes again) calls »career professionals«. My God we were nervous during that screening in Berlin … and how happy and relieved we were after the warm exchange which came about with the audience.*

Today, CENTRAL DO BRASIL *has won 50 international awards, and the film has found resonance with audiences from many different latitudes. But I'll never forget that first time, nor the courage required to select a film emerging from a convalescing cinematography, by an unknown director for the Official Competition of the Berlinale. This taste for risk, in fact, is perhaps the main reason so many cinematographies and directors have been discovered in Berlin. Yilmaz Guney and Turkish cinema, the new Asian cinema, the North American independents and Mexican cinema, among many others. May there be many more discoveries.*

A sense of melancholy still lingers in the streets

By Arthur Cohn

Why, I have often asked myself, is Berlin such a completely different festival? Why, I have often asked myself, is the atmosphere, are the discussions as well as the reactions in Berlin so completely different from anywhere else in the world? Of course, the sun does not shine here like it does in Cannes and there is no mundane Croisette; there is not the harsh beat of a city like Chicago, nor the intimate talks of Sundance. Berlin is completely different and I think I know why.

In 1951 when the Film Festival was first launched in post-war Berlin, it was not founded for the same reasons as other festivals in Europe or the New World. For it was the wish of the Americans, in the broadest sense of the Western Allies, to establish such a festival in Berlin. Only six years after the Second World War had decimated Europe and left new borders, the »showcase of the free world« came into being.

Such roots don't disappear. Berlin – today once again the capital of a united Germany – still breathes the air of those times. The borders to the East are still constantly present in people's minds, the shots of the border guards have not died away completely. And even when one leaves the best-humored party, or has experienced the most magnificent premiere: a sense of melancholy can still be felt and seen in the streets. Wherever one goes, memories are evoked – even of times before 1933. »Ufa« – these letters are a symbol of German film history. Names suddenly come to mind, those who helped establish the world of film. Yes – the world of film, not just of Germany. And they fled from the Nazis to many countries, some making big movies in Hollywood. And many were forced to take that route which ended in an extermination camp …

In other words, the International Film Festival in Berlin has developed at a site that has known both tremendous brilliance and gloom. It came into being in a political environment after the war which often left one feeling breathless and speechless.

I have had the honor of accepting the Golden Bear in Berlin twice. For IL GIARDINO DEI FINZI-CONTINI *(»The Garden of the Finzi-Continis«) filmed by my mentor Vittorio De Sica, and just recently for the film* CENTRAL DO BRASIL *(»Central Station«). The fact that I received the »Bear« directly from Moritz de Hadeln made me especially happy. He directs this Festival with great wisdom and visions, and*

CENTRAL DO BRASIL:
Vinicius de Oliveira

above all with the rare talent for making Berlin a meeting place for film people who often could not be more different. If this Festival can be seen as a UN of film today, then it is thanks to de Hadeln.

Twice I have been able to experience how high esteem for these »Bears« is worldwide. I know no other film award – aside from the Oscar and Cannes' Palme d'or – to which so much attention and tribute is paid internationally. Which is certainly the most beautiful compliment that can be made to the Festival in Berlin after 50 years and, I hope, in the future, too.

Shakespeare in Love:
Gwyneth Paltrow

The red shawl

1999

Feb. 10th-21st, 1999 (Competition)
Feb. 11th-21st, 1999 (Forum)

It was a magnificent, radiant start. Crowds gathered in front of the Zoo Palast just like in the old days. The atmosphere was relaxed and cheerful, onlookers applauding warmly as good-humored stars and starlets, and other Berlinale guests strolled up the red carpet. This year, there were no demonstrations to distract from the Festival. And the perplexed frowns caused by Michael Naumann, Federal Minister of State for Cultural Affairs and the Media, before the Festival, when he stated that the Berlinale had to adopt a style more fitting for a capital and finally show Cannes who was tops, had long been forgotten – as had all ironic commentary in response. The snow covering Berlin glittered; everything else seemed dull and remote.

Politics and culture

Politics and culture – one had the impression that Berlin and the Berlinale were rehearsing metropolitan flair. For the first time in the history of the Festival, the opening was attended by the German Chancellor. Gerhard Schröder did the Festival the honor, although admittedly only briefly, as he had to fly directly on to Washington that same evening. In any case, the political note struck by him went over well with the opening night audience. Many would have liked to have heard the speech which Michael Naumann had written for him, but Schröder had forgotten it (as well as his glasses), and so there were three minutes of »Schröder straight« – in which he paid tribute to the city and the Festival, and made a few marginal remarks on film policy and promotion, and international festival rivalry. Then there was Mayor Eberhard Diepgen with his opening speech, who made a dig at Cannes, the Festival's competitor, in a humorous couplet, Berlin cannot boast »the Mediterranean Sea, but Europe so very centrally« and insisted on coining a new name for the Berlin Film Festival: the »Bearinale«, as sturdy and as strong as Berlin's heraldic animal, the bear. Et voilà!

From Moritz de Hadeln's opening speech: »The Berlinale has no special orientation or specific motto. It is a German festival, therefore somehow reflecting a particular sensibility, deeply influenced by the cultural atmosphere surrounding it and the recent history of this town, not to mention the multi-cultural reality of its public. The only thing which animates us is our love of film and our understanding of its complex nature.«

Next, Angela Molina came on stage, president of the International Jury. Vivaciously, she whirled about, throwing the official protocol into confusion, effervescent with joy and good spirits, she was not to be restrained. She flung a fiery red stole competently around her shoulders, over and over again, because it just would not stay where she had put it. A colorful streak, she sparkled, laughed and introduced her colleagues – as if it were an evening on a southern piazza and not a stiff celebration in wintry, icy-cold Berlin. The magic of the red shawl pervaded the Festival. It was a Berlinale with señora. Days later, another American lady joined in the festivities, and she was just as vivacious, just as charming, popular and high-spirited: Shirley MacLaine. This year's Film Festival was sure looking good.

One might even go so far as to claim it turned out to be a Berlinale of the women. In fact, the opening film AIMÉE & JAGUAR by Max Färberböck – which had been expected to participate a year earlier – succeeded primarily due to the brilliant and intense interaction of two actresses. Maria Schrader and Juliane Köhler portrayed the true-life love story between two women in Nazi Germany of the forties, and they did so without misplaced sentimentality or false feelings. Their performance was suffused with honesty, it was not merely the assertion of a life which had been lived, but approval of it. Both the tumultuous applause which they received after the premiere, and the Silver Bear as the best actresses at the end of the Festival, were for them, and for Lilly Wust. Now an old lady, the historical figure of the film was visibly moved when she stood on the stage and softly said, »I still love Felice: Felice Schragenheim, she was a Jew and killed in a concentration camp.«

Moritz de Hadeln, Angela Molina

Steven Spielberg, Moritz de Hadeln

German Chancellor Gerhard Schröder, Angela Molina

It had been ages since the atmosphere at a Berlinale had been so impressive. European and American stars put in appearances, and there was a positive response to the films in all sections. Of course, opinions and preferences differed. However, the fact that in the paper »Freitag«, under the flashy but feeble headline »Between Hollywood and the Holocaust«, director and author Dietmar Hochmuth criticized everything on all counts could hardly be understood as anything but absolute subjectivism. There were also pre-judgments in the »post-commentary«: apparently the Berlinale had in the nineties seldom been »so dull and colorless as in this February, when it was a matter of saying farewell to a part of Berlin's film and festival history at and around the Zoo Palast. Now it was time to give that ever so longed-for and now apparently dreaded new start a go: in the Sony and Daimler-Benz Cities at Potsdamer Platz. Such a great deal of uncontested routine and apparent material fatigue is at play in the ›Festival machinery‹ that it is difficult to imagine how both are to be packaged in one new wrapping.« (Feb. 26, 1999) True, there were other voices demanding a new context for the Berlinale, and one of these voices was the Festivals Ltd. director Ulrich Eckhardt. He spoke of a »historic turning point« for the Berlinale and believed that the Festival had to communicate its international appeal more vividly. He pointed out that at the Sony grounds at Potsdamer Platz, a unique center was emerging with the Film House, in which the Deutsche Kinemathek with its Film Museum, the Freunde der Deutschen Kinemathek with the Arsenal movie theater, and the Deutsche Film- und Fernsehakademie (German Film and Television Academy) would all take up residence. (Die tageszeitung, March 15, 1999) Links that might evolve from this development for the Festival had long been established: i. e., the Deutsche Kinemathek was jointly responsible for the film-historical Retrospectives, and the Freunde der Deutschen Kinemathek for the International Forum. Yet it was right to urge everyone not to overlook the opportunities for expansion, as well as all the other dramaturgical connections that might result for the Festival

Jennifer Jason Leigh

Alan Rudolph

Claude Chabrol

Shirley MacLaine

Maria Schrader, Michael Naumann (Federal Minister of State for Cultural Affairs and the Media)

due to the spatial proximity of these institutions. Apropos the Festival résumé: if one was inclined to share its reservations, one could agree with Jan Schulz-Ojala: »One has no right to find fault with a festival that for a half a century has ranked amongst the three greatest in the world, especially in a year that has three nines and hence numerically so visibly gravitates toward the very nearest of futures. This year has turned out to be a phase-out model par excellence: indeed, it continued running and running and running on a well-tried course which one could have almost managed in one's sleep, with well-tried drivers, not to mention, well-tried technology, but it is, after all, a bit out of fashion. The new model – and we are in the mood for it despite all traces of melancholy – is already on display, only a few doors down, a few kilometers away, in a year's time.« (Der Tagesspiegel, Feb. 22, 1999) These »drivers« need to realize: all new models have teething troubles; and just as one had been willing to brave the »moose test« and had not immediately declared the new model a flop, the Festival management could set out toward the future not only with optimism but also knowing that there were tail winds that would not throw them off the road in a curve.

A Competition of contrasts

And this year's films? People spoke of a »Competition of contrasts«: majors vs. newcomers, mainstream vs. innovation, America vs. Europe vs. Asia. For the selection of the Competition program, approximately 550 features had been viewed in Germany and abroad (and 180 short films); 25 films were chosen, amongst them were 13 world premieres and six debuts. Scandinavia, France, and Spain were strongly represented. The German entries in the Competition program this year proved quite state-of-the-art, whether screened in competition or at special showings. As in the previous year, there were films from the US majors: UIP, 20th Century Fox, Buena Vista; as well as the ›mini‹-majors: Miramax and PolyGram. However, the quality of the films submitted for selection by former Eastern bloc nations was disappointing. In the selection committee it was noted with some disquiet that

Mikhalkov & Sokurov

not a single film from Eastern Europe was included in the Competition. Nikita Mikhalkov's film, The Barber of Siberia, which had been invited to participate in the early stages of the selection process, and was to be shown as the Festival's final film, was withdrawn by its French co-producers; the new film by Aleksandr Sokurov, Moloch – a very original scenario which traces Hitler, Eva Braun and other Nazis up the Obersalzberg, achieving a psychotic, claustrophobic atmosphere – kindled a controversial debate amongst the members of the selection committee, ranging from the film's adamant but well-founded rejection to enthusiastic approval. The final vote was a stalemate. In the end, Moritz de Hadeln decided to invite the film to the Competition, knowing that its German producers were also hoping it would participate in Cannes. Yet, following its invitation to Berlin, the film was submitted for viewing in Cannes. It was asked to participate there and the producers agreed. The absence of Eastern European films in the Competition was, however, balanced out by the large number of Eastern European productions in the Panorama as well as in the Forum. Ultimately, the program that crystallized united both big and famous names, such as Bertrand Tavernier, Robert, Altman, Alan Rudolph, Terrence Malick, Claude Chabrol, David Cronenberg, Ann Hui or Stephen Frears, and many new promising talents, such as Andreas Dresen, Max Färberböck, Tony Bui, Ben Hopkins, Yeşim Ustaoğlu or Manuel Viegas: it was truly a Competition of contrasts.

Especially noticeable had been how coolly American cinema was received, except for Terrence Malick's anti-war film The Thin Red Line, an intense apocalyptic portrayal of war experiences, a film which leaves no one who sees it untouched. »You can reject, yes, even hate its poetry, its meditative atmosphere, all held in the solitude of its protagonists' innermost feelings of imminent disaster, protagonists who are virtually damned (and damn others) to die at the next second – nevertheless, it does not allow you to look away, like for instance Stephen Spielberg's conven-

The Thin Red Line: Sean Penn

Cookie's Fortune: Glenn Close

tionally slushy battlefield film ›Saving Private Ryan‹.« (Jan Schulz-Ojala, Der Tagesspiegel, Feb. 22, 1999) Another exception was Robert Altman's masterly latest work COOKIE'S FORTUNE: »the horror story of a family, humorous and – for a sarcastic man like Altman – amazingly compassionate«, as Peter von Becker stated in the »Tagesspiegel« on February 21st. The film also owed its intense humanity to its leading actress Glenn Close. At the end of the Festival, astonishment was great when the Jury completely omitted Altman's film from the awards. Malick's film, on the other hand, received – quite justifiably – the Golden Bear; while another favorite, John Madden's SHAKESPEARE IN LOVE, had to make do with a consolation prize: a Silver Bear for best script. Many believed that this film – with its sophisticated dramaturgy that interlaced the past and the present, and its experimental profusion of allusions that gently and ingeniously concealed cultural-historical ironies beneath the narrative surface, light-heartedly but not light-mindedly – deserved all the prizes.

Social realism

Many films depicted the trials of daily life with wit and great seriousness, in small, episodic stories, so that some critics discerned a new social realism. Yet, the spectrum of the films was in fact vastly colorful, ranging from the Danish entry, a summery, ironic film, MIFUNES SIDSTE SANG – DOGME 3 (»Mifune – Dogma 3«) to Andreas Dresen's moral and comic Berlin tales NACHTGESTALTEN (»Nightshapes«) and Bertrand Tavernier's committed and stringent social reportage ÇA COMMENCE AUJOURD'HUI (»It All Starts Today«) to the Portuguese film GLÓRIA by Manuela Viegas, with its sparse and haunting urgency, and Tony Bui's American-Vietnamese production THREE SEASONS, whose suspended world of imagery from a foreign and distant land stuck in one's mind. The Turkish film GÜNEŞE YOLCULUK (»Journey to the Sun«) by Yeşim Ustaoğlu also ranked among these new discoveries. The film had initially not been submitted to the Competition or any other program section, but then, shortly before the selection process was completed, its producer personally brought by a print to the Film Festival's offices and requested a viewing. The

Turks and Kurds

THE THIN RED LINE: Nick Nolte

eXISTENZ: Jennifer Jason Leigh

Lola & Bilidikid: Baki Davrak (in the Panorama)

members of the selection committee immediately and unanimously voted to include this film in the Competition, and Moritz de Hadeln announced its invitation. The fact that Kurdish protest against the arrest of their leader Abdullah Öçalan's escalated in Berlin on the very day of the film's premiere in the Zoo Palast lent the film – which quietly depicts Kurd life (and survival) in Turkey – additional significance and caused tension at the screening of this sensitive portrait of a dying culture. »At no point does criticism of the Turkish government become explicit«, Ariane Heimbach wrote in the »Deutsches Allgemeines Sonntagsblatt«. »Filmed on location in Istanbul and southeast Anatolia, the second half of the film turns into a melancholic road movie across a devastated countryside. It is here that young Mehmet journeys with the coffin of his dead friend Berzan, a Kurd. First by car, then by train and in the end by horse-and-cart, he drives as if in a trance through karstic landscapes and villages laid to waste, finally arriving in front of Berzan's sunken home. A dam caused the village to be flooded.« (Feb. 26, 1999)

An independent Panorama

The Panorama wisely stuck to its program policy: complementing the Competition, a playground for independent productions (here in competition with the Forum), but also a place for documentary films dealing primarily with racism, such as Greta Schiller's film The Man Who Drove with Mandela, or with the Nazi era, such as Ilona Ziok's portrait Kurt Gerrons Karussell. Wieland Speck and his team had primarily chosen films from Europe, and American films did not dominate quite as much as in previous years. The films in the Panorama also exhibited that keen perception of reality which distinguished so many Competition films. Tim Roth's directing debut The War Zone, a drama about relationships between teenagers and their parents, was among these films: »What initially appears to be a kind of bizarre English family film, soon turns into a tragedy, which Tim Roth stages with a grim naturalism. (…) The War Zone is a family idyll in Roth's uncompromising film, despair and horror are revived in a theme that has been watered

Aimée & Jaguar: Maria Schrader, Juliane Köhler (in the Competition)

down by so many TV films.« (Hans Schifferle, Süddeutsche Zeitung, Feb. 16, 1999) In a different way – cheeky, naive and irreverent, and in uncomplicated pictures – the Swedish film FUCKING ÅMÅL (»Show Me Love«) by Lukas Moodysson brings to life the world of teenagers growing-up in a small provincial nest. The perfidy of adolescence is revealed and a first love that fails to live up to the two girls expectations, until they realize that they are in fact in love with one another. Moodysson's film received the Teddy award.

Berlin in film

There was a noticeable link between a number of films in the different sections of the program. Berlin was the setting for Andreas Dresen's and Max Färberböck's entries in the Competition, it was also the scene of Oscar Roehler's existential and emotional film GIERIG (»Greedy«) and the gay melodrama LOLA & BILIDIKID (»Lola and Bilidikid«) by Kutlug Ataman, both in the Panorama. In the Forum, Thomas Arslan's film DEALER, a story set in the world of Turkish drug dealers in Berlin Kreuzberg, was neither »pseudo-authentic« nor a »milieu report«, as Mark Siemons wrote in the »Frankfurter Allgemeinen Zeitung«, »but an austere minimalistic and intimate work à la Bresson«. (Feb. 20, 1999) There was also a rather experimental Berlin film shown in the Forum, KILLER.BERLIN.DOC by Bettina Ellerkamp and Jörg Heitmann.

Known and unknown cinematographies

In keeping with its tradition of focusing on unknown cinematographies, the Forum presented a series of films from Morocco. Emphasis was also on Asia and Western Europe, especially France and Italy. A film from Cuba was in the program too: LA VIDA ES SILBAR (»Life Is to Whistle«) by Fernando Pérez, turned out to be a melodramatic and comical view of a country, that used genre elements to spark critique. »The metaphor of fainting, which is what the people in the streets of Havana do when they hear words like freedom, truth, sex or opportunism, speaks volumes. The surreal sweep of the plot, which revolves round three figures, burdened by complexes, seems to be just a pleasant variant of the general state of emergency.«

FUCKING ÅMÅL: Alexandra Dahlström (in the Panorama)

JUHA: Kati Outinen, André Wilms (in the Forum)

(Hans-Jörg Rother, Frankfurter Allgemeine Zeitung, Feb. 22, 1999) From the USA, two documentaries left their mark: AN AMERICAN LOVE STORY by Jennifer Fox, a portrait of a married couple, she white and he black; and THE CRUISE by Bennett Miller, a cinematic declaration of love to Manhattan, presented by tourist guide Timothy »Speed« Levitch, master in the art of living and philosopher on everyday life in New York City. Another highlight in the Forum was the screening of Aki Kaurismäki's silent film JUHA, a story of a triangular relationship: a farmer's wife lives peacefully and modestly carefree with her aging husband who has a bad leg, until one day, a man from the city walks into her life. He awakens in her a desire for a new life, and so she leaves with him, yet she is then forced to work in a brothel. The film evokes shining examples of cinematic history. Murnau and Griffith are cited, images in an expressive black-and-white, the essence of silent film; although Kaurismäki also utilizes the flat shades of gray from the movies of the fifties. In contrast to these qualities, the story's simple vitality pales – as does the protagonists' overly stiff interaction.

Recollections of the Holocaust

Beyond the many attempts made by films in the different Festival sections to capture – with social exactitude – contemporary reality in fictive images, there were two documentaries which concentrated on and revealed history: THE LAST DAYS, produced by Steven Spielberg and presented at the Berlinale (in the Competition hors concours), and Volker Koepp's documentary HERR ZWILLING UND FRAU ZUCKERMANN (in the Forum). Koepp portrayed »the two last remaining Jews to be born in the old town of Czernovitz. At the age of ninety, Herr Zwilling and Frau Zuckermann are all too aware that they survived the war and the turmoils of the twentieth century not because of an act of divine providence but by sheer coincidence.« (Christiane Peitz, Die Zeit, Feb. 25, 1999) Spielberg's production, on the other hand, is »dedicated to five survivors of a Hungarian concentration camp, whose return to the sites of their childhood – they now all live in the USA – is recorded by the di-

Banoo (in the Forum)

International Jury
Angela Molina
(Spain, president)
Ken Adam (Great Britain)
Paulo Branco (Portugal)
Pierre-Henri Deleau
(France)
Katja von Garnier (Germany)
Hellmuth Karasek (Germany)
Jeroen Krabbé (Netherlands)
Michelle Yeoh (Malaysia)

rector, as is their shock and tearful confrontation with the barracks, gas chambers, crematoriums of the extermination camp – a film so horrific that surely every audience is left aghast«. (Ruprecht Skasa-Weiß, Stuttgarter Zeitung, Feb. 13, 1999) Both films caused the busy Festival to stop a moment and reflect.

Star guest of the Berlinale was Shirley MacLaine, who was awarded a Golden Honorary Bear. She received standing ovations at the Zoo Palast, where she played with her audience, recounting pointed anecdotes as well as giving insights into life. At the press conference she fluctuated between warm responses and pert dismissals. Nevertheless, she did it all with a smile. And she continued smiling from her seat at the gala in the evening, while she watched the entire length of her film Being There, even though a dinner had been scheduled with the International Jury. She couldn't have cared less about protocol, nor about her colleagues' hunger. The audience had priority. And then there was Sandrine Bonnaire, who played a role in Claude Chabrol's film Au cœur du mensonge (»The Color of Lies«): a woman of gentle sternness, with eyes that left no room for lies.

It was as if the Berlinale had attempted a dry run – on a small scale – for Michael Naumann's appeal for an »Alliance for Film«. With the magic of a red shawl, this year's Festival had been able to keep a promise. And it promised even more for next year.

The Awards of the
International Jury

Feature Films
Grand Prix of the 49th IFB
Golden Berlin Bear
The Thin Red Line
USA
directed by Terrence Malick

Silver Berlin Bear
Special Prize of the Jury
Mifunes sidste sang –
Dogme 3
Denmark/Sweden
directed by Søren Kragh-Jacobsen

Silver Berlin Bear
for the best actress
Juliane Köhler
ex aequo
Maria Schrader
in Aimée & Jaguar
Germany

Silver Berlin Bear
for the best actor
Michael Gwisdek
in Nachtgestalten
Germany

Silver Berlin Bear
for the best director
Stephen Frears
The Hi-Lo Country
Great Britain/USA

Silver Berlin Bear
for his remarkable artistic achievements
David Cronenberg
eXistenZ
Canada/Great Britain

The Blue Angel
Güneşe yolculuk
directed by Yeşim Ustaoğlu
Turkey/Netherlands/Germany

Alfred Bauer Prize
Karnaval
directed by Thomas Vincent
France/Belgium/Switzerland

Special Mention
for his excellent camerawork
to John Toll
The Thin Red Line
USA

Special Mention
for an outstanding young actress
Iben Hjejle
Mifunes sidste sang – Dogme 3
Denmark/Sweden

Special Mention
for its special thematic qualities
Ça commence aujourd'hui
directed by Bertrand Tavernier
France

Short Films
Golden Berlin Bear
Faraon
Russia
directed by Sergei Ovcharov
ex aequo
Masks
Germany/Poland
directed by Piotr Karwas

Silver Berlin Bear
Desserts
Great Britain
directed by Jeff Stark

Au cœur du mensonge: Sandrine Bonnaire

On the verge of an exciting journey

By Yeşim Ustaoğlu

Then and now, I remember the 1999 Berlin Film Festival as the first important stop on the long road of my film, GÜNEŞE YOLCULUK *(»Journey to the Sun«) – a three-year project, often difficult, but never without a fulfilling exchange of emotions and ideas.*

Everyone who joined this journey, with me and producer Behrooz Hashemian, found themselves with the same feelings and goals. Berlin was a very important moment for us all, a breaking away from the silent efforts of shooting and finally sharing the results with others.

When I first had the idea of making GÜNEŞE YOLCULUK, *I knew that I was on the verge of an exciting journey. A journey that I would share with my film's characters: Mehmet, Berzan and Arzu. To look closely at their lives, I knew that I was going to have to look at another face of Turkey, to go into the insides of Istanbul – to a place that too many of us try to ignore.*

The system has a way of dictating and defining lives; exactly what I wanted to react against. The world's conflicts do not directly touch everyone. The sad result of this is that the untouched are usually not very interested in those problems. At least not interested enough to look at the streets' water puddles for reflections of life's other faces. With GÜNEŞE YOLCULUK, *one can see clearly that this too-often ignored other life is just right around the corner.*

The subject and characters of :my film arose from the real suffering of the past 15 years of struggle in Turkey. GÜNEŞE YOLCULUK *tells the story of pure friendship. A purity resulting from survival against the pressures of the growing nationalist trend in a country with a history rich because of its multi-cultural identity. The characters are simply longing for their right to basic human existence amongst the unpredictable rules of life in contemporary Turkey. The world is filled with real-life Mehmets, Berzans and Arzus. I wondered how many of them would be in the audience at my official screening in Berlin. How many of them would have similar stories to tell? How many would discover things they were unable to see before?*

The day of the official screening, a series of events with respect to the Turkish-Kurdish situation developed to the point where no longer only Turkey alone could be involved. Events that put the eyes of the world on Turkey for an examination of its democracy, human rights and peace. Such issues are crucial to the relationship between Turkey and the rest of Europe. Answers would take time and would not be found easily.

So there I was in Berlin, a filmmaker about to present her film for its world premiere amidst all those events and questions. A film whose subject was directly linked to those dramatic and painful events. As if worries about how my film would be received for its artistic values were not difficult enough. Adding also to that pressure was the fact that GÜNEŞE YOLCULUK, *only my second feature, was the first Turkish entry in many years to be shown in the Berlin Film Festival Competition.*

Despite the warm and sympathetic interest of the Festival organizers. the atmosphere remained tense due to questions arising from the recent events. When the situation resulted in those devastatingly sad events in Berlin, the Festival was forced to call in additional security for the official screening. Spectators had to walk through a wall of policemen to get into the Zoo Palast auditorium for the world premiere of my film.

Güneşe Yolculuk
by Yeşim Ustaoğlu (in the Competition): Newroz Baz

I hope that I have not given the impression that the 1999 Berlin Film Festival was without joy for me. Watching the film for the first time with my actors, emotional comments from spectators, and, of course, receiving two prizes in Berlin brought great joy for all of us involved. Especially two prizes of such significance: The Blue Angel Prize for Best European Film and the Heinrich Böll Foundation's Peace Prize.

The answer has always been clear and simple to me: a filmmaker simply has to believe in what she wants to tell – and tell this story with all of her soul. This realization I will forever associate with the Berlin Film Festival.

Where will things go from here?

By Monika Treut

As the person responsible for a student movie theater in Marburg and since the mid-eighties as a film director, the Berlinale has been for me from the start a mixture of inspiration, market place and amusement park, a place to catch the flu and to make contacts.

Like most students, we spent our first years camping out at the Academy of the Arts: stocked with provisions, we were there from early afternoon until the wee hours of the morning. We wanted to see cinematographic rarities, which we would then later show at our movie theater in the province. Bleary-eyed, pumped full of nicotine and caffeine, we watched extremely long programs and engaged in heated discussions, for instance, about Syberberg's HITLER, EIN FILM AUS DEUTSCHLAND *(»Hitler – A Film from Germany«).*

Since the mid-eighties, I have been making films of my own, and they have been shown at the Berlinale. As a consequence, my arena slowly shifted more to Budapester Straße in the CineCenter. My first film, VERFÜHRUNG: DIE GRAUSAME FRAU *(»Seduction: the Cruel Woman«), premiered worldwide at the Delphi within the framework of the Forum.*

Now, it was my own work that was being heatedly debated. This first work, realized with Elfi Mikesch, elicited conflicting reactions from German viewers; nevertheless, via international friends, it was invited to festivals around the world. It was a life-saving strategy of the Berlin Film Festival: we were able to travel with the film from Edinburgh via Montreal and Toronto, to many important festivals, found distributors abroad, and so were able to put the harsh critique we had received at home back in perspective.

A few years later, I was able to experience the presentation of my second feature film at the Berlinale, DIE JUNGFRAUENMASCHINE *(»Virgin Machine«), in a more protected atmosphere since Manfred Salzgeber had taken me under his wing. My next films were first shown by my loving friends from the Panorama program section, aside from Manfred, these included above all Wieland Speck and Margaret von Schiller, and their experienced team. The Atelier am Zoo became my favorite Festival theater and the Panorama my Festival nest.*

My most dramatic premiere took place during the Gulf War in 1991, when there was a bomb threat at the Zoo Palast and the entire complex was evacuated by the police. The audience for the 11 p.m. screening of MY FATHER IS COMING *were driven out into the icy cold, and waited obediently in snow flurries for a whole hour until the all-clear signal and they were allowed to go back into the warm movie house.*

The nineties were more relaxed, especially the audience at the Panorama was more international and less inhibited. And from premiere to premiere it was more and more fun. The last time I was there, I was pleased to be able to present the entire family of the Norwegian icon of sixties Mexican cinema, Eva Norvind, who was portrayed in the documentary DIDN'T DO IT FOR LOVE. *After the screening, the film continued on the stage of the Atelier am Zoo. To the audience's amusement, Eva tried to strangle her sister-in-law. After the premiere of* GENDERNAUTS, *my last film, the protagonist, the »Goddess of Cyberspace«, Sandy Stone, forced me to simulate a collective orgasm with her in front of the large audience – and that with me, who enjoys hiding behind the camera most and is actually shy, although, at least in Germany, I have never been able to rid myself of my reputation as the »cruel woman«.*

Where will things go from here? I am not the only one to wonder. As of February 2000, the Berlinale will be held at Potsdamer Platz. I have nothing against changes: the medium with which we work as well as we who are its makers have to constantly re-invent ourselves. But I do now feel nostalgic when I think of the many talks and encounters at all those places related to the Festival for me: for instance, breakfasts at dawn at the Schwarzes Café with African, Brazilian and Finnish filmmakers; Peter Kern's birthday parties at Florian's; dinners with the Canadian festival organizers at the Paris Bar. A feeling of loss, because some close friends are no longer with us, especially for Manfred Salzgeber, Dieter Schidor and Michael McLernon, my cutter and friend Steve Brown from New York, eccentric Alfred Edel and David Overbee who, never tiring, scouted out new cinema talents for Toronto. Let us take a moment's break to think of the friends we miss.

And where will things go from here in Berlin-Mitte? Where will the new centers of night life be for the bohemian film scene, removed from the receptions of the Deutsche Bank? So asks a woman, who lives in Hamburg by choice, and swears by it; and she commutes between Hamburg and the world, visiting the capital only in February – for there is no other German film festival that is so wonderfully international and such a mix. Here's to wishing the Festival the best of luck at its new locations, and hoping it succeeds in bringing forth just as much creativity, internationality and liberality as it did at its old locations.

In the year 2000, and beyond ...

By Moritz de Hadeln

2000

Feb. 9th–20st, 2000

Historians don't like speculations. But in requesting that I write the last chapter of our Festival's history, Wolfgang Jacobsen has asked me nothing less than to speculate on how the future might me. In this fast changing film world, it's a mighty dangerous exercise indeed to venture into the future of any festival, and even more so a festival like Berlin's.

February 2000 is not only the 50th anniversary of the event, but also the 10th anniversary of the first Festival on »both sides« of the still divided town. And I shall never forget when, after months of secret negotiations with the GDR authorities, we felt we had to inform the »West-Berlin« Minister of Culture of what was going on. »But, Mr. de Hadeln, that's not correct what you are doing« – was the first reaction of Anke Martiny in a tone full of reproach – »While we are still thinking over what we should do, you are already negotiating!« For a long time such an attitude was almost symbolic for much of what was going on in town. Pondering and planning, but hardly taking the risk of deciding. The Festival's history is full of those moments, some justified, others less. But things are changing. A new Berlin is coming spectacularly to birth, amazing the whole world as some sort of second German miracle. And the Film Festival is on the move too!

The decision to move

For almost three years now we have been planning the 50th Berlin International Film Festival, the first one to take place at Potsdamer Platz. Nevertheless, only a few months before its inauguration, still many elements of its organization are unclear. But the pieces are coming together nicely, one by one, on a daily basis. At this stage, however, it's still impossible to depict what the 50th Festival will really look like. It will be a great festival, a new festival: of that we are convinced. But who really knows what it will be like?

The Festival's move after 49 years to Potsdamer Platz – the new town center built by Mercedes Benz and Sony – was not, initially, the Festival's choice. It was a political decision, for which today no single politician seems willing to take responsibility. »It comes from very high up«, I was once told by the town's cultural minister, Peter Radunski (Senator for Cultural Affairs from 1994 to 1999) with a gesture pointing to the sky. And he added: »Neither you nor I can avoid the move taking place, so we'd better do everything to make it work!«

But life was indeed becoming quite unbearable in the old buildings surrounding the Zoo Palast. Prof. Ulrich Eckhardt, head of the Berlin Festivals Ltd. – of which the Film Festival is part, was at a very early stage convinced that Potsdamer Platz was the right place to go and a guarantee for the Festival's future. His arguments included the modern architecture, a theater with a large capacity, the proximity of many cultural landmarks (several museums, the national library, the philharmonic hall, and above all the film museum, the film school, the film archives not to mention the many restaurants and entertainment facilities), and above all that Potsdamer Platz was again to become the heart of reborn Berlin. I agreed with all his arguments, but I was nevertheless worried – and the future proved me right – that not everything at Potsdamer Platz is ideal for a film festival. When the Festival organizers were faced with the decision to move, construction plans had already been finalized and there was little flexibility left to adapt what was available to our specific needs.

One could write a whole chapter alone on the saga of the Festival's film depot, wandering from one building to another, or on the Festival's press center being in a provisional setup at the very last moment. One could tell of our endless meetings with the architects and bureaucrats of the Mercedes real estate company – all of them recorded in impressive memos, of the many promises that were made of the endless struggles to get things ready in time or obtain the necessary permits from the different authorities. One could tell of our lost battle to obtain larger film theaters or the many plans to move the Tinguely sculpture throning in the middle of our market premises out of the way ... And what about the Sony theaters just across the road, ready – if everything goes as planned – just in time for the Festival. But hopefully all this will be forgotten history by the time the 50th Festival opens its doors.

A dream that never came true

Generosity has its limits. No one could expect, neither from Mercedes nor from Sony, our partners in this new venture, that they substitute for the town or federal government in what should have been their duty. But they both had neither the money nor the will to invest in the building of a real Festival center, a dream which all those who have headed this event have had ever since it began. Already, in the 1960s, Dr. Bauer had had detailed plans for the construction of a Festival center on Kurfürstendamm, but even then no one came forward with the necessary financing. Wolf Donner was more lucky in at least being able to build the market screening facilities on Budapester Strasse, meanwhile dismantled. I myself dreamed for a while of converting the GDR »Palace of the Republic« to Festival needs – only to be looked at as a lunatic. So in the end, unlike Cannes or Venice – with their own palace and generous public funding, we just had to take more or less what was offered to us and make the best of it. And indeed, for three years no effort has been spared on our side to conceive and plan a festival adapted to its new location and ready for the many challenges promised by the new millennium.

Building a new festival

If stripped to the bone, a film festival is made essentially out of three elements: its program, its organization and its atmosphere and – if I may say – by the way, all three are developed and delivered.

Of course, a good program is not achieved just by lining up films in different sections: their choice has to aim – within the limits of what is made available at a given moment – at giving the event a »raison d'être«. And this is, due to the complex nature of film production and distributions, and the multiple expectations of conflicting interests behind the scenes, the first stumbling block. Sometimes, I think of a festival like some giant radar screen monitoring the film production from one end of the earth to the other, trying to detect in time and give an early warning of what's coming up: trends, talents, but also moods and exceptional achievements. It's a scout's game, loaded with speculations, risks, illusions and hopes. And, I admit, the radar screen is often difficult to read!

By saying farewell to Budapester Strasse, we have also had to clean up our appearance, and somehow renew our corporate identity. With the help of MetaDesign, a major Berlin company specialized in this field, we went through a brain storming process aimed at finding out and defining »who we were« and »who we should be« – or »how we would like to be«! Maybe a mountain was made out of a molehill, but this learning process, to my knowledge quite unique in the history of film festivals, can only be the starting point for a deeper awareness of the need to constantly question ourselves in what we do and update our actions year after year. There is, in the business, no place left for routine!

In redefining our corporate identity, a new corporate design has resulted and plans on how to mark the presence of the Festival at its new locations. Every festival has its geography, the path used daily by its users. It was essential for us that the short distances existing at Potsdamer Platz between the different Festival facilities should be made obvious and used in an optimal way, and everything done to make the Festival-goer feel at home right from the beginning. From experience we know that every change in the organization of a festival raises suspicions and leads to comparisons with the past. The fear of change is human, but changes were needed to modernize the Festival to the many new expectations and to the new needs of Berlin, now the German capital. But ultimately, all this boils down to creating the necessary framework for a good festival atmosphere, indeed something not easy to achieve when one knows the explosive mixture – and often moody attitude – of the public, the media, the filmmakers and Festival guests during those crazy twelve orgiastic cinematic days.

At the opening ceremony of the 49th Festival at the Zoo Palast on February 10, 1999, I mentioned what the »Berlinale« could and should be: »a festival like this one cannot and must not be reduced to a few formulas ... Film is a living art, always on the move, and so is the industry behind it ... The Berlinale has no orientation or specific motto. It is a German festival, therefore somehow reflecting a particular sensibility, deeply influenced by the cultural atmosphere surrounding it ... not to mention the multi-cultural reality of its public ... Let's all together see that it does not become an arrogant festival, but remains the festival it is now: a festival with a human face.« In saying this I was of course primarily thinking of the coming Festival at Potsdamer Platz.

Beyond 2000

The Festival of the year 2000 will be what it will be. More interesting for me, at this stage, is to look ahead beyond this date. There are some permanent questions that every festival head asks himself: What form and structure should a modern festival have? Where is film production going? Are new technologies going to replace traditional film presentation – if not the making of films themselves? Where is filmmaking heading? Will filmmaking retain enough independence and originality to truly remain a »cultural exception«? I would like to add some thoughts to this debate .

Ever since the first film festival was established in 1931 in Venice, voices have been heard suggesting there were other ways of doing it better. Many have tried, but they soon turned back to more classical structures. By experimenting with alternative forms of the festival, the Venice film festival almost disappeared between 1972 and 1978. Years ago, in his usual radical way, Jean-Luc Godard suggested to me during a visit to his village on the Swiss Riviera in 1986 that a film festival should show no more than 10 films – the best of course! He did not, however, explain what the best films were ...

In search of the impossible

In the wake of May 1968, many thought alternative formulas for festivals were within reach, a dream that Alberto Barbera, the newly appointed director in Venice, still has today: »What we all have to do is ... find a new formula, something more modern« and he adds: »I am still trying to figure out what this can be«. May 1968: »Power to the Imagination!« was the slogan written on the walls of Paris. From it were born, so to say, the germs that led to the creation in Cannes of the *Directors Fortnight* and in Berlin to the *International Forum of Young Cinema*, that has meanwhile become *of New Cinema*. Both were to radically open the road to a new form of festival. New films and new filmmakers were indeed discovered and a more human approach to the role of the artists within the industry was achieved, but a new convincing form of festival had hardly been attained. With time, both had to resort to a more pragmatic integration into given structures of film presentation. The reality is that film production has radically changed over the past 20 years and with it the tastes and demands of the public. No festival whatsoever can change this reality, unless it becomes some sort of a laboratory for a few happy fanatics. And with such an attitude, no one will ever fill the screening rooms available at Potsdamer Platz.

In an interview given to *The Hollywood Reporter* in a special issue on Cannes in May 1999, Alberto Barbera admits that »increasingly (we) have less control over our own events. To a large extent these are determined by the promotional strategies of major movie studios« and he adds: »All major festivals are starting to look the same ... Today, these rival events (Cannes, Berlin and Venice) have started looking like each other because their movie selections are largely determined by the same contingencies. They all choose among the same array of films. What determines their choices are just time factors and studio strategy decisions.« And Stephen Galloway, author of this article, concludes: »Whatever the individual festival's tastes, with few really good films in any given year, the festival directors themselves are left to scramble for the best films they can get. They know that many will fall through ....« In a recent meeting with Gilles Jacob, responsible for the Cannes event since 1976, we both agreed that the dilemma as it is presented by Alberto Barbera seems for the time being to have no solution. As Pia Horlacher in the *Neue Zürcher Zeitung* put it on September 1, 1999: »... experienced people know that there are not so many alternatives for new forms of festivals, as some new festival directors would like to believe there are«.

Revolutions to come

Frightening indeed is the production and distribution concentration we presently observe. Never before, especially on the German scene, can I remember there being so many companies buying up others to create major conglomerates. Alternatives are rapidly disappearing as things are put into fewer hands. Money games are not innocent games when it is a matter of guaranteeing the freedom of creation. In such an environment festivals like ours will be more and more subject to the will of a happy few controlling the market. They will become dependent, exposed to all sorts of pressures and somehow lose the freedom of choice they still have. The next century will certainly be dominated by visual media, but their source could well be tightly controlled by a small group imposing their tastes on the whole world. In a society in which more and more time is left for entertainment, this perspective is far from exciting!

Film is a child of our technological world. It depends heavily on technical progress. And it is in this field where most spectacular advances are to be expected. Not a single step will be spared, from the making of a film to its distribution. But fortunately computers and technical engineers will never succeed in replacing the talent of an artist, but only give him further means to express himself. For this reason alone, there is no risk that film festivals will become obsolete events. The need to discover and uncover will remain.

Already now, with the advent of high definition video and modern computer technology, special effects can be achieved that one could only dream of when everything could only be done through photographic effects. Film is still two dimensional, which facilitates the creation of illusions. But refined 3D technology is now being exploited on the market, for instance by IMAX (polarized images), opening up a new dimension to creativity. Sound effects and sound quality have made giant leaps forward, making film entertainment an extraordinary event. Image sharpness and color rendering have never been so accurate, while inventors are working on still better quality.

It is in the field of distribution where the most spectacular changes are probably to be expected within the next decade, and they will certainly influence the making of festivals. While some are working on a 48 ratio of projection (Max/Vision Cinema Technology, Los Angeles) versus today's 24 frames per second, others are concentrating on digital high-definition images and satellite distribution. One of the pioneers in this field is George Lucas (Lucasfilm, San Francisco) who has proudly announced that the second episode of his STAR WARS will only be distributed electronically. The industry remains however sceptical, and for good reasons: not everybody is yet convinced of the projection quality, copyright protection is not guaranteed and above all equipment size and costs are still beyond tolerable limits. In this high-tech field Europe is for once not behind and among others, Berlin and Babelsberg are to be counted on. One day, the Berlin Film Festival will probably also have to update its screening facilities, invest still more money, but that day has not come yet!

If we look into the crystal ball once more, what other surprises could the future have in store for us? I am still concerned about our own European film production that yet has to conquer a larger share of our markets, about our authors who too seldom come up with convincing scripts and finally that we find ways to make films within reasonable budgets in order to keep filmmaking within reach for many. But I am not concerned about talent as there is plenty around, and there are still many good stories to tell. We still have to find ways to create viable alternatives to the Hollywood movie-making machine. Competition never hurts.

More questions and hopes

As for the future of the Berlin International Film Festival? If we keep on believing in what we are doing and nourishing our love for this fascinating art, if we receive the necessary financial support and if solutions are found in time to the pending structural problems, I have little doubt that it will continue on its road to success in spite of a few bumps here and there. But there are still some ghosts haunting the event that need to be put at rest, one being the illusion among civil servants concerned with the Festival's financing, that it will cost no more money at Potsdamer Platz than it has up to now. The Festival has rapidly grown, especially since 1989. But its managing team has remained just as small as it was before. Despite all good will, this can of course not continue. Finally, decisions will have to be made about the future of the Berlin Festivals Ltd. – that company owned jointly by the federal government and the city state of Berlin and which organizes, among other activities, the Festwochen and Theatertreffen each year – and if the Festival continues to be part of it, once Prof. Ulrich Eckhardt has retired as he has announced he will at the end of the year 2000. Neither myself nor my team will be around forever, and certainly not in a leading position for the 60th anniversary!

Money invested in a film festival is never lost. It falls largely back on the local economy and provides an indispensable podium for an art and the industry behind it. But the Berlin Film Festival has always been, alongside its function as a trade fair and an exhibition opportunity, a public festival. In our age of saturating home entertainment, more and more people feel the need to gather and experience common emotions, or just discover together other worlds or ways of thinking. Film, both as art and entertainment, has an assured future ahead, and with it our Festival – but I must apologize for not being able to give any simple answers as to how this future will really be. At the end of this century, everything is on the move, and who really knows where we shall be tomorrow.

Thanks

In 1989, Moritz de Hadeln asked me to write a history of the Berlin International Film Festival. The book which was written then about the Berlinale has now been continued and expanded in a review of the past ten years. Without Moritz de Hadeln's superior support, this book could not have been realized. He assisted me in obtaining unrestricted access to the files of the Berlinale and answered all my questions patiently and extensively. Erika de Hadeln was able to fill me in on a wide variety of additional details. I have not presented everything I have read and learned in this book.

Wolfgang Linke, who died in 1990, helped me to organize the first volume. His recollections of the Festival were also a great aid. I would like to remember him here.

I would also like to thank Werner Gondolf and Wilhelm Faber for all the information they gave me in many friendly talks as well as for all other assistance.

Manfred Salzgeber and Wolf Donner, who have both died in the meantime, deserve my thanks. They gave me much useful and interesting information.

Wieland Speck and Margaret von Schiller were of great help in pointing out many aspects pertinent to the history of the Panorama.

Ulrich Gregor from the International Forum of New Cinema, who supported the project from the very start, aided me in reconstructing the history of the Forum.

My warmest thanks also go to Helga Belach who accompanied the book with her astute and critical editing.

For a multitude of other tips and assistance, I would like to thank: Ruth Bauer, Berlin; Volker Baer, Berlin; Melenke Böhme, International Film Festival, Berlin; Dr. Hans Borgelt, Berlin; Klara Engl, Berlin; Rainer Geist, Berlin and elsewhere; Erika Gregor, International Forum of New Cinema, Berlin; Frauke Greiner, International Film Festival, Berlin; Dorothea und Ron Holloway, Berlin; Karin Hoffinger, International Film Festival, Berlin; Peter Latta, Filmmuseum Berlin-Deutsche Kinemathek, Berlin; Edmund Luft †; Christa Maerker, Berlin; Oscar Martay †; Karin Meßlinger, International Forum of New Cinema, Berlin; Karen Möller, International Forum of New Cinema, Berlin; Michael Müller, Bundesarchiv, Berlin; Al Newman, Los Angeles; Hans Helmut Prinzler, Filmmuseum Berlin-Deutsche Kinemathek, Berlin; Heiner Roß, Hamburg; Christa Schahbaz, Filmmuseum Berlin-Deutsche Kinemathek, Berlin; Hans-Joachim Schlegel, Berlin; Dieter Schmidt, International Film Festival, Berlin; Peter B. Schumann, Berlin; Wolfgang Theis, Filmmuseum Berlin-Deutsche Kinemathek, Berlin; the staff of the Bundesarchiv Berlin, the Landesarchiv Berlin, the Landesbildstelle Berlin, the library of the Filmmuseum Berlin-Deutsche Kinemathek, Berlin, Berlin's Senator for Science, Research and Culture (formerly: Senator for Cultural Affairs). I would also like to express my gratitude to the Stiftung Deutsche Klassenlotterie Berlin for its financial support. A great part of the manuscript was written by the author during a period of scholarship at the Villa Aurora (Pacific Palisades).

What would this book have been without the recollections of Festival guests? I would like to take the opportunity here to thank all those who have participated in this »play of memory«.

Last not least, I would like to thank my wife, Dietlinde Pardey, who read the manuscript as it took on form and made so many helpful comments.

Photos

dpa (1; p.31, bottom right). – Filmmuseum Berlin – Deutsche Kinemathek: archive (192), Heinz Köster Collection (30). – Freunde der Deutschen Kinemathek/International Forum of New Cinema: archive (34), Ekko von Schwichow (28), Marian Stefanowski (1). – International Film Festival Berlin: archive (69), Harry Croner (7), Joachim Diederichs (1), Kindermann (7), Heinz Köster (1), Max Kullmann (4), Mario Mach (4), Erika Rabau (114), Ronald Siemoneit (34), Wimmer (3). – Landesarchiv Berlin (1). – Landesbildstelle Berlin (15). – Ullstein Bilderdienst (10; p.83 on the right, 92, 148 at top, 154, 166 top right, 211 on the left, 364, 365). – Private collections: Sylvia Andresen (1), Moritz de Hadeln (3), Ulrich Gregor (1), Wolfgang Jacobsen (6), Steven Klain (2), Toshiro Mifune (1), Oscar Martay (1), Horst Pehnert (1), Ulrike Ottinger (1).

Notes

Round brackets and *quotation marks* designate American distribution titles. Film titles in *square brackets* are Festival titles or unofficial translations of the original language titles. This differentiation has no longer been made for the years 1990–1999, as films were seldom presented with special Festival titles, but directly with their distribution or television titles.

The *Russian-English transcriptions of names and film titles* generally follow the recommendations given in »The Chicago Manual of Style« (Chicago and London: University of Chicago Press, 1982) or are those most commonly in use.

Bibliography

All documents and letters cited in this book are to be found in the archives of the Berlin International Film Festival. The final reports of the Festival directors and numerous Festival journals, program brochures and documentations were also examined and evaluated. Unfortunately, most of the documents from the International Forum of Young Cinema were lost in a fire; just the same, the final reports and some other material pertaining to the Forum were available. For the chapter »Flashback«, diverse materials from the Bundesarchiv in Berlin were utilized, including the minutes of the Politburo of the ZK of the SED, files from the Office of ZK Secretary Kurt Hager and from the GDR Central Department of Film.

Presentations of the history of the Berlin International Film Festival have been few and largely for internal purposes. The first overview was given by the journalist Felix Henseleit: Zehn Jahre im Zeitraffer. Tatsachen und Eindrücke. In: Film in Berlin. Offizieller Festspiel-Almanach. Berlin 1960. – For the 25th jubilee celebration, a book was published about the Film Festival by Dr. Hans Borgelt, long-standing head of the IFB press office: Stars und Stories. Munich: Herbig 1975. – The Indian journalist Devendra Kumar also brought out a jubilee volume: 25 Years Berlinale. Delhi: Festival Press n.d. [1975]. – In Jahrbuch Film 78/79, edited by Hans Günther Pflaum, there are three essays on the Film Festival: Wolf Donner: Perspektiven der Berlinale. Thesen zum Thema Internationale Filmfestspiele; Patricia Highsmith: Filmfestspiele und Jurydienst; Ulrich Gregor: Auf der Suche nach Alternativen. Das Internationale Forum des jungen Films. Munich, Vienna: Hanser 1978. – Thorsten Ochs: Die Berichterstattung über die Berlinale seit dem Mauerfall. Dissertation. Otto-Friedrich-Universität Bamberg 1999. – Ulrich & Erika Gregor (editors): Zwischen Barrikade und Elfenbeinturm. Berlin: Henschel 2000. – An overview of films presented at the Berlin International Film Festival and the award-winners can be found in the following brochures: Paul Otto Schulz (editor): Die preisgekrönten Filme und Künstler 1951–1975. IFB 1976. – Axel Marquardt (editor): 1951–1984. Filme, Namen, Zahlen. IFB 1984. Supplement 1985. – Wolfgang Jacobsen (editor): 1985 – 1990. Filme, Namen, Zahlen. IFB 1990. – Sylvia Andresen (editor): Internationales Forum des jungen Films. Index 1971–1980. Freunde der Deutschen Kinemathek 1980.

The author

Wolfgang Jacobsen was born in 1953. He is a film historian and head of the department of publications/events at the Filmmuseum Berlin – Deutsche Kinemathek. He is a member of the Berlin International Film Festival staff and responsible for the film historical Retrospective and Homage sections. He is editor of the film lexicon »CineGraph«. He lives in Berlin.

Film

Name